T0331741

Intelligent Techniques for Data Analysis in Diverse Settings

Numan Celebi
Sakarya University, Turkey

A volume in the Advances in Data Mining and
Database Management (ADMDM) Book Series

An Imprint of IGI Global

Published in the United States of America by
Information Science Reference (an imprint of IGI Global)
701 E. Chocolate Avenue
Hershey PA, USA 17033
Tel: 717-533-8845
Fax: 717-533-8661
E-mail: cust@igi-global.com
Web site: http://www.igi-global.com

Library of Congress Cataloging-in-Publication Data

Names: Celebi, Numan, editor.
Title: Intelligent techniques for data analysis in diverse settings / Numan
  Celebi, editor.
Description: Hershey, PA : Information Science Reference, [2016] | Includes
  bibliographical references and index.
Identifiers: LCCN 2015051293| ISBN 9781522500759 (hardcover) | ISBN
  9781522500766 (ebook)
Subjects: LCSH: Quantitative research.
Classification: LCC QA76.9.Q36 I57 2016 | DDC 001.4/2--dc23 LC record available at http://lccn.loc.gov/2015051293

This book is published in the IGI Global book series Advances in Data Mining and Database Management (ADMDM) (ISSN: 2327-1981; eISSN: 2327-199X)

British Cataloguing in Publication Data
A Cataloguing in Publication record for this book is available from the British Library.

For electronic access to this publication, please contact: eresources@igi-global.com.

Advances in Data Mining and Database Management (ADMDM) Book Series

David Taniar
Monash University, Australia

ISSN: 2327-1981
EISSN: 2327-199X

MISSION

With the large amounts of information available to organizations in today's digital world, there is a need for continual research surrounding emerging methods and tools for collecting, analyzing, and storing data.

The **Advances in Data Mining & Database Management (ADMDM)** series aims to bring together research in information retrieval, data analysis, data warehousing, and related areas in order to become an ideal resource for those working and studying in these fields. IT professionals, software engineers, academicians and upper-level students will find titles within the ADMDM book series particularly useful for staying up-to-date on emerging research, theories, and applications in the fields of data mining and database management.

COVERAGE

- Neural Networks
- Factor Analysis
- Information Extraction
- Educational Data Mining
- Quantitative Structure–Activity Relationship
- Profiling Practices
- Text Mining
- Data warehousing
- Sequence Analysis
- Database Testing

IGI Global is currently accepting manuscripts for publication within this series. To submit a proposal for a volume in this series, please contact our Acquisition Editors at Acquisitions@igi-global.com or visit: http://www.igi-global.com/publish/.

Titles in this Series

For a list of additional titles in this series, please visit: www.igi-global.com

Managing and Processing Big Data in Cloud Computing
Rajkumar Kannan (King Faisal University, Saudi Arabia) Raihan Ur Rasool (King Faisal University, Saudi Arabia)
Hai Jin (Huazhong University of Science and Technology, China) and S.R. Balasundaram (National Institute of
Technology, Tiruchirappalli, India)
Information Science Reference • copyright 2016 • 307pp • H/C (ISBN: 9781466697676) • US $200.00 (our price)

Handbook of Research on Innovative Database Query Processing Techniques
Li Yan (Nanjing University of Aeronautics and Astronautics, China)
Information Science Reference • copyright 2016 • 625pp • H/C (ISBN: 9781466687677) • US $335.00 (our price)

Handbook of Research on Trends and Future Directions in Big Data and Web Intelligence
Noor Zaman (King Faisal University, Saudi Arabia) Mohamed Elhassan Seliaman (King Faisal University, Saudi
Arabia) Mohd Fadzil Hassan (Universiti Teknologi PETRONAS, Malaysia) and Fausto Pedro Garcia Marquez
(Campus Universitario s/n ETSII of Ciudad Real, Spain)
Information Science Reference • copyright 2015 • 500pp • H/C (ISBN: 9781466685055) • US $285.00 (our price)

Improving Knowledge Discovery through the Integration of Data Mining Techniques
Muhammad Usman (Shaheed Zulfikar Ali Bhutto Institute of Science and Technology, Pakistan)
Information Science Reference • copyright 2015 • 391pp • H/C (ISBN: 9781466685130) • US $225.00 (our price)

Modern Computational Models of Semantic Discovery in Natural Language
Jan Žižka (Mendel University in Brno, Czech Republic) and František Dařena (Mendel University in Brno, Czech
Republic)
Information Science Reference • copyright 2015 • 335pp • H/C (ISBN: 9781466686908) • US $215.00 (our price)

Mobile Technologies for Activity-Travel Data Collection and Analysis
Soora Rasouli (Eindhoven University of Technology, The Netherlands) and Harry Timmermans (Eindhoven University of Technology, The Netherlands)
Information Science Reference • copyright 2014 • 325pp • H/C (ISBN: 9781466661707) • US $225.00 (our price)

Biologically-Inspired Techniques for Knowledge Discovery and Data Mining
Shafiq Alam (University of Auckland, New Zealand) Gillian Dobbie (University of Auckland, New Zealand) Yun
Sing Koh (University of Auckland, New Zealand) and Saeed ur Rehman (Unitec Institute of Technology, New
Zealand)
Information Science Reference • copyright 2014 • 375pp • H/C (ISBN: 9781466660786) • US $265.00 (our price)

DISSEMINATOR OF KNOWLEDGE

www.igi-global.com

701 E. Chocolate Ave., Hershey, PA 17033
Order online at www.igi-global.com or call 717-533-8845 x100
To place a standing order for titles released in this series, contact: cust@igi-global.com
Mon-Fri 8:00 am - 5:00 pm (est) or fax 24 hours a day 717-533-8661

Editorial Advisory Board

Table of Contents

Detailed Table of Contents

In biomedical signal processing, wavelet transform has gained an edge over other existing methods due to its highly efficient transforming capabilities. Relative wavelet energy is a technique used to extract meaningful and concise information from wavelet coefficients for signal classification. The possibility of classifying large datasets combined with the simplicity of the process makes this technique very attractive for many applications. The focus is on testing and validating the use of this technique on different signals keeping in view the specific needs for various biomedical applications. The importance of this unified technique is highlighted with statistical results and validation on several benchmark datasets.

The efficient management of shelf space carries critical importance on both the reduction of operational costs and improvement of financial performance. In this context, which products to display among the available products (assortment decision), how much shelf space to allocate the displayed products (allocation decision) and which shelves to display of each product (location decision) can be defined as main problems of shelf space management. In this paper, allocation problem of shelf space management is examined. To this end, a model which includes linear profit function is used for the shelf space allocation decision. Then, heuristic approaches are developed based on particle swarm optimization and artificial bee colony for this model. Finally, the performance analysis of these approaches is realized with problem instances including different number of products and shelves. Experimental results show that the proposed swarm intelligence approaches are superior to Yang's heuristics for the shelf space allocation model.

Chapter 3

Miraç Eren, Atatürk University, Turkey
Ali Kemal Çelik, Atatürk University, Turkey
İbrahim Huseyni, Şirnak University, Turkey

Housing sector is commonly considered as a very strong economic industry in terms of both its contribution to creating employment and its impact on other associated sectors. By means of its featured characteristics, the sector also plays an important role on economic growth and development of emerging countries. In this respect, any evidence that determines factors affecting housing investments and future demand behavior may be remarkably valuable for monitoring possible future excess supply and deficits. This chapter attempts to determine factors affecting housing demand in Turkey during a sample period of 2003-2011 using a genetic algorithm-based multivariate grey model. Housing demand forecasts are also employed until the year 2020. Results reveal that several factors including M2 money supply, consumer price index and urbanization rate have an impact on housing demand. According to housing demand forecasts, a significant housing demand increase is expected in Turkey.

Chapter 4

Tuğrul Taşci, Sakarya University, Turkey

In today's World, huge multi-media databases have become evident due to the fact that Internet usage has reached at a very-high level via various types of smart devices. Both willingness to come into prominence commercially and to increase the quality of services in leading areas such as education, health, security and transportation imply querying on those huge multi-media databases. It is clear that description-based querying is almost impossible on such a big unstructured data. Image mining has emerged to that end as a multi-disciplinary field of research which provides example-based querying on image databases. Image mining allows a wide variety of image retrieval and image matching applications intensely required for certain sectors including production, marketing, medicine and web publishing by combining the classical data mining techniques with the implementations of underlying fields such as computer vision, image processing, pattern recognition, machine learning and artificial intelligence.

Chapter 5

Tuncay Ozcan, Istanbul University, Turkey
Tarik Küçükdeniz, Istanbul University, Turkey
Funda Hatice Sezgin, Istanbul University, Turkey

Electricity load forecasting is crucial for electricity generation companies, distributors and other electricity market participants. In this study, several forecasting techniques are applied to time series modeling and forecasting of the hourly loads. Seasonal grey model, support vector regression, random forests, seasonal ARIMA and linear regression are benchmarked on seven data sets. A rolling forecasting model is developed and 24 hours of the next day is predicted for the last 14 days of each data set. This day-ahead forecasting model is especially important in day-ahead market activities and plant scheduling operations. Experimental results indicate that support vector regression and seasonal grey model outperforms other approaches in terms of forecast accuracy for day-ahead load forecasting.

Chapter 6

Abdulkadir Hiziroglu, Yildirim Beyazit University, Turkey

There are a number of traditional models designed to segment customers, however none of them have the ability to establish non-strict customer segments. One crucial area that can meet this requirement is known as soft computing. Although there have been studies related to the usage of soft computing techniques for segmentation, they are not based on the effective two-stage methodology. The aim of this study is to propose a two-stage segmentation model based on soft computing using the purchasing behaviours of customers in a data mining framework and to make a comparison of the proposed model with a traditional two-stage segmentation model. Segmentation was performed via neuro-fuzzy two stage-clustering approach for a secondary data set, which included more than 300,000 unique customer records, from a UK retail company. The findings indicated that the model provided stronger insights and has greater managerial implications in comparison with the traditional two-stage method with respect to six segmentation effectiveness indicators.

Chapter 7

Seda Tolun, Istanbul University, Turkey
Halit Alper Tayalı, Istanbul University, Turkey

This chapter focuses on available data analysis and data mining techniques to find the optimal location of the Multicriteria Single Facility Location Problem (MSFLP) at diverse business settings. Solving for the optimal of an MSFLP, there exists numerous multicriteria decision analysis techniques. Mainstream models are mentioned in this chapter, while presenting a general classification of the MSFLP and its framework. Besides, topics from machine learning with respect to decision analysis are covered: Unsupervised Principal Components Analysis ranking (PCA-rank) and supervised Support Vector Machines ranking (SVM-rank). This chapter proposes a data mining perspective for the multicriteria single facility location problem and proposes a new approach to the facility location problem with the combination of the PCA-rank and ranking SVMs.

Chapter 8

Tarık Küçükdeniz, Istanbul University, Turkey
Şakir Esnaf, Istanbul University, Turkey

Facility location-allocation problems are one of the most important decision making areas in the supply chain management. Determining the location of the facilities and the assignment of customers to these facilities affect the cap of achievable profitability for most of the companies' supply chains. Geographical clustering of the customers, while considering their demands, has been proved to be an effective method for the facility location problem. Heuristic optimization algorithms employ an objective function that is provided by user, therefore when the total transportation cost is selected as the objective function, their performance on facility location problems is considered to be promising. The disadvantage of population based heuristic optimization algorithms on clustering analysis is their requirement of the increased number of dimensions to represent the complete solution in a single member of the population. Thus in two-dimensional geographical clustering, number of dimensions required for each population member is double of the number of required facility. In this study, a new neighborhood structure for the standard particle swarm optimization algorithm is presented for uncapacitated planar multiple facility location problem. This new approach obsoletes the need for higher number of dimensions in particles. Proposed method is benchmarked against k-means, fuzzy c-means, fuzzy c-means & center of gravity hybrid method, revised weighted fuzzy c-means and the standard particle swarm optimization algorithms on several large data sets from the literature. The results indicate that the proposed approach achieves lower total transportation cost within less computational time in facility location problems compared with the standard particle swarm optimization algorithm.

Chapter 9

Halil Ibrahim Cebeci, Sakarya University, Turkey
Abdulkadir Hiziroglu, Yıldırım Beyazıt University, Turkey

Business intelligence and corresponding intelligent components and tools have been one of those instruments that receive significant attention from health community. In order to raise more awareness on the potentials of business intelligence and intelligent systems, this paper aims to provide an overview of business intelligence in healthcare context by specifically focusing on the applications of intelligent systems. This study reviewed the current applications into three main categories and presented some important findings of that research in a systematic manner. The literature is wide with respect to the applications of business intelligence covering the issues from health management and policy related topics to more operational and tactical ones such as disease treatment, diagnostics, and hospital management. The discussions made in this article can also facilitate the researchers in that area to generate a research agenda for future work in applied health science, particularly within the context of health management and policy and health analytics.

Chapter 10

Alper Ozpinar, Istanbul Commerce University, Turkey
Emel Seyma Kucukasci, Istanbul Commerce University, Turkey

The timeless search for optimizing the demand and supply of any resource is one of the main issues for humanity nearly from the beginning of time. The relevant cost of adding an extra resource reacts by means of more energy requirement, more emissions, interaction with policies and market status makes is even more complicated. Optimization of demand and supply is the key to successfully solve the problem. There are various optimization algorithms in the literature and most of them uses various algorithms of iteration and some degree of randomness to find the optimum solution. Most of the metaheuristic and artificial intelligence algorithms require the randomness where to make a new decision to go forward. So this chapter is about the possible use of chaotic random numbers in the metaheuristic and artificial intelligence algorithms that requires random numbers. The authors only provide the necessary information about the algorithms instead of providing full detailed explanation of the subjects assuming the readers already have theoretical basic information.

Chapter 11

Today, suppliers of companies are no longer local. Companies have to offer their products to the market just in time and as fast as possible in order to compete. This situation is possible by establishing an effective supply chain for the goods and services they need in the manufacturing system. Finding the right suppliers who are able to provide the companies with the high quality products and services at the reasonable price, at just on time and in the right quantities is an important issue concerned in the process of supply chains concept. There are certain techniques developed in this respect. Some of such methods are approaches developed for situations unmindful of fuzziness and vagueness. Nonetheless, the process of supplier selection contains both vagueness and fuzziness. This study improves the Grey Relational Analysis and VIKOR methods, to fuzzy and ambiguous environments. Then, these approaches are applied to a supplier selection problem, which is previously solved through fuzzy logic and AHP method in literature, and the comparative results of both techniques are given.

Chapter 12

Document clustering, which involves concepts from the fields of information retrieval, automatic topic extraction, natural language processing, and machine learning, is one of the most popular research areas in data mining. Due to the large amount of information in electronic form, fast and high-quality cluster analysis plays an important role in helping users to effectively navigate, summarize and organise this information for useful data. There are a number of techniques in the literature, which efficiently provide solutions for document clustering. However, during the last decade, researchers started to use metaheuristic algorithms for the document clustering problem because of the limitations of the existing traditional clustering algorithms. In this chapter, the authors will give a brief review of various research papers that present the area of document or text clustering approaches with different metaheuristic algorithms.

Chapter 13

As a basic standard of life, internet connects millions of computers in a global network. People use, participate, or access the internet with the help of internet service providers (ISPs). To have better quality of connection, customers are prone to change their ISPs. In the competitive environment, ISPs endeavor to prevent losing their customers which are referred as churn. Thus, churn management takes an important place for ISPs. To investigate customer loyalty status, behavior, and information of the churn possibility in Turkey, a questionnaire is implemented. By using a real data obtained from a survey, promising and applicable results are obtained to predict the churn behavior of ISP customers in Turkey. As an extension of the study, the questionnaire will be applied for a larger population to find accurate results about churn situations. This study will help ISP companies to determine the required advertising campaigns for the customers.

Chapter 14

Adil Gürsel Karaçor, Atilim University, Turkey
Turan Erman Erkan, Atilim University, Turkey

Huge amount of liquidity flows into a number of financial instruments such as stocks, commodities, currencies, futures, and so on every day. Investment decisions are mainly based on predicting the future movements of the instrument(s) in question. However, high frequency financial data are somewhat hard to model or predict. It would be valuable information for the investor if he or she knew which financial instruments were quantitatively more predictable. The data used in the model consisted of intraday frequencies covering the period between 1993 and 2013. An Artificial Neural Network model using Radial Basis Functions containing only past data of three different types of instruments (stocks, currencies, and commodities) to predict future high values on six different frequencies was applied. A total of 72 different artificial neural networks representing 12 different instruments were trained five times each, and their prediction performances were recorded on average. Considerably clear distinctions were observed on prediction performances of different financial instruments.

Chapter 15

Girisha Garg, BBDIT, India
Vijander Singh, NSIT, India

Signal processing problems require feature extraction and selection techniques. A novel Wavelet Feature Selection algorithm is proposed for ranking and selecting the features from the wavelet decompositions. The algorithm makes use of support vector machine to rank the features and backward feature elimination to remove the features. The finally selected features are used as patterns for the classification system. Two EEG datasets are used to test the algorithm. The results confirm that the algorithm is able to improve the efficiency of wavelet features in terms of accuracy and feature space.

Foreword

Large quantities of digital data are accumulated in the databases of enterprises that actively use computer technology in every phase of their operations. These unproductive data can now be transformed into a useful form using new techniques and tools. This process is known as database information extraction.

Rapid developments and changes are seen today in computer science and informatics. We encounter innovations especially in computer and communication technologies field every day. These developments in information technologies (data collection sensors, satellites, social media tools and real-time integration and the use of smart phone data) make it possible to record all data in a digital environment. Customer data in a store, patient data in a hospital, the phone calls of the customers of a telephone operator and any kind of data from users accessing a host computer (server) on the internet are collected in digital environments. For example, the daily accumulated data for the packages a bank uses for its credit card transactions or on the internet and which is routed over routing devices can be quite large. How can these accumulated data be used? Can information that will be useful to solve real world problems be obtained from these data?

Useful information for enterprises can be extracted from the data accumulated by creating structures called intelligent decision support systems thanks to a variety of techniques. Various statistical and mathematical methods and artificial intelligence tools are used to analyze data. However, this analysis is hard to perform on today's databases. Therefore, data warehouses have been developed to manage the data easily, and intelligent data analysis approaches that access the useful information by analyzing the data have been developed.

Intelligent data analysis extracts useful information from the large quantities of data that is accumulated in the databases of enterprises using algorithms, statistics, mathematical disciplines, modeling techniques, database technology, artificial intelligence tools and computer programs. It uses these methods to extract hidden information from the data produced by an enterprise. It is also not a solution on its own, but is a tool that supports the decision-making processes seeking solutions and helps to find the models, patterns and relationships among the data. This book includes fifteen studies of practices that use these techniques to solve real-world problems.

Numan Çelebi
Sakarya University, Turkey

Preface

Data production and collection is rapidly increasing today. The quantity of data is approximately doubled each year. This increase is caused by using computers in the business world and scientific developments as well as the data obtained from tools such as smart cards, cameras, satellite systems and more. In addition, using the internet as a global information system requires large quantities of data. The daily processing data that accumulate electronically due to shopping processes in markets and is known as market basket analysis (Agraval & Sirkatan, 1994), and log data which traces the users interacting with websites and information systems (Bucklin & Sismeiro, 2003) are examples of this data accumulation. Information systems collect and accumulate large quantities of data in various formats such as texts, videos, images and more. The collected data may be entirely regular, semi-regular or entirely text. Data in this format make it difficult for researchers to make correct decisions. This has led to the need for new technical and automatic tools. Newly developed computer science theories and tools help researchers extract information quickly from large quantities of data (Berthold, Borgelt, Hoppner, & Klawonn, 2010). This has led to the development of an interdisciplinary research area known by names such as database information extraction and intelligent data analysis. This area is closely related to the techniques such as statistics, machine learning, artificial intelligence, fuzzy logic, rough sets, grey theory, heuristic algorithms and computer science. These techniques complement each other. Many statistical methods need computers for especially large data sets. However, the power of computers alone cannot be replaced by statistical information.

Intelligent Data Analysis (IDA) is associated with Knowledge Discovery from Databases (KDD) (Frawley, Piatetsky-Shapiro, & Matheus, 1991), which is frequently defined as a process, and consists of the following steps (Fayyad, Piatetsky-Shapiro, & Smyth, 1996): Understanding the problem, cleaning the data and making them available for processing, extracting the information hidden in the data and expressing this information in pattern and rule forms. This last step is usually defined as Data Mining (DM) in KDD.

These intelligent techniques help us to obtain useful information from large quantities of data. A research area called database information extraction or data mining has been developed in computer science to achieve this purpose. These fields discover the patterns that are hidden in large quantities of data and include information. These intelligent methods have emerged recently. Twenty years ago, researchers in artificial intelligence and computer science increasingly began to take interest in the processing, analysis and interpretation of large quantities of data. The main reason for this was that large quantities of data were hard to process with the methods of the time such as statistics and conventional methods.

We used the term, Intelligent Data Analysis (IDA), instead of Knowledge Discovery from Databases (KDD), although these two terms have a lot in common. Intelligent data analysis is an approach that performs data analysis with artificial intelligence methods (Mohammadzadeh, Safdari, & Mohammadzadeh, 2014). This tool allows the extraction of useful information hidden in large quantities of data. It also helps decision makers make quick decisions. Intelligent data analysis is very similar to data mining; however, it uses the initial information area to analyze the data using iterative and interactive methods. This initial information area increases the effectiveness of the information extraction process and prevents researchers and users from receiving useless results. Probability methods such as statistical classifications, hidden Markov models, Bayesian classification and rule extracting methods are used in traditional data analysis (Holmes & Peek, 2007). Intelligent data analysis tries to solve real world problems using techniques from various fields such as statistics, artificial intelligence, data mining, computational statistics, machine learning and optimization. Thus, intelligent data analysis is useful for researchers and decision makers in many different fields (Vučenović, Trivić, & Kos, 2015).

Therefore, in this book we describe studies of the application of intelligent data analysis techniques in a variety of fields. This book includes a variety of research subjects and practical techniques of data analysis based on theories and various intelligent methods. These subjects include the basic subjects of exploratory data analysis, classification and feature selection, soft computing, information extraction, decision making, data mining, estimation and clustering.

ORGANIZATION OF THE BOOK

The book is organized into fifteen chapters. A brief description of each of the chapters follows:

Chapter 1 presents the notion of 'wavelet transform', which has gained an edge over other existing methods due to its highly efficient transforming capabilities in biomedical signal processing. The authors focused on testing and validating the use of this technique on different signals keeping in view the specific needs for various biomedical applications. The importance of this unified technique is highlighted with statistical results and validation on several benchmark datasets

Chapter 2 examines the allocation problem of shelf space management. The chapter first sets the Yang's model which includes linear profit function for the shelf space allocation. Then, The authors developed heuristic approaches both based on particle swarm optimization and artificial bee colony algorithm to solve the problem. They showed the heuristics approcahes are superior than Yang's heuristics for the shelf space allocation model by using performance analysis.

Chapter 3 attempts to determine the factors affecting housing demand in Turkey. The authors of this chapter establishesed a genetic algorithm-based multivariate grey model in order to reveal their aims. They showed that several factors including M2 money supply, consumer price index and urbanization rate have an impact on housing demand.

Chapter 4 gives an image mining approach. It is an evidence that a huge amount of data is continuously accumulated in databases through internet and various types of smart devices. It is also clear that description-based querying is almost impossible on such a big unstructured data. The author proposed an image mining which provides example-based querying on image databases.

Chapter 5 tries to predict the electricity load. The day-ahead forecasting model is especially important in day-ahead market activities and plant scheduling operations. This chapter's authors developed several forecasting model in order to predict the hourly loads. Their experimental results indicated that support vector regression and seasonal grey model outperforms other approaches in terms of forecast accuracy for day-ahead load forecasting.

Chapter 6 presents a two-stage segmentation model based on soft computing using the purchasing behaviours of customers in a data mining framework. Segmentation was performed via neuro-fuzzy two stage-clustering approach for a secondary data set, which included more than 300,000 unique customer records, from a UK retail company. The findings indicated that the model provided stronger insights and has greater managerial implications in comparison to the traditional two-stage method with respect to six segmentation effectiveness indicators.

Chapter 7 focuses on available data analysis and data mining techniques to find the optimal location of the Multicriteria Single Facility Location Problem (MSFLP) at diverse business settings. The authors proposed a new approach to the facility location problem with the combination of the PCA-rank and ranking SVMs while presenting a general classification of the MSFLP and its framework.

Chapter 8 addresses the issue of facility location problem with geographical clustering of the customers while considering their demands. The author proposed a new neighborhood structure for the standard particle swarm optimization algorithm to solve the problem. They compared their approach with k-means, fuzzy c-means, fuzzy c-means and center of gravity hybrid method, revised weighted fuzzy c-means algorithm and the standard particle swarm optimization algorithms on several large data sets from the literature. The results indicate that the proposed approach achieves less total transportation cost with less computational cost requirement in facility location problems.

Chapter 9 aims to provide an overview of business intelligence in healthcare context by specifically focusing on the applications of intelligent systems. The author reviewed the current applications into three main categories and presented some important findings of that research in a systematic manner. The discussions made in this chapter can also facilitate the researchers in that area to generate a research agenda for future work in applied health science, particularly within the context of health management and policy and health analytics.

Chapter 10 is about the possible use of chaotic random numbers in the metaheuristic and artificial intelligence algorithms that requires random numbers. The authors only provide the necessary information about the algorithms instead of providing full detailed explanation of the subjects assuming the readers already have theoretical basic information.

Chapter 11 reviews the issue of supplier selection which is an important problem in business. The authors argued that it is possible to solve it by improving the traditional grey relation analysis and VIKOR methods in fuzzy environment. They took a problem from literature and compared their solution with fuzzy and AHP methods.

Chapter 12 analyzes several numbers of techniques in literature, which efficiently provide solutions for document clustering. The author proposed metaheuristic algorithms for document clustering problem because of the limitations of the existing traditional clustering algorithms. They also gave a brief review over various research papers that present the area of document or text clustering approaches with different metaheuristic algorithms.

Chapter 13 addresses the issue of churn with particular reference to Internet Service Providers (ISPs). The authors implemented a questionnaire to investigate customer loyalty status, behavior, and information of the churn possibility in Turkey. They used a real data collected from a survey and obtained a promising and applicable results. It is believed that it will help ISP companies to determine the required advertising campaigns for the customers

Chapter 14 analyzes liquidity flows into a number of financial instruments such as stocks, commodities, currencies, futures. The authors tried to identify which financial instruments were quantitatively more predictable. They used the data for their model intraday frequencies covering the period between

1993 and 2013. They analysed 72 different artifical neural networks to observe distinction on prediction peformances of different financial instrument.

Chapter 15 proposed a novel Wavelet Feature Selection algorithm for ranking and selecting the features from the wavelet decompositions. The authors used support vector machine to rank the features and backward feature elimination to remove the features. The EEG datasets are used to test the algorithm. The results confirmed that the algorithm is able to improve the efficiency of wavelet features in terms of accuracy and feature space.

Numan Çelebi
Sakarya University, Turkey

REFERENCES

Agrawal, R., & Srikant, R. (1994). Fast algorithms for mining association rules. In *Proc. of the Int. Conf. Very Large Data Bases* (VLDB'94), (pp. 487–499). Academic Press.

Berthold, M., Borgelt, C., Hoppner, F., & Klawonn, F. (2010). *Guide to intelligent data analysis*. Springer. doi:10.1007/978-1-84882-260-3

Bucklin, R. E., & Sismeiro, C. (2003). A model of web site browsing behavior estimated on clickstream data. *JMR, Journal of Marketing Research*, *40*(3), 249–267. doi:10.1509/jmkr.40.3.249.19241

Fayyad, U. M., Piatetsky-Shapiro, G., & Smyth, P. (1996). The KDD process for extracting useful knowledge from volumes of data. *Communications of the ACM*, *39*(11), 27–41. doi:10.1145/240455.240464

Frawley, W., Piatetsky-Shapiro, G., & Matheus, C. (1991). Knowledge discovery in databases: An overview. In *Knowledge discovery in databases*. The AAAI Press.

Holmes, J. H., & Peek, K. (2007). Intelligent data analysis in biomedicine. *Journal of Biomedical Informatics*, *40*(6), 605–608. doi:10.1016/j.jbi.2007.10.001 PMID:17959422

Mohammadzadeh, N., & Safdar, İ, R., & Mohammadzadeh, F. (2014). Using intelligent data analysis in cancer care: Benefits and challenges. *Journal of Health Informatics in Developing Countries*, *8*(2).

Vučenović, D., Trivić, I., & Kos, D. (2015). *Intelligent data analysis – From data to knowledge*. Retrieved from http://www.astro.hr/s3/izvjestaji/s3pp2009/WebReport_IntelligentDataAnalysis.pdf

Chapter 1
Unified Wavelet Transform Analysis Adapted to Different Biomedical Applications

Girisha Garg
BBDIT, India

Vijander Singh
NSIT, India

ABSTRACT

In biomedical signal processing, wavelet transform has gained an edge over other existing methods due to its highly efficient transforming capabilities. Relative wavelet energy is a technique used to extract meaningful and concise information from wavelet coefficients for signal classification. The possibility of classifying large datasets combined with the simplicity of the process makes this technique very attractive for many applications. The focus is on testing and validating the use of this technique on different signals keeping in view the specific needs for various biomedical applications. The importance of this unified technique is highlighted with statistical results and validation on several benchmark datasets.

1. INTRODUCTION

Feature transformation is used to obtain a new feature space from the raw biomedical signals. There are various transformations which are applied to the biomedical signals (Hu, Wang, Ren, 2005; Ciaccio, Dunn, & Akay, 1993; Tsipourasemail, & Fotiadis, 2004). In order to obtain an efficient feature space, biomedical signals require time-frequency transformation. Discrete Wavelet Transform (DWT) and Wavelet Packet Transform (WPT) are the most efficient and frequently used time-frequency based techniques for feature transformation of biomedical signals. The DWT is attractive primarily because the Mallat algorithm (Mallat, 1997) is a computationally efficient implementation of the WT and, depending on the mother wavelets; it can be used as an orthogonal or bi-orthogonal transform.

The coefficients derived from the DWT decomposition are too large (usually the same as the number of samples in the biomedical signal) to be used as feature space for classification; therefore many

DOI: 10.4018/978-1-5225-0075-9.ch001

algorithms have been proposed for extracting relevant features from the wavelet coefficients (Khadra, Al Fahoum, & Al-nashah, 1997; Englehart, Hudgins, & Parker, 2001; Subasi, & Gursov, 2010). The statistical measures like standard deviation, mean, chaotic measures, etc. have been used extensively for this purpose (Dastidar, Adeli, & Dadmehr, 2007). The major problem with these measures is the lesser consensus among them. The other commonly used techniques for wavelet features extraction are Principal Component Analysis (PCA) (Hu, Wang, Ren, 2005) and Linear Discriminant Analysis (LDA) (Subasi, & Gursov, 2010), but these are not optimal for biomedical signal processing because the features extracted by these methods only utilize the averaged feature variations over time, and ignore the detailed status in each time slot, frequency band and the feature variation, and thus may lead to inaccurate results. The other reasons due to which these methods are avoided for this study are:

- PCA does not take into account the vector's classes so it cannot look at the classes' separability.
- PCA assumes linear transformation which is inappropriate for nonlinear biomedical data.
- LDA involves eigen decomposition and matrix inversions which may lead to computationally expensive programs and numerical instability respectively.
- LDA suffers from small sample size problem. It shows poor generalization ability and degrades the classification performance when the sample dimensionality is larger than the number of available training samples per subject, which is normally the case for biomedical signals.

The direct use of DWT coefficients results in inaccurate classification not only because of the large number of coefficients but also due to much discussed disadvantage of wavelet transform known as shift invariance. The DWT coefficients of a signal are sensitive to the location of the signal, and the energy distribution of wavelet coefficients of two signals may be quite different even if the two signals just differ by a time (or space) shift. In literature the problem is addressed by finding a best set of DWT coefficients among all time (or space) shifts to represent the signal (G. Wang, Z. Wang, Chen, Zhuang, 2006). Wang et al. (Garg, Singh, Gupta, Mittal, & Chandra, 2011) reported that the feature set constructed using energy of wavelet coefficients within each sub band can provide features with translational invariant property. Thus the energy representation of the wavelet coefficients overcome the problem of shift invariance as well as produce a reduced and efficient representation of the feature set. Based on the above observations, we are motivated to test the energy representation (of wavelet coefficients) method for the following solutions:

- A general feature extraction approach for performing classification on datasets of different origin and applications.
- A method which extracts non redundant and robust features from high dimension biomedical signals while retaining the diagnostically important information.
- Consistent performance for different problems.

In our previous works (Garg, Singh, Gupta, Mittal, Chandra, 2011; Garg, Singh, Gupta, Mittal, 2012) the energy representation method was used for feature extraction of EEG signals in sleep scoring and epilepsy detection. This paper will examine Relative Wavelet Energy (RWE) as a generalized feature extractor for harnessing the diagnostically important information from different biomedical signals. The focus will be on investigating consistency in the performance of RWE over a range of diverse classification problems. The aim is to determine the effectiveness of RWE in discriminating the biomedical data into different groups based on their intrinsic properties. In pursuance of achieving this aim of investigating underlying discrimination mechanism, three different methods are adopted based on the following measures: visual distinction, statistical grouping and classification accuracy. The different datasets are selected on the basis of following criterion:

- Selection of biomedical signals from different origin e.g. Electroencephalogram from brain, electrocardiogram from heart, gait signals from foot movement and electromyogram from muscle movement.
- Selection of binary as well as multiclass classification tasks.
- Selection of clean as well as noisy signals.

Rest of the paper is organized as follows. First a brief discussion on RWE is given in section 2, and then distance similarity measures used for evaluation are presented. The theoretical explanation of wavelet transform and DWT is omitted and can be referred from (Mallat, 1989). The approach is tested on 8 benchmark datasets and computer simulation results are presented in section 4. Section 5 is dedicated for discussion of the results presented and section 6 concludes the paper.

2. RELATIVE WAVELET ENERGY

The main objective of using a feature extraction technique in signal processing is to obtain a small number of relevant features from the wavelet coefficients. Since the feature sets obtained are used for diagnostic classification, the wavelet power spectrum will be different for all the diagnostic categories. Therefore spectrum based feature extraction methods are most appropriate and simple, to select important features relevant to each category.

The biomedical signals are highly subjective; the characteristic information for different diagnostic classes can appear at random scales. Therefore it is important to use a method that can harness the frequency variation of the signals with respect to time, to accurately detect and characterize the specific phenomenon related to the biomedical signals. Relative Wavelet Energy (RWE) is a feature extraction method which can capture the inherent properties of the biomedical signal frequency spectrum in the form of informative energy features. It has been successfully used in previous works related to feature extraction of wavelet based applications (Manikandan, & Dhandapat, 2007; Guo, Rivero, Seoane, & Pazos, 2009; Shepard, 1987). The underlying idea is to use RWE to filter out the irrelevant data, which makes it easier to mine knowledge from the remaining data. RWE is defined by the ratio of detail energy at the specific decomposition level to the total energy. The energy of DWT detail coefficients $d_{j,k}$ at each level, j is given by:

$$E_j = \sum_{k-1}^{N} |d_{j,k}|^2 \ j = 1 \text{ to } n \tag{1}$$

where

n: Decomposition level

N: Number of detail coefficients

The raw energy of detailed signals cannot necessarily characterize the normal/abnormal activity. In different patients similar energy values can represent different states. Therefore raw energy index cannot clearly describe the level of abnormality. To eliminate this shortcoming, the energy values are divided by the energy of the whole spectrum, and the total energy for all the levels is given by:

$$E_{total} = \sum_j E_j \tag{2}$$

Thus the relative wavelet energy is given by:

$$RWE = \frac{E_j}{E_{total}} \tag{3}$$

This gives the relative index which considers the background spectrum of the biomedical signal to differentiate between the normal and abnormal activity. Some of the biomedical signals have their important characteristics represented by the low frequencies that the approximation energy may capture. But approximation energy is ignored as they don't produce relevant changes with difference in classes. This can be proved with the RWE processing on signals of Dataset I explained in the Appendix. The wavelet energy patterns for both approximation and detail energy features are given below. Figure 1(a) shows the patterns for normal EEG and Figure 1(b) shows the patterns for epileptic EEG. On comparing both the figures, it can be seen that the variations in the patterns occur only in the detail energy features.

RWE extracts the energy of each sub band and can detect the degree of similarity between segments of a signal. Thus this method accurately detects and characterizes the specific phenomenon related to the different frequency bands of the biomedical signals such that only the useful information is extracted from

Figure 1. (a): Energy Patterns for normal EEG (b): Energy Patterns for epileptic EEG

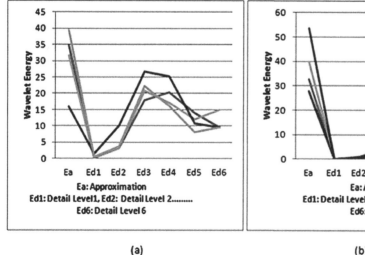
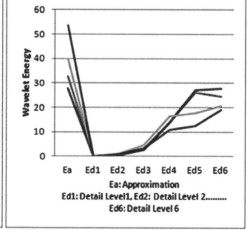

(a)   (b)

the signal about the process under study. Since RWE captures the energy of the system that generated the original biomedical signal, the RWE energy reflects the abnormalities in the system that generated the biomedical signal. Thus the features extracted have a physiological meaning, are simple to compute and are robust to the typical kind of noises present in the biomedical signals. The reduction in the feature set dimension by using RWE can be explained using the following example:

The Dataset I explained in the Appendix has EEG signals with 4097 samples each. The DWT decomposition performed on the signal using db4 wavelet at decomposition level 5 produces 4129 wavelet coefficients. The number of wavelet coefficients is greater than the number of samples in the EEG signal due to the convolution process involved in calculation of the coefficients. This number can be equalized to the number of samples in the EEG signal by padding. Using 4129 features per pattern for classification is not possible. Therefore, feature extraction is performed using RWE, which gives a feature set of cardinality equal to the decomposition level, i.e. 5, for this example. Thus a feature space of 4097 in the original EEG signal is reduced to 5 in the RWE feature set as shown in Figure 2.

3. DISTANCE SIMILARITY MEASURES

The aim of using RWE as features extraction technique for this work is that this method is signal independent and fits for a wide range of datasets. A multidatabase validation approach is followed to ensure the better generalization properties of this technique. For validation purposes, the distance based similarity measures are used. These methods are generally used for comparing two or more patterns to discover their likeness or differences. The distance methods are preferred here for validation, for their simple approach and also due to the fact that they can be used to measure the proximity with a high degree of accuracy, when the describing features are quantitative. The following distance metrics are used for the validation of RWE as a generic feature extraction technique which can cope up with a variety of data. The following metrics calculate the distance d_{rs} between two samples x_r and x_s.

I.   Euclidean Distance

$$d_{rs}^2 = (x_r - x_s)(x_r - x_s)^T \tag{4}$$

Figure 2. Example for depicting the reduction in the feature dimension using RWE

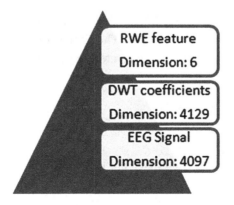

II.   Mahalanobis Distance:

$$d_{rs}^2 = (x_r - x_s)V^{-1}(x_r - x_s)^T \tag{5}$$

where V is the sample covariance matrix

III.   City Block Metric:

$$d_{rs} = \sum_{j=1}^{n} | x_{rj} - x_{sj} | \tag{6}$$

IV.   Minkowski Metric:

$$d_{rs} = \left\{ \sum_{j=1}^{n} | x_{rj} - x_{sj} |^p \right\}^{1/p} \tag{7}$$

V.   Cosine Distance:

$$d_{rs} = \left(1 - x_r x_s^T / (x_r^T x_r)^{1/2} (x_s^T x_s)^{1/2} \right) \tag{8}$$

VI.   Correlation Distance:

$$d_{rs} = 1 - \frac{(x_r - \bar{x}_r)(x_s - \bar{x}_s)^T}{[(x_r - \bar{x}_r)(x_r - \bar{x}_r)^T]^{1/2}[(x_s - \bar{x}_s)(x_s - \bar{x}_s)^T]^{1/2}} \tag{9}$$

where

$$\bar{x}_r = \frac{1}{n}\sum_j x_{rj} \text{ and } \bar{x}_s = \frac{1}{n}\sum_j x_{sj}$$

The performance of RWE as a feature extraction technique is evaluated on different biomedical datasets using the above mentioned distance metrics. The similarity is found on the basis of the universal law proposed by Shepard (Shepard, 1987) which states that the distance and similarity are related via an exponential function as follows:

$$sim_{r,s} = e^{-d_{r,s}} \tag{10}$$

Thus using this law, the following statements are to be verified for the RWE feature sets extracted from different biomedical datasets:

- In order to have similar patterns in a group, the features should produce a high intraclass grouping. Therefore the value of d_{rs} for RWE patterns belonging to same class should be as low as possible.
- In order to have different patterns for different groups, the features should produce a low interclass grouping; therefore the value of d_{rs} for RWE patterns belonging to different classes should be as high as possible.

This concept can be explained with the help of visual analysis of the RWE patterns which are explained in the next section.

4. SIMULATION RESULTS

The feature extraction method adopted using DWT and RWE can be explained using the flow chart shown in Figure 3. The biomedical signal in time domain is first transformed into time-frequency domain using DWT.

The DWT coefficients at each level are then used to calculate the relative wavelet energy at each level. The feature vector obtained after applying RWE will consist of 1 x n features for each signal, where n is the decomposition level.

4.1. Visual analysis of RWE distributions

The discrimination capability of the RWE feature extraction method can be evaluated by analyzing the RWE patterns obtained for different datasets. For producing optimal classification accuracy, the signals

Figure 3. Flow diagram for feature extraction

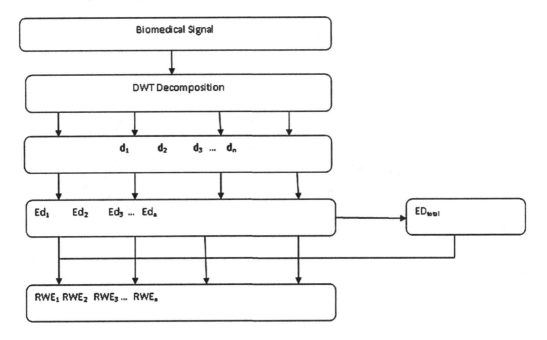

belonging to same class should have similar RWE patterns, and there should a distinction between the RWE patterns of signals belonging to different classes. The visual analysis is performed on the biomedical datasets with binary classification. The RWE patterns Figure 4(a) & (b) shows the RWE distributions of EEG signals (Dataset I) of normal and pre-ictal activity respectively.

Figure 5 (a) & (b) shows the RWE distributions for different ECG signals (Dataset III) belonging to the control class and apnoea class respectively.

Figure 6 (a) & (b) show the RWE distribution for EMG (Dataset V) signals from term deliveries and pre-term deliveries respectively. Figure 7(a) & (b) show the RWE distribution for snoring signals (Dataset VII) of apnoea class and hypopnoea class respectively.

Figure 4. (a): RWE distributions for EEG signals of normal activity (Dataset I) (b): RWE distributions for EEG signals of preictal activity(Dataset I)

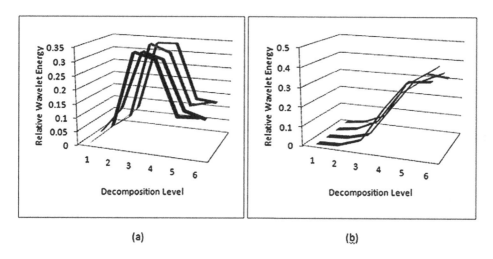

(a)   (b)

Figure 5. (a): RWE distributions for ECG signals of control class (Dataset III) (b): RWE distributions for ECG signals of apnoea class (Dataset III)

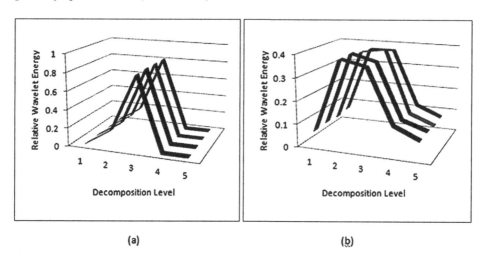

(a)   (b)

Figure 6. (a): RWE distributions for EMG signals from term deliveries (Dataset V) (b): RWE distributions for EMG signals from pre term deliveries (Dataset V)

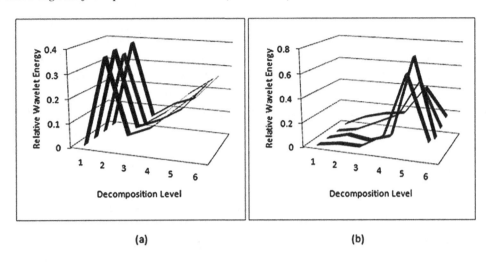

(a)   (b)

Figure 7. (a): RWE distributions for snoring signals of apnoea class (Dataset VII) (b): RWE distributions for snoring signals of hypopnoea class (Dataset VII)

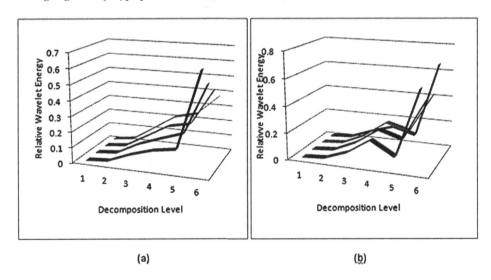

(a)   (b)

It is observed from Figure 4 (a) that RWE distributions for EEG signals of normal activity have almost the same patterns. It is also observed from Figure 4(a) & Figure 4(b) that the RWE distributions for normal and pre ictal have different patterns. Similar observations can be made from all the above shown figures for RWE distributions of different datasets. Thus RWE can discriminate between the biomedical signals of different classes accurately. The discrimination ability of RWE can be proved to be applicable to different other biomedical datasets by performing similarity analysis using the distance metrics.

4.2. Similarity Analysis of RWE distributions

The performance evaluation of RWE using similarity analysis is performed on three different datasets of different biomedical signals. The datasets chosen are Dataset I for EEG signals, Dataset IV for ECG signals, and Database VI for EMG signals. Detailed information of these datasets is given in the Appendix. The DWT decomposition is performed using db4 wavelet at decomposition level 5. Therefore for every biomedical signal the RWE feature set will have a cardinality of 5 features. The RWE values are calculated using the Equations (1) to (3), and then Equations (4) to (9) are used to find the value of d_{rs} using different distance metrics.

4.2.1. ECG Signals

Dataset IV has normal ECG signals and ECG signals of patients suffering from different arrhythmias. Although the distance metrics were calculated for 20 signals from each class, for evaluation purposes RWE feature sets of 5 normal ECG signal (N1 to N5) and 5 arrhythmia (RBBB) ECG signals (A1 to A5) are used. The values of distance metric using different distance measures calculated for different combinations of these RWE sets are shown in Table 1, e.g. the distance between feature set of signal N1 and A1 is represented by combination N1-A1.

The values calculated for different RWE sets of Dataset IV are shown in Table 1. It can be seen from the Table 1 that the distance values for RWE sets of similar classes (highlighted) like N1-N2, N2-N3, A1-A2 etc. are very small. Thus RWE is able to extract features of high similarity from the signals belonging to the same class. Whereas the distance values for RWE sets of different classes like N1-A2, N3-A4 etc. are very large as compared to the values of sets like N1-N2, A1-A2 etc. This confirms that RWE has accurately discriminated the signals belonging to the different classes.

4.2.2. EEG Signals

The evaluation is performed using only EEG signals of two major classes from Dataset I, namely normal class (Set A) and pre-ictal class (Set C). RWE sets of 5 normal EEG signals (N1 to N5) and 5 pre-ictal EEG signals (E1 to E5) are used for evaluation. The results of this evaluation are presented in Table 2.

Table 2 shows the values of distance metrics calculated for RWE feature sets for EEG signals. Although there is a difference in the values of distance metrics for patterns of same classes and different classes, but this discrimination is not as clear as for ECG signals and EMG signals. The justification is that the EEG signals are very chaotic in nature and the random nature of the variation of the EEG signals doesn't give a clear discrimination using statistical measures.

4.2.3. EMG Signals

Dataset VI has EMG signals of three different classes; the evaluation is performed using all three classes for proving the capability of RWE to discriminate between more than two diagnostic classes. RWE patterns from 4 EMG signals from each class are used i.e. Healthy class (H1-H4), Myopathy class (M1-M4) and Neuropathy class (N1-N4). The results of this evaluation are presented in Table 3.

Table 1. Distance values calculated using different metrics for RWE patterns of Dataset IV

Sets	Distance Measure					
	Euclidean	Mahalanobis	City block	Minkowski	Cosine	Correlation
N1-N2	0.0064073	2.087	0.011011	0.0054115	1.6458e-005	1.5629e-005
N1-N3	0.011384	3.4129	0.020394	0.0094437	5.6538e-005	5.0465e-005
N1-N4	0.012927	3.8233	0.026409	0.0096135	0.0001125	0.00010014
N1-N5	0.011096	3.6101	0.022968	0.0082474	0.0001067	0.00011046
N1-A1	0.63296	3.96	0.694	0.63099	0.12063	0.16683
N1-A2	0.64158	2.8107	0.71144	0.63894	0.11547	0.15494
N1-A3	0.64947	3.1816	0.72539	0.64618	0.11321	0.14436
N1-A4	0.65408	3.3506	0.73422	0.65023	0.10796	0.12972
N1-A5	0.65617	3.9751	0.73913	0.65203	0.10411	0.12272
N2-N3	0.0050509	1.4724	0.0094796	0.0040838	1.256e-005	1.0662e-005
N2-N4	0.0073222	2.6415	0.015494	0.0053983	4.5256e-005	3.9897e-005
N2-N5	0.0083263	3.6175	0.018179	0.0058722	4.5931e-005	5.2236e-005
N2-A1	0.62791	3.029	0.69301	0.62575	0.11855	0.16483
N2-A2	0.63657	2.4953	0.71045	0.63369	0.11343	0.15304
N2-A3	0.64447	3.1665	0.72441	0.64093	0.11116	0.1425
N2-A4	0.6491	2.8348	0.73323	0.64498	0.10591	0.12788
N2-A5	0.6512	3.1785	0.73815	0.64679	0.10208	0.1209
N3-N4	0.0040121	1.7923	0.0086581	0.0028725	1.1192e-005	1.082e-005
N3-N5	0.0086966	3.802	0.016196	0.0070746	1.7537e-005	2.4272e-005
N3-A1	0.6243	3.1117	0.69303	0.622	0.11707	0.16378
N3-A2	0.63299	2.9623	0.70924	0.62995	0.11197	0.15206
N3-A3	0.6409	3.3228	0.72319	0.63719	0.10965	0.14153
N3-A4	0.64553	2.7899	0.73202	0.64124	0.10437	0.12689
N3-A5	0.64764	3.3431	0.73694	0.64304	0.10055	0.1199
N4-N5	0.006128	2.9829	0.010782	0.0055134	5.398e-006	6.0792e-006
N4-A1	0.62587	3.433	0.69913	0.62333	0.11546	0.16227
N4-A2	0.63458	3.0349	0.71428	0.63127	0.1104	0.15062
N4-A3	0.64252	2.7798	0.72613	0.63851	0.10805	0.14011
N4-A4	0.64716	2.5864	0.73495	0.64256	0.10277	0.1255
N4-A5	0.64928	3.9181	0.73987	0.64437	0.098961	0.11851
N5-A1	0.63142	3.8495	0.70391	0.62882	0.1154	0.16147
N5-A2	0.64015	3.1478	0.71905	0.63676	0.11036	0.14983
N5-A3	0.6481	3.7229	0.72993	0.644	0.10807	0.13933
N5-A4	0.65276	3.6763	0.73817	0.64806	0.10285	0.12478
N5-A5	0.65488	3.7913	0.74308	0.64986	0.099044	0.11782
A1-A2	0.011896	1.6345	0.019923	0.0098881	0.00024582	0.00028506
A1-A3	0.022368	3.4521	0.036387	0.018578	0.0012536	0.00091564

continued on following page

Table 1. Continued

Sets	Distance Measure					
	Euclidean	**Mahalanobis**	**City block**	**Minkowski**	**Cosine**	**Correlation**
A1-A4	0.029422	3.5931	0.048561	0.024535	0.0028865	0.0026679
A1-A5	0.03261	3.8395	0.052576	0.027351	0.0035088	0.0039918
A2-A3	0.01057	2.1294	0.018369	0.0086981	0.00044171	0.00022985
A2-A4	0.017691	2.3837	0.030543	0.014659	0.0015895	0.0014754
A2-A5	0.020875	3.1716	0.034558	0.017492	0.0020801	0.0025354
A3-A4	0.0072028	1.4184	0.012174	0.0060922	0.00038898	0.00055307
A3-A5	0.010446	3.9098	0.016363	0.0089748	0.00070409	0.0012562
A4-A5	0.0033415	2.7815	0.0051976	0.0028879	6.2828e-005	0.00014389

Table 2. Distance values calculated using different metrics for RWE patterns of Database I

Sets	Distance Measure					
	Euclidean	**Mahalanobis**	**Cityblock**	**Minkowski**	**Cosine**	**Correlation**
N1-N2	0.12566	1.6552	0.2183	0.11021	0.025157	0.069156
N1-N3	0.13634	1.5001	0.23022	0.11738	0.024469	0.049981
N1-N4	0.14059	1.6644	0.24409	0.12314	0.031711	0.088506
N1-N5	0.14497	1.2524	0.24521	0.12524	0.033844	0.095253
N1-E1	0.55727	3.2398	1.0813	0.42855	0.42401	0.9557
N1-E2	0.34041	3.4809	0.68309	0.26354	0.19715	0.63593
N1-E3	0.22542	2.6559	0.41367	0.19199	0.083911	0.25004
N1-E4	0.48437	1.3611	0.98674	0.35992	0.36017	0.93493
N1-E5	0.36641	2.7179	0.7234	0.29278	0.23258	0.80229
N2-N3	0.2604	2.7684	0.44851	0.22713	0.096943	0.22809
N2-N4	0.021754	0.16721	0.03561	0.018362	0.00081803	0.0026509
N2-N5	0.043809	1.2264	0.076651	0.03866	0.0032613	0.010179
N2-E1	0.50584	2.7372	0.94901	0.39953	0.35726	0.84651
N2-E2	0.26173	2.1036	0.55078	0.18818	0.12326	0.44487
N2-E3	0.26335	2.8355	0.46384	0.23373	0.1233	0.42867
N2-E4	0.43992	2.5305	0.85442	0.34254	0.30811	0.85975
N2-E5	0.37876	2.8312	0.6429	0.32948	0.26489	1.0483
N3-N4	0.27542	2.8641	0.47431	0.23998	0.10928	0.26098
N3-N5	0.27944	2.8752	0.47542	0.24156	0.11268	0.26991
N3-E1	0.63489	2.4305	1.1965	0.50047	0.51904	1.0737
N3-E2	0.44511	3.8415	0.79829	0.37314	0.30532	0.8497
N3-E3	0.24724	1.6245	0.52887	0.17533	0.085385	0.18784
N3-E4	0.55785	3.3386	1.1019	0.4303	0.44263	1.0301
N3-E5	0.38748	3.4654	0.8386	0.27239	0.22953	0.63759

continued on following page

Table 2. Continued

Sets	Distance Measure					
	Euclidean	**Mahalanobis**	**Cityblock**	**Minkowski**	**Cosine**	**Correlation**
N4-N5	0.026299	1.0734	0.042413	0.022373	0.0011435	0.003343
N4-E1	0.48732	3.0865	0.91669	0.38465	0.33078	0.78141
N4-E2	0.24395	1.7605	0.51845	0.17401	0.10718	0.38737
N4-E3	0.26217	2.7994	0.45731	0.23135	0.12244	0.4277
N4-E4	0.42317	2.7798	0.8221	0.33048	0.28525	0.79718
N4-E5	0.37548	3.117	0.63637	0.32668	0.26084	1.0369
N5-E1	0.4721	2.6569	0.90636	0.36796	0.30806	0.71605
N5-E2	0.23581	3.2288	0.50812	0.16557	0.098606	0.34366
N5-E3	0.25787	3.3293	0.4481	0.22696	0.11699	0.39738
N5-E4	0.40931	1.9931	0.81177	0.31712	0.26482	0.72754
N5-E5	0.37289	2.9614	0.62715	0.32274	0.25401	0.9803
E1-E2	0.26596	3.0472	0.42318	0.22536	0.083245	0.12021
E1-E3	0.41186	2.5384	0.68552	0.34134	0.23377	0.54833
E1-E4	0.10051	1.7877	0.18557	0.081377	0.0087406	0.0064474
E1-E5	0.39112	3.7222	0.68621	0.31931	0.20901	0.48256
E2-E3	0.26558	2.7166	0.46289	0.23007	0.13226	0.53031
E2-E4	0.20564	3.3993	0.34945	0.16898	0.063737	0.15363
E2-E5	0.29204	3.6923	0.58794	0.21536	0.16712	0.77783
E3-E4	0.32812	2.9581	0.57307	0.2693	0.17299	0.4973
E3-E5	0.17153	3.358	0.31196	0.13681	0.055737	0.23231
E4-E5	0.29413	2.9335	0.51309	0.23971	0.13871	0.40039

Table 3. Distance values calculated using different metrics for RWE patterns of Database VI

Sets	Distance Measure				
	Euclidean	**Mahalanobis**	**Cityblock**	**Minkowski**	**Cosine**
H1-H2	0.030936	1.1329	0.055829	0.024707	0.0017199
H1-H3	0.036651	1.2373	0.062792	0.030153	0.0023881
H1-H4	0.055615	1.5763	0.093958	0.046586	0.0055713
H1-M1	0.24607	2.7599	0.37985	0.20633	0.089189
H1-M2	0.24024	3.4097	0.37833	0.20369	0.081883
H1-M3	0.26193	3.1356	0.42702	0.21797	0.10019
H1-M4	0.25741	2.88	0.45062	0.2103	0.10139
H1-N1	0.25849	2.5562	0.40467	0.21806	0.098945
H1-N2	0.24855	3.9518	0.44891	0.20212	0.10041
H1-N3	0.23744	3.603	0.40567	0.19736	0.084347
H1-N4	0.25125	3.7502	0.41483	0.20863	0.093105

continued on following page

Table 3. Continued

Sets	Distance Measure				
	Euclidean	**Mahalanobis**	**Cityblock**	**Minkowski**	**Cosine**
H2-H3	0.030799	0.76545	0.051535	0.026507	0.0017001
H2-H4	0.052511	1.0782	0.087133	0.044813	0.0049625
H2-M1	0.23383	2.5974	0.38144	0.19513	0.079959
H2-M2	0.22459	3.2155	0.34687	0.18888	0.070667
H2-M3	0.24455	2.7006	0.38263	0.20447	0.086371
H2-M4	0.23965	2.7779	0.40623	0.19831	0.087116
H2-N1	0.25109	3.5208	0.42161	0.21132	0.093035
H2-N2	0.23438	3.7458	0.40452	0.19403	0.088849
H2-N3	0.22103	3.5386	0.37877	0.18309	0.072362
H2-N4	0.23309	2.4522	0.36593	0.19491	0.079211
H3-H4	0.022988	0.44047	0.041247	0.018559	0.00094735
H3-M1	0.26253	2.788	0.41891	0.22025	0.10276
H3-M2	0.25212	2.4456	0.3778	0.21182	0.091483
H3-M3	0.27293	2.8353	0.42761	0.2284	0.10968
H3-M4	0.26851	3.2121	0.45121	0.22314	0.11083
H3-N1	0.28057	4.3787	0.45908	0.2376	0.11803
H3-N2	0.26329	3.6819	0.44951	0.22003	0.11275
H3-N3	0.24833	2.76	0.4097	0.20654	0.093052
H4-M1	0.28415	3.5779	0.45846	0.23828	0.12159
H4-M2	0.27299	3.1162	0.41533	0.22898	0.1087
H4-M3	0.29306	2.8382	0.4452	0.24595	0.12769
H4-M4	0.28819	3.3346	0.4688	0.24105	0.12855
H4-N1	0.30302	4.5215	0.49862	0.25601	0.1389
H4-N2	0.28316	3.8937	0.46709	0.23828	0.13092
H4-N3	0.26845	3.1166	0.43196	0.22392	0.10976
H4-N4	0.28165	3.2956	0.42851	0.23626	0.1191
M1-M2	0.037676	1.5498	0.076453	0.028167	0.00191
M1-M3	0.049568	2.0456	0.090714	0.04072	0.0034159
M1-M4	0.061722	2.9837	0.094479	0.052065	0.0053738
M1-N1	0.052329	2.3466	0.096746	0.042086	0.0038682
M1-N2	0.063476	3.2047	0.13243	0.045901	0.0049568
M1-N3	0.045819	1.9172	0.076843	0.038796	0.0029585
M1-N4	0.055337	2.8665	0.11079	0.043111	0.0043278
M2-M3	0.041312	1.8837	0.084861	0.030436	0.0023578
M2-M4	0.060944	3.2425	0.12234	0.046565	0.0049372
M2-N1	0.08654	3.52	0.16717	0.067539	0.010395
M2-N2	0.080497	4.2598	0.17184	0.057992	0.0078471

continued on following page

Table 3. Continued

Sets	Distance Measure				
	Euclidean	**Mahalanobis**	**Cityblock**	**Minkowski**	**Cosine**
M2-N3	0.031467	1.9808	0.052976	0.025991	0.0011785
M2-N4	0.042466	2.6444	0.069013	0.035791	0.0024554
M3-M4	0.025453	1.4109	0.051558	0.019355	0.00069389
M3-N1	0.093062	3.238	0.16267	0.079681	0.012116
M3-N2	0.060024	3.2946	0.1066	0.048694	0.0038892
M3-N3	0.038328	2.5064	0.077316	0.02808	0.0019395
M3-N4	0.017353	1.0764	0.035	0.012357	0.000397
M4-N1	0.098426	3.5264	0.1724	0.086885	0.013764
M4-N2	0.045697	2.885	0.088979	0.036398	0.0026331
M4-N3	0.049725	3.4414	0.084293	0.042407	0.0035654
M4-N4	0.025606	1.3711	0.053326	0.019311	0.00083794
N1-N2	0.089689	4.0472	0.15878	0.076944	0.010821
N1-N3	0.09714	4.255	0.17359	0.080676	0.013399
N1-N4	0.096742	3.4863	0.18275	0.080636	0.013211
N2-N3	0.060201	3.1428	0.11957	0.043371	0.0047563
N2-N4	0.064933	3.9641	0.10973	0.053896	0.0051844
N3-N4	0.043013	3.566	0.079819	0.034619	0.0025914

Table 3 summarizes the discrimination between the RWE patterns of same class and different classes on the basis of distance metrics. The distance values for RWE patterns of same class are too low as compared to the distance values for the RWE patterns of different classes.

5. DISCUSSIONS

On the basis of the results shown in Table 1, Table 2 and Table 3, it is verified that RWE can accurately extract features for discrimination of different types of biomedical signals into two or more than two classes. Another observation made is that the Mahalanobis distance is the only distance measure which is not able to accurately discriminate between the different classes of RWE patterns. All other measures give similar results. Therefore RWE is a generalized method for extracting features from the wavelet coefficients of the biomedical signals. The reasons for choosing RWE as a feature extraction technique can be summarized as follows:

- **Generalization:** The technique can be generalized for all types of biomedical signals without any modifications.

- **Computationally Efficient:** The technique doesn't require computational load to be executed. Among the various other methods used for extracting features from the wavelet coefficients like PCA, statistical measures, LDA, etc, it is the most computationally efficient method.

- **Low Complexity:** As compared to other methods, the implementation of RWE doesn't require use of complex equations or changing of any parameters to obtain accurate results.

- **Robust:** The technique is robust to the noises present in the biomedical signals and requires no preprocessing techniques for removing the noises which is a generally used step for feature processing of biomedical signals. This is due to the fact that technique is based on capturing the frequency spectrum information in terms of energy features.

- **High Feature Reduction:** The reduction in the feature space using the technique is very high. As seen from the example explained in section 2, the original feature space of 4097 features is reduced to a feature space of only 5 features.

Although methods like PCA, LDA, log of wavelet features, moments of wavelet features etc, have also been implemented successfully for feature extraction, each method suffers from one or another drawback. The reasons for choosing RWE over PCA and LDA have been summarized in section 1. For comparison purposes, the accuracy of two other methods proposed in (Carreno, & Vuskovic, 2007; Andrzejak, 2001) have been compared with the results obtained using RWE on some datasets. The accuracies shown in Table 4 below are calculated by implementing the respective methods on same training and test data. The datasets have been chosen according to different types of biomedical signals (EEG, ECG, EMG and GAIT signals) and classification (binary and multiclass).

It should be noted here that the RWE features used for comparison purposes were further selected using unified wavelet feature optimization algorithm explained in [14]. The RWE technique can also be used for feature extraction of WPT coefficients. In the case of WPT, a tree of nodes is generated using the concept of approximation and decomposition coefficients. For implementing RWE on WPT coefficients, the relative energy is calculated for every node of the wavelet tree. Thus the number of features decreases to the number of nodes in the WPT tree. In both the cases of WPT and DWT, many of the features computed using RWE may be irrelevant and only certain features will contain discriminatory information to distinguish between the different classes under consideration. Many of the computed features may also be correlated and therefore adding one feature to another strongly correlated feature does not necessarily result in a significant change in performance to discriminate between different classes. This problem can be solved by evaluating the performance of the features while searching for the optimal energy features. In practice this can be achieved by including a feature selection to select the optimal energy feature subset while providing better classification results.

Table 4. Comparison of relative wavelet energy with different methods on different datasets

Datasets	RWE Features	Log Features	Moment Features
Dataset I	97.44%	98.98%	51.02%
Dataset IV	98.33%	96.24%	50.5%
Dataset V	99.2%	96.44%	83.71%
Dataset VIII	95%	91%	80%

6. CONCLUSION

DWT used for feature transformation of biomedical signals, produces a large number of coefficients which are shift variant. Therefore a feature extraction technique is required to extract a compressed shift invariant feature vector to perform the classification task easily and accurately. RWE is a computationally efficient feature extraction method which is used to extract features from the wavelet coefficients based on the frequency content of the biomedical signals. The generalization capability of this method is evaluated on various datasets using the pattern based and distance based similarity measures. Experiments show that RWE works better than the other existing methods and correlates well with the subjective assessment. It is also seen that the presented methodology is independent from occurrence of disturbances. From the results, it is concluded that RWE can easily discriminate between different classes of the biomedical datasets. The method eliminates the problem of curse of dimensionality by reducing the number of features to be used for classification without requiring the prior knowledge of the behaviour of the dataset under study.

REFERENCES

Andrzejak, R. G., Lehnertz, K., Mormann, F., Rieke, C., David, P., & Elger, C. E. (2001). Indications of nonlinear deterministic and finite-dimensional structures in time series of brain electrical activity: Dependance on recording region and brain state. *Physical Review*, *64*, 1–8. PMID:11736210

Bradley A. P. (2003).Shift Invariance in Discrete Wavelet Transform. In *Proceeding of 7th Digital Image Computing: Techniques and Applications*, (pp. 29-38). Academic Press.

Carreño, I. R., & Vuskovic, M. (2007). Wavelet Transform Moments for Feature Extraction from Temporal Signals. In *Proceedings of Informatics in Control, Automation and Robotics II* (pp. 235–242). Netherlands: Springer. doi:10.1007/978-1-4020-5626-0_28

Ciaccio, E. J., Dunn, S. M., & Akay, M. (1993). Biosignal pattern recognition and interpretation systems, Methods for feature extraction and selection. *IEEE Engineering in Medicine and Biology Magazine*, *12*(4), 106–113. doi:10.1109/51.248173

Englehart, K., Hudgins, B., & Parker, P. A. (2001). A wavelet-based continuous classification scheme for multifunction myoelectric control. *IEEE Transactions on Bio-Medical Engineering*, *48*(3), 302–311. doi:10.1109/10.914793 PMID:11327498

Englehart, K., Hudgins, B., Parker, P. A., & Stevenson, M. (1999). Classification of the myoelectric signal using time frequency based representations. *Medical Engineering & Physics*, *21*(6-7), 431–438. doi:10.1016/S1350-4533(99)00066-1 PMID:10624739

Garg, G., Singh, V., Gupta, J. R. P., & Mittal, A. P. (2012). Relative Wavelet Energy As A New Feature Extractor for Sleep Classification using EEG Signals. *International Journal of Biomedical Signal Processing*, *2*, 75–79.

Garg, G., Singh, V., Gupta, J. R. P., & Mittal, A. P. (2012). Wrapper Based Wavelet Feature Optimization for EEG signals, *Springer. Biomedical Engineering Letters*, *2*(1), 24–37. doi:10.1007/s13534-012-0044-0

Garg, G., Singh, V., Gupta, J. R. P., Mittal, A. P., & Chandra, S. (2011). Computer Assisted Automatic Sleep Scoring System Using Relative Wavelet Energy Based Neuro Fuzzy Model. *WSEAS Transaction on Biology and Biomedicine*, *8*, 12–24.

Ghosh-Dastidar, S., Adeli, H., & Dadmehr, N. (2007). Mixed band wavelet-chaos-neural network methodology for epilepsy and epileptic seizure detection. *IEEE Transactions on Bio-Medical Engineering*, *54*(9), 1545–1551. doi:10.1109/TBME.2007.891945 PMID:17867346

Guo L., Rivero D., Seoane J. A., & Pazos A. (2009). Classification of EEG signals using relative wavelet energy and artificial neural networks. In *Proceeding of 1st ACM/SIGEVO Summit on Genetic and Eutionary Computation*, (pp. 177-184). ACM.

Hausdorff, J. M. (n.d.). *Gait in Aging and Disease Database*. Available on: http://physionet.org/physiobank/database/gaitdb/ doi:10.13026/C2C889

Heneghan, C. (n.d.). *St. Vincent's University Hospital / University College Dublin Sleep Apnea Database*. Available on: http://physionet.org/physiobank/database/ucddb/ doi:10.13026/C26C7D

Hu, X., Wang, Z., & Ren, X. (2005). Classification of surface EMG signal using relative wavelet packet energy. *Computer Methods and Programs in Biomedicine*, *79*(3), 189–195. doi:10.1016/j.cmpb.2005.04.001 PMID:15913836

Kemp, B., Zwinderman, A. H., Tuk, B., Kamphuisen, H. A. C., & Oberyé, J. J. L. (2000). Analysis of a sleep-dependent neuronal feedback loop: The slow-wave microcontinuity of the EEG. *IEEE Transactions on Bio-Medical Engineering*, *47*(9), 1185–1194. doi:10.1109/10.867928 PMID:11008419

Khadra, L., Al-Fahoum, A. S., & Al-Nashash, H. (1997). Detection of life-threatening cardiac arrhythmias using the wavelet transformation. *Medical & Biological Engineering & Computing*, *35*(6), 626–632. doi:10.1007/BF02510970 PMID:9538538

Khushaba, R. N., Kodagoa, S., Lal, S., & Dissanayake, G. (2011). Driver drowsiness classification using fuzzy wavelet packet based feature extraction algorithm. *IEEE Transactions on Bio-Medical Engineering*, *58*(1), 121–131. doi:10.1109/TBME.2010.2077291 PMID:20858575

Mallat, S. G. (1989). A Theory for Multiresolution Signal Decomposition: The Wavelet Representation. *IEEE Transactions on Pattern Analysis and Machine Intelligence*, *11*(7), 674–693. doi:10.1109/34.192463

Manikandan, M. S., & Dandapat, S. (2007). Wavelet energy based diagnostic distortion measure for ECG. *Biomedical Signal Processing and Control*, *2*(2), 80–96. doi:10.1016/j.bspc.2007.05.001

Moody, G. B., & Mark, R. G. (2001). The impact of the MIT-BIH Arrhythmia Database. *IEEE Engineering in Medicine and Biology*, *20*(3), 45–50. doi:10.1109/51.932724 PMID:11446209

Penzel, T., Moody, G. B., Mark, R. G., Goldberger, A. L., & Peter, J. H. (2000). The Apnea-ECG Database. *Computers in Cardiology*, *27*, 255–258.

Rosso, O. A., Martin, M. T., Figliola, A., Keller, K., & Plastino, A. (2006). EEG analysis using wavelet-based information tools. *Journal of Neuroscience Methods*, *153*(2), 163–182. doi:10.1016/j.jneumeth.2005.10.009 PMID:16675027

Rutkove, S. (n.d.). *Examples of Electromyograms*. Available on: http://physionet.org/physiobank/database/emgdb/ doi:10.13026/C24S3D

Shepard, R. N. (1987). Toward a universal law of generalization for psychological science. *Science*, *237*(4820), 1317–1323. doi:10.1126/science.3629243 PMID:3629243

Subasi, A., & Gursoy, M. I. (2010). EEG Signal classification using PCA, ICA, LDA and support vector machine. *Expert Systems with Applications*, *37*(12), 8659–8666. doi:10.1016/j.eswa.2010.06.065

Tsipourasemail, M. G., & Fotiadis, D. I. (2004). Automatic arrhythmia detection based on time and time–frequency analysis of heart rate variability. *Computer Methods and Programs in Biomedicine*, *74*(2), 95–108. doi:10.1016/S0169-2607(03)00079-8 PMID:15013592

Wang, G., Wang, Z., Chen, W., & Zhuang, J. (2006). Classification of surface EMG signals using optimal wavelet packet method based on Davies-Bouldin criterion. *Medical & Biological Engineering & Computing*, *44*(10), 865–872. doi:10.1007/s11517-006-0100-y PMID:16951931

Žorž, G. F., Kavšek, G., Antolič, Ž. N., & Jager, F. (2008). A comparison of various linear and non-linear signal processing techniques to separate uterine EMG records of term and pre-term delivery groups. *Medical & Biological Engineering & Computing*, *46*(9), 911–922. doi:10.1007/s11517-008-0350-y PMID:18437439

APPENDIX

1. Dataset I

Data described in (Andrzejak et al., 2001) which is publicly available, is used for epilepsy detection. The complete dataset consists of five sets (denoted A–E), each containing 100 single-channel Electro-EncephaloGram (EEG) signals of 23.6 s. Sets A and B have been taken from surface EEG recordings of five healthy volunteers with eyes open and closed, respectively. Signals in two sets have been measured in seizure-free intervals from five patients in the epileptogenic zone (D) and from the hippocampal formation of the opposite hemisphere of the brain (C). Set E contains seizure activity, selected from all recording sites exhibiting ictal activity. EEG signals from Set A and Set C representing normal and pre-ictal brain activities respectively are used for epilepsy detection. Instead of Set E, Set C is used for the application since in practical situation it is not viable to detect epilepsy at the time of seizure from the ictal activity EEG.

2. Dataset II

In this case the sleep EEG Dataset provided by physiobank (Kemp, Zwinderman, Tuk, Kamphuisen, 2000) is used. The recordings were obtained from Caucasian males and females (21 - 35 years old) without any medication; they contain horizontal EOG, Fpz-Cz and Pz-Oz EEG, each sampled at 100 Hz. Sleep scoring is done using Fpz-Cz EEG signals and the hypnogram is used as the target output for training and evaluating the performance of the classifier. The scoring is done in three classes, namely, waking, REM sleep and NREM sleep.

3. Dataset III

Data contributed by Dr. Thomas Penzel of Phillips-University, Marburg, Germany for physionet bank is used for apnea detection using ECG signals (Penzel. Moody, Mark, Goldberg, Peter, 2000). The data consist of 70 records, divided into a *learning set* of 35 record and a *test set* of 35 records. The ECG signals are digitized at 100 samples per second, and the gain is 200 A/D units per mV. ECG signals of 10 sec duration are used for this study.

4. Dataset IV

The ECG data collected from MIT-BIH arrhythmia database (Moody, Mark, 2001) is used for multiclass classification of different types of arrhythmia namely, Normal Sinus Rhythm, Right Bundle Branch Block (RBBB), Left Bundle Branch Block (LBBB), and Atrial Fibrillation (AF). The recordings were digitized at 360 samples per second per channel with 11-bit resolution over a 10 mV range and gain of 200 A/D per unit mV. The ECG segments from MLII signals of records 101, 109, 212, and 202 are used for NSR, LBBB, RBBB and AF respectively.

5. Dataset V

The ElectroHysteroGram (EHG) records (uterine EMG records) included in the Term-Preterm Electro-HysteroGram Database obtained at the University Medical Centre Ljubljana, Department of Obstetrics and Gynecology are used for classification of term pre-term deliveries using EHG signals (Zorz, Kavsek, Antolic, 2008). The records were obtained during regular check-ups either around the 22nd week of gestation or around the 32nd week of gestation. Each record is composed of three channels, recorded from 4 electrodes. The differences in the electrical potentials of the electrodes were recorded, producing 3 channels:

- S1 = E2–E1 (first channel);
- S2 = E2–E3 (second channel);
- S3 = E4–E3 (third channel).

Each signal has been digitized at 20 samples per second per channel and the gain is 13107 A/D units per mV. For classification purposes, signal S3 is used as the EHG signal without any filtering.

6. Dataset VI

The EMG data provided by Department of Neurology, Beth Israel Deaconess Medical Center is used to classify between Healthy, Neuropathic and Myopathic EMG signals from emgdb dataset on physiobank. The data were recorded at 50 KHz and then down sampled to 4 KHz. During the recording process two analog filters were used: a 20 Hz high-pass filter and a 5 KHz low-pass filter.

7. Dataset VII

The physionet UCD Sleep Apnea Database is used for classification of apnea and hypopnoea using sound / snoring signals from ucddb database on physiobank. This database contains 25 full overnight polysomnograms with simultaneous three-channel Holter ECG, from adult subjects with suspected sleep-disordered breathing. The Snoring signals were obtained using a tracheal microphone. The classification is done between apnea (central apnea) and hypopnoea patients using snoring signals. The signals are sampled as 1 Hz with a gain of 2047 A/D per unit mV.

8. Dataset VIII

The classification of healthy, elderly and Parkinson disease subjects is done using the gait signals from the physionet Gait in Aging and Disease Database. Walking stride interval time series included are from 15 subjects: 5 healthy young adults (23 - 29 years old), 5 healthy old adults (71 - 77 years old), and 5 older adults (60 - 77 years old) with Parkinson's disease. The sampling frequency of the signals is 250 Hz. The signals are classified as young, elderly and Parkinson disease gait signals.

Chapter 2
Swarm Intelligence Approaches to Shelf Space Allocation Problem with Linear Profit Function

Tuncay Ozcan
Istanbul University, Turkey

Şakir Esnaf
Istanbul University, Turkey

ABSTRACT

The efficient management of shelf space carries critical importance on both the reduction of operational costs and improvement of financial performance. In this context, which products to display among the available products (assortment decision), how much shelf space to allocate the displayed products (allocation decision) and which shelves to display of each product (location decision) can be defined as main problems of shelf space management. In this paper, allocation problem of shelf space management is examined. To this end, a model which includes linear profit function is used for the shelf space allocation decision. Then, heuristic approaches are developed based on particle swarm optimization and artificial bee colony for this model. Finally, the performance analysis of these approaches is realized with problem instances including different number of products and shelves. Experimental results show that the proposed swarm intelligence approaches are superior to Yang's heuristics for the shelf space allocation model.

INTRODUCTION

As the number of brand lines continually increases, shelf space is scarce and fixed resource for a retailer. This limitation of shelf space causes some decision problems such as which products should be displayed, how much shelf space should be allocated to the displayed products. These decisions have an important role on both the optimization of financial performance of the retailer and improvement of customer

DOI: 10.4018/978-1-5225-0075-9.ch002

service level. On the other hand, marketing research show that most customer decisions are made at the point of purchase and product selection by customers may be influenced through in-store factors such as display locations (Irion et al., 2004). The observed behavior of customers indicates tendency to purchase more visible products. In particular, this would be valid under the assumption that customers do not have the tendency of purchasing a specific product before walking in to the store. However, the research shows that unplanned purchases by customers are rather common and they constitute at least one third of the overall sales of many retailers (Buttle, 1984). This behavior pattern emphasizes that shelf space is a significant resource of retail management for increasing sales.

Retail management aims to develop a retail mix that is able to effect customer purchasing decisions and satisfy their demands (Chen & Lin, 2007). To this end, shelf space management plays an important role in satisfying customer demand and changing their purchasing preferences. A retailer's success depends on its ability to match its changing environment by continually deciding between how much of which products to shelve where and when (Hansen et al., 2010).

Having achieved an effective shelf space management, retailers are able to attract customer interest as well as preventing stock-outs and more importantly reducing operational costs while improving their financial performances (Irion et al., 2004). Retailers are most often confronted by these basic decision problems on the shelf space management:

- **Product Assortment:** Which products to choose in display amongst other potential product ranges?
- **Shelf Space Allocation:** How much shelf space should be allocated for the displayed products?
- **Shelf Location:** Which shelves should be allocated in the store for the displayed products?
- **Inventory:** What would be the best order time and order quantity for the displayed products?

The remainder of this study is organized as follows: the next section provides a detailed review of relevant theoretical literature. In the third part, a mathematical model used for shelf space allocation developed by Yang (2001) is explained. In the fourth part, the developed approaches based on artificial bee colony and particle swarm optimization for solving the model are detailed. The fifth part shows experimental results for different problems to compare the performances of the developed approaches. In the final part, the results of experimental design are discussed.

LITERATURE REVIEW

Many studies can be found in the literature for the last 40 years on decision problems of retail shelf space management such as space allocation, product assortment, store layout and inventory. While some of these studies were focused on single particular problem of shelf space management; others suggested integrated models for the solution of two or more decision problems. The classification of these studies in the literature based on the type of decision problem is shown in Table 1. As could be seen in Table 1, a considerable part of the studies on the shelf space management are on shelf space allocation and product assortment decisions.

Alternatively, these studies can also be basically classified into two groups according to their structures: experimental studies and optimization models.

Table 1. The classification of shelf space management literature

Study	Space Allocation	Product Assortment	Location / Shop Layout	Inventory Decision
Abbott and Palekar (2008)				✓
Anderson and Amato (1974)	✓			
Anderson (1979)	✓			
Bai et al. (2008)	✓		✓	
Bai et al. (2013)	✓		✓	
Bookbinder and Zarour (2001)	✓			
Borin et al. (1994)	✓	✓		
Borin and Farris (1995)	✓	✓		
Brijs et al. (1999)		✓		
Brijs et al. (2000)		✓		
Bultez and Naert (1988)	✓			
Chen and Lin (2007)	✓	✓	✓	
Cl (2012)			✓	
Crstjens and Doyle (1981)	✓			
Dreze et al. (1995)			✓	
Gjjar and Adil (2010)	✓			
Gajjar and Adil (2011)	✓			
Geismar (2015)	✓		✓	
Gn and Badur (2008)		✓		
Hansen and Heinsbroek (1979)	✓	✓		
Hansen et al. (2010)	✓		✓	
Hriga et al. (2007)	✓	✓	✓	✓
Hwang et al. (2005)	✓		✓	✓
Hwang et al. (2009)	✓		✓	
Iion et al. (2004)	✓	✓		
Liang et al. (2007)	✓			
Lim et al. (2002)	✓			
Lim et al. (2004)	✓			
McIntyre and Miller (1999)		✓		
Miller et al. (2010)		✓		
Murray et al. (2010)	✓		✓	
Nfari and Shahrabi (2010)	✓	✓		
Ozcan and Esnaf (2011)	✓			
Ozcan and Esnaf (2013)			✓	
Rmaseshan et al. (2009)	✓	✓		✓
Reyes and Frazier (2005)	✓			
Reyes and Frazier (2007)	✓			
Russell and Urban (2010)	✓	✓	✓	

continued on following page

Table 1. Continued

Study	Space Allocation	Product Assortment	Location / Shop Layout	Inventory Decision
Tai and Huang (2015)	✓		✓	
Uban (1998)	✓	✓		
Yang and Chen (1999)	✓		✓	
Yng (2001)	✓		✓	
Zfryden (1986)	✓			

Experimental Studies

The majority of prior research related to the experimental studies has been conducted in the relationship between shelf space and product sales (Cox, 1964; Cox, 1970; Curhan, 1972). In these studies, space elasticity has been widely used in order to measure this relationship. Space elasticity can be defined as the ratio of relative change in unit sales to relative change in shelf-space (Curhan, 1972). Using this method, Curhan (1972) assumed the space elasticity as a function of variables, which contain merchandising, use and physical characteristics for a product. In this study, Curhan (1972) developed a regression model for estimating space elasticity and this model showed a positive relationship between shelf space and unit sales. Similarly, in another study, Anderson (1979) developed a theoretical model which is based on the relationship between the market share and the shelf space of the product and suggested the market-space elasticity as an experimental measure. Eisend (2014) performed an experimental study about shelf space elasticity at the category or brand level.

The experimental studies based on space elasticity displayed that unit sales increase at a decreasing rate while shelf space is increased. The relationship between shelf space and product sales is characterized with an exponential parameter changing between 0 and 1. The value of the space elasticity may show difference depending on the products, store types and in-store layout. For example; Curhan (1972), Hansen and Heinsborek (1979) and Corstjent and Doyle (1981), Eisend (2014) found the space elasticity as 0.212, 0.15, 0.086, 0.17 respectively. The average value of the space elasticity was about 0.2; that is, a doubling of facings or shelf spaces led to a 20% increase in sales (Dreze et al., 1995). The concept of cross elasticity was introduced in the literature as an improvement to space elasticity. The relative change in the sales of one product depending on the change in the shelf space of another product is defined as cross elasticity. This value is defined in the range from -1 to +1 (Urban, 1998). Positive values are indicated the complementary effects while negative values are showed the substitute effects. In another experimental study, Dreze et al. (1995) investigated on the relationship between shelf location and product sales. This study concluded that the shelf location had more effect on sales than space allocation provided that a threshold value was used to prevent the stock-out case.

Optimization Models

Literature review about optimization models in the shelf space management is presented in three sections. The first section deals with the space elasticity. Second section reviews the literature on the data mining models. Finally, other mathematical modeling approaches are provided. These studies can be detailed as follows.

The Models Based on Space Elasticity

In a considerable amount of studies in the literature, optimization models are proposed by using mathematical forms of the space elasticity and cross elasticity in the demand function. In these studies, the available shelf space, supply and quantity constraints of the retailer are added to the mathematical model. In this context, one of the earliest optimization models was developed by Hansen and Heinsbroek (1979). In this study, Hansen and Heinsbroek (1979) suggested a model which combined the main demand effect with the respective costs and used a polynomial demand function. On the other hand, the cross sales effect between product items inside the store is not considered, but only the relationship between the product demand and the shelf space is taken into account.

Cross elasticity was first used by Corstjens and Doyle (1981). In their study, they developed a non-linear programming model which includes the cross elasticity and space elasticity of the demand function for shelf space allocation. The upper and lower bounds for space allocated to product items are considered in the model. Amongst the studies on shelf space allocation, the most well-known is that of Cortjens and Doyle's (1981) model which is taken as base for multiple models developed to solve shelf space allocation problems (Zufryden, 1986; Bultez & Naert, 1988; Bookbinder & Zarour, 2001; Irion et al., 2004). Zufryden (1986) extended the model of Corstjens and Doyle (1981) by incorporating space elasticity and non-space factors such as price, advertising, and promotion. Bultez and Naert (1988) developed a model that focuses on demand dependence between products. Borin et al. (1994) and Borin and Farris (1995) designed a model for an integrated solution of the shelf space allocation and product assortment problems by taking into account the direct and cross sales elasticity. Irion et al. (2004) developed a non-linear integer programming model which integrated space elasticity, cross elasticity and instore costs for shelf space allocation and used the piecewise linearization technique for their model solution.

Abbott and Palekar (2008) developed a replenishment model for retail stores integrating space and cross elasticities. Urban (1998) and Hariga et al. (2007) designed integrated models based on space elasticity for space allocation, product assortment and inventory decisions. In some studies, the location effect of shelves has been included into the demand function based on space elasticity and cross elasticity (Hwang et al., 2005; Hariga et al., 2007; Hwang et al., 2009). Hwang et al. (2005) proposed a mathematical model for the space allocation and inventory control problem considering shelf location and inventory level effect on demand. Hariga et al. (2007) designed a mixed integer nonlinear programming model for shelf space allocation, inventory replenishment and product assortment under shelf space and backroom storage constraints. Hwang et al. (2009) developed an integer programming model for shelf space design and allocation. Hansen et al. (2010) presented a retail shelf space decision model, which integrates non-linear profit function, the effects of horizontal and vertical location and product cross elasticity. Murray et al. (2010) developed a model for product prices, display facing areas, display orientations and shelf-space location decisions. In this model, products can be stacked and demand is influenced by each product's two-dimensional facing area. Bai et al. (2013) developed an integer nonlinear programming model based on space elasticity, cross elasticity and location effect for two dimensional shelf space allocation problem. Due to NP-Hard nature of the developed model, Bai et el. (2013) presented a multiple neighborhood based on simulated annealing and hyper-heuristic learning mechanism.

The classification of the studies that consider space elasticity, cross elasticity and location effect in literature is presented in Table 2.

The Models Based on Data Mining Algorithms

The space elasticity based models require calculation of large number of parameters. For example; a shelf-space allocation problem with n number of products, $2n+n^2$ parameters must be calculated. It is necessary to conduct a series of experiments to estimate of parameters in the space elasticity based models. These experiments have a high cost in terms of financial and time resources. Another difficulty is that ever-changing market conditions and parameter values need to be updated accordingly (Borin & Farris, 1994). Due to the difficulties of estimating these parameters, the efficiency of these models in large scaled shelf space allocation problems is inferior. Thus, instead of models based on space elasticity and cross elasticity, models based on data mining present important opportunities for shelf space management. Studies based on the use of data mining for shelf space management problems could be summarized as below:

Brijis et al. (1999) proposed an approach based on association rule mining on product selection. Brijis et al. (2000) developed this study later on and included category management constraints and presented the model's application for larger baskets. Chen and Lin (2007) developed a shelf space allocation model for sub categories and product categories on the basis of multi-level association rule mining. Gun and Badur (2008) proposed another model for product selection by improving on Brijis et al.'s (2000) study. However, in this study the capacity of the shelf space and product dimensions were not considered. Nafari and Shahrabi (2010) proposed a new approach based on data mining for shelf space allocation and product assortment which also takes product price into the account. In another study, Cil (2012) developed a new approach to supermarket layout using association rule mining and multidimensional

Table 2. The classification of the studies based on space elasticity

Study	Space Elasticity	Cross Elasticity	Location Effect
Abbott and Palekar (2008)	✓	✓	
Bai et al. (2013)	✓	✓	✓
Bookbinder and Zarour (2001)	✓	✓	
Bultez and Naert (1988)	✓	✓	
Cortsjens and Doyle (1981)	✓	✓	
Hansen and Heinsbroek (1979)	✓		
Hansen et al. (2010)	✓	✓	✓
Hariga et al. (2007)	✓	✓	✓
Hwang et al. (2005)	✓	✓	✓
Hwang et al. (2009)	✓	✓	✓
Irion et al. (2004)	✓	✓	
Murray et al. (2010)	✓		✓
Zufryden (1986)	✓		

scaling. Tsai and Huang (2015) proposed a method using association rules mining and sequential pattern mining algorithms for solving the shelf space allocation problem. The proposed method considers customer transactions and moving records and increases cross-selling opportunities.

The Other Mathematical Modeling Approaches

There is a limited number of approaches on the solution of shelf space management problems that are developed without the use of space elasticity and cross elasticity. In these studies, Anderson and Amato (1974) developed an optimization model in order to optimize the product variety and shelf space allocation simultaneously on the base of profitability of the retailer. In the one of the most well-known studies, Yang (2001) developed a shelf space allocation model as a multi-constraint knapsack problem. Many studies have been carried out by using Yang's (2001) model (Lim et al., 2002; Lim et al., 2004; Liang et al., 2007; Gajjar & Adil, 2011, Castelli & Vanneschi, 2014).

In the other studies, Reyes and Frazier (2005) have focused on shelf space allocation with the help of a demand function that models consumer purchasing behaviors in a retail store. Reyes and Frazier (2007) have dealt with the problem of how much shelf space will be assigned to the products when total shelf space is known for a certain product category and they proposed a nonlinear integer goal programming model that balances customer service factors and profitability.

The Heuristic and Metaheuristic Approaches

Amongst the studies in the literature, majority present a single product or a small product group in their numerical examples rather than large scale real life examples due to the complexity of model structures. For example; a 10 shelf x 100 product shelf space allocation problem contains more than a nonillion (10^{30}) different configurations (Hansen et al., 2010). At this point, heuristic and meta-heuristic algorithms are needed so that developed models could be used in large scaled applications. In this context, many approaches have also been proposed, including simulated annealing (Borin et al., 1994; Borin, & Farris, 1995; Bai et al., 2008; Bai et al., 2013), genetic algorithm (Urban, 1998; Hwang et al., 2005, Liang et al., 2007, Hwang et al., 2009, Castelli & Vanneschi, 2014), variable neighborhood search (Castelli & Vanneschi, 2014), tabu search (Lim et al., 2004), particle swarm optimization (Ozcan & Esnaf, 2011) and artificial bee colony (Ozcan & Esnaf, 2011). Furthermore, Yang (2001) suggested a heuristic approach that is based on earnings per display area. Similarly, in some studies, specialized heuristics are proposed for solution of the shelf space allocation problem (Gajjar & Adil, 2010; Gajjar & Adil, 2011; Hansen et al., 2010).

A classification of heuristic and meta-heuristic approaches in literature on retail shelf space management is given in Table 3.

MATHEMATICAL MODEL

In this paper, Yang's model (2001) is used as the shelf space allocation model. In this model; following notation is used where n denotes the number of product items ($i=1,2,..,n$), m denotes the number of shelves ($k=1,2,..,m$) (Yang, 2001).

Table 3. Heuristic and metaheuristic approaches in the shelf space allocation literature

Proposed Approach	Study
Simulated annealing	Borin et al. (1994), Borin and Farris (1995), Bai et al. (2008), Bai et al. (2013)
Genetic algorithm	Urban (1998), Hwang et al. (2005), Liang et al. (2007), Hwang et al. (2009), Castelli and Vanneschi (2014)
Tabu search	Lim et al. (2004)
Particle swarm optimization	Ozcan and Esnaf (2011)
Artificial bee colony	Ozcan and Esnaf (2011)
Variable neighborhood search	Castelli and Vanneschi (2014)
Specialized heuristics	Yang (2001), Gajjar and Adil (2010), Gajjar and Adil (2011), Hansen et al. (2010)

p_{ik}: The profit per facing of product i displayed on shelf k

x_{ik}: The allocated amount of facings of product i on shelf k

a_i: The length of the facing of product i

L_i: The lower bound for the amount of facings of product i

U_i: The upper bound for the amount of facings of product i

T_k: The length of shelf k

The objective function and the constraints of the model can be expressed as the following, where P is the total profit of the store and N denotes the set of natural numbers.

$$\max\ P = \sum_{i=1}^{n}\sum_{k=1}^{m} p_{ik} x_{ik} \tag{1}$$

subject to

$$\sum_{i=1}^{n} a_i x_{ik} \leq T_k, \quad k = 1, \ldots, m \tag{2}$$

$$L_i \leq \sum_{k=1}^{m} x_{ik} \leq U_i, \quad i = 1, \ldots, n \tag{3}$$

$$x_{ik} \in N \cup \{0\}, \quad i = 1, \ldots, n, \ k = 1, \ldots, m \tag{4}$$

In the model; as can be seen from (1), the objective function value is obtained by multiplying the allocated amount and the unit profit. Equation (2) is a capacity constraint which ensures that the length of one shelf is greater than the total length of the facings allocated to this shelf. Equation (3) are control constraints which guarantee that the upper and lower bounds of each product are satisfied. Equation (4) ensures that the shelf space allocated for each item is a positive integer and zero.

Metaheuristic Approaches for Shelf Space Allocation Problem

Heuristic approaches are required to solve large shelf space allocation problems. At this point, Yang (2001) proposed a heuristic approach for the solution of the shelf space allocation model. The steps of this approach are described as follows:

Step 1: Sort the elements of S=$\{(i,k)|i=1,...,n, k=1,...,m\}$ according to the descending order of weight p_{ik}/a_i .

Step 2: For successive $(i,k)\in$ S, $R_i=L_i$, $x_{ik}=\min(R_i,[T_k/a_i]$, update $R_i=R_i-x_{i,k}$, $T_k=T_k-a_ix_{ik}$, where [] is the symbol of Guass integer.

Step 3: If not EOF of S, then next (i,k) and repeat step 2, else go to Step 4.

Step 4: If $T_k=0$ for all k, go to Step 8, else reset S and go to Step 5.

Step 5: For successive $(i,k)\in$ S, $R_i= U_i-L_i$, $x_{ik}= x_{ik} + \min(R_i,[T_k/a_i])$, update $R_i=R_i-x_{ik}$, $T_k=T_k-a_ix_{ik}$

Step 6: If $T_k>0$ for some k and not EOF of S, then next (i,k) and repeat step 5, else go to Step 7.

Step 7: Compute the total profit using Equation (1) for the final solution $\{x_{ik}\}$.

The proposed heuristic allocates shelf-space item by item according to the descending order of profit for each item per display area considering the given constraints (Castelli & Vanneschi, 2014). Yang (2001) performed some modifications to improve the solution performance of this heuristic algorithm using the neighbor operators such as swap and insert. Readers may refer to the Yang (2001) for a detailed information on the improved Yang's heuristic. In this chapter; metaheuristic algorithms are proposed by using artificial bee colony (ABC) algorithm and particle swarm optimization (PSO). The effectiveness of these proposed approaches are compared with heuristics developed by Yang (2001).

Solution Encoding

Selecting an appropriate coding structure is an important process in applying metaheuristic algorithms to an optimization problem. There are three main types of solution representation which are bit string, permutation and real value encoding. In this study, real value encoding is used. Any element in an individual presents the shelf space allocated to product item i on shelf k (X_{ik}). An individual consists of nxm (the number of product items x the number of shelves) elements. In other words, an individual (solution) is represented by the X=$(x_{11},x_{12},...,x_{1m},x_{21},x_{22},...,x_{2m},...,x_{n1},x_{n2},...,x_{nm})$.

An Artificial Bee Colony Based Approach for Shelf Space Allocation Model

The artificial bee colony is a population based stochastic metahuristic algorithm and was developed by Karaboga (2005). This algorithm is inspired from the intelligent foraging behavior of honey bee swarm. In the ABC algorithm, the colony of artificial bees is consist of three bee groups: employed bees, onlooker bees and scout bees. The first half of the colony consists of the employed bees and the second half includes the onlooker bees. For every food source, there is only one employed bee. In other words, the number of employed bees is equal to the number of food sources (Karaboga, 2005). The position of a food source represents a feasible solution of the optimization problem and the nectar amount of a food source corresponds to the fitness value of the associated solution.

The basic steps of the original ABC algorithm can be summarized as follows (Zhang et al., 2010):

Step 1: Initialize the population of solutions and evaluate them.

Step 2: Produce new solutions for the employed bees, evaluate them and apply the greedy selection process.

Step 3: Calculate the probabilities of the current sources with which they are preferred by the onlookers.

Step 4: Assign onlooker bees to employed bees according to probabilities, produce new solutions and apply the greedy selection process.

Step 5: Stop the exploitation process of the sources abandoned by bees and send the scouts in the search area for discovering new food sources, randomly.

Step 6: Memorize the best food source found so far.

Step 7: If the termination condition is not satisfied, go to step 2, otherwise stop the algorithm.

After initialization, the colony is evaluated and is subjected to repeated cycles of the search processes of the employed bees, the onlooker bees and scout bees.

The ABC based algorithm is developed to solve the shelf space allocation model. In this algorithm; following notation is used where *SN* denotes the size of population and *SN/2* denotes the number of food sources. The number of employed bees or onlooker bees is set equal to the number of food sources (*SN/2*).

The steps of the ABC based approach can be detailed as follows:

Step 1: Generation of the initial solution which satisfies the model constraints and calculation of the fitness values

    I.   Sort the elements of $S=\{(i,k)|i=1,\ldots,n, k=1,\ldots,m\}$ according to the descending order of weight p_{ik}/a_i.

    II.   Generate random facings by using equation (5) for successive $(i,k) \in$ S. In this equation, $\lfloor \cdot \rfloor$ denotes the floor integer.

$$X_{ik}^t = \left\lfloor L_i^t + rand(0,1)(U_i^t - L_i^t) + 0.5 \right\rfloor \qquad (5)$$

The random creation of the initial solution in the original ABC is caused to non-feasible food sources. Because of this case, the generation of the initial solution is arranged as follows.

Sub-Step 1: Satisfaction of the control constraint.

    I.   Calculate $G_i = (\sum_{k=1}^{m} X_{ik}) - U_i$ for each product in each food source. Find product items which are $G_i > 0$.

    II.   For each product item *i*, generate a selection set. $S=\{(i,k)|X_{ik}>0, G_i>0\}$.

    III. Select the element which has minimum p_{ik}. Delete the selected element (i,k) from the selection set.

    IV. For the selected element, update x_{ik} using Equation (6)

$$x_{ik} = x_{ik} - \min(\sum_{k=1}^{m} x_{ik} - U_i, x_{ik}) \qquad (6)$$

    V.   Update G_i, if $G_i > 0$ then repeat steps (iii)-(iv).

VI.   Calculate $H_i = L_i - (\sum_{k=1}^{m} X_{ik})$ for each product in each food source. Find product items which are $H_i > 0$.

VII. For each product item i, select the element which has maximum p_{ik}. For the selected element, update x_{ik} using Equation (7)

$$x_{ik} = x_{ik} + L_i - \sum_{k=1}^{m} x_{ik} \tag{7}$$

The control constraint expressed by Equation (3) is satisfied with the sub-step 1.

Sub-Step 2: Satisfaction of the capacity constraint.

I.   Calculate $E_k = (\sum_{i=1}^{n} X_{ik} a_i) - T_k$ for each shelf in each food source. Find shelves which are $E_k > 0$.

II.   For each shelf i, generate a selection set. S={$(i,k)|X_{ik} > 0, E_k > 0$}.

III. Select the element which has minimum p_{ik}/a_i. Delete the selected element (i,k) from the selection set.

IV. For the selected element, update x_{ik} using Equation (8).

$$x_{ik} = x_{ik} - \min(x_{ik}, \sum_{k=1}^{m} x_{ik} - L_i, \left\lceil \frac{\sum_{i=1}^{n} a_i x_{ik} - T_k}{a_i} \right\rceil) \tag{8}$$

V.   Update E_k for all shelves, if $E_k > 0$ for any shelf then repeat steps (iii)-(iv), otherwise go to next sub-step 3.

The capacity constraint defined by Equation (2) is satisfied with the sub-step 2. After sub-step 2, the feasible food sources which provide all constraints are obtained.

Sub-Step 3: Calculation of the fitness values of the food sources.

Evaluate the fitness values of each food source of the initial solution by using equation (1).

Step 2: Employed bees phase.

I.   Produce a new food source for the employed bee of the food source by the equation (9).

$$S_{it}^{new} = \begin{cases} S_{it} + \varphi_{it}(S_{it} - S_{ik}), & R_i < MR \\ S_{it}, & \text{otherwise} \end{cases} \tag{9}$$

where S_{it} denotes the position of the element i of the food source t, $k \in \{1,2,...,SN\}$ is randomly chosen index that has to be different from t and φ_{it} is uniformly distributed random real number in the range of $[-1,1]$. Ri is uniformly distributed random real number in the range of $[0,1]$ and MR is a control parameter of ABC algorithm in the range of $[0,1]$ which controls the number of parameters to be modified (Karaboga and Akay,2011).

II.   If no element position in each food source is changed, change one random parameter of the food source by the following equation.

$$S_{it}^{new} = S_{it} + \varphi_{it}(S_{it} - S_{ik})$$ (10)

III.   Check the control constraint. Repeat the sub-step 1.
IV.   Check the capacity constraint. Repeat the sub-step 2.
V.   Calculate the new fitness values of each food source by using equation (1).
VI.   Apply the selection process between new and old position based on greedy heuristics. If *new fitness t >fitness t* update *fitness t = new fitness t*, $S_{it} = S_{it}^{new}$ and *failure t = 0* otherwise update *failure t = failure t + 1*. *failure t* is the non-improvement number of the food source *t*.
VII.   Calculate the selection probability (*SPt*) of each food source by the following equation.

$$SP_t = \frac{fitness_t}{\sum\limits_{t=1}^{SN} fitness_t}$$ (11)

Step 3: Onlooker bees phase.
   I.   Select a food source based on the selection probabilities (*SP_t*) for each onlooker bee.
   II.   Produce a new food source for the onlooker bee of the food source by using equation (9).
   III.   Check the control constraint. Repeat the sub-step 1.
   IV.   Check the capacity constraint. Repeat the sub-step 2.
   V.   Calculate the new fitness values of each food source by using equation (1).
   VI.   Apply the selection process between new and old position based on greedy heuristics. If *new fitness t >fitness t* update *fitness t = new fitness t*, $S_{it} = S_{it}^{new}$ and *failure t = 0* otherwise update *failure t = failure t + 1*.
Step 4: Scout bees phase.

Check the iteration number. If *iteration number mod SPP = 0* and max(*failure t*) > limit, replace food source *t* with a new randomly produced solution by using equation (9). Here, limit is a bound value for production of the scout bee and SPP is scout production period.

Step 5: Repeat of Step 2-4 until a stopping criterion is satisfied.

Repeat Step 2-4 until the determined iteration number or the target fitness value is satisfied.

An Particle Swarm Optimization Based Approach for Shelf Space Allocation Model

Particle swarm optimization (PSO) is a population based stochastic swarm intelligence algorithm and was introduced by Eberhart and Kennedy (1995). This algorithm is inspired by social behaviour of bird flocking.

The steps of the basic PSO algorithm can be described as the following (Shi & Eberhart, 1998):

Step 1: Initial solution is generated using position vector and velocity vector.

Step 2: Fitness value is calculated for each particle.

Step 3: The obtained fitness value of each particle is compared with the best value of each particle. If the obtained value is better, the best value of each particle is updated to this value.

Step 4: The obtained fitness value of the population is compared with the fitness value of previous population. If the obtained value is better, the global best value of the population is updated to this value.

Step 5: Position and velocity values of each particle are updated using equation (12)-(14).

Step 6: Step 2-5 is repeated until a sufficiently good fitness value or a maximum number of iterations is reached.

In PSO, following notations and formulations are used for movement in the solution space of particles.

v_i^k: The velocity of particle i in iteration k

x_i^k: The position of particle i in iteration k

p_i^k: The local best of particle i in iteration k

g^k: The global best in iteration k

c_1, c_2: The acceleration coefficients

r_1, r_2: Random numbers U[0,1]

w_k: The inertia weight of iteration k

w_{max}: The maximum inertia force

w_{min}: The minimum inertia force

$iter_{max}$: The maximum iteration number

$$v_i^{k+1} = w_k . v_i^k + c_1 . r_1 . (p_i^k - x_i^k) + c_2 . r_2 . (g^k - x_i^k) \qquad (12)$$

$$x_i^{k+1} = x_i^k + v_i^{k+1} \qquad (13)$$

$$w_k = w_{max} - \left(\frac{w_{max} - w_{min}}{iter_{max}} \right) . k \qquad (14)$$

Generation of the initial solution in the PSO based heuristic is the same with the Step 1 of the ABC based heuristic. Only, food source number must be replaced with particle number. The other steps of the algorithm can be detailed as follows:

Step 2: Updating the position values of the particles and creation of the new swarm
 I.   Update the position of each particle and the velocity of each particle using Equation (12)-(14).
 II.   Generate the new particles and swarms with the updated values.
 III. Repeat the sub-step 1 and sub-step 2 in order to satisfy the model constraints.
Step 3: Calculation of the fitness value, the local best and the global best of the particles
 I.   Calculate the fitness value of the particles using equation (1).
 II.   Determine the local best position (p_i^k) visited so far by each particle.
 III. Determine the global best position (g^k) visited so far by all the particles.
Step 4: Repeat of Step 2-3 until a stopping criterion is satisfied

Repeat Steps 2-3 until the determined iteration number or the target fitness value is satisfied.

EXPERIMENTAL DESIGN AND RESULTS

The developed approaches are coded in MATLAB 2015B. For performance analysis of the developed approaches and Yang's heuristics, three different problem sizes with 2x2x2=8 test cases are considered (see Table 4) and 20 randomly data sets are generated for each problem size. Thus, 480 different instances are solved in total. For each instance, 10 independent replications are carried out. All tests were performed on Intel i7 2.4 Ghz CPU with 8 GB RAM. The values of model parameters and their ranges for the problem instances were generated based on Lim et al. (2004). These values are shown in Table 4.

In the developed approaches, the ABC parameters are given in Table 5. For these parameters, Karaboga and Akay (2011) recommend the range [0.3-0.8] for the control parameter *MR*, the range [0.5xSNxD-SNxD] for the control parameter *Limit* and the range [0.1xSNxD-2xSNxD] for the control parameter *SPP*. The PSO parameters adopted from Shi and Eberhart (1998). These values are given in Table 6. The stopping criterion of the developed approaches is maximum iteration number.

Finally, performance comparison of the developed approaches for three different problem sizes is given in Table 7. At this point, for each problem size, the average performance gap, maximum performance

Table 4. Parameter values and ranges for shelf space allocation problem instances

Parameter	Random Value	Range
(n,m)	-	(10,5), (30,10), (100, 20)
Pi	U[0,10]	-
Ai	U[1,A]	A=50,100 2 values
Li	U[0,L]	L=5, 10 2 values
Δ	U[0,Δ]	Δ=5,10 2 values
Ui	Li+Δi	-
Tk	U[Tl,Tu]	Tl=$\sum$ Li Ai /k, Tu=$\sum$ Ui.Ai /k

Table 5. ABC parameter values

Parameter	Value
Food source number	20
Max. iteration number	1000
MR	0.5
Limit	0.5xSNxD
SPP	0.1xSNxD

Table 6. PSO parameter values

Parameter	Value
Particle number	20
Max. iteration number	1000
c_1, c_2	2
v_i	U[0,4]
w_{min}	0.4
w_{max}	0.9

Table 7. Statistics of the performance gaps of the proposed approaches

Approach	Statistics	(10,5)	(30,10)	(100,20)
ABC Based Heuristic	Average performance gap (%)	0.32	0.25	0.20
PSO Based Heuristic		0.54	0.42	0.31
Yang's Original Heuristic		1.85	4.58	12.25
Yang's Heuristic with Improvements		1.24	2.12	4.37
ABC Based Heuristic	Maximum performance gap (%)	0.46	0.37	0.28
PSO Based Heuristic		1.40	1.09	0.86
Yang's Original Heuristic		13.62	18.14	26.79
Yang's Heuristic with Improvements		4.34	8.23	12.18
ABC Based Heuristic	Standard deviation performance gap (%)	0.05	0.04	0.02
PSO Based Heuristic		0.28	0.22	0.18
Yang's Original Heuristic		3.25	4.26	4.73
Yang's Heuristic with Improvements		1.14	2.04	2.56

gap and the standard deviation of the performance gap of the proposed approaches and Yang's heuristic are calculated. The performance gap is calculated by the difference between the solution obtained with an approach and the best solution of all the approaches (Castelli & Vanneschi, 2014).

These values are showed that the ABC based and PSO based approaches are superior than Yang's heuristics for the shelf space allocation model. In addition, when the size of the problem is increased, the difference between the performances of the proposed approaches increases.

CONCLUSION

Retailers face difficulties such as to promptly responding to the continuously changing customer demands and adopting themselves to the dynamic market competition. Given this situation, one of the basic decision processes of retailing management is that of shelf space allocation aiming to maximize the profitability of the retailer. A retailer's success depends on its ability to match its changing environment by continually deciding between how much of which products to shelve where and when (Hansen *et al.*, 2010).

These decisions, that are covered by shelf space management, become more critical under conditions of rapid increase in number of new products and limited shelf space area (Anderson & Amato, 1974).

In this study, firstly a detailed classification of studies in literature about retail shelf space management has been presented. Later, a shelf space allocation model developed by Yang (2001) is analyzed. Metaheuristic algorithms based on artificial bee colony and particle swarm optimization have been designed for the solution of large-scale real-life problems of this model. Finally, the efficiency of the developed approaches have been presented with problem instances including different product items and shelf. The experimental results showed that the developed ABC and PSO based approaches outperform the Yang's heuristics.

REFERENCES

Abbott, H., & Palekar, U. S. (2008). Retail replenishment models with display-space elastic demand. *European Journal of Operational Research*, *186*(2), 586–607. doi:10.1016/j.ejor.2006.12.067

Anderson, E. E. (1979). An analysis of retail display space: Theory and methods. *The Journal of Business*, *52*(1), 103–118. doi:10.1086/296036

Anderson, E. E., & Amato, H. N. (1974). A mathematical model for simultaneously determining the optimal brand-collection and display-area allocation. *Operations Research*, *22*(1), 13–21. doi:10.1287/opre.22.1.13

Bai, R., Burke, E. K., & Kendall, G. (2008). Heuristic, meta-heuristic and hyper-heuristic approaches for fresh produce inventory control and shelf space allocation. *The Journal of the Operational Research Society*, *59*(10), 1387–1397. doi:10.1057/palgrave.jors.2602463

Bai, R., Van Woensel, T., Kendall, G., & Burke, E. K. (2013). A new model and a hyper-heuristic approach for two-dimensional shelf space allocation. *4OR, 11*(1), 31-55.

Bookbinder, J. H., & Zarour, F. H. (2001). Direct product profitability and retail shelf-space allocation models. *Journal of Business Logistics, 22*(2), 183-208.

Borin, N., & Farris, P. (1995). A sensitivity analysis of retailer shelf management models. *Journal of Retailing*, *71*(2), 153–171. doi:10.1016/0022-4359(95)90005-5

Borin, N., Farris, P. W., & Freeland, J. R. (1994). A model for determining retail product category assortment and shelf space allocation. *Decision Sciences*, *25*(3), 359–384. doi:10.1111/j.1540-5915.1994.tb01848.x

Brijs, T., Goethals, B., Swinnen, G., Vanhoof, K., & Wets, G. (2000, August). A data mining framework for optimal product selection in retail supermarket data: the generalized PROFSET model. In *Proceedings of the sixth ACM SIGKDD international conference on Knowledge discovery and data mining* (pp. 300-304). ACM. doi:10.1145/347090.347156

Brijs, T., Swinnen, G., Vanhoof, K., & Wets, G. (1999, August). Using association rules for product assortment decisions: A case study. In *Proceedings of the fifth ACM SIGKDD international conference on Knowledge discovery and data mining* (pp. 254-260). ACM. doi:10.1145/312129.312241

Bultez, A., & Naert, P. (1988). SH.ARP: Shelf allocation for retailers' profit. *Marketing Science, 7*(3), 211–231. doi:10.1287/mksc.7.3.211

Buttle, F. (1984). Merchandising. *European Journal of Marketing, 18*(6/7), 104–123. doi:10.1108/EUM0000000004795

Castelli, M., & Vanneschi, L. (2014). Genetic algorithm with variable neighborhood search for the optimal allocation of goods in shop shelves. *Operations Research Letters, 42*(5), 355–360. doi:10.1016/j.orl.2014.06.002

Chen, M. C., & Lin, C. P. (2007). A data mining approach to product assortment and shelf space allocation. *Expert Systems with Applications, 32*(4), 976–986. doi:10.1016/j.eswa.2006.02.001

Cil, I. (2012). Consumption universes based supermarket layout through association rule mining and multidimensional scaling. *Expert Systems with Applications, 39*(10), 8611–8625. doi:10.1016/j.eswa.2012.01.192

Corstjens, M., & Doyle, P. (1981). A model for optimizing retail space allocations. *Management Science, 27*(7), 822–833. doi:10.1287/mnsc.27.7.822

Cox, K. (1964). The responsiveness of food sales to shelf space changes in supermarkets. *JMR, Journal of Marketing Research, 1*(2), 63–67. doi:10.2307/3149924

Cox, K. K. (1970). The effect of shelf space upon sales of branded products. *JMR, Journal of Marketing Research, 7*(1), 55–58. doi:10.2307/3149507

Curhan, R. C. (1972). The relationship between shelf space and unit sales in supermarkets. *JMR, Journal of Marketing Research, 9*(4), 406–412. doi:10.2307/3149304

Dreze, X., Hoch, S. J., & Purk, M. E. (1995). Shelf management and space elasticity. *Journal of Retailing, 70*(4), 301–326. doi:10.1016/0022-4359(94)90002-7

Eberhart, R. C., & Kennedy, J. (1995, October). A new optimizer using particle swarm theory. In *Proceedings of the sixth international symposium on micro machine and human science* (Vol. 1, pp. 39-43). doi:10.1109/MHS.1995.494215

Eisend, M. (2014). Shelf space elasticity: A meta-analysis. *Journal of Retailing, 90*(2), 168–181. doi:10.1016/j.jretai.2013.03.003

Gajjar, H. K., & Adil, G. K. (2010). A piecewise linearization for retail shelf space allocation problem and a local search heuristic. *Annals of Operations Research, 179*(1), 149–167. doi:10.1007/s10479-008-0455-6

Gajjar, H. K., & Adil, G. K. (2011). Heuristics for retail shelf space allocation problem with linear profit function. *International Journal of Retail & Distribution Management, 39*(2), 144–155. doi:10.1108/09590551111109094

Geismar, H. N., Dawande, M., Murthi, B. P. S., & Sriskandarajah, C. (2015). Maximizing Revenue Through Two-Dimensional Shelf-Space Allocation. *Production and Operations Management, 24*(7), 1148–1163. doi:10.1111/poms.12316

Gun, A. N., & Badur, B. (2008, July). Assortment planning using data mining algorithms. In *Management of Engineering & Technology, 2008. PICMET 2008. Portland International Conference on* (pp. 2312-2322). IEEE. doi:10.1109/PICMET.2008.4599855

Hansen, J. M., Raut, S., & Swami, S. (2010). Retail shelf allocation: A comparative analysis of heuristic and meta-heuristic approaches. *Journal of Retailing, 86*(1), 94–105. doi:10.1016/j.jretai.2010.01.004

Hansen, P., & Heinsbroek, H. (1979). Product selection and space allocation in supermarkets. *European Journal of Operational Research, 3*(6), 474–484. doi:10.1016/0377-2217(79)90030-4

Hariga, M. A., Al-Ahmari, A., & Mohamed, A. R. A. (2007). A joint optimisation model for inventory replenishment, product assortment, shelf space and display area allocation decisions. *European Journal of Operational Research, 181*(1), 239–251. doi:10.1016/j.ejor.2006.06.025

Hwang, H., Choi, B., & Lee, G. (2009). A genetic algorithm approach to an integrated problem of shelf space design and item allocation. *Computers & Industrial Engineering, 56*(3), 809–820. doi:10.1016/j.cie.2008.09.012

Hwang, H., Choi, B., & Lee, M. J. (2005). A model for shelf space allocation and inventory control considering location and inventory level effects on demand. *International Journal of Production Economics, 97*(2), 185–195. doi:10.1016/j.ijpe.2004.07.003

Irion, J., Al-Khayyal, F., & Lu, J. C. (2004). *A piecewise linearization framework for retail shelf space management models*. Academic Press.

Karaboga, D. (2005). *An idea based on honey bee swarm for numerical optimization* (Vol. 200). Technical report-tr06. Erciyes University, Engineering Faculty, Computer Engineering Department.

Karaboga, D., & Akay, B. (2011). A modified artificial bee colony (ABC) algorithm for constrained optimization problems. *Applied Soft Computing, 11*(3), 3021–3031. doi:10.1016/j.asoc.2010.12.001

Liang, C., Cheung, Y. M., & Wang, Y. (2007, August). A bi-objective model for shelf space allocation using a hybrid genetic algorithm. In *Neural Networks, 2007. IJCNN 2007. International Joint Conference on* (pp. 2460-2465). IEEE. doi:10.1109/IJCNN.2007.4371344

Lim, A., Rodrigues, B., Xiao, F., & Zhang, X. (2002). Adjusted network flow for the shelf-space allocation problem. In *Tools with Artificial Intelligence, 2002. (ICTAI 2002). Proceedings. 14th IEEE International Conference on* (pp. 224-229). IEEE. doi:10.1109/TAI.2002.1180808

Lim, A., Rodrigues, B., & Zhang, X. (2004). Metaheuristics with local search techniques for retail shelf-space optimization. *Management Science, 50*(1), 117–131. doi:10.1287/mnsc.1030.0165

McIntyre, S. H., & Miller, C. M. (1999). The selection and pricing of retail assortments: An empirical approach. *Journal of Retailing, 75*(3), 295–318. doi:10.1016/S0022-4359(99)00010-X

Miller, C. M., Smith, S. A., McIntyre, S. H., & Achabal, D. D. (2010). Optimizing and evaluating retail assortments for infrequently purchased products. *Journal of Retailing, 86*(2), 159–171. doi:10.1016/j.jretai.2010.02.004

Murray, C. C., Talukdar, D., & Gosavi, A. (2010). Joint optimization of product price, display orientation and shelf-space allocation in retail category management. *Journal of Retailing*, *86*(2), 125–136. doi:10.1016/j.jretai.2010.02.008

Nafari, M., & Shahrabi, J. (2010). A temporal data mining approach for shelf-space allocation with consideration of product price. *Expert Systems with Applications*, *37*(6), 4066–4072. doi:10.1016/j. eswa.2009.11.045

Ozcan, T., & Esnaf, S. (2011, June). A heuristic approach based on artificial bee colony algorithm for retail shelf space optimization. In *Evolutionary Computation (CEC), 2011 IEEE Congress on* (pp. 95-101). IEEE. doi:10.1109/CEC.2011.5949604

Ozcan, T., & Esnaf, S. (2013). A discrete constrained optimization using genetic algorithms for a bookstore layout. *International Journal of Computational Intelligence Systems*, *6*(2), 261–278. doi:10.1080 /18756891.2013.768447

Ramaseshan, B., Achuthan, N. R., & Collinson, R. (2009). A retail category management model integrating shelf space and inventory levels. *Asia-Pacific Journal of Operational Research*, *26*(04), 457–478. doi:10.1142/S0217595909002304

Reyes, P. M., & Frazier, G. V. (2005). Initial Shelf Space Considerations at New Grocery Stores: An Allocation Problem With Product Switching and Substitution. *The International Entrepreneurship and Management Journal*, *1*(2), 183–202. doi:10.1007/s11365-005-1128-4

Reyes, P. M., & Frazier, G. V. (2007). Goal programming model for grocery shelf space allocation. *European Journal of Operational Research*, *181*(2), 634–644. doi:10.1016/j.ejor.2006.07.004

Russell, R. A., & Urban, T. L. (2010). The location and allocation of products and product families on retail shelves. *Annals of Operations Research*, *179*(1), 131–147. doi:10.1007/s10479-008-0450-y

Shi, Y., & Eberhart, R. C. (1998, January). Parameter selection in particle swarm optimization. In *Evolutionary programming VII* (pp. 591–600). Springer Berlin Heidelberg. doi:10.1007/BFb0040810

Tsai, C. Y., & Huang, S. H. (2015). A data mining approach to optimise shelf space allocation in consideration of customer purchase and moving behaviours. *International Journal of Production Research*, *53*(3), 850–866. doi:10.1080/00207543.2014.937011

Urban, T. L. (1998). An inventory-theoretic approach to product assortment and shelf-space allocation. *Journal of Retailing*, *74*(1), 15–35. doi:10.1016/S0022-4359(99)80086-4

Yang, M. H. (2001). An efficient algorithm to allocate shelf space. *European Journal of Operational Research*, *131*(1), 107–118. doi:10.1016/S0377-2217(99)00448-8

Yang, M. H., & Chen, W. C. (1999). A study on shelf space allocation and management. *International Journal of Production Economics*, *60*, 309–317. doi:10.1016/S0925-5273(98)00134-0

Zhang, C., Ouyang, D., & Ning, J. (2010). An artificial bee colony approach for clustering. *Expert Systems with Applications*, *37*(7), 4761–4767. doi:10.1016/j.eswa.2009.11.003

Zufryden, F. S. (1986). A dynamic programming approach for product selection and supermarket shelf-space allocation. *The Journal of the Operational Research Society, 37*(4), 413–422. doi:10.1057/jors.1986.69

KEY TERMS AND DEFINITIONS

Artificial Bee Colony: A swarm intelligence algorithm that inspires from the intelligent foraging behavior of honey bee swarm.

Cross Elasticity: The relative change in the sales of one product depending on the change in the shelf space of another product.

Particle Swarm Optimization: A population based swarm intelligence algorithm that inspires by social behavior of bird flocking.

Retailing: The selling of the products or services of producers to customers through different channels of distribution.

Shelf Space Allocation: The decision problem of determining the amount of shelf space to each product according to the capacity and operational constraints for retailers.

Space Elasticity: The relative change in unit sales to relative change in shelf-space.

Swarm Intelligence: A collection of metaheuristic algorithms inspired by the collective behavior of social insects such as ants, bees, birds.

Chapter 3
A Genetic Algorithm–Based Multivariate Grey Model in Housing Demand Forecast in Turkey

Miraç Eren
Atatürk University, Turkey

Ali Kemal Çelik
Atatürk University, Turkey

İbrahim Huseyni
Şırnak University, Turkey

ABSTRACT

Housing sector is commonly considered as a very strong economic industry in terms of both its contribution to creating employment and its impact on other associated sectors. By means of its featured characteristics, the sector also plays an important role on economic growth and development of emerging countries. In this respect, any evidence that determines factors affecting housing investments and future demand behavior may be remarkably valuable for monitoring possible future excess supply and deficits. This chapter attempts to determine factors affecting housing demand in Turkey during a sample period of 2003-2011 using a genetic algorithm-based multivariate grey model. Housing demand forecasts are also employed until the year 2020. Results reveal that several factors including M2 money supply, consumer price index and urbanization rate have an impact on housing demand. According to housing demand forecasts, a significant housing demand increase is expected in Turkey.

INTRODUCTION

Nowadays, housing investments have been emerged as one of the most valuable components of housing sector by substantially increasing capital flows along with financial globalization. Indeed, housing investments assure the development of all other sectors which provide various inputs to the housing

DOI: 10.4018/978-1-5225-0075-9.ch003

sector. Since the multiplier effect of housing expenditures is relatively high, a possible increase in this entry will automatically accelerate the growth of other sectors with an increase on the demand for some products (e.g. home appliances, furniture, home textiles, etc). Housing sector is adopted as a leading sector by courtesy of dominant domestic capital production, higher employment potential and more frequent input-output association with other sectors such as manufacturing (Fitöz, 2008). Moreover, earlier studies (Greenwood & Hercowitz, 1991) highlight the importance of housing market in the economy as a significant indicator of consumer expenditures and social welfare.

The number of studies concerning the housing industry have been significantly increased with the most recent global economic events such as housing price balloons occurred in South Asian countries and the United States. In this respect, a more comprehensive investigation of the Turkish housing market is intensively required. An earlier survey (Kargi, 2013) that examines housing market in Turkey and its impact on the Turkish economic growth for the sample period 2000-2012 suggests that enlargement of housing loans volume and housing expenditures are considerably sensitive to Gross Domestic Product (GDP). Additionally, any housing price balloons are observed during the sample period. Specifically, housing loans enlargement and housing expenditures are in line with GDP until the third quarter of 2008 and they are also significantly sensitive to GDP decline after that period. In this circumstance, price inflation would be unavoidable since a relatively high demand depending on a GDP increase and economic stability and a possible supply contraction due to the behavior of interests. In the light of this progress, the major objective of this chapter is to examine housing demand forecast in Turkey and to determine how the housing supply should behave to avoid both price inflation and inactive housing problem. The study also investigates the share of the housing industry in GDP and the ranking of the housing investments in other fixed assets investments such as manufacturing and transportation. For these purposes, a housing demand forecasting will be employed using the housing demand data of the Housing Development Administration in Turkey during the sample period from the implementation of 2003 Urgent Action Plan declared by the current Turkish government to the present.

Time series analysis has always been a relatively popular topic for researchers both in the past and at present. However, the lack of ability of conventional analysis methods to forecast time series that are not smooth leads researchers to employ various forecasting models that have different mathematical backgrounds including artificial neural networks, fuzzy predictors, evolutionary and genetic algorithms. Statistical and artificial intelligence-based approaches are considered as the two main techniques for time series analysis in the existing literature. Nevertheless, both techniques require higher mathematical background and more complex data. In some circumstances, researchers can make future decisions regarding their predictions with a relatively simpler datasets. In this study, predictions for future periods of basic indicators between the years of 2003-2014 related to the housing demand and its determinants in turkey is aimed to make by using of the Grey Forecasting model (GM), being a branch of grey system theory and a beneficial when dealing with prediction by minimum data according to Ju-Long (1982).

The rest of the chapter is organized as the following. Methodology section gives detailed information about the conceptual background of the forecast models used in the study. Application section presents the corresponding forecast results. The chapter concludes with the discussion of the results and recommendation for future policy making.

METHODOLOGY

In the multivariable grey optimization models, the determination of input variables that may possible influence the output variable is performed. Afterwards, the quantitative analysis related to the initial qualitative analysis is established. Thus, system modeling takes place in four steps:

Step 1: Determination of the input variables affecting output variable

At this stage, factors which may affect the output variable to be estimated are theoretically determined. Afterwards, the data related to output variable and their determinants are collected.

Step 2: Examine any relationship between the factors determined in Step 1 to find causes and effects affecting the development of the system under consideration.

In order to give more precise results of the grey prediction model to be established, there must exist a high correlation between the output sequences and its associated sequences.

Many methods in statistics, such as regression analysis, variance analysis, and principal component analysis, are all commonly used in the analysis of systems. However, these methods have the following shortcomings (Liu & Lin, 2006):

1. A large amount of data is required. Otherwise it would be difficult to draw statistical conclusions with reasonable confidence and reliability.
2. It is required that all samples or populations satisfy certain typical probability distribution(s), that the relation between the main characteristic variable of the system and factor variables is roughly linear. Unfortunately, these requirements are frequently not satisfied in real-life practice.
3. Heavy mathematical computations are often needed.
4. Quantitative conclusions generally may not agree with qualitative analysis results that causes misunderstandings about the systems under consideration.

Therefore, applying statistical methods can hardly achieve many useful conclusions. Grey incidence analysis remedies this defect when applied in the content of systems analysis. It can be applied to cases of various sample sizes and distributions with a relatively small amount of computation. In general, each application of grey incidence analysis does not result in situations of disagreement between quantitative analysis and qualitative analysis (Liu & Lin, 2006).

Grey Incidence Analysis

The basic logic of grey incidence analysis is that the closeness of a relationship is based on the similarity level of the geometric patterns of sequence curves. The more similar the curves are, the higher the degree of incidence between sequences, and vice versa. Assume that X_i is a systems' factor with the kth observation value being $x_i(k), \quad k = 1, 2, ..., n$. Then

$$X_i = \left(x_i(1), x_i(2), ..., x_i(\mathrm{n})\right)$$

is called a behavioral sequence of the factor X_i. If index i is equal to 0, then X_0 represents a sequence of dependent (output) variable. Accordingly, main stages of grey incidence analysis are as follows:

1. Compute the absolute degree of incidence. Let

$$
\begin{aligned}
X_i^0 &= \left(x_i(1) - x_i(1), x_i(2) - x_i(1), x_i(3) - x_i(1), ..., x_i(n) - x_i(1) \right) \\
&= (x_i^0(1), x_i^0(2), ..., x_i^0(n))
\end{aligned}
\tag{1}
$$

Then,

$$
\varepsilon_{0i} = \frac{1 + |s_0| + |s_i|}{1 + |s_0| + |s_i| + |s_i - s_0|}, \quad i = 1, 2, ..., N
\tag{2}
$$

Here,

$$
|s_i| = \left| \sum_{k=2}^{n-1} x_i^0(k) + \frac{1}{2} x_i^0(n) \right|, \quad i = 0, 1, 2, ..., N
\tag{3}
$$

and

$$
|s_i - s_0| = \left| \sum_{k=2}^{n-1} \left[x_i^0(k) - x_0^0(k) \right] + \frac{1}{2} \left[x_i^0(n) - x_0^0(n) \right] \right|, \quad i = 1, 2, ..., N
\tag{4}
$$

Compute the relative degree of incidence. The relevant stages of X_i, $i = 1, 2, ..., n$ are initially computed. From

$$
\begin{aligned}
X_i' &= \left(\frac{x_i(1)}{x_i(1)}, \frac{x_i(2)}{x_i(1)}, \frac{x_i(3)}{x_i(1)}, ..., \frac{x_i(n)}{x_i(1)} \right) \\
&= \left(x_i'(1), x_i'(2), x_i'(3), ..., x_i'(n), \right)
\end{aligned}
\tag{5}
$$

The images of X_i, $i = 1, 2, ..., n$ of zero starting points are given as follows:

$$
\begin{aligned}
X_i^0 &= \left(x_i'(1) - x_i'(1), x_i'(2) - x_i'(1), x_i'(3) - x_i'(1), ..., x_i'(n) - x_i'(1) \right) \\
&= (x_i'^0(1), x_i'^0(2), ..., x_i'^0(n))
\end{aligned}
$$

Then,

$$r_{0i} = \frac{1 + \left|s_0'\right| + \left|s_i'\right|}{1 + \left|s_0'\right| + \left|s_i'\right| + \left|s_i' - s_0'\right|}, \quad i = 1, 2, ..., N \tag{6}$$

Here,

$$\left|s_i'\right| = \left|\sum_{k=2}^{n-1} x_i'^0(k) + \frac{1}{2} x_i'^0(n)\right|, \quad i = 0, 1, 2, ..., N \tag{7}$$

and,

$$\left|s_i' - s_0'\right| = \left|\sum_{k=2}^{n-1} \left[x_i'^0(k) - x_0'^0(k)\right] + \frac{1}{2}\left[x_i'^0(n) - x_0'^0(n)\right]\right|, \quad i = 1, 2, ..., N \tag{8}$$

2. Compute the synthetic degree of incidence.

$$\rho_{0i} = \theta\varepsilon_{0i} + (1 - \theta)r_{0i}, \quad i = 1, 2, 3, ..., N \tag{9}$$

In this equation, the theta is generally preferred as 0.5.

Step 3: Make estimates by determining the most appropriate mathematical models with regard to each independent variable

The basic data for grey modeling are sequence generations. Therefore, the most appropriate grey differential equations should be essentially determined for the estimation of both input and output sequences.

Grey Differential Models

The grey models encompass a group of differential equations adapted to determine the most appropriate parameters for prediction. The accumulated generating operation (AGO) is the most important characteristic of the grey system theory and purposes to reduce the randomness of the data(Tien, 2012). Accordingly, the mathematical operations associated with AGO sequences are as follows:

Let $X_i^{(0)} = \left\{x_i^{(0)}(1), x_i^{(0)}(2), ..., x_i^{(0)}(n)\right\}$ $i = 1, 2, ..., N$ be all of the original input and output sequences. Then, a one-order accumulated generating operation (1-AGO) to assemble the collected time sequences data, and to obtain internal regularity in order to manage the random original data is

$$\begin{aligned}X_i^{(1)} &= \left\{x_i^{(1)}(1), x_i^{(1)}(2), ..., x_i^{(1)}(n)\right\}\\ &= \left\{x_i^{(0)}(1), x_i^{(0)}(1) + x_i^{(0)}(2), ..., x_i^{(0)}(1) + x_i^{(0)}(2) + ... + x_i^{(0)}(n)\right\}\end{aligned} \quad i = 1, 2, ..., N \tag{9}$$

The general form of the grey model GM (k, N), where k stands for the kth order derivative of the AGO sequences of dependent variables, and N stands for N variables (i.e. one dependent variable and N-1 independent variables) in the model is defined as a linear differential equation(Tsaur, 2006):

$$\frac{d^k X_1^{(1)}(t)}{dt^k} + a_1 \frac{d^{k-1} X_1^{(1)}(t)}{dt^{k-1}} + ... + a_{k-1} \frac{dX_1^{(1)}(t)}{dt} + a_k X_1^{(1)}(t)$$
$$= b_2 X_2^{(1)}(t) + b_3 X_3^{(1)}(t) + ... + b_N X_N^{(1)}(t) t = 1, 2, ..., n \qquad (10)$$

where $x_1^{(1)}(t)$ is AGO values of the dependent variable; $x_2^{(1)}(t), x_3^{(1)}(t), ..., x_N^{(1)}(t)$ are AGO values of independent variables. $a_1, a_2, ..., a_k$ are called the grey developmental coefficients, and $b_2, b_3, ..., b_N$ are called the associated coefficients corresponding to associated sequences (Wu & Chen, 2005).

If $k = 1$ and $N = 1$, then the grey model GM(1,1) with one order differential equation and one dependent variable model can be defined as

$$\frac{dX_1^{(1)}(t)}{dt} + aX_1^{(1)}(t) = b \quad t = 1, 2, ..., n \qquad (11)$$

where a and b are referred to as developed and control parameters, respectively (Tsaur, 2006).

GM (1, 1) is useful for sequences almost satisfying the law of exponentiality, and can only be applied to describe monotonic processes of change. For non-monotonic wavelike development sequences, or saturated sigmoid sequences, GM (1, 1) model may not be appropriate. Therefore, it is necessary to check whether original sequences satisfy a quasi-smoothness, and a one-order accumulated generating operation sequences satisfy the law of quasi-exponentiality for predicting and forecasting the output sequence depending on the associated sequences.

Quasi-Smooth Sequence

If an original sequence, $X^{(0)} = \left\{ x^{(0)}(1), x^{(0)}(2), ..., x^{(0)}(n) \right\}$ satisfies that

1. For $k = 2,3,...,$n,

$$\rho(k) = \frac{x^{(0)}(k)}{x^{(1)}(k-1)} \qquad (12)$$

For $k = 3,4,...,$n, $\rho(k) \in \left[0, \varepsilon \right]$ and

2. $\varepsilon < 0.5$,

then $X^{(0)}$ is referred to be a quasi-smooth sequence.

If $X^{(0)}$ is a non-negative quasi-smooth sequence, the sequence, generated by applying accumulating generation once on $X^{(0)}$, satisfies the law of quasi-exponent (Liu & Lin, 2006). So, there is no need to examine whether $X^{(1)}$ sequence is quasi-exponent. If an original sequence $X^{(0)}$ doesn't satisfy the conditions for being quasi-smooth, various grey differential models can be established. Models like GM (2, 1) and Verhulst can be considered as building (Liu & Lin, 2006).

GM (2, 1) and Verhulst Models

According to the grey differential in Equation (8), the equation,

$$\frac{d^2 X_1^{(1)}(t)}{dt^2} + a_1 \frac{d^1 X_1^{(1)}(t)}{dt^1} a_2 X_1^{(1)}(t) = b \quad t = 1, 2, ..., n \tag{13}$$

is called a whitenization equation of a GM (2, 1) grey differential equation. Furthermore, the equation,

$$\frac{d^1 X_1^{(1)}(t)}{dt^1} + a_1 X_1^{(1)}(t) = b \left[X_1^{(1)}(t) \right]^r \quad t = 1, 2, ..., n \tag{14}$$

is called the whitenization equation of the GM (2, 1) power model. If r is equal to 2, then Equation (14) is called the grey Verhulst model.

Step 4: Prediction and forecasting of the dependent variable according to factors relevant by optimizing the system.

Grey prediction models are generally the models based on the GM (1, 1) model. Only the GM (1, 1) model is widely used at present. However, the existing GM (1, 1) model cannot be used for accurate prediction for many actual systems, while the system behaviors are affected more or less by other relative factors and their characteristic values do not completely follow the grey exponential law. Therefore, the prediction model GM (1, N) with n-1 relative factors being acted as the associated series including the predicted series is presented(Tien, 2012).

Grey Prediction Model, GM (1, N)

Assume that $X_1^{(0)} = \left\{ x_1^{(0)}(1), x_1^{(0)}(2), ..., x_1^{(0)}(n) \right\}$ is a sequence of data of a system's characteristics, $X_i^{(0)} = \left\{ x_i^{(0)}(1), x_i^{(0)}(2), ..., x_i^{(0)}(n) \right\}$ $i = 1, 2, ..., N$ sequences of relevant factors, $X_i^{(1)}$ the 1-AGO sequence of $X_i^{(0)}$, $i = 1, 2, ..., N$. If a linear differential equation in the Equation (8) is rearranged according to the first order derivative, then, the resulting

$$\frac{dX_1^{(1)}(t)}{dt} + a_1 X_1^{(1)}(t) = b_2 X_2^{(1)}(t) + b_3 X_3^{(1)}(t) + ... + b_N X_N^{(1)}(t) \quad t = 1, 2, ..., n \tag{15}$$

is called as a whitenization equation of a GM (1, N) grey differential equation. The derivative $\dfrac{dX_1^{(1)}(t)}{dt}$ for the dependent variable is represented as

$$\frac{dX_1^{(1)}(t)}{dt} = \lim_{h \to 0} \frac{X_1^{(1)}(t+h) - X_1^{(1)}(t)}{h}, \quad \forall t \geq 1 \tag{16}$$

Since the collected data is a time-series data, the sampling time interval between period t and $t+1$ is assumed to be one unit. Then, the derivative $\dfrac{dX_1^{(1)}(t)}{dt}$ can be approximated to an inverse accumulated generating operation (IAGO) variable $X_1^{(0)}(t)$ of the original dependent time series data as

$$\frac{dX_1^{(1)}(t)}{dt} \approx \frac{X_1^{(1)}(t+1) - X_1^{(1)}(t)}{1} = X_1^{(0)}(t), \quad \forall t \geq 1 \tag{17}$$

In order to have more steady value for the dependent variable $X_1^{(1)}(t)$, the second part of the Equation (15) is suggested to be expressed as the background value $Z_1^{(1)}(t)$ based on consecutive neighbors of $X_1^{(1)}(t)$. Let be the background value

$$Z_1^{(1)}(t) = \alpha X_1^{(1)}(t) + (1-\alpha)X_1^{(1)}(t-1), \quad t = 2,3,...,n \quad and \quad 0 \leq \alpha \leq 1.$$

If Equation (13) is rearranged, then

$$X_1^{(0)}(t) + a_1 Z_1^{(1)}(t) = b_2 X_2^{(1)}(t) + b_3 X_3^{(1)}(t) + ... + b_N X_N^{(1)}(t) \quad t = 1,2,...,n \tag{18}$$

In the original GM (1, N) model, the α value is usually set to 0.5 and the background value $Z_1^{(1)}(t)$ is named the sequence mean generated based on consecutive neighbors of $X_1^{(1)}(t)$ (Liu & Lin, 2006).

In the grey difference equation, the values of the development coefficient "a_1" and grey input coefficients "$b_1, b_2, ..., b_N$" are generally obtained by the least square method (Tzeng & Chiang, 1998). According to this, if $\hat{a} = \begin{bmatrix} a & b \end{bmatrix}^T$ is sequence of parameters, and

$$Y = \begin{bmatrix} x_1^{(0)}(2) \\ x_1^{(0)}(3) \\ \vdots \\ x_1^{(0)}(n) \end{bmatrix}, \ B = \begin{bmatrix} -z_1^{(1)}(2) & x_2^{(1)}(2) & \cdots & x_N^{(1)}(2) \\ -z_1^{(1)}(3) & x_2^{(1)}(3) & \cdots & x_N^{(1)}(3) \\ \vdots & \vdots & & \vdots \\ -z_1^{(1)}(n) & x_2^{(1)}(n) & \cdots & x_N^{(1)}(n) \end{bmatrix},$$

Then the least square estimate sequence of the grey differential equation satisfies

$$\hat{a} = \left[B^T B \right]^{-1} B^T Y \tag{19}$$

or, let ε be an error sequence. Thus, the objective is

$$\min \quad z = \varepsilon^T \varepsilon = \left[Y - B\hat{a} \right]^T \left[Y - B\hat{a} \right]^T$$
$$= \sum_{t=2}^{n} \left[x_1^{(0)}(t) + a_1 z_1^{(1)}(t) - \sum_{k=2}^{N} b_k x_k^{(1)}(t) \right]^2 \tag{20}$$

The development coefficient "a_1" and grey input coefficients "$b_1, b_2, ..., b_N$ "in the grey differential equation are important parameters in the grey forecasting model (Lu & Yeh, 1997).

After the solution of grey differential equation, the obtained parameter values are placed into the whitening equation of the solution. Thus, the solution of the grey differential equation is given by

$$\hat{X}_1^{(1)}(t+1) = \left[x_1^{(1)}(0) - \frac{1}{\hat{a}_1} \sum_{k=2}^{N} \hat{b}_k X_i^{(1)}(t+1) \right] e^{-\hat{a}t} + \frac{1}{\hat{a}_1} \sum_{k=2}^{N} \hat{b}_k X_i^{(1)}(t+1), \quad where \;\; x_1^{(1)}(0) = x_1^{(0)}(1) \tag{21}$$

when $N = 1$, then the solution of GM (1, 1) is rewritten as

$$\hat{X}_1^{(1)}(t+1) = \left[x_1^{(1)}(0) - \frac{\hat{b}}{\hat{a}} \right] e^{-\hat{a}t} + \frac{\hat{b}}{\hat{a}}, \quad where \qquad x_1^{(1)}(0) = x_1^{(0)}(1). \tag{22}$$

Thus, GM (1, 1) is essentially a kind of exponential prediction model.

After the obtained parameter values are placed into the whitening equation of the solution, the predicted result $\hat{X}_1^{(0)}(t)$ from inverse accumulated generating operation by $\hat{X}_1^{(0)}(t+1) = \hat{X}_1^{(1)}(t+1) - \hat{X}_1^{(1)}(t)$ is obtained and $\hat{X}_1^{(0)}(t)$ is the prediction result for the next observation.

The original grey model uses the least square method to estimate the coefficients. Furthermore, the use of this method requires a large number of data and good behavior of distribution data in order to estimate the parameters. However, when a grey forecasting model uses a limited sampled data (about four sample data), such estimates would result in a significant error. Particularly, for data with obvious fluctuation, the least square method used to estimate the coefficients will have a considerable error (Hsu & Wang, 2009). Therefore, both to improve mentioned shortcomings and to provide a better performance prediction, an improved multivariable grey forecasting models GAGM(1, N) solved by genetic algorithm approach with the global search and rapid convergence is more suitable to estimate the grey differential equation coefficients for both improving the relevant shortcomings and providing a better performance prediction.

Genetic Algorithm Grey Prediction Model, GAGM(1, *N*)

In order to solve the development coefficient "a_1" and grey input coefficients "$b_1, b_2, ..., b_N$ ", Genetic Algorithm (GA) is adopted to the GM(1, N) model. GA uses crossover, reproduction, and mutation, and evaluates the advantage of model on each generation to produce a better target optimal solution (Hsu & Wang, 2009). The performance of each solution to the problem is evaluated by a fitness function, which corresponds to the objective function of the optimization problem. The fitness function in this study is Mean Absolute Percentage Error (MAPE), which is defined as the minimum of in sample-average error, which is

$$min \quad MAPE = \frac{1}{N-1} \sum_{t=2}^{N} \left| \frac{X_1^{(0)}(t) - \hat{X}_1^{(0)}(t)}{X_1^{(0)}(t)} \right| \times 100 \tag{23}$$

subject to

$$\hat{X}_1^{(1)}(t+1) =$$
$$\left[x_1^{(0)}(1) - \frac{1}{\hat{a}_1} \sum_{k=2}^{N} \hat{b}_k X_i^{(1)}(t+1) \right] e^{-\hat{a}_1 t} + \frac{1}{\hat{a}_1} \sum_{k=2}^{N} \hat{b}_k X_i^{(1)}(t+1), \quad \forall t = 1, 2, ..., N-1$$

$$\hat{X}_1^{(0)}(t+1) = \hat{X}_1^{(1)}(t+1) - \hat{X}_1^{(1)}(t) \quad \forall t = 1, 2, ..., N-1$$

APPLICATION

Numerous researchers have presented a wide range of forecasting techniques. Most of these methods are based on statistical studies that involve the use of univariate time series data. However, these models usually lacks to clearly explain the insights of forecast results(Hsu & Wang, 2009). Therefore, this study uses a multivariate grey prediction model GM(1, N) (where, N is the number of independent variables), which incorporates grey relational analysis for housing demand forecasting of Turkey. In the process, the study has initially evaluated the importance of influencing variables, and then ranked the variables using the grey relational method. These important variables has been finally substituted into the multivariate grey prediction model. In the multivariable grey optimization models, the qualitative analysis that was determined of the input variables affecting output variable (that is demand for housing in Turkey) is initially performed. Later, a quantitative analysis is performed with respect to the initial qualitative analysis. Thus, system modeling takes place in four steps:

Step 1: Determination of the input variables affecting output variable

In the literature review based on the demand theory in economics, the demand for housing has been observed to be affected disposable income (Y_t), current housing price (P_t), the rate of interest (r), the expected future house price (P_e), easy access to finance (F_t), economic growth (G_t), taxes or subsidies (TS_t), and demographic factors (*DEM*) like population growth and or household formation (Fitöz, 2008; Kargi, 2013; Öztürk & Fitöz, 2009; Rahman et al., 2012; Thomas Ng et al., 2008). Accordingly, when considering the availability of data, as factors that influence the demand for housing in Turkey: national income per capita, the CPI rate (for housing price index), the Gini coefficient, interest rate, urbanization rate, the M2/ GDP ratio (for the monetary indicator) variables were taken into account. Thus, inputs and output are presented in Figure 1.

Step 2: Examine any relationship between the factors determined in Step 1 to find causes and effects affecting the development of the system under consideration.

In order to give more precise results of the grey prediction model to be established, there must exist a high correlation between the output sequences and its associated sequences theoretically determined. Since many methods in statistics, such as regression analysis, variance analysis, and principal component analysis commonly used in the analysis of systems contains some shortcomings as mentioned earlier for the output sequences and its associated sequences in this study, the use of grey incidence analysis has been found as the most appropriate method.

Grey Incidence Analysis

The basic logic of grey incidence analysis is that the closeness of a relationship is based on the similarity level of the geometric patterns of sequence curves. The more similar the curves are, the higher the degree of incidence between sequences, and vice versa. To determine the closeness of a relationship between the number of residential dwelling the output variable and its associated variables such as M2 Money Supply, Interest Rate, Consumer Price Index (CPI), Gini Coefficient, Urbanization Rate, GDP Per Capita, PPP (Nominal $), the sequence of the number of residential dwellings, and its relevant factors are firstly given in the following Table 1.

Compute the absolute degree of incidence. For the 9 years, from

$$X_i^0 = \left(x_i(1) - x_i(1), x_i(2) - x_i(1), x_i(3) - x_i(1), ..., x_i(9) - x_i(1) \right)$$
$$= (x_i^0(1), x_i^0(2), ..., x_i^0(9))$$

$i = 0, 1, 2, ..., 6$; then

Figure 1. Inputs and output used in the analysis

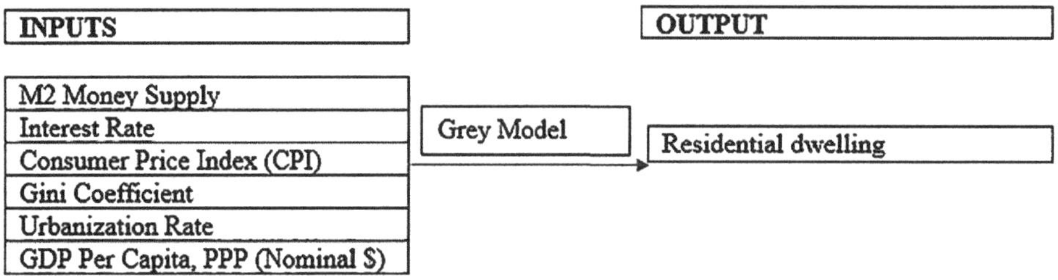

Table 1. Recorded values of variables for the years 2003 to 2011

	2003	2004	2005	2006	2007	2008	2009	2010	2011
X_0 (The number of residential dwelling)	162,781	164,734	249336	294269	325255	356358	468133	428045	554459
X_1 (M2 Money Supply)	82,712,966	108539246	238801378	297734743	344376752	436380326	493060975	587261177	674409579
X_2 (Interest Rate)	29,330	25,190	15,100	21,450	16,800	20,670	12,060	9,530	14,400
X_3 (Consumer Price Index (CPI))	100,020	108,610	117,500	128,780	140,050	154,670	164,350	178,410	189,980
X_4 (GDP Per Capita, PPP (Nominal \$))	8931,250	10301,370	11532,450	13049,320	14040,020	15177,530	14659,950	16193,370	17908,130
X_5 (Urbanization Rate)	66,570	67,180	67,780	68,380	68,980	69,560	70,140	70,720	71,280
X_6 (Gini Coefficient)	0,420	0,400	0,380	0,428	0,406	0,405	0,415	0,402	0,404

$$X_0^0 = \left(x_0^0(1), x_0^0(2), x_0^0(3), ..., x_0^0(9) \right) = \left(0, 1953, 84602, ..., 156890 \right),$$

$$X_1^0 = \left(x_1^0(1), x_1^0(2), x_1^0(3), ..., x_1^0(9) \right) = \left(0, 25826280, 130262100, ..., 164961400 \right),$$

$$X_2^0 = \left(x_2^0(1), x_2^0(2), x_2^0(3), ..., x_2^0(9) \right) = \left(0, -4.140, -10.090, ..., 0.790 \right),$$

$$X_3^0 = \left(x_3^0(1), x_3^0(2), x_3^0(3), ..., x_3^0(9) \right) = \left(0, 8.590, 8.890, ..., 15.520 \right),$$

$$X_4^0 = \left(x_4^0(1), x_4^0(2), x_4^0(3), ..., x_4^0(9) \right) = \left(0, 1370.120, 1231.080, ..., 561.720 \right),$$

$$X_5^0 = \left(x_5^0(1), x_5^0(2), x_5^0(3), ..., x_5^0(9) \right) = \left(0, 0.610, 0.600, ..., 0.540 \right),$$

$$X_6^0 = \left(x_6^0(1), x_6^0(2), x_6^0(3), ..., x_6^0(9) \right) = \left(0, -0.020, 0.048, ..., -0.002 \right).$$

From

$$\left| s_i \right| = \left| \sum_{k=2}^{8} x_i^0(k) + \frac{1}{2} x_i^0(9) \right|,$$

$i = 0, 1, 2, ..., 6$, it follows that

$$\left| s_0 \right| = \left| 1953 + 84602 + \ldots + \frac{1}{2} 156890 \right|,$$

$$\left| s_1 \right| = \left| 25826280 + 130262100 + \ldots + \frac{1}{2} 164961400 \right|,$$

$$\left| s_3 \right| = \left| 8.590 + 8.890 + \ldots + \frac{1}{2} 15.520 \right|,$$

$$\left| s_4 \right| = \left| 1370.120 + 1231.080 + \ldots + \frac{1}{2} 561.720 \right|,$$

$$\left| s_5 \right| = \left| 0.610 + 0.600 + \ldots + \frac{1}{2} 0.540 \right|,$$

$$\left| s_6 \right| = \left| (-0.020) + 0.048 + \ldots + \frac{1}{2} (-0.002) \right|,$$

From

$$\left| s_i - s_0 \right| = \left| \sum_{k=2}^{8} \left[x_i^0(k) - x_0^0(k) \right] + \frac{1}{2} \left[x_i^0(9) - x_0^0(9) \right] \right|,$$

$i = 1, 2, \ldots, 6$, it follows that

$$\left| s_1 - s_0 \right| = 907146100, \quad \left| s_2 - s_0 \right| = 626411.245, \quad \left| s_3 - s_0 \right| = 626262.900,$$

$$\left| s_4 - s_0 \right| = 616260.540, \quad \left| s_5 - s_0 \right| = 626386.930, \quad \left| s_6 - s_0 \right| = 626393.021.$$

From

$$\varepsilon_{0i} = \frac{1 + \left| s_0 \right| + \left| s_i \right|}{1 + \left| s_0 \right| + \left| s_i \right| + \left| s_i - s_0 \right|},$$

$i = 1, 2, \ldots, 6$, it follows that

$$\varepsilon_{01} = 0.500, \quad \varepsilon_{02} = 0.500, \quad \varepsilon_{03} = 0.500, \quad \varepsilon_{04} = 0.508, \quad \varepsilon_{05} = 0.500, \quad \varepsilon_{06} = 0.500.$$

Compute the relative degree of incidence. The initial images of X_i, $i = 1, 2, ..., n$ firstly computed. For the 9 years, from

$$X_i' = \left(\frac{x_i(1)}{x_i(1)}, \frac{x_i(2)}{x_i(1)}, \frac{x_i(3)}{x_i(1)}, ..., \frac{x_i(9)}{x_i(1)} \right)$$
$$= \left(x_i'(1), x_i'(2), x_i'(3), ..., x_i'(9), \right)$$

$i = 0, 1, 2, ..., 6$, it follows that

$$X_1' = \left(x_1'(1), x_1'(2), x_1'(3), ..., x_1'(9) \right) = \left(1, 1.012, 1.514, ..., 1.283 \right),$$

$$X_2' = \left(x_2'(1), x_2'(2), x_2'(3), ..., x_2'(9) \right) = \left(1, 1.312, 2.200, ..., 1.222 \right),$$

$$X_3' = \left(x_3'(1), x_3'(2), x_3'(3), ..., x_3'(9) \right) = \left(1, 1.086, 1.082, ..., 1.075 \right),$$

$$X_4' = \left(x_4'(1), x_4'(2), x_4'(3), ..., x_4'(9) \right) = \left(1, 1.153, 1.120, ..., 1.031 \right),$$

$$X_5' = \left(x_5'(1), x_5'(2), x_5'(3), ..., x_5'(9) \right) = \left(1, 1.009, 1.009, ..., 1.008 \right),$$

$$X_6' = \left(x_6'(1), x_6'(2), x_6'(3), ..., x_6'(9) \right) = \left(1, 0.952, 0.950, ..., 0.995 \right).$$

The images of X_i, $i = 1, 2, ..., 9$ of zero starting points are given as follows:

From
$$X_i'^0 = \left(x_i'(1) - x_i'(1), x_i'(2) - x_i'(1), x_i'(3) - x_i'(1), ..., x_i'(9) - x_i'(1) \right)$$
$$= (x_i'^0(1), x_i'^0(2), ..., x_i'^0(9))$$

$i = 0, 1, 2, ..., 6$, it follows that

$$X_0'^0 = (x_0'^0(1), x_0'^0(2), ..., x_0'^0(9)) = \left(0, 0.012, 0.502, ..., 0.284 \right),$$

$$X_1'^0 = (x_1'^0(1), x_1'^0(2), ..., x_1'^0(9)) = \left(0, 0.312, 0.888, ..., 0.120 \right),$$

$$X_2^{'0} = (x_2^{'0}(1), x_2^{'0}(2),..., x_2^{'0}(9)) = \left(0, -0.141, -0.259, ..., 0.392\right),$$

$$X_3^{'0} = (x_3^{'0}(1), x_3^{'0}(2),..., x_3^{'0}(9)) = \left(0, 0.086, -0.004, ..., -0.014\right),$$

$$X_4^{'0} = (x_4^{'0}(1), x_4^{'0}(2),..., x_4^{'0}(9)) = \left(0, 0.153, -0.034, ..., 0.013\right),$$

$$X_5^{'0} = (x_5^{'0}(1), x_5^{'0}(2),..., x_5^{'0}(9)) = \left(0, 0.009, -0.00023, ..., -0.0002\right),$$

$$X_6^{'0} = (x_6^{'0}(1), x_6^{'0}(2),..., x_6^{'0}(9)) = \left(0, -0.048, -0.002, ..., -0.0000246\right).$$

From

$$\left|s_i^{'}\right| = \left|\sum_{k=2}^{8} x_i^{'0}(k) + \frac{1}{2} x_i^{'0}(9)\right|,$$

$i = 0, 1, 2, ..., 6$, it follows that

$$\left|s_0^{'}\right| = 0.425 \quad \left|s_1^{'}\right| = 0.282 \quad \left|s_2^{'}\right| = 0.276 \quad \left|s_3^{'}\right| = 0.068$$

$$\left|s_4^{'}\right| = 0.038 \quad \left|s_5^{'}\right| = 0.007 \quad \left|s_6^{'}\right| = -0.005$$

From

$$\left|s_i^{'} - s_0^{'}\right| = \left|\sum_{k=2}^{8} \left[x_i^{'0}(k) - x_0^{'0}(k)\right] + \frac{1}{2}\left[x_i^{'0}(9) - x_0^{'0}(9)\right]\right|,$$

$i = 1, 2, ..., 6$, it follows that

$$\left|s_1^{'} - s_0^{'}\right| = 0.923 \quad \left|s_2^{'} - s_0^{'}\right| = 0.919 \quad \left|s_3^{'} - s_0^{'}\right| = 0.357$$

$$\left|s_4^{'} - s_0^{'}\right| = 0.388 \quad \left|s_5^{'} - s_0^{'}\right| = 0.418 \quad \left|s_6^{'} - s_0^{'}\right| = 0.430$$

From

$$r_{0i} = \frac{1 + \left|s_0'\right| + \left|s_i'\right|}{1 + \left|s_0'\right| + \left|s_i'\right| + \left|s_i' - s_0'\right|},$$

$i = 1, 2, ..., 6$, it follows that

$$r_{01} = 0.923, \quad r_{02} = 0.919, \quad r_{03} = 0.807, \quad r_{04} = 0.790, \quad r_{05} = 0.774, \quad r_{06} = 0.769.$$

Compute the synthetic degree of incidence.

From $\rho_{0i} = \theta\varepsilon_{0i} + (1 - \theta)r_{0i,}$

$i = 1, 2, ..., 6$, for $\theta = 0.5$, it follows that

$$\rho_{01} = 0.711, \quad \rho_{02} = 0.710, \quad \rho_{03} = 0.654, \quad \rho_{04} = 0.649, \quad \rho_{05} = 0.637, \quad \rho_{06} = 0.634.$$

Final analysis. From

$$\rho_{01} > \rho_{02} > \rho_{03} > \rho_{04} > \rho_{05} > \rho_{06},$$

it can be suggested that

$$X_1 > X_2 > X_3 > X_4 > X_5 > X_6$$

with X_1 (M2 Money Supply) being the most favorable factor, X_2 (Interest Rate) the second, X_3 (Consumer Price Index (CPI)) the third, X_4 (GDP Per Capita, PPP (Nominal $)) the fourth, X_5 (Urbanization Rate) the fifth, and X_6 (Gini Coefficient) the last. That is to say, the M2 Money Supply have the greatest effect on The number of residential dwellings, Interest Rate have the second greatest effect, and the Gini Coefficient has the least effect.

Step 3: Make estimates by determining the most appropriate mathematical models with regard to each independent variable

The basic data for grey modeling are sequence generations. So, for estimation of both input and output sequences, it needs to determine the most appropriate grey differential equations. GM (1, 1) is useful for sequences almost satisfying the law of exponentiality, and can only be applied to describe monotonic processes of change. For non-monotonic wavelike development sequences, or saturated sigmoid sequences, GM (1, 1) model may not be appropriate. Therefore, for predicting and forecasting the output sequence depending on the associated sequences, it is necessary to check whether original sequences satisfy a quasi-smoothness, and a one-order accumulated generating operation sequences satisfy the law of quasi-exponentiality. But, if $X^{(0)}$ is a non-negative quasi-smooth sequence, the sequence $X^{(1)}$, generated by applying accumulating generation once on $X^{(0)}$ satisfies the law of quasi-exponent(Liu & Lin, 2006). In this sense, there is no need to examine whether $X^{(1)}$ sequence is quasi-exponent. It is sufficient to determine whether it satisfies the quasi-smoothness conditions of both X_0 (The number of residential dwellings) which is output sequence and X_1 (M2 Money Supply), X_2 (Interest Rate), X_3 (Consumer Price Index (CPI)), X_4 (GDP Per Capita, PPP (Nominal $)), X_5 (Urbanization Rate), and X_6 (Gini Coefficient) which are input sequences. Accordingly, let $X_0^{(0)} = \{162781, 164734, ..., 710729\}$ be an original sequence of the number of residential dwellings which is output sequence. If a quasi-smoothness check is checked on $X_0^{(0)}$ from

$$\rho(k) = \frac{x_0^{(0)}(k)}{x_0^{(1)}(k-1)} \quad , k = 1, 2, ..., 11,$$

$$\rho(2) = \frac{x_0^{(0)}(2)}{x_0^{(1)}(1)} = \frac{164734}{162781} = 1.012,$$

$$\rho(3) = \frac{x_0^{(0)}(3)}{x_0^{(1)}(2)} = \frac{249336}{327515} = 0.761,$$

...

$$\rho(11) = \frac{x_0^{(0)}(11)}{x_0^{(1)}(10)} = \frac{710729}{4267938} = 0.2$$

will be obtained. In similar lines, the following table is obtained for associated sequences (see Table 2).

$\rho(4) > 0.5$, for both "The number of residential dwellings" sequence and "M2 Money Supply" sequence. That is, for the case of $k > 3$, the condition of being quasi-smooth is not satisfied. Then, GM (1, 1) model may not be appropriate for these two sequences. So, various grey differential models can be established. Models like GM (2, 1) and Verhulst can be considered as building for these two sequences predict and forecast.

Step 4: Prediction and forecasting of the dependent variable according to factors relevant by optimizing the system.

Grey prediction models are generally the models based on the GM (1, 1) model. However, GM (1, 1) model cannot be used for accurate prediction for many actual systems, while the system behaviors are affected more or less by other relative factors and their characteristic values do not completely follow the grey exponential law. Therefore, the prediction model GM (1, N) with n-1 relative factors being

Table 2. Quasi-smoothness values for each sequence $\rho(k)$

Years	k	The Number of Residential Dwellings	M2 Money Supply	Interest Rate	Consumer Price Index (CPI)	GDP Per Capita, PPP (Nominal $)	Urbanization Rate	Gini Coefficient
2003	1							
2004	2	1.012	1.312	0.859	1.086	1.153	1.009	0.952
2005	3	0.761	1.249	0.277	0.563	0.600	0.507	0.463
2006	4	0.510	0.692	0.308	0.395	0.424	0.339	0.357
2007	5	0.373	0.473	0.184	0.308	0.320	0.256	0.249
2008	6	0.298	0.407	0.192	0.26	0.262	0.205	0.199
2009	7	0.301	0.327	0.094	0.219	0.201	0.172	0.170
2010	8	0.212	0.293	0.068	0.195	0.185	0.148	0.141
2011	9	0.226	0.261	0.096	0.174	0.172	0.13	0.124
2012	10	0.184	0.228	0.060	0.161	0.150	0.116	0.110
2013	11	0.200	0.227	0.061	0.149	0.134	0.105	0.098

acted as the associated series besides the predicted series is presented (Tien, 2012). In this study, grey incidence analysis showed that the number of residential dwellings is affected by M2 Money Supply, Interest Rate, Consumer Price Index (CPI), GDP Per Capita, PPP (Nominal $), Urbanization Rate, and Gini Coefficient, respectively. Then, let $X_1^{(0)}, X_2^{(0)}, X_3^{(0)}, X_4^{(0)}, X_5^{(0)}, X_6^{(0)}$ and $X_7^{(0)}$ be respectively, original sequences of the number of residential dwellings, M2 Money Supply, Interest Rate, Consumer Price Index (CPI), GDP Per Capita, PPP (Nominal $), Urbanization Rate, and Gini Coefficient variables. According to this, firstly, If Genetic Algorithm Grey Prediction Model GAGM (1, 1) is applied for the prediction of the number of residential dwellings variable,

$$min \quad \text{MAPEp} = \frac{1}{9-1} \sum_{t=2}^{N=9} \left| \frac{X_1^{(0)}(t) - \hat{X}_1^{(0)}(t)}{X_1^{(0)}(t)} \right| \times 100 ,$$

subject to

$$\hat{X}_1^{(1)}(t+1) = \left[x_1^{(0)}(0) - \frac{\hat{b}_1}{\hat{a}_1} \right] e^{-\hat{a}_1 t} + \frac{\hat{b}_1}{\hat{a}_1} , \quad \forall t = 1, 2, ..., 9-1 ,$$

$$\hat{X}_1^{(0)}(t+1) = \hat{X}_1^{(1)}(t+1) - \hat{X}_1^{(1)}(t) \quad \forall t = 1, 2, ..., 9-1$$

where *N* is number of years in the period 2003-2011.

If the genetic algorithm used to solve the above-mentioned nonlinear constrained systems of equations (here, Matlab R2012a software program has been used to find the optimum coefficient of model, and set the parameters of GA as follows: population size: 20, crossover rate: 0.8, mutation rate: 0.1, and iteration number: 10000, in the simulation optimization process), values of the whitening equation would be obtained, yielding the following matrix:

$$\hat{a} = \begin{bmatrix} \hat{a}_1 & \hat{b}_1 \end{bmatrix} = \begin{bmatrix} -0.133 & 182097.7 \end{bmatrix}$$

According to this parameter values, it has been found that Mean Absolute Percentage Error of the prediction (MAPEp) is %7.866. If obtained values is substituted in the whitening equation defined as the time response function, predictions and forecasts would be generated. Then,

$$\hat{X}_1^{(1)}(t+1) = \left[x_1^{(0)}(0) - \frac{182097.7}{(-0.133)} \right] e^{-(-0.133)t} + \frac{182097.7}{(-0.133)}, \quad \forall t = 1, 2, ..., 9-1.$$

After the obtained parameter values are placed into the whitening equation of the solution, get the predictedresult $\hat{X}_1^{(0)}(t)$ frominverseaccumulatedgeneratingoperationby $\hat{X}_1^{(0)}(t+1) = \hat{X}_1^{(1)}(t+1) - \hat{X}_1^{(1)}(t)$, $\hat{X}_1^{(0)}(t)$ is prediction result for the next observation. In this context, it is found that Mean Absolute Percentage Error of the forecast (MAPEf) is %7.759. Finally, if all independent variables, from the variable having the greatest effect on "the number of residential dwellings" to the variable having the least effect, are resolved by including a step by step model, parameter results in the following table is obtained (see Table 3).

Table 3. GAGM (1, N) parameter values

	Original Associated Sequences	Parameter Values						
		a1	b1	b2	b3	b4	b5	b6
GAGM(1,1)		-0.133	182097.7					
GAGM(1,2)	$X_2^{(0)}$	30.545	0.029					
GAGM(1,3)	$X_2^{(0)}, X_3^{(0)}$	2.041	0.001	8000.133				
GAGM(1,4)	$X_2^{(0)}, X_3^{(0)}, X_4^{(0)}$	5.783	0.004	7817.506	3834.672			
GAGM(1,5)	$X_2^{(0)}, X_3^{(0)}, X_4^{(0)}, X_5^{(0)}$	5.680	0.002	-110.427	70.580	72.865		
GAGM(1,6)	$X_2^{(0)}, X_3^{(0)}, X_4^{(0)}, X_5^{(0)}, X_6^{(0)}$	5.646	0.002	-4.773	-107.794	73.677	45.469	
GAGM(1,7)	$X_2^{(0)}, X_3^{(0)}, X_4^{(0)}, X_5^{(0)}, X_6^{(0)}, X_7^{(0)}$	8.018	0.003	2147.371	803.174	101.013	134.46	3423.461

After the obtained parameter values are placed into the whitening equation of the solution, the predicted result $\hat{X}_1^{(0)}(t)$ from inverse accumulated generating operation by $\hat{X}_1^{(0)}(t+1) = \hat{X}_1^{(1)}(t+1) - \hat{X}_1^{(1)}(t)$, for the next observation is performed. Thus, MAPEp and MAPEf values are obtained. Lewis (1982) interprets the MAPE results as a convenient way to judge the accuracy of the forecast, where less than 10% is a highly accurate forecast; 10%-20% is a good forecast; 20%-50% is a reasonable forecast; and more than 50% is an inaccurate forecast. Results indicate that there are four different model type that both MAPEp (for the in-sample) values and MAPEf (for out-of-sample) values are less than 10% (namely, having an excellent forecasting power), including GAGM(1,1), GAGM(1,5), GAGM(1,6), and GAGM(1,7). So, the projection results obtained according to these four different models are as depicted in Figure 2 and Figure 3 (see Table 4).

According to these four different models, the number of residential dwellings in 2020 is expected to be between 1,830,087 and 4,023,885. As a result, while the number of residential dwellings in 2013 is 710,729, this number is approximately expected to be around from 2.6 to 5.7 times in 2020.

CONCLUSION

Housing sector is commonly considered as a very strong economic industry in terms of both its contribution to creating employment and its impact on other associated sectors. By means of its featured

Figure 2. GAGM(1,1) and GAGM(1,5) results

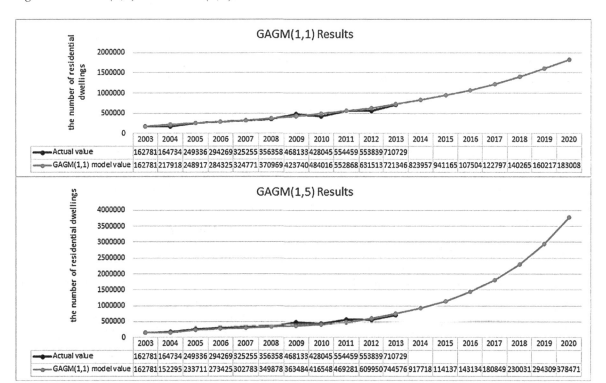

Figure 3. GAGM(1,6) and GAGM(1,7) results

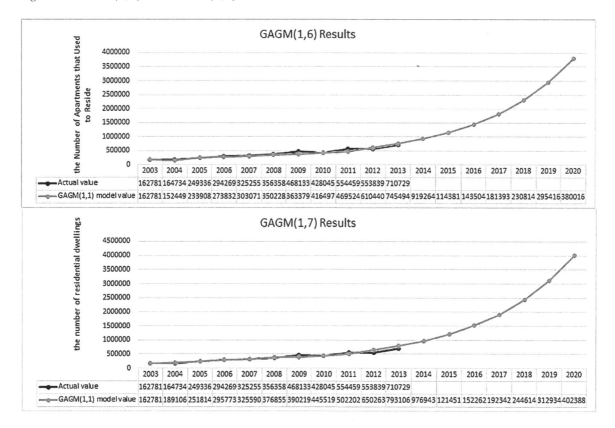

characteristics, the sector also plays an important role on economic growth and development of emerging countries. In this respect, any evidence that determines factors affecting housing investments and future demand behavior may be remarkably valuable for monitoring possible future excess supply and deficits. This chapter attempts to determine factors affecting housing demand in Turkey using a sample period of 2004-2011. Furthermore, a housing demand forecast of Turkey until 2020 was also established using grey model. Results indicate that M2 money supply of housing demand was found to be associated with interest ratios between 0.710 and 0.710. This high relationship is in line with the existing literature, since many earlier studies consider housing demand as housing investments. Particularly, money supply is considered as the most important variable that explains interest rates. In this sense, a close relationship between these two variables can be inherently interpreted as an explanatory indirect contributor of M2 money supply and housing demand.

Housing demand is significantly affected by a change in consumer price index since prices of construction sector has naturally a high input. Forecasting results reveal that this variable is highly associated with housing demand. When houses are considered as normal commodities, a change on income is expected to have an impact on housing. On the other hand, this study finds evidence about a high relationship between GDP and housing demand. In line with the existing literature, urbanization rate and Gini coefficient are also highly associated with housing demand. According to forecasting results, 2012

Table 4. Predicted and Forecasted Values, MAPEp and MAPEf Values

Years	Actual Value	GAGM(1,1)		GAGM(1,2)		GAGM(1,3)		GAGM(1,4)		GAGM(1,5)		GAGM(1,6)		GAGM(1,7)	
		Model value	Absolute Percentage Error	Model value	Absolute Percentage Error	Model value	Absolute Percentage Error	Model value	Absolute Percentage Error	Model value	Absolute Percentage Error	Model value	Absolute Percentage Error	Model value	Absolute Percentage Error
2003	162781	162781.0		162781.0		162781.0		162781.0		162781.0		162781.0		162781.0	
2004	164734	217918.0	32.28	18797.5	88.59	125840.0	23.61	180987.6	9.87	152294.9	7.55	152448.9	7.46	189106.4	14.80
2005	249336	248916.9	0.17	226722.5	9.07	189563.3	23.97	264055.4	5.90	233710.8	6.27	233908.3	6.19	251813.9	0.99
2006	294269	284325.3	3.38	282675.0	3.94	234160.9	20.43	320331.6	8.86	273425.1	7.08	273832.2	6.94	295773.2	0.51
2007	325255	324770.6	0.15	326957.8	0.52	235564.2	27.58	353776.1	8.77	302783.4	6.91	303071.2	6.82	325589.9	0.10
2008	356358	370969.2	4.10	414307.7	16.26	295011.2	17.21	432239.2	21.32	349877.7	1.82	350227.9	1.72	376854.7	5.75
2009	468133	423739.5	9.48	468121.4	0.00	288883.2	38.29	466323.9	0.39	363483.7	22.35	363379.2	22.38	390219.4	16.64
2010	428045	484016.5	13.08	557556.9	30.26	325092.5	24.05	537383.6	25.54	416547.9	2.69	416496.6	2.70	445518.6	4.08
2011	554459	552867.8	0.29	640297.2	15.48	386875.7	30.22	611917.9	10.36	469280.6	15.36	469523.6	15.32	502202.5	9.42
MAPEp (2003-2011)			7.87		20.52		25.67		11.38		8.75		8.69		6.54
2012	553839	631513.3	14.02	973568.2	54.16	532895.4	15.62	8859736.9	36.14	609950.1		610439.9	3.34	650262.6	2.97
2013	710729	721346.0	1.49	1285583.4	78.22	689747.1	4.38	1097724.7	52.18	744576.1		745493.5	3.35	793106.1	9.95
MAPEf (2012-2013)			7.76		66.19		10.00		44.16		3.32		3.34		6.46

and 2013 forecast were closely illustrated with real housing demand in Turkey which positively affects forecasting reliability. Forecast of 2020 expects that housing demand in Turkey would be increased by five times with respect to current demand. With respect to housing demand forecasts, housing sector will greatly contribute to GDP and employment.

REFERENCES

Fitöz, E. (2008). *Türkiye'de konut piyasasının belirleyicileri: Ampirik bir uygulama*. (Unpublished master thesis). Zonguldak Karaelmas University, Graduate School of Social Sciences.

Greenwood, J., & Hercowitz, Z. (1991). The allocation of capital and time over the business cycle. *Journal of Political Economy*, *99*(6), 1188–1214. doi:10.1086/261797

Hsu, L.-C., & Wang, C.-H. (2009). Forecasting integrated circuit output using multivariate grey model and grey relational analysis. *Expert Systems with Applications*, *36*(2), 1403–1409. doi:10.1016/j.eswa.2007.11.015

Ju-Long, D. (1982). Control problems of grey systems. *Systems & Control Letters*, *1*(5), 288–294. doi:10.1016/S0167-6911(82)80025-X

Kargi, B. (2013). Konut piyasası ve ekonomik büyüme ilişkisi: Türkiye üzerine zaman serileri analizi (2000-2012) [in Turkish]. *International Journal of Human Sciences*, *10*(1), 897–892.

Lewis, C. D. (1982). *Industrial and business forecasting methods: A practical guide to exponential smoothing and curve fitting*. London: Butterworth-Heinemann.

Liu, S., & Lin, Y. (2006). *Grey information: theory and practical applications*. London: Springer Science & Business Media.

Lu, H.-C., & Yeh, M.-F. (1997). Some basic features of GM (1, 1) model (II). *Journal of Grey System*, *4*, 307–321.

Öztürk, N., & Fitöz, E. (2009). Türkiye'de konut piyasasının belirleyicileri: Ampirik bir uygulama. *ZKÜ Sosyal Bilimler Dergisi*, *5*(10), 21-46. Available from http://ijmeb.org/index.php/zkesbe/article/view/197

Rahman, M. M., Khanam, R., & Xu, S. (2012). The factors affecting housing price in Hangzhou: An empirical analysis. *International Journal of Economic Perspectives*, *6*(4), 57–66.

Thomas Ng, S., Skitmore, M., & Wong, K. F. (2008). Using genetic algorithms and linear regression analysis for private housing demand forecast. *Building and Environment*, *43*(6), 1171–1184. doi:10.1016/j.buildenv.2007.02.017

Tien, T.-L. (2012). A research on the grey prediction model GM (1, n). *Applied Mathematics and Computation*, *218*(9), 4903–4916. doi:10.1016/j.amc.2011.10.055

Tsaur, R.-C. (2006). Forecasting analysis by fuzzy grey model GM (1, 1). *Journal of the Chinese Institute of Industrial Engineers*, *23*(5), 415–422. doi:10.1080/10170660609509337

Tzeng, G., & Chiang, C. (1998). Applying possibility regression to grey model. *Journal of Grey System*, *1*(1), 19–31.

Wu, W.-Y., & Chen, S.-P. (2005). A prediction method using the grey model GMC (1, n) combined with the grey relational analysis: A case study on Internet access population forecast. *Applied Mathematics and Computation*, *169*(1), 198–217. doi:10.1016/j.amc.2004.10.087

KEY TERMS AND DEFINITIONS

Forecasting: The process of making predictions of the future based on past and present data and analysis of trends.

Genetic Algorithm: A search heuristic that mimics the process of natural selection, and being routinely used to generate useful solutions to optimization and search problems in the field of artificial intelligence.

Grey Differential Models: The grey models encompass a group of differential equations adapted to determine the most appropriate parameters for prediction.

Grey Incidence Analysis: A technique measuring the similarity level of the geometric patterns of sequence curves.

Mean Absolute Percentage Error (MAPE): It is also known as mean absolute percentage deviation (MAPD), is a measure of prediction accuracy of a forecasting method in statistics, for example in trend estimation.

Stepwise Grey Model: In statistics, stepwise grey prediction model includes regression models in which the choice of predictive variables is carried out by an automatic procedure.

The Prediction Methods: A statistical method that is analyzed the properties of the system by using a large number history data.

Chapter 4
Image Mining:
Techniques for Feature Extraction

Tuğrul Taşci
Sakarya University, Turkey

ABSTRACT

In today's World, huge multi-media databases have become evident due to the fact that Internet usage has reached at a very-high level via various types of smart devices. Both willingness to come into prominence commercially and to increase the quality of services in leading areas such as education, health, security and transportation imply querying on those huge multi-media databases. It is clear that description-based querying is almost impossible on such a big unstructured data. Image mining has emerged to that end as a multi-disciplinary field of research which provides example-based querying on image databases. Image mining allows a wide variety of image retrieval and image matching applications intensely required for certain sectors including production, marketing, medicine and web publishing by combining the classical data mining techniques with the implementations of underlying fields such as computer vision, image processing, pattern recognition, machine learning and artificial intelligence.

INTRODUCTION

Aggregation of information is undoubtedly the key element inspring to the progress of humankind. Information has been increasing until today with an accelerated manner. The main reason for that is obviously the tendency of utilizing all kinds of information and experience regarding human life in order to deepen knowledge in the same areas or to explore novel ideas in various different areas. For instance, observing the notably silent flight of owl by the virtue of its wings nature can allow engineers to apply such a structure in aircraft design to enable more comfortable and noise-free landing and takeoffs. Also, storage and transfer of information to the new generations gained along the ages through the techonological equipments and methods of each particular age may be evaluated as the complementary factor for the formation of ever-increasing information process.

The rapid advancements of technology today provide an opportunity to acquire massive amount of data in diverse fields including natural and applied sciences, social and human sciences, life and health

DOI: 10.4018/978-1-5225-0075-9.ch004

sciences and various other fields related to daily life experiences. The becoming of internet, mobile connectivity and highly-portable digital image and video storage devices as an integral part of our daily life leads to permanently growing data in almost all fields of daily life. In this context, the convenient analysis of this data in order to obtain useful information for the purpose of facilitating human life may be fairly considered as a usual result of humankind evolution.

Data mining is a method of knowledge discovery with a rather broad definition. To become more specific, data mining can be defined as a process of extraction of understandable and purposive information and associations from massive amount of data in order to utilize in diversified applications. According to Zaki & Meira (2014), the emergence of data mining as a research field has allowed the analysis of all type of patterns and models to be performed with the applications ranging from scientific discovery to business intelligence and analytics. In their study, Linoff & Berry (2011) define data mining as a process of huge data investigation in order to discover significant patterns and rules. Data mining is quotted as one of the most important phases of a knowledge discovery process comprising data cleaning, data integration, data selection and transformation, data mining, pattern evaluation and knowledge representation in the work of Jiawei et.al. (2012).

In today's world, data related to different areas including scientific research, education, economy and demography is stored digitally in databases, especially in the developed countries. Obtaining useful information from those huge databases is a quite complicated problem and implies efficient methods to be applied. Within this context, data mining is a well-established field of research involving various powerful methods and offers availed solutions. However, images and videos accepted as non-standard forms of data have been intensively in use especially in the past decade. Multimedia databases have dramatically grown in association with widely available Internet based services, intensive use of digital recording mobile devices and the large size of images and videos because of high definition file formats. Data mining with traditional methods has become inadequate in handling multi-media data and extracting information efficiently. Thus, a new research field has been formed namely image mining which derives methods and techniques of data mining and other related fields such as image processing, pattern recognition and machine learning in order to discover information robustly from non-standard data sources containing high portion of data produced more particularly in recent past.

Joseph & Wilson (2014) define image mining as the process of information discovery on the image databases. The ultimate purpose in an image mining application is the retrieval of similar images and linking associated data semantically with an example image which can be visually queried from database. For instance, the information of whether the people living in different regions have similar diseases can be obtained by analyzing regional weather satellite images through an image mining system. Ever-increasing information obtained from images and videos implies existence of efficient methods allowing such a visual query to be performed. Hence in their work, Singhai & Shandilya (2010) highlight the claim that tendency to the multi-media retrieval sytems has been increasing collateraly with the rapidly increasing demand of accurate and fast content-based querying.

Image mining is investigated in this chapter by briefly revising the studies referring to the field's place in the literature and revealing the relationship between image and traditional data mining. A generic image mining process algorithm is given with the phases containing the principle operations. The existing applications of image mining are summarized by emphasizing their prominent attributes. A descriptive overview of content-based image retrieval systems is also introduced in terms of functional requirements and the facilities and benefits provided in case of using such a system. The main focus of this chapter is providing a comprehensive review of image features and extraction methods. Commonly used image clustering and indexing methods are also covered shortly.

IMAGE MINING

Through the rapid developments in information techonologies in the recent years, it becomes more practical to obtain data from an arbitrary system using suitable sensors including mechanic, optic, acoustic, haptic, environmental or navigational devices. In the case that such huge data sources are available, it can not be considered as an extraordinary activity to search the way of developing methods allowing to extract useful information based on this data. Image mining which aims to extract information from visual data is the exact achievement reached on the way of such efforts. In this context, image mining methods have been frequently applied recently in order to provide solutions to real-world problems requiring analysis of image data such as machine based surveillance and control. Image mining, is a field of research focusing on extracting relationships and patterns from images that are not explicitly storred in database. In the work of Zhang et.al. (2001), the authors claim that image mining methods can be used to provide solution to the issue of existence of efficient methods extracting meaningful information from images that are not adequate. Hema & Annasaro (2013) indicate that image mining is a novel field of research dealing with the analysis and interpretation of images in a more straightforward manner. Missaoui & Palenichka (2005) state that image mining is a multidisciplinary field of research based on data mining, artificial intelligence, machine learning, image retrieval, image processing, databases, computer vision and pattern recognition. Dey et.al. (2015) on the other hand, highlight the idea that the capability of image mining methods in detecting useful image patterns opens new horizons in various reseach fields.

There is a sequence of challenging issues in the process of image mining. Non-standard and unstructured data, scalability, data inaccessibility and privacy particularly in some areas such as medical, and the lack of robust general methods can be stated as the most remarkable challenges. However, there are some image mining appications intended to overcome those challlanges in specific areas.

Although the origins of image mining come from traditional data mining there exist some differences in application between those. For example, specification of the products bought from a retailer market by a particular customer group is a desirable case since this information can be used to associate different products in the same basket which allows market managers to organize sale promotions. Such a specifiacation can be performed by querying sales database which explicitly contains each product sold. On the other hand, because of manuel labelling or categorization of images is not a practical way in most cases due to the enourmous size of non-standard image data it is not reasonable to execute a similar query. Accordingly, a system having certain fuctions to extract information from images either in basic or abstact levels is required in an image mining system. Such a system can tangibly be defined as content-based image retrieval (CBIR) system. One of the earliest works in the field literature, Ordonez & Omiecinski (1998), reveal the idea that CBIR is a system using the properties and methods of data mining, image analysis and databases efficiently.

A recent study, Gajjar & Chauhan (2012), state that image mining has diverse applications including natural scene recognition, weather forecasting, criminal investigation, image segmentation and image watermarking. Conci & Castro (2002) which is an earlier work, project the application areas of image mining in a way to involve scientific and biomedical imaging, geographic information systems, stock photo databases; fabric and fashion design, art galleries and museum management, architectural and engineering design and WWW search engines. Ordonez & Omiecinski (1998) also mention about image mining applications such as military reconnaissance, the management of earth's resources and medical imaging. Biological data management and mining, medical imagery, decision tree based image processing and navigational help for blind people are some of the other applications indicated in Gholap et.al. (2005), Caperna et.al. (2009) ve Lu & Yang (2009).

The aim of image mining, as indicated in Tahoun et.al. (2005), is to make query from image database depending on features and similarities and to retrieve the corresponding images. From this point of view, it can readily be stated that a generic image mining algoritm has pre-processing, feature extraction, storage, data mining, evaluation and interpretation and knowledge representation steps. In the pre-processing step, the images are cleaned from noise, enhanced in terms of appearance and contrast and prepared to feature extraction step by performing a sequence of transformations associate with the proposed feature extraction methods. In the feature extraction step, image features are extracted through image analysis methods at spatial, logical or sematic levels based on the application area and proposed methods. The next step is related to image clustering. Images are categorized by implementation of some particular clustering methods in which the image features are compared with reference to some similarity criteria. Another important function belonging to storage step is image indexing which aims providing fast access to the requested images. Images are indexed by using some indexing methods mostly based on tree structure as well as some dimension reduction techniques. The most significant step of image mining step is probably the data mining step which aims associating the images with the existing data. Data mining step contains building association rules. An additional step called evaluation and interpretation refers to obtaining robust association rules that are valid almost every case. The final step of image mining algorithm is the knowledge representation. In this step, the requested information obtained through robust association rules are displayed and presented in a preferred format. A shematic diagram of generic image mining algoritm is given by Figure 1.

Figure 1. Image mining algorithm schematic diagram

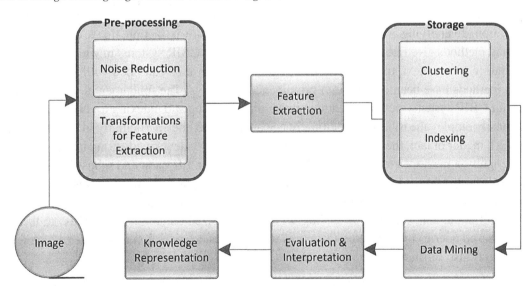

CONTENT BASED IMAGE RETRIEVAL

The requirement of extracting hidden information which is the main difference of image mining from traditional data mining leads to the emergence of content based image retrieval systems. CBIR system is deemed as the skeleton of image mining. The most prominent attribute of CBIR systems is their effective and efficient use of image databases. CBIR systems also focus on developing successful searching and browsing techniques. In their work, Kannan et.al. (2010), the authors claim that CBIR systems are located on the intersection of databases, information retrieval, ve computer vision fields and the attention directed to CBIR systems has been increasing in the recent years. When the applications in the field are examined, it can be stated that there exist two type of methods in which the first type of methods are based on manual attributing images and storing them in relational databases while the methods in the latter group deal with automatic extraction of image features and clustering. There are both advantages and disadvantages of each type of methods. The first group of methods require too much manual operations and the cases of incompatible labelling and definition inadequacy can be met to a large extent due to the fact that each human being has a unique type of image perception. Another remarkable disadvantage of this group of methods is the language dependency. On the other hand, manual attributing mehods offer a domain-free applications which can be considered as their powerful aspect. Although it is a lengthy and troublesome process, manual but proper image attributing enables various applications to be performed in diverse fields. When the second group of methods aiming automatic extraction of image features are evaluated, it can easily be seen that the produced number of features are limited and depends upon the method used. However, the obtained features always remain fixed after each extraction process. Also, a significant amount of processing time is gained due to the computerized process by using this group of methods. In both of the studies, Balan & Devi (2012) and Alghamdi et.al. (2014) the authors have an alternative approach which can be accepted as a separate group of methods aiming to combine manual image attributing with automatic feature extraction in order to eliminate the weaknesses while utilizing the powerful aspects of each particular type of methods.

The manual image attributing methods tend to draw less attention and drop out of being a preference recently because of the fact that the image databases of many fields increase non-linearly at each passing day. In addition, diversifying and enhancement of automatic feature extraction, image clustering and image indexing methods give rise to the reliability and stability of CBIR systems in which those methods are essential. In this context, the applications based on CBIR sytems equipped with automatic feature extraction methods have been coming into prominence nowadays. The fundamental problems that are still valid for CBIR systems are image feature extraction, clustering and indexing for faster access. CBIR systems mostly employ the robustly operating image analysis methods particularly in feature extraction process. As a matter of fact, the most widely used as well as newly developed strong image analysis and pattern recognition methods are the primary focus of this chapter. Efficient and robust extraction of image features is just one step for CBIR systems implementation. Another important task is the accurate clustering of images without being highly affected by image noise and deformations, applied transformations and illumination. Because of dealing with massive-sized databases, fast access to the results of example based queries by using tree structures with dimension reduction techniques which refers to indexing step is also substantial among the other steps of image mining algorithm.

Data and Image Data Representation

The principal problem in both data and image mining is the mathematical representation of data. Data is mostly represented by a $n \times d$ matrix structure where n refers to the size of data and d is the dimensionality. Rows are the records in data set, columns are the usable attributes of data. Depending on the application area, rows may represent records, samples, feature vectors or tuples. Similarly, columns may denote attributes, features or fields. The task of selection from extracted data features is used to reduce dimensionality via specifying the most significant features. On the other side, the discretizion methods are operated in order to determine the required amount of data for covering an attribute sufficiently. Another way of reducing the size of data is to utilize statistical sampling techniques.

Most of the image processing software today use matrix form to handle image related manipulations. On the other hand, any data set under the evaluation of a mining application may be in list, text, time-series, image, sound or video form requiring special techniques to be analyzed rather than being just in matrix form. However, no matter what the form of data is, it can be converted to matrix form by using various transforms. For instance, a transform may be applied to a data set so as to make rows to represent images while the columns display color, texture or intensity. Data may also be numerical such as integer and real or categorical which may be nominal like gender or ordinal allowing to make logical comparisons. An alternative representation type for data is using graphs that enable specification of topological attributes.

In a matrix-based image representation system, the height of an image may be considered as the number of rows in a matrix while the width stands for the number of columns. In such a representation, each element of the matrix corresponds to a pixel of the image. For example, $I(1,1)$ may indicate the left-top pixel of the image I where the value of $I(1,1)$ is the intensity of that pixel in along a single dimension. Images may be in binary, grayscale or color form. The binary image are the easiest processed type of images, but they usually don't be used in real-world applications. The most commonly used type is color images due to the fact that they have more detail thus they have high potential to contain more information. A color space such as RGB, CMYK or YUV is used in the storage process of a color image supported by the recording device. In the digitalization phase of a color image, a single matrix is used for each component of the color space selected. For example, a 320×240 sized RGB color image is represented by a matrix having dimensions of $3 \times 320 \times 240$.

In image analysis, it is a time-consuming process to manuplate color images because of the high dimensionality. Depending on the implementation requirements, images are frequently converted to grayscale or binary form to operate on. Grayscale images are formed to assign a gray tone for each distinc color between black and white. Therefore, a more detailed grayscale image requires more gray tones to be represented. The number of gray tones in a grayscale image is calculated by the *bit* depth of that image. For instance, a grayscale image having 8 bit depth is required to represent an image with 256 gray tones.

Image Features and Extraction

The main requirement for applying image mining is to extract meaningful information from images. However, as highlighted in She (2006), images contain enourmous number of features and it may not be feasible to label them manually due to some reasons target recognition difficulty, point of view inequality, illumination conditions, occlusions, deformations, wideness of object classes and background clutter. Image feature extraction is based on detection of distinct and unique attributes of a complete image, region or object that make that it is different from others. However, according to Wilson & Ritter (2000), a sequence of tranforms may be applied to an image in order to make it prepared to feature extraction step including logical, arithmetic and matrix or set-based operations for image enhancement, analysis and understanding. Image features extraction is actually the operation of reducing the number of labels and definitions required to identify objects within huge amount of data. Although the feature extraction is a mostly solved problem today there exist still challenging sub-problems arising from requirements related to the quality of features and real-time considerations. In most cases, a robust operating CBIR system is strictly required for automatic extraction of image features.

Image features may be categorized in three levels. The basic features such as spatial locations of image elements, color, shape and texture fall into the lowest level. Detection of certain objects or people is deemed as a logical feature which appears in the middle level and implies a number of image analysis methods applied together or substantially. Top level image features are accepted as the abstract features larglely require reasoning and heuristic techniques to be employed. The aim of this work is primarily focusing on giving referral information about general-purpose methods comprehended by extensive literature study. The rest of this part is formed by the listing of well-known and widely used image features with their intended purpose and the methods utilized for extraction of those.

Histogram Operations

Image histogram is graphic chart displaying the total number of each colored-pixel which gives general information about the image associated. If the histogram is narrow it means that the image has a weak appearance, otherwise it refers to that image contains more distinct colors and has a strong contrast. Histogram operations are accepted as the pre-processing operations that make the image features to be detected more easily and efficiently. An example of histogram acquiring process is given by figures 2, 3 and 4 respectively. Original Peppers image is depicted in Figure 2. Figure 3, is the grayscale form of original image which is the source of histogram image given in Figure 4. The Peppers image intensively contains various tones of red and green colors. Therefore, its histogram has an outspread form so as to cover nearly all grayscale colors.

The operations on histograms are mostly performed for image calibration, contrasting or intensity normalizing. Histogram thresholding, stretching and equalization are among the most prominent histogram methods. Histogram thresholding may be applied to an image in order to segment regions or objects by detecting the approximate values that the pixel intensities are centered. A simple test image and its grayscale form which allows the lower and upper threshold values to be easily detected through its histogram are given in Figure 5 and 6 respectively. Figure 7 is a logical image which is obtained by thresholding intensity values outside the interval of $[20, 30]$.

Histogram stretching is used to increase image contrast and thus helps for a smoother segmentation operation. The other popular histogram operation is the histogram equalization which satisfies that the image has a better contrast and appearance by making the distinct colors in the image have a uniform-like distribution. In Figure 8, histogram equalization is applied on grayscale Peppers image to make its colors fall into 16 groups with same number of occurances. On the other hand, Figure 9 is obtained by

Figure 2. Original Peppers image Source: Mc-Guire, 2011

Figure 3. Peppers as grayscale

Figure 4. Histogram of the image

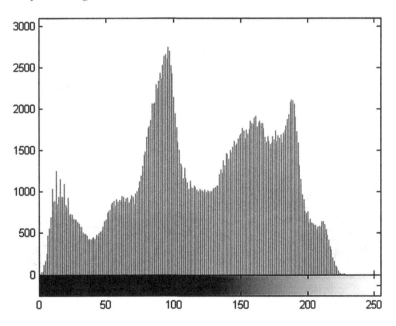

applying histogram stretching on grayscale Peppers image which provides to propagate its colors through the entire 256-colored grayscale spectrum. The effect of histogram stretching operation can easily be distinguished by comparing original image histogram given in Figure 4 and Figure 10 which is the histogram of stretched image.

Figure 5. Original Color Bars image, Source: McGuire, 2011

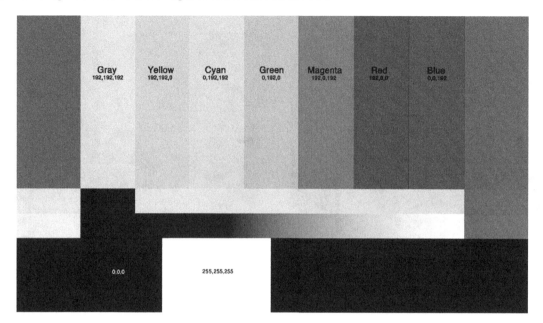

Figure 6. Color Bars as grayscale

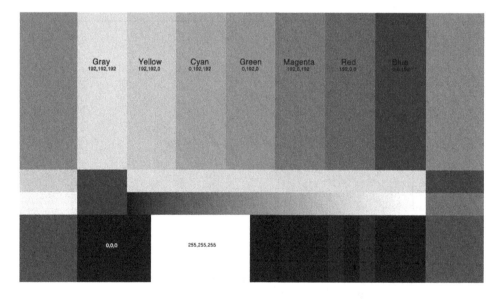

Image Arithmetic

A number of mathematical manuplations may be performed on images by doing the operations on their representative matrices. Among all, the basic addition, subtracting, multiplication and division operations are the leading ones. Addition is usually applied to overlap two or more images while multiplication is done for obtaining the region outlines more sharply. Another intensive use of image multiplication is in

Figure 7. Histogram thresholding applied Color Bars image

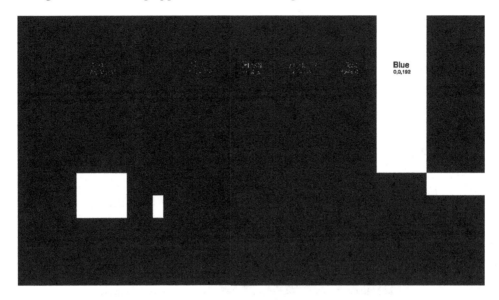

Figure 8. Peppers image with histogram equalization into 16 bins

Figure 9. Peppers image with histogram stretching

frequency domain which corresponds image filtering. On the other hand, image subtraction and division are generally implemented in order to detect differences between images and changes occured in the subsequent time steps for a single imge sequence or video. The change detection is an extremely important case in various problems such as target tracking, unusual activity surveillance and navigational control. A change detection example is given by the figures 11, 12 and 13. The images in Figure 11 and 12 are

Figure 10. Histogram of the stretched Peppers image

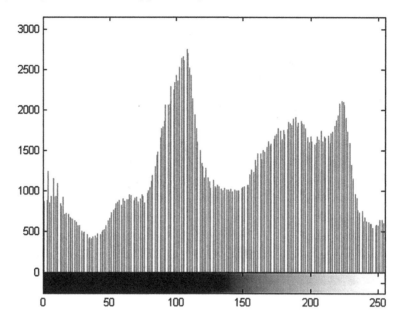

Figure 11. Moving Post It Notes video frame 65

extracted frames of a test video. The image given in Figure 13 is the result of the subtraction operation between these two. As it can be seen on the figure, the changes in a sequence of images or between the consecutive frames of a video can be obtained with a relatively basic calculation.

The basic arithmetic operations may also be applied between images and constant numbers. This operations are usually done for increasing and decreasing brightness values in images. An example of

Figure 12. Moving Post It Notes video frame 70

Figure 13. Difference image

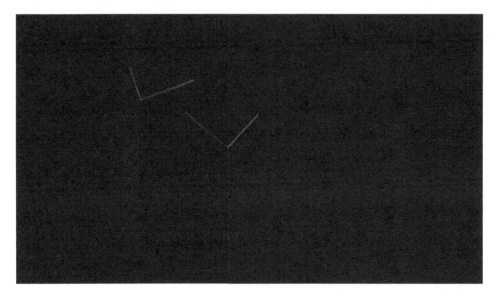

brightness reduction is depicted in Figure 15 which is obtained by multiplying the intensity values of orginal Peppers image (Figure 14) by a constant, 0.60 in this case.

There are so many other algebraic operations applied to images such as rotation, cropping, resizing and translation so as to make the images ready to the next operation such as image registration which aims matching the reference pixels in two or more images located in the same stage.

Figure 14. Original Peppers image

Figure 15. Peppers image multiplied by 0.60

Neighborhood Operations

Neighborhood operations stand for the operation within a certain window in an image affecting a group of connected pixels. Neighborhood operations are often applied for eliminating or reducing image noise, enhancing image appearance, overlapping or registering images, detecting inter-image relationships and manuplating certain portions of images. There exist so many neighborhood operations applicable to images. The fundamental two of those operations are undoubtedly image convolution and correlation.

Convolution is one of the most significant method in signal processing which theoretically aims to make a digital signal pass through a different one in order to obtain a third signal that fits the requested constraints. Convolution is identified as a linear filtering operation in image analysis and it is usually applied to sharpening the edges of objects, reducing random noise, correcting illumination and clarifying motion blur. Correlation, on the other hand, is mainly used to detect similarities between images or image parts. An example of convolution is shown in Figure 17 which is used to thicken the edges in the source image, Figure 16, by employing a filtering core.

Thresholding

Thresholding is probably the most well-known and commonly applied technique in image analysis because of its ease of use and reasonable solutions for a wide variety of applications in several areas such as document image analysis, map processing, scene processing, quality inspection of materials, knowledge representation, extraction of edge field and image segmentation according to Sezgin (2004). There

Figure 16. Difference image of Moving Post It Notes video frames 70 and 65

Figure 17. Difference image with convolution

exist so many methods for thresholding implementation. In clustering-based methods, foreground and background objects are separated with respect to some criterion. Another group of thresholding methods use image entropy which is calculated depending on the connected pixels and their colors. Also, there are some different thresholding methods using inter-pixel relationships and local image properties. A basic thresholding application is performed on Figure 18 and resulted with Figure 19. In this example, Otsu's thresholding algorithm which is based on calculating a generic threshold value by examining the intensity values of the image is used.

Figure 18. Difference image of Moving Post It Notes video frames 70 and 65

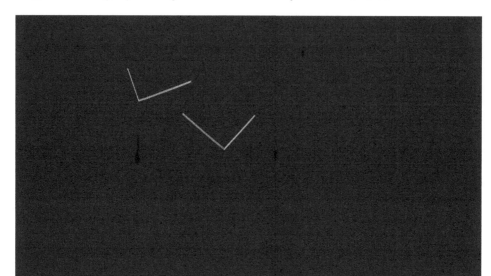

Figure 19. Difference image with Otsu thresholding

Image Filtering

Image filtering is a definition for the operations manipulating a group connected pixels instead of a single one. The underlying idea of image filtering is to obtain a new value for a pixel via calculating a factoral sum using that pixel and a filtering kernel. Although this idea is very basic, image filtering has a considerable place in image processing and analysis. Image filtering is categorized under the neighborhood operations and is mainly applied in pre-processing step for reducing noise and sharp crossings and detecting important image features such as edges and corners. The fundamental issue in image filtering is to specify the coefficients properly in the filtering kernel. Otherwise, a number of negative results can be met such as bluring at image edges, unlinking the connected regions and merging distinct parts of image. Average, median and box filters can be stated among the popular filtering methods. In average filter for instance, the new values of the pixels in a specified neighborhood window are updated by the mean of all pixels covered with that window which results a smoother image appearance. A demonstration of median filtering is illustrated by Figure 20 and Figure 21. In this example, "salt and pepper" type noise contained by the source image, Figure 20, is eliminated by median filtering which aims to update the intensity values with the median within a window.

Morphological Operations

Mathemetical morphology is used to apply thinning, pruning, outline or skeleton detection on image regions. Noise reduction, feature extraction, multi-scale decomposition and image segmentation are other applications of morphology based methods as stated in Serra et.al. (2012). While morphological operations applicable on grayscale images, they are nominately performed on binary images. Morphological operations are based on basic set operations suc as union, intersection, difference and complement. The most widely used morphological operations are erosion, dilation, opening, closing. There are also other methods that can be obtained by any combination of popular operations.

Erosion is defined the process of thinning image regions from their edges using primitive structuring elements such as star, square or diamond. Thanks to erosion operation small and unwanted regions in a binary image can be eliminated. Dilation is the opposite of erosion operation which is used to enlarge existing regions. With the use of dilation operator, a requested region can be concretized in order to be detected more easily. Opening operation is the application of erosion and dilation respectively while closing is the opposite of that. While opening is used to clean small regions, closing is executed for filling gaps within the regions. The examples of morphological erosion and dilation operations are given

Figure 20. Histogram thresholding applied Color Bars image

Figure 21. Median filtering applied image

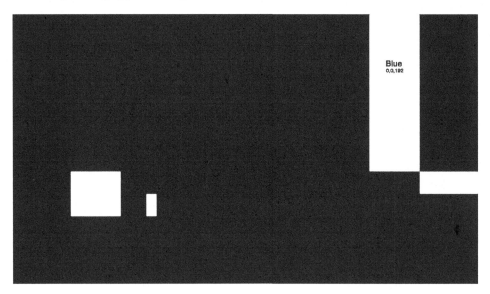

by figures 22, 23, 24 and 25 respectively. Since these two operations have opposite effects of eachother, a source image with its complement are used in Figure 22 and Figure 24 in order to provide a basis for visually comparing the effects of both operations simultaneously. On the other hand, erosion and dilation applied images are depicted in figures 23 and 25. As shown in the figures, the tiny regions that can be evaluated as noises in this case are cleaned by using erosion and dilation operators.

Hit and miss transform is one of the basic operations in mathematical morphology which is used to detect same pattern in multiple images or the variations of a unique pattern in a single image. Another

Figure 22. Difference image of Moving Post It Notes video frames 70 and 65

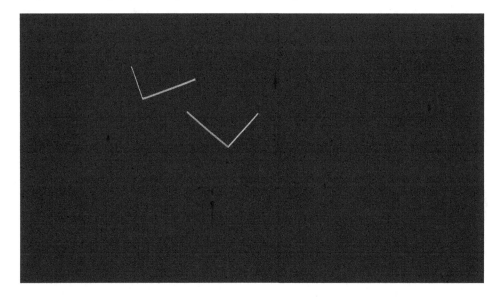

Figure 23. Morphological erosion applied image

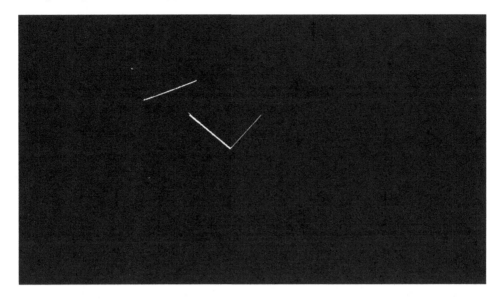

Figure 24. Complement of difference image of Moving Post It Notes video frames 70 and 65

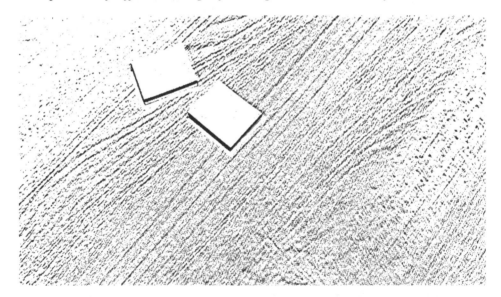

usable morphological method is edge cleaning which is used to eliminate edges that generally appear in obtaining successive frame differences when dealing with videos.

Image-Moments

Having the same definition in physics moments are used as the representative values of images independent from translation, rotation ans scaling processes. Moments can be calculated for first, second or higher orders. First order moments refer to centroid of the image or region and the second order

Figure 25. Morphological dilation applied image

moments explain how the region change around the centroid. The higher order moments are used to ensure independency from image deformations and transforms. Image moments are utilized in pattern recognition and classification.

Edge Detection

Edges in images are defined by the discontinuities or abrupt changes in intensity values. The methods aiming to identify those pixels are called edge detection methods. Edge detection is one of the key methods in feature extraction. There exist a number of well-known edge detection methods in the literatue including Canny, Sobel, Robert, Prevwitt methods. As highlighted in Maini & Aggarwal (2009), edge detection methods are applicable in almost all type of computer vision applications due to providing very convenient information for any case. The most wel-known edge detection techniques are applied on Figure 26 and the results are depicted by figures 27, 28, 29 and 30 respectively. As it can be seen on these figures, the best edge detection method among all is the Canny's method. However, it may need more calculations to be performed which is restricted in wide variety of real-time depended applications. Therefore, the edge detection method is mostly selected according to the result of a trade-off evaluation between restrictions and required accuracy level.

Another popular method used in edge and line detection in images is Hough transform. With the use of this method, straight, circular or eliptic lines can be detected. Traditional edge detection methods may fail because of the discontinuities on edge pixels. However, Hough transform is able to overcome this problem by grouping pixels and thus it is capable of capturing more information from images. Effect of Hough transform method is depicted in Figure 32. The lines are detected by Hough transform in the grayscale Color Bars image, Figure 31, with their starting and ending points.

Figure 26. Color Bars grayscale image

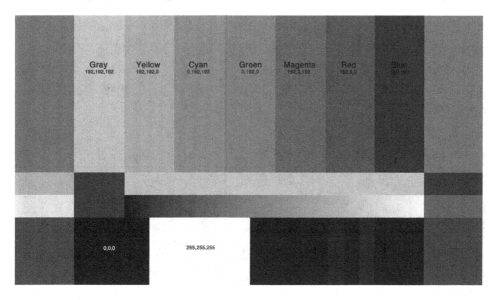

Figure 27. Canny edge detection

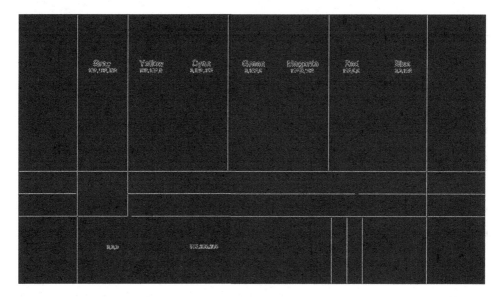

Corner Detection

Corners are the spatial locations in an image where the color passings become highly apparent. For this reason, it is considered as one of the image features detected easily. Corners are useful features especially in image matching applications. Corner detection is illustrated by figures 33, 34 and 35 using the method of He & Yung (2008) based on global and local curvature properties. The marked corners by the method is shown in Figure 34 and the lines is displayed in Figure 35 obtained by unifying the same values and combining these corners on the image.

Figure 28. Sobel edge detection

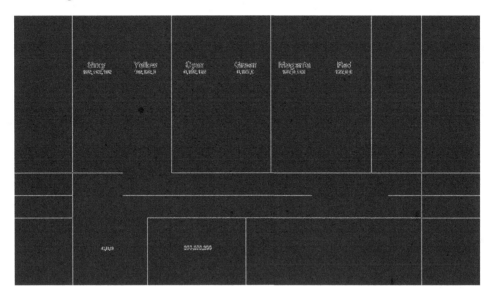

Figure 29. Roberts edge detection

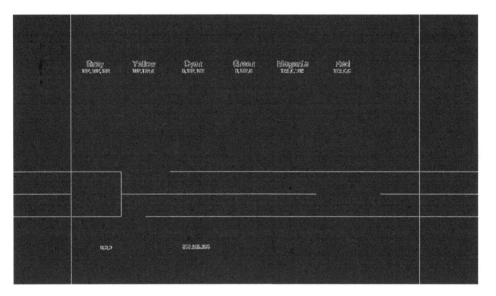

Texture Detection

Texture is defined as a tiny repeating pattern in the image formed by primitive shapes such as rectangle, circle or square. Texture is a significant feature which can be used in image segmentation. Examples of texture detection using different approaches are given by the figures 36, 37 and 38. A repeating pattern on source image, Figure 36, is detected by using two different implementations including range filtering (Figure 37) and entropy based filtering (Figure 38).

Figure 30. Prewitt edge detection

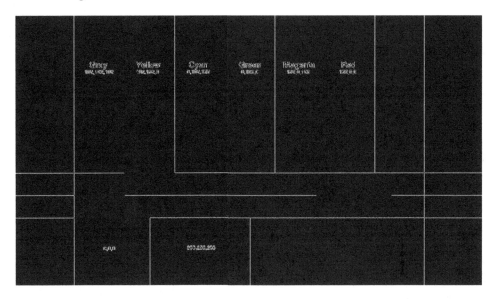

Figure 32. Hough line detection applied image

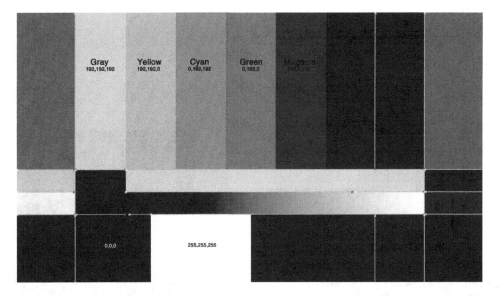

Boundary Detection

Boundary is defined as the minimum primitive shape covering a region or object in the image. However, the own edges of a region may be accepted as a boundary. Boundary detection is generally used for tracking objects in which high accuracy is not very critical. A simple boundary detection example is shown by Figure 39 and Figure 40. In this example, the region having the largest area value is detected first and it is visually highlighted by marking it with its bounding box.

Figure 31. Color Bars grayscale image

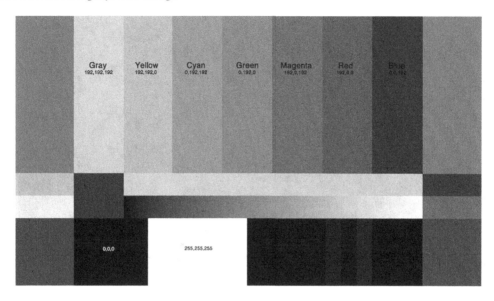

Figure 33. Part of grayscale Color Bars Image   *Figure 34. Corners detected on the image*

Optical-Flow

Optical flow is the observable motion of an object, region or element in the image. Optical flow may give information about spatial locations of tracked objects. Also, the discontinuities in optical flow may be used in segmenting objects by calculating the differences of successive frames. Vidal & Ravichandran

Figure 35. Lines through detected corners

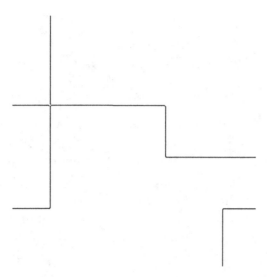

Figure 36. Image with a texture pattern

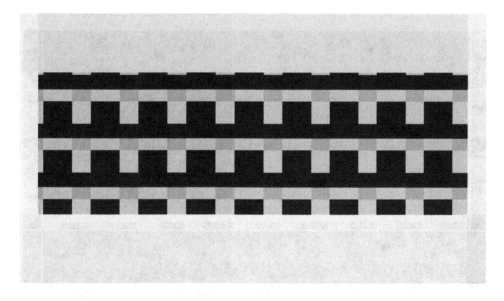

(2005) indicate that optical flow is used for motion detection and tracking, object segmentation, image processing and navigational control.

Level Set Methods and Active-Contours

Active contour or snake in other terms stands for a deformable curve aiming energy minimization calculated by using various image features. Active contour can be employed to detect boundaries of an object in a noisy image. According to Airouche et.al. (2009), active contours are used in several applications including object tracking, shape recognition, image segmentation, edge detection and stereo

Figure 37. Range filtering based texture detection

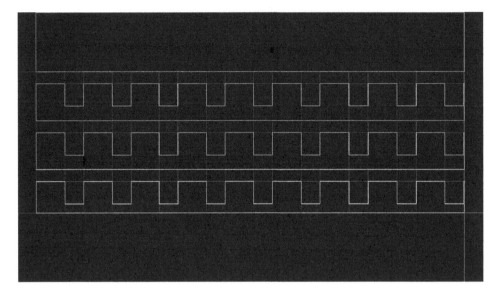

Figure 38. Entropy based texture detection

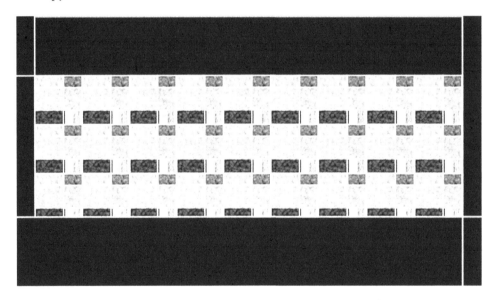

image matching. Level set methods can be deemed as general form of active contours such that they can be used for multiple objects and shapes without implying initial conditions.

Probabilistic-Models

Probabilistic models have a wide variety application in computer vision such as object recognition, classification, alignment and tracking. Probilistic models based methods define the relationship between noisy real-world and hidden parameters of the model. It is frequently applied probabilistic methods in

Figure 39. Resolution Chart binary image. Source: McGuire, 2011

Figure 40. Bounding box applied image

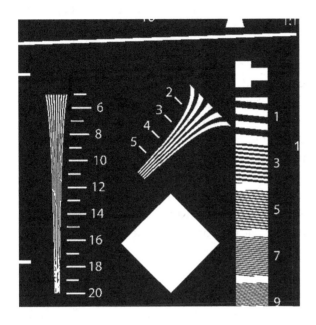

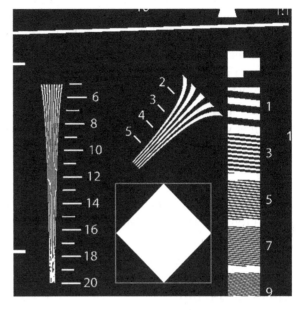

case of object detection and tracking. There are two main phases in this type of methods: prediction, update. In the prediction phase, a prediction is made about the requested object which contains uncertainity. In the update phase, the prediction is corrected using information obtained from image based on extracted features. There exist competent probabilistic model based methods in the literature such as Kalman filter, Markov Chain Monte Carlo and particle filter.

Image Registration

Image registration methods are categorized into two groups: feature based, intensity value based. The first type of methods are required the features such as points, lines and regions to be detected initially and to be matched with the features in other images substantially. The second type of methods are based on matching objects, regions or elements in the source and target images according to the intensity values.

There are also other feature extraction methods that are not explained separately in this part. Detecting shapes using graph-based representation, shading information, kinematic constraints and antropometric information can be stated among these methods. In addition, SURF and SIFT methods can be given as examples of specific applications that are based on extracting special features from images. Both of these methods are mainly used for image matching.

Image Clustering

Image clustering is a method of providing multi-dimensional non-standard data organization and described as the process of collecting similar images into individual groups. Detecting similar images is generally applied by using features extracted from images and considering the recurrence numbers and matching rates of features in different images. A number of problems are encountered in image clustering such as existence of extraordinary data, difference forms of relationship between images and high dimensionality. Additionally, image clustering is sensitive to parameters and it is hard to perform fine-tuning. Therefore, it is not expected image clustering methods to exhibit same performance in different applications. There exist so many image clustering methods implemented in the literature. K-means, nearest neighborhood, K-Nearest Neighbors ve Fuzzy-C means, least squaresi maximum likelihood estimation and coefficient of correlation methods can be regarded among the the most widely used methods in image clustering. There are also other less known methods used for image clustering such as optimization-based simulated annealing ve genetic algorithms and artificial neural network based self-organizing maps.

The most significant issue in an image clustering algorithm is to define the similarity measure accurately. Depending on the applications entropy, contrast, standard deviation, correlation, mean, and variance can be used as a similarity measure. Besides, a number of distance measures are at present such as Euclidean, manhattan, Earthmover's, Minkowski-form and quadratic form distances. On the other hand, probability based distance measures such as Bhattacharya distance, Kullback–Leibler divergence and Mahalanobis distance are used to determine the similarity rate of two distinct probability distribution which can be used as a decision criteria in measuring image similarities.

Image Indexing

In image mining, it is an important issue to retrieve the query result as fast as possible. Feature vectors often have high dimensions. In such a case, dimension reduction and image indexing methods are executed to achive better solutions. Support vector machines, principal component analysis, KL transform and artificial neural network algorithms are among the popular dimension reduction methods.

In relational databases indexing is performed by using primary and secondary keys. However, this is not a valid case for image mining. Indexing has to be done by taking the similarity of images into account which already depends on extracted features from images. There are many methods in the literature used for image indexing such that most of them are tree-based. KD-B tree, R-tree and its variants, TV-tree, linear quad-trees and iMinMax can be accounted as the most commonly used image indexing methods. There are also some indexing methods utilizing feautes based on colors and spatial-locations of image elements.

CONCLUSION AND FUTURE RESEARCH DIRECTIONS

In today's world information and communication technologies are intensively used in so many fields such as scientific research, education, health, security and nearly all aspects of daily life. Nowadays, almost each individual particularly in developed countries has mobile internet connectivity and digital image and video recording device. At the present time, a significant part of humankind lives in big cities in which the life passes rapidly because of the implications. So, time itself becomes extremely valuable. In such a condition, it can easily be claimed that the demand for visual information is a must. Therefore, the requirement for analyzing visual data which contains much more information than the data in tabular or text form has been ever-increasing. Image mining is the most important tool at present at this point in order to handle such an issue. It is possible to extract information from visual data and to introduce use of people in almost every field. Within this context, it is obvious that researching and developing applications related to image mining is strictly required. From this perspective, it is aimed to give a brief information by this chapter to especially new field researchers about image mining so as to be used as a source of reference.

In this chapter, the theoretical base of image mining which refers to knowledge discovery and data mining is briefly explained with prominent aspects and applications. Image mining is also covered with its detailed definition, properties and literature as well as the components. A generic image mining algorithm is introduced step by step with a schematic block diagram. Additionally, the fundamental part of image mining system called content-based image retrieval system is also examined by revealing the attributes and advantages. The applications of content-based image retrieval systems are also mentioned by associating them to the underlying functions including feature extraction, image clustering and image indexing. Although the image clustering and indexing methods are matured the most important group of methods namely feature extraction methods are not robust for now. So, this chapter is focused on the feature extraction methods with examples which refers to the image processing area. Image data representation is reviewed with covering a wide variety of image feature extraction methods. The definition of methods are given with indicating the purposes and application areas.

The image feature extraction methods which form the most important component of content-based image retrieval systems are open to developments in terms of method enhancements and expanding and diversifying the application areas. For method enhancements, it can be argued that there are some reseach and development efforts by the researchers of image analysis, computer vision and pattern recognition society. However, there is a gap in content-based image retrieval systems and applications. A number of applications may be developed in this field such as search engines supporting example-based querying, recognition of face and other parts of humans, text mining and criminal profile construction of people by examining their shared images on social media platforms.

REFERENCES

Airouche, M., Bentabet, L., & Zelmat, M. (2009, July). Image segmentation using active contour model and level set method applied to detect oil spills. In *Proceedings of the World Congress on Engineering* (Vol. 1, pp. 1-3).

Alghamdi, R., Taileb, M., & Ameen, M. (2014, April). A new multimodal fusion method based on association rules mining for image retrieval. In *Mediterranean Electrotechnical Conference (MELECON), 2014 17th IEEE* (pp. 493-499). IEEE. doi:10.1109/MELCON.2014.6820584

Balan, S., & Devi, T. (2012). Design and Development of an Algorithm for Image Clustering In Textile Image Retrieval Using Color Descriptors. *International Journal of Computer Science, Engineering and Applications, 2*(3).

Conci, A., & Castro, E. M. M. (2002). Image mining by content. *Expert Systems with Applications, 23*(4), 377–383. doi:10.1016/S0957-4174(02)00073-8

Dey, N., & Kar, Á. (2015). Image mining framework and techniques: A review. *International Journal of Image Mining, 1*(1), 45–64. doi:10.1504/IJIM.2015.070028

Gajjar, T. Y., & Chauhan, N. C. (2012). A review on image mining frameworks and techniques. *International Journal of Computer Science and Information Technologies, 3*(3).

Gholap, A., Naik, G., Joshi, A., & Rao, C. K. (2005, August). Content-based tissue image mining. In Computational Systems Bioinformatics Conference, 2005. Workshops and Poster Abstracts. IEEE (pp. 359-363). IEEE. doi:10.1109/CSBW.2005.45

Han, J., Kamber, M., & Pei, J. (2012). Data Mining: Concepts and Techniques (3rd ed.). Morgan Kaufmann.

He, X. C., & Yung, N. H. (2008). Corner detector based on global and local curvature properties. *Optical Engineering (Redondo Beach, Calif.), 47*(5), 057008–057008. doi:10.1117/1.2931681

Hema, A., & Annasaro, E. (2013). A survey in need of image mining techniques. *International Journal of Advanced Research in Computer and Communication Engineering*, 2319-5940.

Joseph, C. N., & Wilson, A. (2014, November). Retrieval of images using data mining techniques. In *Contemporary Computing and Informatics (IC3I), 2014 International Conference on* (pp. 204-208). IEEE.

Kannan, A., Mohan, V., & Anbazhagan, N. (2010). Image clustering and retrieval using image mining techniques. In *IEEE International Conference on Computational Intelligence and Computing Research* (Vol. 2).

Lu, K. C., & Yang, D. L. (2009). Image Processing and Image Mining using Decision Trees. *J. Inf. Sci. Eng., 25*(4), 989–1003.

Maini, R., & Aggarwal, H. (2009). Study and comparison of various image edge detection techniques. *International Journal of Image Processing, 3*(1), 1-11.

McGuire, M. (2011, August 26). *Computer Graphics Archive*. Retrieved September 16, 2015.

Missaoui, R., & Palenichka, R. M. (2005, August). Effective image and video mining: an overview of model-based approaches. In *Proceedings of the 6th international workshop on Multimedia data mining: mining integrated media and complex data* (pp. 43-52). ACM. doi:10.1145/1133890.1133895

Ordonez, C., & Omiecinski, E. R. (1998). *Image mining: A new approach for data mining*. Academic Press.

Serra, J., & Soille, P. (Eds.). (2012). *Mathematical morphology and its applications to image processing* (Vol. 2). Springer Science & Business Media.

Sezgin, M. (2004). Survey over image thresholding techniques and quantitative performance evaluation. *Journal of Electronic Imaging, 13*(1), 146–168. doi:10.1117/1.1631315

She, Y. Y. (2006). *Real-time animation of walking and running using inverse kinematics*. (Doctoral dissertation). Concordia University.

Singhai, N., & Shandilya, S. K. (2010). A survey on: Content based image retrieval systems. *International Journal of Computers and Applications, 4*(2), 22–26. doi:10.5120/802-1139

Tahoun, M., Nagaty, K., & El-Arief, T. (2005, March). A robust content-based image retrieval system using multiple features representations. In Networking, Sensing and Control, 2005. Proceedings. 2005 IEEE (pp. 116-122). IEEE.

Vidal, R., & Ravichandran, A. (2005, June). Optical flow estimation & segmentation of multiple moving dynamic textures. In *Computer Vision and Pattern Recognition, 2005. CVPR 2005. IEEE Computer Society Conference on* (Vol. 2, pp. 516-521). IEEE. doi:10.1109/CVPR.2005.263

Wilson, J. N., & Ritter, G. X. (2000). *Handbook of computer vision algorithms in image algebra*. CRC Press.

Zaki, M. J., & Meira, W. Jr. (2014). *Data mining and analysis: fundamental concepts and algorithms*. Cambridge University Press.

Zhang, J., Hsu, W., & Lee, M. L. (2001). Image mining: Issues, frameworks and techniques. In *Proceedings of the 2nd ACM SIGKDD International Workshop on Multimedia Data Mining (MDM/KDD'01)*. University of Alberta.

KEY TERMS AND DEFINITIONS

Antropometric Data: Data related to the relative locations and distances between articulated objects, mainly human images.

Image Feature: Valuable spatial, chromatic or semantic information about image pixels, objects or regions.

Image Histogram: Graphic chart displaying the total tumber of distinct-colored pixels of a grayscale image.

Image Morphology: Technical concept covering a sequence of logical operations on binary image data.

Knowledge Discovery: The overall process of reaching significant and practicable information about a system or a fact.

Multimedia Database: Database containing non-standard forms of data such as image and videos instead of traditional alpha-numeric data.

Similarity Measure: The comparable magnitude of the likeness of images or image parts.

Texture: Definition for a tiny repeating pattern as in an image formed by mixture of certain colors and primitive shapes such as rectangle, circle or square.

Chapter 5

Comparative Analysis of Statistical, Machine Learning, and Grey Methods for Short-Term Electricity Load Forecasting

Tuncay Ozcan
Istanbul University, Turkey

Tarik Küçükdeniz
Istanbul University, Turkey

Funda Hatice Sezgin
Istanbul University, Turkey

ABSTRACT

Electricity load forecasting is crucial for electricity generation companies, distributors and other electricity market participants. In this study, several forecasting techniques are applied to time series modeling and forecasting of the hourly loads. Seasonal grey model, support vector regression, random forests, seasonal ARIMA and linear regression are benchmarked on seven data sets. A rolling forecasting model is developed and 24 hours of the next day is predicted for the last 14 days of each data set. This day-ahead forecasting model is especially important in day-ahead market activities and plant scheduling operations. Experimental results indicate that support vector regression and seasonal grey model outperforms other approaches in terms of forecast accuracy for day-ahead load forecasting.

INTRODUCTION

Electricity is an unstorable energy resource. This increases the importance of timely and accurate management in the electricity market. As well as the profitability of the electricity market as a social obligation it must be operated properly. In this context, load forecasting has become a process that must be performed successfully for the companies. Jabbour et al. (1988) identifies several areas of usage for load forecasting, including;

DOI: 10.4018/978-1-5225-0075-9.ch005

- Setting the spinning reserve
- Maintenance scheduling
- Economically operating the generators and the transmission system
- System security studies
- Contingency planning and load management scheduling
- Determining the tie and interchange schedules among interconnected utilities
- Demand side management
- Preparing for unusual events
- Optimizing the cost of fuel inventory
- Load flow studies

In literature electricity load forecasting is divided into three categories in terms of the time horizon under consideration. These are long, medium and short terms. The first category includes long term load forecasting. The time span in consideration can be six months, one year or longer. It is particularly important for growth strategies at the government level and also it has importance on the strategic decision making process of the electricity market operators. The second category deals with medium term load forecasting. The time span is weeks or months. It is vital for electricity generation companies because the stock levels and resource management decisions need this information (Hoffman & Wood, 1976). The last category is short term, hourly load forecasts. The short-term forecasts refer to hourly prediction of electricity load demand for a lead time ranging from 1 hour to several days ahead. In certain instances, the prediction of the daily peak load is the objective of short-term load forecasting, since it is the most important load during any given day (Niu et al., 2010). Hourly load forecasting of the next day is a crucial operation in electricity markets. All market players need this information to make a bidding decision on the market. Also, this information is vital for electricity production and distribution companies.

These requirements to the load forecasting have led to the development of many load forecasting methods. Basic and advanced statistical methods, artificial intelligence based methods, grey theory based methods and recently machine learning methods are applied to the load forecasting. Because of its difficulty due to the complexity of the prediction of the variables that effect the demand (such as temperature) and the high cost of the mistakes, load forecasting is still an area being heavily worked on where new algorithms developed constantly. This study will investigate the performances of the prominent forecasting techniques on short-term load forecasting. Literature shows that the statistical models are dominant in the past. However, today these statistical models have left their places to the more sophisticated statistical techniques, machine learning techniques and to advanced methods such as grey systems. There are very few studies about these methods in load forecasting. In this study performances of the grey models and support vector regression (SVR) and random forest techniques which are known to be very strong forecasting algorithms in the field of machine learning, will be investigated.

This remainder of this chapter is organized as follows: The next section provides a detailed review of the literature on the electricity load forecasting problem. In the third part, detailed information on seasonal grey forecasting model, support vector regression, random forests and seasonal ARIMA are presented. The fourth part shows experimental results on seven data sets to assess the efficiency of the proposed forecasting algorithms. In the final part, the comparative results of the proposed algorithms are discussed.

LITERATURE REVIEW

There are numerous studies about load forecasting in literature. Statistics based methods like multiple linear regression, time series methods, the state space model and general exponential smoothing approaches try to formulate the mathematical relations among input variables and the electricity load. However, high complexity of the load data makes it extremely difficult to establish a mathematical forecasting model. Machine learning algorithms play a prominent role to deal with this high complexity. Expert systems, artificial neural networks, fuzzy inference and more recent machine learning algorithms like support vector machines are more complex solution approaches to the load forecasting problem. Advanced statistical methods like ARIMA and generalized autoregressive conditional heteroscedasticity (GARCH) and grey forecasting models are also offer new approaches to load forecasting.

Forecasting algorithms can be classified with respect to the forecast period (hourly, daily, monthly, annual), employed algorithm (basic and advanced statistics based, machine learning based) and the variables used (time series data, temperature, humidity, population). A successful algorithm on a specific dataset may not be that good on another.

The review of electricity load forecasting models presented in this chapter is categorized as follows:

- Statistical models
- Neural network, expert systems and fuzzy models
- Support vector machine (SVM) models
- Grey forecasting models

Statistical Models

Rahman (1990) states that extensive computerization of the electric power industry has resulted in the application of various statistics and signal processing techniques, which include state estimation techniques, spectral expansion techniques, load weather regression models, exponential smoothing techniques, and Box and Jenkins modeling concepts. Moghram and Rahman (1989) evaluates five short-term load forecasting techniques: multiple linear regression, stochastic time series, general exponential smoothing, state space and Kalman filters and expert systems. Christiaanse (1971), Hagan and Behr (1987), Papalexopoulos and Hesterberg (1990), Ho et al. (1990), Hubele and Cheng (1990), Haida and Muto (1994), Huang and Shih (2003), Ahmed (2005), Taylor and McSharry (2007), Mirasgedis et al. (2006) have successfully applied statistical methods for load forecasting. Also, Hor et al. (2005), Parkpoom et al. (2004), Taylor and Buizza (2003) and Teisberg et al. (2005) analyzed effects of weather conditions and temperature on electricity load.

GARCH models have been in use to analyze time series data. However its use in electricity load forecasting is limited. Garcia et al. (2005) uses GARCH model to predict day-ahead electricity prices. Hor et al. (2006) estimated maximum electricity demand using load and temperature data with ARIMA and GARCH models. Their model concerns the risk of under-demand prediction. The authors claim that their model not only can predict the short term load pattern but also reliable for longer range forecasts. GARCH models are further applied to electricity price forecasting. Khosravi et al. (2013) applied GARCH models with neural networks to electricity price interval prediction.

Neural Network, Expert Systems, and Fuzzy Models

With the increasing popularity of the artificial intelligence and expert systems; these approaches also find their place in load forecasting. Rahman and Bhatnagar (1988), Ho et al. (1990), Rahman (1990), Peng et al. (1992), Chen et al. (1992), Papalexopoulos et al. (1994), Piras et al. (1996), Bakirtzis et al. (1996), Chow and Leung (1996a), Vermaak and Botha (1998), Papadakis et al. (1998), Kim et al. (2000), Kim et al. (2002), Senjyu et al. (2002), Kermanshahi and Iwamiya (2002), Kandil and Debeiky (2002), Taylor and Buizza (2002), Khotanzad et al. (2002) are the studies about applying artificial intelligence and expert system methods on load forecasting.

Artificial neural network model has been intensely applied to time series modeling and prediction. Hsu and Chen (2003) predicted the annual regional peak load of Taiwan using an artificial neural network model. Hippert et al. (2005) examines the effectiveness of large neural networks for short-term electric load forecasting. At this point, large neural networks are compared with conventional regression-based methods. Their results show that large neural networks seem to perform at least as well as the standard linear methods. Azadeh et al. (2007) presented an Artificial Neural Network (ANN) approach based on supervised multi-layer perceptron (MLP) network for the electrical consumption forecasting. Hamzacebi (2007) proposed an artificial neural network model for electricity consumption forecasting on sectoral basis in Turkey. Mamlook et al. (2009) developed a fuzzy inference model for short term load forecasting problem in Jordan. Yadav and Srinivasan (2011) proposed a SOM-based hybrid linear-neural model for short-term load forecasting. Chang et al. (2011) proposed a weighted evolving fuzzy neural network for monthly electricity demand forecasting in Taiwan. Proposed model is compared with other approaches such as backpropagation neural network, winter's exponential smoothing, multiple regression analysis and evolving neural network. Chen (2012) developed a collaborative fuzzy-neural approach for long term load forecasting. In this methodology, fuzzy back propagation networks and a radial basis function network is used. Li et al. (2013) proposed a hybrid model based on the generalized regression neural network and fruit fly optimization algorithm for the annual power load forecasting. In this study, fruit fly optimization algorithm is used to optimize parameters of generalized regression neural network. Kulkarni et al. (2013) used spiking neural networks for short term load forecasting. Hooshmand et al. (2013) presented a new two-step hybrid algorithm which combines wavelet transform (WT), artificial neural network (ANN) and adaptive neural fuzzy inference system (ANFIS) for short-term load fore-casting (STLF). Ko and Lee (2013) developed a hybrid algorithm which combines SVR (support vector regression), RBFNN (radial basis function neural network) and DEKF (dual extended Kalman filter) for short-term load forecasting.

Wavelets are applied to time series modelling of hourly load data. Kim et al. (2002) applied wavelet transform procedure with Kohonen neural network for short-time load forecasting. They classified seasonal load data into four patterns using Kohonen neural network and then wavelet transform is adopted in order to forecast the hourly data. They concluded that seasonal classification and wavelet transformation is essential in short-term load forecasting to achieve good forecasting results.

In many studies, optimization techniques are applied to fine tune the forecasting algorithms. Hyperparameter optimization of forecasting algorithms, feature selection and training set size optimization are primary areas of application of optimization algorithms in load forecasting. Niu et al. (2010) employed ant colony optimization heuristic for feature selection in hourly load forecasting. Initially they have identified several variables like daily maximum, minimum and average temperature, rainfall, wind speed, humidity and cloud cover, and then used ant colony optimization to select the best variables among them. This method reduced the number of attributes from 38 to 21.

Special days like holidays are a different area of study in load forecasting. There are several studies committed to load forecasting at the special days. Kim et al. (2000) applied fuzzy inference and neural networks for special days in anomalous load conditions. In their study special days are classified into five different day types and maximum and minimum loads of special days are forecasted.

Support Vector Machine (SVM) Models

Based on the statistical learning theory, support vector machines (SVM) is a robust and promising machine learning algorithm. SVM is especially suitable for solving problems of small sample size (Chen et al., 2004). SVM is grounded in the framework of statistical learning theory, which has been developed by Vapnik and Chervonenkis (1974). A version of SVM for regression was proposed in Drucker et al. (1997). This method is called support vector regression (SVR). References Alpaydin (2004), Che et al. (2012), Gao et al. (2007) and Pai and Hong (2005a) show details of the support vector regression algorithm. There are various applications of the SVR model to the short term load forecasting in the literature.

Mohandes (2002) applies support vector machines to short term electrical load forecasting and compares its performance with autoregression model. Espinoza et al. (2005) uses fixed size least squares support vector machines to forecast hourly load. Yuancheng et al. (2002) forecast electricity load with least squares SVM by using temperature and load data in the dataset.

In recent studies, Che et al. (2012) examines the optimal training subset in a SVR model for load forecasting problem. A full training set increases complexity and may increase the risk of overfitting due to the mass amount of data. Gu and Hu (2012) divide daily load curve into clusters and forecast each part on its own dataset. They suggest that this method improves forecasting performance due to the decreased complexity. Hsu et al. (2006) also tries to optimize the parameters of the SVR. They use real valued genetic algorithms for this purpose. Jain and Satish (2009) includes seasonal indexes in the dataset to train a SVR model, and then forecasts the half-hourly electricity load for the next day.

In the literature, many studies which combines SVR and metaheuristic algorithms can be found for electricity load forecasting problem. In these studies, metaheuristic algorithms are used for the selection of optimum parameters of support vector regression. In this context, many approaches have also been proposed, including simulated annealing (Pai & Hong, 2005a), genetic algorithms (Pai & Hong, 2005b; Hsu et al., 2006), chaotic genetic algorithms (Hong, 2009c; Hong, 2013), immune algorithm (Hong, 2000; Hong, 2009a), chaotic particle swarm optimization (Hong, 2009b), chaotic artificial bee colony (Hong, 2011). In these studies, the developed models are compared with artificial neural networks and statistical methods such as ARIMA, regression based models.

Grey Forecasting Models

Many studies can be found in the literature concerning the application of grey prediction models for electricity load forecasting problem. These studies are summarized as follows:

Yao et al. (2003) developed an improved GM (1, 1) based prediction approach to forecast short term electric load. In this study, the forecast accuracy is improved by using adaptive model parameters. Li et al. (2006) presented a GM (2, 1) model for short term load forecasting. Zhou et al. (2006) proposed GM (1, 1) model with the trigonometric residual modification technique to predict electricity demand. Niu et al. (2008) developed an improved genetic algorithm – GM (1, 1) model to solve the problem of short-term load forecasting. In the proposed model, the value of parameter α in the GM (1, 1) is determined by using genetic algorithm. Bianco et al. (2010) applied a trigonometric grey model with rolling mechanism for nonresidential electricity consumption in Romania. Li et al. (2012) used the adaptive grey model for forecasting short term load. In this study, the performance of the proposed grey model is compared with other methods based on back propagation neural networks and support vector regression. Jin et al. (2012) proposed a hybrid optimization grey model using grey correlation contest for short-term load forecasting. The efficiency of developed model is showed by comparing with the results of basic grey models. Bahrami et al. (2014) developed a new model which is based on combination of the wavelet transform and GM (1, N) model. In this paper, to reduce the forecast inaccuracy, the parameters of GM (1, N) model are determined using particle swarm optimization.

In the recent decades advances in the computation power of the computers and the factor of easier and cheaper data retrieval and storage effected the load forecasting methods. As it can be seen in Table 1, load forecasting techniques are moving away from statistics based methods to machine learning based methods. Readers may refer to the Alfares and Nazeeruddin (2002) for a detailed survey and classification on load forecasting methods.

Table 1. The classification of the electricity load forecasting literature

Author(s)	Method	Forecast Horizon	Data Type	Model Variables	Train Size	Test Size
Hong et al. (2013)	Support Vector Regression with Genetic Algorithm	Medium Term	Monthly	Time series data	32 months	7 months
Li et al. (2013)	Generalized Regression Neural Network with Fruit Fly Algorithm	Long Term	Annually	Time series data	25 years	5 years
Ko and Lee (2013)	Support vector regression, radial basis function neural network, dual extended Kalamn filter	Short Term	Hourly	Time series data	600 hours	24 hours, 72 hours, 168 hours
Hooshmand et al. (2013)	Artificial neural network with wavelet transform, adaptive neural fuzzy inference system	Short Term	Hourly, Daily	Temperature, Humidity, Wind speed	Different cases	Different cases
Chen (2012)	Fuzzy back propagation network, Radial basis function network	Long Term	Annually	Time series data	48 years	16 years
Gu and Hu (2012)	Support Vector Regression	Short Term	Hourly	Time series data	2 months	6 days
Che et al. (2012)	Support Vector Regression	Short Term	Hourly	Time series data	29 days	2 days
Li et al. (2012)	Grey Model, Back propagation neural networks, support vector regression	Short Term, Medium Term, Long Term	Hourly	Time series data	4 years	1 year
Taylor (2012)	Exponentially Weighted Methods, Spline Methods, ARMA	Short Term	Hourly	Time series data	2 years	1 year

continued on following page

Table 1. Continued

Author(s)	Method	Forecast Horizon	Data Type	Model Variables	Train Size	Test Size
Hong (2011)	Support Vector Regression with Artificial Bee Colony	Medium Term	Monthly	Time series data	32 months	7 months
Chang et al. (2011)	Fuzzy Neural Network	Medium Term	Monthly	Air pressure, temperature, wind velocity, rainfall, rainy time, relative humidity and daylight time	96 months	24 months
Yadav and Srinivasan (2011)	Neuro-coefficient smooth transition autoregressive model and self-organized map	Short Term	Hourly	Time series data	Different cases	Different cases
Niu et al. (2010)	Support Vector Machine with Ant Colony Optimization	Short Term	Hourly	Time series data, daily maximum, minimum and average temperature, rainfall, wind speed, humidity, cloud cover	2 years	2 months
Taylor (2010)	Seasonal ARIMA, Holt-Winters, Artificial Neural Networks	Short Term	Hourly	Time series data	5 years	1 year
Hong (2009a)	Support Vector Regression with Immune Algorithm	Long Term	Annually	Time series data	12 years	4 years
Hong (2009b)	Support Vector Regression with Particle Swarm Optimization	Long Term	Annually	Time series data	12 years	4 years
Hong (2009c)	Support Vector Regression with Genetic Algorithm	Long Term	Annually	Time series data	12 years	4years
Mamlook et al. (2009)	Fuzzy Inference Model	Short Term	Hourly	Temperature, weather	7 years	
Jain and Satish (2009)	Support Vector Regression	Short Term	Hourly	Time series data, temperature	91 days	13 days
Shareef et al. (2008)	Artificial Neural Networks	Short Term	Hourly	Time series data, temperature, humidity, special events	3 years	1 year
Taylor (2008)	Holt-Winters, Seasonal ARMA	Very short term (10-30 minutes)	Minutely	Time series data, temperature	20 weeks	10 weeks
Mirasgedis et al. (2006)	Autoregressive Models	Mid Term	Daily	Time series data, temperature	8 years	1 year
Azadeh et al. (2007)	Artificial Neural Network	Medium Term	Monthly	Time series data	94 months	12 months
Hamzacebi (2007)	Artificial Neural Network	Long Term	Annually	Time series data	28 years	2 years
Taylor and McSharry (2007)	AR, ARIMA, Holt-Winters, PCA based method	Short Term	Hourly, Half Hourly	Time series data	6720 half hours, 3360 hours	3360 half hours, 1680 hours

continued on following page

Table 1. Continued

Author(s)	Method	Forecast Horizon	Data Type	Model Variables	Train Size	Test Size
Hor et al. (2006)	ARIMA, GARCH	Short Term, Long Term	Hourly, Daily	Time series data, temperature	28 years	4 years
Hsu et al. (2006)	Support Vector Regression with genetic algorithm	Short Term	Hourly	Time series data, temperature	2 years	1 month
Espinoza et al. (2006)	Least Squares Support Vector Machines	Short Term	Hourly	Time series data, temperature	1500 days	500 days
Fan and Chen (2006)	Self-Organizing Maps and Support Vector Machines	Short Term	Hourly	Time series data, temperature	1 year	1 month
Mandal et al. (2006)	Artificial Neural Networks	Short Term	Hourly	Time series data, temperature	135 days	7 days
Ghiassi et al. (2006)	Dynamic ANN	Medium Term	Monthly	Time series data	180 months	12 months
Hippert et al. (2005)	Neural networks, Linear Regression	Short Term	Hourly, Daily, Weekly	Temperature	40 weeks	30 weeks
Ahmed (2005)	Regression type models, smoothing based models and multiplicative decomposition model	Medium Term	Monthly	Time series data	132 months	12 months
Pai and Hong (2005a)	Support Vector Regression with Simulated Annealing, General regression neural networks (GRNN), ARIMA	Long Term	Annually	Time series data	40 years	9 years
Pai and Hong (2005b)	Support Vector Regression with Genetic Algorithm	Long Term	Annually	Time series data	12 years	4 years
Espinoza et al. (2005)	Least Squares Support Vector Machines	Short Term	Hourly	Time series data, temperature	3 years	6 months
Hor et al. (2005)	Multiple Regression	Mid Term	Monthly	Time series data, gross domestic product, population growth	6 years	7 years
Parkpoom et al. (2004)	Linear Regression	Short Term	Hourly	Time series data, temperature		
Chen et al. (2004)	Support Vector Machines	Short Term	Hourly	Time series data, temperature	2 years	1 month
Hsu and Chen (2003)	Artificial Neural Network	Long Term	Annually	Time series data	16 years	4 years
Yuancheng et al. (2002)	Least Squares Support Vector Machines	Short Term	Hourly	Time series data	1 year	
Mohandes (2002)	Support Vector Machines	Short Term	Hourly	Time series data	5 years	1 year
Khontanzad et al. (2002)	Neuro-Fuzzy Method	Short Term	Hourly	Time series data, temperature, price	2 years	1 year
Taylor and Buizza (2002)	Neural Network with Weather Ensemble	Short term	Hourly	Time series data, temperature	12 months	1 month
Kandil and Debeiky (2002)	Expert Systems	Long Term	Annual	Time series data	12 years	4 years
Kermanshahi and Iwamiya (2002)	Artificial Neural Networks	Long term	Annual	Econometric data	20 years	3 years

continued on following page

Table 1. Continued

Author(s)	Method	Forecast Horizon	Data Type	Model Variables	Train Size	Test Size
Senjyu et al. (2002)	Artificial Neural Networks	Short Term	Hourly	Time series data	150 days	1 day
Kim et al. (2002)	Kohonen Neural Network and Wavelet Transform	Short Term	Hourly	Time series data	1 year	1 year
Kim et al. (2000)	Artificial Neural Networks and Fuzzy Inference	Short Term (Special days)	Hourly	Time series data	4 years	1 year
Douglas et al. (1998)	Bayesian Estimation	Short Term	Hourly	Time series data temperature		
Papadakis et al. (1998)	Fuzzy Neural Networks	Short Term	Hourly	Time series data, temperature	1 year	1 year
Vermaak and Botha (1998)	Recurrent Neural Networks	Short Term	Hourly	Time series data, temperature	21 weeks	1 week
Chow and Leung (1996b)	Nonlinear autoregressive integrated neural network	Short Term	Hourly	Time series data, temperature, humidity, rainfall	1 year	6 months
Bakirtzis et al. (1996)	Artificial Neural Network	Short Term	Hourly	Time series data, temperature	1 year	1 week
Piras et al. (1996)	Artificial Neural Network	Short Term	Hourly	Time series data, temperature	2 years	1 year
Papalexopoulos et al. (1994)	Artificial Neural Network	Short Term	Hourly	Time series data, temperature	5 years	1 year
Haida and Muto (1994)	Multivariate Regression	Short Term	Hourly	Time series data, temperature	2 years	1 year
Chen et al. (1992)	Artificial Neural Networks	Short Term	Hourly	Time series data	2 weeks	1 week
Peng et al. (1992)	Artificial Neural Networks	Short Term	Hourly	Time series data, temperature	2 weeks	1 week
Hubele and Cheng (1990)	Statistical Decision Functions	Short Term	Hourly	Time series date, temperature	3 years	1 month
Rahman (1990)	Rule-Based Forecasting	Short Term	Hourly	Humidity, wind speed, temperature	2 years	2 years
Ho et al. (1990)	Linear regression, Expert Systems	Short Term	Hourly	Time series data, temperature, humidity	4 years	1 year
Papalexopoulos and Hesterberg (1990)	Linear Regression, ARMA	Short Term	Hourly	Time series data, temperature	5 years	1 year
Rahman and Bhatnagar (1988)	Expert System	Short Term	Hourly	Time series data, temperature	5 weeks	1 day

FORECASTING ALGORITHMS

Seasonal grey model, support vector machines, random forests and seasonal ARIMA are introduced in this section.

Seasonal Grey Model

Grey systems theory was first introduced by Deng (1982) and can be used to solve uncertainty problems in cases with discrete data and incomplete information. The grey theory consists of five parts: grey prediction, grey relational analysis, grey decision making, grey programming and grey control (1982). Grey prediction is one of the major parts of the grey theory. Grey prediction models have been used in many forecasting problems.

GM (1, 1) model is the basic grey prediction model. GM (1, 1) indicates one variable and one order grey forecasting model (Wang and Hsu, 2008). But, short term electricity load data has multiple seasonal patterns such as weekly, daily and hourly periodicity. The use of the GM (1, 1) model without considering of seasonal factors leads to inaccuracy load forecasting. At this point, Xia and Wong (2014) proposed a seasonal grey model (SGM). In this study, SGM can be used to solve the problem of short-term load forecasting.

The calculation steps of the SGM can be summarized below (Xia & Wong, 2014):

Step 1: Assume $X^{(0)} = \{x^{(0)}(1), x^{(0)}(2),\ldots, x^{(0)}(i),\ldots, x^{(0)}(n)\}$ be an original time series data. A new sequence $X^{(1)}$ is obtained by cycle truncation accumulated generating operation (CTAGO).

$$x^{(1)}(k) = CTAGO(\mathrm{x}^{(0)}(k)) = \sum_{j=1}^{q} x^{(0)}(k+j-1) \quad \forall k = 1, 2, \ldots, n-q+1 \tag{1}$$

where q is the periodicity of the time series.

Step 2: The seasonal grey forecasting model is established as follows.

$$\hat{x}^{(1)}(k+1) = d_1(x^{(1)}(k) + \lambda) + d_2, \qquad \forall k = 1, 2, \ldots, n - q \tag{2}$$

Step 3: In the Equation (2), the values of parameter d_1, d_2 and λ can be calculated as follows using the least square method.

$$d = \left[d_1, d_2 \right]^T = (A^T A)^{-1} A^T Q \tag{3}$$

where

$$A = \begin{bmatrix} x^{(1)}(1) & x^{(1)}(2) & x^{(1)}(3) & \ldots & x^{(1)}(n-q) \\ 1 & 1 & 1 & \ldots & 1 \end{bmatrix}^T \tag{4}$$

$$Q = \left[x^{(1)}(2), x^{(1)}(3), \ldots, x^{(1)}(n-q+1) \right]^T \tag{5}$$

$$\lambda = \frac{\sum_{i=1}^{k-1}(x^{(1)}(i+1) - d_1 x^{(1)}(i) - d_2)}{d_1(k-1)} \tag{6}$$

Step 4: Finally, the predicted values of the original sequence are calculated by using Equation (7).

$$\hat{x}^{(0)}(k+1) = \hat{x}^{(1)}(k-q+2) - x^{(1)}(k-q+1) + x^{(0)}(k-q+1) \quad \forall k = q, q+1, ..., n \tag{7}$$

Support Vector Regression

SVM is especially suitable for solving problems of small sample size (Chen, 2004). SVM is grounded in the framework of statistical learning theory, which has been developed by Vapnik and Chervonenkis (Vapnik & Chervonenkis, 1974).

SVR maps the input data x into a higher dimensional feature space through a nonlinear mapping Φ and then a linear regression problem is obtained and solved in this feature space (Gao et al., 2007). With the given training data $\{(x_1, y_1), ..., (x_i, y_i), ..., (x_n, y_n)\}$, the mapping function can be formulates as;

$$f(x) = \sum_{i=1}^{n} \omega_i \Phi_i x_i + b \tag{8}$$

where ω_i and b are the parameters that need to be defined. SVR is to find a function $f(x)$ that has at most ε deviation from the actually obtained targets y_i for all the training data and at the same time is as flat as possible. Flatness in this case means to reduce the model complexity by minimizing $\|\omega\|^2$, so that this problem can be written as an optimization problem;

$$Min \frac{1}{2}\|\omega\|^2$$
$$s.t \begin{cases} y_i - \Phi(\omega, x_i) - b \leq \varepsilon \\ \Phi(\omega, x_i) + b_i - y \leq \varepsilon \end{cases} \tag{9}$$

Formula 9 defines a constrained optimization problem. Formula 10 shows the solution of this problem.

$$Max \ W(\alpha) = \sum_{i=1}^{n} \alpha_i - \frac{1}{2} \sum_{i=1,j=1}^{n} \alpha_i \alpha_j y_i y_j x_i^T x_j \tag{10}$$

$$s.t. \ C \geq \alpha_i \geq 0, \ \sum_{i=1}^{n} \alpha_i y_i = 0$$

Random Forests

Random forests (Breiman, 2001) is a substantial modification of bagging that builds a large collection of de-correlated trees, and then averages them. The essential idea in bagging is to average many noisy but approximately unbiased models, and hence reduces the variance. Since each tree generated in bagging is identically distributed, the expectation of an average of B such trees is the same as the expectation of any one of them. This means the bias of bagged trees is the same as that of the individual trees, and the only hope of improvement is through variance reduction. The idea in random forests is to improve the variance reduction of bagging by reducing the correlation between the trees, without increasing the variance too much. This is achieved in the tree-growing process through random selection of the input variables. Hastie et al. (2005) gives detailed information about random forests.

Seasonal ARIMA

Autoregressive integrated moving average (ARIMA) model is insufficient for forecasting a time series with seasonality. At this point, seasonal autoregressive integrated moving average (SARIMA) is the widely used statistical model for forecasting stochastic seasonal time series.

Let a time series $\{X_t | t = 1, 2,...,k\}$ be generated by SARIMA (p,d,q) $(P,D,Q)_s$ process of Box and Jenkins time series model. The seasonal ARIMA model can be defined as follows (Box and Jenkins, 1976):

$$\phi_p(B)\Phi_p(\mathrm{B}^s)(1-B)^d(1-B^s)^D X_t = \theta_q(B)\Theta_Q(B^s)\varepsilon_t, \tag{11}$$

where p, d, q, P, D, Q are integers, s is the season period;

$$\phi_p(B) = 1 - \phi_1 B - \phi_2 B^2 - ... - \phi_p B^p,$$

$$\Phi_P(B^s) = 1 - \Phi_s B^s - \Phi_{2s} B^{2s} - ... - \Phi_{ps} B^{Ps},$$

$$\theta_q(B) = 1 - \theta_1 B - \theta_2 B^2 - ... - \theta_q B^q,$$

$$\Theta_Q(B^s) = 1 - \Theta_s B^s - \Theta_{2s} B^{2s} - ... - \Theta_{Qs} B^{Qs}$$

are polynomials in B of degree p, q, P, and Q. B is the backward shift operator, and ε_t is the estimated residual at time t. d is the number of regular differences, D is the number of seasonal differences.

The SARIMA model includes following four steps (Tseng and Tzeng, 2002):

- Identify the SARIMA (p,d,q) $(P,D,Q)_s$ structure,
- Estimate unknown parameters,
- Goodness-of-fit tests on the estimated residuals,
- Forecast future outcomes based on the known data.

SHORT-TERM LOAD FORECASTING WITH PROPOSED ALGORITHMS

Data Sets

In this study forecasting performance of these novel techniques, namely support vector regression, random forests, seasonal grey model, seasonal ARIMA and linear regression are benchmarked against each other on seven data sets. The details of these data sets are given in Table 2.

Table 2. Properties of the seven data sets used for short term load forecasting

No	Data Set	Type	Data Range	Test Range
1	BSE Dataset	General	10.10.2008 – 31.12.2008	18.12.2008 – 31.12.2008
2	GS2 Dataset	Industry	10.10.2011 – 30.12.2011	17.12-2011 – 30.12.2011
3	NGCOM Dataset	Commercial	30.05.2010 – 19.08.2010	06.08.2010 – 19.08.2010
4	NGIND Dataset	Industrial	30.05.2010 – 19.08.2010	06.08.2010 – 19.08.2010
5	National Grid Dataset	General	10.03.2011 – 31.05.2011	18.05.2011 – 31.05.2011
6	PJM-AEP Dataset	General	19.08.2011 – 09.11.2011	27.10.2011 – 09.11.2011
7	PJM-E Dataset	General	19.08.2011 – 09.11.2011	27.10.2011 – 09.11.2011

Average hourly electricity load for each dataset can be seen in Figure 1. Each dataset outlines a different consumption characteristic. The performance of the proposed forecasting model is analyzed on these different datasets.

Methodology

Data sets are divided into training and test sets. Each method is trained on the static training size and then 24 hours of the next period is forecasted with each algorithm. Totally, all hours are predicted for the last 14 days (14x24=336 hours) of each data set.

In this study, each hour is modeled separately; consequently 24 different models are trained for each algorithm. Predictions for each hour are done with its own trained model.

All forecasting models follow similar steps in a forecasting process. Firstly, separate models for separate hours are generated. Then, each hour of the target day is forecasted with the generated model from the training stage. Rolling mechanism is used in this study. With a rolling mechanism, each 24 hours is predicted by expanding the training dataset for each day. In this procedure, a part of the data is employed as training data, and the model generated by this training data is used in forecasting (test) phase. Then for each new day, training data is shifted, thus, the actual values of the previously forecasted day become the last line of the training dataset.

Linear regression, random forests and support vector regression methods uses time lags to represent the time series model. We have used *t-1* (previous day), *t-2* (the day before), *t-7* (the same day in the previous week) if we model each hour separately. In the seasonal grey model and seasonal ARIMA model, the values of the seasonal length of the data sets are taken as 7. The other model parameters are optimized based on minimum MAPE value using MATLAB optimization toolbox.

Figure 1. Average electricity load for each hour of the seven data sets

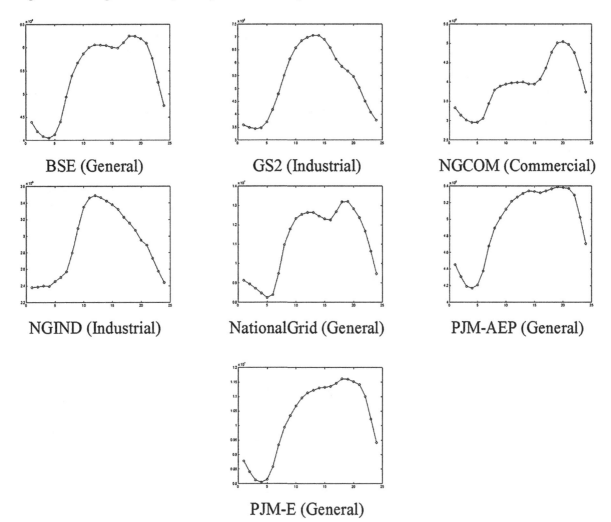

Results

In this study, the mean absolute percentage error (MAPE) is used for comparing the forecasting accuracy of the proposed algorithms. Its formula can be seen in (12). Here, A_i is the actual load value and F_i is the forecasted value for the same hour.

$$MAPE = \frac{100\%}{n} \sum_{i=1}^{n} \frac{|A_i - F_i|}{A_i} \tag{12}$$

Proposed algorithms are coded in MATLAB 2014a. For each dataset, the obtained MAPE values of the proposed forecasting algorithms are given in Table 3. Forecasting results of BSE data set and National Grid data set are also represented in Figures 2 and Figure 3.

Table 3. MAPE values of the proposed algorithms on seven data sets

Data Set	SGM	SVR	Random Forests	S-ARIMA	Linear Regression
BSE	**6.304%**	6.328%	6.912%	8.681%	6.654%
GS2	7.567%	**4.892%**	7.304%	5.236%	7.620%
NGCOM	9.122%	**9.002%**	10.992%	11.678%	13.229%
NGIND	5.882%	6.928%	5.477%	**4.952%**	5.453%
National Grid	**2.244%**	3.106%	3.448%	2.285%	5.836%
PJM-AEP	3.981%	4.243%	4.306%	**3.555%**	4.258%
PJM-E	**3.902%**	5.254%	4.159%	4.279%	5.532%
Average MAPE	**5.572%**	5.679%	6.085%	5.809%	6.940%

Figure 2. Forecasting results of the proposed algorithms for BSE dataset

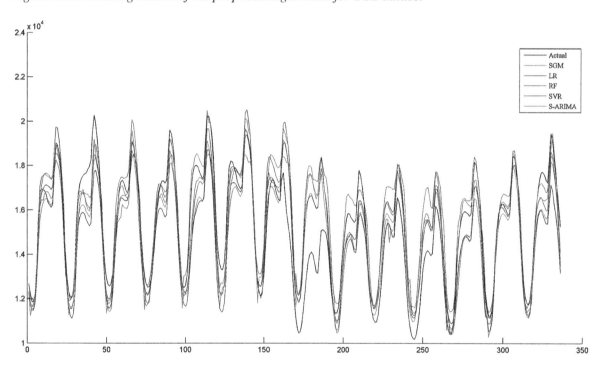

The empirical results indicate that the SGM and SVR model results in better forecasting accuracy than the other methods, especially linear regression and random forests.

CONCLUSION

In this paper, five models were employed, namely, seasonal grey model, support vector machines, random forests, seasonal ARIMA and linear regression to forecast the short-term electricity load. The effectiveness of these methods is illustrated on seven well-known data sets. On the average support vec-

Figure 3. Forecasting results of the proposed algorithms for National Grid dataset

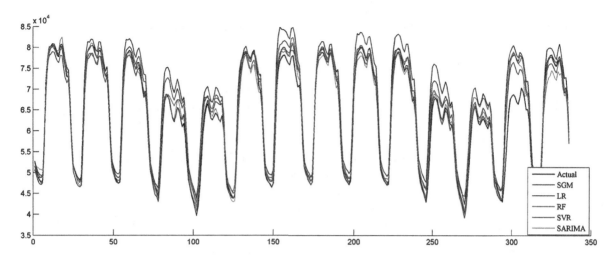

tor regression and the seasonal grey model were the most successful methods, with the average MAPEs of 5.679% and 5.572% respectively. Among these data sets, NGCOM, which has a commercial profile, was very hard to forecast. MAPE value of the linear regression on this data set was as low as 13.229%. Support vector regression performed better than other algorithms on this data set. The smallest MAPE value obtained among all tests was on National Grid data set with seasonal grey method, with a MAPE of 2.244%. Seasonal ARIMA has achieved the minimum error rates on two data sets, but its performance was very poor on other datasets therefore its variance is higher and it can be said that seasonal ARIMA is highly affected by the structure of the data set. Numerical results show that the seasonal grey model is the most efficient model through its better forecast accuracy.

First time in literature, statistical models, grey forecasting models and machine learning models are compared on the same dataset with this study. As results indicate, there is not a significant difference between the performances of the support vector regression and seasonal grey model.

Further studies may include modeling impacts of holidays and other special days in load data by applying outlier analysis. Metaheuristic algorithms are used to improve the forecast accuracy of the proposed algorithms. Also, hybridizing the support vector regression and grey forecasting model may yield to better predictions.

REFERENCES

Ahmed, S. (2005). Seasonal models of peak electric load demand. *Technological Forecasting and Social Change*, *72*(5), 609–622. doi:10.1016/j.techfore.2004.02.003

Al-Shareef, A. J., Mohamed, E. A., & Al-Judaibi, E. (2008). One hour ahead load forecasting using artificial neural network for the western area of Saudi Arabia. *International Journal of Electrical Systems Science and Engineering*, *1*(1), 35–40.

Alfares, H. K., & Nazeeruddin, M. (2002). Electric load forecasting: Literature survey and classification of methods. *International Journal of Systems Science*, *33*(1), 23–34. doi:10.1080/00207720110067421

Alpaydin, E. (2004). *Introduction to machine learning*. Cambridge, MA: MIT Press.

Azadeh, A., Ghaderi, S. F., Tarverdian, S., & Saberi, M. (2007). Integration of artificial neural networks and genetic algorithm to predict electrical energy consumption. *Applied Mathematics and Computation, 186*(2), 1731–1741. doi:10.1016/j.amc.2006.08.093

Bahrami, S., Hooshmand, R. A., & Parastegari, M. (2014). Short term electric load forecasting by wavelet transform and grey model improved by PSO (particle swarm optimization) algorithm. *Energy, 72*, 434–442. doi:10.1016/j.energy.2014.05.065

Bakirtzis, A. G., Petridis, V., Kiartzis, S. J., & Alexiadis, M. C. (1996). A neural network short term load forecasting model for the Greek power system. *Power Systems. IEEE Transactions on, 11*(2), 858–863.

Bianco, V., Manca, O., Nardini, S., & Minea, A. A. (2010). Analysis and forecasting of nonresidential electricity consumption in Romania. *Applied Energy, 87*(11), 3584–3590. doi:10.1016/j.apenergy.2010.05.018

Box, G. E., & Jenkins, G. M. (1976). *Time series analysis: forecasting and control*. Holden-Day.

Breiman, L. (2001). Random forests. *Machine Learning, 45*(1), 5–32. doi:10.1023/A:1010933404324

Chang, P. C., Fan, C. Y., & Lin, J. J. (2011). Monthly electricity demand forecasting based on a weighted evolving fuzzy neural network approach. *International Journal of Electrical Power & Energy Systems, 33*(1), 17–27. doi:10.1016/j.ijepes.2010.08.008

Che, J., Wang, J., & Tang, Y. (2012). Optimal training subset in a support vector regression electric load forecasting model. *Applied Soft Computing, 12*(5), 1523–1531. doi:10.1016/j.asoc.2011.12.017

Chen, B., Chang, M., & Lin, C. (2004). Load forecasting using support vector machines: A study on EUNITE competition 2001. *IEEE Transactions on Power Systems, 19*(4), 1821–1830. doi:10.1109/TPWRS.2004.835679

Chen, N., Lu, W., Yang, J., & Li, G. (2004). *Support vector machine in chemistry* (Vol. 11). Singapore: World Scientific.

Chen, S. T., Yu, D. C., & Moghaddamjo, A. R. (1992). Weather sensitive short-term load forecasting using nonfully connected artificial neural network. *Power Systems. IEEE Transactions on, 7*(3), 1098–1105. doi:10.1109/26.142800

Chen, T. (2012). A collaborative fuzzy-neural approach for long-term load forecasting in Taiwan. *Computers & Industrial Engineering, 63*(3), 663–670. doi:10.1016/j.cie.2011.06.003

Chow, T. W. S., & Leung, C. T. (1996a). Neural network based short-term load forecasting using weather compensation. *Power Systems. IEEE Transactions on, 11*(4), 1736–1742.

Chow, T. W. S., & Leung, C. T. (1996b). Nonlinear autoregressive integrated neural network model for short-term load forecasting. In *Generation, transmission and distribution, IEE proceedings-* (Vol. 143, pp. 500-506). doi:10.1049/ip-gtd:19960600

Christiaanse, W. R. (1971). Short-term load forecasting using general exponential smoothing. *Power Apparatus and Systems, IEEE Transactions on*, (2), 900-911.

Douglas, A. P., Breipohl, A. M., Lee, F. N., & Adapa, R. (1998). The impacts of temperature forecast uncertainty on Bayesian load forecasting. *Power Systems. IEEE Transactions on, 13*(4), 1507–1513.

Drucker, H., Burges, C. J. C., Kaufman, L., Smola, A., & Vapnik, V. (1997). Support vector regression machines. *Advances in Neural Information Processing Systems*, 155–161.

Espinoza, M., Suykens, J., & De Moor, B. (2005). Load forecasting using fixed-size least squares support vector machines. *Computational Intelligence and Bioinspired Systems*, 488-527.

Espinoza, M., Suykens, J. A., & De Moor, B. (2006). Fixed-size least squares support vector machines: A large scale application in electrical load forecasting. *Computational Management Science, 3*(2), 113–129. doi:10.1007/s10287-005-0003-7

Fan, S., & Chen, L. (2006). Short-term load forecasting based on an adaptive hybrid method. *Power Systems. IEEE Transactions on, 21*(1), 392–401.

Gao, C., Bompard, E., Napoli, R., & Cheng, H. (2007). Price forecast in the competitive electricity market by support vector machine. *Physica A: Statistical Mechanics and its Applications, 382*(1), 98-113.

Garcia, R. C., Contreras, J., Van Akkeren, M., & Garcia, J. B. C. (2005). A GARCH forecasting model to predict day-ahead electricity prices. *Power Systems. IEEE Transactions on, 20*(2), 867–874.

Ghiassi, M., Zimbra, D. K., & Saidane, H. (2006). Medium term system load forecasting with a dynamic artificial neural network model. *Electric Power Systems Research, 76*(5), 302–316. doi:10.1016/j.epsr.2005.06.010

Gu, Y., & Hu, F. (2012). An intelligent forecasting method for short term electric power load based on partitioned support vector regression. In *2012 IEEE International Conference on Cyber Technology in Automation, Control, and Intelligent Systems (CYBER)*. doi:10.1109/CYBER.2012.6320044

Hagan, M. T., & Behr, S. M. (1987). The time series approach to short term load forecasting. *Power Systems. IEEE Transactions on, 2*(3), 785–791.

Haida, T., & Muto, S. (1994). Regression based peak load forecasting using a transformation technique. *Power Systems. IEEE Transactions on, 9*(4), 1788–1794.

Hamzaçebi, C. (2007). Forecasting of Turkey's net electricity energy consumption on sectoral bases. *Energy Policy, 35*(3), 2009–2016. doi:10.1016/j.enpol.2006.03.014

Hastie, T., Tibshirani, R., Friedman, J., & Franklin, J. (2005). The elements of statistical learning: Data mining, inference and prediction. *The Mathematical Intelligencer, 27*(2), 83–85. doi:10.1007/BF02985802

Hippert, H. S., Bunn, D. W., & Souza, R. C. (2005). Large neural networks for electricity load forecasting: Are they overfitted? *International Journal of Forecasting, 21*(3), 425–434. doi:10.1016/j.ijforecast.2004.12.004

Ho, K. L., Hsu, Y. Y., Chen, C. F., Lee, T. E., Liang, C. C., Lai, T. S., & Chen, K. K. (1990). Short term load forecasting of Taiwan power system using a knowledge-based expert system. *Power Systems. IEEE Transactions on, 5*(4), 1214–1221.

Hoffman, K. C., & Wood, D. O. (1976). Energy system modeling and forecasting. *Annual Review of Energy, 1*(1), 423-453.

Hong, W. C. (2009a). Electric load forecasting by support vector model. *Applied Mathematical Modelling, 33*(5), 2444–2454. doi:10.1016/j.apm.2008.07.010

Hong, W. C. (2009b). Chaotic particle swarm optimization algorithm in a support vector regression electric load forecasting model. *Energy Conversion and Management, 50*(1), 105–117. doi:10.1016/j.enconman.2008.08.031

Hong, W. C. (2009c). Hybrid evolutionary algorithms in a SVR-based electric load forecasting model. *International Journal of Electrical Power & Energy Systems, 31*(7), 409–417. doi:10.1016/j.ijepes.2009.03.020

Hong, W. C. (2011). Electric load forecasting by seasonal recurrent SVR (support vector regression) with chaotic artificial bee colony algorithm. *Energy, 36*(9), 5568–5578. doi:10.1016/j.energy.2011.07.015

Hong, W. C., Dong, Y., Zhang, W. Y., Chen, L. Y., & Panigrahi, B. K. (2013). Cyclic electric load forecasting by seasonal SVR with chaotic genetic algorithm. *International Journal of Electrical Power & Energy Systems, 44*(1), 604–614. doi:10.1016/j.ijepes.2012.08.010

Hooshmand, R. A., Amooshahi, H., & Parastegari, M. (2013). A hybrid intelligent algorithm based short-term load forecasting approach. *International Journal of Electrical Power & Energy Systems, 45*(1), 313–324. doi:10.1016/j.ijepes.2012.09.002

Hor, C. L., Watson, S. J., & Majithia, S. (2005). Analyzing the impact of weather variables on monthly electricity demand. *Power Systems. IEEE Transactions on, 20*(4), 2078–2085.

Hor, C. L., Watson, S. J., & Majithia, S. (2006, June). Daily load forecasting and maximum demand estimation using ARIMA and GARCH. In *Probabilistic Methods Applied to Power Systems, 2006. PMAPS 2006. International Conference on* (pp. 1-6). IEEE. doi:10.1109/PMAPS.2006.360237

Hsu, C. C., & Chen, C. Y. (2003). Regional load forecasting in Taiwan—applications of artificial neural networks. *Energy Conversion and Management, 44*(12), 1941–1949. doi:10.1016/S0196-8904(02)00225-X

Hsu, C. C., Wu, C. H., Chen, S. C., & Peng, K. L. (2006, January). Dynamically optimizing parameters in support vector regression: An application of electricity load forecasting. In *System Sciences, 2006. HICSS'06. Proceedings of the 39th Annual Hawaii International Conference on* (Vol. 2, pp. 30c-30c). IEEE.

Huang, S. J., & Shih, K. R. (2003). Short-term load forecasting via ARMA model identification including non-Gaussian process considerations. *Power Systems. IEEE Transactions on, 18*(2), 673–679.

Hubele, N. F., & Cheng, C. S. (1990). Identification of seasonal short-term load forecasting models using statistical decision functions. *Power Systems. IEEE Transactions on, 5*(1), 40–45.

Jabbour, K., Riveros, J. F. V., Landsbergen, D., & Meyer, W. (1988). ALFA: Automated load forecasting assistant. *Power Systems. IEEE Transactions on, 3*(3), 908–914.

Jain, A., & Satish, B. (2009, June). Clustering based short term load forecasting using support vector machines. In *PowerTech, 2009 IEEE Bucharest* (pp. 1-8). IEEE. doi:10.1109/PTC.2009.5282144

Jin, M., Zhou, X., Zhang, Z. M., & Tentzeris, M. M. (2012). Short-term power load forecasting using grey correlation contest modeling. *Expert Systems with Applications*, *39*(1), 773–779. doi:10.1016/j.eswa.2011.07.072

Ju-Long, D. (1982). Control problems of grey systems. *Systems & Control Letters*, *1*(5), 288–294. doi:10.1016/S0167-6911(82)80025-X

Kandil, M. S., El-Debeiky, S. M., & Hasanien, N. E. (2002). Long-term load forecasting for fast developing utility using a knowledge-based expert system. *Power Systems. IEEE Transactions on*, *17*(2), 491–496.

Kermanshahi, B., & Iwamiya, H. (2002). Up to year 2020 load forecasting using neural nets. *International Journal of Electrical Power & Energy Systems*, *24*(9), 789–797. doi:10.1016/S0142-0615(01)00086-2

Khosravi, A., Nahavandi, S., & Creighton, D. (2013). A neural network-GARCH-based method for construction of Prediction Intervals. *Electric Power Systems Research*, *96*, 185–193. doi:10.1016/j.epsr.2012.11.007

Khotanzad, A., Zhou, E., & Elragal, H. (2002). A neuro-fuzzy approach to short-term load forecasting in a price-sensitive environment. *Power Systems. IEEE Transactions on*, *17*(4), 1273–1282.

Kim, C. I., Yu, I. K., & Song, Y. H. (2002). Kohonen neural network and wavelet transform based approach to short-term load forecasting. *Electric Power Systems Research*, *63*(3), 169–176. doi:10.1016/S0378-7796(02)00097-4

Kim, K. H., Youn, H. S., & Kang, Y. C. (2000). Short-term load forecasting for special days in anomalous load conditions using neural networks and fuzzy inference method. *Power Systems. IEEE Transactions on*, *15*(2), 559–565.

Ko, C. N., & Lee, C. M. (2013). Short-term load forecasting using SVR (support vector regression)-based radial basis function neural network with dual extended Kalman filter. *Energy*, *49*, 413–422. doi:10.1016/j.energy.2012.11.015

Kulkarni, S., Simon, S. P., & Sundareswaran, K. (2013). A spiking neural network (SNN) forecast engine for short-term electrical load forecasting. *Applied Soft Computing*, *13*(8), 3628–3635. doi:10.1016/j.asoc.2013.04.007

Li, D., Chang, C., Chen, C., & Chen, W. (2012). Forecasting short-term electricity consumption using the adaptive grey-based approach – An Asian case. *Omega*, *40*(6), 767–773. doi:10.1016/j.omega.2011.07.007

Li, G. D., Yamaguchi, D., & Nagai, M. (2006). Application of improved grey prediction model to short term load forecasting. *Proceedings of International Conference on Electrical Engineering*, 1-6.

Li, H. Z., Guo, S., Li, C. J., & Sun, J. Q. (2013). A hybrid annual power load forecasting model based on generalized regression neural network with fruit fly optimization algorithm. *Knowledge-Based Systems*, *37*, 378–387. doi:10.1016/j.knosys.2012.08.015

Mamlook, R., Badran, O., & Abdulhadi, E. (2009). A fuzzy inference model for short-term load forecasting. *Energy Policy*, *37*(4), 1239–1248. doi:10.1016/j.enpol.2008.10.051

Mandal, P., Senjyu, T., Urasaki, N., & Funabashi, T. (2006). A neural network based several-hour-ahead electric load forecasting using similar days approach. *International Journal of Electrical Power & Energy Systems*, *28*(6), 367–373. doi:10.1016/j.ijepes.2005.12.007

Mirasgedis, S., Sarafidis, Y., Georgopoulou, E., Lalas, D. P., Moschovits, M., Karagiannis, F., & Papakonstantinou, D. (2006). Models for mid-term electricity demand forecasting incorporating weather influences. *Energy*, *31*(2), 208–227. doi:10.1016/j.energy.2005.02.016

Moghram, I., & Rahman, S. (1989). Analysis and evaluation of five short-term load forecasting techniques. *Power Systems. IEEE Transactions on*, *4*(4), 1484–1491.

Mohandes, M. (2002). Support vector machines for short-term electrical load forecasting. *International Journal of Energy Research*, *26*(4), 335–345. doi:10.1002/er.787

Niu, D., Wang, Y., & Wu, D. D. (2010). Power load forecasting using support vector machine and ant colony optimization. *Expert Systems with Applications*, *37*(3), 2531–2539. doi:10.1016/j.eswa.2009.08.019

Niu, D. X., Li, W., Han, Z. H., & Yuan, X. E. (2008, October). Power Load Forecasting based on Improved Genetic Algorithm–GM (1, 1) Model. In *Natural Computation, 2008. ICNC'08. Fourth International Conference on* (Vol. 1, pp. 630-634). IEEE.

Pai, P. F., & Hong, W. C. (2005a). Support vector machines with simulated annealing algorithms in electricity load forecasting. *Energy Conversion and Management*, *46*(17), 2669–2688. doi:10.1016/j.enconman.2005.02.004

Pai, P. F., & Hong, W. C. (2005b). Forecasting regional electricity load based on recurrent support vector machines with genetic algorithms. *Electric Power Systems Research*, *74*(3), 417–425. doi:10.1016/j.epsr.2005.01.006

Papadakis, S. E., Theocharis, J. B., Kiartzis, S. J., & Bakirtzis, A. G. (1998). A novel approach to short-term load forecasting using fuzzy neural networks. *Power Systems. IEEE Transactions on*, *13*(2), 480–492.

Papalexopoulos, A. D., Hao, S., & Peng, T. M. (1994). An implementation of a neural network based load forecasting model for the EMS. *Power Systems. IEEE Transactions on*, *9*(4), 1956–1962.

Papalexopoulos, A. D., & Hesterberg, T. C. (1990). A regression-based approach to short-term system load forecasting. *Power Systems. IEEE Transactions on*, *5*(4), 1535–1547.

Parkpoom, S., Harrison, G. P., & Bialek, J. W. (2004, September). Climate change impacts on electricity demand. In *Universities Power Engineering Conference, 2004. UPEC 2004. 39th International* (Vol. 3, pp. 1342-1346). IEEE.

Peng, T. M., Hubele, N. F., & Karady, G. G. (1992). Advancement in the application of neural networks for short-term load forecasting. *Power Systems. IEEE Transactions on*, *7*(1), 250–257.

Piras, A., Germond, A., Buchenel, B., Imhof, K., & Jaccard, Y. (1996). Heterogeneous artificial neural network for short term electrical load forecasting. *Power Systems. IEEE Transactions on*, *11*(1), 397–402.

Rahman, S. (1990). Formulation and analysis of a rule-based short-term load forecasting algorithm. *Proceedings of the IEEE*, *78*(5), 805–816. doi:10.1109/5.53400

Rahman, S., & Bhatnagar, R. (1988). An expert system based algorithm for short term load forecast. *Power Systems. IEEE Transactions on, 3*(2), 392–399.

Senjyu, T., Takara, H., Uezato, K., & Funabashi, T. (2002). One-hour-ahead load forecasting using neural network. *Power Systems. IEEE Transactions on, 17*(1), 113–118.

Taylor, J. W. (2008). An evaluation of methods for very short-term load forecasting using minute-by-minute British data. *International Journal of Forecasting, 24*(4), 645–658. doi:10.1016/j.ijforecast.2008.07.007

Taylor, J. W. (2010). Triple seasonal methods for short-term electricity demand forecasting. *European Journal of Operational Research, 204*(1), 139–152. doi:10.1016/j.ejor.2009.10.003

Taylor, J. W. (2012). Short-term load forecasting with exponentially weighted methods. *Power Systems. IEEE Transactions on, 27*(1), 458–464.

Taylor, J. W., & Buizza, R. (2002). Neural network load forecasting with weather ensemble predictions. *Power Systems. IEEE Transactions on, 17*(3), 626–632.

Taylor, J. W., & Buizza, R. (2003). Using weather ensemble predictions in electricity demand forecasting. *International Journal of Forecasting, 19*(1), 57–70. doi:10.1016/S0169-2070(01)00123-6

Taylor, J. W., & McSharry, P. E. (2007). Short-term load forecasting methods: An evaluation based on european data. *Power Systems. IEEE Transactions on, 22*(4), 2213–2219.

Teisberg, T. J., Weiher, R. F., & Khotanzad, A. (2005). The economic value of temperature forecasts in electricity generation. *Bulletin of the American Meteorological Society, 86*(12), 1765–1771. doi:10.1175/BAMS-86-12-1765

Tseng, F. M., & Tzeng, G. H. (2002). A fuzzy seasonal ARIMA model for forecasting. *Fuzzy Sets and Systems, 126*(3), 367–376. doi:10.1016/S0165-0114(01)00047-1

Vapnik, V. N., & Chervonenkis, A. J. (1974). *Theory of pattern recognition*. Academic Press.

Vermaak, J., & Botha, E. C. (1998). Recurrent neural networks for short-term load forecasting. *Power Systems. IEEE Transactions on, 13*(1), 126–132.

Wang, C., & Hsu, L. (2008). Using genetic algorithms grey theory to forecast high technology industrial output. *Applied Mathematics and Computation, 195*(1), 256–263. doi:10.1016/j.amc.2007.04.080

Xia, M., & Wong, W. K. (2014). A seasonal discrete grey forecasting model for fashion retailing. *Knowledge-Based Systems, 57*, 119–126. doi:10.1016/j.knosys.2013.12.014

Yadav, V., & Srinivasan, D. (2011). A SOM-based hybrid linear-neural model for short-term load forecasting. *Neurocomputing, 74*(17), 2874–2885. doi:10.1016/j.neucom.2011.03.039

Yao, A. W. L., Chi, S. C., & Chen, J. H. (2003). An improved grey based approach for electricity demand forecasting. *Electric Power Systems Research, 67*(3), 217–224. doi:10.1016/S0378-7796(03)00112-3

Yuancheng, L., Tingjian, F., & Erkeng, Y. (2002, October). Short-term electrical load forecasting using least squares support vector machines. In *Power System Technology, 2002. Proceedings. PowerCon 2002. International Conference on* (Vol. 1, pp. 230-233). IEEE. doi:10.1109/ICPST.2002.1053540

Zhou, P., Ang, B. W., & Poh, K. L. (2006). A trigonometric grey prediction approach to forecasting electricity demand. *Energy*, *31*(14), 2839–2847. doi:10.1016/j.energy.2005.12.002

KEY TERMS AND DEFINITIONS

Day-Ahead Market: A market for virtual electricity transaction among buyers and sellers. A buy or sell bid is placed for each hour of the next day, then final prices are calculated according to these bids.

Grey Forecasting: One of the major parts of grey system theory and an effective tool for estimating with limited and discrete time series data.

Grey Theory: A methodology that can be used to solve uncertainty problems in cases with discrete data and incomplete information.

Load Profile: A graph of hourly load values of a single entity.

MAPE (Mean Absolute Percentage Error): A widely used measure that evaluates prediction inaccuracy as a percentage of forecasting methods.

Random Forests: A method for forecasting by using a model generated with many noisy but approximately unbiased models.

Seasonal ARIMA: A class of autoregressive integrated moving average (ARIMA) forecasting models that can capture seasonality in a time series.

Support Vector Regression: A version of support vector machines for regression.

Chapter 6
A Soft Computing Approach to Customer Segmentation

Abdulkadir Hiziroglu
Yildirim Beyazit University, Turkey

ABSTRACT

There are a number of traditional models designed to segment customers, however none of them have the ability to establish non-strict customer segments. One crucial area that can meet this requirement is known as soft computing. Although there have been studies related to the usage of soft computing techniques for segmentation, they are not based on the effective two-stage methodology. The aim of this study is to propose a two-stage segmentation model based on soft computing using the purchasing behaviours of customers in a data mining framework and to make a comparison of the proposed model with a traditional two-stage segmentation model. Segmentation was performed via neuro-fuzzy two stage-clustering approach for a secondary data set, which included more than 300,000 unique customer records, from a UK retail company. The findings indicated that the model provided stronger insights and has greater managerial implications in comparison with the traditional two-stage method with respect to six segmentation effectiveness indicators.

1. INTRODUCTION

Segmentation strategy is an important method to achieve more targeted communication with customers by classifying them according to previously defined characteristics. In order to build a close relationship with customers and arrange the right resources to serve a target customer segment, it is crucial to establish appropriate customer segmentation models. The selection of segmentation techniques is one of the most important issues in segmentation, because the improper selection of classification or clustering tools may have an effect on segmentation results and may cause a negative financial impact (Tsai & Chiu, 2004). In order to avoid this problem, marketing managers should decide which segmentation tools are suitable to adopt.

The vast availability of data and the inefficient performance of traditional statistical techniques (or statistics-oriented segmentation tools) on such voluminous data have stimulated researchers to find effec-

DOI: 10.4018/978-1-5225-0075-9.ch006

tive segmentation tools in order to discover useful insights about their markets and customers. Cluster-based segmentation methods, particularly hierarchical and non-hierarchical methods, have been widely used in the field. But, the hierarchical methods are criticised for non-recovery, while the non-hierarchical methods for their inability to determine the number of clusters initially (Lien, 2005). Hence, the integration of hierarchical and partitioning methods is suggested to make the clustering results powerful for large databases (Kuo et al., 2002a). None of those approaches, however, have the ability to establish non-strict customer segments that could play a significant role in today's competitive consumer markets. Soft computing can be seen as an emerging topic that could tackle this problem (Mitra et al., 2002). Pertaining to segmentation problem, although several individual applications of soft computing techniques can be found in the related literature, they are not based on the effective two-stage methodology. The usage of soft computing techniques in business-related problems, particularly in segmentation, makes segmentation problems more attractive, since these techniques are very effective and applicable (Kuo et al., 2006). This aim of this study is to propose a segmentation model in which the two-stage clustering methodology is used through utilising select soft computing techniques, Artificial Neural Networks (ANN) and Fuzzy Logic (FL). In addition, the model was compared with the select traditional two-stage clustering approaches based on selected indicators regarding segmentation effectiveness.

The rest of the paper is organised as follows. Section 2 discusses key issues in customer segmentation and the applications of soft computing in segmentation, while the research methodology including the associated research questions and hypotheses are described in Section 3. Empirical results of a real-world data are presented in Section 4. Section 5 includes key conclusions and discussions that can be drawn from this study and Section 6 concludes the paper with limitations and future work.

2. LITERATURE REVIEW

The conceptual usage of the term "segmentation" has been attributed to Wendell R. Smith (1956), and in his pioneering article, he considered the differences between the strategies of differentiation and segmentation. Following his work, some other authors, such as Wind (1978), Myers and Tauber (1977), Wilkie and Cohen (1977), Beane and Ennis (1987), Yankelovich and Meer (2006), Dolnicar (2004), Sun (2009) and Tynan and Drayton (1987) also provided broad reviews of segmentation research. The main idea of segmentation or clustering is to group similar customers. A segment can be described as a set of customers who have similar characteristics of demography, behaviours, values, and so on (Nairn and Berthon, 2003, Bailey et al., 2009).

For customer segmentation, a wide variety of data analysis techniques, such as cluster analysis (Hruschka et al., 2004, Li et al., 2009, Liu and Shih, 2005, Wang, 2009, Xia et al., 2010), clusterwise regression (Desarbo et al., 2008), AID(Automatic Interaction Detection)/CHAID(Chi-squared Automatic Interaction Detection) (Gil-Saura & Ruiz-Molina, 2008, Jonker et al., 2004), multiple regression (Suh et al., 1999), discriminant analysis (Tsiotsou, 2006), latent class structure (Wu and Chou, 2011) and sophisticated soft computing techniques such as ANN and FL have been used in the related literature. Even though it is very difficult to provide a clear classification for segmentation techniques, Figure 1 is proposed as a baseline scheme for the classification of those techniques. In this figure, while some techniques are classified under data preparation, others are considered as classification or clustering data analysis techniques.

Figure 1. A classification of segmentation techniques

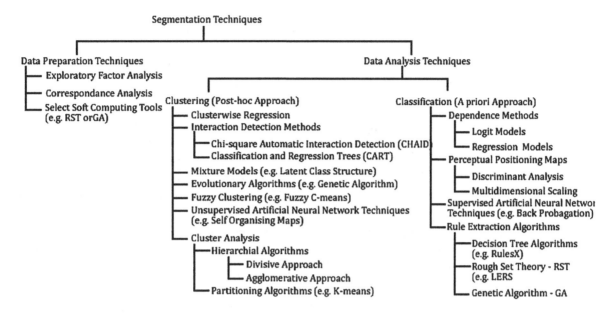

With the growing awareness of soft computing technologies, these techniques are being increasingly utilised for modelling market/customer segmentation problems as in either classification or in clusters form. Table 1 shows the application of soft computing techniques in customer segmentation by illustrating which techniques and variables were used in which industry together with a citation. Most of the fuzzy-oriented applications utilised fuzzy c-means algorithm (Crespo & Weber, 2005, Hsu et al., 2012, Hu & Sheu, 2003, Kaymak, 2001, Ozer, 2001, Shin & Sohn, 2004) in order to segment customers. As far as the applications of ANN in the area of segmentation is concerned, only the backpropagation algorithm (Bloom, 2005, Potharst et al., 2001) was used for classification while the other ANN algorithms (eg., Self-Organizing Maps-SOM) were used for clustering (Chiu et al., 2009, Diez et al., 2008, Ha, 2007, Hsieh, 2004, Hung & Tsai, 2008, Kuo et al., 2006, Lee & Park, 2005, Shin & Sohn, 2004). Some of the techniques in the table run with hierarchical logic (e.g., fuzzy clustering), while some of them are non-hierarchical such as self-organizing maps. It is clearly mentioned that there is a requirement for efficient integration or hybridisation of these techniques in the related literature (Mitra et al., 2002). However, in customer segmentation literature most of them were used individually rather than integrated or hybridised.

The table also shows that many segmentation variables, such as demographic, socio-demographic, and behavioural (e.g., RFM and shopping products, benefits, and product usage), are used in order to segment customers. Some researchers argue that demographics and socio-economic variables are not sufficient for an effective segmentation study (Yankelovich, 1964, Barnett, 1969, Sharma & Lambert, 1994, Greenberg & McDonald, 1989, Haley, 1968, Dhalla & Mahatoo, 1976, Peltier & Schribrowsky, 1997). Also, one of the most valuable pieces of information is their behavioural characteristics, especially past customer purchases and value-oriented attributes (Bayer, 2010, Kim et al., 2006, Wind & Lerner, 1979). In fact, customer analytics related technological advances have facilitated performing segmentation studies based on those characteristics (Bailey et al., 2009).

Table 1. Empirical studies of soft computing in customer segmentation

Techniques	Cite (Year)	Variables	Industry
Fuzzy Clustering	(Crespo and Weber, 2005)	Demographic and policy information	Insurance
	(Hsu, 2000)	Benefit variables	Banking
	(Shin and Sohn, 2004)	Transactions made on both representative assisted trading and online Home Trading System	Stock Market
	(Hu and Sheu, 2003)	Demand attributes	Logistic
	(Kaymak, 2001)	RFM values	Charity Organisation
	(Wedel and Steenkamp, 1989)	Consumer benefit attributes	Food
	(Weber, 1996)	Demographic and socio-economic features	N/A
	(Hruschka, 1986)	Product usage	Universal Products
	(Ozer, 2001)	Interests in music, usage situation, attitudes towards music and computers, consumption, computer usage, demographics	Online Music Industry
	(Hsu et al., 2000)	Benefit attributes	Property
Self Organizing Maps (SOM)	(Kuo et al., 2002b)	Benefit attributes	Store
	(Hsieh, 2004)	Repayment ability, RFM values	Banking
	(Lee et al., 2004)	The convenience of operator, the suitability of feedback, the reality of design, the precision of information and the involvement of virtual community	Online Game Industry
	(Changchien and Lu, 2001)	Job, education and gender	E-store
	(Vellido et al., 1999)	E-shopping characteristics	E-store
	(Kim et al., 2003)	Demographic and travel attributes	Tourism
	(Bloom, 2004, Bloom, 2005)	Travel trip characteristics, perceptions, demographic, socio-economic and geographic characteristics	Tourism
	(Ha et al., 2002)	RFM values	Retail
	(Ha and Park, 1998)	RFM values	Tourism
	(Shin and Sohn, 2004)	Trade amounts	Stock market
	(Lee and Park, 2005)	Costs of customers for the company (marketing, inventory, production, delivery, and service costs)	Automotive
	(Kiang et al., 2004)	Attitudinal characteristics	Telecommunication
	(Kuo et al., 2006, Kuo et al., 2004)	Benefit variables	Transportation
	(Ha, 2007)	RFM values	Retail
	(Hung and Tsai, 2008)	Demographics, Psychographics, Buying attitudes	Multimedia on Demand Service
	(Lien et al., 2006)	Benefit variables	Heating Systems
	(Chiu et al., 2009)	RFM values	Consumer Electronics

continued on following page

Table 1. Continued

Techniques	Cite (Year)	Variables	Industry
Backpropagation	(Natter, 1999)	Psychographics/ socio-demographics, purchase behaviours	N/A
	(Potharst et al., 2001)	RFM variables	Charity Organisation
	(Hruschka and Natter, 1999)	Usage situations, demographic and attitude variables	Household Cleaners
	(Bloom, 2004, Bloom, 2005)	Travel trip characteristics, perceptions, demographic, socio-economic and geographic characteristics	Tourism
	(Mazanec, 1992)	Demographic, socio-economic and behavioural characteristics	Tourism
	(Fish et al., 1995)	Demographics, delivery speed, price level and flexibility, company image, service, sales force's image, product quality	Manufacturing
FSCL (Frequency-Sensitive Competitive Learning) Algorithm)	(Balakrishnan et al., 1996)	Brand switching possibilities	Universal Products
Vector Quantisation	(Dolnicar and Leisch, 2004)	Psychographic variables related to travel activities	Tourism
	(Mazanec, 2001)	Brand image attributes	Transportation
	(Diez et al., 2008)	Product specific variables	Food
Hopfield-Kagmar	(Boone and Roehm, 2002a)	Purchase behaviour variables	Retail
	(Boone and Roehm, 2002b)	N/A (Hypothetically generated data with 8 variables)	N/A
Other ANN algorithms (names are N/A)	(Suh et al., 1999)	Personal and membership information	Social Club
	(Smith et al., 2002)	Policy holder characteristics, claim behaviour	Insurance
	(Hwang et al., 2004)	Lifetime value	Telecommunication
Evolutionary Methods	(Tsai and Chiu, 2004)	Product specific variables(purchased items and the associative monetary expenses)	Retail
	(Chiu, 2002)	Customer demographics	Insurance
	(Jonker et al., 2004)	RFM values	Charity Organisation
	(Kim and Ahn, 2008)	Demographics and personal characteristics	E-store
	(Chan, 2008)	Customer value	Automotive
	(Chiu et al., 2009)	RFM values	Consumer Electronics
Rough Sets	(Voges et al., 2003)	Shopping orientation (enjoyment, personalization, convenience, loyalty, and price)	E-store
	(Cheng and Chen, 2009)	Demographics, RFM values	E-business

3. RESEARCH METHODOLOGY

This study utilises data mining methodology. The previous segmentation studies that used large-scale customer data (Chan, 2008, Cheng & Chen, 2009, Crespo & Weber, 2005, Ha, 2007, Ha et al., 2002, Ha & Park, 1998, Hsieh, 2004, Lee & Park, 2005, Lee et al., 2004, Smith et al., 2002), demonstrate the broad usage of data mining methodology for the segmentation problem and the usefulness of such methodology. The main aim of this study is to propose and develop a customer segmentation model which includes the two-stage segmentation approach in data mining framework through making use of soft computing techniques and to compare the results of it with a traditional two-stage segmentation model according to select segmentation effectiveness criteria.

In the proposed model, a two-stage clustering process was carried out through a combination of soft computing techniques. Although there are few studies proposed to combine two clustering methods together (Hsu et al., 2012, Punj & Stewart, 1983, Vesanto & Alhoniemi, 2000) and some researchers adapted these methodologies in different application domains (Al-Khatib et al., 2005, Amiri & Fathian, 2007, Chiu et al., 2009, D'urso et al., 2013, Lee et al., 2004,, Li et al., 2011, Lien et al., 2006, Kuo et al., 2002a, Kuo et al., 2002b, Mo et al., 2010), the literature does not provide any study that has attempted to develop a methodology both based on soft computing and two-stage clustering. The suggestion of Kuo and his colleagues (2002b), who recommended that a fuzzy-oriented algorithm should replace k-means with the combination of the self-organising maps method for future studies, makes this claim even stronger. Therefore, a combination of self-organizing maps and fuzzy c-means will be used for clustering. Since fuzzy c-means is not able to determine the cluster number, the SOM algorithm will be followed in order to overcome this problem. The traditional two-stage clustering method selected to compare the clustering results of the proposed model includes Ward's minimum variance and k-means methods.

The data was procured from a supermarket retail chain in the UK that includes four consecutive months of customer transactions during the year 2003. Three behavioural characteristics of customers (RFM values) were used as segmentation bases and different weights were given to each variable as an indication of their importance. The weights for RFM values were determined intuitively in this study (0.5-0.25-0.25 respectively). The operationalization of the RFM values is as follows: Recency (R) was measured as the value since a customer made their last transaction. Frequency (F) was measured as the average number of transactions made by a customer during a specified period of time. Monetary (M) value was measured as the average total monetary value of a customer in an average transaction. A normalisation process was followed to prepare data for clustering. Also, before implementing the clustering analyses, the need to address the normality of the variables used in the study was accomplished.

A simple random sampling methodology was employed to extract the research sample. As far as the size of the sample is concerned, approximately 1% of the database was used as the study sample. A sample of 2,981 customers was obtained for conducting the analyses.

The results of the comparative approaches were evaluated using two sets of segmentation effectiveness indicators: assurance of clusters and segmentability criteria. The segmentability criteria used in this study are the most common ones suggested in the literature (Kotler, 2003, Wedel & Kamakura, 2000) and consist of the following indicators: homogeneity, substantiality, identifiability, measurability, actionability, and differentiability. In order to understand whether the model successfully employed or not the specific research questions and hypotheses that address these indicators are presented in Table 2.

In order to perform the analyses, the author used five different software applications. Minitab software was used to perform Ward's minimum variance method; SOM was carried out using IBM SPSS Modeller software; fuzzy c-means and k-means analyses were conducted in NCSS Data; finally both IBM SPSS Modeller and Microsoft Excel were used to obtain descriptive statistics and to test the hypotheses.

Table 2. Research questions and hypotheses

Segmentation Effectiveness Indicators	Research Questions	Research Hypotheses	Measurement Method
Assurance of Clusters	Can the neuro-fuzzy and the traditional clustering approaches identify real clusters in the data?	$H1_0$: The data plots tend to concentrate on one point. $H2_0$: The data plots are uniformly distributed.	C-test by Arnold (1979)
Segmentability Criteria	Are the customers in the clusters homogenous enough to form segments? If so, how homogenous are they compared to the traditional two-stage clustering approach?	$H3_0$: The homogeneity of the clusters obtained using the existing two-stage clustering approach is better than the homogeneity obtained by the proposed two-stage clustering approach.	Cluster validity indices: "intra-class inertia" (Chiu et al., 2009) and "Xie-Beni index" (Kaymak and Setnes, 2000)
	Compared to the two-stage clustering approach, how substantial are the clusters that were obtained through the proposed clustering approach?	$H4_0$: The proposed two-stage clustering approach does not produce a substantial amount of clusters in terms of the size and the total monetary level of the clusters compared to the traditional approach.	Descriptive statistics: the actual size and the total monetary level of the clusters
	Are the clusters identifiable in terms of the segmentation variables being used to form the clusters? How does this identification differ from the traditional method?	$H5_0$: The average RFM values of the clusters obtained by the proposed clustering approach do not differ among them. $H6_0$: There is no difference between the proposed clustering approach and the traditional two-stage method in terms of the resulting cluster structures.	Comparing means: Chi-Square and ANOVA analyses
	Compared to the traditional clustering approach, how measurable are the clusters?	$H7_0$: There is no difference between the proposed clustering approach and the traditional method on the basis of the results they produced in terms of the belongingness to the clusters.	Subjective evaluation through the degree of memberships to different clusters.
	How are the profiles of the clusters? Do the profiles provide actionable information in terms of being able to develop effective marketing programmes? How do these profiles differ from the profiles extracted using the traditional method?	$H8_0$: The proposed two-stage clustering approach does not produce actionable clusters in terms of the variety of the profiles compared to the clustering results of the traditional method.	Subjective evaluation through the possible profiles of the clusters obtained
	Can the clusters be differentiated among themselves in terms of the response rate they exhibit for different marketing programmes? Does this differentiability level differ from the results of the traditional method?	$H9_0$: The average response rate to different marketing programmes among the clusters produced by the proposed clustering approach is the same with the results of the traditional method.	Few hypothetical scenarios based on hypothetical data

4. RESULTS OF THE ANALYSES

4.1. Clustering Results

It was ascertained that the prerequisite for clustering is that the data used should not be normally distributed. Hence, it is imperative to verify that the data employed in this study do not follow a normal distribution. This was observed by conducting Kolmogorov-Smirnov test. The results of Kolmogorov-

Smirnov analysis indicated that the RFM values are not normally distributed as the Z values were found to be 12.3 (p<.05), 8.57 (p<.05), and 7.8 (p<.05) respectively. In fact, the histograms obtained for each variable (see Figure 2 in the Appendix) also demonstrate that all three variables are skewed, hence not normal. The symmetry of the distribution of the R variable was slightly right-skewed while it is moderately left-skewed for F and M variables.

The first stage of clustering produces results to get the initial number of clusters for the clustering methods used in the second stage. Ward's minimum variance and SOM methods were used to obtain initial clustering structures for k-means and fuzzy c-means, respectively. Having the results of those methods as initial cluster numbers, k-means and fuzzy c-means methods were performed to obtain final clustering solutions.

4.1.1. Initial Clusters Obtained by Ward's Minimum Variance and SOM Method

Ward's minimum variance method produces a dendogram based on a certain distance measure (Squared Euclidean Distance). By observing the changes in the distance levels it is possible to observe where the break point is for the possible number of clusters suitable for the data. A cluster cut-off value (number of clusters) can also be determined from this plot by drawing a horizontal line at that value and counting the number of lines that the horizontal line intersects. After applying Ward's method on the dataset, this horizontal line should be drawn between the first two scales (0-47.49), much closer to the zero scale. One can see that four vertical lines appear and these lead us to form four clusters in the data. The dendogram obtained through analysing the data using Ward's method can be seen in Figure 3 in the Appendix.

Through the implementation of SOM the customers are mapped into a 3-by-3 output layer. Figure 4 in the Appendix shows the visualisation of nine output neurons. In the 3-by-3 output layer, the rows indicate the input neurons, the variables (RFM) used to cluster the customers, while the columns represent each output neuron. Each neuron is labelled through a number in the X-Y coordinate. One of the most convenient ways to understand the results of the SOM is to visualise the potential number of clusters. Although each neuron can represent a separate cluster, this may not necessarily be the appropriate approach, because having carefully analysed the results provided, it is possible to observe that some of the neurons (the neurons that have close centroid RFM values) can be merged together to form a cluster. After analysing the above results, three clusters were obtained. Both visualising the SOM result and dendogram for the determination of initial number of clusters could be subjective, although they both give us a clear picture about the potential number of clusters.

4.1.2. Final Clusters Obtained by K-Means and Fuzzy C-Means Methods

By setting the number of clusters as four the final clustering results obtained by k-means were produced. Table 3 provides the average RFM values of each cluster and the corresponding number of observations assigned to those clusters. As the table indicates, 47% of the customers were assigned to cluster 2. In terms of the number of clusters assigned to each cluster, cluster 4 is the second most assigned cluster with an observation of 988. Cluster 4 was followed by cluster 1 and cluster 3, those being assigned 354 and 236 customers respectively. The average RFM values of each cluster were compared with the overall RFM average. At each variable level, if the average RFM value of a cluster exceeded the overall average

Table 3. Average RFM values of the clusters obtained by k-means method

Variables/Clusters	Cluster1	Cluster2	Cluster3	Cluster4
R	.51	.57	.48	.35
F	.15	.08	.32	.08
M	.21	.06	.15	.06
Number of Customers	354	1,403	236	988
RFM Status	H, H, H	H, L, L	L, H, H	L, L, L

RFM, then this particular variable was labelled as high or low depending on the comparison. The last row of the table indicates the status of each cluster in terms of being high (H) or low (L) at each variable level in comparison with the overall average RFM values.

By employing the fuzzy c-means algorithm based on a cluster-structure, the last clustering results can be obtained. Table 4 represents the RFM values and assignments for fuzzy c-means method. Please note that the number of customers assigned to each cluster indicated as integer were the crisp assignments of the fuzzy clustering method where the assignments were made based on the highest belongingness. However, the assignment to the clusters can be achieved by taking into account the bigger the member-ship degree of any one customer among the corresponding clusters. The number of customers was also provided as real values by calculating the sum of the associated membership degree of every customer in the sample. According to the results, cluster 1 and 3 have more than 1/3 of the total customer popula-tion each and RFM label of those clusters were found as H, L, L and L, L, L respectively. In addition, 734 customers were assigned to dominantly belong to cluster 2 that have the RFM status of L, H, H.

4.2. Hypotheses Testing

So far, it was ascertained that if the prerequisite for clustering is met and then the clustering results under the two approaches have been presented. The results of the proposed two-stage clustering model were compared with the traditional two-stage method. To simplify the presentation of the results the traditional approach will be called as "crisp" or "k-means" and the proposed approach will be named as the "fuzzy" approach. It is essential to determine if the clusters (or segments) obtained are different in terms of the indicators regarding segmentation effectiveness as specified in the research hypotheses.

Table 4. Average RFM values of the clusters obtained by fuzzy c-means method

Variables/Clusters	Cluster1	Cluster2	Cluster3
R	.61	.48	.36
F	.07	.18	.10
M	.06	.13	.08
Number of Customers(Integer)	1,103	734	1,144
Number of Customers(Real)	1,119.76	724.54	1,136.68
RFM Status	H, L, L	L, H, H	L, L, L

4.2.1. Hypothesis Test for Assurance of the Clusters

There were two research hypotheses ($H1_0$, $H2_0$) associated with this and for both approaches those hypotheses were tested using the C-test. Having applied C-test on fuzzy and crisp clustering results at 0.05 level of significance yields significant unimodal C-test values of 0.24 (<C=log-max{2.1}=0.32) and 0.31 (<C=log-max{5.18}=0.71), respectively. Therefore, the first hypothesis was rejected. That means the population entities are either uniformly distributed or grouped into clusters for both approaches. Since the first null hypothesis was rejected in both cases, this will lead us to test the second null hypothesis. Applying the same parameters to check C-statistics for the uniform distribution, the results (0.31<0.32 for fuzzy; 0.41<0.71 for crisp) were found to be significant. This shows that there are clusters in the population sample and it can be said that the clusters found through these approaches exist in the sample.

4.2.2. Hypothesis Test for Homogeneity

The homogeneity of a cluster is directly associated with cluster efficiency. The efficiency of the clustering results was measured based on two cluster validity indices, namely, intraclass inertia index and Xie-Beni index. For a clustering solution to be efficient, it needs to be compact and separate at the same time. The intraclass inertia only measures the compactness (Shin and Sohn, 2004), while the Xie-Beni considers both (Kaymak and Setnes, 2000). The compactness measures how close the members of each cluster are to each other, while the separation measures the distance between the different clusters. Therefore, for both approaches these two cluster validity indices were calculated. The intraclass inertia and Xie-Beni indices were found to be .03 and 1.16 for fuzzy approach while those values were .06 and 1.21 for crisp approach. Therefore, in terms of the clustering efficiency of the approaches, fuzzy approach performed slightly better and produced more homogenous clusters than the crisp approach. Should one want to scrutinise whether the difference between the two approaches in terms of "the compactness" of both cluster validity indices are significant or not, a paired-samples t-test analysis will be the answer to that question. According to the paired-samples t-test there was a statistically significant difference in compactness scores of both intraclass inertia (t=-16.81; p<.05) and Xie-Beni (t=-17.98; p<.05) indices for fuzzy and crisp approaches. Also, the differences obtained were unlikely to occur by chance as the effect size of both paired tests were found to be moderate (0.09 and 0.10>0.06).

4.2.3. Hypothesis Test for Substantiality

With regards to the fourth research hypothesis, the substantiality of the segments produced by two approaches was scrutinized. Substantiality can be seen as a combination of both segment size and total value. To test the above hypothesis the segment size and the total monetary levels of each segment were calculated for both approaches. The results were given in Table 5 and Table 6.

The row with the integer numbers only takes into account being a member of a certain segment with a specified alpha-cut value. Setting an Alpha-cut value that acts as a benchmark level does this and customers with membership degrees higher than the alpha-cut value are considered a part of the cluster. The determination of the alpha cut value is subjective but this gives the organizations the freedom to set their own alpha cut values depending on the specific conditions. There exist two generic approaches to setting the alpha cut values. One rule is to set alpha cut value equal to the smallest value of the average membership degrees of each segment. The second approach is to set alpha cut at a value greater or equal

Table 5. Monetary levels and size of each segment for fuzzy approach

Fuzzy Approach (with Alpha-Cut=.24)	FS1	FS2	FS3	Total	Average
Number of Customers(Integer)	1,325	958	1,171	3,454	1,151
Number of Customers(Real)	1,073.42	674.72	1,120.62	2,867.76	956
Total Monetary Level(Integer)	84.82	110.13	87.94	282.89	94.30
Total Monetary Level(Real)	68.71	77.56	84.16	230.43	76.81

Table 6. Monetary levels and segment size of each segment for crisp approach

Crisp Approach	S1	S2	S3	S4	Total	Average
Number of Customers	1,403	236	988	354	2,981	994
Total Monetary Level	79.02	36.04	56	74.83	245.89	61.47

to 1/c where c is the number of clusters. It was decided to choose an alpha-cut value by taking into account the first alternative. As per this rule, the relevant alpha cut value in our case should be greater or equal to 0.24. For example, customers belonging to fuzzy segment 1 are the ones whose membership degrees are more than .24 for that particular segment. However, the row with the real numbers also takes into account the alpha-cut value but when counting the number of customers in each fuzzy segment only total belongingness is considered. In another words, for fuzzy segment 1 the total membership degrees in that segment was taken as the number of assignments to it. In fact, both rows are an indication of the total size of a fuzzy segment in a way, as one constitutes the lower limit while the other is the upper limit of that particular segment. If one considers each fuzzy segment as a market this will show how dynamic the markets are, in a sense. Another conclusion that can be made by looking at the upper and lower limits of the segments is that the smaller the difference, the more stable the market is. Therefore, the third fuzzy segment is more stable compared to the other two fuzzy segments. It should also be noted that it is possible to catch upper and lower limits of the segments without taking the alpha-cut value account, as this issue is directly an implication of membership degrees. However, if the alpha-cut value is increased, the size of the segments will decrease in both rows.

For the select alpha-cut level (.24), the size of each segment compared to the k-means approach is higher. Also, the k-means result does not provide any information regarding the upper and the lower limits of each segment. Similarly, there is no implication of k-means results associated with the stability as opposed to fuzzy approach.

On comparing the two approaches based on the monetary levels, it was found that the total monetary level of the fuzzy approach is 282.89 (based on integer value calculations) while k-means approach yielded a total monetary level of 245.89. Therefore, the total market value of the fuzzy approach is bigger than the crisp approach. Even when the comparison base was taken as the average monetary level shared by each segment, the fuzzy approach's per segment average value is higher than the k-means approach's. However, one issue has to be addressed here, which is that finding that the total or the average monetary level of fuzzy segments is higher than the crisp approach is not the point to be highlighted. Having quite a big alpha-cut value, it may not be practical, but let us say .8, will decrease the number of customers in the segments substantially to a level where even the total integer number of customers may be much less than the actual number of customers, which is 2,981. As a result of this, the total or the average monetary level of the fuzzy segments might be less than the crisp approach. What needs to be highlighted here is the fact that marketing managers would be aware of the substantiality of the segments far better with different alpha-cut values.

4.2.4. Hypothesis Test for Identifiability

To shed light on the fifth hypothesis, a one-way variance (ANOVA) and post-hoc analyses were conducted for both approaches. Please note that the fuzzy results with no alpha-cut were taken into account to conduct the analysis as one cannot perform such analysis having a customer belonging to more than one segment.

As an assumption for ANOVA, Levene's statistics for testing homogeneity of variances among groups for RFM variables were found significant ($p<0.05$) for fuzzy and crisp approaches which indicated that the variances were not homogenous and the assumption was violated. Therefore, instead of checking ANOVA F-statistics another test for equality of means (Welch and Brown-Forsythe measures) was performed for more robust examination. All variables' significance levels were smaller than .05 for both approaches in terms of these measures. Therefore, the first hypothesis was rejected and it can be concluded that the average RFM values were found to be different across segments in each approach. In addition to the above analyses, a post-hoc analysis (Tamhane test) for both approaches was conducted due to the fact that variances are not equal. According to the results, while all the paired differences between the segments in terms of the variables were significant in fuzzy approach, a few differences between k-means segments with regard to F and M variables were found to be insignificant. For k-means results, in terms of F and M variable segment 1 and 3 were not significantly different providing results as $p=.94>.05$ for F and $p=1>.05$ for M.

With regard to the sixth hypothesis, it should be sufficient to look at the cluster centroids of both approaches. Referring to the final cluster results of both approaches, the fuzzy approach produced a three-cluster structure while k-means method appeared to have four clusters. Should one looks at the cluster centroids of both approaches it can be seen that segment 1,2,3 of the fuzzy approach have matched with segment 2,3,4 of k-means method. In fact, RFM status of those clusters is a proof for that match (see Table 4-5). The only non-matching cluster was the first cluster in k-means method as this cluster did not appear in the fuzzy approach at all. In order to statistically capture how different the assignments of customers in the two approaches are, Chi-Square test for independence was conducted. The Chi-Square analysis (Pearson $\chi2=3184.59$ and two-tailed asymptotic significance value$<.05$) indicated that there is a significant difference in terms of the assignments of customers to the segments. Thus, a combined examination of ANOVA and Chi-Square analyses together with the analysis of the cluster centroids and RFM status of the segments in two approaches can bring us a conclusion that there is a substantial difference between the comparative approaches in terms of their resulted segment structures.

4.2.5. Hypothesis Test for Measurability

The above results do not indicate anything with regard to a possible difference between the two approaches in terms of the measurability. Therefore, the measurability capability of two approaches needs to be addressed. Measurability can be defined as the representativeness capability of each individual customer to the corresponding segments. Let us first consider the k-means approach (see Table 3). There are 1,403 customers for segment 1, 236 for segment 2, 988 for segment 3, and 354 for segment 4. In terms of the belongingness to the segments, every single customer belongs to only one single segment. However, looking at the fuzzy approach's results through its membership reports (a sample is provided in Table 7), one can see a completely different picture. This report includes the degree of belongingness information of each segment for every single customer. One can make use of that report in terms of extracting the information related to what extent each customer represents or belongs to different segments, particularly to the segment he/she sharply assigned.

Customer 46 and 340 were assigned to segment 1 while customer id number 1,911 was assigned to segment 2, according to the k-means approach. The representativeness or belongingness of these customers to their corresponding segments is equal to one. However, according to the fuzzy approach although those customers were sharply assigned to segment 1, 2 and 3 respectively, the representativeness of those customers to their corresponding fuzzy segments is not equal to one. For example, customer 46 represents segment 1 with a percentage of 51% approximately but he/she also represents segment 2 by 48%. Similarly, for customer 1,911 the ability of him/her to represent segment 3 is 74% while the belongingness to segment 2 was found to be 20%. Interestingly, customer 340 has almost an equal representativeness to all segments with the degree ranging from 28% to 38%.

4.2.6. Hypothesis Test for Actionability

Actionability is the degree to which the identification of the segments provides guidance for marketing decisions or programmes or campaigns. Therefore, one can try to measure the actionability of the segments through the profiles that the segments possess. Table 8 provides some potential profiles that could be extracted using the fuzzy approach. Creating these profiles totally depends on the issue of what sort of actions a company wants to use to persuade customers. Should the company wish to perform a targeted marketing campaign for each segment then the first six potential profiles could be a consideration. The first of those profiles takes into account only the core members of each segment, and the customers are crisply assigned to the fuzzy segments. However, should the company want to promote a certain marketing campaign then it can put the fuzzy memberships into action and could consider the customers who belong to a particular segment with a minimum level of alpha-cut associated with each fuzzy segment. In addition, if the company wants to employ a marketing campaign with more than one segment then it is possible to create a combinatorial profile of the involved segments based on a certain alpha-cut value. The last four potential profiles represent this type of profile extraction. There could be other possible potential profiles that can be created using the membership concept. Consequently, one can easily claim that the results obtained through the fuzzy approach would provide different types of customer profiles

Table 7. Crisp and fuzzy assignments of three representative customers

Customer ID	Fuzzy	Membership1	Membership2	Membership3	K-Means
46	1	.52	.48	.00	1
340	2	.29	.38	.33	1
1,911	3	.06	.20	.74	2

Table 8. Some potential profiles that could possibly be extracted through the fuzzy approach

Potential Profiles	Explanation
Profile for S1	Core members of S1 by having no alpha-cut
Profile for S2	Core members of S2 by having no alpha-cut
Profile for S3	Core members of S3 by having no alpha-cut
Profile for S1	Members of S1 with a certain value of alpha-cut
Profile for S2	Members of S2 with a certain value of alpha-cut
Profile for S3	Members of S3 with a certain value of alpha-cut
Profile for S1 and S2	Members of a combination of S1 and S2 with a certain alpha-cut value
Profile for S2 and S3	Members of a combination of S1 and S2 with a certain alpha-cut value
Profile for S1 and S3	Members of a combination of S1 and S2 with a certain alpha-cut value
Profile for S1 and S2 and S3	Members of a combination of S1 and S2 and S3 with a certain alpha-cut value

going beyond the available segment structures. As far as the implications are concerned, the results of the fuzzy approach would enable the marketing managers to look at the segments from different angles and that would lead them to come up much more applicable ideas or actions.

4.2.7. Hypothesis Test for Differentiability

For any segmentation study to be considered that produces differentiable segments is associated with the issue of obtaining segments that are conceptually distinguishable and respond differently to different marketing mix elements or programmes. One possible way to test differentiability is to create few hypothetical scenarios and generate some hypothetical data and measure the differentiability capability of both approaches based on these scenarios.

Let us assume that four different marketing campaigns appropriate for each segment are proposed as shown in Table 9. The main objective of implementing the above campaigns could be to increase the value of the customers. In order to simplify the problem, a simple formula was adapted from the existing literature (Hwang et al., 2004) for calculating values at segment level, which can be formulated as Total Value (TV) = Current Value (CV) + Potential Value (PV). The total value of a segment is defined as the summation of its current and potential values. The current value of a segment is assumed to be calculated based on its existing total monetary value. For the potential values the total future contribution of the customers can be taken into account together with the certain probability of reacting to the marketing campaigns.

Table 9. Marketing campaigns and strategies for the obtained segments

RFM Status	Segment Description	Segments	Marketing Strategy	Marketing Campaign
H, L, L	Vulnerable customers	S1, FS1	Customer reactivation	Price discount
L, H, H	Loyal customers	S2, FS2	Customer retention	Up-selling
L, L, L	New customers	S3, FS3	Customer maturity	Buy 1 get 1 free
H, H, H	Vulnerable customers	S4	Customer retention	Shopping voucher

Three scenarios based on some assumptions can be provided. The first scenario is the simplest one and assumes that the probability of a customer reaction to a certain campaign would be either 0 or 1. The first scenario also takes for granted that there would be no cost involved in the calculation of the profit function for running the corresponding campaigns. The second scenario takes the first scenario to a further level and assumes that a customer reacting to a certain campaign would occur under a certain probability between 0 and 1. In the second scenarios, the assumptions made with regard to the profit calculation would be the same as in the first one. The third scenario is the most complicated one and has the same assumption as the second one in terms of the probability of the reaction to the campaigns. It also supposes that a certain amount of cost would be involved in the profit calculation. Associated with the three scenarios above, some hypothetical data was generated for each campaign. Having considered all customers in the sample, a different campaign reaction probability with binary values (0 or 1), as well as continuous probability values with the interval of (0,1), was generated for each campaign. Also, a potential revenue value ranging from 0 to .6 was hypothetically generated for each campaign. The reason for this is simply due to the fact that the overall existing monetary level of customers is within that range. With regard to the cost included into the profit function, 20 percent of the average hypothetical potential revenue value was considered as a constant cost value per customer for any campaign. Since the average hypothetical potential revenue values were found to be 0.276 the constant cost was calculated as .056 (.28*20%) per customer. Using the existing RFM values, the formulas provided and the hypothetical data generated, the current, the potential, and the total value of each segment were calculated based on each scenario for both comparative approaches. These results are presented in Table 10 and Table 11, respectively.

Table 10. Results of three scenarios for fuzzy approach

Fuzzy Approach (with alpha-cut=0.2431)	Scenario 1			Scenario 2			Scenario 3		
	CV	PV	TV	CV	PV	TV	CV	PV	TV
FS1	84.82	186	270.82	84.82	164.45	249.27	84.82	133.68	218.49
FS2	110.13	125.35	235.47	110.13	117.24	227.37	110.13	95.24	205.37
FS3	87.94	163.03	250.97	87.94	153.48	241.42	87.94	125.97	213.91
Total	282.89	474.38	757.26	282.89	435.18	718.06	282.89	354.88	637.77
Per Segment Average	94.30	158.13	252.42	94.30	145.06	239.35	94.30	118.29	212.59

Table 11. Results of three scenarios for crisp approach

Crisp Approach	Scenario 1			Scenario 2			Scenario 3		
	CV	PV	TV	CV	PV	TV	CV	PV	TV
S1	79.02	192.96	271.98	79.02	177.83	256.84	79.02	144.75	223.77
S2	36.04	30.73	66.77	36.04	29.69	65.73	36.04	24.06	60.11
S3	56.00	139.50	195.51	56.00	129.20	185.20	56.00	106.19	162.19
S4	74.83	49.30	124.13	74.83	43.16	117.99	74.83	34.82	109.65
Total	245.89	412.50	658.39	245.89	379.87	625.76	245.89	309.82	555.72
Per Segment Average	61.47	103.12	164.60	61.47	94.97	156.44	61.47	77.46	138.93

Calculations for the fuzzy approach indicated that the total values of the segments increased from 282.89 to approximately 757 in scenario 1, while the same figure went up to around 718 and 637 for scenario 2 and 3 respectively. Also, through taking into account the potential values of the segments the total per segment average values were found to be 252.42 for the first scenario, 239.35 for the second scenario and 212.59 for the third scenario where the current per segment average was 94.3. Likewise, a certain level of increase was obtained according to the k-means scenario results. In fact, for all three scenarios, by using the fuzzy approach the total monetary values and the total per segment average values were found to be higher than the k-means approach. However, as was addressed when the discussions were made regarding the substantiality of the segments, the results that have been found might change depending on the different alpha-cut values used to construct the fuzzy approach. The real conclusion that can be made associated with the above results is that the figures found through the usage of the fuzzy approach are much more sensitive than the results obtained by the k-means method. Therefore, having more sensitive results would enable the marketing managers to better understand the changes in values of the customer segments stimulated by different marketing campaigns in a way that reflects the real-world more appropriately.

5. CONCLUSION AND DISCUSSIONS

Both data mining and marketing research study similar marketing problems such as market segmentation. However, while these research communities share the same research interests, the way that they approach the problems may be different. By doing so, this study sheds light on the differences between the two research disciplines by indicating how data mining methodology using soft computing technologies can be useful to solve customer segmentation problems in a rich data environment. The study showed step by step how a data mining methodology can be applied to do segmentation. Also, using the refined customer transactions in the first period, customers were clustered into homogenous groups so that the customers in the same clusters share similar characteristics and they can be delineated from other customers in different clusters. Furthermore, a comparison between the proposed clustering approach and the traditional clustering model was made and the results were provided through some research hypotheses.

There are two main contributions of this study. The first contribution stems from the potential benefits and implications of having fuzzy segments, which enables us to have flexible segments through the availability of membership degrees of each customer to the corresponding customer segments. The second is the development of a new two-stage clustering model that is expected to be superior to its peer. To be more specific, the following discussions can be made for this study:

- Through the usage of some performance measurements that refer to segmentation effectiveness, the clustering stage of the proposed model successfully created customer segments with the following indicators:
  - The clusters found in the data proved to be real clusters, and this was supported via a statistical research procedure (C-test).
  - A successful evaluation was completed regarding whether the obtained clusters can be considered as customer segments or not. Based on the criteria of homogeneity, substantiality, identifiability, measurability, actionability, and differentiability it was proved that the clusters were segments which constitute effective segmentation results. Within this scope, the following conclusions can be made:

- Homogeneity inside the segments and heterogeneity between the segments were satisfied, and these were proved using two different clustering validity indices.
- In terms of the size and the monetary level of the customers the segments were found to be substantial enough. Also, a lower and an upper level associated with substantiality were obtained using the fuzzy concept. This provided a very valuable insight regarding the dynamism and stability of the market.
- The segments were found to be identifiable from each other based on the attributes used during the clustering process. It was proven that there were significant differences between the segments.
- The measurability of the segments was assessed based on the customers' assignments to the segments. It was found that with different membership degrees the belongingness of the customers varies from each other. This provided the information regarding the extent to which customers belong to the segments, and this can be considered quite crucial when performing different marketing programmes.
- Actionability of the clusters was subjectively evaluated based on the possible number of profiles that the model was able to produce. This would enable marketing managers to produce the different combinations of marketing programmes.
- Differentiability of the segments was measured based on some hypothetical scenarios by taking into account the response rate of the clusters. The proposed model provided really sensitive results in terms of obtaining the real reactions of the customers.

- Another conclusion can be drawn through the comparison of the clustering stage of the proposed model with select segmentation approaches based on the aforementioned segmentability criteria. First of all, the results obtained through the comparative approaches were found to be different in a variety of aspects:
  - Regarding clustering efficiency, the model performed better than the traditional approach. This can only be argued for the data set on which the study was employed. Certainly, no generalisation can be made as this issue somewhat depends on the characteristics of the data. However, what could be argued is that in other application domains the model can produce results as efficient as the traditional one. From this point, the study contributed to the existing body of knowledge in two aspects. First, combining a neural network technique to the fuzzy clustering method in order to overcome the key limitation of fuzzy approaches (not being able to determine the initial number of clusters) provided an easy to use means and reduced difficulties for researchers and practitioners. Second, with the data set have been chosen and in terms of the selected clustering efficiency indicators the model confirmed the findings of the above studies by achieving better clustering efficiency rates, and outperformed the traditional approach.
  - For the current study, it could be concluded that the model produced more identifiable segments compared to the traditional approaches. Moreover, similar to the issue of homogeneity, it may not be appropriate to make a generalisation on this matter.
  - With regard to substantiality, measurability, actionability, and differentiability criteria it can be argued that the proposed model produced more applicable and insightful results in comparison with the traditional approach. The proposed model helped us gain different perspectives for managerial implications in terms of the segmentability criteria used in this study. These angles are mainly related to the ability of fuzzy-based approaches producing flex-

ible segment structures. However, in comparison with the previous fuzzy-based approaches within this respect this study has two main contributions. First, none of the existing studies measured the effectiveness of their models in terms of the whole set of segmentability criteria that were taken into consideration in this study. Mainly one or two of the criteria were discussed in those studies. Second, in the previous studies that used fuzzy-based approaches, the potential managerial implications in relation to the segmentability criteria were not extensively discussed as they have been in this study. Therefore, it could be argued that a clustering methodology based on the fuzzy concept, as in the proposed model, would provide certain advantages and create segmentation structures which other approaches are not capable of having or constructing.

- From a practitioner's point of view, the proposed model has the following advantages that may provide managerial implications:

  - When calculating the level of substantiality of the segments, more accurate measurements are obtained. In terms of both the size and the total value of the segments through the availability of the membership degrees, it is possible to see what the lower and upper levels of a segment would be. This is important, especially if one wants to have an idea of a particular segment as a total market overall, because the range of the segment size through the lower and the upper limits is an indicator for how dynamic the market is. Also, the difference between the upper and the lower levels of a segment is an indication of the likely stability of this particular segment.

  - The above implication can be expanded for considering the measurability of the segments. With the customers belonging to different segments with different membership values, it enables managers to realise how measurable the segments are in the reality.

  - Through the usage of different alpha-cut threshold values, fuzzy clustering results enable marketing managers to produce different types of customer profiles for different purposes going beyond the available classic segment structure which could lead them to utilise better applicable ideas and actions for developing different marketing tactics.

  - The membership concept also enables managers to observe the actual customer response or reactions in a more sensitive way should different marketing campaigns be implemented towards customers within the context of customer relationship management programmes.

  - Obtaining a fuzzy-based segmentation using recency, frequency, and monetary values of customers facilitates managers to rank the value of each segment in a more sensitive way and to help them easily visualise the position of each segment strategically on 2- or 3-dimensional maps (Recency-Monetary, Frequency-Monetary, or Recency-Frequency-Monetary).

6. LIMITATIONS AND FUTURE WORK

Some limitations and associated future work were identified as the followings:

- Firstly, due to technical constraints as well as considerations of confidentiality of the data, the demographics, socioeconomic, and product characteristics could not be obtained. Therefore, the actual profiling of the customer segments was not created to indicate some of the implications on a real dataset. It might be very interesting to observe some of the implications of the study in an environment where there would be access to such customer information.

- Secondly, the model used Recency, Frequency, and Monetary values of customers to conduct segmentation and perform the comparative analyses, and the data were procured from a retail company in the UK. Therefore, the findings and conclusions are limited to the variables selected and the application domain, and it can be said that the external validity of the study remains a limitation. Conducting similar analyses on different segmentation bases (e.g., benefit variables, loyalty status, product characteristics, etc.) as well as on different application domains (i.e., data obtained from different sectors or countries) would be complementary future studies to this study.

- Thirdly, some of the technical parameters associated with the select soft computing techniques used in the study were chosen either based on the recommendations from the related literature or they were arbitrary. This creates a limitation of the study to generalise the results in a broader sense. Further studies can be conducted on this issue through selecting different technical parameters and assumptions.

- Fourthly, in the two-stage clustering of the proposed model, the self-organising maps algorithm was utilised to determine the initial number of clusters. In some cases, it might be difficult to observe the number of clusters using this method. Therefore, in future, other neural network techniques that are able to perform the same task (e.g., adaptive resonance theory) might be used to work complementarily with the fuzzy c-means algorithm.

- Fifthly, for the fuzzy c-means algorithm the initial number of clusters was provided by self-organising maps. However, initial cluster centres could also be provided to increase the effectiveness of the fuzzy c-means method. Therefore, this aspect can be considered as another limitation or assumption of this study. Future work can be done on the same data set (or in different application domains) by providing initial cluster centre information to observe whether the results of this study would be confirmed or not.

- Finally, the segmentability criteria were formulated in a way that they would be appropriate for comparative purposes in this study. However, the formulations may not be applicable in every circumstance; therefore, developing new formulations regarding the segmentability criteria remains a future study.

In conclusion, thanks to the insights provided in this study, the authors anticipate that further contributions regarding the application of soft computing to the problems in strategic marketing, particularly in segmentation and predictive marketing, would be conducted by other researchers. More specifically, some customer characteristics which are intangible in nature and may cause discrepancies in terms of their measurements such as value, loyalty, satisfaction, profitability, and so on could be modelled and measured using the ability of soft computing to deal with imprecision and uncertainty. Many organisations may also benefit from such a modelling facility through gaining more robust solutions at lower costs.

REFERENCES

Al-Khatib, J. A., Stanton, A. A., & Rawwas, M. Y. A. (2005). Ethical segmentation of consumers in developing countries: A comparative analysis. *International Marketing Review*, 22(2), 225–246. doi:10.1108/02651330510593287

Amiri, B., & Fathian, M. (2007). Integration of self organizing feature maps and honey bee mating optimization for market segmentation. *Journal of Theoretical and Applied Information Technology*, *3*(3), 70–86.

Arnold, S. J. (1979). A test for clusters. *JMR, Journal of Marketing Research*, *16*(4), 545–551. doi:10.2307/3150815

Bailey, C., Baines, P. R., Wilson, H., & Clark, M. (2009). Segmentation and customer insight in contemporary services marketing practice: Why grouping customers is no longer enough. *Journal of Marketing Management*, *25*(3-4), 227–252. doi:10.1362/026725709X429737

Balakrishnan, P. V. S., Cooper, M. C., Jacob, V. S., & Lewis, P. A. (1996). Comparative performance of the FSCL neural net and k-means algorithm for market segmentation. *European Journal of Operational Research*, *93*(2), 346–357. doi:10.1016/0377-2217(96)00046-X

Barnett, N. L. (1969). Beyond market segmentation. *Harvard Business Review*, *47*, 152–166.

Bayer, J. (2010). Customer segmentation in the telecommunications industry. *Database Marketing & Customer Strategy Management*, *17*(3), 247–256. doi:10.1057/dbm.2010.21

Beane, T. P., & Ennis, D. M. (1987). Market segmentation: A review. *European Journal of Marketing*, *21*(5), 20–42. doi:10.1108/EUM0000000004695

Bloom, J. Z. (2004). Tourist market segmentation with linear and non-linear techniques. *Tourism Management*, *25*(6), 723–733. doi:10.1016/j.tourman.2003.07.004

Bloom, J. Z. (2005). Market segmentation: A neural network application. *Annals of Tourism Research*, *32*(1), 93–111. doi:10.1016/j.annals.2004.05.001

Boone, D. S., & Roehm, M. (2002a). Evaluating the appropriateness of market segmentation solutions using artificial neural networks and the membership clustering criterion. *Marketing Letters*, *13*(4), 317–333. doi:10.1023/A:1020321132568

Boone, D. S., & Roehm, M. (2002b). Retail segmentation using artificial neural networks. *International Journal of Research in Marketing*, *19*(3), 287–301. doi:10.1016/S0167-8116(02)00080-0

Chan, C. C. (2008). Intelligent value-based customer segmentation method for campaign management: A case study of automobile retailer. *Expert Systems with Applications*, *34*(4), 2754–2762. doi:10.1016/j.eswa.2007.05.043

Changchien, S. W., & Lu, T. Z. (2001). Mining association rules procedure to support on-line recommendation by customers and products fragmentation. *Expert Systems with Applications*, *20*(4), 325–335. doi:10.1016/S0957-4174(01)00017-3

Cheng, C.-H., & Chen, Y.-S. (2009). Classifying the segmentation of customer value via RFM model and RS theory. *Expert Systems with Applications*, *36*(3), 4176–4184. doi:10.1016/j.eswa.2008.04.003

Chiu, C. (2002). A case-based customer classification approach for direct marketing. *Expert Systems with Applications*, *22*(2), 163–168. doi:10.1016/S0957-4174(01)00052-5

Chiu, C.-Y., Chen, Y.-F., Kuo, I., & Kun, H. C. (2009). An intelligent market segmentation system using k-means and particle swarm optimization. *Expert Systems with Applications*, *36*(3), 4558–4565. doi:10.1016/j.eswa.2008.05.029

Crespo, F., & Weber, R. (2005). A methodology for dynamic data mining based on fuzzy clustering. *Fuzzy Sets and Systems*, *150*(2), 267–284. doi:10.1016/j.fss.2004.03.028

D'Urso, P., Giovanni, L. D., Disegna, M., & Massari, R. (2013). Bagged clustering and its application to tourism market segmentation. *Expert Systems with Applications*, *40*(12), 4944–4956. doi:10.1016/j.eswa.2013.03.005

Desarbo, W. S., Atalay, A. S., Lebaron, D., & Blanchard, S. J. (2008). Estimating multiple consumer segment ideal points from context-dependent survey data. *The Journal of Consumer Research*, *35*(1), 142–153. doi:10.1086/529534

Dhalla, N. K., & Mahatoo, W. H. (1976). Expanding the scope of segmentation research. *Journal of Marketing*, *40*(2), 34–41. doi:10.2307/1251004

Diez, J., Coz, J. J., Luacez, O., & Bahamonde, A. (2008). Clustering people according to their preference criteria. *Expert Systems with Applications*, *34*(2), 1274–1284. doi:10.1016/j.eswa.2006.12.005

Dolnicar, S. (2004). Beyond commonsense segmentation: A systematics of segmentation approaches in tourism. *Journal of Travel Research*, *42*(3), 244–250. doi:10.1177/0047287503258830

Dolnicar, S., & Leisch, F. (2004). Segmenting markets by bagged clustering. *Australasian Marketing Journal*, *12*(1), 51–65. doi:10.1016/S1441-3582(04)70088-9

Dunn, J. C. (1974). Well-separated clusters and the optimal fuzzy partitions. *Journal of Cybernetics*, *4*(1), 95–104. doi:10.1080/01969727408546059

Fish, K., Barnes, J., & Aiken, M. (1995). Artificial neural networks: A new methodology for industrial market segmentation. *Industrial Marketing Management*, *24*(5), 432–438. doi:10.1016/0019-8501(95)00033-7

Gil-Saura, I., & Ruiz-Molina, M.-E. (2008). Customer segmentation based on commitment and ICT use. *Industrial Management & Data Systems*, *109*(2), 206–223. doi:10.1108/02635570910930109

Greenberg, M., & Mcdonald, S. S. (1989). Successful needs/benefits segmentation: A user's guide. *Journal of Consumer Marketing*, *6*(3), 29–36. doi:10.1108/EUM0000000002552

Ha, S. H. (2007). Applying knowledge engineering techniques to customer analysis in the service industry. *Advanced Engineering Informatics*, *21*(3), 293–301. doi:10.1016/j.aei.2006.12.001

Ha, S. H., Bae, S. M., & Park, S. C. (2002). Customers time-variant purchase behavior and corresponding marketing strategies: An online retailer's case. *Computers & Industrial Engineering*, *43*(4), 801–820. doi:10.1016/S0360-8352(02)00141-9

Ha, S. H., & Park, S. C. (1998). Application of data mining tools to hotel data mart on the intranet for database marketing. *Expert Systems with Applications*, *15*(1), 1–31. doi:10.1016/S0957-4174(98)00008-6

Haley, R. I. (1968). Benefit segmentation: A decision-oriented research tool. *Journal of Marketing*, *32*(3), 30–35. doi:10.2307/1249759

Hruschka, H. (1986). Market definition and segmentation using fuzzy clustering methods. *International Journal of Research in Marketing, 3*(2), 117–134. doi:10.1016/0167-8116(86)90015-7

Hruschka, H., Fettes, W., & Probst, M. (2004). Market segmentation by maximum likelihood clustering using choice elasticities. *European Journal of Operational Research, 154*(3), 779–786. doi:10.1016/S0377-2217(02)00807-X

Hruschka, H., & Natter, M. (1999). Comparing performance of feed-forward neural nets and k-means for cluster-based market segmentation. *European Journal of Operational Research, 114*(2), 346–353. doi:10.1016/S0377-2217(98)00170-2

Hsieh, N. (2004). An integrated data mining and behavioural scoring model for analysing bank customers. *Expert Systems with Applications, 27*(4), 623–633. doi:10.1016/j.eswa.2004.06.007

Hsu, S. C. (2012). The RFM-based institutional customers clustering: Case study of a digital content provider. *Information Technology Journal, 11*(9), 1193–1201. doi:10.3923/itj.2012.1193.1201

Hsu, T. (2000). An application of fuzzy clustering in group-positioning analysis. *Proc. Natl. Sci, 10*, 157–167.

Hsu, T., Chu, K., & Chan, H. (2000). *The fuzzy clustering on market segment*. The 9th IEEE Int. Conference on Fuzzy Systems.

Hu, T., & Sheu, J. (2003). A fuzzy-based customer classification method for demand-responsive logistical distribution operations. *Fuzzy Sets and Systems, 139*(2), 431–459. doi:10.1016/S0165-0114(02)00516-X

Hung, C., & Tsai, C.-F. (2008). Market segmentation based on hierarchical self-organizing map for markets of multimedia on demand. *Expert Systems with Applications, 34*(1), 780–787. doi:10.1016/j.eswa.2006.10.012

Hwang, H., Jung, T., & Suh, E. (2004). A LTV model and customer segmentation based on customer value: A case study on the wireless telecommunication industry. *Expert Systems with Applications, 26*(2), 181–188. doi:10.1016/S0957-4174(03)00133-7

Jain, A. K., & Dubes, R. C. (1948). *Algorithms for clustering data*. Prentice Hall.

Jonker, J., Piersma, N., & Poel, D. V. (2004). Joint optimization of customer segmentation and marketing policy to maximize long-term profitability. *Expert Systems with Applications, 27*(2), 159–168. doi:10.1016/j.eswa.2004.01.010

Kaufman, L., & Rousseeuw, P. J. (2005). *Finding groups in data: An introduction to cluster analysis*. New York: John Wiley & Sons Inc.

Kaymak, U. & Setnes, M. (2000). *Extended fuzzy clustering algorithms*. ERIM Report Series Research in Management, No: ERS-2000-51-LIS, Rotterdam, Netherlands.

Kaymak, U. Fuzzy target selection using RFM variables. *Proceedings of Joint 9th IFSA World Congress and 20th NAFIPS Int. Conference*. doi:10.1109/NAFIPS.2001.944748

Kiang, M. Y., Hu, M. Y., & Fisher, D. M. (2004). An extended self-organizing map network for market segmentation—a telecommunication example. *Decision Support Systems*, *42*(1), 36–47. doi:10.1016/j.dss.2004.09.012

Kim, J., Wei, S., & Ruys, H. (2003). Segmenting the market of western Australia senior tourists using artificial neural networks. *Tourism Management*, *24*(1), 25–34. doi:10.1016/S0261-5177(02)00050-X

Kim, K., & Ahn, H. (2008). A recommender system using GA *k*-means clustering in an online shopping market. *Expert Systems with Applications*, *34*(2), 1200–1209. doi:10.1016/j.eswa.2006.12.025

Kim, S.-Y., Jung, T.-S., Suh, E.-H., & Hwang, H.-S. (2006). Customer segmentation and strategy development based on customer lifetime value: A case study. *Expert Systems with Applications*, *31*(1), 101–107. doi:10.1016/j.eswa.2005.09.004

Kotler, P. (2003). *Marketing management*. Prentice-Hall.

Kuo, R. J., an, Y., Wang, H., & Chung, W. (2006). Integration of self-organizing feature maps neural network and genetic K-means algorithm for market segmentation. *Expert Systems with Applications*, *30*(2), 313–324. doi:10.1016/j.eswa.2005.07.036

Kuo, R. J., Chang, K., & Chien, S. Y. (2004). Integration of self-organizing feature maps and generic algorithm-based clustering method for market segmentation. *Journal of Organizational Computing and Electronic Commerce*, *14*(1), 43–60. doi:10.1207/s15327744joce1401_3

Kuo, R. J., Ho, L. M., & Hu, C. M. (2002a). Cluster analysis in industrial market segmentation through artificial neural network. *Computers & Industrial Engineering*, *42*(2), 391–399. doi:10.1016/S0360-8352(02)00048-7

Kuo, R. J., Ho, L. M., & Hu, C. M. (2002b). And data mining for product recommendation based on customer lifetime value. *Information & Management*, *42*(3), 387-400.

Mazanec, J. A. (1992). Classifying tourists into market segments: A neural network approach. *Journal of Travel & Tourism Marketing*, *1*(1), 39–59. doi:10.1300/J073v01n01_04

Mazanec, J. A. (2001). Neural market structure analysis: Novel topology-sensitive methodology. *European Journal of Marketing*, *35*(7/8), 894–914. doi:10.1108/EUM0000000005730

Mitra, S., Pal, S. K., & Mitra, P. (2002). Data mining in soft computing framework: A survey. *IEEE Transactions on Neural Networks*, *13*(1), 3–14. doi:10.1109/72.977258 PMID:18244404

Mo, J., Kiang, M., Zou, P., & Li, Y. (2010). A two-stage clustering approach for multi-region segmentation. *Expert Systems with Applications*, *37*(10), 7120–7131. doi:10.1016/j.eswa.2010.03.003

Myers, J. H., & Tauber, E. (1977). *Market structure analysis*. Chicago: American Marketing Association.

Nairn, A., & Berthon, P. (2003). Creating the customer: The influence of advertising on consumer market segments. *Journal of Business Ethics*, *42*(1), 83–99. doi:10.1023/A:1021620825950

Natter, M. (1999). Conditional market segmentation by neural networks: A monte-carlo study. *Journal of Retailing and Consumer Services*, *6*(4), 237–248. doi:10.1016/S0969-6989(98)00008-3

Ozer, M. (2001). User segmentation of online music services using fuzzy clustering. *Omega*, *29*(2), 193–206. doi:10.1016/S0305-0483(00)00042-6

Peltier, J. M., & Schribrowsky, J. A. (1997). The use of need-based segmentation for developing segment-specific direct marketing strategies. *Journal of Direct Marketing*, *11*(4), 54–62. doi:10.1002/(SICI)1522-7138(199723)11:4<53::AID-DIR8>3.0.CO;2-V

Potharst, R., Kaymak, U., & Pijls, W. (2001). *Neural networks for target selection in direct marketing*. ERIM Report Series Research in Management, No: ERS-2001-14-LIS, Rotterdam, Netherlands, March, 1-15.

Punj, G., & Stewart, D. W. (1983). Cluster analysis in marketing research: Review and suggestions for applications. *JMR, Journal of Marketing Research*, *20*(2), 134–148. doi:10.2307/3151680

Sharma, A., & Lambert, D. M. (1994). Segmentation of markets based on customer service. *Int. Journal of Physical Distribution & Logistics Management*, *24*(4), 50–58. doi:10.1108/09600039410757649

Shin, H. W., & Sohn, S. Y. (2004). Segmentation of stock trading customers according to potential value. *Expert Systems with Applications*, *27*(1), 27–33. doi:10.1016/j.eswa.2003.12.002

Smith, K. A., Willis, R. J., & Brooks, M. (2002). An analysis of customer retention and insurance claim patterns using data mining: A case study. *The Journal of the Operational Research Society*, *51*(5), 532–541. doi:10.1057/palgrave.jors.2600941

Smith, W. R. (1956). Product differentiation and market segmentation as an alternative marketing strategy. *Journal of Marketing*, *21*(1), 3–8. doi:10.2307/1247695

Suh, E. H., Noh, K. C., & Suh, C. K. (1999). Customer list segmentation using the combined response model. *Expert Systems with Applications*, *17*(2), 89–97. doi:10.1016/S0957-4174(99)00026-3

Sun, S. (2009). An analysis on the conditions and methods of market segmentation. *International Journal of Business and Management*, *4*(2), 63–70. doi:10.5539/ijbm.v4n2p63

Tsai, C. Y., & Chiu, C. C. (2004). A purchase-based market segmentation methodology. *Expert Systems with Applications*, *27*(2), 265–276. doi:10.1016/j.eswa.2004.02.005

Tsiotsou, R. (2006). Using visit frequency to segment ski resorts customers. *Journal of Vacation Marketing*, *12*(1), 15–26. doi:10.1177/1356766706059029

Tynan, A. C., & Drayton, J. (1987). Market segmentation. *Journal of Marketing Management*, *1*(3), 301–335. doi:10.1080/0267257X.1987.9964020

Vellido, A., Lisboa, P. J., & Meehan, K. (1999). Segmentation of the online shopping market using neural networks. *Expert Systems with Applications*, *17*(4), 303–314. doi:10.1016/S0957-4174(99)00042-1

Vesanto, J., & Alhoniemi, E. (2000). Clustering of the self-organizing map. *IEEE Transactions on Neural Networks*, *11*(3), 586–600. doi:10.1109/72.846731 PMID:18249787

Voges, K., Pope, N., & Brown, M. (2003). A rough cluster analysis of shopping orientation data. In *ANZMAC Proceedings*.

Wang, C. H. (2009). Outlier identification and market segmentation using kernel-based clustering techniques. *Expert Systems with Applications*, *36*(2), 3744–3750. doi:10.1016/j.eswa.2008.02.037

Weber, R. (1996). Customer segmentation for banks and insurance groups with fuzzy clustering techniques. In J. F. Baldwin (Ed.), *Fuzzy Logic*. New York: John Wiley & Sons.

Wedel, M., & Kamakura, W. (2000). *Market segmentation: Conceptual and methodological foundations*. Norwell, MA: Kluwer Academic Publishing. doi:10.1007/978-1-4615-4651-1

Wedel, M., & Steenkamp, J. E. M. (1989). Fuzzy clusterwise regression approach to benefit segmentation. *International Journal of Research in Marketing*, *6*(4), 241–258. doi:10.1016/0167-8116(89)90052-9

Wilkie, W. L., & Cohen, J. B. (1977). *An overview of market segmentation: Behavioral concepts and research approaches*. Cambridge, MA: Marketing Science Institute.

Wind, Y. (1978). Issues and advances in segmentation research. *JMR, Journal of Marketing Research*, *15*(3), 317–337. doi:10.2307/3150580

Wind, Y., & Lerner, D. (1979). On the measurement of purchase data: Surveys versus purchase diaries. *JMR, Journal of Marketing Research*, *16*(1), 39–47. doi:10.2307/3150872

Wu, R.-S., & Chou, P.-H. (2011). Customer segmentation of multiple category data in e-commerce using a soft-clustering approach. *Electronic Commerce Research and Applications*, *10*(3), 331–341. doi:10.1016/j.elerap.2010.11.002

Xia, J., Evans, F. H., Spilsbury, K., Ciesielski, V., Arrowsmith, C., & Wright, G. (2010). Market segments based on the dominant movement patterns of tourists. *Tourism Management*, *31*(4), 464–469. doi:10.1016/j.tourman.2009.04.013

Yankelovich, D. (1964). New criteria for market segmentation. *Harvard Business Review*, *42*(2), 83–90.

Yankelovich, D., & Meer, D. (2006). Rediscovering market segmentation. *Harvard Business Review*, *84*(2), 122–131. PMID:16485810

KEY TERMS AND DEFINITIONS

Back-Propagation: Backpropagation, or propagation of error, is a common method of teaching artificial neural networks how to perform a given task. It is a supervised learning method, and is an implementation of the Delta rule. It requires a teacher that knows, or can calculate, the desired output for any given input.

Customer Segmentation: The process of classifying a market consists of individual customers or consumers into distinct subsets (segments) that behave in similar ways or have similar needs and characteristics.

Fuzzy Clustering: In hard clustering, data are divided into distinct clusters, where each data element belongs to exactly one cluster. In fuzzy clustering, data elements can belong to more than one cluster, and associated with each element is a set of membership levels. These indicate the strength of the association between that data element and a particular cluster. Fuzzy clustering is a process of assigning these membership levels, and then using them to assign data elements to one or more clusters.

Segmentability: The term "segmentability" questions when it is possible to segment a market, and under what conditions this should be done. It is related to what characteristics an effective segmentation study should possess. A common agreement is that measurability, accessibility, substantiality, differentiability, and actionability are five criteria for effective segmentation.

Soft Computing: It refers to a collection of computational techniques in computer science, machine learning and some engineering disciplines, which study, model, and analyse very complex phenomena: those for which more conventional methods have not yielded low cost, analytic, and complete solutions. Soft Computing uses soft techniques contrasting it with classical artificial intelligence hard computing techniques.

Two-Stage Clustering Approach: Combining a hierarchical and a non-hierarchical clustering technique to carry out clustering where initial clusters (the number of clusters) are determined by a hierarchical method, and then a partitional method is employed to find the final clusters.

APPENDIX

Figure 2. Histogram representation of variables

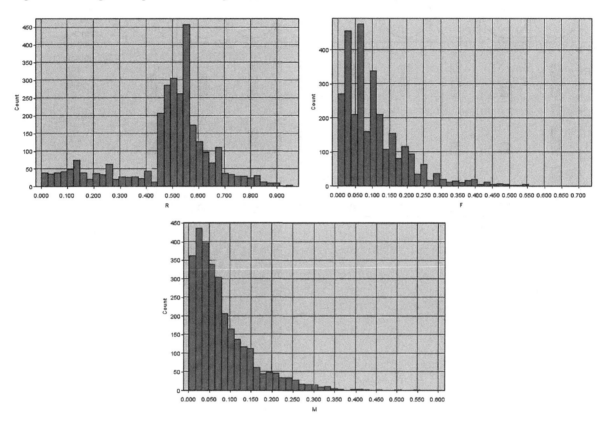

Figure 3. Dendogram representation of Ward's results

Figure 4. Visualisation of SOM results

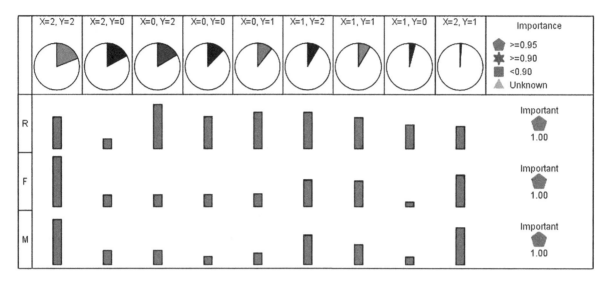

Chapter 7
Data Mining for Multicriteria Single Facility Location Problems

Seda Tolun
Istanbul University, Turkey

Halit Alper Tayalı
Istanbul University, Turkey

ABSTRACT

This chapter focuses on available data analysis and data mining techniques to find the optimal location of the Multicriteria Single Facility Location Problem (MSFLP) at diverse business settings. Solving for the optimal of an MSFLP, there exists numerous multicriteria decision analysis techniques. Mainstream models are mentioned in this chapter, while presenting a general classification of the MSFLP and its framework. Besides, topics from machine learning with respect to decision analysis are covered: Unsupervised Principal Components Analysis ranking (PCA-rank) and supervised Support Vector Machines ranking (SVM-rank). This chapter proposes a data mining perspective for the multicriteria single facility location problem and proposes a new approach to the facility location problem with the combination of the PCA-rank and ranking SVMs.

INTRODUCTION

Businesses encounter selection problems all the time. Selecting the right machine or selecting a type of layout to increase the shop floor performance is a typical problem related to operational research. With its deterministic nature, facility location is among the most studious topics of business, operational research and related fields. Broadly, the facility location problem (FLP) can be defined as selecting the optimal location on where an operation is going to be run.

Location decisions are strategic by all means and they can be based on various needs such as the renewal of the facility or capacity improvement. Structural and long-term decisions tend to have immea-

DOI: 10.4018/978-1-5225-0075-9.ch007

surable impact on the overall efficiency of the systems; meaning that while a good decision can boost the system, a poor decision may have ramifications for all parties in the end.

Decision analysis models can be used to determine the optimal selection by ranking the alternatives of a dataset that contains multiple criteria. Ranking (used interchangeably for ordination) constitutes a significant amount of research in the field of multicriteria decision making (MCDM). The background section of this chapter puts forward the mainstream facility location models used in business management and operational research.

This chapter tackles the facility location selection problem from a quantitative data analysis and data mining perspective. Data mining -a developing sub-category of data analysis that draws attention from both industry and academia- is the extraction of meaningful information and useful patterns from data using data analysis methods and machine learning algorithms. The importance of emerging techniques for the machine learning and business community is emphasized throughout the chapter. The idea of adapting contemporary methods from data analysis and data mining to facility location selection models is introduced in the background section. The aim is to equip readers with a detailed perspective on the facility location selection problem while centering on diverse business applications.

Machine learning literature classifies data mining models basically as supervised and unsupervised learning methods, according to the presence of a pre-assigned response variable within a dataset. Supervised data analysis is used to estimate an unknown dependency from a known input-output data; the learning system is modified so that the error between the model output and training data is minimized. Unsupervised data analysis, on the other hand, does not involve any supervision of an external source and hence any fine-tuning (Ahlemeyer-Stubbe & Coleman, 2014).

While analyzing multicriteria single facility location problem (MSFLP) through the unsupervised learning perspective, this chapter focuses on an exploratory data analysis technique called the principal components analysis (PCA). PCA is based on a mathematically elegant concept, namely the eigenanalysis. Through eigenanalysis, the variance of a dataset is expressed algebraically in a different way, yet the structure of the data cloud is preserved. After unfolding the connection between the variance and the optimal selection of a dataset, PCA-rank is applied to an MSFLP.

First proposed by Herbrich et al. (1999) ranking by support vector machines (SVM) is applied in this chapter for learning the ranking of facility locations. SVM-rank section provides a supervised data analysis perspective for the optimal selection in an MSFLP. Since learning to rank is a supervised learning task, and accordingly is the ranking SVM algorithm, there has to be a training set and that is considered to be the results obtained from the unsupervised PCA-rank.

This chapter approaches the optimal FLP using a combined ranking approach which includes supervised and unsupervised machine learning methods. This hybrid approach is tested on a real life dataset.

BACKGROUND

Business research literature refers to various techniques to solve facility location selection problems and related models such as factor-rating, transportation method of linear programming, center of gravity method, median method, volume-cost analysis, and Ardalan method (Chase et al., 2001; Ozcakar, 2015). An internet-based service provided by NEOS Server ("network-enabled optimization solver") offers valuable resource at their website ("NEOS Guide", 2015) about solvers for numerical optimization and also puts forward a broad classification of the optimization problems. While these solution approaches are mainstream; state-of-the-art techniques such as simulation, heuristics, and geographical information systems (GIS) are also used to determine the optimal facility locations (Ballou, 2004).

Facility location models can be classified in many ways. A popular approach is to classify them according to the concepts from mathematical programming, such as objective functions (cost minimization or profit maximization), constraints of capacity (unlimited or capacitated resource conditions), etc. Farahani et al. (2010) choose to classify the facility location models as multiobjective and multicriteria and further as single and multi-facility location models. The study also presents a summary of the available heuristics and meta-heuristics for the solution of the facility location models. Figure 1 illustrates a suggestion for the classification of the facility location selection problem (Ouenniche, 2011).

Data mining techniques are mostly concerned with the multicriteria multiple facility location problem (MMFLP). The objective of an MMFLP is to optimally locate the facilities to serve a given set of cus-

Figure 1. A suggestion for the classification of the facility location selection problems (Ouenniche, 2011)

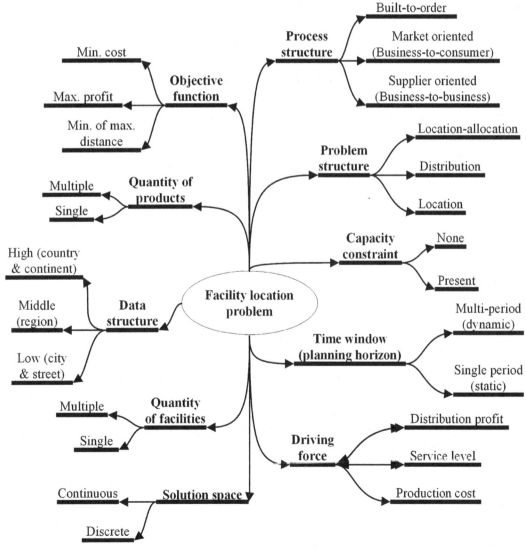

tomers. This location-allocation problem also involves the assignment of customers to facilities (Lozano et al., 1998). Cluster analysis and Kohonen networks, also called the self-organizing maps (SOMs), are two popular algorithms in unsupervised learning. These algorithms do not use external information such as class labels to uncover structures in data (Wu, 2012). The MMFLP is defined as a special clustering problem, where each cluster is composed of a set of customers served by the same facility (Levin & Ben-Israel, 2004). Lozano et al. (1998) propose to use SOMs to solve location-allocation problems in which the demand centers are independently served from a given number of independent, unlimited supply centers. Input patterns are the multi-dimensional location vectors of demand centers and are randomly presented to the network according to a probability distribution. The output layer corresponds to alternative facilities to be located. Apart from industrial applications, there are studies concerned with the FLP with respect to environmental systems, such as the study on the optimization of location of remediation plants by using the k-means and SOMs clustering models with the GIS (Gomes et al., 2007). Esnaf and Kucukdeniz (2009) present a fuzzy clustering-based hybrid method for a multi-facility location problem under unlimited resource constraint. The method uses different approaches sequentially: Based on their geographical locations the customers are initially grouped by fuzzy cluster analysis, then the facilities are located at the proposed cluster centers where each cluster is treated as a single FLP.

Data mining techniques available in the literature are generally for MMFLPs. There is also a considerable amount of study on MSFLPs which are solved by techniques other than those primarily related with data mining. The classical single facility location model is called the Weber model with a minisum objective function, minimizing the weighted sum of the distances between a facility and its demand points. Using only the distance criterion, Weber model aims to determine the optimal location of a single facility to serve a set of demand points, clients or regions. Noble (1967) frames the methodology for engineering applications with respect to the FLP of a power plant and a machine-location problem for a manufacturing shop.

Literature on MSFLPs using multicriteria decision analysis models also spreads out over a broad area of application. Tektas and Hortacsu (2003) apply the analytic hierarchy process (AHP) method to a chocolate store location selection in Istanbul. Ozdagoglu (2008) determines the criteria weight and compares four alternatives for a MSFLP by using analytic network process method. Uyan (2013) investigates the optimal location of renewable solar energy plants by multicriteria decision analysis techniques combined with the GIS.

A general tendency in the MSFLP literature is to compare the results obtained by different multicriteria decision analysis models that rank objects. Ozcan et al. (2011) specify that TOPSIS, ELECTRE and grey theory are among the notable methods and compare and contrast these techniques with regards to the multicriteria decision theory. The study also includes the application of a warehouse location problem. Azadeh et al. (2011) compare the ranking results by using data envelopment analysis, PCA, and numerical taxonomy. Uludag and Deveci (2013) compare the ranking results of VIKOR and fuzzy TOPSIS methods for an airport location selection problem. MSFLP is also recognized in the service sector. Soba (2014) aims solving the location selection problem of banks within a city in Turkey by using AHP and ELECTRE methods.

A procedure to follow for an MSFLP is given by Stevenson (1996):

Step 1: Determine the criteria that affect location selection.
Step 2: Determine the weight of the criteria.
Step 3: Evaluate the alternative locations that meet the criteria set.

In general, criteria is a synonym of factor and both are accounted as the independent variables that affect the location selection. Timor (2011) identifies a set of problem criteria to consider for a retail shop selection: Costs (rent and fitting expenses, and contract length), physical properties (availability of car park, shop size and visibility), geographical position (proximity to business centers, main streets or recreational areas, traffic flow), competitors (number of competitors, proximity to competitors, competitors' strength).

The following sections respectively introduce the theoretical background of the PCA-rank and the ranking SVM, and then discuss the solutions of the analysis conducted for an MSFLP.

PCA-RANK

Application of data mining techniques on MSFLPs is not vast, yet the multicriteria nature of these problems makes them suitable for such applications. Principal components analysis is a preprocessing tool and a statistical technique used in multivariate data analysis. Although it is sometimes regarded as a form of factor analysis, they are different models. It was first introduced by Karl Pearson in 1901 and computationally improved by Hotelling in 1933. (Nardo et al., 2008; Nelson, 2008; Alpaydin, 2014)

PCA is an exploratory quantitative data analysis technique, especially used for feature (dimension or variable) reduction. The objective of the analysis is to explain the variance of the observed data through fewer linear combinations of the original data so that the dataset gets simpler to interpret with less variables (number of dimensions). Rencher (2002) states that PCA seeks to maximize the variance of a linear combination of the variables and further explains the aim of using PCA in ranking problems with an intuitive example: A class of students are expected to be ranked according to their grades from various courses. The students' ranking is reflected better with the PCA-rank framework, rather than sorting their achievement according to an average score of equally weighted grades. In other words, course grades with unequal weights may lead to a better ranking of students' performances (Rencher, 2002; Alpar, 2013). Alpaydin (2014) elaborates Rencher's case and states that PCA can be used to project the whole dataset onto a single dimension so that the differences between the data points become most apparent. The principal eigenvector has the highest variance (eigenvalue) and thus the students are most spread out in this eigenvector's direction. PCA-rank algorithm takes the differences in variances of each course (dimension) into account, so, it performs better in the task of ranking the students' performance rather than using equal weights for each course.

PCA is best known for its feature reduction ability yet its contribution to data analysis extends from assisting the emergence of some MCDM methods -e.g. GAIA (Herngren et al., 2006), AHP (Saaty, 2003; Scala et al., 2014), etc.- to data mining techniques for unsupervised feature selection (Boutsidis et al., 2008). PCA also finds various application areas in signal decomposition, data visualization, pattern recognition, noise reduction, image compression, etc. (Smith, 2002).

PCA is a tool of projection that maps the original dataset to a new coordinate system whose axes are all perpendicular to each other. As a result of the transformation through eigenanalysis and the rotation of the observations of the original dataset, the new coordinate system's axes are composed of a new set of linearly independent eigenvectors. The instances of the rotated variables with the maximum eigenvalue or variance are loaded onto the first eigenvector, the ones with the second greatest eigenvalue are loaded onto the second eigenvector, and so on. This approach leads to the idea that PCA can be solved by tools of mathematical programming with an objective function subject to constraints (Pichette and

Rennison, 2011). The two resulting matrices obtained at the end of PCA are the coefficients and basis matrices. These matrices are expressed in terms of the newly reconstructed set of linearly independent vectors called the bases.

What PCA basically does is to analyze the structure of a dataset through a measure of statistical dispersion. In the literature one can find studies that use either correlation, covariance or the sum of squares and products (SSCP) matrices to initiate the algorithm. Due to lack of consensus on which statistical dispersion measure to use at the initiation phase, a universal scaling problem is considered to be disadvantageous. While using the covariance matrix is preferable in analyses where the metric variables are measured in same units, commonly used statistical software packages prefer to use the correlation matrix of the original dataset, since it carries less information regarding the relative importance of the variables measured in different units (Alpar, 2013). To overcome the obstacle of scaling, it is recommended to use z-standardization for all variables; that is dividing the mean-adjusted observation values by the standard deviation of the related series: $z_i = (x_i - \bar{x}) / s$. Note that without centering the data around the origin by mean adjustment, singular value decomposition is equivalent to PCA (Gillis, 2014). Authors of this chapter prefer to use the SSCP matrix, since both the correlation and covariance matrices are constructed using this matrix (Namboodiri, 1984).

PCA is a multivariate analysis, thus it is expected that the observations to be analyzed are obtained from a normally distributed multivariate space. For the multivariate normality assumption of PCA, there exists many statistical tests, such as Mardia's or Henze-Zirkler's multivariate normality tests. For example, Mardia's test -which can be computed using 'multivariateNormalityCheck.svb' script in STATISTICA software package- analyzes the assumptions regarding the skewness and kurtosis of the variables.

Prior to initializing PCA, one should also run Bartlett's test of sphericity that examines the linear interdependency in the dataset, hence the need for PCA. If the variables are already linearly independent, then there is no need for implementing PCA. Mainstream statistical software packages perform this process by finding the determinant of the correlation matrix of the dataset and checking whether the resulting Bartlett's sphericity test statistic is greater than the corresponding chi-squared value. If so, the null hypothesis that the correlation matrix is equal to the identity matrix is rejected, hence the dataset is suitable for PCA.

Consider a decision matrix $\left[\mathbf{D}\right]_{n \times p}$ (training set), with n input instances (alternative facility locations for the scope of this chapter, yet in general observations or objects) and p features (variables or criteria) that conforms to the assumptions or prerequisites of PCA, the steps of the analysis is then as follows:

Step 1: Compute a new data matrix as $\left[\mathbf{E}\right]_{n \times p}$ from $\left[\mathbf{D}\right]$ by calculating the z-standard scores of each element of $\left[\mathbf{D}\right]$. First, subtract the mean value of each feature $\bar{p}_j$ from each observation value, where $\mathbf{p} = [p_1, p_2, ..., p_j]_{1 \times j}$. Dividing each mean-adjusted value of instances by the related feature's standard deviation constructs each element of $\left[\mathbf{E}\right]$ as $\left(\dfrac{d_{ij} - \bar{p}_j}{s_{p_j}}\right)$.

Step 2: Compute the sum of squares and products matrix, $\left[\text{SSCP}\right] = \mathbf{E}^{\mathrm{T}}\mathbf{E} = \left[\mathbf{A}\right]_{p \times p}$

Step 3: Compute the feature matrix, $\begin{bmatrix} \mathbf{F} \end{bmatrix}_{p \times p}$ by solving the eigenvalue problem, $\mathbf{AX} = \lambda \mathbf{X}$. In order to find p number of eigenvalues λ, so $(\mathbf{A} - \lambda \mathbf{I})\mathbf{X} = \mathbf{0}$ holds for any nonzero $\mathbf{X}$; the characteristic equation of $\mathbf{A}$ is given as $|\mathbf{A} - \lambda \mathbf{I}| = \mathbf{0}$.

Eigenvalues found solving the characteristic equation represent the variance and the corresponding eigenvectors are in unit length. By finding the eigenvalues of the SSCP matrix obtained from the original dataset, new linearly independent variable sets and orthonormal eigenvectors are generated. As a result, the structure of the original dataset is revealed through new variables' variance and the feature set $\begin{bmatrix} \mathbf{F} \end{bmatrix}$ (factors, principal components, or eigenvectors) becomes the new basis for the original dataset.

Full information of the variance of the data is preserved once all the principal components are taken into consideration, meaning that the dimension of dataset is not reduced, and so no information is lost. A detailed explanation about the process of constructing the new bases and the corresponding coordinates of the observations is given in Rajaraman and Ullman (2012).

Ranking the observed elements according to their newly constructed coordinates is called PCA-rank. Since the original observations are standardized by using the z-scores within the PCA-rank framework, the corresponding eigenvectors of the regenerated data are free of measurement units and become comparable. This transformation enables one to use the PCA-rank as an objective ranking method (Kardiyen & Orkcu, 2006; Azadeh & Izadbakhsh, 2008; Gu et al., 2010; Goodarzi & Freitas, 2010; Hochbaum et al., 2012; Alpar, 2013). Decision on selection problems with the PCA-rank has started to take its place in the literature recently. Petroni and Braglia (2000) use PCA-rank for the supplier selection problem at a middle-sized bottling manufacturer firm in Italy.

As a multicriteria decision analysis technique that ranks objects, PCA-rank has been applied to an MSFLP (Azadeh et al, 2011). However, to the authors' knowledge, there is no prior study with regards to the MSFLP using SVM-rank nor a proposal for integrating unsupervised PCA-rank and supervised SVM-rank. The next section explains the ranking of objects based on the ranking SVMs.

SVM-RANK

Learning to rank, or machine-learned ranking, performs the ranking of objects or tasks. A major developing research field within the machine learning community, machine-learned ranking has gained importance with applications on data mining and information retrieval. Existing methods for learning to rank can be classified into different categories such as pointwise training, pairwise training, and listwise training. Further details on these approaches can be found in Cao (2007) and Li (2011).

SVMs are developed for classification tasks. Later they are extended for regression and recently they have been used to learn ranking (or preference) functions. Ranking SVMs have been mainly used in information retrieval and related applications (Joachims, 2002; Cao et al., 2006; Chapelle & Keerthi, 2010). Ranking SVMs are also used in the prediction of rankings as in an online fantasy football league game (Bookman, 2012). This chapter proposes to use ranking SVMs for the prediction of the ranking of alternative facility locations with respect to several related features.

Pairwise training based ranking SVMs, proposed by Herbrich et al. (1999), formulates learning to rank as learning for classification by SVMs on pairs of instances. In learning to rank, each instance is represented by a feature vector and each label corresponds to a rank. Let $\mathbf{x}$ be a vector that consists of elements taking numerical values with respect to each feature in the input space. Since learning to rank is a supervised task, there is also an output space $Y = \{r_1, r_2, ..., r_m\}$ with ordered ranks $r_m \succ_Y r_{m-1} \succ_Y ... \succ_Y r_1$; where $\succ$ symbolizes a preference or a ranking relation.

A training set for ranking SVMs is denoted as $R = \{(\mathbf{x}_1, r_1), ..., (\mathbf{x}_m, r_m)\}$ where r_i is the ranking label of $\mathbf{x}_i$ and R is assumed to be a strict ordering. If $\mathbf{x}_i \succ \mathbf{x}_j$ then $r_i < r_j$; so, if an instance $(\mathbf{x}_i)$ is preferred to another instance $(\mathbf{x}_j)$, then the ranking value of $(\mathbf{x}_j)$ denoted by (r_j) is higher than the ranking value of $(\mathbf{x}_i)$ denoted by (r_i). In other words; the most preferred instance is going to be at the top of the ranking with a ranking value of 1.

Let R^* be the optimal ranking of data in which the instances are ordered perfectly according to preferences. A ranking or the target function $F(\mathbf{x}_i)$ outputs a score for each instance, from which a global ordering of data is constructed such that $F(\mathbf{x}_i) > F(\mathbf{x}_j)$ for any $\mathbf{x}_i \succ \mathbf{x}_j$. If the data is linearly rankable by function F such that:

$$\forall \{(\mathbf{x}_i, \mathbf{x}_j) : r_i < r_j \in R\} : F(\mathbf{x}_i) > F(\mathbf{x}_j) \Leftrightarrow \mathbf{w} \cdot \mathbf{x}_i > \mathbf{w} \cdot \mathbf{x}_j$$

The objective is to learn a global ranking function R^F that is concordant with R^*. This selection of the best linear R^F, which is the best approximation to R^*, is possible by minimizing the loss function with respect to the given ranked instances.

Herbrich et al. (1999) propose a solution to this NP-hard problem by adding slack variables ξ_{ij} into the SVM model. In order for the model to have a good generalization capability the upper bound $\sum \xi_{ij}$ is minimized and the weight vector $\mathbf{w}$ is adjusted. The formulation of this problem leads to the minimization of the loss function as follows:

$$Min : L_1(\mathbf{w}, \xi_{ij}) = \frac{1}{2}\|\mathbf{w}\|^2 + C\sum \xi_{ij}$$
$$subject\ to : \forall(\mathbf{x}_i, \mathbf{x}_j) \in R : \mathbf{w} \cdot \mathbf{x}_i \geq \mathbf{w} \cdot \mathbf{x}_j + 1 - \xi_{ij}$$
$$\forall(i, j) : \xi_{ij} \geq 0$$

The quadratic programming problem above satisfies orderings on the training set with minimal error. C is the soft margin parameter that controls the trade-off between the margin size and the training error.

This optimization problem is similar to the SVM for classification when the constraint is rewritten as $\mathbf{w}(\mathbf{x}_i - \mathbf{x}_j) \geq 1 - \xi_{ij}$. In the ranking case, SVM classifies the pairwise difference vectors, $(\mathbf{x}_i - \mathbf{x}_j)$. As in the task of classification, the target function in the ranking task is also expressed by the support vectors that can be called as the ranking vectors. The ranking vectors in the optimization problem are the data pairs $(\mathbf{x}_i^s, \mathbf{x}_j^s)$ such that the above constraint is satisfied with the equality sign; $\mathbf{w}(\mathbf{x}_i - \mathbf{x}_j) = 1 - \xi_{ij}$. When the data are linearly rankable, the slack variables are equal to $0 (\xi_{ij} = 0)$.

Ranking objects with the linear ranking function $F(\mathbf{x})$ is the projection of the data points onto the separating hyperplane $\mathbf{w}$ so that the data points (objects) can be sorted according to their position on w. Support (ranking) vectors are the closest data pairs when projected to the weight vector, $\mathbf{w}$. The geometrical distance of two vectors $\left(\mathbf{x}_i, \mathbf{x}_j\right)$ projected onto $\mathbf{w}$ is calculated as $\delta = \dfrac{\mathbf{w}\left(\mathbf{x}_i - \mathbf{x}_j\right)}{\|\mathbf{w}\|}$ and is called the margin -the distance between the closest two projections. Generalization is achieved by minimizing $\|\mathbf{w}\|$ in order to maximize this margin.

In Figure 2, on a two dimensional space, two different linear functions $F_{\mathbf{w}_1}$ and $F_{\mathbf{w}_2}$ project four data vectors $\left\{\mathbf{x}_1, \mathbf{x}_2, \mathbf{x}_3, \mathbf{x}_4\right\}$ onto $\mathbf{w}_1$ and $\mathbf{w}_2$ respectively. The distance between the closest two projections onto $\mathbf{w}_1$ is the margin $\delta_1 = \dfrac{1}{\|\mathbf{w}_1\|}$, whereas the distance between the closest two projections onto $\mathbf{w}_2$ is the margin, $\delta_2 = \dfrac{1}{\|\mathbf{w}_2\|}$.

According to the large-margin principle, the separating line producing the largest margin has the best generalization capability for an SVM and for this reason is preferred. Although both of the weight vectors make the same ordering, $\mathbf{x}_1 >_R \mathbf{x}_2 >_R \mathbf{x}_3 >_R \mathbf{x}_4$; $\mathbf{w}_1$ generalizes better than $\mathbf{w}_2$ since margin δ_1 is larger than margin δ_2 (large-margin principle). Hence the ranking SVM performs a good generalization capability by maximizing the minimal ranking difference. Note that the ranking problem can also be formulated in its dual form to handle nonlinear ranking functions (Yu and Kim, 2012).

The next section integrates the output of the unsupervised PCA-rank as an input for the supervised SVM-rank on a real-life dataset.

SOLUTIONS AND RECOMMENDATIONS

The proposed machine learning based ranking approach for the MSFLP is simply a combination of PCA-rank and SVM-rank models that have been explained theoretically in the previous sections.

A multicriteria facility location dataset provided by Azadeh et al. (2011) is used to test the model. The full dataset consists of 25 instances (alternative locations for renewable wind energy plants) and

Figure 2. Linear projection of four data points (Yu and Kim, 2012)

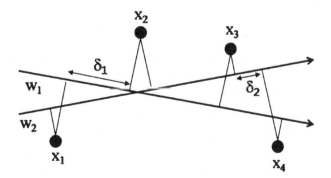

18 features (criteria or indicators). The four core features of the dataset are "intensity of natural disasters occurrence", "average blow wind", "quantity of proper geological areas" and "quantity of proper topographical areas". These features are considered as the criteria that affect the location selection of wind energy plants. Table 1 presents the original input values of 25 alternative locations for wind energy plants with respect to these four core features included in the analysis. This dataset is used to test the performance of the analysis that integrates PCA-rank and SVM-rank.

SVM-rank is a supervised learning algorithm and therefore the analysis needs a response (output) feature (variable), which is the ranking of the locations in this case that the model is expected to learn from. Since there is no previously known ranking of the locations, a ranking that can be taken as a reference is determined by the help of PCA-rank. Hence a sequential analysis of PCA-rank and SVM-rank combination is implemented. As the first step of the analysis, PCA-rank is used to find the rankings. The standardized values of the dataset and PCA-rank results are provided in Table 2. In the next step, given

Table 1. The dataset (Azadeh et al., 2011)

Locations	Intensity of natural disasters occurrence	Average blow wind	Quantity of proper geological areas	Quantity of proper topographical areas
L1	19.40	9.70	36490.30	691.10
L2	19.40	7.20	36490.30	691.10
L3	7.30	11.10	80296.30	10484.10
L4	14.90	9.10	55862.60	2854.00
L5	20.40	16.10	226316.20	80892.00
L6	8.70	8.90	15747.90	891.20
L7	3.00	10.40	14928.70	274.50
L8	5.60	8.10	27784.60	2898.40
L9	12.90	9.60	153426.30	3154.40
L10	4.20	8.00	16738.30	1745.70
L11	2.00	11.00	18064.10	1560.90
L12	5.10	8.30	17827.00	1378.90
L13	8.90	10.50	24081.10	1755.20
L14	7.70	23.90	10655.80	280.30
L15	8.30	10.50	80296.30	10484.10
L16	20.40	8.40	226316.20	80892.00
L17	12.00	6.30	24081.10	1755.20
L18	18.00	9.60	226316.20	80892.00
L19	3.70	8.60	11281.00	6.50
L20	24.30	6.40	83693.90	5725.90
L21	7.80	8.60	31271.00	1797.30
L22	5.60	11.00	27784.60	2898.40
L23	3.60	8.80	56358.90	11761.90
L24	7.60	17.20	154642.30	10857.50
L25	7.60	9.70	154642.30	10857.50

Table 2. Standardized values of the dataset and the PCA-rankings

Locations	Intensity of natural disasters occurrence	Average blow wind	Quantity of proper geological areas	Quantity of proper topographical areas	PCA-rank results
L1	1.4	-0.2	-0.5	-0.5	5
L2	1.4	-0.8	-0.5	-0.5	6
L3	-0.5	0.2	0.1	-0.1	12
L4	0.7	-0.3	-0.2	-0.4	9
L5	1.5	1.5	2.1	2.6	1
L6	-0.3	-0.4	-0.8	-0.5	16
L7	-1.1	0.0	-0.8	-0.5	22
L8	-0.7	-0.6	-0.6	-0.4	20
L9	0.4	-0.2	1.1	-0.4	10
L10	-0.9	-0.6	-0.8	-0.4	23
L11	-1.3	0.2	-0.7	-0.4	24
L12	-0.8	-0.5	-0.7	-0.5	21
L13	-0.2	0.1	-0.7	-0.4	15
L14	-0.4	3.6	-0.8	-0.5	7
L15	-0.3	0.1	0.1	-0.1	11
L16	1.5	-0.5	2.1	2.6	2
L17	0.3	-1.1	-0.7	-0.4	14
L18	1.2	-0.2	2.1	2.6	3
L19	-1.0	-0.4	-0.8	-0.5	25
L20	2.1	-1.0	0.2	-0.3	4
L21	-0.4	-0.4	-0.6	-0.4	17
L22	-0.7	0.2	-0.6	-0.4	18
L23	-1.0	-0.4	-0.2	-0.1	19
L24	-0.4	1.8	1.1	-0.1	8
L25	-0.4	-0.2	1.1	-0.1	13

the ranking determined by the PCA-rank, SVM-rank is run to learn this reference ranking; in other words, the ranking determined by the PCA-rank is included in the SVM-rank analysis as the target (output) value. It is important to note that for both PCA-rank and SVM-rank analyses the standardized values of the features are used due to the existence of different units of measurements in the original dataset.

In machine learning algorithms the dataset to be analyzed is usually divided as training and validation sets. A way to partition the dataset is taking the majority (usually taken as about 70%-80% of the dataset) of the dataset as the training set, which the learning algorithm is going to learn from, and the rest (20%-30% of the dataset) as the validation set to test the performance of the learned model on a different dataset that the model has not seen before. This is important to see the generalization capability of the model since overfitting can be an issue. In order for a machine learning algorithm to learn better, it is recommended to feed it with more data. In this basic data partition approach though, there is a loss of data for training the model because a specific percentage or amount of data is spared as the validation set at the beginning of the process. Therefore it is generally used when the dataset at hand is large enough. Otherwise, if the dataset is scarce, a technique called cross-validation is widely used. Cross-validation is an approach to evaluate the performance of a learning algorithm and select a prediction model. In this approach the instances (examples) in the dataset are both included in the training set and the validation set with repetition without any loss of data.

Since the sample size of the dataset is small, consisting of only 25 instances, rather than splitting the dataset as training and validation set in the first place, cross-validation is preferred in order to prevent the data loss in the training phase as well as to avoid overfitting. In the learning to rank task, the performance measure of a learning algorithm is calculated based on the orderings.

For the ranking problem at hand, two different approaches of cross-validation are implemented; leave-one-block-out (LOBO) cross-validation and a modified k-fold stratified cross-validation. LOBO for ranking tasks is proposed by Chen et al (2011) as an extension to the traditional leave-one-out (LOO) cross-validation. LOO uses one instance for validation and the remaining instances for training whereas in LOBO the dataset is divided in blocks based on the orderings of the instances: One block is spared aside to be used as the validation set and the other remaining blocks are used for training. This step is repeated until each block is processed as a validation set and an average performance measure is calculated in the end.

To apply LOBO cross-validation to the MSFLP, the dataset with 25 instances is divided into 5 blocks such that the locations' PCA rankings and each block contains 5 instances: The first block consists of the top 5 PCA-ranked instances and the training set includes the 20 instances in the remaining 4 blocks. This process is iterated until each block is processed as a validation set. Finally the average performance of the LOBO cross-validation is evaluated.

The second approach is a modification of k-fold stratified cross-validation for ranking tasks. The k-fold stratified cross-validation divides the dataset into k number of subsets of equal size and $k-1$ number of subsets are spared aside as the training set while the remaining fold becomes the validation set. The key point in the stratified cross-validation is to ensure that each fold is a good representation of the whole dataset. The validation subsets are sequentially tested until each fold is processed as a validation set. In this chapter a modified version of k-fold stratified cross-validation for the ranking task is proposed.

The MSFLP dataset is initially divided into $k = 5$ blocks based on their PCA-rank results, as in the LOBO cross-validation. Then $k = 5$ folds are generated by including an instance from each block to maintain the stratified structure: The first fold is made up of the best ranking instances of each block {1, 6, 11, 16, 21}, the second fold is made up of the second best ranking instances of each block {2, 7, 12, 17, 22}, and so on. This process is repeated until all k (in this case, 5) separate folds are considered as the validation set and the average performance measure is calculated in the end.

The ranking predictions are obtained running the SVM[rank] software by Joachims (2009) with default parameters. It is worth mentioning here again that SVM[rank] provides prediction scores for the instances, yet these scores do not have any meaning in terms of their values. The only meaning that these scores carry is their relative ranking. This is in alignment with the aim and scope of this study, which is the prediction of instances' ranking rather than the prediction of the instances' scores.

SVM-rank is run with both the LOBO cross-validation, proposed by Chen et al (2011), and the 5-fold stratified cross-validation, proposed by the authors of this chapter for ranking tasks. The training results of the ranking SVM, together with the reference rankings calculated by the PCA-rank are illustrated in Figure 3 through Figure 12.

Figure 3. SVM-rank predictions for training set 1, LOBO cross-validation

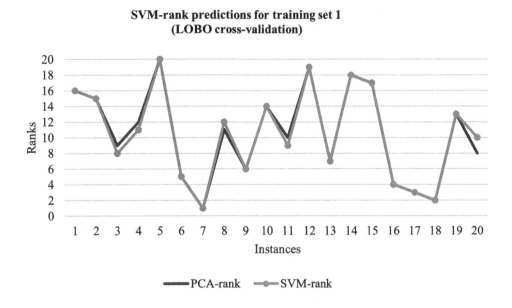

Figure 4. SVM-rank predictions for training set 2, LOBO cross-validation

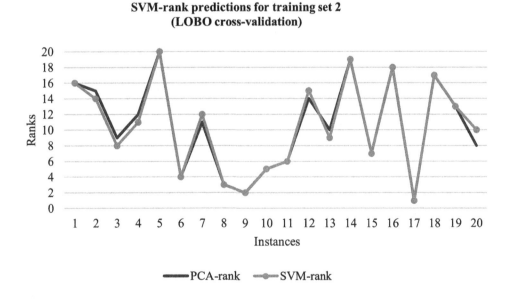

Figure 3 through Figure 7 illustrate the SVM-rank predictions of the alternative locations for the training sets, respectively performed by the LOBO cross-validation. The graphs also depict the original PCA-ranks of the instances (facility locations) in the training sets to provide a comparative visualization.

Figure 8 through Figure 12 illustrate the SVM-rank predictions of the alternative locations for the training sets, respectively performed by the $k = 5$ fold stratified cross-validation for ranking. The graphs, as in Figure 3 through Figure 7, depict the original PCA-ranks of the instances (facility locations) in the training sets.

Figure 5. SVM-rank predictions for training set 3, LOBO cross-validation

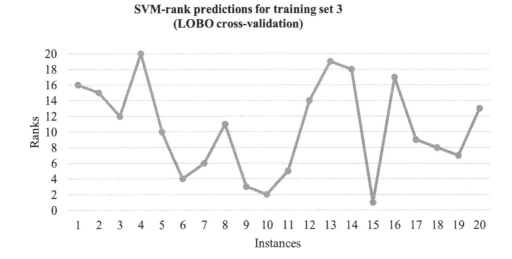

Figure 6. SVM-rank predictions for training set 4, LOBO cross-validation

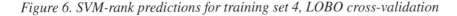

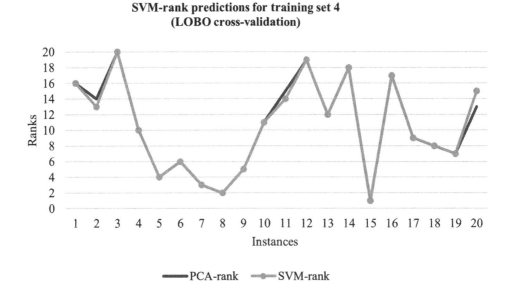

The performance of a supervised learning algorithm is considered to be good if the results obtained are close to the observed values, in other words the predictions of the learning algorithm are accurate. In the above dataset, the ranking of the facility locations obtained by the SVM-rank algorithm are expected to be parallel to the ranking computed by PCA-rank. For both cross-validation approaches, Kendall and Spearman rank correlation tests are carried out to compare the results of SVM-rank and PCA-rank in order to evaluate the learning performance of SVM-rank algorithm for a MSFLP.

Figure 7. SVM-rank predictions for training set 5, LOBO cross-validation

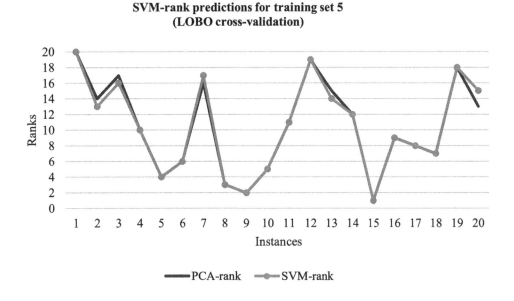

Figure 8. SVM-rank predictions for training set 1, 5-fold stratified cross-validation for ranking

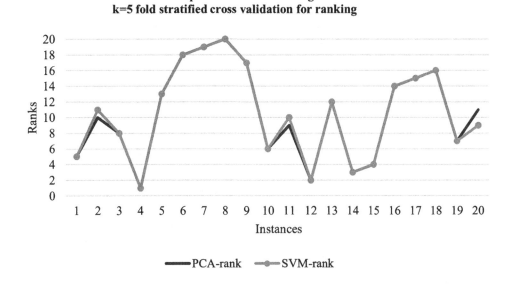

The results are presented in Table 3 for LOBO and in Table 4 for 5-fold stratified cross-validation. The correlation coefficients of the training sets are all very close to 1 in average performance for both tests (Table 3 and Table 4), meaning that SVM-rank could learn to rank from the PCA results. The reason that the Spearman's rho correlation coefficients are relatively higher than the Kendall's tau correlation stems from the fact that there is no significant discrepancy with respect to the orderings of instances of the PCA rankings and the SVM-rank prediction results.

Figure 9. SVM-rank predictions for training set 2, 5-fold stratified cross-validation for ranking

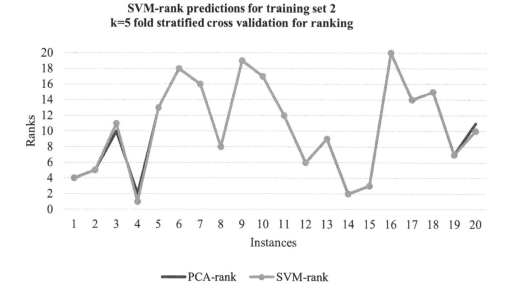

Figure 10. SVM-rank predictions for training set 3, 5-fold stratified cross-validation for ranking

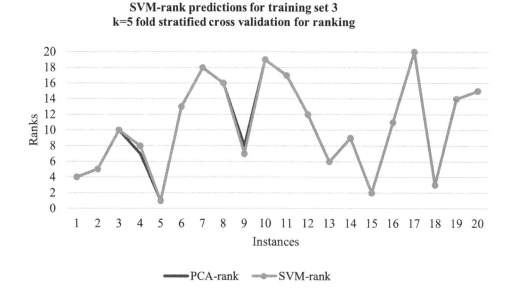

The average performance of the SVM-rank for validation sets using the LOBO cross-validation (Table 3) is close to 1 indicating good prediction results with only one exception of validation set 4, which is 0,4 for Kendall's tau and 0,5 for Spearman's rho. The reason for the low performance of validation set 4 can be further investigated. On the other hand, using the proposed stratified 5-fold cross-validation rankings of the validation sets leads to perfect predictions by the SVM-rank -the average performance measure equals to 1 (Table 4).

Figure 11. SVM-rank predictions for training set 4, 5-fold stratified cross-validation for ranking

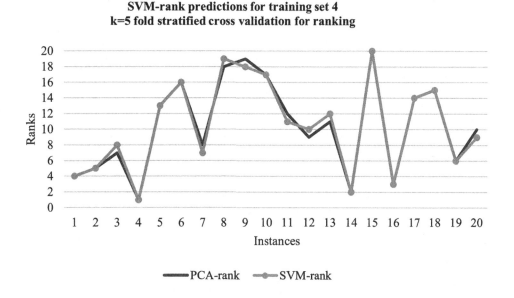

Figure 12. SVM-rank predictions for training set 5, 5-fold stratified cross-validation for ranking

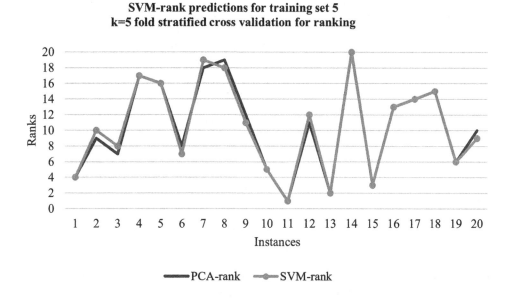

FUTURE RESEARCH DIRECTIONS

Facility location is a strategic area that always bears special interest to management science and businesses. There are several criteria that could affect where a business should be run. The multicriteria structure of the problem in most cases has led researchers to the application of MCDM techniques. Collection of training samples involves conducting questionnaires and this costly process needs repetition when a new set of alternatives is to be evaluated. As defined in the MCDM literature, this is an issue of

Table 3. Evaluation of ranking results for the LOBO cross-validation

	Correlation Coefficients	
	Kendall's tau*	Spearman's rho*
Training Set-1	0,968	0,994
Training Set-2	0,958	0,992
Training Set-3	1,000	1,000
Training Set-4	0,979	0,995
Training Set-5	0,968	0,994
Average Performance Measure for Training Sets	0,975	0,995
Validation Set 1	1,000	1,000
Validation Set 2	1,000	1,000
Validation Set 3	0,800	0,900
Validation Set 4	0,400	0,500
Validation Set 5	1,000	1,000
Average Performance Measure for Validation Sets	0,840	0,880
*Correlations are significant at the 0,01 level (2-tailed)		

Table 4. Evaluation of ranking results for the proposed stratified 5-fold cross-validation

	Correlation Coefficients	
	Kendall's tau*	Spearman's rho*
Training Set-1	0,979	0,995
Training Set-2	0,987	0,998
Training Set-3	0,989	0,998
Training Set-4	0,958	0,994
Training Set-5	0,958	0,994
Average Performance Measure for Training Sets	0,974	0,996
Validation Set (1-2-3-4-5)	1,000	1,000
Average Performance Measure for Validation Sets	1,000	1,000
*Correlations are significant at the 0,01 level (2-tailed)		

rank reversal (Charilas et al., 2008). Emerging research that may address this issue should combine the use of various types of dimensionality reduction with multicriteria decision techniques.

Criteria weights used in an MCDM technique affect the optimal results of the analysis, apart from a setting where the decision framework requires equal or no weights. Behold that the explanatory ratios obtained from the eigenvalues of the SSCP matrix can be used as the criteria weights in a multicriteria decision setting. For example, the variance of measurements are used as defining the decisive criteria weights within a framework consisting of PCA, AHP and ELECTRE methods (Charilas et al., 2014). Although there are several studies proposing the use of explanatory ratios as criteria weights, to the authors' knowledge, there is no prior study that tests and verifies this hypothesis. The main purpose of data mining is to discover meaningful information by data analysis, and it is clear that the relation between ranking and variance requires further research for future works. Moreover, the findings could be used as the output vector of a preference learning algorithm, such as the ranking SVM explained in this chapter.

Despite the fact that PCA-rank is beneficial as an MCDM approach, it is controversial since the signs of the eigenvectors (principal components) that can be obtained with different matrices (correlation or covariance) may vary (James et al., 2014). The signs of the corresponding components may alter the results and thus the interpretation of the analyses. In other words, results may differ from a parametric eigenvector calculation to another. It seems that there is no research on PCA-rank framework with regards to the affected scores and thus different rankings of the objects due to the changing signs of the eigenvectors. This limitation within the PCA-rank framework may be related with the issue of axis rotation. In the factor analysis framework, axis rotation may be required until interpretable analysis results are achieved, however Alpar (2013) states that there is no valid statistical test procedure in the scientific literature to determine the optimal rotation technique amongst varimax, quartimax, equimax, oblimin, promax, etc. -all axis rotation techniques within the factor analysis framework. Until disproven theoretically, a scientific ranking technique should always yield the same result. Future research towards investigating the relation between variance and optimality can use this controversy within the PCA-rank framework as a stepping stone for developing experiments that would lead to concrete results.

CONCLUSION

As the world gets more connected the decision makers' need for cognition increase and so does the need for precise learning algorithms to assist the enterprises in making better decisions. In this era of big data, businesses keep large databases; reaching vast amount of data gets easier day by day, yet the large scale problems are getting harder to tackle. Intelligent algorithms increase the efficiency and the quality of businesses by extracting knowledge from data. The algorithm proposed in this chapter is suitable to be used in circumstances where such data is present.

In the business research literature, the evaluation of the alternative locations and the selection of the optimal location within a multicriteria single facility location model is generally solved using MCDM techniques. Some of these techniques require subjective evaluations. However, the collection of training samples involves conducting questionnaires, which is time consuming and often expensive. Especially the whole process starts from the beginning when there is a new set of alternatives to be evaluated. Critiques on such MCDM techniques focus on the objectivity of the results, triggering further research for intelligent algorithms. The advantage of the proposed algorithm in this chapter stems from its source of information. Instead of collecting and using subjective judgements to compare alternatives and make a decision; the proposed algorithm is based on the dataset constructed by observed values of entities. This notion of objectivity differentiates the proposed approach from the mainstream MCDM techniques.

This chapter proposes a new ranking method to the MSFLP based on the sequential combination of the unsupervised PCA-rank (a multivariate data analysis and an exploratory data mining method) and a supervised machine learning algorithm, ranking SVM. The application data consists of alternative locations available for renewable wind energy plants. There are four features (criteria or indicators) -intensity of natural disasters occurrence, average blow wind, quantity of proper geological areas and quantity of proper topographical areas- that are considered to be effective in the location selection of wind energy plants. Embedded in the ranking SVM, PCA is a preprocessing tool that can reduce the computing time by decreasing the number of features. However, since there are only four features, all the principal components are taken into account and so the total variance of the data is preserved.

Given a reference ranking, the proposed algorithm shows a good learning performance of alternative locations' ranking with a high generalization capability. While introducing the adaptation of PCA-rank into SVM-rank with an application on MSFLP, two different strategies of cross-validation -a common approach in evaluating a learning algorithm and selecting a prediction model- are applied. The results obtained are satisfactory in terms of the performance measures.

Companies continuously seek to lower their costs and create competitive advantage. Choosing the best facility location is an opportunity to realize this goal. Application of this study should enable professionals to select optimal facility locations in a precise way. Furthermore, the proposed ranking approach is suitable for use in various disciplines where a decision is required to rank a set of alternatives.

REFERENCES

Ahlemeyer-Stubbe, A., & Coleman, S. (2014). *A practical guide to data mining for business and industry*. Wiley. doi:10.1002/9781118763704

Alpar, R. (2013). *Uygulamali cok degiskenli istatistiksel yontemler* [Applied multivariate statistical methods]. Ankara: Detay Yayincilik.

Alpaydin, E. (2014). *Introduction to machine learning*. MIT Press.

Azadeh, A., Ghaderi, S. F., & Nasrollahi, M. R. (2011). Location optimization of wind plants in Iran by an integrated hierarchical Data Envelopment Analysis. *Renewable Energy*, *36*(5), 1621–1631. doi:10.1016/j.renene.2010.11.004

Azadeh, A., & Izadbakhsh, H. R. (2008). A multi-variate/multi-attribute approach for plant layout design. *International Journal of Industrial Engineering: Theory. Applications and Practice*, *15*(2), 143–154.

Ballou, R. (2004). *Business logistics / Supply Chain Management*. Pearson Prentice Hall.

Bookman, M. (2012). *Predicting fantasy football - truth in data*. Retrieved May 25, 2015, from http://cs229.stanford.edu/proj2012/Bookman-PredictingFantasyFootball.pdf

Boutsidis, C., Mahoney, M. W., & Drineas, P. (2008, August). Unsupervised feature selection for principal components analysis. In *Proceedings of the 14th ACM SIGKDD international conference on Knowledge discovery and data mining* (pp. 61-69). ACM. doi:10.1145/1401890.1401903

Cao, Y., Xu, J., Liu, T. Y., Li, H., Huang, Y., & Hon, H. W. (2006, August). Adapting ranking SVM to document retrieval, In *Proceedings of the 29th annual international ACM SIGIR conference on Research and development in information retrieval* (pp. 186-193). ACM.

Cao, Z., Qin, T., Liu, T. Y., Tsai, M. F., & Li, H. (2007, June). Learning to rank: from pairwise approach to listwise approach. In *Proceedings of the 24th international conference on Machine learning* (pp. 129-136). ACM. doi:10.1145/1273496.1273513

Chapelle, O., & Keerthi, S. S. (2010). Efficient algorithms for ranking with SVMs. *Information Retrieval Journal*, *13*(3), 201–215. doi:10.1007/s10791-009-9109-9

Charilas, D., Markaki, O., Nikitopoulos, D., & Theologou, M. (2008). Packet-switched network selection with the highest QoS in 4G networks. *Computer Networks*, *52*(1), 248–258. doi:10.1016/j.comnet.2007.09.005

Charilas, D., Panagopoulos, A., & Markaki, O. (2014). A unified network selection framework using principal component analysis and multi attribute decision making. *Wireless Personal Communications*, *74*(1), 147–165. doi:10.1007/s11277-012-0905-y

Chase, R., Aquilano, N., & Jacobs, R. (2001). *Operations management for competitive advantage*. New York: McGraw-Hill/Irwin.

Chen, J., Wang, J., & Zelikovsky, A. (2011). Bioinformatics Research and Application. In *7th International Symposium, ISBRA 2011, Proceedings* (*Vol. 6674*). Springer Science & Business Media.

Esnaf, S., & Kucukdeniz, T. (2009). A fuzzy clustering-based hybrid method for a multi-facility location problem. *Journal of Intelligent Manufacturing*, *20*(2), 259–265. doi:10.1007/s10845-008-0233-y

Evans, J. R., & Olson, D. L. (2007). *Statistics, data analysis, and decision modeling*. Pearson/Prentice Hall.

Farahani, R. Z., SteadieSeifi, M., & Asgari, N. (2010). Multiple criteria facility location problems: A survey. *Applied Mathematical Modelling*, *34*(7), 1689–1709. doi:10.1016/j.apm.2009.10.005

Gillis, N. (2014). The why and how of nonnegative matrix factorization. *Regularization, Optimization, Kernels, and Support Vector Machines*, *12*, 257.

Gomes, H., Ribeiro, A., & Lobo, V. (2007). Location model for CCA-treated wood waste remediation units using GIS and clustering methods. *Environmental Modelling & Software*, *22*(12), 1788–1795. doi:10.1016/j.envsoft.2007.03.004

Goodarzi, M., & Freitas, M. (2010). MIA-QSAR, PCA-ranking and least-squares support-vector machines in the accurate prediction of the activities of phosphodiesterase type 5 (PDE-5) inhibitors. *Molecular Simulation*, *36*(11), 871–877. doi:10.1080/08927022.2010.490261

Gu, F., Greensmith, J., Oates, R., & Aickelin, U. (2010). *Pca 4 dca: The application of principal component analysis to the dendritic cell algorithm*. arXiv preprint arXiv:1004.3460

Herbrich, R., Graepel, T., & Obermayer, K. (1999). Large margin rank boundaries for ordinal regression. *Advances in Neural Information Processing Systems*, 115–132.

Herngren, L., Goonetilleke, A., & Ayoko, G. A. (2006). Analysis of heavy metals in road-deposited sediments. *Analytica Chimica Acta*, *571*(2), 270–278. doi:10.1016/j.aca.2006.04.064 PMID:17723448

Hochbaum, D. S., Hsu, C. N., & Yang, Y. T. (2012). Ranking of multidimensional drug profiling data by fractional-adjusted bi-partitional scores. *Bioinformatics (Oxford, England)*, *28*(12), i106–i114. doi:10.1093/bioinformatics/bts232 PMID:22689749

James, G., Witten, D., Hastie, T., & Tibshirani, R. (2014). *An introduction to statistical learning with applications in R*. New York: Springer.

Joachims, T. (2002, July). Optimizing search engines using clickthrough data. In *Proceedings of the eighth ACM SIGKDD international conference on Knowledge discovery and data mining* (pp. 133-142). ACM. doi:10.1145/775047.775067

Joachims, T. (2009). *Support vector machines for ranking.* Retrieved May 10, 2015, from http://www. cs.cornell.edu/People/tj/svm_light/svm_rank.html

Kardiyen, F., & Orkcu, H. H. (2006). The Comparison of Principal Component Analysis and Data Envelopment Analysis in Ranking of Decision Making Units. *Gazi University Journal of Science, 19*(2), 127–133.

Levin, Y., & Ben-Israel, A. (2004). A heuristic method for large-scale multi-facility location problems. *Computers & Operations Research, 31*(2), 257–272. doi:10.1016/S0305-0548(02)00191-0

Li, H. (2011). A short introduction to learning to rank. *IEICE Transactions on Information and Systems, E94-D*(10), 1–9. doi:10.1587/transinf.E94.D.1854

Lozano, S., Guerrero, F., Onieva, L., & Larraneta, J. (1998). Kohonen maps for solving a class of location-allocation problems. *European Journal of Operational Research, 108*(1), 106–117. doi:10.1016/S0377-2217(97)00046-5

Namboodiri, K. (1984). *Matrix algebra an introduction.* Sage University Papers.

Nardo, M., Saisana, M., Saltelli, A., Tarantola, S., Hoffmann, A., & Giovannini, E. (2008). *Handbook on constructing composite indicators: Methodology and user guide.* Paris: OECD publications.

Nelson, D. (2008). *The Penguin dictionary of mathematics.* UK: Penguin.

NEOS Guide. (2015). *Companion Site to the NEOS Server.* Retrieved July 29, 2015. http://neos-guide.org/

Noble, B. (1967). *Applications of undergraduate mathematics in engineering.* New York: Macmillan.

Ouenniche, J. (2011). *Unpublished lecture notes for design and operational management of supply chains of products and services.* Lecture at ESC Rennes School of Business.

Ozcakar, N. (2015). *Unpublished lecture notes for production management at Istanbul University.*

Ozcan, T., Celebi, N., & Esnaf, S. (2011). Comparative analysis of multi-criteria decision making methodologies and implementation of a warehouse location selection problem. *Expert Systems with Applications, 38*(8), 9773–9779. doi:10.1016/j.eswa.2011.02.022

Ozdagoglu, A. (2008). Tesis yeri seciminde farkli bir yaklasim: Bulanik analitik serim sureci [A different approach in facility location selection: Fuzzy analytical network process]. *Ataturk University Journal of Economics and Administrative Sciences, 22*(1).

Petroni, A., & Braglia, M. (2000). Vendor selection using principal component analysis. *The Journal of Supply Chain Management, 36*(1), 63–69. doi:10.1111/j.1745-493X.2000.tb00078.x

Pichette, L., & Rennison, L. (2011). *Extracting Information from the Business Outlook Survey: A Principal-Component Approach, Canadian Economic Analysis* [PDF document]. Retrieved from http://www.bankofcanada.ca/wp-content/uploads/2011/11/pichette.pdf

Rajaraman, A., & Ullman, J. D. (2012). *Mining of massive datasets* (Vol. 77). Cambridge, UK: Cambridge University Press.

Rencher, A. C. (2002). *Methods of multivariate analysis*. John Wiley & Sons. doi:10.1002/0471271357

Saaty, T. L. (2003). Decision-making with the AHP: Why is the principal eigenvector necessary. *European Journal of Operational Research*, *145*(1), 85–91. doi:10.1016/S0377-2217(02)00227-8

Scala, N., Rajgopal, J., Vargas, L., & Needy, K. (2014). *Using principal components analysis for aggregating judgments in the analytic hierarchy process*. International Symposium of the Analytic Hierarchy Process 2014, Washington, DC.

Smith, L. (2002). *A tutorial on principal components analysis* [PDF document]. Retrieved from http://www.cs.otago.ac.nz/cosc453/student_tutorials/principal_components.pdf

Soba, M. (2014). Banka yeri seçiminin Analitik Hiyerarsi Sureci ve Electre metodu ile belirlenmesi, Usak ilceleri ornegi [Determining the selection of the bank location through Analytical Hierarchy Process and Electre methods: The case of Usak towns]. *Mustafa Kemal University Journal of Graduate School of Social Sciences*, *11*(25), 459–473.

Stevenson, W. (1996). *Production/Operations Management*. Irwin.

Tektas, A., & Hortacsu, A. (2003). Karar vermede etkinliği artıran bir yöntem: Analitik hiyerarsi sureci ve magaza secimine uygulanmasi [A tool for effective decision making: Analytic hierarchy process and application to store location selection]. *Iktisat Isletme ve Finans*, *18*(209), 52–61.

Timor, M. (2011). *Analitik hiyerarsi prosesi* [Analytical hierarchy process]. Istanbul: Turkmen Kitabevi.

Uludag, A. S., & Deveci, M. E. (2013). Using the multi-criteria decision making methods in facility location selection problems and an application. *Abant Izzet Baysal University Graduate School of Social Sciences*, *13*(1), 257–287.

Uyan, M. (2013). GIS-based solar farms site selection using analytic hierarchy process (AHP) in Karapinar region, Konya/Turkey. *Renewable & Sustainable Energy Reviews*, *28*, 11–17. doi:10.1016/j.rser.2013.07.042

Wu, J. (2012). Cluster analysis and K-means clustering: An introduction. In *Advances in K-means Clustering* (pp. 1–16). Springer Berlin Heidelberg. doi:10.1007/978-3-642-29807-3_1

Yu, H., & Kim, S. (2012). SVM Tutorial-Classification, Regression, and Ranking. In *Handbook of Natural Computing* (pp. 479–506). Springer Berlin Heidelberg. doi:10.1007/978-3-540-92910-9_15

KEY TERMS AND DEFINITIONS

Cross-Validation: The process of testing and evaluating the performance of a learning algorithm to select a prediction model.

Decision Analysis Models: Techniques that quantify the decision making processes and help the decision makers compare alternatives.

Learning to Rank: A machine learning application to perform the orderings of objects or tasks.

Machine Learning: A field of computer science that studies any change in a system allowing the machine to re-perform better by learning from data.

PCA-Rank: A decision analysis model that ranks instances, after transforming the dataset via principal components analysis.

Principal Components Analysis: An unsupervised statistical analysis technique mainly used for feature reduction.

Ranking SVMs: A supervised ranking algorithm based on the pairwise trainings of instances.

Support Vector Machines: A family of supervised machine learning methods using the structural risk minimization principle for classification and regression tasks.

Chapter 8
Heuristic Optimization–Based Clustering Solution for Large Facility Location Problems

Tarık Küçükdeniz
Istanbul University, Turkey

Şakir Esnaf
Istanbul University, Turkey

ABSTRACT

Facility location-allocation problems are one of the most important decision making areas in the supply chain management. Determining the location of the facilities and the assignment of customers to these facilities affect the cap of achievable profitability for most of the companies' supply chains. Geographical clustering of the customers, while considering their demands, has been proved to be an effective method for the facility location problem. Heuristic optimization algorithms employ an objective function that is provided by user, therefore when the total transportation cost is selected as the objective function, their performance on facility location problems is considered to be promising. The disadvantage of population based heuristic optimization algorithms on clustering analysis is their requirement of the increased number of dimensions to represent the complete solution in a single member of the population. Thus in two-dimensional geographical clustering, number of dimensions required for each population member is double of the number of required facility. In this study, a new neighborhood structure for the standard particle swarm optimization algorithm is presented for uncapacitated planar multiple facility location problem. This new approach obsoletes the need for higher number of dimensions in particles. Proposed method is benchmarked against k-means, fuzzy c-means, fuzzy c-means & center of gravity hybrid method, revised weighted fuzzy c-means and the standard particle swarm optimization algorithms on several large data sets from the literature. The results indicate that the proposed approach achieves lower total transportation cost within less computational time in facility location problems compared with the standard particle swarm optimization algorithm.

DOI: 10.4018/978-1-5225-0075-9.ch008

INTRODUCTION

Facility location problem is one of the most studied areas of NP-Hard optimization problems (Guner, 2008). It is defined as determining the number, location and the capacities of the facilities when the locations and the demands of the customers are known. Besides, facility location problem involves the assignment of the customers to these facilities after determining the facilities' locations. Objective function includes the setup and transportation costs. Although mathematical modeling based approaches are defined and applied to this problem, the computational cost of these models increases exponentially when the size of the problem increases. In some situations, especially when the dataset is very large, mathematical programming may not be able to calculate the optimal solution within an acceptable time. Heuristic optimization methods are developed and applied to Multiple Facility Location Problem (MFLP) to overcome this problem. Although heuristic algorithms do not guarantee an absolute optimal solution, they can reach to a near optimal solution within an acceptable time.

Another solution approach for the placement of multiple new facilities on a two dimensional plane, which is called planar MFLP, is clustering analysis. Clustering analysis is a principal data analysis tool, which has a wide application area. It is the process of dividing data into several subsets while maintaining maximum similarity among the data within the same cluster and keeping minimum similarity among different clusters. Its applications can be seen in customer segmentation, document clustering and information retrieval, web data analysis, image segmentation, anomaly detection, biology, medicine and many other areas. Clustering is an unsupervised process, thus true knowledge about the class that each data object belongs to is not known by the clustering algorithm. In the clustering analysis models for the planar multiple facility location problem, the set of locations of customers is fed into the algorithm and a facility location set is calculated for which the total transportation cost between these facility locations and the customers is minimum. It is also called centroid clustering problem (Taillard, 2003). It should be noted that both uncapacitated and capacitated planar multiple facility location problems can be handled by using clustering.

In this chapter a particle swarm optimization based clustering technique will be applied to the planar multiple facility location problem on large datasets. The proposed particle swarm optimization (PSO) algorithm uses focal particles as the final representations of the facilities. The usage of multiple focal particles in a way that reduces the dimensionality of the problem is the main contribution and the distinctiveness of the proposed method.

In the following sections, first background information about facility location problems and the clustering approaches to this problem is given. Then particle swarm optimization technique is introduced and method of data clustering with particle swarm optimization is explained. In the fourth section particle swarm optimization with focal particles method is introduced. This method is applied on four location datasets of planar multiple facility location problems, and results and conclusion are given in the final sections.

BACKGROUND

Facility location problem on a logistics networks is a decision that affects the performance of the whole supply chain. The problem is classified into two main categories, namely single and multiple facility location problems. Single facility location problems (SFLPs) and multiple facility location problems

(MFLPs) are investigated under limited and unlimited capacity assumptions. MFLPs, unlike the SFLPs, are not limited to determining the location of the facilities but also handle the assignment of the demand (customers) to these facilities. In the single facility Weber problem (SFWP), the aim is to find the optimal location for a single facility in the Euclidean space, which minimizes the total transportation cost. Similar to SFWP, in the multi-facility Weber Problem (MFWP), cost of opening a facility is not included in the objective; the only cost dealt with is the transportation cost. In addition to that, the number of facilities is predetermined, given as a parameter and facilities can be located anywhere in the continuous Euclidean space.

In the literature, assignment methods based on choosing among alternative locations or numerical optimization methods based on finding locations on a geographical plane are defined for the solution of the MFLP's. Conventional optimization based solutions for the MFLP's are investigated by Sule (2001) and ReVelle and Eiselt (2005). Furthermore Arabani and Farahani (2012) gives detailed information about types of facility location problems. Based on several assumptions, Sule (2001) categorized the problems of location analysis under five basic classes:

1. *p*-median problem (PMP)
2. *p*-center problem (PCP)
3. Uncapacitated facility location problem
4. Capacitated facility location problem
5. Quadratic assignment problem

p-median problem is assigning *p* number of facilities into *p* locations. *p*-center problems are for-mulized as finding the minimum value of the greatest distance between any facility and the customers assigned to that facility. Objective function of the uncapacitated facility location problems is also a minisum function but, here, a setup cost associated with the location of the facility is also added to the cost calculations. Capacitated facility location problems are similar to the uncapacitated version but each facility has a limited capacity, therefore assigning customers to facilities gains importance in these problems. Quadratic assignment problems are the synchronized assignment of *n* number of facilities into *n* locations while maintaining minimum total cost.

Since 1960's, linear programming, dynamic programming, p-median, p-center, minimum and La-grangean relaxation based methods are developed for the uncapacitated MFL problem (Galvao, 2004).

When the history of clustering techniques is investigated, it can be seen that many unsupervised clustering algorithms have been developed. K-means is one of the well known of them. K-means is easy to implement and very efficient, however suffers from several drawbacks. The objective function of the K-means is not convex hence it may contain many local minima. The outcome of the K-means algorithm is heavily dependent on the initial choice of the centroids (Ahmadyfard & Modares, 2008). In order to achieve better clustering performance, fuzzy c-means (FCM) clustering algorithm is introduced by Bezdek (1973).

If customers and facilities can be displayed in *x-y* coordinates, MFLP is defined as a special clus-tering problem when the customers are handled as clusters (Levin and Ben-Israel, 2004). Levin and Ben-Israel (2004) used conventional clustering analysis to solve the MFLP. We call this specific type of MFLP is a planar MFLP. Ruan *et al.* (2010) developed a method for the location of multi-logistics centers, which has three sequential mechanisms including: determining the logistics centers' layout with improved clustering methods based on spatial equilibrium principle firstly, then finding solutions of location problem with the centroid method respectively, finally comparing the solutions and obtaining the best result. Esnaf and Küçükdeniz (2009) combined clustering and center of gravity approaches in an hybrid model for uncapacitated MFLP by transforming the MLFP into SFLP by using Bezdek and Dunn's (1975) Fuzzy C-Means (FCM), which is circular, and Gustafson and Kessel's (1978) elliptical clustering algorithms and then solve the SFLP with center of gravity method. Esnaf and Küçükdeniz (2012), then, applied a similar approach to the capacitated facility location problem. They proposed an assignment algorithm for the capacity constraint, which uses the membership values for this purpose. Instead of center of gravity approach, they use convex programming for the SFLP. Software, which assigns the demand to the most suitable facility dynamically, is developed. Later, Esnaf et al. (2014) designed a single iterated fuzzy c-means algorithm, which uses fixed cluster center solution approach to the facility location-allocation problem.

As the studies in the literature indicate clustering approaches alone are not achieving good performance on the facility location problems. They give better solutions in a hybrid fashion, when combined with a heuristic or weighted algorithm to handle not only the geographical locations but also the demand of the customers. Esnaf and Küçükdeniz (2013) altered the classical fuzzy c-means algorithm to employ the demand of the customers as the weight factor in the calculations for uncapacitated planar MFLP. This eliminated the unnecessary computations and the usage of different algorithms sequentially in hybrid or combined manner.

In this study a particle swarm optimization based new clustering algorithm will be applied to the uncapacitated planar MFLP under large instances and their results are analyzed. When the number of customers and facilities increases, the computational cost of the uncapacitated planar MFLP also increases. High computational costs make heuristics preferable than the exact algorithms. There are several studies in the literature that investigate the solution of the facility location problem with particle swarm optimization technique. Guner and Sevkli (2008) and Sevkli and Guner (2006) proposed a PSO based solution to the uncapacitated facility location problem. Their study employs the classical PSO algorithm with a binary assignment structure, in which each particle's number of dimensions equals to the number of facilities. At each dimension, "0" means closed facility and "1" means open facility. Their approach needs a predefined candidate facilities set, to choose among them. Yapıcıoğlu *et al.* (2004) used PSO for the semi-desirable facility location problem. Yano *et al.* (2008) developed a hybrid PSO algorithm and distributed the customers among facilities equally with their algorithm. Gong *et al.* (2007) developed a facility assignment model for the perishable food distribution centers using particle swarm optimization method. Li (2011) used particle swarm optimization technique to choose the location of a remanufacturing factory among several alternatives. Wang *et al.* (2008) developed a multi swarm approach for uncapacitated facility location problem. They used a binary approach to choose the facilities, which will be opened among alternatives.

As the literature shows, current studies of the PSO algorithm on the facility location problem only employs an assignment approach, which is choosing facilities among a set of predefined candidate facilities. When the literature investigated it seems that few studies on geographical solution to the facility location problem using PSO. In the method proposed here, locations of predetermined number of facilities are to be determined on a geographical plane. Ghaderi *et al.* (2012) proposed a similar approach, and applied a hybrid particle swarm optimization algorithm for solving the uncapacitated continuous location-allocation problem. They benchmarked their method's performance on two datasets from literature by varying the number of clusters (number of facilities). But the standard structure of the PSO algorithm handles each particle as a candidate solution to the optimization problem under consideration. This means, if the locations of 10 facilities are to be found, then each particle should have 10 x 2 (X and Y coordinates) = 20 dimensions. As it can be seen, especially for the large datasets, when the number of the facilities is big, the dimensions of the solution space increase. Küçükdeniz (2009) proposed the particle swarm optimization with focal particles (PSOFP) algorithm as a doctoral dissertation. His work overcomes this issue by a unique approach for the structure of the particles and therefore only needs 2 dimensions for each particle to solve the small facility location problems. Küçükdeniz and Esnaf (2015) then applied the PSOFP to solve data clustering problem on large datasets.

There is limited number of studies about the solution of the facility location problems in large datasets. Taillard (2003) investigated the planar MFLP on several large datasets and applied several heuristic approaches to solve the problem.

This study tries to prove that proposed PSO variant achieves lower total cost than the standard and hybrid PSO algorithms with less computational time requirement by decreasing the number of dimensions with the help of multiple focal particle topologies for large uncapacitated planar MFLPs.

Particle Swarm Optimization Based Clustering Algorithm

Clustering is considered an application field in mathematical optimization when it is done by searching for the global minima of a clustering criteria function. This approach makes it possible to apply heuristic algorithms to clustering analysis. Particle swarm optimization (PSO) is a population based heuristic algorithm, which maintains a population of particles where each particle represents a potential (candidate) solution to an optimization problem.

Swarm optimization algorithms are inspired by the approaches to model the social systems of birds and bees. Particle swarm optimization is developed by Eberhart & Kennedy in 1995 (Eberhart & Kennedy, 1995). In this algorithm, two types of information are open to the particles. These are particle's own former best experience and the best experience of the other particles that this particle is connected to. These two information affect the behavior of the particle and represent a kind of cognitive flow in the swarm.

In PSO, each particle represents a position in N_d dimensional space. PSO algorithm moves these particles through this multi-dimensional search space to search for optimal solution. A particle's movement is affected by three factors;

1. Particle's own velocity vector, v_i
2. Particle's best position found thus far, p_i
3. Best position found by the particles in the neighborhood of that particle, y_i.

In the first step of this algorithm, new velocity is calculated as in (1) and then this value is added to the current position of the particle as given in (2). If x_i is the current position, v_i is the current velocity, p_i is the personal best position and y_i is the global best position of the particle, then the velocity of the particle for the next iteration is;

$$v_i(t+1) = wv_i(t) + c_1 r_1 (p_i(t) - x_i(t)) + c_2 r_2 (y_i(t) - x_i(t))$$ (1)

$$x_i(t+1) = x_i(t) + v_i(t+1) \tag{2}$$

where w is the inertia weight, c_1, c_2 are positive constants, called the cognitive and social acceleration factors respectively, $r_{1,k}(t)$, $r_{2,k}(t) \sim U(0, 1)$, and $k = 1, ..., N_d$ (Merwe & Engelbrecht, 2003).

Merwe and Engelbrecht used PSO in data clustering (Merwe & Engelbrecht, 2003). They also developed a hybrid approach, which combines PSO and K-means algorithms to achieve better clustering performance. Each particle represents a candidate-complete solution. Therefore in a two dimensional problem with three clusters, each particle should have six dimensions. These dimensions are virtually divided to represent a position in the search space.

There are several other studies that involve the application of PSO algorithm to clustering analysis. Ji *et al.* (2004) applied PSO to the mobile networks. Correa *et al.* (2006) categorized biological sample data with PSO. In their study, each position vector represents characteristics of the inspected sample. Chen and Ye (2004) tested the performance of the PSO clustering on four datasets. Cui *et al.* (2005) applied PSO to the document-clustering problem. Attributes of the documents are defined as the dimensions of the search space; therefore each document represents a point in this space. Their algorithm tries to find the best positions for the clusters centers in this search space that represent the documents belong to that cluster. To reduce the computational time of the PSO algorithms, authors limited the run time of the PSO to a predefined point and then they applied K-Means clustering algorithm to the result of the PSO clustering phase. Omran *et al.* (2002, 2006) developed a pattern recognition method based on PSO clustering. Their algorithm dynamically adjusts the number of clusters, yet the number of clusters in an image file is not known beforehand.

Although each of these studies provide a number of improvements and innovations for clustering applications of PSO, all of them remains faithful to the Merwe and Engelbrecht's standard particle representation. But this representation creates a disadvantage by increasing the dimensions of the particles by the number of features of a data vector times the number of desired clusters (Figure 1). Most stochastic optimization algorithms, including particle swarm optimization, suffer from this "curse of dimensionality", which simply put, implies that their performance deteriorates as the dimensionality of the search space increases (Bergh & Engelbrecht, 2004).

Bouveyron *et al.* (2007) advise dimension reduction or subspace clustering as the primary ways of avoiding the curse of dimensionality. Feature extraction and feature selection are the primary methods of dimension reduction (Alpaydin, 2014). Feature extraction removes current variables and builds new variables which carry a proportion of the original information. One of the most well-known feature extraction methods is Principal Component Analysis (PCA). Feature selection methods, in contrary, do

Figure 1. Particle structure of the standard PSO. Each particle contains the centroids for all clusters

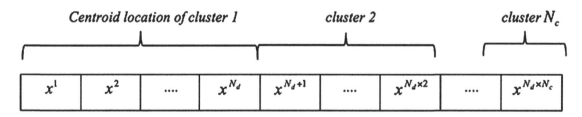

not build new variables, but find a subset of the original variables which represent a specific proportion of the original information. Both feature extraction and feature selection methods lose some part of the original information in order to obtain lower number of dimensions in the solution space.

"PSO with Focal Particles" Clustering Algorithm

The proposed method called PSO with Focal Particles (PSOFP) in this study, unlike the standard PSO approach, allows the achievement of the high quality clustering results without increasing the number of dimensions. To do so, instead of a whole representation of a candidate solution by a particle (including all centroids of all clusters as in Figure 1), In the PSOFP, each particle represents only one centroid in the search space. Therefore the number of dimensions of a particle equals to the number of data vector features. Despite this major change in the particle representation, the PSOFP's adherence to the standard PSO principles is provided by the changes made in the structure of the communication between particles.

One of the main configurational properties of PSO is topology or structure of connections between particles. Several approaches are developed to obtain good performance. In the gbest model, each particle is connected to all other particles (Figure 2a) (Küçükdeniz, 2009). In the lbest model, each particle is connected to a predefined number of other particles (Figure 2b). In star topology, which is a *lbest* model, one of the particles in the swarm become the focal particle and all other particles are connected to this focal particle (Figure 2c). Therefore, all communication in the swarm is transmitted through this focal particle.

The PSOFP addresses the application of a star topology based new PSO clustering method. In this method there are several focal particles in the swarm. Other particles are connected to their nearest focal particle and all communication passes through these focal particles. There are several studies about focal particles in PSO (Kennedy & Mender, 2002; Reyes & Coello, 2006).

Figure 2. Swarm topologies

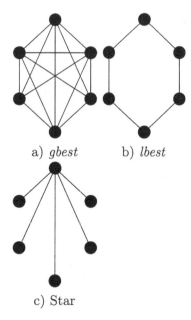

a) *gbest*   b) *lbest*

c) Star

In the PSOFP method, each particle represents only one centroid in the search space. If N_c is the number of clusters, then same number of particles is chosen as the final representatives of clustering solution. These particles are the focal particles to which all other particles in the swarm are connected to their nearest. This neighborhood structure is similar to Figure 3 (Küçükdeniz, 2009). This approach results in less dimensionality in particles. Therefore, it is expected to have less computational costs than the standard approaches.

Algorithm 1 displays the pseudo code of the PSOFP algorithm. To start PSOFP, a swarm with l particles is initialized. Swarm initialization of PSOFP is similar to the standard PSO. Then, randomly selected N_c number of these particles is labeled as focal particles. The swarm size should be bigger than N_c. At each iteration, fitness value of each particle is calculated. To do this calculation, first centroid locations represented by the focal particles are combined together to make a candidate solution. Then, for each non-focal particle, the particle's position vector (the centroid it represents) is overwritten to the corresponding place in the candidate solution. This process is illustrated in the Table 1.

In this illustrative example, a swarm with 8 particles is initialized. The data is to be partitioned into three clusters. Thus, the first three particles are assigned as the focal particles. The data vectors are in two dimensions therefore each particle has two dimensions. To calculate the fitness value of the fourth particle,

Figure 3. f_0 and f_1 are the focal particles. There are 13 particles in total. This is an example of a two-cluster problem

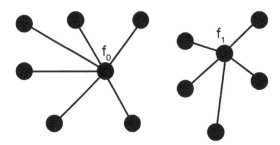

Table 1. Illustrative example for the PSOFP fitness calculation process

Particle Nr.	Focal Particle?	Vector $(x_1; x_2)$
1	True	10; 18
2	True	45; 26
3	True	21; 34
4	False	38; 30
5	False	12; 22
6	False	5; 52
7	False	15; 42
8	False	45; 22

- First a candidate solution is built by the focal particles as: {10; 18 - 45; 26 - 21; 34}. The first two columns of the candidate solution is the centroid of the first cluster and the third and the fourth terms are the centroid of the second cluster, the last part is the centroid of the third cluster.
- Then, the nearest focal particle to the fourth particle is calculated using the selected distance metric. It is the second focal particle in this example.
- In the candidate solution, the place belonging to the second focal particle are replaced with the current particle's position: {10; 18; 38; 30; 21; 34}. Fitness of the fourth particle is calculated by using this final candidate solution.

Another difference from the standard PSO is, focal particles in the PSOFP will not have their own inertia weight component. Focal particles are only affected by their own personal best and the best performances of the other particles that are connected to this focal particle. At the end of each iteration, particles, including the focals, move in the search space. When these movements finish, the neighborhood structure of the swarm is to be updated. Each particle, except focals, will be connected to its nearest focal particle. To do this, the distances among focal and non-focal particles are calculated again.

PSOFP for Uncapacitated Planar Multiple Facility Location Problem

In this study, the PSOFP method is employed to cluster the customers (demand points). Resulting cluster centers are the locations of the facilities. Customers in a cluster are assigned to the facility, which is at the cluster center. The objective function of the PSOFP algorithm is chosen as the total transportation cost (Equation 3), therefore the proposed algorithm tries to find the best location of the facilities that minimizes the total transportation cost between facilities and the customers.

$$\min_{\bar{v}_1, \bar{v}_2, \dots, \bar{v}_c} \sum_{i=1}^{c} \sum_{\bar{x}_k \in V_i} w_k d\left(\bar{x}_k, \bar{v}_i\right) \tag{3}$$

where,

$\bar{x}_k = \left(x_k, y_k\right)$ =The location of customer k in a plane, $k=1,2\dots n$

w_k =The demand of customer k, $w_k > 0$, $k=1,2\dots n$

$\bar{v}_i = \left(p_i, q_i\right)$ = The location or center of facility i

V_i = Cluster of the customer that is assigned to the ith facility

$d\left(\bar{x}_k, \bar{v}_i\right)$ = Distance between the facility i and customer k

$d\left(\bar{x}_k, \bar{v}_i\right)$ is Euclidean distance and formulated as follows:

Algorithm 1. Pseudo code for PSOFP algorithm

Require:
 · Dataset: $D = \{x_1, x_2, \ldots, x_m\}$
 · Number of clusters: N_c
Initialization:
 · Initialize the position x_i and velocity v_i of $l > N_c$ number of particles randomly. Each particle contains one randomly generated centroid vector (o_i) in the search space.
 · Define the set of focal particles S_F, where the number of focal particles, N_p
equal to N_c
 $N_p = N_c$
foreach *iteration* **do**
 forall the *particle i* **do**
 · x_i: Position of the particle i
 · f_i: The index of the focal particle that particle i is connected to
 · x_{fi}: Position of the focal particle that particle i is connected to
 · x_{SF}: All focal particles' positions
 · generate a candidate solution by replacing the x_{fi} in the x_{SF} with the x_i
 · calculate the fitness of particle: $J(x_i)$ by an objective function
 // Compare the particles current fitness with its *pbest*:
 if $J(x_i) < J(p_i)$ **then**
 $p_i = x_i$
 end
 end

 forall the *particle i* **do**
 · *Define neighborhood*: If i is non-focal then assign i to its nearest focal particle
 · $y_i = \text{MIN}(p_i \in S_{neigh} \, i)$ where $S_{neigh} \, i$ is the neighborhood of i
 · Change the velocity of the particle i according to the equation (1)
 if $v_i > v_{max}$ **then**
 $v_i = v_{max}$ // Check if the velocity is out of limits
 end
 Calculate the position of i according to the equation (2)
 if $x_i > x_{max}$ **then**
 $x_i = x_{max}$ // Check if the position is out of limits
 end
 if $x_i < x_{min}$ **then**
 $x_i = x_{min}$ // Check if the position is out of limits
 end
 end
end

$$d_k\left(\overline{x}_k, \overline{v}_i\right) = \sqrt{\left(x_k - p_i\right)^2 + \left(y_k - q_i\right)^2}$$

EXPERIMENTAL RESULTS

In the literature, there is a limited number of studies about facility location problems on large datasets. Taillard (2003) investigated MFLP on several large datasets. In this study Taillard's large datasets are chosen for the benchmarking. The Proposed PSOFP clustering method's performance on facility location problems is benchmarked against these algorithms:

- **K-Means:** Standard k-means algorithm, customer locations are clustered and final cluster centers are accepted as the location of the facilities. Each customer assigned to its nearest facility.
- **Fuzzy C-Means (FCM):** Bezdek's fuzzy c-means clustering algorithm is applied. The procedure is similar to the k-means algorithm.
- **Fuzzy C-Means and Center Of Gravity (FCM & COG- Esnaf and Küçükdeniz, 2009):** Center of gravity of each cluster is calculated after determining the clusters by using FCM. Customer demands are used for gravity calculations. This approach shifts the location of the facilities considering the demand of the customers. Therefore it gives better solutions than the FCM algorithm.
- **Revised Weighted Fuzzy C-Means (RWFCM - Esnaf and Küçükdeniz, 2013):** FCM & COG method is a two-phase hybrid approach, which, firstly, clusters the customers then applies COG to each cluster. RWFCM approach handles the demand of the customers in the FCM phase. The clustering is done in a single phase without requiring any fine-tuning method such as COG.
- **Standard PSO:** Total transportation cost function is supplied to the PSO. At each iteration, the algorithms tries to converge this objective function by finding better positions for the cluster centers.

Table 2 shows the datasets used for benchmarking.

CH2863 dataset (Figure 4) is from Taillard (2003). It has 2863 entities built on real data. The entities are the cities of Switzerland and the weight of each city is the number of inhabitants. PCB3038 (Figure 5), BRD14051 (Figure 6) and PLA85900 (Figure 7) can be found in the TSPLIB compiled by Reinelt (1995). PLA85900 consist of 85900 cities and used as a benchmark dataset in traveling salesman problem (TSP) in various studies. BRD14051 is a dataset used in symmetric TSP problems. Both BRD14051 and PLA85900 data sets do not include demand data originally, therefore randomly generated data is used as the demand data for these datasets.

Table 2. Benchmark data sets

Dataset	Number of Customers	Number of Facilities
CH2863	2,863	100 – 500 – 1,000
PCB3038	3038	500 - 1000
BRD14051	14,051	1,000
PLA85900	85,900	1,000

Figure 4. CH2863 data set

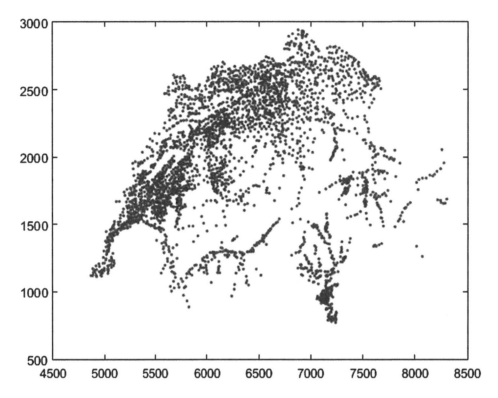

Figure 5. PCB3038 data set

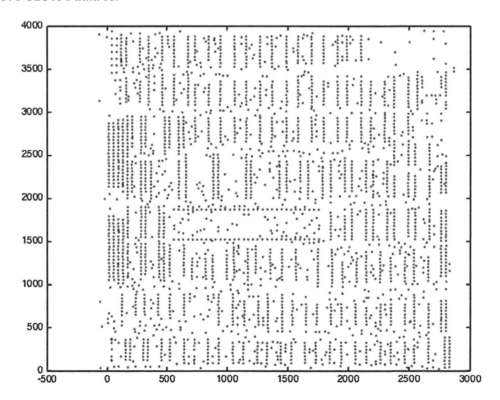

Figure 6. BRD14051 data set

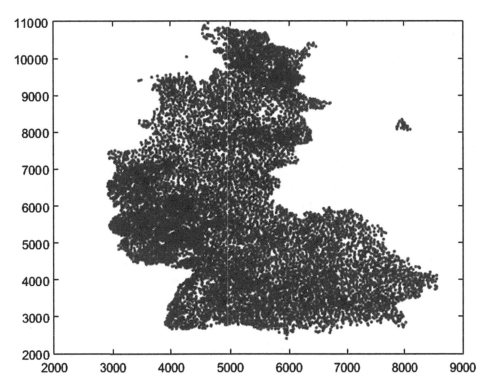

Figure 7. PLA85900 data set

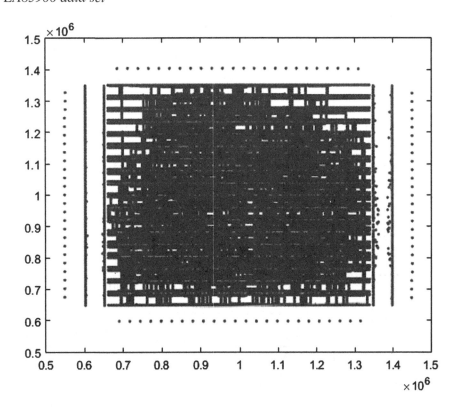

The benchmarking tests are parallelized on a 16-processor computer. Due to the random nature of K-means and particle swarm algorithms, all methods have been run 16 times. The test computer had 16 Intel Xeon E5 2.90 Ghz processors with 30 GB of RAM. 8 parallel runs are done at the same time.

Fitness evaluation process in a single run for the PSO and the PSOFP algorithms is also parallelized. The test computer was on Amazon EC2 cloud computing servers. Garcia and Garcia (2012) can be referred for a discussion on parallelization in data mining applications. The PSO and the PSOFP algorithms are initialized with (5 x number of clusters) particles. Permitted maximum iteration count is 2000, and maximum permitted computation time is 2000 seconds, but iterations stop when there is less than 0.0001 improvement in the global best value during the last 250 iterations. Equation 1 is used for velocity calculations with the default values of w=0.90, c_1=c_2=1.49 from Kennedy and Mendes (2002). In the standard PSO, *gbest* model is chosen. Total transportation cost (3) is chosen as the fitness function. CPU time column is the average CPU time for 16 runs. Mean and Min. columns of transportation cost represent the average and the best value obtained from the 16 runs. Std.Dev. column reports the standard deviation of the test runs.

Table 3 and Table 4 summarize the results obtained from the experimental studies. The FCM, the FCM & COG and the RWFCM algorithms converge to the same solution every time, therefore they don't have a variance in their results. The stars in the Table 3 indicate this situation.

Table 3. Total transportation cost results of the experimental study

Data Set	Number of Facilities	Method	Mean Cost	Min. Cost	Std.Dev.
CH2863	100	K-MEANS	438,934,900.60	427,708,138.55	8,918,034.07
		FCM	456,456,205.09	*	*
		FCM & COG	332,979,312.87	*	*
		RWFCM	302,172,906.74	*	*
		PSO	373,823,417.14	360,650,000.71	8,234,970,19
		PSOFP	304,129,550.19	293,931,603.36	7,646,112,25
CH2863	500	K-MEANS	174,514,648.88	169,067,693.91	6,840,446.05
		FCM	231,899,354.89	*	*
		FCM & COG	131,954,003.67	*	*
		RWFCM	109,083,059.14	*	*
		PSO	131,300,014.81	124,268,300.71	5,015,560.76
		PSOFP	109,558,153.26	104,829,025.88	4,604,789.90
CH2863	1000	K-MEANS	87,796,821.41	86,026,017.31	1,615,270.94
		FCM	129,988,262.75	*	*
		FCM & COG	76,494,475.39	*	*
		RWFCM	59,603,820.43	*	*
		PSO	99,735,790.01	93,793,291.92	1,912,098.45

continued on following page

Table 3. Continued

Data Set	Number of Facilities	Method	Mean Cost	Min. Cost	Std.Dev.
		PSOFP	60,914,080.23	60,488,077.43	1,160,744.19
PCB3038	500	**K-MEANS**	7,136,102.55	6,898,519.29	346,996.67
		FCM	7,780,763.57	*	*
		FCM & COG	7,099,873.97	*	*
		RWFCM	7,066,293.37	*	*
		PSO	8,126,307.32	7,797,656.23	416,712.33
		PSOFP	6,885,999.28	6,847,101.21	226,705.90
PCB3038	1000	**K-MEANS**	4,305,665.87	4,221,701.53	305,716.12
		FCM	5,271,828.65	*	*
		FCM & COG	4,238,594.91	*	*
		RWFCM	4,577,759.43	*	*
		PSO	4,058,415.87	3,963,217.51	298,906.43
		PSOFP	3,868,589.64	3,764,607.96	269,780.67
BRD14051	1000	**K-MEANS**	38,164,802.13	36,597,352.14	1,562,298.31
		FCM	42,527,785.75	*	*
		FCM & COG	40,648,691.64	*	*
		RWFCM	42,994,616.84	*	*
		PSO	65,551,351.36	62,126,820.17	1,980,341.86
		PSOFP	55,239,036.28	53,509,101.67	1,697,246.48
PLA85900	1000	**KMEANS**	33,488,924,293.93	33,444,314,764.05	233,180,961.76
		FCM	38,082,595,356.20	*	*
		FCM & COG	37,648,144,183.17	*	*
		RWFCM	37,012,982,112.24	*	*
		PSO	44,128,096,101.12	43,908,765,108.40	303,782,308.30
		PSOFP	33,008,124,212.01	31,712,744,058.65	269,012,788.26

In the CH2863 data set, with 100 and 500 facilities the PSOFP and the RWFCM methods are giving the best results. When the standard PSO is compared with the proposed PSOFP method, the PSOFP completes the same amount of iterations in a shorter time while finding 18.64% and 16.5% better solutions in terms of total transportation cost respectively.

If the number of facilities increased to 1000, the PSOFP and the RWFCM are still giving the best results, while the cost of the PSOFP solution is 38.92% better than the PSO. The PSOFP completes 256

Table 4. CPU time and completed number of iterations at the termination for the experimental study

Data Set	Number of Facilities	Method	CPU Time	Completed Nr. of Iterations
CH2863	100	K-MEANS	0.32	
		FCM	6.41	
		FCM & COG	7.94	
		RWFCM	2.59	
		PSO	224.76	2000
		PSOFP	128.22	2000
CH2863	500	K-MEANS	4.40	
		FCM	12.58	
		FCM & COG	21.46	
		RWFCM	10.15	
		PSO	774.69	2000
		PSOFP	467.19	2000
CH2863	1000	K-MEANS	15.84	
		FCM	13.11	
		FCM & COG	29.58	
		RWFCM	11.81	
		PSO	1,479.95	2000
		PSOFP	2,003.28	256
PCB3038	500	K-MEANS	49.69	
		FCM	40.14	
		FCM & COG	54.27	
		RWFCM	29.06	
		PSO	5,718.64	
		PSOFP	2,116.36	240
PCB3038	1000	K-MEANS	112.19	
		FCM	64.53	
		FCM & COG	94.22	
		RWFCM	25.25	
		PSO	5,006.82	265
		PSOFP	5,019.73	327
BRD14051	1000	K-MEANS	94.15	
		FCM	356.43	
		FCM & COG	440.73	
		RWFCM	220.54	

continued on following page

Table 4. Continued

Data Set	Number of Facilities	Method	CPU Time	Completed Nr. of Iterations
		PSO	2,027.08	32
		PSOFP	2,037.61	43
PLA85900	1000	K-MEANS	744.65	
		FCM	5,005.57	
		FCM & COG	2,457.43	
		RWFCM	2,319.67	
		PSO	2,001.12	23
		PSOFP	2,018.24	31

iterations in the permitted computation time while the PSO reaches its iteration number constraint before completing the 2000 seconds which is the permitted computation time.

In the PCB3038 data set with 500 facilities, the standard PSO has been run for 5000 seconds, to see if it gets near the PSOFP or the RWFCM solutions. The results show that the increased computation time availability does not provide the standard PSO to reach to the performance of the RWFCM. Also the proposed PSOFP, with its computation time restricted to 2000 seconds, is still 15.26% better than the standard PSO. In the next experiment on the same data set with 1000 facilities, this time the PSOFP has been run for 5000 seconds to analyze its performance on increased computation time. The results show that the PSOFP achieves 4.67% better cost than the PSO, giving the best total transportation cost among the benchmark data sets.

Interestingly, k-means has given the best results in BRD14051 data set with 1000 facilities. Both the PSO and the PSOFP completed in the maximum permitted CPU time of 2000 seconds, while the PSOFP completed 43 iterations, 11 iterations more than the PSO, within the same amount of computation time. The performance of the PSOFP was 15.73% better than the standard PSO.

In the PLA85900 data set, the PSOFP has achieved the best total transportation cost. It is 25.19% less than the PSO and its cost is 10.82% better than the cost of the RWFCM.

CONCLUSION

A novel neighborhood structure for particle swarm optimization technique is applied in this study. This new approach obsoletes the requirement for increased number of dimensions in the standard PSO algorithm when doing clustering analysis. This improvement particularly favors the continuous facility location problems. To analyze the PSOFP algorithm's performance on planar uncapacitated multiple facility location problems, a benchmark study is done. Several large datasets from the literature are used and different number of facilities is considered. The K-means, the fuzzy c-means, the fuzzy c-means & center of gravity hybrid method, the revised weighted fuzzy c-means algorithm and the standard particle swarm optimization algorithms are selected for the benchmarking. The total transportation cost is chosen as the performance criteria.

For the PSO and the PSOFP heuristics, maximum CPU time and maximum number of iterations are limited to 2000 seconds and 2000 iterations. The size of large data sets, with increased number of demand points and facilities affects the performance of the solution algorithm. Benchmark analysis shows that the proposed PSOFP algorithm, with its unique type of handling clustering problems, reduces this negative impact when compared to the standard PSO algorithm. On all data sets, the PSOFP achieves better total transportation cost values than the PSO algorithm while completing higher number of iterations in the same amount of time. Experimental studies indicate that reducing the number of dimensions in particle swarm optimization based clustering method improves the performance of the algorithm in terms of both objective value and the computational cost.

Further studies may include dividing larger data sets into smaller parts for clustering analysis of larger number of demand points and customers. Also parallelization of the proposed PSOFP algorithm, in context of focal points could further be analyzed.

REFERENCES

Ahmadyfard, A., & Modares, H. (2008, August). Combining PSO and k-means to enhance data clustering. In *Telecommunications, 2008. IST 2008. International Symposium on* (pp. 688-691). IEEE. doi:10.1109/ISTEL.2008.4651388

Alpaydin, E. (2014). *Introduction to machine learning*. MIT Press.

Arabani, A. B., & Farahani, R. Z. (2012). Facility location dynamics: An overview of classifications and applications. *Computers & Industrial Engineering*, 62(1), 408–420. doi:10.1016/j.cie.2011.09.018

Bezdek, J. C. (1973). *Fuzzy mathematics in pattern classification*. Academic Press.

Bezdek, J. C., & Dunn, J. C. (1975). Optimal fuzzy partitions: A heuristic for estimating the parameters in a mixture of normal distributions. *Computers. IEEE Transactions on*, 100(8), 835–838.

Bouveyron, C., Girard, S., & Schmid, C. (2007). High-dimensional data clustering. *Computational Statistics & Data Analysis*, 52(1), 502–519. doi:10.1016/j.csda.2007.02.009

Chen, C. Y., & Ye, F. (2004). Particle swarm optimization algorithm and its application to clustering analysis. In *Networking, Sensing and Control, 2004 IEEE International Conference on* (Vol. 2, pp. 789-794). IEEE.

Correa, E. S., Freitas, A. A., & Johnson, C. G. (2006, July). A new discrete particle swarm algorithm applied to attribute selection in a bioinformatics data set. In *Proceedings of the 8th annual conference on Genetic and evolutionary computation* (pp. 35-42). ACM. doi:10.1145/1143997.1144003

Cui, X., Potok, T. E., & Palathingal, P. (2005, June). Document clustering using particle swarm optimization. In *Swarm Intelligence Symposium, 2005. SIS 2005. Proceedings 2005 IEEE* (pp. 185-191). IEEE.

Eberhart, R. C., & Kennedy, J. (1995, October). A new optimizer using particle swarm theory. In *Proceedings of the sixth international symposium on micro machine and human science*. doi:10.1109/MHS.1995.494215

Esnaf, Ş., & Küçükdeniz, T. (2009). A fuzzy clustering-based hybrid method for a multi-facility location problem. *Journal of Intelligent Manufacturing, 20*(2), 259–265. doi:10.1007/s10845-008-0233-y

Esnaf, S., & Küçükdeniz, T. (2013). Solving Uncapacitated Planar Multi-facility Location Problems by a Revised Weighted Fuzzy c-means Clustering Algorithm. *Multiple-Valued Logic and Soft Computing, 21*(1-2), 147–164.

Esnaf, Ş., Küçükdeniz, T., & Tunçbilek, N. (2014). Fuzzy C-Means Algorithm with Fixed Cluster Centers for Uncapacitated Facility Location Problems: Turkish Case Study. In Supply Chain Management Under Fuzziness (pp. 489-516). Springer Berlin Heidelberg.

Galvão, R. D. (2004). Uncapacitated facility location problems: Contributions. *Pesquisa Operacional, 24*(1), 7–38. doi:10.1590/S0101-74382004000100003

García-Pedrajas, N., & de Haro-García, A. (2012). Scaling up data mining algorithms: Review and taxonomy. *Progress in Artificial Intelligence, 1*(1), 71–87. doi:10.1007/s13748-011-0004-4

Ghaderi, A., Jabalameli, M. S., Barzinpour, F., & Rahmaniani, R. (2012). An efficient hybrid particle swarm optimization algorithm for solving the uncapacitated continuous location-allocation problem. *Networks and Spatial Economics, 12*(3), 421–439. doi:10.1007/s11067-011-9162-y

Gong, W., Li, D., Liu, X., Yue, J., & Fu, Z. (2007). Improved two-grade delayed particle swarm optimisation (TGDPSO) for inventory facility location for perishable food distribution centres in Beijing. New Zealand. *Journal of Agricultural Research, 50*(5), 771–779.

Guner, A. R., & Sevkli, M. (2008). A discrete particle swarm optimization algorithm for uncapacitated facility location problem. *Journal of Artificial Evolution and Applications, 2008*, 10. doi:10.1155/2008/861512

Gustafson, D., & Kessel, W. (1978). Fuzzy clustering with a fuzzy covariance matrix. In *1978 IEEE conference on decision and control including the 17th symposium on adaptive processes* (No. 17, pp. 761-766). doi:10.1109/CDC.1978.268028

Ji, C., Zhang, Y., Gao, S., Yuan, P., & Li, Z. (2004, March). Particle swarm optimization for mobile ad hoc networks clustering. In *Networking, Sensing and Control, 2004 IEEE International Conference on* (Vol. 1, pp. 372-375). IEEE.

Kennedy, J., & Mendes, R. (2002). *Population structure and particle swarm performance*. Academic Press.

Küçükdeniz, T. (2009). *Sürü Zekası Optimizasyon Yöntemi ve Tedarik Zinciri Yönetiminde Bir Uygulama*. (Doctoral Dissertation). İstanbul Üniversitesi Fen Bilimleri Enstitüsü.

Küçükdeniz, T., Baray, A., Ecerkale, K., & Esnaf, Ş. (2012). Integrated use of fuzzy c-means and convex programming for capacitated multi-facility location problem. *Expert Systems with Applications, 39*(4), 4306–4314. doi:10.1016/j.eswa.2011.09.102

Küçükdeniz, T., & Esnaf, Ş. (2015). Data clustering by particle swarm optimization with the focal particles. In P. Pardalos, M. Pavone, G. M. Farinella, & V. Cutello (Eds.), Lecture Notes in Computer Science: Vol. 9432. *Machine Learning, Optimization, and Big Data* (pp. 280–292). Switzerland: Springer Publishing International; doi:10.1007/978-3-319-27926-8_25

Levin, Y., & Ben-Israel, A. (2004). A heuristic method for large-scale multi-facility location problems. *Computers & Operations Research*, *31*(2), 257–272. doi:10.1016/S0305-0548(02)00191-0

Li, N. (2011, January). Research on location of remanufacturing factory based on particle swarm optimization. In *Management Science and Industrial Engineering (MSIE), 2011 International Conference on* (pp. 1016-1019). IEEE.

Omran, M., Salman, A., & Engelbrecht, A. P. (2002, November). Image classification using particle swarm optimization. In *Proceedings of the 4th Asia-Pacific conference on simulated evolution and learning* (Vol. 1, pp. 18-22).

Omran, M. G., Salman, A., & Engelbrecht, A. P. (2006). Dynamic clustering using particle swarm optimization with application in image segmentation. *Pattern Analysis & Applications*, *8*(4), 332–344. doi:10.1007/s10044-005-0015-5

Reinelt, G. (1995). *Tsplib95. Interdisziplinäres Zentrum für Wissenschaftliches Rechnen*. Heidelberg, Germany: IWR.

ReVelle, C. S., & Eiselt, H. A. (2005). Location analysis: A synthesis and survey. *European Journal of Operational Research*, *165*(1), 1–19. doi:10.1016/j.ejor.2003.11.032

Reyes-Sierra, M., & Coello, C. C. (2006). Multi-objective particle swarm optimizers: A survey of the state-of-the-art. *International Journal of Computational Intelligence Research*, *2*(3), 287-308.

Ruan, Q., Miao, L., & Zheng, Z. (2010, October). A novel clustering-based approach for the location of multi-logistics centers. In *Supply Chain Management and Information Systems (SCMIS), 2010 8th International Conference on* (pp. 1-5). IEEE.

Sevkli, M., & Guner, A. R. (2006). A continuous particle swarm optimization algorithm for uncapacitated facility location problem. In *Ant colony optimization and swarm intelligence* (pp. 316–323). Springer Berlin Heidelberg. doi:10.1007/11839088_28

Sule, D. R. (2001). *Logistics of facility location and allocation*. New York: CRC Press. doi:10.1201/9780203910405

Taillard, É. D. (2003). Heuristic methods for large centroid clustering problems. *Journal of Heuristics*, *9*(1), 51–73. doi:10.1023/A:1021841728075

Van den Bergh, F., & Engelbrecht, A. P. (2004). A cooperative approach to particle swarm optimization. Evolutionary Computation. *IEEE Transactions on*, *8*(3), 225–239.

Van der Merwe, D. W., & Engelbrecht, A. P. (2003, December). Data clustering using particle swarm optimization. In Evolutionary Computation, 2003. CEC'03. The 2003 Congress on (Vol. 1, pp. 215-220). IEEE. doi:10.1109/CEC.2003.1299577

Wang, D., Wu, C. H., Ip, A., Wang, D., & Yan, Y. (2008, June). Parallel multi-population particle swarm optimization algorithm for the uncapacitated facility location problem using openMP. In *Evolutionary Computation, 2008. CEC 2008.(IEEE World Congress on Computational Intelligence). IEEE Congress on* (pp. 1214-1218). IEEE.

Yano, F., Shohdohji, T., & Toyoda, Y. (2008). Modification of hybridized particle swarm optimization algorithms applying to facility location problems. In *Proceedings of the 9th Asia Pacific Industrial Engineering & Management Systems Conference* (pp. 2278-2287).

Yapıcıoğlu, H., Dozier, G., & Smith, A. E. (2004, June). Bi-criteria model for locating a semi-desirable facility on a plane using particle swarm optimization. In Evolutionary Computation, 2004. CEC2004. Congress on (Vol. 2, pp. 2328-2334). IEEE. doi:10.1109/CEC.2004.1331188

KEY TERMS AND DEFINITIONS

Clustering: Defining similar sets among a number of objects.

Heuristic Optimization: Finding a near-optimal solution of an objective function using a specific algorithm.

Large Data: A data with too many instances and/or dimensions.

Planar Facility Location Problem: Determining the place of facilities like factories, warehouses, distribution centers, retailer on a plane.

Chapter 9
Review of Business Intelligence and Intelligent Systems in Healthcare Domain

Halil Ibrahim Cebeci
Sakarya University, Turkey

Abdulkadir Hiziroglu
Yıldırım Beyazıt University, Turkey

ABSTRACT

Business intelligence and corresponding intelligent components and tools have been one of those instruments that receive significant attention from health community. In order to raise more awareness on the potentials of business intelligence and intelligent systems, this paper aims to provide an overview of business intelligence in healthcare context by specifically focusing on the applications of intelligent systems. This study reviewed the current applications into three main categories and presented some important findings of that research in a systematic manner. The literature is wide with respect to the applications of business intelligence covering the issues from health management and policy related topics to more operational and tactical ones such as disease treatment, diagnostics, and hospital management. The discussions made in this article can also facilitate the researchers in that area to generate a research agenda for future work in applied health science, particularly within the context of health management and policy and health analytics.

1. INTRODUCTION

Healthcare information systems generate massive amounts of healthcare and medical data pertaining to several health processes including inpatient/out-patient registration, patient care, billing, payroll, budget, medical treatment and etc. (Cios & Moore, 2002; Wasan, Bhatnagar & Kaur, 2006). Although healthcare environment can be considered to be "information rich and wealthy", yet, making the most of health and medical data in obtaining strategic knowledge has not been fully accomplished (Abidi, 2001; Bose, 2003; Srinivas, Rani & Govrdhan, 2010). A healthcare organization can gain competitive advantage via

DOI: 10.4018/978-1-5225-0075-9.ch009

turning the health/medical data into knowledge using data-oriented decision support systems and tools, aka business intelligence (BI) or analytics.

BI is an umbrella term and can be defined as a set of technologies that enable companies to acquire the competency of making accurate, timely and effective decisions at all levels of organizations (Turban, Sharda, Delen & King, 2011). These technologies consist of solutions for gathering, consolidating, analyzing and providing access to data and they are used to discover various patterns, generalizations, regularities or anomalies and rules hidden inside the data. BI refers to applying various analytics techniques to organizational data which may be generated through the internal business processes (e.g., clinical or medical processes or health-related administrative business (core or support) processes) or could be acquired from external and open data sources (Vercellis, 2009). The main components of business intelligence can be categorized under four elements (Turban et al., 2011), namely Data Warehouse (data mart in small scale) and associated technologies such as ETL (Extraction-Transformation-Load), business analytics (simple ad-hoc reporting, online analytical processing, data mining, web/text mining), performance and strategy (business performance management components such as dashboards and scorecards), and user interface (other visualization tools).

BI have been implemented in variety of industries where the majority of these applications exists in services industries including transportation, banking, retail, pharmaceuticals, and health care (Chee et al., 2009). One of the main reasons that those applications appear in service-oriented organizations is that the volume and diversity of data in those industries can be considered rather big and complex, hence, so as to process and analyze them. Although health and medical data possesses similar characteristics, the characteristics and roles of different processes (medical, administrative, and support services) in healthcare industry vary compared to other service industries (Mettler & Vimarlund, 2009). Therefore, the considerations regarding data collection, processing and analyses might be different as part of healthcare processes. In fact, the necessity of taking the patients at the center of attention may pose different challenges when modeling the data throughout business intelligence activities.

Although BI is useful for managing the massive amount of data generated by healthcare information systems, the unstructured characteristics of these data have forced decision makers to use more sophisticated approaches within the context of business intelligence applications. In fact, intelligent systems or the techniques within the area of artificial intelligence are considered to be a family of BI methods and tools that have been of use in modelling data for variety of application areas. Intelligent techniques such as; expert systems, fuzzy logic, neural networks, genetic algorithms, agent-based systems provide some advantages for processing and extraction of knowledge from structured and as well as unstructured data sets. Therefore these intelligent techniques have used for analyzing and interpreting the medical and healthcare data in healthcare decision support systems, especially in diagnostics.

Taking into account the massive data sources unique to the healthcare and the potential knowledge that can be derived for various health organizations, it would be of significant importance for researchers working solely in the area of healthcare management to comprehend the potential research that can be conducted together with the research circles working in the area of data analytics and knowledge discovery where the focal practice is making the most of that rich data environment. This study, in fact, aims at increasing the awareness of healthcare research community on potential applications of wealthy health and medical data when appropriately processed and mined using business intelligence technologies, alongside with intelligent techniques, to extract strategic healthcare knowledge. The study tries to accomplish that by providing an overview of the current applications of business intelligence and intelligent technologies in healthcare context.

The rest of the paper is organized as followings. Similar work related to business intelligence in health context is provided in Section 2, while search methodology regarding the review is provided in Section 3. Section 4 presents the applications of business intelligence and intelligent systems within the scope of healthcare management in a categorized manner. Section 5 concludes the paper with discussions on the potential use of business intelligence tools in healthcare domain.

2. SIMILAR WORK ON BUSINESS INTELLIGENCE AND INTELLIGENT SYSTEMS IN HEALTH CONTEXT

This study cannot be considered the only review article as the existing literature also sheds a light on the topic by providing resembling work or reviews. For example, Koh and Tan (2011) presented a review of data mining in healthcare and categorized the current applications into four titles, healthcare management, treatment effectiveness, customer relationship management, fraud and abuse. Jakob and Ramani (2012) also provided a review of data mining applications in healthcare domain according to the associated techniques being utilized via paying a special attention to clinical data mining. The review conducted by Wasan et al. (2006) focuses on data mining techniques in medical diagnosis in which an illustrative example was also provided. Bellazzi and Zupan (2008)'s discussions can be considered more like a guideline regarding the implementation of predictive data mining in clinical medicine. There are also some other work in the related literature which can be regarded as studies that locate at the intersection of business intelligence and healthcare management. Kaur and Wasan (2006) discussed the applications of data mining in public health informatics, e-governance structures in health care, executive information system for health care, forecasting treatment costs and demand of resources and anticipation of patient's future behavior. Bath (2004) also provided discussions on potential use of data mining specifically in the area of healthcare management and treatment effectiveness. Wilson, Thabane & Holbrook (2003) and Ting, Shum, Kwok, Tsang & Lee (2009) highlighted the potential of various business intelligence technologies that could be beneficial in different areas of bio-medicine, including genomics, proteomics, medical diagnosis, effective drug design, adverse drug effects and pharmaceutical industry. Obenshain (2004) reviewed some work pertaining to mining healthcare data under three headings, namely hospital infection control, ranking hospitals, identifying high-risk patients.

When evaluating the current review articles in the literature, two main conclusions can be made. First, some of the reviews identify where to use business intelligence and intelligent systems in health context and differentiate various application areas of healthcare management. Second, the remaining part of the reviews address on how to utilize business intelligence and intelligent techniques or technologies in health domain. The review that will be presented in this article determines the application areas from a macro perspective by presenting categorization on different application domains. It also provides discussions on the utilization of business intelligence and intelligent systems for healthcare management.

3. SEARCH METHODOLOGY

When conducting the review study, the methodology that was followed consists of three main tasks; identification of the relevant studies, establishing a coding procedure, and maintaining the reliability of this coding procedure. The search was carried out using Google Scholar search engine via ensuring a thorough check on journal articles that are accessible on the main databases, namely, sciencedirect, proquest, jstor, and ebsco. It can be said that the majority of the well-known science and social/health science journals were searched. The following key words were used during the search, namely "data mining in health", "business intelligence in health", "health data warehouse/datamart", "health analytics", "intelligent systems in healthcare" and "dashboard and scorecard health applications". Since the analytics applications in health area is relatively new, no year limitation was put in place in the search. Review articles and the articles that are empirical in nature and consist of hypothetical (or simulated) or real-world data were examined separately. At the end of the search, 13 review articles and 41 empirical studies were obtained covering the period between from 1998 to 2014. 43% studies were published in science or social science related journals, while 57% of them were in health-related journals. The review areas (main review themes) were determined via a discussion made by two evaluators based on the examination of the review articles that was carried out. As far as the empirical articles are concerned only the studies that utilize business intelligence techniques as an analytics component were taken into consideration (see Table 1). Only journal articles were examined, and publications in other forms, such as conference paper, book chapters and research reports were not included in the study. All of the selected empirical studies were examined and coded into specified review areas independently by the two evaluators. The consistency between the two evaluators was measured via inter-rater reliability, which was calculated as 90%. The discrepancies were resolved by the evaluators through reviewing the differences again and consequently a joint decision was obtained.

4. BUSINESS INTELLIGENCE AND INTELLIGENT SYSTEMS APPLICATIONS IN HEALTHCARE

The majority of the literature consists of studies on (i) determination of government health policies and development of healthcare decision support systems (ii) analytical business process management type of work for a more effective hospital management system (iii) analytics on medical diagnostics and disease/treatment monitoring. In this context, the review provided in this study will be presented (see Table 1) and evaluated under these categories of work in the remaining sub-sections. Also, each study that was taken into consideration for review was assessed according to the BI components used in that particular work as well as the corresponding objective of the study as it can be seen in Table 1.

4.1. Health Management and Policy

The discovered knowledge that were extracted by business intelligence technologies through analyzing or mining the health data can be used by the healthcare administrators to improve the quality of service. In fact, some recent work focused on the usage business intelligence for a more effective health management and policy specific issues such as achieving better patient service and satisfaction levels, ensuring effective healthcare operations and policies in financial, marketing and human development. The literature in this context can be summarized into four main areas of applications:

- The research that try to establish a system which facilitates the acquisition of knowledge specific to a disease in a single knowledge warehouse or repository in order to make certain policies about

Table 1. Applications of business intelligence and intelligent systems in healthcare

Cite	BI Component or Technique	Description (Objective) of the Study	Application Area
Castañeda-Méndez, Mangan & Lavery, (1998)	Balance Scorecards	List and explain different perspectives of balance scorecards, defines the role and the application of it for healthcare quality management systems	2
Bohanec, Zupan & Rajkovič, (2000)	Expert Systems, Decision Tree Analysis (DTA)	Present an approach to the development and application of qualitative hierarchical decision models that is based on Expert Systems	3
Delesie & Croes, (2000)	Multidimensional scaling, Hill-climbing, Clustering	Present a model to exploit a health insurance databank in order to evaluate the performance of cardiovascular surgery nationwide	1
Abidi, (2001)	Data Mining, Data Warehouse	Offer an integrated architecture of knowledge-driven decision-support system that includes Knowledge Management and Data Mining techniques and technologies.	2
Chae, Ho, Cho, Lee & Ji, (2001)	DTA, Logistic Regression, CHAID	Examine the characteristics of the knowledge discovery and data mining algorithms to demonstrate how they can be used to predict health outcomes and provide policy information	1
Coulter, Bate, Meyboom, Lindquist & Edwards, (2001)	Data Mining, Artificial Neural Networks (ANN)	Examine the relation between antipsychotic drugs and *myocarditis* and cardiomyopathy with Neural network and Bayesian Data mining methods	3
Voelker, Rakich & French, (2001)	Balance Scorecards	Discuss applicability of Balance Scorecards in healthcare industry as a performance measurement tool	2
Breault, Goodall & Fos, (2002)	Data Warehouse, CART	Design a *diabetic* data warehouse and to analyze the data with the classification and regression tree approach (CART) with two variables	1, 3
Inamdar, Kaplan, Bowr & Reynolds, (2002)	Balance Scorecards	Discuss the value of Balance Scorecards applications for different health provider organizations	2
Rafalski, (2002)	Descriptive Data Mining, Data Warehouse	Use patient satisfaction indicators gathering from telephone surveys, to evaluate general hospital quality improvements	2
Pineno, (2002)	Balance Scorecards	Present a specific Balance Scorecard model, which includes both financial and nonfinancial aspect, in healthcare management	2
Berndt, Hevner & Studnicki, (2003)	Data Warehouse	Focus on the technical challenges of designing and implementing an effective data warehouse for health care information	1
Castellani & Castellani, (2003)	Self-Organizing Map, DTA	Describe the use of two different data mining techniques as a qualitative assessment tool in healthcare context	2
Chae, Kim, Tark, Park & Ho, (2003)	DTA, CHAID	Present an analysis of healthcare quality indicators using Decision Tree Analysis technique for developing quality improvement strategies.	2
Zelman, Pink & Mathias, (2003)	Balance Scorecards	Review of the usage of balance scorecard to healthcare	2
Li et al., (2004)	Genetic Algorithm	Present novel data mining architecture with different feature selection methods, and compare the results in terms of detection performance and selected proteomic patterns.	3
Obenshain, (2004)	Data Mining	Present the use of Data Mining techniques in healthcare context, and demonstrates some examples of these	2
Delen, Walker & Kadam, (2005)	ANN, DTA, Logistics Regression	Develop prediction models for *breast cancer* survivability, and compare prediction ability of three analytical mode	3
Kaur & Wasan, (2006)	ANN, DTA, Logistics Regression	Examine the potential use of classification based data mining techniques such as Rule based, decision tree and Artificial Neural Network to massive volume of healthcare data.	3

continued on following page

Table 1. Continued

Cite	BI Component or Technique	Description (Objective) of the Study	Application Area
Madigan & Curet, (2006)	CART	Examine the applicability data mining techniques to home healthcare data, for monitoring three different condition	3
Su, Yang, Hsu & Chiu, (2006)	ANN, DTA, Logistics Regression, Rough Sets	Construct a prediction model for Type II diabetes using anthropometrical body surface scanning data	3
Wasan et al.,(2006)	ANN	Examine the impact of data mining techniques, including ANN, on medical diagnostics	3
Lavrac et al., (2007)	Hierarchical Clustering, DTA	Present an innovative use of visualization techniques of data mining classification reports to support decision makers in planning and Slovenian public healthcare.	1
Phillips-Wren, Sharkey & Dy, (2008)	Descriptive Data Mining, ANN, DTA	Evaluate lung cancer patient dataset with data mining techniques fort o guide medical decision making and public policy.	3
Delen, Fuller, McCann & Ray, (2009)	ANN, DTA	Examine the healthcare coverage of individuals by applying Decision Tree Analysis and Artificial Neural Networks on 23 predictive factors.	1
Zhuang, Churilov, Burstein & Sikaris, (2009)	Case Based Reasoning, Self-Organizing Map,	Present a novel methodology for integrating data mining and case-based reasoning for intelligent decision support for pathology ordering by general practitioners	2, 3
Oh & Kim, (2010)	Predictive Data Mining, DTA	Perform the prediction for the demands of health meteorological information using a decision tree method	1
Srinivas et al., (2010)	ANN, DTA, Rule-based systems, Naïve Bayes,	Examine the potential use of classification based data mining techniques such as Rule based, Decision tree, Naïve Bayes and Artificial Neural Networks to *Hearth disease* related healthcare data	3
Duan, Street & Xu, (2011)	Association Rules, Prefix Tree	Offer a new nursing care plan recommender systems for providing clinical decision support with use of correlations among nursing diagnoses, outcomes and interventions	2, 3
Koh & Tan, (2011)	DTA	Present a systematic review of data mining applications usability over clinical data sets. Presents a case which includes using of DM techniques for to identify high-risk individuals	1
Sæbø, Kossi, Titlestad, Tohouri & Braa, (2011)	Data Warehouse	Investigate the health management systems of four different African countries	1
Booney, (2013)	Rule Based Systems, Decision Support Systems	Present a systematic review of literature with the aspect of key benefits and challenges of incorporating BI technology into Electronic Health and Medical datasets	2
Brossette et al., (2013)	Association Rules	Identify patterns in hospital infection control and public health surveillance data, they offer a new data analysis process based on association rules	2
Hung, Chen, Yang & Deng, (2013)	Association Rules, ANN, Markov Chains	Analyze real-world data for elder self-care service by applying Web usage mining methodology, including association analysis. They thought their results to assist in policy-making in the health care domain	1
Santos, Malheiros, Cavalheiro & De Oliveira, (2013)	Data Mining, Data Warehouse	Present an automated data mining system that allows public health decision makers to access information regarding brain tumors	1, 3
Bose, (2003)	Data Warehouse, OLAP, Data Mining	Presents a knowledge management-enabled system that would help integrate clinical, administrative, and financial processes in healthcare through a common technical architecture	2

continued on following page

Table 1. Continued

Cite	BI Component or Technique	Description (Objective) of the Study	Application Area
Cubillas, Ramos, Feito & Urena, (2014)	Linear and Non-Linear Regression	Present a predictive data mining model for daily patients number to use in healthcare centre administration	2
Diawani & Sam, (2014)	Statistical Methods	Explore the awareness and readiness of data mining technology within healthcare in Tanzania public sector	1
Solanki, (2014)	DTA (J48 and Random Tree)	Present a data mining based estimation method for predict the highly affected troubled zone for Sickle Cell Disease	3
Easton, Stephens & Angelova, (2014)	Linear Regression, Classification Techniques	Illustrate the benefits of a data mining inspired approach to statistically analysing different Healthcare data sets	3
Spruit, Vroon & Batenburg, (2014)	CRISP-DM	Try to create DM based management model to managed both quality and cost of the healthcare management In Netherlands	1,2

1- Health Management and Policy, 2- Hospital Management, 3- Medical Diagnostics and Disease/Treatment Monitoring or Control

the corresponding treatment process. The applications of such effort were in brain tumor (Santos et al., 2013), diabetes (Breult et al., 2002; Koh & Tan, 2011), and hypertension (Chae et al., 2001).

- The work that focus on the determination of variables that could be useful for policy making using predictive data mining techniques in specific areas such as health coverage (Delen et al., 2009), health meteorological information (Oh & Kim, 2010), the success of cardiovascular surgeries (Delesie & Croes, 2000).
- The studies that assess the qualifications of national health services according to different variables or attributes including the ability to access health services (Lavrač et al., 2007), health information systems infrastructure (Sæbø et al, 2011), elderly homecare service (Hung et al., 2013), healthcare quality and costs (Spruit, Vroon & Batenburg, 2014).
- The difficulties and challenges of establishing a healthcare data warehouse (Berndt et al., 2003).
- Explore the awareness and readiness of data mining technology within healthcare (Diawani & Sam, 2014)

4.2. Hospital Management

Applying BI technologies on clinical datasets could be of beneficial with regards to improving the quality and safety of healthcare delivery (Bonney, 2013). The related literature underlines the potential of data mining within this context and highlights the applications of data mining in achieving better assessment of patient needs and superior ideas regarding patient outcomes, more accurate information on clinical fidelity, and effective discovery of association between interventions and outcomes (Jacob & Ramani, 2012). The current work in that specific field focus on illustrative examples on hospital quality improvement (Chae et al., 2003; Rafalski, 2002; Spruit, Vroon & Batenburg, 2014) and strategic planning and managerial reports/dashboards using business performance management tools (Castañeda-Méndez et al., 1998; Inamdar et al., 2002; Pineno, 2002 ; Voelker et al., 2001; Zelman et al., 2003), system proposals on advanced business intelligence technologies (e.g., data mining, intelligent systems) supported hospital management systems (Abidi, 2001; Bose, 2003; Duan et al., 2011; Zhuang et al., 2009), usage of analytical decision making tools in managerial issues of hospitals (Castellani & Castellani, 2003 ; Obenshain, 2004; Cubillas, Ramos, Feito & Urena, 2014), and hospital infection control (Brossette et al., 1998).

4.3. Medical Diagnostics and Disease/Treatment Monitoring or Control

Some business intelligence technologies, in particular predictive data mining techniques, could be considered the most appropriate tool to cope with clinical prediction problems and may also be applied to create decision models regarding certain procedures such as prognosis, diagnosis and treatment planning (Bellazzi & Zupan, 2008). For example, business intelligence can generate structured knowledge on questions such as "what patients need to be targeted for specific evaluations while admitted to a facility given particular symptoms" (Sæbø et al, 2011). Also, the extracted knowledge can be a remedy for medical practitioners to reduce the number of adverse drug effect (Kaur & Wasan, 2006). Similarly, the related literature underline the power of predictive data mining that could useful for prediction of pattern of a disease, proposition of drug combination, identification of determinants for hospitalization and prediction of the likely recovery time of patients (Jacob & Ramani, 2012, Easton, Stephens & Angelova, 2014). It should be also mentioned that business intelligence is not only applicable for problems associated with clinical diagnostics and treatment but also for different areas of bio-medicine and pharmaceutical industry, in particular, for genomics, proteomics, and effective drug design (Ting et al., 2009). The existing work on the applications of business intelligence in medical diagnostics and treatment processes can be categorized into three areas. The first group of studies focuses on development of a data mining system that helps extraction of hidden rules regarding a disease such as brain tumor, diabetes, breast cancer, lung cancer myocarditis, chronic obstructive pulmonary disease, heart failure, hip replacement, Sickle Cell Disease, and etc. (Breault et al., 2002; Bohanec et al., 2000; Chae et al., 2001; Delen et al., 2005; Kaur & Wasan, 2006; Madigan & Curet, 2006; Phillips-Wren et al., 2008; Santos et al., 2013; Solanki, 2014; Srinivas et al., 2010; Su et al., 2006). The second stream of research is mainly related to treatment management e.g., effectiveness of processes or activities such as pathology ordering (Zhuang et al., 2009), development of a recommender system for nursing diagnoses (Duan et al., 2011) and detection of diseases using the samples collected from the organs (Li et al., 2004). The final group can attributed to the conceptual work that being conducted on the effects of business intelligence components or tools on medical diagnostics using intelligent systems (Wasan et al., 2006).

5. CONCLUSION AND FUTURE RESEARCH DIRECTIONS

There have been some challenges that the healthcare community has been facing which could be achieved to some extent through the use of business intelligence and intelligent systems. Classifying the challenging areas that business intelligence could be a remedy for might be a difficult task, but this study reviewed the current applications into three main categories and presented some important findings of that research in a systematic manner. Having examined the current work of the related literature on the applications of business intelligence and intelligent systems in the area of healthcare, some findings can be highlighted as the following:

1.	Some of the studies that are empirical in nature try to use data mining as a business intelligence technology. Also, the type of work those are more like conceptual and theoretical anticipate and discuss significant conclusions pertaining to the potential use of business intelligence and associated technologies in different areas within the scope of healthcare.

2. The majority of the empirical work utilized some common predictive data mining techniques (e.g., decision tree analysis, artificial neural networks, multivariate statistical techniques) that are suitable for structured health data. However, the applications those make use of the techniques that can tackle with unstructured health data were limited.

3. Around %75 of the empirical studies focus on micro-level health management issues while only a small portion of the remaining work concentrate on strategic topics pertaining to health management and policy.

Based on these findings, the following discussions can be made as future work regarding the applications in the context of health management and policy.

First, healthcare data may not just be quantitative in nature but could be in unstructured form which may require special attention to model and deal with. Therefore, it is necessary to further explore more advanced techniques and their capabilities, in particular text mining, to cope with unstructured health data including digital diagnostic images and graphics, documents and audios/videos (Koh & Tan, 2011). Although there have been successful applications in the related literature regarding text mining (Bohanec et al., 2009; Castellani & Castellani, 2003; Jacob & Ramani, 2012), yet the discovery and potential applications of text mining technologies that are capable of performing multimedia and image mining could be considered limited (Koh & Tan, 2011; Ting et al., 2009). Second, intelligent systems can be a remedy to the challenges related to medical and health data. Although it is possible to come across some studies which exploited variety of intelligent techniques including expert and other intelligent decision support systems (Bohanec et al., 2000; Duan et al., 2011; Zhuang et al., 2009), genetic algorithms (Li et al., 2004), artificial neural networks (Chae et al., 2001; Castellani & Castellani, 2003; Delen et al., 2005; Delen et al., 2009; Hung et al., 2013; Kaur & Wasan, 2006; Phillips-Wren et al., 2008; Srinivas et al., 2010; Su et al., 2006; Wasan et al., 2006; Zhuang et al., 2009) and intelligent agents (Corchado, Bajo, De Paz & Tapia, 2008; Hashmi, Cheah, Hassan, Lim & Abidi, 2003; Hein et al., 2006; Lee & Wang, 2007) in the healthcare analytics literature, however, acceptance and dissemination levels of such fine work among the healthcare community can be considered low. Also, utilization of these intelligent techniques in hybrid form (AKA soft computing) for designing decision support systems to resolve the problems associated with hospital management and health management and policy could also be an area for future work. Third, as far as the application areas are concerned, health analytics applications that could (1) tackle with global health problems and health coverage disparity issues and (2) facilitate establishing integrated national health systems should receive attention from the health community (Delen et al., 2009; Sæbø et al., 2011).

As a result of information technology evolution, Healthcare information systems generates high volume (petabytes) of heterogeneous, complex and most of the time unstructured data sets. It is not possible to manage these massive data with traditional software and hardware and to analyze conventional tools or methods (Kamal, Wiebe, Engbers & Hill, 2014; Raghupathi & Raghupathi, 2014; Wang, Ranjan, Kołodziej & Zomaya, 2015). In this context, concept of big data analytics emerges as a new approach in healthcare. It is envisaged that big data analytics provide some advantages for healthcare decision makers in context of; patient centric services, spreading disease detection, hospital quality monitoring, treatment method improvement, public health, genomic analytics, evidence based medicine, pre-adjudication fraud analysis, patient profile analytics (Raghupathi & Raghupathi, 2014; Archenaa & Anita, 2015;)

It should also be noted that the success of any business intelligence practice in healthcare context depends on the availability of clean/processed health and medical data (Koh & Tan, 2011). Therefore, the following issues can be considered to be of great importance (Bath, 2004; Berndt et al., 2003; Breault et al., 2002; Haux, Ammenwerth, Herzog & Knaup, 2002; Koh & Tan, 2011; Santos et al., 2013):

- Efficient configuration of metadata (automatic selection of relevant attributes),
- Managing changes in ontology,
- Using data squashing to reduce the size of massive data sets,
- Synchronization of data mining models,
- Standardization of clinical vocabulary,
- Efficient Data warehouse design (maintaining historical data accuracy, managing the impact of dimensional table changes),
- Ensuring data quality as well as validity, usability and acceptance of BI techniques,
- More scalable algorithms for processing and mining big data
- Utilization of mobile and cloud technologies.

In conclusion, it seems obvious that health community will exploit and benefit business intelligence and intelligent technologies much more in the near future. To be able to conduct successful applications and increase their effectiveness, collaboration between medical/health disciplines with other technical/ engineering oriented areas might be rather important. Sharing of data across organizations to create integrated systems and handling medical and health data due to its forms and settings may require a specific strategy to follow (Breault et al., 2002; Jacob & Ramani, 2012; Koh & Tan, 2011) not just for data acquisition and integration but also for building up a competent team who have expertise in business intelligence tools, intelligent technologies as well as health/medical domain knowledge.

REFERENCES

Abidi, S. S. R. (2001). Knowledge management in healthcare: Towards 'knowledge-driven' decision-support services. *International Journal of Medical Informatics*, *63*(1), 5–18. doi:10.1016/S1386-5056(01)00167-8 PMID:11518661

Archenaa, J., & Anita, E. M. (2015). A Survey of Big Data Analytics in Healthcare and Government. *Procedia Computer Science*, *50*, 408–413. doi:10.1016/j.procs.2015.04.021

Bath, P. A. (2004). Data mining in health and medical information. *Annual Review of Information Science & Technology*, *38*(1), 331–369. doi:10.1002/aris.1440380108

Bellazzi, R., & Zupan, B. (2008). Predictive data mining in clinical medicine: Current issues and guidelines. *International Journal of Medical Informatics*, *77*(2), 81–97. doi:10.1016/j.ijmedinf.2006.11.006 PMID:17188928

Berndt, D. J., Hevner, A. R., & Studnicki, J. (2003). The Catch data warehouse: Support for community health care decision-making. *Decision Support Systems*, *35*(3), 367–384. doi:10.1016/S0167-9236(02)00114-8

Bohanec, M., Zupan, B., & Rajkovič, V. (2000). Applications of qualitative multi-attribute decision models in health care. *International Journal of Medical Informatics*, *58*, 191–205. doi:10.1016/S1386-5056(00)00087-3 PMID:10978921

Bonney, W. (2013). Applicability of business intelligence in electronic health record. *Procedia: Social and Behavioral Sciences*, *73*, 257–262. doi:10.1016/j.sbspro.2013.02.050

Bose, R. (2003). Knowledge management-enabled health care management systems: Capabilities, infrastructure, and decision-support. *Expert Systems with Applications*, *24*(1), 59–71. doi:10.1016/S0957-4174(02)00083-0

Breault, J. L., Goodall, C. R., & Fos, P. J. (2002). Data mining a diabetic data warehouse. *Artificial Intelligence in Medicine*, *26*(1), 37–54. doi:10.1016/S0933-3657(02)00051-9 PMID:12234716

Brossette, S. E., Sprague, A. P., Hardin, J. M., Waites, K. B., Jones, W. T., & Moser, S. A. (1998). Association rules and data mining in hospital infection control and public health surveillance. *Journal of the American Medical Informatics Association*, *5*(4), 373–381. doi:10.1136/jamia.1998.0050373 PMID:9670134

Castaeda-Méndez, K., Mangan, K., & Lavery, A. M. (1998). The role and application of the balanced scorecard in healthcare quality management. *Journal for Healthcare Quality*, *20*(1), 10–13. doi:10.1111/j.1945-1474.1998.tb00243.x PMID:10177013

Castellani, B., & Castellani, J. (2003). Data mining: Qualitative analysis with health informatics data. *Qualitative Health Research*, *13*(7), 1005–1018. doi:10.1177/1049732303253523 PMID:14502965

Chae, Y. M., Ho, S. H., Cho, K. W., Lee, D. H., & Ji, S. H. (2001). Data mining approach to policy analysis in a health insurance domain. *International Journal of Medical Informatics*, *62*(2), 103–111. doi:10.1016/S1386-5056(01)00154-X PMID:11470613

Chae, Y. M., Kim, H. S., Tark, K. C., Park, H. J., & Ho, S. H. (2003). Analysis of healthcare quality indicator using data mining and decision support system. *Expert Systems with Applications*, *24*(2), 167–172. doi:10.1016/S0957-4174(02)00139-2

Chee, T., Chan, L. K., Chuah, M. H., Tan, C. S., Wong, S. F., & Yeoh, W. (2009). Business intelligence systems: state-of-the-art review and contemporary applications. In *Symposium on Progress in Information & Technology*.

Cios, K. J., & Moore, G. W. (2002). Uniqueness of medical data mining. *Artificial Intelligence in Medicine*, *26*(1), 1–24. doi:10.1016/S0933-3657(02)00049-0 PMID:12234714

Corchado, J. M., Bajo, J., De Paz, Y., & Tapia, D. I. (2008). Intelligent environment for monitoring Alzheimer patients, agent technology for health care. *Decision Support Systems*, *44*(2), 382–396. doi:10.1016/j.dss.2007.04.008

Coulter, D. M., Bate, A., Meyboom, R. H., Lindquist, M., & Edwards, I. R. (2001). Antipsychotic drugs and heart muscle disorder in international pharmacovigilance: Data mining study. *BMJ (Clinical Research Ed.)*, *322*(7296), 1207–1209. doi:10.1136/bmj.322.7296.1207 PMID:11358771

Cubillas, J. J., Ramos, M. I., Feito, F. R., & Ureña, T. (2014). An improvement in the appointment scheduling in primary health care centers using data mining. *Journal of Medical Systems*, *38*(8), 1–10. doi:10.1007/s10916-014-0089-y PMID:24964781

Delen, D., Fuller, C., McCann, C., & Ray, D. (2009). Analysis of healthcare coverage: A data mining approach. *Expert Systems with Applications*, *36*(2), 995–1003. doi:10.1016/j.eswa.2007.10.041

Delen, D., Walker, G., & Kadam, A. (2005). Predicting breast cancer survivability: A comparison of three data mining methods. *Artificial Intelligence in Medicine*, *34*(2), 113–127. doi:10.1016/j.artmed.2004.07.002 PMID:15894176

Delesie, L., & Croes, L. (2000). Operations research and knowledge discovery: A data mining method applied to health care management. *International Transactions in Operational Research*, *7*(2), 159–170. doi:10.1111/j.1475-3995.2000.tb00192.x

Diwani, S. A., & Sam, A. (2014). Data Mining Awareness and Readiness in Healthcare Sector: A case of Tanzania. *Advances in Computer Science: an International Journal*, *3*(1), 37–43.

Duan, L., Street, W. N., & Xu, E. (2011). Healthcare information systems: Data mining methods in the creation of a clinical recommender system. *Enterprise Information Systems*, *5*(2), 169–181. doi:10.1080/17517575.2010.541287

Easton, J. F., Stephens, C. R., & Angelova, M. (2014). Risk factors and prediction of very short term versus short/intermediate term post-stroke mortality: A data mining approach. *Computers in Biology and Medicine*, *54*, 199–210. doi:10.1016/j.compbiomed.2014.09.003 PMID:25303114

Hashmi, Z. I., Cheah, Y. N., Hassan, S. Z., Lim, K. G., & Abidi, S. S. R. (2003). *Intelligent Agent Modeling and Generic Architecture Towards a Multi-Agent Healthcare Knowledge Management System* (pp. 941–944). ICWI.

Haux, R., Ammenwerth, E., Herzog, W., & Knaup, P. (2002). Health care in the information society. A prognosis for the year 2013. *International Journal of Medical Informatics*, *66*(1), 3–21. doi:10.1016/S1386-5056(02)00030-8 PMID:12453552

Hein, A., Nee, O., Willemsen, D., Scheffold, T., Dogac, A., & Laleci, G. (2006). *SAPHIRE-Intelligent Healthcare Monitoring based on Semantic Interoperability Platform-The Homecare Scenario*. ECEH.

Hung, Y. S., Chen, K. L. B., Yang, C. T., & Deng, G. F. (2013). Web usage mining for analysing elder self-care behavior patterns. *Expert Systems with Applications*, *40*(2), 775–783. doi:10.1016/j.eswa.2012.08.037

Inamdar, N., Kaplan, R. S., Bower, M., & Reynolds, K. (2002). Applying the balanced scorecard in healthcare provider organizations. *Journal of Healthcare Management*, *47*(3), 179–196. PMID:12055900

Jacob, S. G., & Ramani, R. G. (2012). Data Mining in Clinical Data Sets: A Review. *International Journal of Applied Information Systems*, *4*(6), 15–26. doi:10.5120/ijais12-450774

Kamal, N., Wiebe, S., Engbers, J. D. T., & Hill, M. D. (2014). Big data and visual analytics in health and medicine: From pipe dream to reality. *J Health Med Informat*, *5*, e125.

Kaur, H., & Wasan, S. K. (2006). Empirical study on applications of data mining techniques in healthcare. *Journal of Computer Science*, 2(2), 194–200. doi:10.3844/jcssp.2006.194.200

Koh, H. C., & Tan, G. (2011). Data mining applications in healthcare. *Journal of Healthcare Information Management*, 19(2), 65. PMID:15869215

Lavrač, N., Bohanec, M., Pur, A., Cestnik, B., Debeljak, M., & Kobler, A. (2007). Data mining and visualization for decision support and modeling of public health-care resources. *Journal of Biomedical Informatics*, 40(4), 438–447. doi:10.1016/j.jbi.2006.10.003 PMID:17157076

Lee, C. S., & Wang, M. H. (2007). Ontology-based intelligent healthcare agent and its application to respiratory waveform recognition. *Expert Systems with Applications*, 33(3), 606–619. doi:10.1016/j.eswa.2006.06.006

Li, L., Tang, H., Wu, Z., Gong, J., Gruidl, M., Zou, J., & Clark, R. A. (2004). Data mining techniques for cancer detection using serum proteomic profiling. *Artificial Intelligence in Medicine*, 32(2), 71–83. doi:10.1016/j.artmed.2004.03.006 PMID:15364092

Madigan, E. A., & Curet, O. L. (2006). A data mining approach in home healthcare: Outcomes and service use. *BMC Health Services Research*, 6(1), 18. doi:10.1186/1472-6963-6-18 PMID:16504115

Mettler, T., & Vimarlund, V. (2009). Understanding business intelligence in the context of healthcare. *Health Informatics Journal*, 15(3), 254–264. doi:10.1177/1460458209337446 PMID:19713399

Obenshain, M. K. (2004). Application of data mining techniques to healthcare data. *Infection Control*, 25(08), 690–695. doi:10.1086/502460 PMID:15357163

Oh, J., & Kim, B. (2010). Prediction model for demands of the health meteorological information using a decision tree method. *Asian Nursing Research*, 4(3), 151-162.

Phillips-Wren, G., Sharkey, P., & Dy, S. M. (2008). Mining lung cancer patient data to assess healthcare resource utilization. *Expert Systems with Applications*, 35(4), 1611–1619. doi:10.1016/j.eswa.2007.08.076

Pineno, C. J. (2002). The balanced scorecard: An incremental approach model to health care management. *Journal of Health Care Finance*, 28(4), 69–80. PMID:12148665

Rafalski, E. (2002). Using data mining/data repository methods to identify marketing opportunities in health care. *Journal of Consumer Marketing*, 19(7), 607–613. doi:10.1108/07363760210451429

Raghupathi, W., & Raghupathi, V. (2014). Big data analytics in healthcare: Promise and potential. *Health Information Science and Systems*, 2(1), 3. doi:10.1186/2047-2501-2-3 PMID:25825667

Sæbø, J. I., Kossi, E. K., Titlestad, O. H., Tohouri, R. R., & Braa, J. (2011). Comparing strategies to integrate health information systems following a data warehouse approach in four countries. *Information Technology for Development*, 17(1), 42–60. doi:10.1080/02681102.2010.511702

Santos, R. S., Malheiros, S. M. F., Cavalheiro, S., & De Oliveira, J. P. (2013). A data mining system for providing analytical information on brain tumors to public health decision makers. *Computer Methods and Programs in Biomedicine*, 109(3), 269–282. doi:10.1016/j.cmpb.2012.10.010 PMID:23122302

Solanki, A. V. (2014). Data Mining Techniques Using WEKA classification for Sickle Cell Disease. *International Journal of Computer Science and Information Technologies, 5*(4), 5857–5860.

Spruit, M., Vroon, R., & Batenburg, R. (2014). Towards healthcare business intelligence in long-term care: An explorative case study in the Netherlands. *Computers in Human Behavior, 30*, 698–707.

Srinivas, K., Rani, B. K., & Govrdhan, A. (2010). Applications of data mining techniques in healthcare and prediction of heart attacks. *International Journal on Computer Science and Engineering, 2*(02), 250–255.

Su, C. T., Yang, C. H., Hsu, K. H., & Chiu, W. K. (2006). Data mining for the diagnosis of type II diabetes from three-dimensional body surface anthropometrical scanning data. *Computers & Mathematics with Applications (Oxford, England), 51*(6), 1075–1092. doi:10.1016/j.camwa.2005.08.034

Ting, S. L., Shum, C. C., Kwok, S. K., Tsang, A. H., & Lee, W. B. (2009). Data mining in biomedicine: Current applications and further directions for research. *Journal of Software Engineering and Applications, 2*(03), 150–159. doi:10.4236/jsea.2009.23022

Turban, E., Sharda, R., Delen, D., & King, D. (2011). *Business Intelligence: A Managerial Approach.* Academic Press.

Vercellis, C. (2009). *Business Intelligence: Data Mining and Optimization for Decision Making.* Editorial John Wiley and Sons. doi:10.1002/9780470753866

Voelker, K. E., Rakich, J. S., & French, G. R. (2001). The balanced scorecard in healthcare organizations: A performance measurement and strategic planning methodology. *Hospital Topics, 79*(3), 13–24. doi:10.1080/00185860109597908 PMID:11794940

Wang, L., Ranjan, R., Kołodziej, J., Zomaya, A., & Alem, L. (2015). Software Tools and Techniques for Big Data Computing in Healthcare Clouds. *Future Generation Computer Systems, 43*, 38–39. doi:10.1016/j.future.2014.11.001

Wasan, S. K., Bhatnagar, V., & Kaur, H. (2006). The impact of data mining techniques on medical diagnostics. *Data Science Journal, 5*, 119–126. doi:10.2481/dsj.5.119

Wilson, A. M., Thabane, L., & Holbrook, A. (2004). Application of data mining techniques in pharmacovigilance. *British Journal of Clinical Pharmacology, 57*(2), 127–134. doi:10.1046/j.1365-2125.2003.01968.x PMID:14748811

Zelman, W. N., Pink, G. H., & Matthias, C. B. (2003). Use of the balanced scorecard in health care. *Journal of Health Care Finance, 29*(4), 1–16. PMID:12908650

Zhuang, Z. Y., Churilov, L., Burstein, F., & Sikaris, K. (2009). Combining data mining and case-based reasoning for intelligent decision support for pathology ordering by general practitioners. *European Journal of Operational Research, 195*(3), 662–675. doi:10.1016/j.ejor.2007.11.003

KEY TERMS AND DEFINITIONS

Big Data Analytics: It comes up because of the inability to process of large amount of data, also called big data, of traditional analytic tools. Big Data Analytics is the process of analyzing big data to uncover useful information such as hidden patterns, unknown correlations.

Business Intelligence: Set of tools, techniques and technologies for handling large amount of, mostly unstructured, data to reveal meaningful and useful information for business analysis purposes. BI also creates comprehensible reports and visual elements to better understanding of the results of the complex techniques for decision makes.

Healthcare Management Systems: An information system with use of the healthcare management purpose. It has the ability to process unstructured medical data with the use of management information systems tool. Most of the time HMS act like a Decision Support System.

Intelligent Systems: Real time systems, which have massive processing power and ability to perform complex applications by embedded intelligent techniques, such as artificial intelligence, agent systems etc.

Medical Data: It is kind of an unstructured medical record which include medical history, symptoms, examination results, diagnostic tests, treatment methods.

Chapter 10
Use of Chaotic Randomness Numbers:
Metaheuristic and Artificial Intelligence Algorithms

Alper Ozpinar
Istanbul Commerce University, Turkey

Emel Seyma Kucukasci
Istanbul Commerce University, Turkey

ABSTRACT

The timeless search for optimizing the demand and supply of any resource is one of the main issues for humanity nearly from the beginning of time. The relevant cost of adding an extra resource reacts by means of more energy requirement, more emissions, interaction with policies and market status makes is even more complicated. Optimization of demand and supply is the key to successfully solve the problem. There are various optimization algorithms in the literature and most of them uses various algorithms of iteration and some degree of randomness to find the optimum solution. Most of the metaheuristic and artificial intelligence algorithms require the randomness where to make a new decision to go forward. So this chapter is about the possible use of chaotic random numbers in the metaheuristic and artificial intelligence algorithms that requires random numbers. The authors only provide the necessary information about the algorithms instead of providing full detailed explanation of the subjects assuming the readers already have theoretical basic information.

INTRODUCTION

Most recent optimization problems of recent years is not only limited to balancing the classical supply and demand problems as well searching for the common optimization problems related with the real-world challenges. Those challenges can be listed as sustainable energy management, logistics, transportation, production, manufacturing, consumption, healthcare, education, financial, telecommunication, cloud

DOI: 10.4018/978-1-5225-0075-9.ch010

computing, smart grids, internet of things and even genetic research. Most of these studies can be solved by using combinatorial optimization problems (COPs) and most of them are classified as NP-hard type problems. These real-life COPs are frequently characterized by their large-scale sizes and the need for obtaining high-quality solutions in short computing times, thus they require the use of metaheuristic and also artificial intelligence algorithms (Juan, Faulin, Grasman, Rabe, & Figueira, 2015).

In practice initializations of the stochastic and combinatorial optimization algorithms are based on the random number sequences and feeds. The modifications on the initialization directly affect the later phases and the success of the applied metaheuristics algorithm. Moreover, some of the algorithms do selections in regard to random numbers to search the solution space during the iterations. The performances of the evolutionary algorithms are asserted to be improved by using qualified random number generators (Bastos-Filho, Oliveira, Nascimento, & Ramos, 2010; Caponetto, Fortuna, Fazzino, & Xibilia, 2003).

In order to solve the complex and big domain complex problems it's a preferred way to solve them in distributed and parallel within high performance computing systems and supercomputers. The main problem steps distributed among those computing machines which are the members of the distributed system. The term computing machine refers either a single computer with multiple core CPU's, a high performance computing cluster, a supercomputer or may be a distributed grid structure formed by many computing nodes. A good distributed computing structure requires the higher level of transparency. In general transparency refers to operation which does not requires a common operation set, synchronized time settings between nodes, share of memory and variables. Many multi-core processors are homogeneous hardware architectures by means of shared-memory and direct memory access properties, meaning that all cores are identical however heterogeneous configurations of multi-core systems also exist in various computing centers (DAngelo & Marzolla, 2014). The required transparency within the high performance computing and cloud computing applications, requires the ideal case that is all the computing inventory acting like a single system even it does not.

A common problem here is increasing the number of devices results in the increasing the coincidences related with the random computing. Due to the logic and circuit system foundations the outcome of the computers is always acting in the same way unless affected by some an external feedback or source. They can create a random number by using an algorithm and mostly by implementing a deterministic function. Without a dynamic input or bias this double team never makes a surprise to its user. For example in most of the programming courses a lecture is generally includes some practical daily examples about generating random numbers with computers for lottery or card games. A simple example for shooting n random numbers with the simplest code in the computer laboratory, all the students in the lab will get the same lucky numbers in the same order. Some programming languages like c, a seeding number can be used to change the process of random number generation however this time the students using the same number for seeding sequence also gets the same numbers.

Using current time as a continuous changing and non-repeating type of seeds also does not solve the uniqueness problem of random numbers. This is the sensitive and crucial point about solving the problems in parallel and distributed. Considering the top list of super computers with more than million cores the probability of coincidence for obtaining same random numbers increase with the decrease of the quality of the random numbers. As a result either computational performance is decreased or limited search domain obtained for solution progress, which is not desired. In conclusion a good quality random number generation progress is required. The following sections explain this idea in detail with definitions and applications.

RANDOM NUMBER GENERATORS

To generate independently identically distributed random variables with good statistical properties there are algorithms which provide random numbers that mimic most features of the truly random numbers. The purpose of these algorithms is to produce sequences of numbers or objects whose behavior is very hard to distinguish from that of their "truly random" counterparts, at least for the application of interest (Gentle, 2004).

There are two main types of random number generators available for use in computational operations. The first one is Pseudo-Random Number Generators (PRNGs), based on algorithms that use mathematical methods like linear congruential method or preset data to produce sequences of numbers. Therefore standard microcontrollers and computers without a special modification or upgrade can be classified as PRNGs type. PRNGs can operate with high performance and speed when required to generate ordinary random numbers which are sufficient enough to use in daily operations that does not require high security, uniqueness and complexity.

A pseudo-random number generator (PRNG) can be defined as an algorithm enabling to generate sequences of numbers with some properties of randomness.(Francois, Grosges, Barchiesi, & Erra, 2014) The TRNG derives its output from a physical noise source whereas a PRNG expands a relatively short key (possibly from a TRNG) into a long sequence of seemingly random bits based on a deterministic algorithm (Tsoi, Leung, & Leong, 2003). This determinism brings about the name pseudo-random instead of random. Additionally, the initial inputs of the equations are the "seeds" which are also random numbers. Let S be a set and $s \in S$ be the randomly selected seed number. Also let f be an invertible function from S to S. The pseudo-random number sequence is such that $\left\{ s, f\left(s\right), f^2\left(s\right), f^3\left(s\right), \dots \right\}$.

Another option is to use True Random Number Generators (TRNGs) as a hardware or as a software service instead of classical random number function of the computers. The need for a true random number generation is not only limited to metaheuristics and artificial intelligence. Another essential are is to secure any type of communication between electronic devices and in cryptography.

TRNGs can be performed based on different sources like electrical noise, jitter, chaos, entropy change, some irrelevant information noise, weather conditions, traffic congestion or even from elliptic curve operations and biometric sources. (Szczepanski, Wajnryb, Amiga, Sanchez-Vives, & Slater, 2004; Lee & Wong, 2004; Cicek, Pusane, & Dundar, 2014) Those sources mostly based on a natural physical phenomenon and the properties of independence as well as the unpredictability of the generated values are guaranteed by physical laws (Marton, Suciu, & Ignat, 2010). Since true randomness and true random generators do not practically exist, the name physical random number generator is also preferred in the literature. Although TRNGs provide non-predictable random sequences which cannot be repeated, the generation process is too slow and it depends on the specifications of hardware.

CHAOTIC RANDOM NUMBER GENERATION

Random numbers are useful for a variety of purposes, such as generating data encryption keys, simulating and modeling complex phenomena and selecting random samples from larger data sets (Kumar, Shukla, Prakash, Mishra, & Kumar, 2011). Additionally, qualified random numbers are also needed in Monte Carlo techniques (Gentle,), system dynamics (Eberhart & Shi, 2001; Uchida, 2012) and metaheuristics

(Alatas, 2010; Bastos-Filho et al., 2010; Jahan & Akbarzadeh, 2012; Mukhopadhyay & Banerjee, 2012; Reese, 2009). Random number generation is to find an independent identically distributed sequence with property of non-repeatability where at each repeat, a different sequence must be obtained.

Recently, different random number generators are proposed in the literature based on quantum devices, elliptic curves, cellular automata and different map functions (Akhshani, Akhavan, Mobaraki, Lim, & Hassan, 2014; dos Santos Coelho, 2009; Karimi, Hosseini, & Jahan, 2013; Pivoluska & Plesch, 2015; Reyad & Kotulski, 2015; Wang, Yu, Ding, & Leng, 2008). Random number generators are selected to be used for these applications based on desired application-specified statistical quality. There are physical generators and computational algorithms that imitate the physical generators. Additionally, random numbers can also be generated exploiting chaos theory, where the chaotic behavior of the output provides necessary statistical and computational properties.

The defined function f can also be a chaotic function and the obtained pseudo-random sequence is a chaotic pseudo-random sequence if and only if f has the following properties (Keller & Wiese, 2007):

- f reacts sensibly to changes in s, i.e. even small changes to the value of s result in large changes of the sequence,
- f is topologically transitive, i.e. almost every element of S can be connected to almost every other element of S by a finite sequence,
- f is topologically dense, i.e. even small intervals of S contain periodic points of f.

Chaotic pseudo-random number generators (CPRNG) are preferred since after a certain period length, a pseudo-random sequence repeats itself. The idea of applying discrete chaotic dynamical systems, intrinsically, exploits the property of extreme sensitivity of trajectories to small changes of initial conditions (Lozi & Taralova, 2014).

Aim of this chapter is to explain he use of Chaotic pseudo-random number generators (CPRNGs) in suitable metaheuristic and artificial intelligence algorithms on the other hand search for new generations, new weights, new distances or new parameters based on a previous step and also a randomized touch to scatter, change, improve, mutate the results for new frontiers to the solution and problem set. (Gilli, Maringer, & Schumann, 2011)

CHAOTIC MAPS

Chaotic dynamic system behavior can be described by using several map functions. The chaotic time series sequences can be obtained by using polynomial nonlinearities or piecewise linear maps (Afrabandpey, Ghaffari, Mirzaei, & Safayani, 2014; Caponetto et al., 2003; Jin & Ryu, 2012; Kim, Bok, & Ryu, 2013; May, 1976). Simple linear equations, the initial random value and the knowledge of the parameters are sufficient to generate the chaotic pseudo-random sequences. The following map functions are the mostly used goal-oriented chaotic sequences.

1. **Logistic Map:** A nonlinear function that describes the dynamic behavior of the biological populations is proposed (May, 1976). The logistic difference equation is

$$x^{t+1} = a \, x^t \, (1 - x^t)$$

where t is the iteration number and $a > 0$ is the biotic potential and the generated sequence is in $(0,1)$ if $x^0 \in (0,1)$.

2. **Tent Map:** Similar to logistic map, tent map is a nonlinear function that takes as an input the previous output and generates chaotic sequences in $(0,1)$ with the following form (Peitgen, Jürgens, & Saupe, 2006)

$$x^{t+1} = \begin{cases} x^t / 0.7, & if \ x^t < 0.7, \\ 10 / 3x^t \left(1 - x^t\right), & otherwise. \end{cases}$$

3. **Cubic Map:** The famous cubic map which has a wide range of applications is formally defined as (Rogers & Whitley, 1983)

$$x^{t+1} = \pi \, x^t \, (1 - \left(x^t\right)^2)$$

with the parameter $\pi = 2.59$. The generated chaotic sequence is in $(0, 1)$.

4. **Gauss Map:** This map is generally utilized for testing the features of the generated sequences by using the following equations

$$x^{t+1} = G\left(x^t\right)$$

$$G\left(x\right) = \begin{cases} 0, & for \ x = 0, \\ \dfrac{1}{x} \, mod\left(1\right), & for \ x\epsilon \left(0,1\right). \end{cases}$$

5. **Circle Map:** This is an iterative nonlinear function that maps the circle onto itself and has the behavior of a simple sinusoidal oscillator (Essl, 2006). The simple circle map function is as follows

$$x^{t+1} = x^t + b - \left(a / 2\pi\right) \sin\left(2\pi x^t\right) mod\left(1\right)$$

6. **Sinusoidal Map:** The equation for the famous sinusoidal iterator is the following (Peitgen et al., 2006)

$$x^{t+1} = a\left(x^t\right)^2 \sin(\pi x^t).$$

If the sequence begins with $x^0 = 0.7$ and we also have $a = 2.3$, then the equation is simplified as

$$x^{t+1} = \sin\left(\pi x^t\right).$$

7. **Henon Map:** This nonlinear map is also used for testing purposes and has two parameters a and b. The representation of the map is described as

$$x^{t+1} = 1 - a\left(x^t\right)^2 + bx^{t-1})$$

where $a = 1.4$ and $b = 0.3$ are the suggested parameters.

8. **Lozi Map:** This map is the simplified version of the Henon map with a two-dimensional piecewise linear function given by

$$(x^{t+1}, y^{t+1}) = H\left(x^t, y^t\right)$$

$$H\left(x^t, y^t\right) = \left(1 + y^t - a\left|x^t\right|, bx^t\right)$$

where $a = 1.7$ and $b = 0.5$ are the suggested parameters.

9. **Baker's Map:** Another two dimensional function represents Baker's map which defined as (Fridrich, 1998)

$$B(x) = \begin{cases} (2x, 2y), & for\, 0 \le x < 0.5, \\ \left(2 - 2x, 1 - \dfrac{y}{2}\right), & for\, 0.5 \le x < 1. \end{cases}$$

A one dimension of the Baker's map gives another representation which is similar to tent map given by

$$x^{t+1} = \begin{cases} 2x^t, & for\, 0 \le x^t < 0.5, \\ 2 - 2x^t, & for\, 0.5 \le x^t < 1. \end{cases}$$

10. **Arnold's Cat Map:** A two dimensional map is proposed in (Arnold & Avez, 1968) where an image of a cat is used to illustrate the chaotic behavior of the map. The representation of this map is

$$x^{t+1} = x^t + y^t mod\left(1\right)$$

$$y^{t+1} = x^t + 2y^t mod\left(1\right)$$

where $x^t \epsilon \left(0,1\right)$ and $y^t \epsilon \left(0,1\right)$.

11. **Lorenz Map (Lorenz Attractor):** Lorenz Map first introduced in (Lorenz, 1963) for a simplified model for atmospheric convection. Lorenz map is similar to logistic map and accepted as a gener-

alization of circle homeomorphisms from zero entropy to positive entropy.(Cui & Ding, 2015) So the Lorenz map has two leaves, or branches, separated by a singular point at y=0.(Gilmore, 2015) Lorenz system based on definition of the system with three non-linear equations

$$\frac{dx}{dt} = a(y-x), \ \frac{dy}{dt} = x(b-z) - y, \frac{dz}{dt} = xy - cz$$

where a, b and c are constants . An example set is (10,28,8/3) and (28,46.92,4).

STATISTICAL TESTS FOR RANDOMNESS

Every PRNG should have a reasonably long period before its output sequence repeats itself, and its output sequence should pass statistical test suites so that it sufficiently resembles a truly random sequence (Keller & Wiese, 2007). The generated random numbers must have forward unpredictability property such that it is not possible to predict the future evolution of the system. Also, it must be shown that the generated pseudo-random numbers cannot be distinguished from truly random numbers. Hence, the statistical tests are proposed to justify the reliability of the generated random bit sequences.

If a pseudo-random number generator passes the next bit test then it passes any statistical test, i.e., no randomized polynomial-time algorithm can distinguish the generated pseudo-random numbers from truly random numbers (Graham, 1995). An ideal random number generator is infinite, aperiodic, uniform, uncorrelated, and computationally efficient (Phatak & Rao, 1995). For each type of algorithm, the selection of the suitable chaotic map and its parameters (i.e. initial values and control parameters) to generate the random numbers must depend on the statistical test results. Quantitative performance measurement of the chaotic driven random selections is provided by incurring most famous statistical tests (Beker & Piper, 1982; Chan, Chan, & Cheng, 2001) which are enumerated below.

1. **Frequency (Monobit) Test:** The frequencies of the 0 and 1 values in a binary sequence are tested such that they must be approximately equal. The frequency test checks that the number of ones in the sequence is not significantly different from half of the length of the sequence (Kanso & Smaoui, 2009)
2. **Serial (Two-Bit) Test:** Random sequences must have the property that value of each element of a sequence must be independent from the value of its predecessor. Hence, the frequencies of the different transitions in a binary sequence such that 11, 10, 01 and 00 must be approximately equal.
3. **Runs Test:** To test the hypothesis of the independence, the arrangement of numbers in a sequence is examined. After the serial test is passed, the number of runs in the sequence also must be checked to be a dichotomous sequence of values.
4. **Poker Test:** This test determines whether the sequences of different lengths each appear approximately the same number of times in the sequence as it is expected from a random sequence (Karimi et al., 2013). Obviously, the frequency test and the serial test are contained in the poker test.

USE OF CHAOTIC RANDOMNESS IN SELECTED ALGORITHMS

In this section of the chapter, the possible use of Chaotic pseudo-random number generators (CPRNG) for proper metaheuristic and artificial intelligence algorithms has explained. As mentioned in the beginning of this chapter there are vast number of research papers and books about different implementations and descriptions of the algorithms therefore instead of providing the detailed technical and theoretical background only sample solutions for adapting CPRNG's is provided. (Draco, Petrowski, Siarry, & Taillard, 2006; Glover & Kochenberger, 2003; Gonzalez, 2007; Luke, 2009; Souza, Omkar, & Senthilnath, 2012; Talbi, 2009; Yegnanarayana, 2009).

Metaheuristic and artificial intelligence optimization algorithms search for an optimum in the problem domain without trapping in to local optimums, avoiding fall in to infinite loops and careful about early victories due to memorization or other issues. The main reason behind those is optimization is different from modelling or learning. Most of the optimizations based on searching for an unknown solution set. This uncertainty in algorithm sometimes gives a candidate optimum with the possibility of the local optimum accepted as a global or searching for the neighbors sometimes results in missing the optimum next to your current location. So there are also optimum parameters in the algorithm which searches the optimum of the problem. Also computational and algorithmic complexity is another concern while working with computers, high performance computing machines as well as the supercomputers and cloud computing where the computational limits far beyond normal acceptance. A balance of amount of resources like CPU, ram and computational time versus the possible algorithms available has to be obtained in order to solve the optimization problem.

In most of the methods two common function types can be used, one of them is to produce a direct random variable with "CPRNG" methods and normalize if necessary and the second one is "CPRNGTweak" method that will change and modify the original or candidate value with a degree of modification and a random number obtained from CPRNG (Box 1).

Box 1. CPRNG Generation

```
CPRNGRandom <- PRNGRandom number from ordinary equations
t <- initialization for chaotic map
repeat
test_status <- true
repeat t times do
 map(t+1) <- chaotic_map_function(map(t))
 CPRNGRandom <-map(t+1)
 repeat all_tests do
 if test fails then
 test_status=false
 break
until test_status is true or time limit reached
return CPRNGRandom
```

Simple Methods and Random Search

Simples search algorithms like Gradient Ascent, Newton's Method, Steepest Ascent Hill-Climbing and Random Search methods are the easy and simple methods to start with. All of these methods start with an initial random point or candidate point within the search domain. The rest is more or less in common, search the optimality and the validity of the candidate, if the stopping criteria is not satisfied then change the candidate a little with a random affect and return to the loop. A search based on pure random candidate for each time is not a good way of searching, instead using a brute force or combinatorial search is better. Searching in in single, parallel or multi node computing adapting by replacing the random number operator with CPRNG will improve the solution diversity and performance (Box 2).

Simulated Annealing (SA)

Simulated Annealing is another global search algorithm for global optimization similar the Hill-Climbing with the difference of changing the candidate and intermediate candidate. Annealing is actually a heat application process in manufacturing and materials science that changes the physical and chemical

Box 2. Improved Hill-Climbing with Random Restarts with CPRNG

```
time_interval <- distribution of possible time intervals
candidate <- A Random CPRNG Candidate
optimum <- candidate
repeat
time <- a random time in near future from time_interval set
repeat
 mid_candidate <- CPRNGTweak (candidate)
if Quality(mid_candidate) > Quality (candidate)
then
candidate <- mid_candidate
 until stopping criteria satisfied with candidate, time is up or timeout
 if Quality(candidate) > Quality (optimum)
then
 optimum <- candidate
 candidate <- A Random CPRNG Candidate
until stopping criteria satisfied with optimum or timeout
Improved Random Search with CPRNG
optimum <- A Random CPRNG Candidate
repeat
candidate <- A random CPRNG Candidate
if quality(candidate) > quality (optimum)
then
optimum <- candidate
until stopping criteria satisfied with optimum or timeout
```

properties of a material in order to obtain harder more ductile products. The Annealing process initially heating up the material above a suitable critical temperature where the material starts recrystallization and forms better bigger crystal structures which provides the ductility and hardness. After that the process continues with waiting for a proper time which allows slowly cooling so the crystal atoms becomes stable and forms new crystal structure (Box 3).

Tabu Search (TS)

Tabu Search is a search algorithm using an imaginary memory of the recently tested candidate solutions by putting them on a list called tabu list with a predefined capacity m of storing them. Like memories, tabu lists are volatile based on the time passed or list fully filled with candidates with FIFO principle. It is based on a local search of the neighbors and checking the list if visited before or not. n modified and tweaked candidate children is generated in each step but the ones in the memory is not considered (Box 4).

Particle Swarm Optimization (PSO)

Almost the same as the inspiration of the nerve cells particle swarm optimization motivated/brought about from the behaviors of the different huge numbers in the nature like birds, fishes, ants. Particle swarm optimization thought about/believed as population based optimization and can be improved by using chaotic random number modified members, crossovers and mutations. In general PSO a set of computer instructions is used for optimization where candidate solution sets or working limits/guidelines for the population modelled according to the general behaviors. These candidate solution sets which are called particles in solution swarm, live together and change and get better at the same time based on knowledge sharing with close-by particles. Each particle acts individually and also in coordination with the other particles. So each particle creates a solution based on the problem statement and initial starting point. In each turn all the particles changes their location, limits/guidelines, settings by using a

Box 3. Improved Simulated Annealing with CPRNG

```
T <- a high temperature value //melting
candidate <- A Random CPRNG Candidate
optimum <- candidate
repeat
mid_candidate <- CPRNGTweak (candidate)
if quality(mid_candidate) > quality(candidate) or
CPRNG[0..1] < exp((quality(mid_candidate)-quality(candidate))/T)
then
candidate <- mid_candidate
decrease t //cooling
if quality(candidate) > quality (optimum)
then
optimum <- candidate
until stopping criteria satisfied with optimum, T<=0 or timeout
```

Box 4. Improved Tabu Search CPRNG

```
m <- tabu list length //memory size
n <- number of tweaked candidates desired for sample the gradient
candidate <- some initial candidate solution CPRNG Candidate
optimum <- candidate
tabu_list <-{} a tabu list of length m //FIFO based
enqueuer candidate to memory
repeat
if tabu_list.LEN = m
then
apply FIFO remove the oldest from tabu_list
mid_candidate <- CPRNGTweak (candidate)
for n-1 times do
dummy_candidate <- CPRNGTweak (candidate)
if dummy_candidate not in tabu_list and
quality(W)> quality(mid_candidate) or mid_candidate is in tabu_list
then
mid_candidate <- dummy_candidate
if mid_candidate is not a member of memory and
quality(mid_candidate)> quality(candidate)
then
candidate <- mid_candidate
 enqueue mid_candidate to memory
if quality(candidate) > quality (optimum)
then
optimum <- candidate
until stopping criteria satisfied with optimum or timeout
```

speed vector to reach its next position in the solution space. Each particle changes its speed in order to reach a better position than the previous one by using its own best previous experience data and also the best previous experience data from the neighbors within the swarm.

Particles update their velocities as shown in equations below

$$v_{t+1}^i = w_t v_t^i + c_1 r_1 \left(p_t^i - x_t^i \right) + c_2 r_2 \left(p_t^g - x_t^i \right)$$

and the new positions according to

$$x_{t+1}^i = x_t^l + v_{t+1}^l$$

where x_t^i represents the current position of particle i in solution space and subscript t indicates an iteration, p_t^i is the best-found position of particle i up to iteration count t and represents the cognitive contribution to the search velocity v. Each component of v_t^i can be limited to the range $[-v_{max}, v_{max}]$ to control excessive roaming of particles within the problem domain and creating unfeasible solutions. p_t^g is the global best-found position among all particles in the problem domain up to iteration count t and forms the swarm information flow to the velocity vector; r_1 and r_2 are random numbers uniformly distributed in the interval $(0,1)$, where the chaotic random numbers will be replaced, while c_1 and c_2 are the cognitive and social scaling parameters depending on the structure of problem. Finally w_t is the particle inertia, which is reduced dynamically to decrease the search area in a gradual fashion. The variable w_t is updated as

$$w_t = \left(w_{max} - w_{min} \right) * \frac{t_{max} - t}{t_{max}} + w_{min}$$

where, w_{max} and w_{min} denote the maximum and minimum of w_t respectively; t_{max} is a given number of maximum iterations. So the swarm members repeated the communication and changed their parameters until a time limit or a stopping criteria values reached (Box 5).

Genetic Algorithms (GA)

Genetic algorithm (GA), is the most widely used version of evolutionary algorithms in the metaheuristic. Similar to the inspiration from the nature as well as ANN and PSO, genetic algorithms used the structure of evolution in order to reach the perfect solution that fits in to the energy environment. As in the nature every individual member of the has set of properties and working parameters which differs that device among the rest of the solutions in the domain.

Box 5. Improved Particle Swarm Optimization

```
for each candidate particle in the candidate particle set
Initialize particle with working parameters
End
repeat
for each particle
Calculate fitness value for better
if the fitness value is better than the best fitness value (p_Best) in history
set current value as the new p_Best
End
Choose the particle with the best fitness value of all the particles as the
g_Best
for each particle
Calculate particle adapting velocity using
update particle working parameters r_1 and r_2 using CPRNG
end
until stopping criteria satisfied with optimum or timeout
```

These properties and working parameters corresponds to the chromosomes or genotypes similar to the ones in the living organisms (John, 1992).

As the nature changes and gets better in the time domain with new generation reproduced or composed of their parents or family relatives or things that existed long, long ago genotypes by crossover and change. Each new next generation member has a possible chance to better fit to its surrounding conditions. The rules of related to tiny chemical assembly instructions inside of living things sets of computer instructions can be changed to fit optimization problems. Most of the numerical adaptations of the problems numerical values decoded as binary strings so easy to make different levels and sources of crossovers and mutations (Kumar & Mohan, 2011). The common steps of genetic algorithm is as follows

1. **Representations:** Proper coding of the optimization problem in to mathematical chromosomes while the decision variables within a solution (chromosome) are genes. The possible values of variables (genes) are the alleles and the position of an element (gene) within a chromosome is named locus. Most common representation is based on bits. Binary, discrete and permutation representations are available in the literature.

2. **Population Initialization:** Using the representation coding an initial state of the problem settings created and represented as defined on the first step. As to continue from the previous step, initial population contains some power stations are operational and some are not in a particular initial timing.

3. **Objective Function:** Proper coding of the optimization problem in to mathematical chromosomes which will be used to calculate the goodness of the solution.

4. **Selection Strategy:** The best parameter sets or working plans which fit in to the objective function selected for the next round of reproduction. In the rank based selections, without looking the proportions best n solutions selected for the reproduction. Roulette Wheel Selection, Stochastic Universal Sampling, Tournament Selection, Rank-Based Selection are common selection methodologies.

5. **Reproduction with CPNRG:** Using the current solutions sets best solutions will produce the next generation alternatives by the use of chaotic random numbers
   a. **Chaotic Crossover:** Crossover is used to increase the diversity of the possible solutions.
   b. **Chaotic Mutations:** New genetic material into the gene at some minor ratio. With a small probability, randomly chosen bits of the offspring genotypes change from '0' to '1' and vice versa for binary coded strings. This will increase the possibility of the new searches in the domain.

6. **Replacement Strategy:** The best solutions which fit in to the objective function selected for the next round of reproduction

7. **Stopping Criteria:** The best solutions which fit in to objective function selected for the next round of reproduction

Like most of the other artificial optimization methods genetic algorithm can be used for complex problems (Box 6).

Ant Colony Algorithm (ACO)

Ant Colony Optimization (ACO) is an another swarm intelligence based metaheuristic algorithm that is inspired by the pheromone trail laying and tracking of the remaining of ants while finding their way to

Box 6. Improved Genetic Algorithms with CPRNG

```
generate an initial population with CPRNG
repeat
Repeat
If crossover condition satisfied Then
select parent chromosomes
choose crossover parameters
perform crossover with CPRNGCrossover
End if
If mutation condition satisfied Then
choose mutation points
perform mutation with CPRNGMutation
End if
evaluate fitness of offspring
Until sufficient offspring created;
select new population;
until stopping criteria satisfied with optimum or timeout
```

food or home. Use of artificial ants in ACO for optimization problems are stochastic solutions that build possible candidate solutions for the optimization settings and parameters of the smart grid by adapting the artificial pheromone in other words fitness information. ACO mostly used for discrete optimization problems. The real ants uses stigmergy which is a form of indirect communication by modifying the environment for further usage or communication. In case of the ACO, stigmergy based on the pheromone trails leaved by the ants while passing through a path or way (Box 7).

Chaotic Crossover

In crossover is the operation of mixing and matching the genes of two parents in to new generations. Mixing and matching is totally random based on some rules. A good quality random numbers will increase the variety of the possible new generations and increase the search domain. In the general application there are three possible crossovers available as one-point, two-point and uniform crossovers. In all of these crossovers random locations selected for crossover (Boxes 8 and 9).

Chaotic Mutation

Mutation is an operator used to maintain many different kinds of possible solutions from one generation of a problem set to the next. It is the same as change of values in a from its initial state. In mutation, the solution may change wholly from the previous solution. Hence GA can come to a better solution or sometimes an unfeasible solution. If the degree of mutation it is set too high, the optimization will turn into a random search. A simple mutation operator is the bit-flip operator for binary coding's (Box 10).

Box 7. Improved Ant Colony Optimization with CPRNG

```
Initialize the base efficiency and fitness (attractiveness), τ, and visibil-
ity, η, for each solution set ;
repeat
for each ant do
choose CPRNGTweak(previous equation) the next state to move into
add that move to the tabu list for each smart agent
repeat until each smart agent completed a solution for dynamic response
End
For each ant that completed a solution do
update fitness τ for each edge that the ant traversed;
End
if (local best solution better than global solution) then
save local best solution as global solution;
End
until stopping criteria satisfied with optimum or timeout
```

Box 8. Improved Single Point Crossover with CPRNG

```
parent_a_dna <- genetic coding of the problem to the representation
parent_b_dna <- genetic coding of the problem to the representation
c <- a CPRNG random integer chosen uniformly from 1 to length of dna
if c<> 1 then
for I from 1 to c-1 do
swap the values of parent_a_dna(i) and parent_a_dna(i)
Improved Two Point Crossover with CPRNG
parent_a_dna <- genetic coding of the problem to the representation
parent_b_dna <- genetic coding of the problem to the representation
c1 <- a CPRNG random integer chosen uniformly from 1 to length of dna
c2 <- a CPRNG random integer chosen uniformly from 1 to length of dna
if c1>c2 then
swap c1,c2
if c1<>c2 then
for i from c1 to c2-1 do
swap the values of parent_a_dna(i) and parent_a_dna(i)
```

FUTURE RESEARCH DIRECTIONS

The application of true random number generations with modified chaotic maps planned by the authors for the future research directions. The main idea behind the progress is to modify the nature inspired events and conditions with chaotic map functions and generate a hybrid version of semi TRNGs and semi CPRNGS.

Box 9. Improved Uniform Crossover with CPRNG

```
swap_probability < - setting a 1/length_of_dna, <=0.5
parent_a_dna <- genetic coding of the problem to the representation
parent_b_dna <- genetic coding of the problem to the representation
for i from 1 to length_of_dna do
if p>= CPRNG[0..1] then
swap the values of parent_a_dna(i)and parent_a_dna(i)
```

Box 10. Improved Bit-Flip Mutation with CPRNG

```
flip_probability < - setting a probability of flipping a bit
parent_dna <- genetic coding of the problem to the representation
for i from 1 to length_of_dna do
if p>= CPRNG[0..1] then
flip the values of parent_a_dna(i) as 1>0, 0>1
```

CONCLUSION

Metaheuristic and artificial intelligence algorithms are widely used in different optimization, modelling and learning problems. Stochastic optimization and search algorithms require the use of random number for initialization of the problem set and tweaks of the current variables to the next calculation step. Increasing the uniqueness and the quality of the random numbers will eventually increase the processing time and the goodness of the solution. This is a more obvious requirement in parallel and grid computing based calculations where the probability of the coincidence of the same random numbers occurring in the system increased in using ordinary PRNGs. The use of TRNG is a possibility with increasing the computational complexity which costs energy and time. This chapter makes a common review of the subjects and gives examples of selected methodologies. As can be seen from the selected examples any algorithm that starts with random initial position, random variables and random modifications within the routine can be modified with chaotic pseudo random number generators and functions.

REFERENCES

Afrabandpey, H., Ghaffari, M., Mirzaei, A., & Safayani, M. (2014). A novel bat algorithm based on chaos for optimization tasks. *Intelligent Systems (ICIS), 2014 Iranian Conference on* (pp. 1-6) IEEE. doi:10.1109/IranianCIS.2014.6802527

Akhshani, A., Akhavan, A., Mobaraki, A., Lim, S. C., & Hassan, Z. (2014). Pseudo random number generator based on quantum chaotic map. *Communications in Nonlinear Science and Numerical Simulation, 19*(1), 101–111. doi:10.1016/j.cnsns.2013.06.017

Alatas, B. (2010). Chaotic bee colony algorithms for global numerical optimization. *Expert Systems with Applications, 37*(8), 5682–5687. doi:10.1016/j.eswa.2010.02.042

Arnold, V. I., & Avez, A. (1968). *Ergodic problems of classical mechanics*. Retrieved from WA Benjamin.

Bastos-Filho, C. J., Oliveira, M. A., Nascimento, D. N., & Ramos, A. D. (2010). Impact of the random number generator quality on particle swarm optimization algorithm running on graphic processor units. *Hybrid Intelligent Systems (HIS), 2010 10th International Conference on* (pp. 85-90) IEEE. doi:10.1109/HIS.2010.5601073

Beker, H., & Piper, F. (1982). *Cipher systems: the protection of communications*. Northwood Books.

Caponetto, R., Fortuna, L., Fazzino, S., & Xibilia, M. G. (2003). Chaotic sequences to improve the performance of evolutionary algorithms. *Evolutionary Computation. IEEE Transactions on*, *7*(3), 289–304.

Chan, C. K., Chan, C. K., & Cheng, L. M. (2001). *Software Generation of Random Numbers by Using Neural Network. Artificial Neural Nets and Genetic Algorithms*. Springer. doi:10.1007/978-3-7091-6230-9_51

Cicek, I., Pusane, A. E., & Dundar, G. (2014). A novel design method for discrete time chaos based true random number generators. *Integration, the VLSI Journal, 47*(1), 38-47. doi:10.1016/j.vlsi.2013.06.003

Cui, H., & Ding, Y. (2015). Renormalization and conjugacy of piecewise linear Lorenz maps. *Advances in Mathematics*, *271*, 235–272. doi:10.1016/j.aim.2014.11.024

D'Angelo, G., & Marzolla, M. (2014). New trends in parallel and distributed simulation: From many-cores to Cloud Computing. *Simulation Modelling Practice and Theory*, *49*, 320–335. doi:10.1016/j.simpat.2014.06.007

dos Santos Coelho, L. (2009). Reliability and redundancy optimization by means of a chaotic differential evolution approach. *Chaos, Solitons, and Fractals*, *41*(2), 594–602. doi:10.1016/j.chaos.2008.02.028

Draco, J., Petrowski, A., Siarry, P., & Taillard, E. (2006). *Metaheuristics for hard optimization: methods and case studies*. Springer Science & Business Media.

Eberhart, R. C., & Shi, Y. (2001). Tracking and optimizing dynamic systems with particle swarms. *Evolutionary Computation, 2001.Proceedings of the 2001 Congress on* (vol. 1, pp. 94-100) IEEE. doi:10.1109/CEC.2001.934376

Essl, G. (2006). Circle maps as a simple oscillators for complex behavior: Ii. experiments. In *Proceedings of the International Conference on Digital Audio Effects (DAFx)*.

Francois, M., Grosges, T., Barchiesi, D., & Erra, R. (2014). Pseudo-random number generator based on mixing of three chaotic maps. *Communications in Nonlinear Science and Numerical Simulation*, *19*(4), 887–895. doi:10.1016/j.cnsns.2013.08.032

Fridrich, J. (1998). Symmetric ciphers based on two-dimensional chaotic maps. *International Journal of Bifurcation and Chaos in Applied Sciences and Engineering*, *8*(6), 1259–1284. doi:10.1142/S021812749800098X

Gentle, J. E., Hardle, W., & Mori, Y. (Eds.). (2004). Handbook of Computational Statistics. Springer.

Gilli, M., Maringer, D., & Schumann, E. (2011). Generating Random Numbers. In M.G.M. Schumann (Ed.), Numerical Methods and Optimization in Finance (pp. 119-158). San Diego, CA: Academic Press.

Gilmore, R. (2015). Explosions in Lorenz maps. *Chaos, Solitons, and Fractals, 76,* 130–140. doi:10.1016/j. chaos.2015.03.020

Glover, F., & Kochenberger, G. A. (2003). *Handbook of metaheuristics Springer Science & Business Media.*

Gonzalez, T. F. (2007). *Handbook of approximation algorithms and metaheuristics CRC Press.* doi:10.1201/9781420010749

Graham, R. L. (1995). *Handbook of combinatorics* (1st ed.). Elsevier.

Jahan, M. V., & Akbarzadeh, T. (2012). Hybrid local search algorithm via evolutionary avalanches for spin glass based portfolio selection. *Egyptian Informatics Journal, 13*(2), 65–73. doi:10.1016/j.eij.2012.04.002

Jin, C. H., & Ryu, H. G. (2012). Performance evaluation of chaotic CDSK modulation system with different chaotic maps. *ICT Convergence (ICTC), 2012 International Conference on* (pp. 603-606) IEEE. doi:10.1109/ICTC.2012.6387115

John, H. H. (1992). *Adaptation in natural and artificial systems: an introductory analysis with applications to biology, control, and artificial intelligence.* MIT Press.

Juan, A. A., Faulin, J., Grasman, S. E., Rabe, M., & Figueira, G. (2015). A review of simheuristics: Extending metaheuristics to deal with stochastic combinatorial optimization problems. *Operations Research Perspectives, 2,* 62–72. doi:10.1016/j.orp.2015.03.001

Kanso, A., & Smaoui, N. (2009). Logistic chaotic maps for binary numbers generations. *Chaos, Solitons, and Fractals, 40*(5), 2557–2568. doi:10.1016/j.chaos.2007.10.049

Karimi, H., Hosseini, S. M., & Jahan, M. V. (2013). On the combination of self-organized systems to generate pseudo-random numbers. *Information Sciences, 221,* 371–388. doi:10.1016/j.ins.2012.09.029

Keller, J. A., & Wiese, H. (2007). Period lengths of chaotic pseudo-random number generators. *Proceedings of the Fourth IASTED International Conference on Communication, Network and Information Security* (pp. 7-11). ACTA Press.

Kim, S., Bok, J., & Ryu, H. G. (2013). Performance evaluation of DCSK system with chaotic maps. *Information Networking (ICOIN), 2013 International Conference on* (pp. 556-559). IEEE.

Kumar, J., Shukla, S., Prakash, D., Mishra, P., & Kumar, S. (2011). Random Number Generator Using Various Techniques Through VHDL. *International Journal of Computer Applications in Engineering Sciences, 1.*

Kumar, V. S., & Mohan, M. R. (2011). A genetic algorithm solution to the optimal short-term hydrothermal scheduling. *International Journal of Electrical Power & Energy Systems, 33*(4), 827–835. doi:10.1016/j.ijepes.2010.11.008

Lee, L. P., & Wong, K. W. (2004). A random number generator based on elliptic curve operations. *Computers & Mathematics with Applications, 47*(2-3), 217-226. doi:10.1016/S0898-1221(04)90018-1

Lorenz, E. N. (1963). Deterministic nonperiodic flow. *Journal of the Atmospheric Sciences, 20*(2), 130–141. doi:10.1175/1520-0469(1963)020<0130:DNF>2.0.CO;2

Lozi, R., & Taralova, I. (2014). From chaos to randomness via geometric undersampling. *ESAIM: Proceedings and Surveys, 46*, 177-195. Retrieved from EDP Sciences.

Luke, S. (2009). *Essentials of Metaheuristics. A Set of Undergraduate Lecture Notes*. Zeroth Edition.

Marton, K., Suciu, A., & Ignat, I. (2010). Randomness in digital cryptography: A survey. Romanian Journal of Information Science and Technology. *ROMJIST, 13*(3), 219–240.

May, R. M. (1976). Simple mathematical models with very complicated dynamics. *Nature, 261*(5560), 459–467. doi:10.1038/261459a0 PMID:934280

Mukhopadhyay, S., & Banerjee, S. (2012). Global optimization of an optical chaotic system by chaotic multi swarm particle swarm optimization. *Expert Systems with Applications, 39*(1), 917–924. doi:10.1016/j.eswa.2011.07.089

Peitgen, H. O., Jürgens, H., & Saupe, D. (2006). *Chaos and fractals: new frontiers of science*. Springer Science & Business Media.

Phatak, S. C., & Rao, S. S. (1995). Logistic map: A possible random-number generator. *Physical Review E: Statistical Physics, Plasmas, Fluids, and Related Interdisciplinary Topics, 51*(4), 3670–3678. doi:10.1103/PhysRevE.51.3670 PMID:9963048

Pivoluska, M., & Plesch, M. (2015). *Device Independent Random Number Generation*. arXiv:1502.06393

Reese, A. (2009). Random number generators in genetic algorithms for unconstrained and constrained optimization. Nonlinear Analysis: Theory. *Methods & Applications, 71*(12), e679–e692.

Reyad, O., & Kotulski, Z. (2015). On Pseudo-Random Number Generators Using Elliptic Curves and Chaotic Systems. *Applications of Mathematics, 9*(1), 31–38.

Rogers, T. D., & Whitley, D. C. (1983). Chaos in the cubic mapping. *Mathematical Modelling, 4*(1), 9–25. doi:10.1016/0270-0255(83)90030-1

Souza, C., Omkar, S. N., & Senthilnath, J. (2012). Pickup and delivery problem using metaheuristics techniques. *Expert Systems with Applications, 39*(1), 328–334. doi:10.1016/j.eswa.2011.07.022

Szczepanski, J., Wajnryb, E., Amiga, J. M., Sanchez-Vives, M. V., & Slater, M. (2004). Biometric random number generators. *Computers & Security, 23*(1), 77–84. doi:10.1016/S0167-4048(04)00064-1

Talbi, E. G. (2009). Metaheuristics: from design to implementation (74th ed.). John Wiley & Sons.

Tsoi, K. H., Leung, K. H., & Leong, P. H. W. (2003). Compact FPGA-based true and pseudo random number generators. *Field-Programmable Custom Computing Machines, 2003. FCCM 2003. 11th Annual IEEE Symposium on* (pp. 51-61). IEEE.

Uchida, A. (2012). *Optical communication with chaotic lasers: applications of nonlinear dynamics and synchronization*. John Wiley & Sons.

Wang, Q., Yu, S., Ding, W., & Leng, M. (2008). Generating high-quality random numbers by cellular automata with PSO. *Natural Computation, 2008. ICNC'08. Fourth International Conference on* (vol. 7, pp. 430-433). IEEE. doi:10.1109/ICNC.2008.560

Yegnanarayana, B. (2009). *Artificial neural networks*. PHI Learning Pvt. Ltd.

ADDITIONAL READING

Afrabandpey, H., Ghaffari, M., Mirzaei, A., & Safayani, M. (2014, February). A novel bat algorithm based on chaos for optimization tasks. In Intelligent Systems (ICIS), 2014 Iranian Conference on (pp. 1-6). IEEE. doi:10.1109/IranianCIS.2014.6802527

Alligood, K. T., Sauer, T. D., & Yorke, J. A. (1997). [Springer Berlin Heidelberg.]. *Chaos (Woodbury, N.Y.)*, 105–147.

Bastos-Filho, C. J., Andrade, J., Pita, M. R., & Ramos, A. D. (2009, October). Impact of the quality of random numbers generators on the performance of particle swarm optimization. In Systems, Man and Cybernetics, 2009. SMC 2009. IEEE International Conference on (pp. 4988-4993). IEEE. doi:10.1109/ICSMC.2009.5346366

Ding, K., & Tan, Y. (2014, July). Comparison of random number generators in Particle Swarm Optimization algorithm. In Evolutionary Computation (CEC), 2014 IEEE Congress on (pp. 2664-2671). IEEE. doi:10.1109/CEC.2014.6900461

Feng, Y., Teng, G. F., Wang, A. X., & Yao, Y. M. (2007, September). Chaotic inertia weight in particle swarm optimization. In Innovative Computing, Information and Control, 2007. ICICIC'07. Second International Conference on(pp. 475-475). IEEE. doi:10.1109/ICICIC.2007.209

Kazimipour, B., Li, X., & Qin, A. K. (2014, July). A review of population initialization techniques for evolutionary algorithms. In Evolutionary Computation (CEC), 2014 IEEE Congress on (pp. 2585-2592). IEEE. doi:10.1109/CEC.2014.6900618

Kromer, P., Snael, V., & Zelinka, I. (2013, October). On the Use of Chaos in Nature-Inspired Optimization Methods. In Systems, Man, and Cybernetics (SMC), 2013 IEEE International Conference on (pp. 1684-1689). IEEE. doi:10.1109/SMC.2013.290

Krömer, P., Zelinka, I., & Snášel, V. (2014). Behaviour of pseudo-random and chaotic sources of stochasticity in nature-inspired optimization methods. *Soft Computing*, *18*(4), 619–629. doi:10.1007/s00500-014-1223-y

Lin, H., & Yim, S. C. S. (1996). Analysis of a nonlinear system exhibiting chaotic, noisy chaotic, and random behaviors. *Journal of Applied Mechanics*, *63*(2), 509–516. doi:10.1115/1.2788897

Niederreiter, H. (1978). Quasi-Monte Carlo methods and pseudo-random numbers. *Bulletin of the American Mathematical Society*, *84*(6), 957–1041. doi:10.1090/S0002-9904-1978-14532-7

Parejo, J. A., Ruiz-Cortés, A., Lozano, S., & Fernandez, P. (2012). Metaheuristic optimization frameworks: A survey and benchmarking. *Soft Computing*, *16*(3), 527–561. doi:10.1007/s00500-011-0754-8

Skiadas, C. H., & Skiadas, C. (2008). *Chaotic modelling and simulation: analysis of chaotic models, attractors and forms*. CRC Press. doi:10.1201/9781420079012

Stojanovski, T., & Kocarev, L. (2001). Chaos-based random number generators-part I: analysis [cryptography]. Circuits and Systems I: Fundamental Theory and Applications. *IEEE Transactions on, 48*(3), 281–288.

Stojanovski, T., Pihl, J., & Kocarev, L. (2001). Chaos-based random number generators. Part II: practical realization. Circuits and Systems I: Fundamental Theory and Applications. *IEEE Transactions on, 48*(3), 382–385.

Timmer, J., Rust, H., Horbelt, W., & Voss, H. U. (2000). Parametric, nonparametric and parametric modelling of a chaotic circuit time series. *Physics Letters. [Part A], 274*(3), 123–134. doi:10.1016/S0375-9601(00)00548-X

Toso, R. F., & Resende, M. G. (2015). A C++ application programming interface for biased random-key genetic algorithms. *Optimization Methods and Software, 30*(1), 81–93. doi:10.1080/10556788.2014.890197

KEY TERMS AND DEFINITIONS

Chaotic Crossover: An evolutionary crossover based on the chaotic random numbers.

Chaotic Mutation: An evolutionary mutation based on the chaotic random numbers.

Chaotic Pseudo-Random Number Generators (CPRNG): PRNG based on chaotic maps and chaotic functions.

CPRNG Tweak Function: A modification function that uses the original value and a random number from CPRNG to tweak and modify the value.

Pseudo-Random Number Generators (PRNGs): A process for generating random numbers based on deterministic algorithms.

Random Number Generation: A process for generating tested random numbers for different purposes.

True-Random Number Generators (TRNGs): A process for generating random numbers based on non-deterministic random number generation.

Chapter 11

An Integrated Grey Relations Analysis and VIKOR Method for Multi Criteria Decision Making under Fuzzy Environment:
Supplier Selection Case

Ihsan Hakan Selvi
Sakarya University, Turkey

Orhan Torkul
Sakarya University, Turkey

Ismail Hakki Cedimoglu
Sakarya University, Turkey

ABSTRACT

Today, suppliers of companies are no longer local. Companies have to offer their products to the market just in time and as fast as possible in order to compete. This situation is possible by establishing an effective supply chain for the goods and services they need in the manufacturing system. Finding the right suppliers who are able to provide the companies with the high quality products and services at the reasonable price, at just on time and in the right quantities is an important issue concerned in the process of supply chains concept. There are certain techniques developed in this respect. Some of such methods are approaches developed for situations unmindful of fuzziness and vagueness. Nonetheless, the process of supplier selection contains both vagueness and fuzziness. This study improves the Grey Relational Analysis and VIKOR methods, to fuzzy and ambiguous environments. Then, these approaches are applied to a supplier selection problem, which is previously solved through fuzzy logic and AHP method in literature, and the comparative results of both techniques are given.

DOI: 10.4018/978-1-5225-0075-9.ch011

1. BACKGROUND AND MOTIVATION

Supplier selection and management is today a means for outclassing opponents, and it is of strategic importance, particularly for production companies. Nowadays, companies tend to establish sound and long-term relationships with their suppliers in the global market. A successful method of supply chain management is directly related to an effective supplier selection method/process. Therefore, for manufacturers, it is really a difficult task to install an effective supplier selection process and to choose the right supplier. Rapid changes of demand in the market urge companies to decrease their production and storage costs, improve quality, enhance customer satisfaction, and leave them face to face with other difficulties such as decreasing product life cycle. In the case where companies can operate their own resources, as well as the outsourced ones, in an integrated way, they can remain competitive and continue their progress. Firms wish to refrain from spending their money, time and energy on unfamiliar goods and services, whereas they want to focus on fundamental production issues. In order to decrease the costs in the supply chain and to minimize related risks, companies have to decide on which supplier to collaborate with. At this stage, the ability to choose the right supplier brings certain advantages for enterprises, such as competitive edge, decrease in costs, and improvement in end product quality. Supplier selection and management also includes issues like commercial experiences of suppliers, their prestige, product prices, quality, and delivery time. In addition, supplier selection is often a difficult period for decision-makers since it contains an ambiguous and varying environment. One has to be careful while making decisions in such an ambiguous and complex environment, and in practice, there is a need for a systematic method. Supplier selection can be described as a multi-criteria decision-making problem owing to the various tangible and intangible criteria it includes by nature. Alternatives, which are determined according to attributes considered within multi-criteria problems, are compared with each other and ranked. Since decision-makers apply their personal attitudes with regard to intangible criteria, a vague and uncertain condition arises. There is not a single appropriate solution for problems involving such circumstances; therefore, the optimal solution may change due to applied methods and chosen criteria. That is, none of the alternatives may be the best solution for the chosen or determined criteria. Nonetheless, it is necessary to obtain the appropriate solution pursuant to selection problems and prescribed criteria. In this respect, various decision support approaches are used in order to determine the most convenient alternative.

Most models used in supplier selection focus firstly on determination of criteria, and then assessment of alternatives depending on these criteria. The common feature of such models consists of how the sequence of these alternatives will be determined. The first study on criteria assessment was realised by Dickson in 1966 (Yucel & Guneri, 2011). He examined a total of 273 companies in the USA and Canada, and determined 23 main criteria. Among these 23, according to him, the most important three criteria were quality, on-time delivery and past performance. Weber et al. (1991) analysed 74 articles on supplier selection issued between 1966 and 1991. According to results of this analysis, quality, on-time delivery and price criteria bore the highest importance; of secondary importance were geographical position, financial situation, capacity, and production facility. In terms of supplier selection, Nydick and Hill (1992) examined quality, price, delivery, and service in 1992, Karpak et al. (2001) and analysed cost, quality and delivery, while Bhutta and Huq (2002) handled costs, quality, technology, and service. Liao and Kao (2011) summarised criteria used in literature since 1966, and expressed that quality, cost, and on-time delivery are proposed as supplier selection criteria in many articles.

In the literature, there are many studies regarding order and assessment of alternatives. Most of these studies concentrate on two factors: the first is to attribute importance weights on specifications; the second is to detect the performances of alternatives (suppliers) according to these specifications (Ordoobadi, 2009). The assessment of these two factors highly depends on the judgments of the decision-maker. That is why the evaluation transaction should be protected from individual judgments as much as possible. For example, the Analytic Hierarchy Process (AHP) method that was developed by Saaty (1980) can be used in order to determine the weight of specifications. Decision-makers are often asked to indicate their preferences via numerical values, in order to designate the performance values of suppliers. In such a case, any compulsion in decision-makers for decisions with numerical values may lead to loss of subjectivity values related to perceptions. To overcome the above mentioned difficulty, there is a need for a mechanism that may take expression of individual preferences into account and that includes subjectivity. Individual assessments and convictions are expressed through linguistic terms the best without any numerical scale restrictions (Ordoobadi, 2009). Fuzzy logic is a methodology that enables the decision-maker to indicate his preferences via linguistic expressions (Onut et al., 2009). This methodology is a powerful means that can be used for solving many real world problems and supplier selection issues that include vagueness and uncertainty.

Recently, many studies have been carried out on methods in the case of fuzziness and vagueness, such as Data Envelopment Analysis (DEA) (Toloo & Nalchigar, 2011), AHP (Sari et al., 2008), Nonlinear Programming (Hadi-Vencheh, 2011), Mathematical Modelling (Fazlollahtabar et al., 2011), fuzzy logic (Ordoobadi, 2009), and fuzzy AHP (Onal & Kilincci, 2011). According to Labib (2011), in many studies within the literature, the treated problem is solved only through developed or recommended models, and there are very few studies in which a single problem is solved and compared by means of various models and techniques. This study intends to make up for this deficiency in the literature. In the wake of the research to that end, a sample problem in technical literature has been handled, it has been solved with methods which will be explained in following sections, and the obtained results have been compared.

The sample problem is cited from a study by Ordoobadi (2009) where supplier criteria are defined in a hierarchy and the values of these criteria are obtained via fuzzy numbers. Ordoobadi formed the following hierarchical structure given in Figure 1 for selecting criteria.

Figure 1. Criteria and sub-criteria for supplier selection (Ordoobadi, 2009)

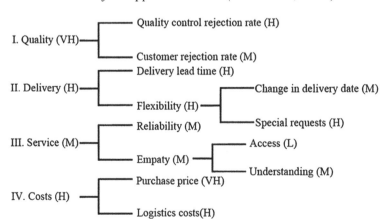

In this structure, decision-makers have given both the criteria and the performance values via linguistic expressions. Fuzzy membership functions and fuzzy mathematical operations are used in order to determine the fuzzy performance rate for each supplier. Following this, these fuzzy values are transformed into crisp values through a defuzzification operation, and the rank of suppliers has been defined.

The remaining part of the study is organised as follows: Fuzzy logic theory and the membership function used in the study, as well as fuzzy arithmetic operations and a general overview on supplier selection application of fuzzy theory are given in the second section. The third section comprises explanations of Grey system theory and development of recommended fuzzy Grey relation analysis method. The fourth section reveals the VIKOR method and phases of the recommended fuzzy VIKOR method. The fifth section details the recommended fuzzy Grey relationship analysis of the considered sample problem for supplier selection cited from literature, as well as solution stages via recommended fuzzy VIKOR methods, and a comparison between proposed models and the method used on the sample problem by the cited study. Finally, the paper concludes with a conclusion and suggestions for future research in section 6.

2. A BRIEF OVERVIEW OF FUZZY LOGIC

The supplier selection problem may include fuzziness and vagueness since it is a multi-criteria problem. Various fuzzy logic based methods have been used in order to solve the problem of fuzziness and vagueness. You can see below an analysis from literature that deals with the fuzzy logic approach and includes the latest integrated or hybrid studies.

Chan et al. (2008) proposed a fuzzy AHP approach in order to eradicate the disadvantages of the AHP method in the course of the global supplier selection problem. Chamodrakas et al. (2010) used fuzzy AHP in the electronics sector, whereas Onal and Kilincci (2011) applied the same method in the supplier selection of a dishwasher manufacturer. Guneri and Kuzu (2009) developed a fuzzy logic approach for JIT environments, in order to reduce the vagueness in supplier selection problems. This approach firstly calculates a fuzzy compatibility index for determination of an effective alternative seller. Then, the best supplier is chosen among alternatives, after ranking fuzzy compatibility indexes. Vahdani and Zandiah (2010) offered a new multi-criteria decision making (MCDM) model, known as fuzzy balancing and ranking. This model enables usage of linguistic variables while forming ranking alternatives of criteria where there is not sufficient information about decision making criteria. Ozkok and Tiryaki (2011) proposed a balancing fuzzy method, using Werners' "fuzzy and" operator, in order to choose the supplier for each product and to determine how much to purchase from every chosen supplier, with respect to the MLSSP-MI (multi-objective linear supplier selection problem with multiple-item) problem. Wang et al. (2009), for the purpose of eliminating the disadvantages of the Fuzzy TOPSIS method by Chen (2000), put forward the fuzzy hierarchical TOPSIS method by means of using simplified parametric distance and the fuzzy AHP method. The recommended model was applied to a sample problem and compared with methods such as AHP, TOPSIS and Chen's TOPSIS (Chen, 2000). Then, the same model was implemented regarding the supplier selection problem for "Lithium-Ion battery protection IC". Vinodh et al. (2011) applied the fuzzy ANP approach for supplier selection by an electronic key manufacturer in India. Liao and Kao (2011) put forth integrated fuzzy TOPSIS and the multiple-choice target program approach. This method allows configuration of multiple threshold value, thus provides convenience for decision-makers during the selection process.

2.1. Fuzzy Logic

The human environment is full of vagueness. Decision-makers have to make decisions under such uncertainties. Decisions via classic approaches are represented with expressions such as yes/no or 0-1, pursuant to Aristotelian logic. Nevertheless, real life is not based on an absolute distinction as is indicated in Aristotelian logic, saying "an element is or is not a member of a set". In other words, many grey hues exist within decision environments between absolute black (0) and absolute white (1). Accordingly, decision processes are full of a vagueness that resembles a grey colour. In order to eliminate these uncertainties as a result of complex systems, we need some logical and mathematical approaches that are different from the ones based on classic logic. The approach with which to meet this requirement is expressed firstly by Zadeh (1965), who defined the new concept as "Fuzzy Logic" in his article issued in the periodical "Fuzzy Sets" back in 1965. Differently from classic logic, in fuzzy logic, an element can be a partial member of more than one set. This method can be used as a powerful means during measurements of vagueness in the course of the decision making processes; moreover, the verbal expressions of an expert can be represented in mathematical terms.

In fuzzy logic, contrary to conventional logic, sets are not objective but subjective. That is, it is determined by a subjectively defined membership function whether an element is a member of a certain set. Thanks to this method, the deduction mechanism in fuzzy logic is used by decision-makers in order to obtain results about current situations. In mathematical terms, a fuzzy U set in universal set E is expressed as $\mu_U(x) : E \rightarrow [0-1]$. The membership degree of an object within the U set varies between 0 and 1, and it is mathematically indicated as follows:

$$U = \{x, \mu_U(x)) : x \in E, \mu_U(x) \in [0,1]\} \tag{1}$$

where, the μ_U function is referred to as the membership function of set U, and it indicates the membership degree of x within set U. As the μ_U value approximates "1", the membership of object to related set increases, whereas approximation towards "0" means a decrease in membership of object to set.

2.2. Definition of Compatible Membership Functions

Membership functions are defined pursuant to the views and value judgments of specialists. Consequently, the form of this function changes depending on specialist (user's) experience and problems. The application usually employs triangular, trapezoidal, piecewise linear and Gaussian membership functions (Mendel, 1995). Importance values of chosen attributes, as well as success (performance) values of suppliers are specified depending on judgments by decision-makers. Two different trapezoidal fuzzy memberships were defined in order to assess the weights of attributes and the performance of suppliers. These membership functions were adopted from the study by Ordoobadi (2009), from which the sample problem is derived, in order to be able to provide the comparative results of recommended the approaches. In equation 2, you can see the mathematical notation of membership function of trapezoidal fuzzy number, defined with $A = (l, m, u, k)$ parameters; also in Figure 2, the graphical expression of this function is given.

Figure 2. Trapezoidal fuzzy number

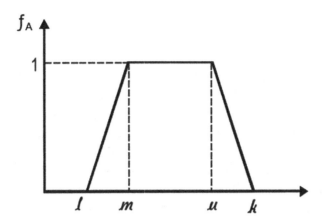

$$f_A(x) = \begin{cases} (x-l)/(m-l), & l \leq x \leq m \\ 1, & m \leq x \leq u \\ (x-k)/(u-k), & u \leq x \leq k \\ 0, & otherwise \end{cases} \tag{2}$$

Importance levels of criteria are assessed as "low importance", "moderate importance", "high importance" and "very high importance". These linguistic values are represented as fuzzy numbers within a 0-1 interval, in the form of a trapezoidal membership function.

Tables 1 and 2 comprise a linguistic scale of weight and performance membership functions, respectively.

Arithmetic operations are needed in order to evaluate fuzzy numbers. With two trapezoidal fuzzy numbers, A (l1, m1, u1, k1) and B (l2, m2, u2, k2), Dubois and Padre defined arithmetic operations of fuzzy numbers as follows (Dubois & Padre, 1980):

$$A \oplus B = [l_1 + l_2, m_1 + m_2, u_2 + u_2, k_1 + k_2] \tag{3}$$

$$A \otimes B = [l_1 l_2, m_1 m_2, u_2 u_2, k_1 k_2] \tag{4}$$

Table 1. Linguistic importance scale (Ordoobadi, 2009)

Low importance (L)	(0.0, 0.0, 0.2, 0.4)
Moderate importance(M)	(0.2, 0.4, 0.4, 0.6)
High importance (H)	(0.4, 0.6, 0.6, 0.8)
Very high importance (VH)	(0.6, 0.8, 1.0, 1.0)

Table 2. Linguistic performance scale (Ordoobadi, 2009)

Poor performance (P)	(0, 0, 2, 4)
Good performance (G)	(2, 4, 4, 6)
Very good performance (VG)	(4, 6, 6, 8)
Excellent performance (EX)	(6, 8, 10, 10)

$$A - B = [l_1 - k_2, m_1 - u_2, u_1 - m_2, k_1 - l_2]$$ (5)

2.3. Defuzzification Method

We need ranging fuzzy numbers in order to compare the alternatives rated by those performances. Ordering alternatives with fuzzy numbers, however, is not as easy and comprehensible as with real numbers. That is why fuzzy numbers should be transformed into real numbers. For this purpose, researchers have recommended various defuzzification approaches, such as including maximum, middle of maximum (MOM), center of gravity (COG), random choice of maxima (RCOM), basic defuzzification distributions (BADD) and many more (Chandramohan et al., 2006). It is the researcher or designing engineer who decides which of these techniques shall be applied depending on the current problem. In this study, we have used the centroid defuzzification method in order to transform fuzzy numbers into real numbers. This method, developed by Sugeno (Runkler, 1996), is one of most common approaches, and it is notated with the below-given equation.

$$x^* = \frac{\int \mu_i(x) \; x \; dx}{\int \mu_i(x) \; dx} x^* = \frac{\int \mu_i(x) \; x \; dx}{\int \mu_i(x) \; dx}$$ (6)

where, x* is defuzzificated output value, μ_i is the collected membership function, and X is linguistic variable value.

3. A BRIEF OVERVIEW OF THE GREY THEORY

The Grey system theory is applied for analysing the relationship between systems, establishing a model, and also for estimation and decision problems (Wen, 2004). Grey theory digitises and thus models situations under vagueness that cannot be overcome through stochastic or fuzzy models. In real life, models are often established under missing information and assumptions, and decisions are taken in this respect. The emergence of grey theory is based on this philosophy. Whenever the operational structure and form of a system are vague, grey system theory lends assistance in revealing the relationship between system parameters. The concept of the colour "grey" in this theory means that information within a system is not exactly known. On the contrary, "white" signifies that all the information is defined and complete, whereas "black" defines that the information within the system is totally unknown (Hsia & Wu, 1998). Grey system theory aims at transforming the black (unknown) part of existing (present) knowledge into white (defined). Instead of dealing with boring (difficult) mathematical calculations and statistical assumptions in order to unfold the characteristic structures of grey systems, Deng (1982) uses grey modelling and examine systems with missing/insufficient information by the help of simple calculation methods.

In statistical analyses, different data structures should be analysed by the relevant methods, since they expose different random attributes. In grey system theory, all different random processes are accepted as grey. Hence, even the problems with no compatible distribution with multivariate statistics, that do not contain sufficient data or that cannot be modelled due to vagueness can be modelled via grey theory.

Grey relational analysis (GRA) is an important application of grey system theory when it comes to estimating a convenient alternative within a set. In GRA, the data set is considered as a sequence that includes the same attributes. GRA can be used for measuring the relationship between two sequences in both quantitative and qualitative terms. To this end, the relationship between these two sequences should be numerically calculated. This calculated relation degree is called grey relation grade (GRG). GRG is notated with a numerical scale between 0 and 1 (Lu et al., 2008). This method has been successfully employed in various studies in order to solve multi-criteria decision making (MCDM) problems (Wu, 2002).

The grey relational analysis method is applied in various domains in order to operate/analyse the processes where ambiguous and uncertain information exists. A brief research on the literature about application areas is given below. Song et al. (2005) used the GRA method for the evaluation of software performance via small data sets. Song and Jamalipour (2005) used the GRA method, along with the Analytical Hierarchy Process. Regarding the supplier selection problem, Yang & Chen. (2006) combined the GRA method with AHP. Tsai et al. (2003) applied GRA for developing a vendor model. Guo-Dong Li et al. (2007) formed a supplier selection approach based on grey theory. In this approach, first of all, linguistic variables were defined in order to be able to express the weight and degree of attributes belonging to all alternative suppliers through grey numbers. Following this, the grey probability degree was proposed for determining the ranking of all alternative suppliers. Huang et al. (2008) combined the GRA method with rough set theory, and applied it to an income distribution problem with respect to a shared portfolio. Kuo and Liang (2011) merged the GRA method with the VIKOR method and assessed service quality of airfields under fuzzy circumstances. Guo-Dong Li et al. (2008) recommended the grey based rough set approach for supplier selection. The recommended approach benefits from mathematical analysis capability of grey system theory, as well as from the power of rough sets used in data mining and knowledge discovery. This approach takes the weights of qualitative and quantitative attributes as equal; nevertheless, it is indicated that it can be used in the decision making process in case of vagueness. Bai and Sarkis (2011) have developed a methodology in which grey system theory and rough aggregation theory operate together in an integrated way for supplier evaluation. Thanks to this methodology, it is possible to analysis qualitative, quantitative, tangible, intangible, and perceptual data. Wu (2009) is grounded in fuzzy numbers for common decision-making problems and proposes grey relation analysis; whereas Dempster-Shafer put forward a new model that solves the problem through theory. The recommended model includes grey relation analysis, individual aggregation, followed by group aggregation phases together with the rule combinations of Dempster-Shafer.

3.1. Proposed Fuzzy Grey Relational Analysis Method (PFGRAM)

Grey relational analysis (GRA), which is one of the sub-methods of Grey theory, enables the determination of relation level between each factor in a vague system (each factor is defined as a line or column sequence) and compared factor (reference) series.

Definition 1: X is a fuzzy number sequence set. $x_0 \in X$ means a reference series, and $x_i \in X$ signifies a comparison sequence $(i = 1, 2, ..., m)$. These series are shown as below:

$$x_0 = (x_0(1), x_0(2), ..., x_0(n)) \ (j = 1, 2, ..., n)$$

$$x_i = (x_i(1), x_i(2), \ldots\ldots\ldots, x_i(n)) \ (j = 1, 2, \ldots\ldots\ldots, n) \tag{7}$$

where $x_0(j)$ and $x_i(j)$ are fuzzy trapezoidal numbers; and they are notated as follows:

$$x_0(j) = (l_j^0, m_j^0, u_j^0, k_j^0)$$

$$x_i(j) = (l_{ij}, m_{ij}, u_{ij}, k_{ij}) \tag{8}$$

Comparison series articulate the performance of alternative no. i. according to criteria no. j. Decision matrices undergo normalisation depending on benefit or cost attributes of criteria. For benefit and cost criteria, equations 9 and 10 are used, respectively.

$$x_i(j) = \left[x_i(j) - \min x_i(j) \right] / \left[\max x_i(j) - \min x_i(j) \right] \tag{9}$$

$$x_i(j) = \left[\max x_i(j) - x_i(j) \right] / \left[\max x_i(j) - \min x_i(j) \right] \tag{10}$$

After the normalisation process, the reference series in the decision table are determined by virtue of the below-given equation 11.

$$x_0(j) = (\max_{1 \le i \le m} l_{ij}, \max_{1 \le i \le m} m_{ij}, \max_{1 \le i \le m} u_{ij}, \max_{1 \le i \le m} k_{ij}) = (l_j^0, m_j^0, u_j^0, k_j^0), \ j = 1, 2, \ldots\ldots, n \tag{11}$$

Then, the difference values between reference series and comparison series are calculated pursuant to the following equations.

$$\Delta_i^L(j) = \left| l_j^0 - l_{ij} \right|, \ \Delta_i^M(j) = \left| m_j^0 - m_{ij} \right|, \ \Delta_i^U(j) = \left| u_j^0 - u_{ij} \right|, \ \Delta_i^K(j) = \left| k_j^0 - k_{ij} \right|$$

$$\Delta_{\max}^L = \max_i \max_j \left| l_j^0 - l_{ij} \right|, \ \Delta_{\min}^L = \min_i \min_j \left| l_j^0 - l_{ij} \right|$$

$$\Delta_{\max}^M = \max_i \max_j \left| m_j^0 - m_{ij} \right|, \ \Delta_{\min}^M = \min_i \min_j \left| m_j^0 - m_{ij} \right|$$

$$\Delta_{\max}^U = \max_i \max_j \left| u_j^0 - u_{ij} \right|, \ \Delta_{\min}^U = \min_i \min_j \left| u_j^0 - u_{ij} \right| \tag{12}$$

$$\Delta_{\max}^K = \max_i \max_j \left| k_j^0 - k_{ij} \right|, \ \Delta_{\min}^K = \min_i \min_j \left| k_j^0 - k_{ij} \right|$$

Definition 2: The influence level between factors is called grey relational degree. Grey relational degree is calculated in consideration of geometric similarity between referential factor series and factor series that will be compared. Function, which defines this grey relational degree, should provide axioms of normality, dual symmetry, wholeness and closeness (Wen, 2004). Grey relational degree between series x_0 and x_i is defined as $r(x_0(j), x_i(j))$. $x_i(j)$ shows value no. j. of series i.. Related explanations on these four axioms are provided as follows:

1. Normality

$$0 < r(x_0(j), x_i(j)) \le 1 \quad \forall_i, \forall_j \tag{13}$$

2. Dual symmetry

$$r(x_0(j), x_i(j)) = r(x_i(j), x_0(j)) \Leftrightarrow X = \{x_0(j), x_i(j)\} \tag{14}$$

3. Wholeness

$$r(x_i, x_j) \ne r(x_j, x_i) \; \forall x_i, x_j \in X = \{x_i \mid i = 0, 1, 2, \dots\dots n\}, \; n > 2 \tag{15}$$

4. Closeness:

The value of $r(x_0, x_i)$ is determined by $|(x_0(j) - x_i(j))|$. As small is $|(x_0(j) - x_i(j))|$, so is the size of the grey relational degree. Consequently, the grey relational degree that will provide the four above mentioned axioms is expressed with the following equation.

$$r(x_0(j), x_i(j)) = \frac{\min_i \min_k |x_0(j) - x_i(j)| + \rho \max_i \max_k |x_0(j) - x_i(j)|}{|x_0(j) - x_i(j)| + \rho \max_i \max_k |x_0(j) - x_i(j)|} \tag{16}$$

where, reference series $x_0(j)$ and comparison series $x_i(j)$ are determined in the wake of normalization of multi-criteria fuzzy decision matrix. $\Delta_i(j)$ is the absolute difference between these two series, and it is notated with the formula $\Delta_i(j) = |x_0(j) - x_i(j)|$.

Definition 3: Equation 16 in definition two is a classic grey relational degree equation. In the present study, the approach in is developed for trapezoidal fuzzy numbers (Liou & Wang, 1992), as follows in equation 17.

$$r_\lambda = \frac{1}{2} \big[(1-\lambda)l + m + u + \lambda k \big] \tag{17}$$

According to this equation, λ signifies the risk coefficient of the decision-maker that undertakes a value in the interval of $0 \le \lambda \le 1$, and in practice, it is often considered as 0.5. Thereby, conventional the grey relation degree equation, which is formed for real numbers, is transformed into an equation by means of which the grey relation degree can be calculated for trapezoid fuzzy numbers. The new equation is expressed as follows (Wang et al., 2007).

$$r_{ij} = r(x_0(j), x_i(j)) = \frac{1}{2} \left[\begin{array}{c} (1-\lambda) \dfrac{\Delta_{\min}^{L} + \rho\Delta_{\max}^{L}}{\Delta_{i}^{L}(j) + \rho\Delta_{\max}^{L}} + \dfrac{\Delta_{\min}^{M} + \rho\Delta_{\max}^{M}}{\Delta_{i}^{M}(j) + \rho\Delta_{\max}^{M}} \\[3mm] + \dfrac{\Delta_{\min}^{U} + \rho\Delta_{\max}^{U}}{\Delta_{i}^{U}(j) + \rho\Delta_{\max}^{U}} + \lambda \dfrac{\Delta_{\min}^{K} + \rho\Delta_{\max}^{K}}{\Delta_{i}^{K}(j) + \rho\Delta_{\max}^{K}} \end{array} \right] \tag{18}$$

According to equation 18, ρ is the differentiation coefficient varying between 0 and 1, and it is often considered as 0.5. This coefficient regulates the difference between Δ_{0i} and $\Delta_{\max}$. Therefore, this equation enables the easy solution of decision-making problems in a vague and fuzzy environment.

Grey relation degree represents the relation level between each criterion and compared reference series in a vague decision table. A greater grey relation degree demonstrates a strong relation between x_0 and x_i. In other words, grey relation degree shows how much the compared series resemble the reference series. Finally, fuzzy grey relation coefficient in a decision table with n criteria is calculated by virtue of below-given equation 19.

$$r_i = r(x_0, x_i) = \frac{1}{n} \sum_{j=1}^{n} r(x_0(j), x_i(j)) \tag{19}$$

4. A BRIEF OVERVIEW OF THE VIKOR PROCESS

VIKOR was first proposed in 1998 by Opricovic (1998), as an algorithm grounded in the ideal solution method, in order to solve multi-criteria decision-making problems. The method was first used for multi-criteria optimisation of complex systems in a study by Opricovic and Tzeng (2004). The VIKOR method targets determining the sequence of alternatives under criteria that contradict with one another and that do not possess the same scale, as well as choosing the most appropriate one. First of all, VIKOR defines positive ideal solution and negative ideal solution. Positive ideal solution is the best among alternatives within evaluated criteria, whereas negative ideal solution is the worst among the same alternatives. This method determines a convenient solution for decision-makers, by ensuring the biggest group benefit for "majority", and the smallest individual regret for "dissidents". VIKOR finds appropriate solutions by means of forming order lists, just as TOPSIS does. The TOPSIS method uses vector normalisation, whereas VIKOR employs linear normalisation (Tzeng et al., 2005). In addition, TOPSIS prefers the alternative which is closest to positive ideal solution and farthest from negative ideal solution as the best option (Chu et al., 2007). Regarding VIKOR, this method calculates ideal positive and negative rates, and designates the proper solution depending on these advantage rates (Tzeng et al., 2005). This is why, according to Opricovic and Tzeng (2004), the VIKOR method can better reflect the ideas of decision-makers. Among suitable solutions of VIKOR, f_1^* represents the positive ideal solution of first criterion, and f_1^- represents the negative ideal solution of the first criterion. The proper solution F^c is closest to the optimal solution, and it is the convenient result between two criteria. Appropriate solutions are calculated as $\Delta f_1 = f_1^* - f_1^c$ and $\Delta f_2 = f_2^* - f_2^c$, as is given in Figure 3 below.

In the existing literature, there are limited numbers of studies with respect to supplier selection by the VIKOR method. You can find below a short analysis on these studies. Tianchang et al. (2008) carried out supplier evaluation and selection by using rough set theory (RST) and VIKOR methods among three alternatives, in consideration of price, on-time delivery rate, qualification rate, geographical position and comprehensive strength. Guo and Zhang (2008) established a model according to which, in the first stage, supplier selection criteria were determined with RST and in the second, best supplier selection was carried out by means of the VIKOR method.

For the purpose of defining and evaluating the best possible supplier and vendor, Chen and Wang (2009) suggested a rational and systematic model that uses a fuzzy VIKOR method in order to develop the best alternative and compromise solution under each selection criterion. In their study, Sanayei et al. (2010) used the VIKOR method for a supplier selection problem in a fuzzy environment. Tarokh et al. (2011) expanded the VIKOR method for supplier selection by using a mechanism that designates target weights grounded in the Shannon entropy concept. In this method, the final decision is obtained through using the results of regret, group benefit, and Q values.

By means of a fuzzy multi-criteria decision-making method, Wu and Liu (2011) offer a solution to supplier selection problems based on the VIKOR algorithm that complies with the entropy method, which ensures integrated TOPSIS and attributes weights to criteria.

4.1. Proposed Fuzzy-VIKOR Model (PFVM)

Multi-criteria decision problems include the calculation of the most useful alternatives from the whole group, and the range these alternatives. An alternative solution that provides the highest benefit is con-

Figure 3. Appropriate and compromise solutions of VIKOR

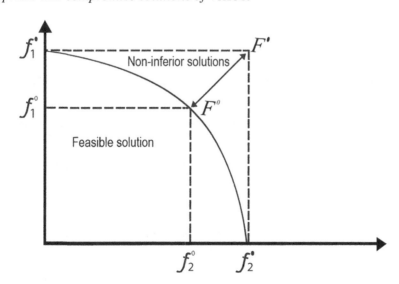

sidered as an optimal solution. Below, you can see the main steps of the VIKOR method, adapted to fuzzy logic.

Representation of fuzzy decision matrix. Fuzzy decision matrix is represented with equation 20 as follows:

$$F = [f_{ij}]_{mxn} \tag{20}$$

where f_{ij} is the fuzzy performance of alternative number $i.$, according to criterion no. $j.$.

Determination of fuzzy positive ideal and fuzzy negative ideal solution. Best fuzzy value f_i^* and worst fuzzy f_i^- values of all criteria functions are defined as follows.

$$A^* = \max_j f_{ij} = \{f_1^*, f_2^*, f_3^*, \ldots\ldots\ldots f_n^*\}$$

$$A^- = \min_j f_{ij} = \{f_1^-, f_2^-, f_3^-, \ldots\ldots\ldots f_n^-\} \tag{21}$$

$$i = 1, 2, \ldots\ldots\ldots, m$$

$$j = 1, 2, \ldots\ldots\ldots, n$$

Calculation of benefit and regret criteria. Fuzzy benefit and regret criteria are determined for each alternative by means of the below-given equations:

$$S_i = \sum_{i=1}^{n} w_j (f_j^* - f_{ij}) / (f_j^* - f_j^-) \tag{22}$$

$$R_i = \max_j [w_j (f_j^* - f_{ij}) / (f_j^* - f_j^-)] \tag{23}$$

where, S_i and R_i represent benefit and regret criteria respectively, and w_j means the weight of criterion no. j.

Calculation of the VIKOR index. Fuzzy VIKOR index is calculated via the following equation:

$$Q_i = v \left[\frac{S_i - S^*}{S^- - S^*} \right] + (1 - v) \left[\frac{R_i - R^*}{R^- - R^*} \right] \tag{24}$$

where Q_i represents the VIKOR value of alternative no. $i.$ ($i = 1, 2, \ldots\ldots\ldots, m$).

$$S^* = \min_i (S_i);\ S^- = \max_i (S_i);\ R^* = \min_i (R_i);\ R^- = \max_i (R_i)$$

and v is the weight of maximum group benefit, and it is often accepted as 0.5. The alternative with the lowest VIKOR value is chosen as the best solution.

5. A NUMERICAL EXAMPLE

In this section, a sample problem in literature (Ordoobadi, 2009) is considered in order to reveal the application steps of the proposed Fuzzy Grey Relational Analysis and Fuzzy VIKOR methods. The linguistic performance rates given by decision-makers to suppliers pursuant to chosen criteria of the problem can be seen in Table 3.

First of all, decision tables of the treated problem should be transformed into a matrix format that can be solved by means of developed methods. For this purpose, the linguistic supplier performance rates in Table 3 are transformed into a fuzzy performance table, as shown in Table 4 by means of using the linguistic scale in given Table 2. For example, linguistic performance of Supplier 1 with respect to sub-criterion customer rejection rate under quality control criteria is determined as (VG). This performance rate is obtained as $(4, 6, 6, 8)$ pursuant to Table 2. The remaining performance rates have been transformed into fuzzy numbers through the same approach. The fuzzy performance grading matrix for all criteria can be as shown Table 4.

Then, linguistic importance weights for each criterion (knot) in Figure 1 are transformed into fuzzy weights thanks to the linguistic scale in Table 1. This operation is calculated by multiplying the weight of each sub-criterion from knot to branches with the weight of the criterion to which it is connected. For example, the quality control rejection rate (H) regarding the first criterion is multiplied with the importance weight of quality criteria, and the values

$$w_1 = (0.4, 0.6, 0.6, 0.8)\ (0.6, 0.8, 1.0, 1.0 = (0.24, 0.48, 0.6, 0.8)$$

Table 3. Linguistic performance rate of suppliers according to chosen criterion (Ordoobadi, 2009)

		S1	**S2**	**S3**
Quality	Customer reject rate	G	EX	VG
	Quality control reject rate	VG	VG	G
Delivery	Delivery lead time	P	G	P
	Change in delivery date	EX	P	VG
	Special request	G	P	VG
Service	Reliability	P	G	EX
	Access	VG	EX	P
	Understanding	G	P	G
Costs	Purchase price	P	G	G
	Logistic cost	VG	G	P

Table 4. Fuzzy performance matrix for suppliers

		S1	S2	S3
Quality	Customer reject rate	(2,4,4,6)	(6,8,10,10)	(4,6,6,8)
	Quality control reject rate	(4,6,6,8)	(4,6,6,8)	(2,4,4,6)
Delivery	Delivery lead time	(0,0,2,4)	(2,4,4,6)	(0,0,2,4)
	Change in delivery date	(6,8,10,10)	(0,0,2,4)	(4,6,6,8)
	Special request	(2,4,4,6)	(0,0,2,4)	(4,6,6,8)
Service	Reliability	(0,0,2,4)	(2,4,4,6)	(6,8,10,10)
	Access	(4,6,6,8)	(6,8,10,10)	(0,0,2,4)
	Understanding	(2,4,4,6)	(0,0,2,4)	(2,4,4,6)
Costs	Purchase price	(0,0,2,4)	(2,4,4,6)	(2,4,4,6)
	Logistic cost	(4,6,6,8)	(2,4,4,6)	(0,0,2,4)

are obtained. Using a similar approach for the rest of the criteria, the fuzzy weight values matrix given in Table 5 is calculated.

5.1. Solution of Proposed Fuzzy Grey Relation Analysis Method

In the fuzzy grey relation analysis method, first of all, the decision matrix is obtained. For this purpose, a weighted fuzzy decision matrix per criterion is calculated for each supplier by multiplying the weights with fuzzy supplier performance values given in Table 5. This matrix is presented in Table 6.

Very big or very small values of criteria in a fuzzy decision matrix prevent the realisation of correct analyses. Therefore, values of criteria should be normalised or standardised by means of a transformation method. For the transformation process, the min-max normalisation method is applied. According to this method, criterion is examined in two aspects: criteria of benefits and those of costs. For enterprises, the aim is to set the benefit criterion value big (the bigger the better), and cost criterion small (the smaller

Table 5. Fuzzy weight values of criteria

		Weight
Quality	Quality control reject rate	(0.24, 0.48, 0.6, 0.8)
	Customer reject rate	(0.12, 0.32, 0.4, 0.6)
Delivery	Delivery lead time	(0.16, 0.36, 0.36, 0.64)
	Change in delivery date	(0.032, 0.144, 0.144, 0.384)
	Special request	(0.064, 0.216, 0.216, 0.512)
Service	Reliability	(0.04, 0.16, 0.16, 0.36)
	Access	(0.0, 0.0, 0.032, 0.144)
	Understanding	(0.008, 0.064, 0.064, 0.216)
Costs	Purchase price	(0.24, 0.36, 0.48, 0.8)
	Logistic cost	(0.16, 0.36, 0.36, 0.64)

Table 6. Weighted fuzzy decision matrix

	S1	S2	S3
Quality	0.96, 3.84, 4.8,9.6	1.92, 5.76, 8.4, 12.8	1.2, 4.16, 5.2, 10
Delivery	0.32, 2.016, 3.024, 9.472	0.32, 1.44, 2.16, 7.424	0.384, 2.16, 2.88, 9.728
Service	0.016, 0.256, 0.768, 3.888	0.08, 0.64, 1.088, 4.464	0.256, 1.536, 1.92, 5.472
Costs	0.64, 2.16, 3.36, 8.32	0.8, 3.36, 3.84, 8.64	0.48, 1.92, 3.12, 7.36

the better). In the fuzzy decision table in Table 6, quality, delivery and service are criteria of benefit, whereas costs criteria constitute the criteria of cost. Using equation 9 for benefit and equation 10 for cost criteria, the normalised fuzzy decision matrix is acquired, as seen in Table 7.

Then, the reference series of the normalised fuzzy decision matrix are obtained as shown below, using equation 11.

$$X(0) = \{(1, 1, 1, 1), (1, 1, 1, 1), (1, 1, 1, 1), (1, 1, 1, 1)\}$$

Distances between normalised values and reference series are calculated via equation 12, and a fuzzy distance matrix is acquired as presented in Table 8.

Fuzzy numbers in distance matrix are calculated by virtue of equation 18. There values are transformed into the crisp values as shown in Table 9, in order to constitute grey relation degree matrix.

Grey relation coefficient matrix, which determines the ranking of each candidate obtained by means of applying equation 19 to values in the grey relation degree matrix, is provided in Table 10.

Table 7. Normalised fuzzy decision matrix

	S1	S2	S3
Quality	(0, 0, 0, 0)	(1, 1, 1, 1)	(0.25, 0.167, 0.111, 0.125)
Delivery	(0, 0.8, 1, 0.889)	(0, 0, 0, 0)	(1, 1, 0.833, 1)
Service	(0, 0, 0, 0)	(0.267, 0.3,0.278,0.364)	(1, 1, 1, 1)
Costs	(0.5, 0.167, 0.333, 0.75)	(1, 1, 1, 1)	(0, 0, 0, 0)

Table 8. Fuzzy distance matrix

	S1	S2	S3
Quality	(1, 1, 1, 1)	(0, 0, 0, 0)	(0.75, 0.833, 0.889, 0.875)
Delivery	(1, 0.2, 0, 0.11)	(1, 1, 1, 1)	(0, 0, 0.167, 0.01)
Service	(1, 1, 1, 1)	(0.733, 0.7, 0.722, 0.636)	(0, 0, 0, 0)
Costs	(0.5, 0.833, 0.667, 0.25)	(0, 0, 0, 0)	(1, 1, 1, 1)

Table 9. Grey relation degree matrix

	S1	S2	S3
Quality	0.5	1.5	0.558
Delivery	1.145	0.5	1.375
Service	0.5	0.624	1.5
Costs	0.693	1.5	0.5

Table 10. Candidate ranking matrix

	S1	S2	S3
$R_i R_i$	0.70962	1.03106	0.98335
Rank	3	1	2

5.2. Solution of Proposed Fuzzy VIKOR Method

In this section, the sample problem which is solved by fuzzy GRA in previous section will be solved by proposed fuzzy VIKOR method. The steps of the proposed method are given as follows:

Step 1: First, the decision matrix is obtained according to the sample problem in fuzzy VIKOR method. In this step, the decision matrix in table 4 is taken into account in order to evaluate the suppliers.

Step 2: Fuzzy positive ideal f_i^* and fuzzy negative ideal f_i^- values are used for each criterion and its sub-criterion, and through equation 21, related values are obtained as shown in Table 11.

Quality, delivery and Service are criteria of benefit, whereas costs criteria constitute the criteria of cost. For companies, the aim is that the benefit criterion value is big (the bigger the better), whereas cost criterion is small (the smaller the better). For this reason, for cost criterion, the minimum fuzzy positive ideal value is taken as $\{(0,0,2,4),(0,0,2,4)\}$, whereas the maximum fuzzy negative value is taken as $\{(2,4,4,6),(4,6,6,8)\}$. In this way, the supplier with low costs will be preferred by the enterprise.

Table 11. Fuzzy ideal best value and fuzzy ideal worst value

	A^*	A^-
Quality	$\{(6,8,10,10),(4,6,6,8)\}$	$\{(2,4,4,6),(2,4,4,6)\}$
Delivery	$\{(2,4,4,6),(6,8,10,10), (4,6,6,8)\}$	$\{(0,0,2,4),(0,0,2,4), (0,0,2,4)\}$
Service	$\{(6,8,10,10),(6,8,10,10), (2,4,4,6)\}$	$\{(0,0,2,4),(0,0,2,4), (0,0,2,4)\}$
Costs	$\{(0,0,2,4),(0,0,2,4)\}$	$\{(2,4,4,6),(4,6,6,8)\}$

Step 3: Fuzzy benefit values are calculated via equation 22 for each criterion and supplier, and the benefit table in Table 12 is obtained.

In order to transform values in the fuzzy benefit table into real numbers, the centroid defuzzification method is used, and the benefit criterion for each alternative is calculated. Similarly, regret criterion is calculated by means of equation 23. Calculated values for both criteria are given in Table 13.

Step 4: The fuzzy VIKOR index is calculated in order to order the alternatives. To this end, first of all, minimum and maximum values of benefit and regret values calculated in the third step are obtained as $S^* = 0.808$, $S^- = 1.753$, $R^* = 0.418$, $R^- = 0.726$, respectively. Then, these values are put into equation 24, and the VIKOR index values are calculated as follows in Table 14.

5.3. Comparative Results

The results of recommended methods are compared with results obtained by Labib (2011), who solves the same problem with the AHP method. Results of this comparison are given in Table 15.

Table 12. Fuzzy benefit table

	S1	S2	S3
Quality	0,178	0.053	0.143
Delivery	0.388	0.156	0.329
Service	0.461	0.181	0.418
Costs	0.726	0.418	0.638

Table 13. Benefit and regret values

	S1	S2	S3
S_i	1.753	0.808	1.516
R_i	0.726	0.418	0.638

Table 14. VIKOR index values

	S1	S2	S3
Q_i	1	0	0.731
Rank	3	1	2

Table 15. Results of comparison between methods

		S1	S2	S3
Ordoobadi's study (Fuzzy)	Result	13.50	15.78	14.44
	Rank	3	1	2
Proposed fuzzy grey relation model	Result	0.71	1.031	0.983
	Rank	3	1	2
Proposed fuzzy VIKOR model	Result	1	0	0.731
	Rank	3	1	2
Labib's study (AHP)	Result	0.407	0.316	0.277
	Rank	1	2	3

Finally, two new methods have been proposed and used in this study: First, the Fuzzy Grey Relational Analysis method; second, the Fuzzy VIKOR method. Application steps of these methods are explained in chapters of the previous sections by means of a sample problem. As seen in the comparison table, the proposed fuzzy grey relation analysis and fuzzy VIKOR methods gave the same results with Ordoobadi's model. But the AHP method, which is proposed by Labib, yielded a different solution from our model and Ordoobadi's model.

6. CONCLUSION AND REMARKS

Developments in communication and technology have rendered all markets global. As a result of this changing environment, customer expectations have increased. Companies have to carry out more rapid and agile production processes in order to meet the expectations of customers. Along with changes they make in production and design, companies are now aware of the importance of materials and services provided by suppliers when it comes to meeting customer requirements. The supply process within the supply chain includes meeting the requirements of raw material and components necessary for manufacturing end product. The problem of choosing supplier or suppliers who will meet the needs of companies is in fact a multi-criteria decision-making problem.

Despite many methodologies with respect to supplier selection problem, there are insufficient studies regarding which one is the most appropriate Wu and Liu (2011). Present studies rather focus on a new method and aim at offering a solution to the treated problem. In the supplier selection problem, chosen criteria are as important as the treating method. Results for similar problems may hugely vary depending on chosen criteria and methods. In this case, it is quite difficult to decide which method and related results should be taken into account. In this study, a sample problem that already exists in literature has been handled in order to carry out a comparative analysis on supplier evaluation models. Then, this problem is separately solved by two models previously recommended. Results via these models are compared with results of the fuzzy logic method used in the study, including related problems. In addition,

- In future studies, comparisons in consideration of the same problem via different methods will contribute to existing literature.

- Having investigated the information provided in table 15, it can be said that the models proposed in selecting the most appropriate suppliers produce similar results as the results of the study suggested by Ordoobadi (2009) while they are different to the ones found in Labib (2011). Therefore, these proposed models should be tested on the problems to which fuzzy-based models were applied and several investigations should be conducted accordingly to observe if the results produced will be similar.

- Solving the same problem using different models and techniques may yield different results. This creates a problem for managers in terms of which model of technique to choose among several alternatives. In order to overcome such a problem, a variety of optimization studies can be conducted that could be considered as a contribution to the existing body of literature.

In addition to this, software should be created for the recommended methods in order to make them available for practical usage in the hands of implementing persons.

REFERENCES

Bai, C., & Sarkis, J. (2011). Evaluating supplier development programs with a grey based rough set methodology. *Expert Systems with Applications*, *38*(11), 13505–13517.

Bhutta, K. S., & Huq, F. (2002). Supplier selection problem: A comparison of the total cost of ownership and analytic hierarchy process approaches. *Supply Chain Management. International Journal (Toronto, Ont.)*, *7*(3), 126–135.

Chamodrakas, I., Batis, D., & Martakos, D. (2010). Supplier selection in electronic marketplaces using satisficing and fuzzy AHP. *Expert Systems with Applications*, *37*(1), 490–498. doi:10.1016/j.eswa.2009.05.043

Chan, N., Felix, T. S., Kumar, M. K., Tiwari, H. C., Lau, W., & Choy, K. L. (2008). Global supplier selection: A fuzzy-AHP approach. *International Journal of Production Research*, *46*(14), 3825–3857. doi:10.1080/00207540600787200

Chandramohan, A., Rao, M. V. C., & Arumugam, S. M. (2006). Two new and useful defuzzification methods based on root mean square value. Soft Computing-A Fusion Of Foundations. *Methodologies And Applications*, *10*(11), 1047–1059.

Chen, C. T. (2000). Extensions of the TOPSIS for group decision-making under fuzzy environment. *Fuzzy Sets and Systems*, *114*(1), 1–9. doi:10.1016/S0165-0114(97)00377-1

Chen, L. Y., & Wang, T. (2009). Optimizing Partners' Choice in IS/IT Outsourcing Process: The Strategic Decision of Fuzzy VIKOR. *Int. J. Produciton Economics*, *120*(1), 233–242. doi:10.1016/j.ijpe.2008.07.022

Chu, M. T., Shyu, J., Tzeng, G. H., & Khosla, R. (2007). Comparison Among Three Analytical Methods For Knowledge Communities Group Decision Analysis. *Expert Systems with Applications*, *33*(4), 1011–1024. doi:10.1016/j.eswa.2006.08.026

Deng, J. L. (1982). Control problems of grey systems. *Systems & Control Letters*, *1*(5), 288–294. doi:10.1016/S0167-6911(82)80025-X

Dubois, D., & Padre, H. (1980). *Fuzzy Sets and Systems: Theory and Applications*. New York: Academic Press.

Fazlollahtabar, H., Mahdavi, I., Ashoori, M. T., Kaviani, S., & Mahdavi-Amiri, N. (2011). A multi-objective decision-making process of supplier selection and order allocation for multi-period scheduling in an electronic market. *International Journal of Advanced Manufacturing Technology*, *52*(9-12), 1039–1052. doi:10.1007/s00170-010-2800-6

Guneri, A. F., & Kuzu, A. (2009). Supplier selection by using a fuzzy approach in just-in-time: A case study. *International Journal of Computer Integrated Manufacturing*, *22*(8), 774–783. doi:10.1080/09511920902741075

Guo, J., & Zhang, W. (2008). Selection of Suppliers Based on Rough Set Theory and VIKOR Algorithm. *Intelligent Information Technology Application Workshops. IITAW '08. International Symposium on*, (pp. 49 – 52).

Guo-Dong, L., Yamaguchi, D., & Nagai, M. (2007). A grey-based decision-making approach to the supplier selection problem. *Mathematical and Computer Modelling*, *46*(3-4), 573–581. doi:10.1016/j.mcm.2006.11.021

Guo-Dong, L., Yamaguchi, D., & Nagai, M. (2008). A grey-based rough decision-making approach to supplier selection. *International Journal of Advanced Manufacturing Technology*, *36*(9-10), 1032–1040. doi:10.1007/s00170-006-0910-y

Hadi-Vencheh, A. (2011). A new nonlinear model for multiple criteria supplier-selection problem. *International Journal of Computer Integrated Manufacturing*, *24*(1), 32–39. doi:10.1080/0951192X.2010.527372

Hsia, K. H., & Wu, J. H. (1998). A study on the data preprocessing in grey relational analysis. *J. Chinese Grey System Association*, *1*(1), 47–53.

Huang, Y. K., Shieh, S. L., Jane, C. J., & Jheng, D. J. (2008). A new Grey Relation Analysis Applied to the Assert Allocation of stock portfolio. *Int. J. Computational Cognition*, *6*(3), 6–12.

Karpak, B., Kumcu, E., & Kasuganti, R. R. (2001). Purchasing materials in the supply chain: Managing a multi-objective task. *European. Journal of Purchasing and Supply Management*, *7*(1), 209–216. doi:10.1016/S0969-7012(01)00002-8

Kuo, M. S., & Liang, G. S. (2011). Combining VIKOR with GRA techniques to evaluate service quality of airports under fuzzy environment. *Expert Systems with Applications*, *38*(3), 304–1312. doi:10.1016/j.eswa.2010.07.003

Labib, A. W. (2011). A supplier selection model: A comparison of fuzzy logic and the analytic hierarchy process. *International Journal of Production Research*, *49*(21), 6287–6299. doi:10.1080/00207543.2010.531776

Liao, C. N., & Kao, H. P. (2011). An integrated fuzzy TOPSIS and MCGP approach to supplier selection in supply chain management. *Expert Systems with Applications*, *38*(9), 10803–10811. doi:10.1016/j.eswa.2011.02.031

Liou, T. S., & Wang, M. J. (1992). Ranking fuzzy numbers with integral value. *Fuzzy Sets and Systems*, *50*(3), 247–255. doi:10.1016/0165-0114(92)90223-Q

Lu, I. J., Lin, S. J., & Lewis, C. (2008). Grey relation analysis of motor vehicular energy consumption in Taiwan. *Energy Policy*, *36*(7), 2556–2561. doi:10.1016/j.enpol.2008.03.015

Mendel, J. (1995). Fuzzy logic systems for engineering: A tutorial. *Proceedings of the IEEE*, *83*(3), 345–377. doi:10.1109/5.364485

Nydick, R. L., & Hill, R. P. (1992). Using the analytic hierarchy process to structure the supplier selection procedure. *Int. J. Purchasing and Materials Management*, *28*(2), 31–36.

Onal, S. A., & Kilincci, O. (2011). Fuzzy AHP approach for supplier selection in a washing machine company. *Expert Systems with Applications*, *38*(8), 9656–9664. doi:10.1016/j.eswa.2011.01.159

Onut, S., & Kara, S. S., & Isik, E. (2009). Long term supplier selection using a combined fuzzy MCDM approach: A case study for a telecommunication company. *Expert Systems with Applications, 36*(2), 3887–3895.

Opricovic, S. (1998). *Multi-Criteria Optimization of Civil Engineering Systems*. Belgrade: Faculty of Civil Engineering.

Opricovic, S., & Tzeng, G. H. (2004). Compromise solution by MCDM methods: A comparative analysis of VIKOR and TOPSIS. *European Journal of Operational Research*, *156*(2), 445–455. doi:10.1016/S0377-2217(03)00020-1

Ordoobadi, S. M. (2009). Development of a supplier selection model using fuzzy logic. *Supply Chain Management. International Journal (Toronto, Ont.)*, *14*(4), 314–327.

Ozkok, B. A., & Tiryaki, F. (2011). A compensatory fuzzy approach to multi-objective linear supplier selection problem with multiple-item. *Expert Systems with Applications*, *38*(9), 11363–11368. doi:10.1016/j.eswa.2011.03.004

Runkler, T. A. (1996). Extended Defuzzification Methods and Their Properties. *IEEE Transactions*, 694-700.

Saaty, T. L. (1980). *The analytic hierarchy process*. New York: McGraw-Hill.

Sanayei, A., Mousavi, S. F., & Yazdankhah, A. (2010). Group Decision Making Process For Supplier Selection With VIKOR Under Fuzzy Environment. *Expert Systems with Applications*, *37*(1), 24–30. doi:10.1016/j.eswa.2009.04.063

Sari, B., Sen, T., & Kilic, S. E. (2008). AHP model for the selection of partner companies in virtual enterprises. *International Journal of Advanced Manufacturing Technology*, *38*(3-4), 367–376. doi:10.1007/s00170-007-1097-6

Song, Q., & Jamalipour, A. (2005). An adaptive quality-of-service network selection mechanism for heterogeneous mobile networks. *Wireless Communications and Mobile Computing*, *5*(6), 697–708. doi:10.1002/wcm.330

Song, Q., Shepperd, M., & Mair, C. (2005). Using grey relational analysis to predict software effort with small data sets. *11th IEEE International Software Metrics Symposium*. doi:10.1109/METRICS.2005.51

Tarokh, M. J., Shemshadi, A., Shirazi, H., & Toreihi, M. (2011). A fuzzy VIKOR method for supplier selection based on entropy measure for objective weighting. *Expert Systems with Applications*, *38*(10), 12160–12167. doi:10.1016/j.eswa.2011.03.027

Tianchang, L., Zhiwei, Z., & Lin, Z. (2008). Evaluation and selection of suppliers in supply chain based on RST and VIKOR algorithm. *Control and Decision Conference, CCDC 2008*. doi:10.1109/CCDC.2008.4597658

Toloo, M., & Nalchigar, S. (2011). A new DEA method for supplier selection in presence of both cardinal and ordinal data. *Expert Systems with Applications*, *38*(12), 14726–14731. doi:10.1016/j.eswa.2011.05.008

Tsai, C. H., Chang, C. L., & Chen, L. (2003). Applying grey relational analysis to the vendor evaluation model. *Int. J. The Computer. The Internet and Management*, *11*(3), 45–53.

Tzeng, G. H., Lin, C. W., & Opricovic, S. (2005). Multi- Criteria Analysis of Alternative-Fuel Buses for Public Transportation. *Energy Policy*, *33*(11), 1373–1383. doi:10.1016/j.enpol.2003.12.014

Vahdani, B., & Zandieh, M. (2010). Selecting suppliers using a new fuzzy multiple criteria decision model: The fuzzy balancing and ranking method. *International Journal of Production Research*, *48*(18), 5307–5326. doi:10.1080/00207540902933155

Vinodh, S., Ramiya, R. A., & Gautham, S. G. (2011). Application of fuzzy analytic network process for supplier selection in a manufacturing organisation. *Expert Systems with Applications*, *38*(1), 272–280. doi:10.1016/j.eswa.2010.06.057

Wang, J. W., Cheng, C. H., & Kun-Cheng, H. (2009). Fuzzy hierarchical TOPSIS for supplier selection. *Applied Soft Computing*, *9*(1), 377–386. doi:10.1016/j.asoc.2008.04.014

Wang, Q. P., Zhang, D. H., & Hu, H. Q. (2007). A method of Grey Incidence Analysis for Group Decision-Making under Fuzzy Information. *Proceedings of International Conference on Grey Systems and Intelligent Services*. doi:10.1109/GSIS.2007.4443263

Weber, C. A., Current, J. R., & Benton, W. C. (1991). Vendor selection criteria and methods. *European Journal of Operational Research*, *50*(1), 2–18. doi:10.1016/0377-2217(91)90033-R

Wen, K. L. (2004). *Grey Systems: Modeling and Prediction*. YangSky Scientific Press.

Wu, D. (2009). Supplier selection in a fuzzy group setting: A method using grey related analysis and Dempster–Shafer theory. *Expert Systems with Applications*, *36*(5), 8892–8899. doi:10.1016/j.eswa.2008.11.010

Wu, H. H. (2002). A comparative study of using grey relational analysis in multiple attribute decision making problems. *Quality Engineering*, *15*(2), 209–217. doi:10.1081/QEN-120015853

Wu, M., & Liu, Z. (2011). The supplier selection application based on two methods: VIKOR algorithm with entropy method and Fuzzy TOPSIS with vague sets method. *Int. J. Management Science and Engineering Management*, *6*(2), 110–116.

Yang, C. C., & Chen, B. S. (2006). Supplier selection using combined analytical hierarchy process and grey relational analysis. *Journal of Manufacturing Technology Management, 17*(7), 926–941. doi:10.1108/17410380610688241

Yucel, A., & Guneri, A. F. (2011). A weighted additive fuzzy programming approach for multi-criteria supplier selection. *Expert Systems with Applications, 38*(5), 6281–6286. doi:10.1016/j.eswa.2010.11.086

Zadeh, L. A. (1965). Fuzzy Sets. *Information and Control, 8*(3), 338–353. doi:10.1016/S0019-9958(65)90241-X

KEY TERMS AND DEFINITIONS

Fuzzy Logic: It was introduced by Lotfi A. Zadeh in 1965. Fuzzy logic is an extension of Boolean logic based on the mathematical theory of fuzzy sets, which is a generalization of the classical set theory.

Grey Relational Analysis: Grey relational analysis (GRA) is an important application of grey system theory when it comes to estimating a convenient alternative within a set.

Multi Criteria Decision Making: Multi criteria decision making is a sub-discipline of operation research that refers to making decisions in the presence of multiple, usually conflicting, criteria.

Supplier Selection Problem: Finding the right suppliers who are able to provide the companies with the high quality products and services at the reasonable price, at just on time and in the right quantities.

VIKOR: It was first proposed in 1998 by Opricovic, as an algorithm grounded in the ideal solution method, in order to solve multi-criteria decision-making problems.

Chapter 12
A Brief Review of Metaheuristics for Document or Text Clustering

Sinem Büyüksaatçı
Istanbul University, Turkey

Alp Baray
Istanbul University, Turkey

ABSTRACT

Document clustering, which involves concepts from the fields of information retrieval, automatic topic extraction, natural language processing, and machine learning, is one of the most popular research areas in data mining. Due to the large amount of information in electronic form, fast and high-quality cluster analysis plays an important role in helping users to effectively navigate, summarize and organise this information for useful data. There are a number of techniques in the literature, which efficiently provide solutions for document clustering. However, during the last decade, researchers started to use metaheuristic algorithms for the document clustering problem because of the limitations of the existing traditional clustering algorithms. In this chapter, the authors will give a brief review of various research papers that present the area of document or text clustering approaches with different metaheuristic algorithms.

INTRODUCTION

Exponential growth of text documents' volumes is accelerated by a noticeable increase in digital libraries and repositories, social networking applications, company-wide intranets, digitized personal information such as blog articles and emails, etc. The effective usage of computers as well as Internet adds billions of electronic documents to the search area. This increase in both the volume and the variety of text documents requires advances in methodology to automatically understand, process, and summarize the data. Fast and high-quality cluster analysis plays an important role in helping users to effectively navigate, summarize and organize the large amount of information.

DOI: 10.4018/978-1-5225-0075-9.ch012

Cluster analysis has been the subject of many disciplines from past to present. Statisticians, engineers, psychologists, biologists, taxonomists, social scientists, mathematicians, computer scientists, medical researchers and others who are interested in real data have all contributed to cluster analysis. The classic definition of clustering is natural grouping of similar objects that exists in a set of patterns or data points while the similarities between objects in different groups are low. Different distance measures are used to quantify the similarity between two objects like euclidean distance, cosine distance, jaccard coefficient etc. Each measure has its own advantages and disadvantages that make it more or less suitable to a given domain or application area such as bioinformatics, document clustering or categorization. Moreover, choosing an appropriate similarity measure is also crucial for cluster analysis.

Clustering is a kind of unsupervised learning and should not be confused with classification, since unlike classification, no labelled documents are provided in clustering. However in some applications, cluster analysis is referred as unsupervised classification.

Document (or text) clustering, which is a subset of data clustering, is one of the most widely used topics in data mining researches. It includes concepts from the fields of information retrieval, automatic topic extraction, natural language processing, and machine learning. In document clustering, each document is considered as a vector in the term-space and according to documents' similarity; each document is assigned to clusters. Although there are several ways to model a document in document clustering, using the frequency of each term as weight is the popular one.

Document-clustering algorithms are divided into a wide variety of different types in literature such as feature selection methods, distance based clustering algorithms, density based clustering algorithms, word and phrase based algorithms, probabilistic document clustering. On the other hand, hierarchical clustering algorithms and partitional clustering algorithms are the most commonly used ones. Different clustering algorithms have different tradeoffs in terms of effectiveness and efficiency.

Besides these traditional clustering algorithms, because of their robust, fast, and close approximate solution, metaheuristic algorithms are being used for document clustering in recent years.

In this study, first of all, a short view about metaheuristics is given. In addition to that, the authors briefly explain some topics related to the general document clustering procedure like document representation, similarity measures and evaluation of clustering solution. Afterwards, a review of various research papers that present the area of document or text clustering approaches with different metaheuristic algorithms will be summarized in a nutshell.

METAHEURISTICS

The solutions of real life problems can be numerous and sometimes an infinite number of solutions may be possible. In such a case, if the problem admits one solution, this will only actualize with a unique set of parameter values and traditional optimization approaches cannot be applied (Antoniou & Lu, 2007). On the other hand, the size of possible solutions that prevents an exhaustive search, the complexity and difficult constraints of the discussed problems, caused the approximate methods to be popular.

Metaheuristic algorithms, which are a class of approximate methods, have emerged in the 1980's. The word *"heuristic"* has its origin in the old Greek word "heuriskein", meaning the art of discovering new strategies (rules) to solve problems. The suffix *"meta"*, also a Greek word, means upper level methodology. Fred Glover (1986) firstly introduced the term metaheuristic in the paper "Future paths for integer programming and links to artificial intelligence" (Talbi, 2009, p.1).

A metaheuristic is formally defined as an iterative generation process which guides a subordinate heuristic by combining intelligently different concepts for exploring and exploiting the search space, learning strategies are used to structure information in order to find efficiently near-optimal solutions (Osman & Laporte, 1996, p.1). In general, metaheuristic algorithms have been specially developed to find a solution that is "good enough" where a processing time is "small enough".

Blum and Roli (2003) summarized nine properties of metaheuristics as follows:

- Metaheuristics are strategies that "guide" the search process.
- The goal is to efficiently explore the search space in order to find (near–) optimal solutions.
- Techniques, which constitute metaheuristic algorithms, range from simple local search procedures to complex learning processes.
- Metaheuristic algorithms are approximate and usually non-deterministic.
- They may incorporate mechanisms to avoid getting trapped in confined areas of the search space.
- The basic concepts of metaheuristics permit an abstract level description.
- Metaheuristics are not problem-specific.
- Metaheuristics may make use of domain-specific knowledge in the form of heuristics that are controlled by the upper level strategy.
- Today's more advanced metaheuristics use search experience (embodied in some form of memory) to guide the search.

The bases of metaheuristic algorithms vary greatly. Some algorithms express the optimization process by using approaches apparently unrelated to optimization, like behavior of swarms (e.g. particle swarm optimization, ant colony optimization, bat algorithm), natural evolution (e.g. genetic algorithm), physical changes (e.g. simulated annealing, harmony search) while some are based on biological fundamentals (neural networks). However, in general all metaheuristics contain a randomness structure.

The solution of an optimization problem with a metaheurstic is initiated by one or more randomly generated solutions. Then, in each iteration step, the current solution(s) is changed by the new solution(s). The new solutions are often created by search operators, which are known as variation operators. In addition, during the solution of the problem, intensification (exploitation) and diversification (exploration) steps are regularly carried out. The goal of intensification is to improve the quality of solutions. In this step, a current good solution found in a local region is improved using variation operators. In contrast, in the diversification step, new areas of the search space are explored on the global scale and this prevents to trap to the local optima (Yang, 2010, Rothlauf, 2011).

In literature, it can be easily seen that metaheuristic algorithms have become more popular in different research areas and industries. There are lot of studies about continuous optimization problems, combinatorial optimization problems, design problems, layout problems, manufacturing problems, routing and transportation problems, scheduling and sequencing problems, multi-objective optimization problems, classification or clustering problems etc. that are handled with metaheuristics. In this chapter, only the document (or text) clustering problem with metaheuristics is studied.

DOCUMENT REPRESENTATION

In the document clustering procedure, each data has to be converted to the digital form from the standard text form. The most common representation of documents in digital form is the "Vector Space Model" which is presented by Salton et al. (1975). The vector space model, also referred to as the term vector model, is actually an algebraic model that allows the representation of text documents as vectors. In this model, the contents of a document are shaped in multi-dimensional space and a document is represented by a vector d. While $i = 1, 2, ..., M$ and $j = 1, 2, ..., N$; w_{ij} shows the weight of the term i in the document j and the document j is expressed as $d_j = \{ w_{1j}, w_{2j}, ..., w_{Mj} \}$.

The term weight value indicates how important a term is in a document. The most common method to calculate the weight of the term is term frequency-inverse document frequency (TD-IDF) method. In this method, each weight is the product of two components referred to as the *term frequency* and *inverse document frequency*.

The number of times a term occurs in a document is called *term frequency* (*tf*). Term frequency is the ratio of the number of times the term is stated in that document to the total number of terms in the document. Thus, a term seen frequently within a document leads to an increase of weight. The term frequency of term i in the document j is defined by Equation 1:

$$tf_{ij} = \frac{n_{ij}}{\sum_{i=1}^{M} n_{ij}} \tag{1}$$

The *inverse document frequency* (*idf*) is a measure of whether a term is discussed commonly or rarely within all of the documents. It is obtained by dividing the total number of documents by the number of documents that contain the term, and then taking the logarithm of this quotient. Due to the high number of documents in many document sets, this number is compressed through the logarithm function. The inverse document frequency of term i is shown in Equation 2,

$$idf_i = \log_2 \left(\frac{N}{df_i} \right) = \log_2 \left(\frac{N}{\left| \left\{ j \in N : t_i \in d_j \right\} \right|} \right) \tag{2}$$

where df_i is frequency of the term i in the document set and N is the total number of documents in the document set.

In fact, the inverse document frequency solves a problem with non-common words that do not have any effect over the clustering process. If a word is found in all of the documents, both the numerator and the denominator are equal in the inverse document frequency and the term weight automatically gets the value of "0". This case eliminates the effect of the words like "and", "but", "an" etc. (Tarczynski, 2011; Shah ve Mahajan, 2012). Therefore, the terms located within just a few documents can be easily separated through the entire set of documents by the inverse document frequency (Premalatha ve Natarajan, 2010a).

The weight value of the term i in the document j is calculated as follows:

$$w_{ij} = tf_{ij} \times idf_i \qquad (3)$$

Equation 3 shows that the terms, which occur frequently in a document but rarely in a document set, have high power in document clustering (Bisht ve Paul, 2013).

The common problem also seen in similar equations is division by "0". To overcome this problem, two approaches are presented. The first approach is the idea of adding denominator 1, but this will change the results. The second more commonly used approach is removing the words that are not included in any of the documents (Tarczynski, 2011).

SIMILARITY MEASURES

Cluster analysis methods are based on measuring the similarity between a pair of objects. Determination of the similarity between a pair of objects comprises three main stages: selection of variables to be used to define objects, selection of a weight chart for variables and selection of a similarity measure for determining the degree of similarity between the document vectors.

The similarity measures are among the most important elements of almost every clustering algorithm. These measures will not only determine the similarity between the two documents, but they can also be used to calculate the similarity between a document and a set or between two sets (Shah and Mahajan, 2012). A similarity, in fact, reflects the proximity of the target object and the degree of separation.

The cosine similarity is the most commonly used measure to calculate the similarities between two documents in vector space. This factor is measured, depending on the cosine angle between document vectors, as given in Equation 4.

$$\cos\left(d_j, d_k\right) = \frac{d_j \cdot d_k}{\left\|d_j\right\| \times \left\|d_k\right\|} = \frac{\sum_{i=1}^{M}\left(w_{ij} \times w_{ik}\right)}{\sqrt{\sum_{i=1}^{M} w_{ij}^2} \times \sqrt{\sum_{i=1}^{M} w_{ik}^2}} \qquad (4)$$

In Equation 4, d_j and d_k are document vectors. This formula is expressed as $\cos\left(d_j, d_k\right) = d_j \cdot d_k$, where d_j and d_k are unit vectors. If the two document vectors are identical to each other, cosine similarity is 1. If the two document vectors are orthogonal, so they do not contain any common terms, cosine similarity takes a value of 0. As a result, cosine similarity is a non-negative value between [0,1].

Other popular measures, which are used to compare the similarity between documents, are Minkowski distance, Euclidean distance, Manhattan distance and Chebyshev distance.

The Minkowski distance is calculated in a M-dimensional vector space as follows:

$$\text{Distance}\left(d_j, d_k\right) = \left(\sqrt{\sum_{t=1}^{M}\left|d_{t,j} - d_{t,k}\right|^n}\right)^{1/n} \qquad (5)$$

For $n = 2$, the Minkowski distance is transformed into the Euclidean distance. The Euclidean distance is a standard measure that is used for geometric problems. Equation 6 shows the formulation of the Euclidean distance.

$$\text{Distance}_2 \left(d_j, d_k \right) = \sqrt{\sum_{t=1}^{M} \left(d_{t,j} - d_{t,k} \right)^2} \tag{6}$$

In Equation 6, $d_{t,j}$ presents the t-th element in document d_j. If the Euclidean distance is 0, it means that the documents are same with each other. If there is no common point between documents, the distance is calculated as $\sqrt{2}$.

The Manhattan and Chebyshev distances are calculated respectively on the basis of Minkowski distance with Equation 7 and 8 (Anastasiu et al., 2013):

$$\text{Distance}_1 \left(d_j, d_k \right) = \sum_{t=1}^{M} \left| d_{t,j} - d_{t,k} \right| \tag{7}$$

$$\text{Distance}_\infty \left(d_j, d_k \right) = \max_{t=1} \left| d_{t,j} - d_{t,k} \right| \tag{8}$$

EVALUATION OF CLUSTERING RESULTS

One of the most important issues of cluster analysis is the evaluation of the clustering results. Evaluation is made to understand how well the outputs represent the structure of the original data.

There are two kinds of indices for evaluation of clustering results:

- **Internal Quality Indices:** These quality indices are based on a general similarity between the pair of documents and there is no need for any information. Dunn index, Davies-Bouldin index, Calinski-Harabasz index, Silhouette index are some examples of these indices.
- **External Quality Indices:** Some external information is required to calculate this kind of indices. Entropy, the F-measure, purity (purity), accuracy etc. are the indices that are examined in this context.

In the literature, external quality indices were used more commonly in scientific papers. Therefore, some of these indices are presented in this section.

Accuracy is the rate of right clustered documents to the total number of documents in a document set. It is calculated as seen in Equation 9.

$$\text{Accuracy} = \left(\frac{\sum_{i=1}^{K} n_i^+}{n} \right) \times 100\% \tag{9}$$

where n_i^+ is the number of documents that are assigned correctly in cluster i, n is the total number of documents in the whole set and K is the number of clusters. Greater accuracy value is required for a successful clustering solution.

One of the most fundamental indices is the F-measure, which is the harmonic mean of two concepts: precision and recall. If we express these concepts clearer on an example, let's assume that a document set is clustered as A, B, C and the confusion matrix that is obtained from the clustering results is as given in Table 1.

The confusion matrix shows how the predictions are made with respect to the actual one by the model. The diagonal elements show the number of correct clustering made for each cluster, and the off-diagonal elements show the errors made. In the light of this information, for example for cluster A, precision, recall and F-measure values are calculated as follows.

$$\text{Precision}(A) = \frac{tp}{tp + fp} = \frac{tp_A}{tp_A + e_{BA} + e_{CA}} \tag{10}$$

$$\text{Recall}(A) = \frac{tp}{tp + fn} = \frac{tp_A}{tp_A + e_{AB} + e_{AC}} \tag{11}$$

$$\text{F-measure=F}(A) = \frac{2 \times \text{Precision}(A) \times \text{Recall}(A)}{\text{Precision}(A) + \text{Recall}(A)} \tag{12}$$

The F-measure value of whole clusters is calculated using Equation 13, which is based on the weighted average of all F-measure value.

Table 1. Confusion matrix example

Predicted clusters			
Known clusters		A	B	C
	A	tp_A	e_{AB}	e_{AC}
	B	e_{BA}	tp_B	e_{BC}
	C	e_{CA}	e_{CB}	tp_C

$$F = \sum_{i=1}^{K} \frac{n_i}{n} \left\{ F(i) \right\}$$
(13)

Higher value of the F-measure indicates better clustering (Tarczynski, 2011).

LITERATURE REVIEW

Document clustering problem has attracted the attention of many research groups in the field of data mining and have been widely studied in the literature. Due to the current limitations of traditional clustering methods, researchers have started to use metaheuristic algorithms to solve this problem. In particular, swarm-intelligence based algorithms, which are more flexible and robust, have achieved better results than the most commonly used clustering algorithms such as the K-means algorithm. In this section, the authors summarize the document or text clustering approaches with different metaheuristic algorithms.

All the studies that are explained below in detail are listed in Table 2.

Particle swarm optimization (PSO) is one of the swarm intelligence-based algorithms that has proven itself as an effective algorithm to solve many optimization problems. If the title of the document clustering is treated as an optimization problem, which aims to find the optimal cluster centers, it is concerned that the PSO algorithm can be applied to the document clustering solutions.

Cui et al. (2005) proposed a hybrid document clustering algorithm that is based on PSO. They combined the global search capability of the K-means algorithm with the convergence property of the PSO algorithm and hereby they avoided the disadvantages of each algorithm. The proposed algorithm was tried on four document sets that exist in the literature and was compared with K-means and PSO algorithms. They used the average distance between the documents and cluster centers as a performance indicator and trials revealed that the hybrid PSO algorithm creates more meaningful clustering results.

Cui and Potok (2005) later expanded the work of Cui et al. (2005). They used the results of the K-means clustering algorithm as a starting solution for the PSO algorithm and made trials on the same document sets that Cui et al. used. The aim of this study was to determine whether the sequence of the algorithms used in the hybrid PSO algorithm is important.

Cui et al. (2006) formed a document clustering algorithm depending on the moving behavior of some animals such as fish and birds that live in groups in nature. As a result of their experiments on the synthetic data set and the real document set, which contains 100 news articles in 12 categories, the authors found that the new algorithm is better than the K-means clustering algorithm and the ant clustering algorithm. The results were compared according to the F-measure.

Machnik (2007) developed an ant colony optimization based clustering algorithm. In order to prove the feasibility of the developed algorithm in the area of document clustering, the author compared it with the most widely used and applied three clustering algorithms in the literature, namely the K-means algorithm, the single link method and the average link method. In the experimental studies, McCallum newsgroups and the Reuter-21578 document were used and the algorithms were evaluated in terms of intra-cluster variance, purity and time.

Mahdavi and Abolhassani (2009) applied the combination of K-means algorithm and harmony search optimization algorithm to document a clustering problem. The authors conducted experiments on 5 document sets and used the average distance of documents to the cluster centers and the F-measure

Table 2. Document clustering approaches with metaheuristics

Year	Author(s)	Algorithm	Data sets	Evaluation indices
2005	Cui, X., Potok, T. E., Palathingal, P	Hybrid PSO algorithm and K-means algorithm	Text Retrieval Conference (TREC) collection	The average distance of documents to the cluster centroid (ADDC)
2005	Cui, X., Potok, T. E.	Hybrid PSO and K-means algorithm	TREC-5, TREC-6 and TREC-7 collections	ADDC
2006	Cui, X., Gao, J., Potok, T. E.	Flocking based algorithm	One synthetic dataset and one real document collection	F-measure
2007	Machnik, Ł.,	Ant colony optimization algorithm	McCallum newsgroups and Reuters-21578	Intra-cluster variance Purity
2009	Mahdavi, M., Abolhassani, H.	Hybrid K-means algorithm and harmony search algorithm	TREC-5, TREC-6, and TREC-7 collections, San Jose Mercury newspaper articles, DMOZ collection, Usenet newsgroups	ADDC F-measure
2010	Premalatha, K., Natarajan, A. M.	Hybrid PSO algorithm and genetic algorithms	Document collections (Acid et al., 2003)	Fitness value
2012	Gao, X., Lu, Y.	PSO algorithm	20 newsgroups TREC collection	Recall Precision F-measure Entropy Accuracy
2013	Zaw, M. M., Mon, E. E	Cuckoo search optimization algorithm	Web pages	Precision Recall F-measure
2013	Karol, S., Mangat, V.	Hybrid fuzzy C-means and PSO algorithm Hybrid K-means and PSO algorithm	20 newsgroups Reuters-21578	F-measure Entropy
2013	Akter, R., Chung, Y.	Genetic algorithm based evolutionary algorithm	Reuters-21578	F-measure
2013	Azaryuon, K., Fakhar, B.	New ant clustering algorithm	Reuters-21578	Precision Recall
2014	Aly, W. M., Kelleny, H. A.	Cuckoo search optimization algorithm	The corpus of contemporary Arabic	Purity
2015	Forsati, R., Keikha, A., Shamsfard, M.	Bee colony optimization algorithm	San Jose Mercury newspaper articles, 20 Newsgroup WebACE project	F-measure

for evaluating K-means and harmony K-means algorithms. They also compared three known partitioning algorithms, namely genetic K-means algorithm, PSO based clustering algorithm and Mises-Fisher Generative Model based algorithm, with the harmony K-means algorithm according to the run time and cluster quality.

Premalath and Natarajan (2010b) worked on the hybrid PSO and genetic algorithms approach for the document clustering problem. In this hybrid approach, the ability of the genetic algorithm to prevent premature convergence is combined with the PSO algorithm. Three different sets of documents were used for this analysis. The authors compared their algorithm with the K-means and PSO + K-means algorithm that was proposed by Cui and Potok (2005) and demonstrated their hybrid algorithm success.

Gao and Lu (2012) developed a PSO-based automatic document clustering algorithm, which makes the distinction between clusters maximum, while minimizing intra-cluster distribution. The authors used cosine similarity as a distance similarity measure and chose various algorithms for experiments such as K-means, bisection K-means, agglomeration clustering algorithm, graph-based clustering algorithm. Experiments were held on ten different subgroups of 20 newsgroups document sets that have different number of clusters, number of instances or category and five subsets obtained from the TREC (Text Retrieval Conference) collection. According to the recall, precision, F-measure, entropy and accuracy indices, the PSO-based automatic document clustering algorithm achieved much better results than K-means, bisection K-means, agglomeration, graph-based clustering algorithms.

Zaw and Mon (2013) clustered the web documents with the cuckoo search optimization algorithm, which was developed by the inspiration from the behaviors of some cuckoo species. In this study, 300 randomly selected web pages were clustered into 3 different clusters in 100 iterations using the cosine similarity as a distance similarity measure. The authors considered the cluster quality value for the different probability parameters of the algorithm. They also calculated the precision, recall and F-measure indices.

Karol and Mangat (2013) presented the hybrid PSO-based document clustering application. The authors combined two different partitional clustering algorithms, namely fuzzy c-means and K-means clustering algorithms, with the PSO algorithm. Hybrid algorithms' performances were tried on 20 news-groups document sets that contain 2000 and 1000 documents and a Reuters-21578 document set. They compared the presented algorithms with the classic fuzzy c-means and K-means algorithm according to the different number of clusters and computed entropy and F-measure indices. As a result, hybrid algorithms gave better results than all other algorithms on both data sets.

Akter and Chung (2013) developed a solution to the document clustering problem by developing a genetic algorithm based evolutionary algorithm. Instead of applying a genetic algorithm to the entire document set, the authors divided the data set into subgroups and applied a genetic algorithm to each of them. Then they used these results as a set and applied the genetic algorithm again. As a result of experiments achieved on 1000 documents from the Reuters-21578 document set, which includes 5 different titles, the evolutionary algorithm yielded better results than the K-means algorithm and the genetic algorithm. In the experiments, the Davies-Bouldin index was used as a criterion function.

Azaryuon and Fakhar (2013) proposed a new ant clustering algorithm for document clustering by changing the movements of ants, which is completely random in standard ant clustering algorithm. In their algorithm, each ant moved towards the region where carried element of the ant was most similar to elements of that region during the clustering process. If there was a non-carrier ant, this moved into the region where an element was surrounded by non-similar elements. For these movements, it was assumed that each ant had a universal map that shows the location of the documents. The authors tested the proposed algorithm performance on the set of 50 documents derived from a Reuters-21578 document set and compared it with a standard ant clustering algorithm and a K-means algorithm.

Aly and Kelleny (2014) used a cuckoo search algorithm for document clustering. The authors studied this algorithm where the number of nests was dynamic so that they searched the space for different values of the number of clusters. The algorithm's performance was tested on the document set of contemporary Arabic that has 12 different categories and was compared with the K-means algorithm using purity evaluation criteria. The results revealed that the proposed approach has a good performance and reached a higher value of clustering purity when compared with the classical K-means clustering algorithm.

Forsati et al. (2015) improved the classic bee colony optimization algorithm by changing some basic characteristics of the algorithm and applied it to both data sets of clustering and document clustering. For document clustering, the analysis was performed on five different document sets with different number of clusters and number of documents. F-measure was used as performance indices. The improved bee colony optimization algorithm demonstrated a successful performance with respect to the K-means algorithm, genetic algorithm and harmony search based clustering algorithms.

CONCLUSION

Document clustering is a fundamental process in data mining that is used for unsupervised document organization, automatic topic extraction, and information retrieval. In this chapter, the authors tried to give a brief review over various research papers that present the area of document or text clustering approaches with different metaheuristic algorithms. The authors also presented some headings such as document representation, similarity measures and evaluation of clustering results, which are associated with document clustering.

Document clustering has been studied and researched upon during the last twenty years, starting from traditional methods, going on to metaheuristic algorithms. Metaheuristics were preferred because of their effective, robust and fast features. Some researchers claim that most of the metaheuristic algorithms rename the existing concepts by being inspired from the behavior of virtually any species of insects, the flow of water, musicians playing together etc. They accept just a few metaheuristics like tabu search, genetic algorithms and simulated annealing, as novel methods. This idea is a matter of debate and it needs to be addressed in future studies.

REFERENCES

Acid, S., De Campos, L. M., Fernández-Luna, J. M., & Huete, J. F. (2003). An information retrieval model based on simple Bayesian networks. *International Journal of Intelligent Systems*, *18*(2), 251–265. doi:10.1002/int.10088

Akter, R., & Chung, Y. (2013). An Evolutionary Approach for Document Clustering. *IERI Procedia*, *4*, 370–375. doi:10.1016/j.ieri.2013.11.053

Aly, W. M., & Kelleny, H. A. (2014). Adaptation Of Cuckoo Search For Documents Clustering. *International Journal of Computers and Applications*, *86*(1), 4–10. doi:10.5120/14947-3041

Anastasiu, D. C., Tagarelli, A., & Karypis, G. (2013). Document Clustering: The Next Frontier. In C. C. Aggarwal & C. K. Reddy (Eds.), *Data Clustering: Algorithms and Applications* (pp. 305–338). CRC Press.

Antoniou, A., & Lu, W.-S. (2007). *Practical Optimization-Algorithms and Engineering Applications*. Springer Science and Business Media, LLC.

Azaryuon, K., & Fakhar, B. (2013). A Novel Document Clustering Algorithm Based on Ant Colony Optimization Algorithm. *Journal of Mathematics and Computer Science*, *7*, 171–180.

Bisht, S., & Paul, A. (2013). Document Clustering: A Review. *International Journal of Computers and Applications*, *73*(11), 26–33. doi:10.5120/12787-0024

Blum, C., & Roli, A. (2003). Metaheuristics in combinatorial optimization: Overview and conceptual comparison. *ACM Computing Surveys*, *35*(3), 268–308. doi:10.1145/937503.937505

Cui, X., Gao, J., & Potok, T. E. (2006). A flocking based algorithm for document clustering analysis. *Journal of Systems Architecture*, *52*(8), 505–515. doi:10.1016/j.sysarc.2006.02.003

Cui, X., & Potok, T. E. (2005). Document clustering analysis based on hybrid PSO+K-means algorithm. *Journal of Computer Sciences*, 27-33.

Cui, X., Potok, T. E., & Palathingal, P. (2005), Document clustering using particle swarm optimization, *Proceedings of IEEE in Swarm Intelligence Symposium.*

Forsati, R., Keikha, A., & Shamsfard, M. (2015). An improved bee colony optimization algorithm with an application to document clustering. *Neurocomputing*, *159*, 9–26. doi:10.1016/j.neucom.2015.02.048

Gao, X., & Lu, Y. (2012). Automatic text clustering via particle swarm optimization. *International Journal of Digital Content Technology and its Applications, 6*(23), 12-21.

Glover, F. (1986). Future paths for integer programming and links to artificial intelligence. *Computers & Operations Research*, *13*(5), 533–549. doi:10.1016/0305-0548(86)90048-1

Karol, S., & Mangat, V. (2013). Evaluation of text document clustering approach based on particle swarm optimization. *Central European Journal of Computer Science*, *3*(2), 69–90.

Machnik, Ł. (2007). A document clustering method based on ant algorithms. *Task Quarterly*, *11*(1-2), 87–102.

Mahdavi, M., & Abolhassani, H. (2009). Harmony K-means algorithm for document clustering. *Data Mining and Knowledge Discovery*, *18*(3), 370–391. doi:10.1007/s10618-008-0123-0

Osman, I. H., & Laporte, G. (1996). Metaheuristics: A bibliography. *Annals of Operations Research*, *63*(5), 511–623. doi:10.1007/BF02125421

Premalatha, K., & Natarajan, A. M. (2010a). A literature review on document clustering. *Information Technology Journal*, *9*(5), 993–1002. doi:10.3923/itj.2010.993.1002

Premalatha, K., & Natarajan, A. M. (2010b). Hybrid PSO and GA models for Document Clustering. *Int. J. Advance. Soft Comput. Appl*, *2*(3), 302–320.

Rothlauf, F. (2011). Design of Modern Heuristics Principles and Application. Springer. doi:10.1007/978-3-540-72962-4

Salton, G., Wong, A., & Yang, C.-S. (1975). A vector space model for automatic indexing. *Communications of the ACM, 18*(11), 613–620. doi:10.1145/361219.361220

Shah, N., & Mahajan, S. (2012). Document Clustering: A Detailed Review. *International Journal of Applied Information Systems*, 2249-0868.

Talbi, E.-G. (2009). *Metaheuristics from Design to Implementation*. Hoboken, NJ: John Wiley & Sons, Inc.

Tarczynski, T. (2011). Document Clustering-Concepts, Metrics and Algorithms. *International Journal of Electronics and Telecommunications, 57*(3), 271-277.

Yang, X.-S. (2010). *Nature-Inspired Metaheuristic Algorithms*. Luniver Press.

Zaw, M. M., & Mon, E. E. (2013). Web document clustering using cuckoo search clustering algorithm based on levy flight. *International Journal of Innovation and Applied Studies*, *4*(1), 182–188.

KEY TERMS AND DEFINITIONS

Accuracy: The rate of correct clustered documents made by the algorithm over a data set.

Clustering: A natural grouping of similar objects that exists in a set of patterns or data points while the similarities between objects in different groups are low.

Document Clustering: An application of cluster analysis, which browses a collection of documents and organizes them in groups that are called as clusters, according to the determinated similarity measures.

F-Measure: The harmonic mean of precision and recall.

Inverse Term Frequency: A measure of whether a term is discussed common or rare among all the documents.

Metaheuristic: A master strategy that guides and modifies other heuristics to produce solutions beyond those that are normally generated in a quest for local optimality.

Term Frequency: A measure that shows the number of times a term is occurred in a document.

Vector Space Model: An algebraic model that allows the representation of text documents as vectors.

Chapter 13
Churn Prediction in Internet Service Provider Companies

İlayda Ülkü
Istanbul Kültür University, Turkey

Mehmet Yahya Durak
Istanbul Kültür University, Turkey

Fadime Üney-Yüksektepe
Istanbul Kültür University, Turkey

ABSTRACT

As a basic standard of life, internet connects millions of computers in a global network. People use, participate, or access the internet with the help of internet service providers (ISPs). To have better quality of connection, customers are prone to change their ISPs. In the competitive environment, ISPs endeavor to prevent losing their customers which are referred as churn. Thus, churn management takes an important place for ISPs. To investigate customer loyalty status, behavior, and information of the churn possibility in Turkey, a questionnaire is implemented. By using a real data obtained from a survey, promising and applicable results are obtained to predict the churn behavior of ISP customers in Turkey. As an extension of the study, the questionnaire will be applied for a larger population to find accurate results about churn situations. This study will help ISP companies to determine the required advertising campaigns for the customers.

INTRODUCTION

Internet is one of the main standards of life and there are a wide variety of service providers to make people trustworthy. In a competitive market, each company tries to give better quality and efficient internet services. Internet Service Providers (ISPs) provide various packages for internet access. They recommend different type of services according to different customer profile to increase the customer within the ISPs. Therefore, the customers decide on ISP between so many options. No doubt, the customers' decision may often change depending on the competitors' ISP campaign. Thus, to acquiring customers, ISPs have too much expense on advertising.

DOI: 10.4018/978-1-5225-0075-9.ch013

In the competitive environment, ISPs endeavor to prevent losing customer. In order to prevent the loss of customers, ISPs must provide proper and timely decisions. No doubt, huge data collection may contain valuable information. However, to discover valuable information or knowledge, data mining as a new technique will be helpful for decision makers.

Today the market is having change almost in a daily basis. During these changes, many factors, such as increase in competition, new cost models and regulatory changes, play an important role. Now, the ISPs have to invest new services, reduce infrastructure costs and cope with the continuous growth in deployment of new technologies (CISKO, 2015). ISPs provide different type of services due to the customers' behavior, to increase potential number of customers. Thus, customers have opportunities to prefer an ISP and they can easily change their current service provider to another service provider. This kind of customer behavior results as a churn which is defined as an index of customer satisfaction. Therefore, companies try to determine the customers who are likely to churn in advance. Companies may offer some challenging campaigns to these customers.

In the business matter, "churn" indicates the customers' migration that is loss volume of the customers. Therefore, "churn rate" mentions the percentage of the customers who do not have any relation with the organization. That's why organizations try to increase their customer volume by offering them appropriate campaigns in the competitive market (Rouse, 2013).

Every company may have worthful knowledge about their customers. However, the important point is to discover valuable information from the obtained data. Therefore, decision makers try to find some new techniques to discover useful knowledge about their customers. In order to make more precise decisions and make predictions based on the information obtained from analyzing those data, ISPs need to analyze the critical data.

In this research, customer information and behavior is analyzed by using a questionnaire. In the process of creating the survey, interviews were done with relevant IPS organizations in Turkey. After discussions during the interviews, required questions for the survey was created. In the survey, not only the customer information and behavior is analyzed, but also loyalty status of the churn situation is discussed. With this study, the important factors for the churn prediction are introduced by using existing data mining algorithms. The rest of this paper is organized as follows. In the next part of this chapter, broad definitions and discussions are included as a literature review. Churn management is considered in different areas such as, in mobile service providers, banking and insurance, and in ISPs. Then problem statement and methodology part is given to represent the selected data mining method to obtain the results. In the next part, computational results are illustrated, and then future research and conclusion parts are described.

BACKGROUND

Data mining applications can be used in various areas such as, medicine, banking/finance, transportation, sale/marketing, health care and insurance, etc. (Brachman *et. al.,* 1996). To identify the prediction of customer churn situation, a paper is studied by M. Owczarczuk (Owczarczuk, 2010) with the help of logistic regression. Likewise, Nie *et al.* studied with logistic regression (Nie, 2011). However, they expand their study and decision tree model is added to find accurate predictions. There is another study proposed by Shim et al where logistic regression and decision tree is used (Shim *et al.,* 2012). They also extend their study by applying neural network to classify the customers. In addition, Binomial logistic regression model is studied by Keramati and Ardabili to predict customer churn (Keramati & Ardabili, 2011).

The main steps to solve a data mining problem are given in Figure 1. First of all, the problem should be defined. After data collection, data preprocessing is applied. Then, a proper data mining method is selected with an appropriate model and training parameters. The next step is to apply the training data to the algorithm, and finally the evaluation is completed of the generated model (Chen, 2001).

Nowadays, to manage the obtained information successfully, data mining is used as a new technique by ISPs. Analyzing large amount of data to find new and hidden information by improving business efficiency is the main process of data mining. There exist many industries which utilizes data mining to their business processes to achieve competitive advantages and provide business to enlarge. By separating information from a data set and also converting this information into a meaningful structure are main goals of the data mining process (ZENTUT, 2015).

ISP Industry in Turkey

Information Technologies and Communications Authority (ICTA, 2012) is a national telecommunications regulatory authority of Turkey. According to ICTA, by the 3th Quarter of 2014, the market data in Turkey is approximately 40 million broadband internet subscribers. Especially, with the 3G services started to be served since 2009, a remarkable rise in the number of broadband subscribers is observed. Due to the mobile broadband internet service, the largest increase in the number of broadband internet subscribers is observed. These data indicate that Turkey is rapidly adopting the Internet and technology that become a part of our lives. According the results in Figure 2, it seems there are 40 million potential internet users in Turkey (TELKODER, 2015).

Churn Management in Mobile Service Providers

Customer churn management is one of main concepts in mobile service providers and it becomes a more critical problem as the market volume is increasing (Hyeon *et. al.* 2006). Customers frequently churn from one ISP to another if they find better service for their usage. In Turkey, there are 67,68 million mobile subscribers corresponding to 89,5% penetration rate. As of December 2012, three operators Turkcell, Vodafone and Avea have market shares of 51,90%, 28,17% and 19,93% respectively, and also churn rates are 2,65% for Turkcell, 3,21% for Vodafone and 3,90% for Avea in mobile market (ICTA, 2012).

Figure 1. Data mining lifecycle (Chen, 2001)

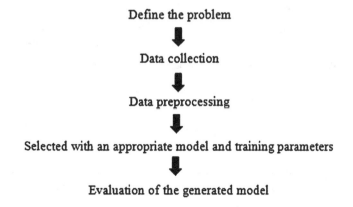

Figure 2. Broadband internet subscribers (TELKODER, 2015)

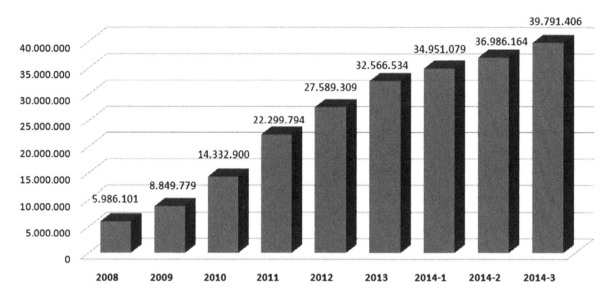

Dividing the number of customers who unsubscribed to the service, by the number of total customers the churn rate can be calculated, Figure 3 represents the churn rates of mobile operators in percentage basis. Numbers of customers are decreasing, when the churn ratio is greater than the customer acquisition ratio. If the churn ratio is high, the companies need to consider that there is a weakness at the competitive environment. During the periods represented in Figure 2, highest churn rate can be seen in Avea, On the other hand, lowest churn rate can be seen in Turkcell among mobile service providers.

Churn Management in Banking and Insurance

As the customer behavior plays an important role to determine campaigns, banking and insurance companies give importance to analyze the churn prediction. Therefore, with the help of churn manage-

Figure 3. Churn Rates of Mobile Operators (ICTA, 2012)

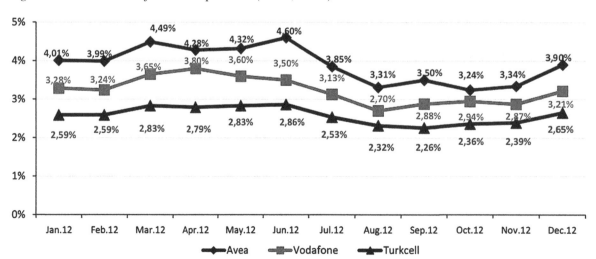

ment, companies can increase customer retention. Bank managers as decision makers can find hidden information by using data mining techniques to discover useful knowledge about their customers (Prasad & Madhavi, 2012).

Churn Management in ISPs

ISP ensures an access to the Internet for a fee. The most common way to connect to an ISP is to use a phone line (dial-up) or broadband connection (cable or DSL). The Internet connection speed is affected with the line capacity of the service provider. Thus, bigger line capacity of service providers will positively affect your connection speed to the Internet. It is one of the most important features while choosing the ISP. In this research, the other important factors for ISP to ensure the customer loyalty are analyzed by applying a questionnaire to observe customer information and behavior. If a customer's current ISP does not satisfy the customer's needs, the customer can easily switch to another ISP. Therefore, to achieve more realistically results, interviews were done with relevant IPS organizations in Turkey.

As, ISPs are interested in customers' churn rate, they try to have such campaigns for specific customers. With the help of data mining, data will be presented in a useful format that will help the decision makers.

Minimum sample size needed for the survey is found as 97 people with %90 confidence level (Roasoft Sample Size Calculator, 2015). In this research, a survey which 150 people attended throughout Istanbul is conducted. As 150 people is greater than minimum sample size which is 97, this research represents with 90% confidence the results are within the margin of error of the correct answer. There are 29 questions in the questionnaire. Some of them are as follows;

- Average Internet Invoice Amount (Monthly)
- How many times did you change your Internet Service Provider?
- Did the old Internet Provider Service call you after churning?

To determine the significance factors for customers, this study will help ISPs to determine the significance factors for customers which will help them to find required advertising campaigns for the customers.

PROBLEM STATEMENT AND METHODOLOGY

There are many industries which utilizes data mining to their business processes to achieve competitive advantages and provide business to enlarge. Because, the important point of having huge amount of data is to find new and hidden information through these huge amount of data. This can be done only by using data mining technique to improve business efficiency. When data mining is used as a technique by ISPs to acquire actual data, understanding customers' behavior in advance will be advantageous for ISPs.

In this research, customer loyalty status of the churn possibility and customer information is analyzed by using a questionnaire. By using a real data obtained from a survey, promising and applicable results are obtained to predict the churn behavior of ISP customers. In the questionnaire, 29 questions related to personal and educational information, income, payment behavior and previous loyalty situation are included. 150 survey results are obtained from the people living in Istanbul.

The Knowledge Discovery in Databases (KDD) process is commonly defined with the stages of selection, pre-processing of the selected data, transformation, data mining, and interpretation. Transforming raw data into understandable format can be done with data pre-processing step in the data mining process. Thus, data pre-processing has an important role in the data mining process (Pyle, 1999). Throughout whole dataset obtained from the survey results, there can be some irrelevant, redundant information, or uncertain data. Therefore, knowledge discovery during the data mining process will be more difficult. Preparation of the data can take considerable amount of time. In this research, feature selection and discretization is used to prepare data for pre-processing step (Kotsiantis *et. al.,* 2006). Many datasets can be studied in many distinct ways for pre-processing step (Janssen, 2015).

- **Data Cleaning:** Data is cleaned through processes such as filling missing values which can be attribute or class value, identifying outliers, and adjusting conflicting data. In the situation of missed class label, the filling missing values process is applied, and to use attribute mean for all samples that are related to the same class is helpful.
- **Data Integration:** By combining data from different sources into a consistent data involves data integration process. These sources can contain multiple databases.
- **Data Transformation:** Normalization, aggregation, generalization, smoothing, and attribute construction are included in data transformation process. In normalization, attribute values are scaled in a specific range or mean and standard deviation is used for scaling the attribute values. Aggregation is used for numeric attributes of multiple analyses of data. On the other hand, generalization is used for nominal attributes. Also, replacing new attributes with existing attributes can be done as attribute construction for data transformation process.
- **Data Reduction:** This step helps to decrease the number of attributes by applying roll-up, slice or dice operations which are data cube aggregation process.
- **Data Discretization:** Transforming numerical variables into categorical variables is done by discretization process. As an example from the survey, there is a question for age categories such as <15, 15-24, 25-34, 35-44, 45-54, 55<. Discretization provides accuracy of the predictive models by decreasing the redundant information. Also, discretization ensures outliers, irrelevant, or redundant information easily of numerical variables.

In the research, feature selection and discretization method is used in the pre-processing step. After that suggested dataset, the results are obtained by running the training and testing dataset in WEKA. Then, best method and dataset is determined as shown in Figure 4.

Data mining can be applied in any organization that needs to find the relationships in larger data. Some data mining methods are such as, classification, cluster analysis, association rule learning, anomaly detection, etc. In this research classification method is used.

CLASSIFICATION

Assigns items in a target class is noted as data classification. The main aim of classification is to estimate the target class in the data. Classification algorithms discover relationships between the values of the target and the values of the predictors. There are different classification algorithms applied with various methods to discover the relationships. The most common methods are Decision Tree Approach, Bayes-

Figure 4. Steps of data mining

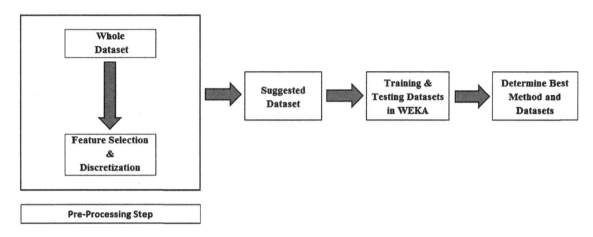

ian Classification, Neural Networks, Support Vector Machines, Genetic Algorithms, and Mathematical Programming (ORACLE, 2015). There are various classification algorithms and the following are helpful to use in churn management.

- **K-Nearest Neighbor (K-NN):** K-Nearest Neighbor (K-NN) is one of the basic instance-based classifiers which determines the undiscovered data by using the closest instance in the known data. The main idea is to decrease computational time while finding the distances, and this is done by dimension reduction techniques. Also, by reviewing the training data set to accelerate the search, some redundant points are removed from the training data set. As, the number of samples in the training data set is getting large, the expected distance to the nearest neighbor is increasing. Therefore, to decrease the dimensionality of the selecting subsets of the predictor variables takes an important step for K-NN (Leung, 2007).
- **Decision Tree (DT):** In a decision tree structure, there is a root node, branches, and leaf nodes (Figure 5). A test on an attribute is represented with an internal node and the outcome of a test is denoted with a branch. A class label is hold by a leaf node. For the churn management, decision trees can be used to identify whether a customer is likely to Churn or Not Churn. Using DT can have some benefits such as, it does not need any domain information, and it is easy to detect as the DT steps are simple and fast.

Figure 5. Decision tree example

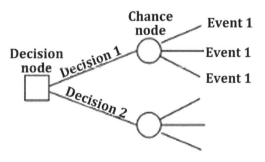

- **Support Vector Machine (SVM):** The support vector machine (SVM) is used to learn classification rules from data. The idea of support vector machine is to take two critical members from different classes where each member defines the channel. Each member is called support vectors. As classification task usually involves training and test sets, every data in the training set has a class label and several attributes. The goal of SVM is to generate a model to predict target values of data in the testing set where only attributes are known. The SVM classification problem can be illustrated as a two class problem as in Figure 6. The straight line in Figure 6 which separates the two classes linearly (Burbidge & Buxton, 2015).
- **Neural Network (NN):** Neural Network (NN) is a mathematical model which has a structure of biological neural networks as shown in Figure 7. NN includes interconnected group of artificial neurons and by using connectionist approach information is gathered. As the external or internal information flows in the network can have some changes, the NN structure can be adapted to these changes (Andonie & Kovalerchuk, 2015).

Evaluation of Classification Methods

A confusion matrix gives information about actual and predicted classifications which are resulted by a classification method. Performance of the systems is determined by using the data in the matrix. In Table 1, confusion matrix for two class classifier is presented.

The terms in Table 1 are listed below to comprehend the information given in the table.

Figure 6. Line that separates two classes

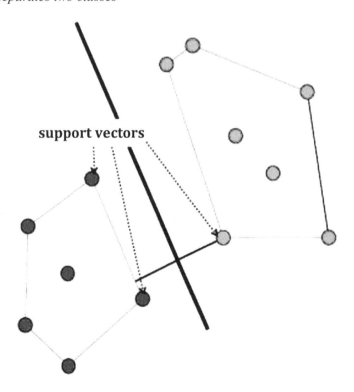

Figure 7. Neural connections in animal vs. Neural Network (Singh and Chauhan, 2009)

Neural Connections in Animals

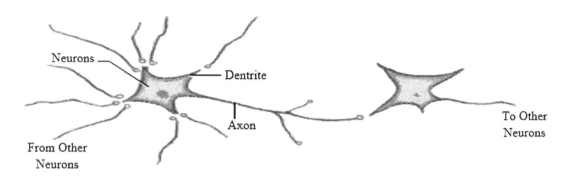

Artificial Neural Network

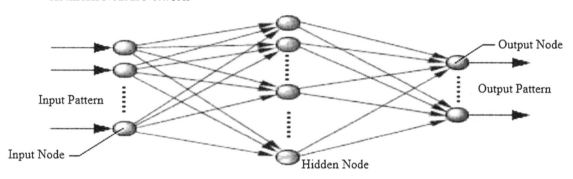

Table 1. Confusion matrix

		Predicted Classifications	
		Yes	No
Actual classifications	**Yes**	True positives	False negatives
	No	False positives	True negatives

- **True Positives:** Positive cases in the test data which are predicted correctly.
- **True Negatives:** Negative cases in the test data which are predicted correctly.
- **False Positives:** Negative cases in the test data which are predicted incorrectly.
- **False Negatives:** Positive cases in the test data which are predicted incorrectly predicted.

The formula given in Eq. (1) represents the accuracy of the total number of predictions that were correct.

$$\text{Accuracy} = \frac{\left(\text{True Positive} + \text{True Negative}\right)}{\text{Total Instances}} \qquad (1)$$

IMPLEMENTATION

WEKA software is developed by the University of Waikato to solve machine learning problems. WEKA includes embedded machine learning algorithms for data mining tasks which can be used for classification, clustering, data pre-processing, regression, association rules, and visualization methods. In this research, WEKA is used, to find the accurate results about churn situations.

By using the data obtained from the survey, a data mining study is developed. In the first step, by the help of preprocessing, attribute values are controlled and some logical adjustments are performed on the data. As a result, 129 attributes (16 numerical and 113 categorical) are generated with 59 Churn and 41 Not Churn instances. In Table 2 some attribute names and types are represented as an example.

In the second step, attribute selection algorithms are used to determine the important features. Among 129 attributes, 9 of them are found to be predominantly affecting the churn prediction. Thus, two different data sets are proposed for classification. One of the data sets consists of all 129 attributes, whereas the second only includes the 9 important features. In Table 3, selected attributes with related attribute selection method is given.

By using the two data sets, 98 different data classification methods are studied to predict the churn situation. Suggested data sets are represented in Table 4.

COMPUTATIONAL RESULTS

Data Set 1

The following data shows a part of data classification results from 41 classification methods. In Table 5, for both classes Churn and Not Churn, the overall accuracy is shown. Data set 1 has highest accuracy

Table 2. Determined attributes (16 numerical and 113 categorical in total)

Attribute No	Attribute Name	Attribute Type
1	Gender	Categorical
2	Age	Categorical
3	Sex	Categorical
4	Marital Status	Categorical
5	Educational Status	Categorical
6	Income	Categorical
7	User Type(Individual, Institutional)	Categorical
8	Currently Used Internet Service Provider	Categorical
.	.	.
.	.	.
.	.	.
126	Lack of Excesses Bill	Numeric
127	Advertising Campaigns	Numeric
128	The Difficulty of Canceling Process	Numeric
129	Constricted Infrastructure of Internet Service Provider	Numeric

Table 3. Attribute selection methods and selected attributes

Attribute Selection Method	Selected Attributes
CfsSubsetEval	16, 17, 19, 108, 109
ConsistencySubsetEval	2, 4, 6, 10, 109
FilteredSubsetEval	16, 109

Table 4. Suggested data sets and characteristics

	Attribute No	Attribute Name	Attribute Type
Data set 1	1-129	All attributes	Categorical
Data set 2	2	Age	Categorical
	4	Education Status	Categorical
	6	Income	Categorical
	10	Average Internet Invoice Amount (Monthly)	Categorical
	16	How many times did you change your Internet Service Provider?	Categorical
	17	The name of the previous Internet Service Provider that you use	Categorical
	19	Churning from TTNET to Turkcell Superonline	Categorical
	108	Did the old Internet Provider Service call you after churning?	Categorical
	109	Did the new Internet Provider Service call you after churning?	Categorical

value (86%) for Bayes BayesNet algorithm, as it can be seen from the Table 5. Among whole classification methods, highest accuracy value (91%) is obtained from Meta Bagging algorithm for Data Set 1.

Data Set 2

The following data shows a part of data classification results from 57 classification methods. In Table 6, for both classes Churn and Not Churn, the overall accuracy is shown. Data set 2 has highest accuracy value (90%) for Bayes Averaged One-Dependence Estimators (AODE) algorithm, as it can be seen from the Table 6. Among whole classification methods, highest accuracy value (91%) is obtained from Lazy Locally Weighted Learning (LWL) algorithm for Data Set 2.

Overall

The following data shows a part of data classification results from 98 classification methods for Data Set 1 and Data Set 2. Among them, Data Set 2 has the highest accuracy value (91%) by Lazy Locally Weighted Learning (LWL) algorithm as represented in Table 7.

Table 5. Accuracy of classification methods for data set 1

	Classification Methods	Overall	Accuracy	
			Churn	Not Churn
Bayes	BayesNet	86.00%	84.70%	87.80%
	NaiveBayes	85.00%	84.70%	85.40%
	NaiveBayesMultinominalText	59.00%	1.00%	0.00%
	NaiveBayesUpdateable	85.00%	84.70%	85.40%
Functions	Logistics	71.00%	72.90%	68.30%
	SGD	82.00%	79.70%	85.40%
	SGDText	59.00%	1.00%	0.00%
	SimpleLogistic	87.00%	84.70%	90.20%
	SMO	83.00%	83.10%	82.90%
	VotedPerceptron	71.00%	88.10%	46.30%
Lazy	IBk	78.00%	71.20%	87.80%
	KSTar	76.00%	72.90%	80.50%
	LWL	91.00%	89.80%	92.70%
Meta	AdaBoostM1	88.00%	89.80%	85.40%
	AttributeSelectedClassifier	91.00%	89.80%	92.70%
	Bagging	91.00%	89.80%	92.70%
	ClassificationViaRegression	85.00%	84.70%	85.40%
	CVParameterSelection	59.00%	1.00%	0.00%
	FilteredClassifier	90.00%	89.80%	90.20%
	LogitBoost	86.00%	86.40%	85.40%
	MultiClassClassifier	71.00%	72.90%	68.30%
	MultiClassClassifierUpdateable	82.00%	79.70%	85.40%

Best Data Set and Method

Data Set 2 has a significant factor to predict the churn situation of the ISP users. The highest accuracy value is obtained by Lazy LWL algorithm which postpone the process of the training data. This usually involves storing the training data in memory, and finding relevant data in the database. LWL method is developed by Eibe Frank, Mark Hall, Bernhard Pfahringer in 2003 [16]. Table 8 shows the most important attributes to determine the churn situation. According to results, when the old ISP called the customer after churning is one of the most significant attributes to recognize the churn situation. Also age categories such as <15, 15-24, 25-34, 35-44, 45-54, 55< can have an important effect on the churn situations. Therefore, ISPs can make efficient campaigns to influence the particular age groups. If ISPs are interested for the target group between 25-34 age which are employees and regular internet users, they need to update their internet package campaigns to prevent churning.

With the selected method, there are 9 misclassifications in 100 samples where 3 instances are misclassified as Not Churn and 6 instances are misclassified as Churn as shown in Table 9.

Table 6. Accuracy of classification methods for data set 2

	Classification Methods	Overall	Accuracy	
			Churn	Not Churn
Bayes	AODE	90.00%	88.10%	92.70%
	AODESr	88.00%	84.70%	92.70%
	BayesNet	87.00%	86.40%	87.80%
	NaiveBayes	88.00%	86.40%	90.20%
	NaiveBayesSimple	88.00%	86.40%	90.20%
	NaiveBayesUpdateable	88.00%	86.40%	90.20%
Functions	Logistics	74.00%	74.60%	73.20%
	RBFNetwork	87.00%	84.60%	87.80%
	SimpleLogistics	85.00%	83.10%	87.80%
	SMO	87.00%	88.10%	85.40%
	Spegasos	80.00%	84.70%	73.20%
	VotedPerceptron	86.00%	86.40%	85.40%
	Winnow	79.00%	74.60%	85.40%
Lazy	IB1	85.00%	83.10%	87.80%
	IBk	88.00%	86.40%	90.20%
	KSTar	88.00%	84.70%	92.70%
	LBR	88.00%	86.40%	90.20%
	LWL	91.00%	89.80%	92.70%
Meta	AdaBoostM1	91.00%	89.80%	92.70%
	AttributeSelectedClassifier	91.00%	89.80%	92.70%
	Bagging	90.00%	88.10%	92.70%
	ClassificationViaClustering	80.00%	72.90%	90.20%

By using a real data obtained from a survey, promising and applicable results are obtained to predict the churn behavior of ISP customers.

FUTURE RESEARCH

As an extension of the study, the questionnaire will be applied for a larger population to find accurate results about churn situations. Also, the questionnaire construction can be improved for specific groups or people to represent better conditions of the ISP users. This study will help to the ISPs to determine the required advertising campaigns for the customers. In this research a classification method is used to identify the class of attributes. However, the relationship between attributes did not considered. As a future work, the method can be changed and relationship between attributes can be considered.

Table 7. Accuracy of classification methods for overall results

Dataset		Classification Methods	Overall	Accuracy	
				Churn	Not Churn
Dataset2	Lazy	LWL	91.00%	89.80%	92.70%
Dataset2	Meta	AdaBoostM1	91.00%	89.80%	92.70%
Dataset2	Meta	AttributeSelectedClassifier	91.00%	89.80%	92.70%
Dataset2	Meta	END	91.00%	89.80%	92.70%
Dataset2	Meta	FilteredClassifier	91.00%	89.80%	92.70%
Dataset2	Meta	MultiBoostAB	91.00%	89.80%	92.70%
Dataset2	Rules	ConjunctiveRule	91.00%	89.80%	92.70%
Dataset2	Rules	JRip	91.00%	89.80%	92.70%
Dataset2	Rules	OneR	91.00%	89.80%	92.70%
Dataset2	Rules	PART	91.00%	89.80%	92.70%
Dataset2	Trees	DecisionStump	91.00%	89.80%	92.70%
Dataset2	Trees	J48	91.00%	89.80%	92.70%
Dataset2	Trees	J48graft	91.00%	89.80%	92.70%
Dataset2	Trees	RandomForest	91.00%	91.50%	90.20%
Dataset2	Trees	SimpleCart	91.00%	89.80%	92.70%
Dataset1	Lazy	LWL	91.00%	89.80%	92.70%
Dataset1	Meta	AttributeSelectedClassifier	91.00%	89.80%	92.70%
Dataset1	Meta	Bagging	91.00%	89.80%	92.70%

Table 8. The most important attributes

Attribute No	Attribute Name
2	Age
4	Education Status
6	Income
10	Average Internet Invoice Amount (Monthly)
16	How many times did you change your Internet Service Provider?
17	The name of the previous Internet Service Provider that you use
19	Churning from TTNET to Turkcell Superonline
108	Did the old Internet Provider Service call you after churning?
109	Did the new Internet Provider Service call you after churning?

Table 9. Confusion matrix of the selected method

		Predicted Classifications	
		Churn	Not Churn
Actual classifications	Churn	53	6
	Not Churn	3	38

CONCLUSION

In this research, churn prediction of customers in ISPs are discussed. After reviewing the literature, understanding customers' behavior becomes an important point to be considered in most of service industries. This paper indicates an implementation to analyze customer information by applying a questionnaire. With the results of questionnaire, customers' behavior and loyalty status of the churn possibility is discovered. A real data is obtained from a survey where applicable results are obtained to predict the churn behavior of ISP customers. The questions are related to personal and educational information, income, payment behavior and previous loyalty situation. The survey results are obtained from the people living in Istanbul. With the data obtained from the survey, a data mining study is developed. After controlling the attribute values, some logical adjustments are performed. By determining data sets, data classification methods are studied to predict the churn situation. The results are promising and applicable. Thus, the decision makers in ISPs may take precautions in order to prevent the loss of customers.

REFERENCES

Andonie, R., & Kovalerchuk, B. (2015). *Neural Networks for Data Mining: Constrains and Open Problems*. Retrieved June 27, 2015, from http://citeseerx.ist.psu.edu/viewdoc/download?doi=10.1.1.91.783 5&rep=rep1&type=pdf

Brachman, R., Khabaza, T., Kloesgen, W., Piatetsky-Shapiro, G., & Simoudis, E. (1996). Mining Business Databases. *Communications of the ACM*, *39*(11), 42–48. doi:10.1145/240455.240468

Burbidge, R., & Buxton, B. (2015). *An Introduction to Support Vector Machines for Data Mining*. Retrieved June 27, 2015, from http://www.cc.gatech.edu/classes/AY2008/cs7641_spring/handouts/ yor12-introsvm.pdf

Chen, Z. (2001). *Data Mining and Uncertain Reasoning: An Integrated Approach*. Wiley.

CISKO. (2015). *İnternet servis sağlayıcılar*. Retrieved June 27, 2015, from http://www.cisco.com/web/ TR/solutions/sp/segments/isp/isp_home.html

Frank, E., Hall, M., & Pfahringer, B. (2003). Locally weighted naive bayes. In *19th Conference in Uncertainty in Artificial Intelligence*.

ICTA. (2012). *Electronic Communications Market in Turkey*. Retrieved June 27, 2015, from http://eng. btk.gov.tr/dosyalar/2012-3-English_25_12_12.pdf

Jae-Hyeon, A., Sang-Pil, H., & Yung-Seop, L. (2006). Customer churn analysis: Churn determinants and mediation effects of partial defection in the Korean mobile telecommunications service industry. *Telecommunications Policy*, *30*(10-11), 552–568. doi:10.1016/j.telpol.2006.09.006

Janssen, C. (2015). *Data Preprocessing*. Retrieved June 27, 2015, from http://www.techopedia.com/ definition/14650/data-preprocessing

Keramati, A., & Ardabili, S. M. S. (2011). Churn analysis for an Iranian mobile operator. *Telecommunications Policy*, *35*(4), 344–356. doi:10.1016/j.telpol.2011.02.009

Kisioglu, P., & Topcu, Y. (2011). Applying Bayesian Belief Network approach to customer churn analysis: A case study on the telecom industry of Turkey. *Expert Systems with Applications*, *38*(6), 7151–7157. doi:10.1016/j.eswa.2010.12.045

Kotsiantis, S., Kanellopoulos, D., & Pintelas, P. (2006). Data Preprocessing for Supervised Leaning. *International Journal of Computer Science*, *1*, 111–117.

Leung, K. M. (2007). *k-Nearest Neighbor Algorithm for Classification*. Retrieved June 27, 2015, from http://cis.poly.edu/mleung/FRE7851/f07/k-NearestNeighbor.pdf

Nie, G., Rowe, W., Zhang, L., Tian, Y., & Shi, Y. (2011). Credit card churn forecasting by logistic regression and decision tree. *Expert Systems with Applications*, *38*(12), 15273–15285. doi:10.1016/j.eswa.2011.06.028

ORACLE. (2015). *Classification*. Retrieved June 27, 2015, from http://docs.oracle.com/cd/B28359_01/datamine.111/b28129/classify.htm#i1005746

Owczarczuk, M. (2010). Churn models for prepaid customers in the cellular telecommunication industry using large data marts. *Expert Systems with Applications*, *37*(6), 4710–4712. doi:10.1016/j.eswa.2009.11.083

Prasad, U. & Madhavi, S. (2012). Prediction of Churn Behavior of Bank Customers. *Business Intelligence Journal, 5*, 96-101.

Pyle, D. (1999). *Data Preparation for Data Mining*. Los Altos, CA: Morgan Kaufmann Publishers.

Roasoft Sample Size Calculator. (2015). Retrieved September 30, 2015, from http://www.raosoft.com/samplesize.html

Rouse, M. (2013). *Churn Rate (Predictive Churn Modeling)*. Retrieved June 27, 2015, from http://searchcrm.techtarget.com/definition/churn-rate

Shim, B., Choi, K., & Suh, Y. (2012). CRM strategies for a small-sized online shopping mall based on association rules and sequential patterns. *Expert Systems with Applications*, *39*(9), 7736–7742. doi:10.1016/j.eswa.2012.01.080

Singh, Y. & Chauhan, A. S. (2009). Neural Networks in Data Mining. *Journal of Theoretical and Applied Information Technology*, 37-42.

TELKODER. (2015). *İnternet Tabanlı Hizmetler (ITH/Ott) Elektronik haberleşme sektörüne etkisi ve düzenleme önerileri*. Retrieved June 27, 2015, from http://www.telkoder.org.tr/core/uploads/page/document/4840_130415306458648.pdf

ZENTUT. (2015). *Data mining applications*. Retrieved June 27, 2015, from http://www.zentut.com/data-mining/data-mining-applications/

KEY TERMS AND DEFINITIONS

Accuracy: The ratio of correct predictions to the total number of test instances.

Bayesian Classifier: Bayesian Classifier is a simple probabilistic classifier based on applying Bayes' Theorem with strong independence assumptions.

Churn Prediction: An anlytical approach to forecast the customers who have the possibility of leaving the company.

Data Classification (DC): DC is a supervised learning strategy that tries to build models which able to assign new instances to a set of well-defined classes.

Decision Tree Induction: It is a predictive model that maps observations of training instances to conclusions using a tree structure.

Internet Service Provider (ISP): A company which is providing internet access, usage and participation to its customers.

Neural Network (NN): A neural network is a data structure that attempts to simulate the behavior of neurons in a biological brain.

Support Vector Machines (SVM): SVM approach operates by finding a hyper surface that will split the classes so that the distance between the hyper surface and the nearest of the points in the groups has the largest value.

Chapter 14
On the Comparison of Quantitative Predictabilities of Different Financial Instruments

Adil Gürsel Karaçor
Atilim University, Turkey

Turan Erman Erkan
Atilim University, Turkey

ABSTRACT

Huge amount of liquidity flows into a number of financial instruments such as stocks, commodities, currencies, futures, and so on every day. Investment decisions are mainly based on predicting the future movements of the instrument(s) in question. However, high frequency financial data are somewhat hard to model or predict. It would be valuable information for the investor if he or she knew which financial instruments were quantitatively more predictable. The data used in the model consisted of intraday frequencies covering the period between 1993 and 2013. An Artificial Neural Network model using Radial Basis Functions containing only past data of three different types of instruments (stocks, currencies, and commodities) to predict future high values on six different frequencies was applied. A total of 72 different artificial neural networks representing 12 different instruments were trained five times each, and their prediction performances were recorded on average. Considerably clear distinctions were observed on prediction performances of different financial instruments.

INTRODUCTION

Price movements of financial instruments, whether they are random, chaotic, or of any other stochastic process, are definitely non-linear. Prior to going further into predictability analysis, it should be a good idea to define some terminology about non-linear dynamics.

First of all, a *dynamic system* can be defined as a deterministic mathematical prescription for evolving the state of a system forward in time where time may be either a continuous or discrete variable. (Ott E. (1993)). A *dissipative system* is a dynamic system, in which the phase space volume contracts along a trajectory.

DOI: 10.4018/978-1-5225-0075-9.ch014

The term *non-linear* is defined as the opposite of linear. In a linear system the variables appear in the first degree, they are not multiplied by one another; they are only multiplied by constants, and are combined only by addition or subtraction, while non-linear systems can occur in various forms such as division, multiplication and powers. The vast majority of systems we come across in real life are actually non-linear.

Collection of all possible states of a dynamic system is called the *phase space*. A *map* is a discrete function in the phase space that gives the next state of the system as a function of its current states. In a similar fashion, a *flow* is a continuous function that describes the time derivative of the state variables as a function of the present state values.

A state $\mathbf{x}^*$ is an *equilibrium point* of the system if once $\mathbf{x}(t)$ is equal to $\mathbf{x}^*$, it remains equal to $\mathbf{x}^*$ for all future times. When the system is exactly on the *periodic orbit* it will move on it forever and pass through the same points periodically. Both flows and maps can have equilibrium points and periodic orbits. Equilibrium points and periodic orbits can be either *stable* (even if the system slightly deviates from the equilibrium point or periodic orbit, it returns), *unstable* (if the system slightly deviates from the equilibrium point or periodic orbit, it does not come back) or *a saddle* (if the system slightly deviates from the equilibrium point or periodic orbit in some direction, it returns; if it deviates in some other direction it diverges; such equilibrium points or periodic orbits are also considered unstable).

As some people call non-linear financial dynamics as chaos, let us explain some more terminology on chaotic systems.

Until the last few decades of 20th century, the term *chaos* only meant disordered formless matter, complete disorder, utter confusion, randomness, or uncertainty. However since then it has gained a special scientific meaning, and started being used designate *deterministic chaos* which is a specific type of behavior that can be observed in non-linear dynamic systems and can be expressed by a set of discrete-time or continuous-time equations. Although its mathematical description is deterministic, a chaotic system has unpredictability in the long run. Another interesting point about chaotic dynamics is that the phase trajectories strongly depend on initial conditions. In addition, a dissipative chaotic system neither converges to a stable point or a stable periodic orbit, nor diverges to infinity; instead it wanders around in a fractal region. Such kind of chaotic behavior can be observed in various systems in different areas ranging from chemistry to electronics. However, it is not usually desired for a non-linear system to exhibit chaotic behavior, this is where control comes into the picture: due to its unpredictable nature chaos can give rise to problems. On the other hand, by taking advantage of certain properties of chaotic behavior, much can be achieved with little control effort. The founders of the OGY method; Ott, Grebogi and Yorke took advantage of the fact that there are quite a number of unstable limit cycles and equilibrium points within the strange attractor once the system comes close enough to one of these points of choice.

As the term *strange attractor* is mentioned, it needs to be explained. A dissipative chaotic system is such a system that neither converges to a stable point or a stable periodic orbit, nor diverges to infinity; instead it wanders around in a fractal region. Such a system contains many unstable or saddle type equilibrium points and so called *strange attractors*. A strange attractor actually consists of an infinitely long single trajectory that does not cross itself, and does not repeat itself periodically. Yet any trajectory attracted to a strange attractor sticks with it forever.

The global stability of a linear, time invariant system is determined by the eigenvalues of the system, which all has to be negative. Similarly, in a non-linear system the *Lyapunov exponent* indicates the exponential divergence or convergence rate (positive exponents correspond to divergence and negative ones to convergence) of the system when it slightly deviates from the equilibrium point or trajectory.

Chaotic systems have at least one positive Lyapunov exponent, which can be thought of as the source of the sensitive dependence on initial conditions, because even small deviations are amplified and nearby trajectories diverge from one another due to the positive Lyapunov exponent.

In a dissipative system, trajectories starting from a finite phase volume tend to occupy smaller and smaller phase volume as time evolves such that in the limit as time goes to infinity the phase volume they occupy becomes zero. It should be noted that only dissipative chaotic systems can have strange attractors with zero phase volume, but due to their fractal structure, these strange attractors are distributed over a finite phase volume.

Embedded into the strange attractor of a dissipative chaotic system there usually are many (sometimes infinite) unstable (saddle-type) equilibrium points and/or periodic orbits. The chaotic system, once it enters the strange attractor, keeps on moving in it and passes from time to time through a close neighborhood of these embedded saddle-like equilibrium points and/or periodic orbits.

BACKGROUND

Huge amount of money flows into the markets all around the world for the trade of various financial instruments such as stocks, commodities, foreign exchange (forex), futures, and so on every day. For example, according to experts and professionals, average daily turnover in forex markets alone is in excess of 4 trillion US dollars (What is Foreign Exchange, 2011). Investment and trading decisions, whether they tend to be long term or short term, are mainly based on predicting the future movements of the financial instrument(s) in question. There has been an ongoing debate among researchers on whether financial markets are predictable or not for a long time. Some think that financial market movements are nothing but random walk, and some findings support that claim: for example VIX futures prices were found to be unpredictable (Konstantinidi, E. & Skiadopoulos G. (2011)). Furthermore, some researchers even claimed that none of the conventional predictive models proposed in the literature on stock prediction seems capable of systematically predicting stock returns in long range of time horizons, and speculators do not earn significant profits in commodity and interest rate futures markets in aggregate (Hartzmark, M. L. (1987)) (Bossaerts, P. & Hillion, P. (1999)) (Goyal, A. Welch, I. (2008)). On the other hand, many researchers disagree with this random walk approach. Some of them claim speculators can gain profits on commodity and currency futures (Yoo, J., & Maddala, G. S. (1991)) (Kearns, J., & Manners, P. (2004)) (Kho, B. C. (1996)) (Taylor, S. J. (1992)) (Wang, C. (2004)) (Strozzi F., Zaldivar J.M. (2005)). Some others believe that financial instruments, commodities in particular, are predictable, at least to a certain extent (Campbell, J. Y., Thompson, S. (2008)) (Zunino Et al (2010)). The debate has not been settled yet, however, it is fair to say that financial instruments are definitely hard to model or predict, if not totally unpredictable. Obviously, it would be valuable information for the investor if he or she knew which financial instrument was quantitatively more predictable. In this chapter the possibility to give the investor a better starting point by trying to answer the following question was investigated: which financial instrument is quantitatively more predictable? We solely used technical (quantitative) analysis i.e. past price movements of the instruments. However fundamental analysis is not in the scope of this study.

Considering the non-linearity of financial price movements, it would be wise to use non-linear modeling tools. Usage of Artificial Neural Networks (ANNs) is quite popular for modeling, prediction, and decision making over financial data, and ANNs are regarded as an excellent tool for the purpose (Lam

M. (2003)) (Cheng Et al (1997)) (S. Dutta, S. Shekhar (1988)). In this chapter ANNs were used as a tool for measuring and comparing predictability. ANNs using RBF (ANN-RBFs) were preferred as they are quite popular and have good performance in financial time series prediction (Dash Et al (2014)) (Yu Et al (2008)) (D.K. Wedding, K.J. Cios (1996)) (Xi Et al (2014)). ANN-RBFs were trained to predict three different types of instruments: currency pairs, commodities, and stocks. As mentioned above there are many research papers on predictability of financial instruments, however, predictability comparison of these instruments in literature is very rare. In fact the only study we came across was the one comparing real estate returns with stock returns (Serrano J., Hoesli M. (2010)). It should be emphasized that the aim of this study is to determine which financial instrument is more predictable. The aim is neither to prove whether financial instruments are indeed predictable or not, nor to improve predicting performance of certain financial instruments.

DATA

The data used in our model consisted of 1-minute (1m), 5-minute (5m), 15-minute (15m), 30-minute (30m), 1-hour (1h), and 4-hour (4h) intraday frequencies covering the period between 1993 and 2013 with approximately 65000 data points for each instrument and frequency. This corresponds to a few months for 1-minute data, and 20 years for 4-hour data. The data were taken from authors' private data accounts. High frequency data were preferred, because in lower frequencies more and more non-technical fundamental factors might start to affect price movements. Three types of instruments were considered in this chapter: stocks, currencies (forex), and commodities. Four individual instruments were chosen to represent each type of instrument; namely Australian Dollar against US Dollar (AUDUSD); Euro against Canadian Dollar (EURCAD); Euro against US Dollar (EURUSD); and US Dollar against Japanese Yen (USDJPY), representing forex, BRENT crude oil; LIGHT crude oil; silver (XAGUSD); and gold (XAUUSD), representing commodities, and finally Amazon.com Inc (AMZN); Cisco Systems Inc. (CSCO); General Motors (GM); and Coca Cola Company (KO), representing stocks.

METHODOLOGY

Feature Selection

The total of fourteen features for the prediction model was chosen; that contained only past data (past high/low values, etc.) of the financial instruments. The output was the prediction of the actual result i.e. the maximum price value into the next eight periods (8x1-minute, 8x5-minutes, 8x15-minutes, and so on).

Prediction Method

ANNs were preferred in this study as a prediction tool, considering ANNs high predictive modeling power. As mentioned before, the aim of this chapter is to determine which financial instrument is more predictable and it is not to improve predicting performance of certain financial instruments, or to compare predicting performances of different tools or methods.

In fact, biological neural networks are much more complicated than the mathematical models we use. Biological neural networks consist of biological neurons while artificial neural networks consist of so-called mathematical neurons (nodes), which contain activation functions.

The way biological neural networks work, can be summarized as follows: each neuron is a part that uses biochemical reactions to receive, process and transmit information. A neuron's dendrites are connected to a vast number of neighboring neurons. As one of those neurons fire, a small electrical charge is received by one of the dendrites. The strengths of all the received charges are added up, and then the total input is passed to the soma. The soma and the enclosed nucleus do not play a significant role in the processing of incoming and outgoing data. Their primary function is to perform the continuous maintenance required to keep the neuron working. The part of the soma that does concern itself with the signal is the axon hillock. If the aggregate input is greater than the axon hillock's threshold value, the neuron fires, and an output signal is transmitted down the axon. The strength of the output is constant, regardless of whether the input was just above the threshold, or a hundred times as great. The output strength is unaffected by the many divisions in the axon; it reaches each terminal button with the same intensity it had at the axon hillock. This uniformity is critical in an analogue device such as a brain where small errors can snowball, and where error correction is more difficult than in a digital system. Each terminal button is connected to other neurons across a small gap called a synapse. The physical and neuro-chemical characteristics of each synapse determine the strength and polarity of the new input signal (Neil F. 1998).

ANNs are inspired from biological neural networks, and are well known for their high approximation and modeling capabilities (Karacor Et al (2007)). ANNs are trained in order that they learn a set of input-output data that represent usually a very complex or even undefined function. With sufficient number of hidden layers and neurons, they can model any given input-output relationship (Hornik Et al (1989)). All nodes (artificial neurons) are interconnected, thus form a massive parallelism, and each connection has a weight that changes as the ANN is trained, and also each node has an activation function. There are numerous activation functions, ranging from simple linear functions to various nonlinear ones. The nonlinearity of activation functions enables the ANN to learn even the most complex patterns.

General structure of a multi-layer artificial neural network is shown in Figure 1. The 'circles' indicate the nodes. A typical artificial neuron or node structure is shown in Figure 2. On the other hand, an artificial neuron is designed to simulate a real neuron with inputs entering the node and then multiplied by corresponding weights (w1, w2,..., wn) to indicate the strength of the synapse. Equation for a single node is given in Equation (1).

Figure 1. General structure of a multi-layer artificial neural network

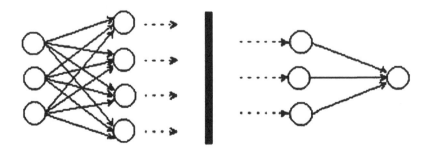

An ANN is a network of many processors (nodes) each possibly having a small amount of local memory. The nodes have activation functions, which describe the output behavior of that node. Activation functions can be of various types such as sigmoid, tangent hyperbolic, Gaussian, etc. Communication channels that usually carry numeric data, encoded by activation functions, connect the nodes. The nodes operate only on their local data and on the inputs they receive via the connections.

Input Layer is the part, which provides external input to the network. *Hidden Layer(s)* is the part, which receives from the input layer or another hidden layer and provides inputs to the output layer or the next hidden layer. *Output Layer* receives inputs from a hidden layer and produces the output(s) of the network. *Weight* is a connection between two nodes with a value that is dynamically changed during a neural networks learning process.

ANNs are meant to be the models of biological neural networks; however, there has been always the desire to produce artificial systems capable of sophisticated, perhaps *intelligent* computations similar to those that the human brain routinely performs. On the other hand, much is yet to be achieved, as an ANN is, at least currently, no match for the human brain, which is a collection of about 85 billion interconnected neurons within itself.

Usually ANNs need to be *trained* where the weights of connections are adjusted according to the input data. In other words, ANNs *learn* from examples and are expected to show some capability for generalization beyond the training data. When the training is performed, there are two types of learning: *supervised* and *unsupervised.* In supervised learning the learning algorithm is carried out with a set of inputs against the corresponding correct outputs, and learning involves comparing produced outputs with the correct or desired outputs, and the weights are adapted accordingly. In contrast, unsupervised learning employs a type of learning where the system is not given the *right answer*, i.e. it is not trained on pairs consisting of an input and the desired output. Instead, the system is given the input patterns and is left to find interesting patterns, regularities, clusters, or relations among the patterns. As an example, a boy learning to skate can be classified as in an unsupervised learning situation while a student learning the multiplication table at school is learning in a supervised manner.

ANNs are known to be related to parallelism, as the computations of the components are mainly independent of each other. In general, ANNs are especially useful for classification and function ap-

Figure 2. Artificial neuron

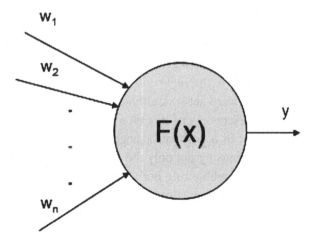

proximation/problems that are somewhat complex and are very hard to model or predict, which have reasonable amount of training data available, yet to which hard and fast rules, like in expert systems, cannot easily be applied. Theoretically any function can be approximated to arbitrary precision by ANNs, if there are sufficient number of neurons, enough data and computing resources.

In other words, ANNs can compute any computable function. They essentially are function approximators, pattern matchers, and classifiers. They do very little outside of these basic functions although these tasks can be employed in a wide variety of powerful and complex applications ranging from several control tasks to stock market prediction.

There are several requirements and conditions a problem must satisfy if it is to be an acceptable candidate for an ANN solution. First and foremost the problem must be tolerant of some level of imprecision. All artificial intelligence techniques sacrifice some small measure of precision in favour of speed and tractability. This imprecision may be very small, much less than one percent or it may be relatively large such as ten percent. ANN error rates tend to be below two percent, but for certain applications error rates can go as low as a very small fraction of one percent, or on the contrary they can go as high as forty percent. Any application that has zero tolerance for imprecision, cannot be solved with any artificial intelligence technique including ANNs.

Another requirement is that abundant high quality data must exist for both training and testing purposes. An ANN must be able to observe the problem at hand. It must also be put to test on that problem once it is trained but before it is put into service. This may require quite a lot of training and testing data depending on the complexity of the problem.

Consequently; complex, ambiguous and nearly unpredictable systems which tend to be difficult to compute or model, yet have enough resources for training data, are very suitable candidates for ANN modeling. Financial instruments fit well into this frame.

There is virtually no limit to the type and variety of ANNs, however in general ANNs are classified according to two factors: the topology or shape of the network and the learning method used. For instance, the most widely used topology is the feed-forward network and the most common learning method is the *backpropagation of errors*. Backpropagation is a form of supervised learning in which a network is given input and then the network's actual output is compared to the correct output. The network's connections (weights) are adjusted to minimize the error between the actual and the correct output. Feed forward networks that use backpropagation learning are so common that these networks are commonly referred to as *backpropagation networks* although this terminology is not correct. *Multi-layer feed-forward* refers to the topology and pattern of information flow in the network. Backpropagation refers to a specific type of learning algorithm. It is possible to use a feed forward architecture without backpropagation, or to use back propagation with another type of structure. In both cases, it has become commonly accepted to call this combination of topology and learning method simply a *back propagation network*.

Another common network structure is the *recurrent or feedback network*. Recurrent networks are usually similar in shape to the feed forward network although data may pass backwards through the net or between nodes in the same layer. Networks of this type operate by allowing neighbouring neurons to adjust other nearby neurons either in a positive or negative direction. This allows the network to reorganize the strength of its connections by not only the comparison of actual output against correct output but also by the interaction of neighbouring nodes. Recurrent networks are generally slower to train and to implement and also derive mathematical models than feed forward networks although they present several interesting possibilities including the idea of unsupervised learning. As discussed earlier, in unsupervised learning the network is only given input with no output and neurons are allowed to work in order to extract meaningful information from the data. This is especially useful when trying to analyse data searching for some pattern but no specific pattern is known to exist beforehand, such as segmentation issues.

A third network structure, also based on the feed forward architecture, is the *functional link network*. This type of network duplicates the input signal with some type of transformation on the input. In a functional link network, additional inputs will also be fed to the network, which are in some form of the original inputs. These additional inputs may be various products of the original inputs, or they may be high and low values from the whole input set, or they may be any combination of mathematical functions that are deemed to contain value for this set of input. In this network the functional link is directly connected to the output layer although the functional link may be directed toward the hidden layer. The idea behind this type of network is to give the network as much information as possible about the original input set by also giving it variations of the input set.

Aside from the fact that the system to be modelled must be error tolerant to a certain extent, there is another somewhat disturbing characteristic of ANNs. Let us explain: an ANN may solve a practical problem, but it is not obvious how it does it. Once the architecture of the network is decided and the training data are fed, the network learns and does everything by itself, without any human intervention. After the learning phase, the network may start to give output that makes sense; however, the designers and users of the network do not have much knowledge about how that output is generated and why it is generated. The knowledge of an ANN resides entirely in its synaptic table, the table that holds the weights for the connections in the network. This table typically holds quite a lot of numbers, but is of little meaning to the onlooker. In a scientific work, knowledge must be accessible.

$$y = F(\sum_j \sum_i (w_j x_i) + \theta) \tag{1}$$

Here; y is the output, w_j is the jth weight connected to the node, x_i is the ith input, F(x) is the activation function, and θ is the bias term. As mentioned before, there are numerous activation functions, and ANN-RBFs are preferred in this work, whose equation is given in (2) below.

$$F(x) = e^{-\frac{(x-c)^2}{r^2}} \tag{2}$$

ANN-RBF is yet another network structure. For RBF networks, Gaussian activation functions are preferred in this study: where c is the centre and r is the radius of the function. Like other types of ANNs, RBF networks can learn arbitrary mappings; however, the primary difference is in the hidden layer. RBF hidden layer units have a receptive field, which has a center: that is, a particular input value at which they have a maximal output. Their output tails off as the input moves away from this point or just the other way round in the case of a multiquadric node function. This hidden layer function could be a Gaussian, Cauchy, multiquadric, and so on. RBFs have the advantage that one can add extra nodes with centers near the parts of the input data that are difficult to classify. This way they take advantage of both supervised and unsupervised learning (Karacor G., Denizhan Y. (2004)). Figure 3 shows a traditional RBF network, in which each of n components of the input vector u feeds forwards to m basis functions whose outputs are linearly combined with weight vector w into the network output f (u).

Figure 3. ANN-RBF

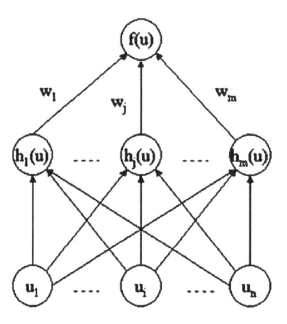

Machine Learning

As mentioned previously, there are two types of learning as far as ANNs are concerned: supervised and unsupervised. Supervised learning requires the programmer to give the network a sufficient number of data sets consisting of input(s) and the corresponding correct output. This way, the network can compare what it has output against what it should output, and it can correct itself. On the other hand, unsupervised learning provides input but no correct output. A network using this type of learning is only given inputs and the network must organize its connections and outputs without direct feedback and try to find possible regularities and relations. This type of learning is well suited to data extraction and analysis in which a pattern is known to exist in some data but the type and location of this pattern is unknown. Managing chaotic systems should be based on data gathered from the system. These data can be used to train the neural network in a supervised manner.

Once the network structure is designed, the input-output relation should be learnt by the network in order to obtain the desired model. In our case, which is mostly a supervised learning problem, the relation between input and output of the system is learned from the examples supplied by a supervisor. The set of the examples is referred to as the training set and it contains pairs of dependent and independent variables. Supervised learning requires the programmer to give the network a sufficient number of data sets consisting of input(s) and the corresponding correct output. This way, the network can compare what it has as output against what it should have as output, and it can correct itself using the difference i.e. error. In this work gradient descent was used as the learning algorithm. Gradient descent is the most widely used method for ANN training. The reason for this popularity is that only simple computation is necessary to apply this method and gradient can be computed with local information. The principle in this method is simple: the values for the weights are changed in a direction opposite to the direction of the gradient. The gradient of a surface indicates the direction of the maximum rate of change. Therefore, provided that the weights are changed in the opposite direction of the gradient, the system state will approach points where the surface is flatter. The weight values that correspond to the point of minimum error are the optimal weights. The change in weights is formulated as:

$$w_{k+1} = w_k + 2\mu e_k x_k \tag{3}$$

where μ is the learning rate parameter i.e. a sufficiently small constant, e_k is the error – the difference between the desired response and the actual system response at iteration step k, x_k is the input value to the weight i at iteration k, and w_k is the value of weight i at iteration k. This method is known as Least Mean Square (LMS) algorithm.

Although there are many learning algorithms such as Hebb rule, Adaline, decision tree, and genetic algorithms; back propagation with LMS is the most widely used method for neural network training because it is easy to implement and to understand and works reasonably well for most problems.

In ANN-RBFs y=f(u), where y is a scalar and u is a vector. Assume that there is a training set $\{(u_i, y_i)\}$, i=1,...,P to be used approximate the function f. The ANN-RBF uses a linear model. In the hidden layer node, for a scalar input, the radial function can be either a Gaussian, Cauchy or multiquadric. Gaussian ones are preferred in our case as mentioned earlier.

With the model in question and a P-pattern training set $\{(\mathbf{u}_i, y_i)\}^P$, the least squares should minimize the sum-squared-error,

$$S = \sum_{i=1}^{P} (y_i - f(\mathbf{u}_i))^2 \tag{4}$$

with respect to the weights of the model. The minimization of the cost function leads to a set of m simultaneous linear equations with m unknown weights. These equations can be written more conveniently as,

$$\underline{\underline{\mathbf{A}}}\mathbf{w} = \mathbf{H}^T y \tag{5}$$

here $\underline{\underline{\mathbf{H}}}$ is the *design matrix*,

$$\underline{\underline{\mathbf{H}}} := \begin{bmatrix} h_1(x_1) & h_2(x_1) & ... & h_m(x_1) \\ h_1(x_2) & h_2(x_2) & ... & h_m(x_2) \\ \vdots & \vdots & \vdots & \vdots \\ h_1(x_p) & h_2(x_p) & ... & h_m(x_p) \end{bmatrix} \tag{6}$$

and $\underline{\underline{\mathbf{A}}}^{-1}$ is the *variance matrix,*

$$\underline{\underline{\mathbf{A}}}^{-1} = (\underline{\underline{\mathbf{H}}}^T \mathbf{H} + \Lambda)^{-1} \tag{7}$$

The elements of the matrix Λ are all zero except for the regularization parameters along its diagonal. The solution is the so-called *normal equation,*

$$\mathbf{w} = \underline{\underline{\mathbf{A}}}^{-1} \underline{\underline{\mathbf{H}}}^{T} y \tag{8}$$

which minimizes the sum-squared error. Hence, the problem is to choose the number of the radial functions in the hidden layer, To obtain the optimal number of Radial Basis Functions in the hidden layer, the so-called *forward selection* procedure is used. In this procedure, the parameters are the centers and the radii of the Radial Basis Functions. The weight vector is computed after the optimal set of these parameters has been selected. The aim of this procedure is to find a subset of the design matrix $\underline{\underline{\mathbf{H}}}$ that consists of fixed parameters. The procedure begins with an empty set. With each iteration a Basis Function, which decreases the predicted error, is added to the subset. During the optimal subset selection, a heuristic *error prediction* is utilized to predict the sum-squared error when the selected Basis Function is added to subset. The so-called projection matrix holds the error prediction,

$$\underline{\underline{\mathbf{P}}} := \underline{\mathbf{I}} - \underline{\underline{\mathbf{H}}}\underline{\underline{\mathbf{A}}}^{-1}\underline{\underline{\mathbf{H}}}^{T} \tag{9}$$

where $\underline{\mathbf{I}}$ is a PxP identity matrix. The matrix $\underline{\underline{\mathbf{P}}}$ projects the vectors in the P-dimensional space to the m-dimensional subspace. Since there are P training patterns, the training set output y is in the P-dimensional space. However, the network consisting of m model is in the m-dimensional subspace. According to the least squares principle, the optimal network is the one which has a minimum distance from the projection of $\mathbf{y}$ onto the m-dimensional subspace. By using the projection matrix, the sum-squared error can be calculated as,

$$S = y^{T}\underline{\underline{\mathbf{P}}}^{2}y \tag{10}$$

The relationship between $\underline{\underline{\mathbf{P}}}_{m}$, the projection matrix for the m units in the hidden layer, and $\underline{\underline{\mathbf{P}}}_{m=1}$, the projection matrix if $\mathbf{f}_{j}$, the jth column of the design matrix $\underline{\underline{\mathbf{H}}}$ is added, is given in (11).

$$\underline{\underline{\mathbf{P}}}_{m=1} = \underline{\underline{\mathbf{P}}}_{m} - \frac{\underline{\underline{\mathbf{P}}}_{m} f_{j} f_{j}^{T} \underline{\underline{\mathbf{P}}}_{m}}{f_{j}^{T} \underline{\underline{\mathbf{P}}}_{m} f_{j}} \tag{11}$$

Forward subset selection utilizes this relationship when selecting the basis function that decreases the prediction sum-squared error. This procedure is terminated when a predetermined error criterion is satisfied. This way, the number of nodes to be used in the hidden layer are not necessarily decided beforehand, instead nodes are added one by one until they contribute to the networks performance no more, which saves one from a cumbersome task (Orr, 1996).

65000 data points for each instrument were time-wise randomly split: approximately 60% was used for training, 15% for cross validation, and the remaining 25% for testing. Each network was trained until no improvement was brought about in the cross validation set for 100 epochs, and the weights were then saved. One of the main issues concerning machine learning is over-learning or over-fitting problem, in which the system memorizes a certain data set rather than learning it, because of too many training epochs. The performance of the system can be excellent on that data set; however it performs poorly on different data due to the lack of generalization. The opposite of this issue is the under-learning or under-fitting problem. Therefore, sufficient number of training epochs is crucial for an optimum system performance. The criterion of training until improvement in the cross validation set stops is a trade off in this study. The inputs to ANNs contained only past data of the financial instruments. The output was the prediction of the actual result i.e. the maximum price value into the next eight periods for each frequency (e.g. 8x1-minute, 8x5-minutes, 8x15-minutes, and so on). A sample of the training process used in this study is shown in Figure 4, displaying the relation between training epochs and the Mean Squared Error (MSE).

RESULTS

ANNs to model each instrument and frequency were trained 5 times starting with randomly different initial weights, and performances on test sets were averaged to obtain Normalized Mean Squared Error (NMSE) values. NMSE is calculated by the formula below:

$$\text{NMSE} = \frac{\sum_{j=0}^{P}\sum_{i=0}^{N}(d_{ij}-y_{ij})^2}{\sum_{j=0}^{P}\dfrac{N\sum_{i=0}^{N}d_{ij}^{2}-(\sum_{i=0}^{N}d_{ij})^2}{N}} \tag{12}$$

where P = number of output processing elements (neurons),

N = number of exemplars in the data set,
y_{ij} = network output for exemplar i at processing element j,
d_{ij} = desired output for exemplar i at processing element j.

Figure 4. Mean squared error as training evolves

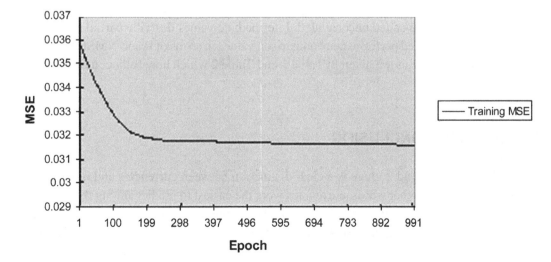

NMSE is actually mean square error divided by variance of desired output. Being a normalized value, it could easily be used for comparing different instruments of different prices and of different frequencies. Since it is an error term, values closer to zero denote better predictability.

Another statistically meaningful variable we used for predictability performance is the correlation coefficient R. Correlation coefficient R is used to measure how well one variable fits on another, linear regression wise. In our case, these variables were predicted against desired, in other words, ANN outputs vs. actual maximum values of the financial instruments in the next 8 periods of corresponding frequencies. R value is calculated by the formula below:

$$R = \frac{\dfrac{\sum_i (x_i - \bar{x})(d_i - \bar{d})}{N}}{\sqrt{\dfrac{\sum_i (d_i - \bar{d})^2}{N}} \sqrt{\dfrac{\sum_i (x_i - \bar{x})^2}{N}}} \tag{13}$$

where P = number of output processing elements (neurons),

N = number of exemplars in the data set,

x = network output,

d_{ij} = desired output.

The size of the mean square error (MSE) can be used to determine how well the network output fits the desired output, but it does not necessarily reflect whether the two sets of data move in the same direction. For instance, by simply scaling the network output, we can change the MSE without changing the directionality of the data. The correlation coefficient R solves this problem. By definition, the correlation coefficient between a network output x and a desired output d is defined by formula (12). The correlation coefficient is confined to the range (-1 1). When R = 1 there is a perfect positive linear correlation between x and d, i.e. they vary accordingly, which means that they vary by the same amount. When R = -1, there is a perfect linear negative correlation between x and d, i.e. they vary in opposite ways (when x increases, d decreases by the same amount). When R =0 there is no correlation between x and d, i.e. the variables are called uncorrelated. Intermediate values describe partial correlations.

All recorded and calculated performance comparison values in terms of R and NMSE for all financial instruments and all frequencies are given in Table 1 and Table 2 which hopefully could enlighten us on predictability.

DISCUSSION AND CONCLUSION

As can be seen in Tables 1 and 2, there is a clear distinction between currencies and other instruments both R and NMSE wise. In other words, currencies were the easiest to predict among the instruments in question. The group of instruments which was the hardest to predict was stocks, however with a narrow margin against commodities. We can also say that 15-minute data were the least technically predictable

Table 1. Detailed performance comparison

Instrument	4h		1h		30m		15m		5m		1m	
	R	NMSE	R	NMSE	R	NMSE	R	NMSE	R	NMSE	R	NMSE
AMZN	0.35	0.88	0.33	0.89	0.25	0.94	0.25	0.94	0.28	0.92	0.27	0.93
CSCO	0.28	0.92	0.26	0.94	0.22	0.96	0.15	0.98	0.33	0.89	0.45	0.80
GM	0.29	0.91	0.30	0.91	0.36	0.87	0.40	0.84	0.41	0.84	0.53	0.73
KO	0.22	0.96	0.21	0.96	0.18	0.97	0.22	0.96	0.21	0.96	0.07	1.01
AUDUSD	0.42	0.82	0.40	0.84	0.46	0.79	0.32	0.90	0.28	0.92	0.25	0.94
EURCAD	0.51	0.74	0.55	0.70	0.35	0.88	0.24	0.94	0.70	0.52	0.80	0.36
EURUSD	0.41	0.83	0.28	0.92	0.31	0.90	0.27	0.92	0.29	0.91	0.36	0.87
USDJPY	0.39	0.85	0.32	0.90	0.36	0.87	0.26	0.93	0.31	0.90	0.25	0.94
BRENT	0.19	0.96	0.22	0.95	0.21	0.96	0.21	0.96	0.40	0.84	0.36	0.87
LIGHT	0.16	0.97	0.13	0.98	0.05	1.02	0.10	1.00	0.39	0.87	0.36	0.87
XAGUSD	0.41	0.84	0.44	0.81	0.46	0.79	0.37	0.86	0.25	0.94	0.27	0.93
XAUUSD	0.40	0.84	0.45	0.80	0.36	0.87	0.36	0.87	0.38	0.85	0.27	0.93

Table 2. Overall performance comparison

		Stocks	Currencies	Commodities	All Instruments
4h	R	0.28643812	0.43200822	0.29237317	0.33693984
	NMSE	0.91880484	0.81166616	0.90663130	0.87903410
1h	R	0.27377488	0.39063054	0.31002520	0.324810208
	NMSE	0.92536862	0.83727909	0.88463085	0.88242618
30m	R	0.25179278	0.37118151	0.26792855	0.29696761
	NMSE	0.93196670	0.85952219	0.90406936	0.89851942
15m	R	0.25615607	0.27153008	0.26154911	0.26307841
	NMSE	0.92765705	0.92566387	0.92063667	0.92465253
5m	R	0.30625493	0.39743173	0.35640030	0.35336232
	NMSE	0.90142611	0.81463511	0.87568382	0.86391501
1m	R	0.33082840	0.41394639	0.31386376	0.35287952
	NMSE	0.86390559	0.77781108	0.90010259	0.84727309
Average	R	0.28420753	0.37945474	0.30035668	0.32133965
	NMSE	0.91152149	0.83776292	0.89862577	0.88263672

among the other frequencies. Nevertheless, the predictability of 30-minute data was not so much better than that of 15-minute data, again both R and NMSE wise. 1-minute data were the most quantitatively predictable in terms of NMSE, on the other hand 5-minute data were the most quantitatively predictable in terms of R. However, neither the predictability performance of 1-minute data nor the predictability performance of 5-minute data is much better than those of 1-hour or 4-hour data. Therefore from the investor's point of view, trading decisions based on 1-hour or 4-hour data could even be more profitable, considering commissions and spread margins are usually more disadvantageous in higher frequencies like 5-minute or 1-minute.

For future work, the addition of more instruments in each category, and addition of different categories such as futures, interest rates, etc. could be considered. Other time periods like daily or weekly data could also be considered, as well as different ANN types or even different methods other than ANNs. The scope of future work could also include profitability instead of or along with predictability, using buy, sell, take profit and stop loss conditions.

Judging by the R values in Tables 1 and 2, one could argue that the prediction performances are somewhat low; however predicting financial instruments technically is indeed such a hard task and again, the aim of this study is to determine which financial instrument is more predictable, and not to prove whether financial instruments are indeed predictable or not, or to improve predicting performance of certain financial instruments. Improvements could be introduced in future work, however, considering the scope of this chapter, at least it was demonstrated that it would be possible to give some hope to the investor and assist him/her in choosing more predictable instruments.

REFERENCES

Bossaerts, P., & Hillion, P. (1999). Implementing Statistical Criteria to Select Return Forecasting Models: What Do We Learn? *Review of Financial Studies*, *12*(2), 405–428. doi:10.1093/rfs/12.2.405

Campbell, J. Y., & Thompson, S. (2008). Predicting the Equity Premium Out of Sample: Can Anything Beat the Historical Average? *Review of Financial Studies*, *21*(4), 1509–1531. doi:10.1093/rfs/hhm055

Cheng W., McClain B.W., Kelly C. (1997). Artificial Neural Networks Make Their Mark as a Powerful Tool for Investors. *Review of Business,* 4 –9.

Dash, R., Dash, P. K., & Bisoi, R. (2014). A self adaptive differential harmony search based optimized extreme learning machine for financial time series prediction. *Swarm and Evolutionary Computation*, *19*, 25–42. doi:10.1016/j.swevo.2014.07.003

Dutta, S., & Shekhar, S. (1988). Bond-rating: a Non-conservative Application of Neural Networks. *Proceedings of the IEEE International Conference on Neural Networks*. doi:10.1109/ICNN.1988.23958

Goyal, A., & Welch, I. (2008). A Comprehensive Look at the Empirical Performance of Equity Premium Prediction. *Review of Financial Studies*, *21*(4), 1455–1508. doi:10.1093/rfs/hhm014

Hartzmark, M. L. (1987). Returns to individual traders of futures: Aggregate results. *Journal of Political Economy*, *95*(6), 1292–1306. doi:10.1086/261516

Hornik, K., Stinchcombe, M., & White, H. (1989). Multilayer Feedforward Networks are Universal Approximators. *Neural Networks*, *2*(5), 359–366. doi:10.1016/0893-6080(89)90020-8

International Business Times AU. (n.d.). *What is Foreign Exchange?* Retrieved February 11, 2011 from http://au.ibtimes.com/forex

Karacor, A. G., Sivri, N., & Ucan, O. N. (2007). Maximum Stream Temperature Estimation of Degirmendere River Using Artificial Neural Network. *Journal of Scientific and Industrial Research*, *66*(5), 363–366.

Karacor, G., & Denizhan, Y. (2004). Advantages of Hierarchical Organisation in Neural Networks. *International Journal Of Computing Anticipatory Systems*, *16*, 48–60.

Kearns, J., & Manners, P. (2004). *The Profitability of Speculators in Currency Futures Markets*. Working Paper. Reserve Bank of Australia.

Kho, B. C. (1996). Time-varying Risk Premia, Volatility, and Technical Trading Rule Profits: Evidence from Foreign Currency Futures Markets. *Journal of Financial Economics*, *41*(2), 249–290. doi:10.1016/0304-405X(95)00861-8

Konstantinidi, E., & Skiadopoulos, G. (2011). Are VIX futures prices predictable? An empirical investigation. *International Journal of Forecasting*, *27*(2), 543–560. doi:10.1016/j.ijforecast.2009.11.004

Lam M. (2003). Neural Network Techniques for Financial Performance Prediction: Integrating Fundamental and Technical Analysis. *Decision Support Systems*, *37*(2004), 567– 581.

Neil, F. (n.d.). *Neuron*. Retrieved June 15, 2015 from http://vv.carleton.ca/~neil/neural/neuron-a.html

NeuroSolutions. (n.d.). NeuroDimension Inc. Retrieved June 15, 2015 from www.nd.com

Orr, M. (1996). *Introduction to Radial Basis Functions,* Retrieved June 15, 2015 from http://www.anc.ed.ac.uk/rbf/intro/intro.html

Ott, E. (1993). *Chaos in Dynamical Systems*. Cambridge University Press.

Serrano, J., & Hoesli, M. (2010). Are Securitized Real Estate Returns more Predictable than Stock Returns? *The Journal of Real Estate Finance and Economics*, *41*(2), 170–192. doi:10.1007/s11146-008-9162-y

Strozzi, F., & Zaldivar, J. M. (2005). Non-linear Forecasting in High-frequency Financial Time Series. *Physica A*, *353*, 463–479. doi:10.1016/j.physa.2005.01.047

Taylor, S. J. (1992). Rewards Available to Currency Futures Speculators: Compensation for Risk or Evidence of Inefficient Pricing? *The Economic Record*, *68*(Supplement), 105–116. doi:10.1111/j.1475-4932.1992.tb02298.x

Wang, C. (2004). Futures Trading Activity and Predictable Foreign Exchange Market Movements. *Journal of Banking & Finance*, *28*(5), 1023–1041. doi:10.1016/S0378-4266(03)00047-5

Wedding, D. K. II, & Cios, K. J. (1996). Time series forecasting by combining RBF networks, certainty factors, and the Box-Jenkins model. *Neurocomputing*, *10*(2), 149–168. doi:10.1016/0925-2312(95)00021-6

Xi, L., Muzhou, H., Lee, M. H., Li, J., Wei, D., Hai, H., & Wu, Y. (2014). A new constructive neural network method for noise processing and its application on stock market prediction. *Applied Soft Computing*, *15*, 57–66. doi:10.1016/j.asoc.2013.10.013

Yoo, J., & Maddala, G. S. (1991). Risk Premia and Price Volatility in Futures Markets. *Journal of Futures Markets*, *11*(2), 165–177. doi:10.1002/fut.3990110204

Yu, L., Lai, K. K., & Wang, S. (2008). Multistage RBF neural network ensemble learning for exchange rates forecasting. *Neurocomputing*, *71*(16-18), 3295–3302. doi:10.1016/j.neucom.2008.04.029

Zunino, L., Tabak, B.M., Serinaldi, F., Zanin, M., Perez, D.G., & Rosso, O.A. (2010). Commodity Predictability Analysis with a Permutation Information Theory Approach. *Physica A*, *390*(2011), 876–890.

KEY TERMS AND DEFINITIONS

Artificial Neural Network: The tool inspired from biological neural networks, and used for modeling any input output relation(s) of any system.

Data Mining: The concept of working on large volumes of data in order to find valuable information.

Financial Instrument: Any type of investment material that can be bought and sold in global markets.

Machine Learning: The process of teaching a device; a function, a relation, or a pattern in a data set by means of an algorithm.

Predictability: The characteristic of a financial instrument in terms of how well it can be predicted.

Quantitative Analysis: The analysis that is built purely upon mathematical calculations of measured values of past price movements.

Radial Basis Function: Any mathematical distribution function with a center and a radius.

Time Series: The representation of data with regard to time in a sequence.

Chapter 15
Selection of Wavelet Features for Biomedical Signals Using SVM Learning

Girisha Garg
BBDIT, India

Vijander Singh
NSIT, India

ABSTRACT

Signal processing problems require feature extraction and selection techniques. A novel Wavelet Feature Selection algorithm is proposed for ranking and selecting the features from the wavelet decompositions. The algorithm makes use of support vector machine to rank the features and backward feature elimination to remove the features. The finally selected features are used as patterns for the classification system. Two EEG datasets are used to test the algorithm. The results confirm that the algorithm is able to improve the efficiency of wavelet features in terms of accuracy and feature space.

1. INTRODUCTION

The subject of wavelets is considered a major breakthrough in mathematical science, and provides a common link between mathematicians and engineers. Because of their interdisciplinary origins, wavelets appeal to scientists and engineers of many different backgrounds. Over the last decade most of the work is based on application of time-frequency transforms to the problem of signal representation and classification. Most recently, the emergence of wavelet theory has motivated a considerable amount of research in transient and nonstationary signal analysis. The wavelet theory is applied to different signal based applications in conjunction with the machine learning. Machine learning provides tools by which large quantities of data can be automatically analyzed. Fundamental processes for machine learning are feature selection and feature ranking. Feature selection identifies the most salient features for learning. It focuses the learning algorithm on those aspects of data which are most useful for analysis and future prediction. This is especially relevant when high dimensional classification domains are

DOI: 10.4018/978-1-5225-0075-9.ch015

being investigated. Feature selection is useful when there are very few labeled training samples relative to the very high dimensionality of the feature measurement available for each sample. Particularly in biomedical engineering, training sets are derived from clinical trials of at the most 50-60 patients. Each training sample is represented by hundreds of features. In this letter Wavelet Feature Selection (WFS) is presented for biomedical signal processing. WFS is a feature selection and ranking algorithm based on machine learning. Application of machine learning based algorithm for feature selection not only helps in dimensionality reduction but also ensures that the features selected can optimally improve the classification accuracy. This algorithm is inspired by the Support Vector Machine Recursive Feature Elimination (SVM RFE) proposed by Isabelle Guyon (Guyon, Weston, Barnhill, & Vapnik, 2002). The goal of introducing WFS algorithm is to eliminate wavelet coefficients redundancy automatically and yield optimal and compact feature subset.

2. METHODS

Wavelet transforms of a signal can be viewed as a step by step transformation of the signal from the time domain to the frequency domain. Discrete Wavelet Transform (DWT) analyses the signal using multi resolution analysis by decomposing the signal into approximations and detail information by employing two functions: scaling and wavelet function. The approximation coefficient is subsequently divided into new approximation and detailed coefficients. This process is carried out iteratively producing a set of approximation coefficients and detailed coefficients at different levels of decomposition.

If the scaling functions and wavelets form an orthogonal basis, Parseval's theorem relates the energy of the signal $x(t)$ to the energy in each of the components and their wavelet coefficients. The energy of the detailed signal at each resolution level, j is given by:

$$E_j = \sum_{k=1}^{N} |d_{j,k}|^2 \quad j = 1 \text{ to } n \tag{1}$$

$$E_{total} = \sum_{j} E_j \tag{2}$$

The wavelet energy can be used to extract only the useful information from the signal about the process under study.

For this work the concept of relative energy is used. Relative Wavelet Energy (RWE) gives information about relative energy with associated frequency bands and can detect the degree of similarity between segments of a signal. RWE is defined by the ratio of detail energy at the specific decomposition level to the total energy. Thus the relative energy is given by:

$$RWE = \frac{E_j}{E_{total}} \tag{3}$$

RWE resolves the wavelet representation of the signal in one wavelet decomposition level corresponding to the representative signal frequency. Thus this method accurately detects and characterizes the specific phenomenon related to the different frequency bands of the EEG signal. RWE gains the advantages over DWT based feature extraction in terms of speed, computation efficiency and classification rate. The RWE features are ranked and selected in order to further improve the computational efficiency. This is done by evaluating how well an individual energy feature contributes to the classification accuracy.

SVM is a binary classifier algorithm that looks for an optimal hyperplane as a decision function in high-dimensional space. For binary SVM every sample is partitioned by a series of optimal hyperplanes. The optimal hyperplane is the one which has maximum distance from the training data and will achieve lowest error when used for classifying the training data. These hyperplane for pattern x_i is modeled as:

$$\mathbf{w}_{st}\mathbf{x}_i^T + b_{st} = 0 \tag{4}$$

and the classification functions are defined as $f_{st} = \mathbf{w}_{st}\mathbf{x}_i^T + b_{st}$, where x_i denotes the i th row of the training matrix x, w is the weight vector, b is a bias term, s and t denote two partitions of two classes (-1 and +1) separated by an optimal hyperplane. SVM determines these hyperplanes using the convex quadratic programming and obtains the optimal solution of $\mathbf{w}_{st}$ and b_{st}. The weight vectors are the functions of a small subset of the training examples called "support vectors". The existence of the support vectors depends upon the computational properties and the classification performance of the SVM. SVM training algorithm can be summarized as follows:

Inputs: Training samples $(x_1, x_2, x_3,.....x_l)$ and class labels $[y_1, y_2, y_3, ... y_l]$
Maximize

$$W(\alpha) = \sum_{i=1}^{l}\alpha_i y_i - \frac{1}{2}\sum_{i=1}^{n}\sum_{j=1}^{n}\alpha_i\alpha_j y_i y_j x_i x_j \tag{5}$$

Subject to

$$\sum_{i=1}^{n}\alpha_i y_i = 0, \ 0 \le \alpha_i \le C$$

where α and C are positive constants and are termed as soft margin parameters.

The decision function for an input vector $\mathbf{x}$ is:

$$D(x) = \mathbf{w}.\mathbf{x} + b \tag{6}$$

where

$$\mathbf{w} = \sum_{i=1}^{l} \alpha_i \mathbf{x_i} y_i$$

$$b = \left(y_i - \mathbf{wx}_i \right)$$

Thus the energy features are ranked using the magnitude of the weights of SVM classifier as the ranking criteria. Further the optimal features are selected and redundant features are eliminated by using the recursive feature elimination procedure which is an instance of backward feature elimination.

The above mentioned techniques are used to design the WFS algorithm. This algorithm is used to obtain a compact and optimal feature subset from the wavelet features. The algorithm is explained in detail in the next section.

2.1. Wavelet Feature Selection Algorithm

The motivation behind this algorithm is to improve the classification robustness by reducing data dimensionality in order to facilitate better generalization as well as reducing the learning and operating complexity of the classifiers. While doing so, classification performance must not be compromised by throwing away components that provide useful information regarding the class labels.

WFS is an application of SVMRFE on wavelet theory. DWT is first utilized to obtain the wavelet coefficients and then the relative wavelet energy is found for each decomposition level. The features obtained by RWE are then ranked and selected using the SVM-RFE algorithm. This is done by finding a subset of size n among m RWE features $(n < m)$ which maximizes the performance of the classifier. The method is based on a backward sequential selection. In this method one starts with all the features and removes one feature at a time until n features are left. The RWE features are removed using weight magnitude as the ranking criteria. The algorithm adopts the first order method for ranking the features wherein the feature is ranked according to its influence on the criterion which is measured with the absolute value of the derivative. The ranking criterion is the sensitivity of ‖w‖2 with respect to the RWE feature. The removed feature is the one whose removal minimizes the variation of ‖w‖2. Hence the ranking criteria Rc for a given RWE feature is given by:

$$R_{ci} = \left(w_i \right)^2 \tag{7}$$

where **w** is the weight vector obtained after training the RWE features using SVM and class labels. Thus the removed variable is the one which has least affect on the variation of the weight vector. WFS algorithm designed using SVMRFE is as follows.

Algorithm WFS:
- ◦ Training EEG Inputs: X0=[x1 x2 x3……xl]^T
- ◦ Class Labels y: [y1 y2 y3 ……..yl]^T
- ◦ Apply DWT on the EEG training samples
- ◦ Calculate the RWE Feature Vector using equation (4)
  - ▪ Eo= [E1 E2 E3………El]^T

- • E1= [Ed1 Ed2 .... Edm]

where m= decomposition level

- ◦ For all RWE feature vectors
- ◦ Initialize
  - • Subset of surviving energy features
  - • e = [1,2 3,.....m]
  - • Feature Ranked List f = [ ] (null vector)
- ◦ Repeat until e = [ ] (null vector)
- ◦ Restrict Energy feature vector to good feature indices
  - • E = E_0(:,e)
- ◦ Train the SVM classifier with the Energy vector E and class label y
- ◦ For all features of E compute the weight vector and the ranking criteria Rc
- ◦ Find the feature with smallest ranking criteria
  - • c = argmin (Rc)
- ◦ Update the feature ranked list
  - • f= [e(c),f]
- ◦ Remove the feature with smallest ranking criteria
  - • e= e(1:c-1,c+1:length(e))
- ◦ Output: Feature ranked list f
- ◦ Use the feature ranked list to select the optimal RWE Feature Vector
  - • Et = [E1 E2 E3.........El]^T
  - • E1 = [Edf (1) Edf(2) .... Edf(n)]

where n= number of features required

The procedure explained above can be used to derive a compact and optimal feature vector from the wavelet decomposition features. The above mentioned algorithm will be applied on two real world EEG Databases for detecting efficiency capabilities of the presented WFS algorithm. The experimental work is explained in the next section.

3. RESULTS

3.1. Data Description

The WFS algorithm is tested on two real world EEG Databases. The first Database, i.e. Database1, is sleep EEG Database provided by Physiobank with six different types of stages (Andrzejak, Lehnertz, & Rieke, 2001). They contain horizontal EOG, Fpz-Cz and Pz-Oz EEG, each sampled at 100 Hz. The second Database, i.e., Database2 is the epilepsy Database (Kemp, Zwinderman, Tuk, Kamphuisen,& Oberyé, 2000), which is publicly available. The complete Database consists of five sets (denoted A–E), each containing 100 single-channel EEG signals of 23.6 s. Although several works have been reported on the classification of both the Databases as mentioned in (Garg, Singh, Gupta, Mittal, & Chandra, 2011; Garg, Behl, & Singh, 2011), these have been chosen for their established results. The separation of the data in different classes for both the cases (Databases) is easy but the WFS make the whole procedure more computationally efficient and fast.

3.2. Experimental Work

The experimental work is done using the system explained in Garg, et al. (2011). DWT is used for feature extraction, WFS algorithm for feature selection and SVM classifier for classification step. For both the Databases the same procedure is adopted. A randomly chosen small portion of the data is used as a training set and rest are included in a test set.

3.2.1. Feature Extraction

The discrete wavelet transform is used in this study to decompose the EEG signals into several frequency bands. One of the most important issues while addressing DWT for signal analysis is to choose the appropriate wavelet and decomposition level. For this study the dabuchies, symmlet and coiflet families are considered. Several experimentations are performed to test the optimal wavelet function for both Databases. The results yield sym4 as the best mother wavelet for Database1 and db4 as the best mother wavelet for Database2. The decomposition level is chosen to be 6 for both the Databases (see Figures 1 and 2).

The RWE features obtained are ranked using the WFS algorithm. The ranking of the features is shown in Table 1. The next step is to decide the value of n. After various experimentations as shown in Figure 3 and Figure 4, the value of n is taken as 2. Therefore after feature ranking and selection, the two top ranked energy features are used to create the optimal RWE feature subset. The WFS algorithm also requires the processing of SVM classifier. The SVM classifier is designed using Spline kernel function (see Figures 3 and 4).

Figure 1. Error comparison for best decomposition level for Database 1

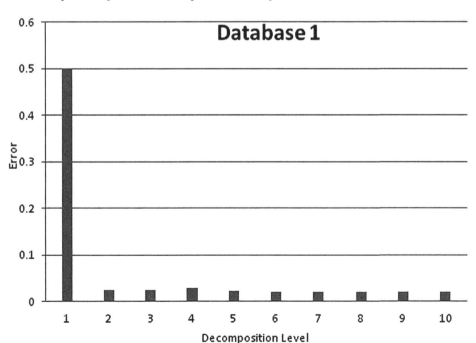

Figure 2. Error comparison for best decomposition level for Database 2

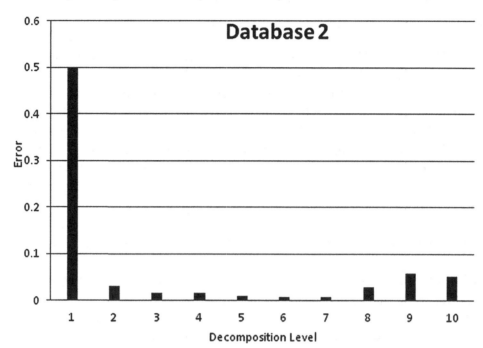

Table 1. Feature ranking using WFS algorithm

Feature	*f1*	*f2*	*f3*	*f4*	*f5*	*f6*	*f7*
Database 1	1	1	3	6	4	5	2
Database 2	2	3	4	2	5	6	1

Figure 3. Error comparison for number of features for Database1

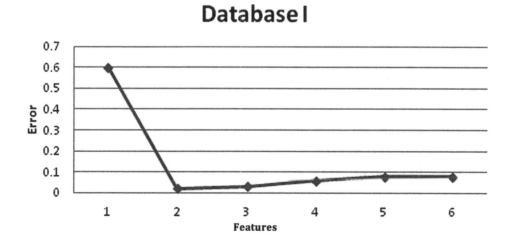

3.2.2. Classification

The SVM classifier is designed using the optimal feature subset selected after applying WFS on the EEG signals from the Database1 and Database2. The classifier designed for the WFS is used for the classification purposes. The accuracy of the classifier is evaluated individually for both the Databases. The training of SVM1 for Database1 is performed by using 30 samples of EEG data from all the six classes. The total number of training features is 180x2=360. The trained classifier is then tested for 300 samples of EEG data. The total number of test features is 300x2=600. The training of SVM2 for Database2 is performed by using 30 EEG signals from all the five sets. The total number of training features is 150x2=300. The test data comprises of 300 EEG signals. The total number of test features is 300x2=600.

3.2.3. Assessment of the Algorithm

In order to assess the quality of the proposed algorithm, the following metrics are used:

1. **Feature Space:** The true benefits of a feature selection algorithm can be investigated by evaluating the reduction in the amount of data needed to achieve learning.
2. **Execution Time:** This is one feature which is correlated with the feature space. As the feature space decreases, the execution time also decreases. But in several cases due to the complexity of the algorithm the execution time increases making the system slow. It is to be noted here that the time considered is the time taken by the trained classifier to classify the test signals.
3. **Accuracy:** The prime requirement of any efficient algorithm is that the accuracy of the system designed using the feature selection algorithm should not be compromised due to the reduction in the feature space.
4. The values of all these metrics are shown in Table 2 and Table 3. The tables describe the value of above mentioned metrics for original feature set and the optimal feature set obtained using WFS algorithm.

Figure 4. Error comparison for number of features for Database2

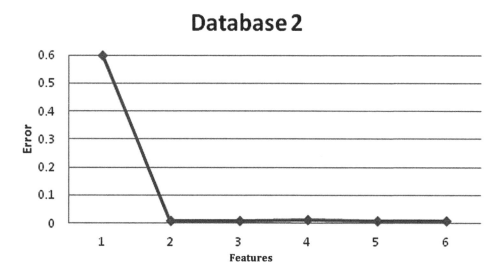

From Table 2 and Table 3 it is verified that in addition to the reduction in the feature space by decreasing the number of features per sample, the algorithm also shows a significant improvement in the classification accuracy and the execution time. Also since the same classifier is used for the feature selection and classification stage, the computational complexity is also within the limits.

4. CONCLUSION

A feature ranking and selection algorithm WFS is developed for the biomedical signal processing based on the machine learning. The inclusion of the machine learning algorithm in the feature ranking stage ensures that only those features are kept which aid in improving the classification accuracy of the final system designed. The ultimate benefits obtained by designing the algorithm are as follows:

1. The memory space required for execution of the program is reduced due to less number of features per sample.
2. Elimination of irrelevant features enhances the generalized performance of the whole system. This is evident from the consistent performance of the system on both the Databases.
3. Minimize the effect of the redundant, noisy and unreliable information.
4. Computational time is reduced significantly.

The algorithm is tested on two EEG Databases and the wavelet features obtained from decomposition are ranked and selected using WFS algorithm. The results demonstrate that the algorithm can produce powerful classification results by using only a small portion of the original wavelet decomposition feature set.

Table 2. Comparisons of metrics for original and WFS features (Database 1)

	Execution Time	**Average Accuracy**	**Feature Space (per Sample)**
Original Features	7 sec	100%	6
WFS Features	1.5 sec	100%	2

Table 3. Comparisons of metrics for original and WFS features (Database 2)

	Execution Time	**Average Accuracy**	**Feature Space (per Sample)**
Original Features	10 sec	92%	6
WFS Features	3sec	98%	2

REFERENCES

Andrzejak, R. G., Lehnertz, K., & Rieke, C. (2001). Indications of non linear deterministic and finite dimensional structures in time series of brain electrical activity: Dependence on recording region and brain state. *Physical Review E: Statistical, Nonlinear, and Soft Matter Physics, 64*(6), 1–8. doi:10.1103/PhysRevE.64.061907

Garg, G., Behl, S., & Singh, V. (2011). Assessment of non-parametric and parametric PSD estimation methods for automated epileptic seizure detection. *Journal of Computing, 3*, 160–166.

Garg, G., Singh, V., Gupta, J. R. P., Mittal, A. P., & Chandra, S. (2011). Computer assisted automatic sleep scoring system using relative wavelet energy based neuro fuzzy model. *WSEAS Transaction on Biology & Biomedicine, 8*, 12–24.

Guyon, I., Weston, J., Barnhill, S., & Vapnik, V. (2002). Gene selection for cancer classification using support vector machines. *Machine Learning, 46*(1/3), 389–422. doi:10.1023/A:1012487302797

Kemp, B., Zwinderman, A. H., Tuk, B., Kamphuisen, H. A. C., & Oberyé, J. J. L. (2000). Analysis of a sleep-dependent neuronal feedback loop, the slow-wave microcontinuity of the EEG. *IEEE Transactions on Bio-Medical Engineering, 47*(9), 1185–1194. doi:10.1109/10.867928 PMID:11008419

Compilation of References

Abbott, H., & Palekar, U. S. (2008). Retail replenishment models with display-space elastic demand. *European Journal of Operational Research*, *186*(2), 586–607. doi:10.1016/j.ejor.2006.12.067

Abidi, S. S. R. (2001). Knowledge management in healthcare: Towards 'knowledge-driven'decision-support services. *International Journal of Medical Informatics*, *63*(1), 5–18. doi:10.1016/S1386-5056(01)00167-8 PMID:11518661

Acid, S., De Campos, L. M., Fernández-Luna, J. M., & Huete, J. F. (2003). An information retrieval model based on simple Bayesian networks. *International Journal of Intelligent Systems*, *18*(2), 251–265. doi:10.1002/int.10088

Afrabandpey, H., Ghaffari, M., Mirzaei, A., & Safayani, M. (2014). A novel bat algorithm based on chaos for optimization tasks. *Intelligent Systems (ICIS), 2014 Iranian Conference on* (pp. 1-6) IEEE. doi:10.1109/IranianCIS.2014.6802527

Agrawal, R., & Srikant, R. (1994). Fast algorithms for mining association rules. In *Proc. of the Int. Conf. Very Large Data Bases* (VLDB'94), (pp. 487–499). Academic Press.

Ahlemeyer-Stubbe, A., & Coleman, S. (2014). *A practical guide to data mining for business and industry*. Wiley. doi:10.1002/9781118763704

Ahmadyfard, A., & Modares, H. (2008, August). Combining PSO and k-means to enhance data clustering. In *Telecommunications, 2008. IST 2008. International Symposium on* (pp. 688-691). IEEE. doi:10.1109/ISTEL.2008.4651388

Ahmed, S. (2005). Seasonal models of peak electric load demand. *Technological Forecasting and Social Change*, *72*(5), 609–622. doi:10.1016/j.techfore.2004.02.003

Airouche, M., Bentabet, L., & Zelmat, M. (2009, July). Image segmentation using active contour model and level set method applied to detect oil spills. In *Proceedings of the World Congress on Engineering* (Vol. 1, pp. 1-3).

Akhshani, A., Akhavan, A., Mobaraki, A., Lim, S. C., & Hassan, Z. (2014). Pseudo random number generator based on quantum chaotic map. *Communications in Nonlinear Science and Numerical Simulation*, *19*(1), 101–111. doi:10.1016/j.cnsns.2013.06.017

Akter, R., & Chung, Y. (2013). An Evolutionary Approach for Document Clustering. *IERI Procedia*, *4*, 370–375. doi:10.1016/j.ieri.2013.11.053

Alatas, B. (2010). Chaotic bee colony algorithms for global numerical optimization. *Expert Systems with Applications*, *37*(8), 5682–5687. doi:10.1016/j.eswa.2010.02.042

Alfares, H. K., & Nazeeruddin, M. (2002). Electric load forecasting: Literature survey and classification of methods. *International Journal of Systems Science*, *33*(1), 23–34. doi:10.1080/00207720110067421

Alghamdi, R., Taileb, M., & Ameen, M. (2014, April). A new multimodal fusion method based on association rules mining for image retrieval. In *Mediterranean Electrotechnical Conference (MELECON), 2014 17th IEEE* (pp. 493-499). IEEE. doi:10.1109/MELCON.2014.6820584

Al-Khatib, J. A., Stanton, A. A., & Rawwas, M. Y. A. (2005). Ethical segmentation of consumers in developing countries: A comparative analysis. *International Marketing Review*, *22*(2), 225–246. doi:10.1108/02651330510593287

Alpar, R. (2013). *Uygulamali cok degiskenli istatistiksel yontemler* [Applied multivariate statistical methods]. Ankara: Detay Yayincilik.

Alpaydin, E. (2004). *Introduction to machine learning*. Cambridge, MA: MIT Press.

Al-Shareef, A. J., Mohamed, E. A., & Al-Judaibi, E. (2008). One hour ahead load forecasting using artificial neural network for the western area of Saudi Arabia. *International Journal of Electrical Systems Science and Engineering*, *1*(1), 35–40.

Aly, W. M., & Kelleny, H. A. (2014). Adaptation Of Cuckoo Search For Documents Clustering. *International Journal of Computers and Applications*, *86*(1), 4–10. doi:10.5120/14947-3041

Amiri, B., & Fathian, M. (2007). Integration of self organizing feature maps and honey bee mating optimization for market segmentation. *Journal of Theoretical and Applied Information Technology*, *3*(3), 70–86.

Anastasiu, D. C., Tagarelli, A., & Karypis, G. (2013). Document Clustering: The Next Frontier. In C. C. Aggarwal & C. K. Reddy (Eds.), *Data Clustering: Algorithms and Applications* (pp. 305–338). CRC Press.

Anderson, E. E. (1979). An analysis of retail display space: Theory and methods. *The Journal of Business*, *52*(1), 103–118. doi:10.1086/296036

Anderson, E. E., & Amato, H. N. (1974). A mathematical model for simultaneously determining the optimal brand-collection and display-area allocation. *Operations Research*, *22*(1), 13–21. doi:10.1287/opre.22.1.13

Andonie, R., & Kovalerchuk, B. (2015). *Neural Networks for Data Mining: Constrains and Open Problems*. Retrieved June 27, 2015, from http://citeseerx.ist.psu.edu/viewdoc/download?doi=10.1.1.91.7835&rep=rep1&type=pdf

Andrzejak, R. G., Lehnertz, K., Mormann, F., Rieke, C., David, P., & Elger, C. E. (2001). Indications of nonlinear deterministic and finite-dimensional structures in time series of brain electrical activity: Dependance on recording region and brain state. *Physical Review*, *64*, 1–8. PMID:11736210

Andrzejak, R. G., Lehnertz, K., & Rieke, C. (2001). Indications of non linear deterministic and finite dimensional structures in time series of brain electrical activity: Dependence on recording region and brain state. *Physical Review E: Statistical, Nonlinear, and Soft Matter Physics*, *64*(6), 1–8. doi:10.1103/PhysRevE.64.061907

Antoniou, A., & Lu, W.-S. (2007). *Practical Optimization-Algorithms and Engineering Applications*. Springer Science and Business Media, LLC.

Arabani, A. B., & Farahani, R. Z. (2012). Facility location dynamics: An overview of classifications and applications. *Computers & Industrial Engineering*, *62*(1), 408–420. doi:10.1016/j.cie.2011.09.018

Archenaa, J., & Anita, E. M. (2015). A Survey of Big Data Analytics in Healthcare and Government. *Procedia Computer Science*, *50*, 408–413. doi:10.1016/j.procs.2015.04.021

Arnold, S. J. (1979). A test for clusters. *JMR, Journal of Marketing Research*, *16*(4), 545–551. doi:10.2307/3150815

Arnold, V. I., & Avez, A. (1968). *Ergodic problems of classical mechanics*. Retrieved from WA Benjamin.

Azadeh, A., Ghaderi, S. F., & Nasrollahi, M. R. (2011). Location optimization of wind plants in Iran by an integrated hierarchical Data Envelopment Analysis. *Renewable Energy*, *36*(5), 1621–1631. doi:10.1016/j.renene.2010.11.004

Azadeh, A., Ghaderi, S. F., Tarverdian, S., & Saberi, M. (2007). Integration of artificial neural networks and genetic algorithm to predict electrical energy consumption. *Applied Mathematics and Computation*, *186*(2), 1731–1741. doi:10.1016/j.amc.2006.08.093

Azadeh, A., & Izadbakhsh, H. R. (2008). A multi-variate/multi-attribute approach for plant layout design. *International Journal of Industrial Engineering: Theory. Applications and Practice*, *15*(2), 143–154.

Azaryuon, K., & Fakhar, B. (2013). A Novel Document Clustering Algorithm Based on Ant Colony Optimization Algorithm. *Journal of Mathematics and Computer Science*, *7*, 171–180.

Bahrami, S., Hooshmand, R. A., & Parastegari, M. (2014). Short term electric load forecasting by wavelet transform and grey model improved by PSO (particle swarm optimization) algorithm. *Energy*, *72*, 434–442. doi:10.1016/j.energy.2014.05.065

Bai, R., Van Woensel, T., Kendall, G., & Burke, E. K. (2013). A new model and a hyper-heuristic approach for two-dimensional shelf space allocation. *4OR*, *11*(1), 31-55.

Bai, C., & Sarkis, J. (2011). Evaluating supplier development programs with a grey based rough set methodology. *Expert Systems with Applications*, *38*(11), 13505–13517.

Bailey, C., Baines, P. R., Wilson, H., & Clark, M. (2009). Segmentation and customer insight in contemporary services marketing practice: Why grouping customers is no longer enough. *Journal of Marketing Management*, *25*(3-4), 227–252. doi:10.1362/026725709X429737

Bai, R., Burke, E. K., & Kendall, G. (2008). Heuristic, meta-heuristic and hyper-heuristic approaches for fresh produce inventory control and shelf space allocation. *The Journal of the Operational Research Society*, *59*(10), 1387–1397. doi:10.1057/palgrave.jors.2602463

Bakirtzis, A. G., Petridis, V., Kiartzis, S. J., & Alexiadis, M. C. (1996). A neural network short term load forecasting model for the Greek power system. *Power Systems. IEEE Transactions on*, *11*(2), 858–863.

Balakrishnan, P. V. S., Cooper, M. C., Jacob, V. S., & Lewis, P. A. (1996). Comparative performance of the FSCL neural net and k-means algorithm for market segmentation. *European Journal of Operational Research*, *93*(2), 346–357. doi:10.1016/0377-2217(96)00046-X

Balan, S., & Devi, T. (2012). Design and Development of an Algorithm for Image Clustering In Textile Image Retrieval Using Color Descriptors. *International Journal of Computer Science, Engineering and Applications, 2*(3).

Ballou, R. (2004). *Business logistics / Supply Chain Management*. Pearson Prentice Hall.

Barnett, N. L. (1969). Beyond market segmentation. *Harvard Business Review*, *47*, 152–166.

Bastos-Filho, C. J., Oliveira, M. A., Nascimento, D. N., & Ramos, A. D. (2010). Impact of the random number generator quality on particle swarm optimization algorithm running on graphic processor units. *Hybrid Intelligent Systems (HIS), 2010 10th International Conference on* (pp. 85-90) IEEE. doi:10.1109/HIS.2010.5601073

Bath, P. A. (2004). Data mining in health and medical information. *Annual Review of Information Science & Technology*, *38*(1), 331–369. doi:10.1002/aris.1440380108

Bayer, J. (2010). Customer segmentation in the telecommunications industry. *Database Marketing & Customer Strategy Management*, *17*(3), 247–256. doi:10.1057/dbm.2010.21

Beane, T. P., & Ennis, D. M. (1987). Market segmentation: A review. *European Journal of Marketing*, *21*(5), 20–42. doi:10.1108/EUM0000000004695

Beker, H., & Piper, F. (1982). *Cipher systems: the protection of communications*. Northwood Books.

Bellazzi, R., & Zupan, B. (2008). Predictive data mining in clinical medicine: Current issues and guidelines. *International Journal of Medical Informatics*, *77*(2), 81–97. doi:10.1016/j.ijmedinf.2006.11.006 PMID:17188928

Berndt, D. J., Hevner, A. R., & Studnicki, J. (2003). The Catch data warehouse: Support for community health care decision-making. *Decision Support Systems*, *35*(3), 367–384. doi:10.1016/S0167-9236(02)00114-8

Berthold, M., Borgelt, C., Hoppner, F., & Klawonn, F. (2010). *Guide to intelligent data analysis*. Springer. doi:10.1007/978-1-84882-260-3

Bezdek, J. C. (1973). *Fuzzy mathematics in pattern classification*. Academic Press.

Bezdek, J. C., & Dunn, J. C. (1975). Optimal fuzzy partitions: A heuristic for estimating the parameters in a mixture of normal distributions. *Computers. IEEE Transactions on*, *100*(8), 835–838.

Bhutta, K. S., & Huq, F. (2002). Supplier selection problem: A comparison of the total cost of ownership and analytic hierarchy process approaches. *Supply Chain Management. International Journal (Toronto, Ont.)*, *7*(3), 126–135.

Bianco, V., Manca, O., Nardini, S., & Minea, A. A. (2010). Analysis and forecasting of nonresidential electricity consumption in Romania. *Applied Energy*, *87*(11), 3584–3590. doi:10.1016/j.apenergy.2010.05.018

Bisht, S., & Paul, A. (2013). Document Clustering: A Review. *International Journal of Computers and Applications*, *73*(11), 26–33. doi:10.5120/12787-0024

Bloom, J. Z. (2004). Tourist market segmentation with linear and non-linear techniques. *Tourism Management*, *25*(6), 723–733. doi:10.1016/j.tourman.2003.07.004

Bloom, J. Z. (2005). Market segmentation: A neural network application. *Annals of Tourism Research*, *32*(1), 93–111. doi:10.1016/j.annals.2004.05.001

Blum, C., & Roli, A. (2003). Metaheuristics in combinatorial optimization: Overview and conceptual comparison. *ACM Computing Surveys*, *35*(3), 268–308. doi:10.1145/937503.937505

Bohanec, M., Zupan, B., & Rajkovič, V. (2000). Applications of qualitative multi-attribute decision models in health care. *International Journal of Medical Informatics*, *58*, 191–205. doi:10.1016/S1386-5056(00)00087-3 PMID:10978921

Bonney, W. (2013). Applicability of business intelligence in electronic health record. *Procedia: Social and Behavioral Sciences*, *73*, 257–262. doi:10.1016/j.sbspro.2013.02.050

Bookbinder, J. H., & Zarour, F. H. (2001). Direct product profitability and retail shelf-space allocation models. *Journal of Business Logistics, 22*(2), 183-208.

Bookman, M. (2012). *Predicting fantasy football - truth in data*. Retrieved May 25, 2015, from http://cs229.stanford.edu/proj2012/Bookman-PredictingFantasyFootball.pdf

Boone, D. S., & Roehm, M. (2002a). Evaluating the appropriateness of market segmentation solutions using artificial neural networks and the membership clustering criterion. *Marketing Letters*, *13*(4), 317–333. doi:10.1023/A:1020321132568

Boone, D. S., & Roehm, M. (2002b). Retail segmentation using artificial neural networks. *International Journal of Research in Marketing*, *19*(3), 287–301. doi:10.1016/S0167-8116(02)00080-0

Borin, N., & Farris, P. (1995). A sensitivity analysis of retailer shelf management models. *Journal of Retailing, 71*(2), 153–171. doi:10.1016/0022-4359(95)90005-5

Borin, N., Farris, P. W., & Freeland, J. R. (1994). A model for determining retail product category assortment and shelf space allocation. *Decision Sciences, 25*(3), 359–384. doi:10.1111/j.1540-5915.1994.tb01848.x

Bose, R. (2003). Knowledge management-enabled health care management systems: Capabilities, infrastructure, and decision-support. *Expert Systems with Applications, 24*(1), 59–71. doi:10.1016/S0957-4174(02)00083-0

Bossaerts, P., & Hillion, P. (1999). Implementing Statistical Criteria to Select Return Forecasting Models: What Do We Learn? *Review of Financial Studies, 12*(2), 405–428. doi:10.1093/rfs/12.2.405

Boutsidis, C., Mahoney, M. W., & Drineas, P. (2008, August). Unsupervised feature selection for principal components analysis. In *Proceedings of the 14th ACM SIGKDD international conference on Knowledge discovery and data mining* (pp. 61-69). ACM. doi:10.1145/1401890.1401903

Bouveyron, C., Girard, S., & Schmid, C. (2007). High-dimensional data clustering. *Computational Statistics & Data Analysis, 52*(1), 502–519. doi:10.1016/j.csda.2007.02.009

Box, G. E., & Jenkins, G. M. (1976). *Time series analysis: forecasting and control.* Holden-Day.

Brachman, R., Khabaza, T., Kloesgen, W., Piatetsky-Shapiro, G., & Simoudis, E. (1996). Mining Business Databases. *Communications of the ACM, 39*(11), 42–48. doi:10.1145/240455.240468

Bradley A. P. (2003).Shift Invariance in Discrete Wavelet Transform. In *Proceeding of 7th Digital Image Computing: Techniques and Applications,* (pp. 29-38). Academic Press.

Breault, J. L., Goodall, C. R., & Fos, P. J. (2002). Data mining a diabetic data warehouse. *Artificial Intelligence in Medicine, 26*(1), 37–54. doi:10.1016/S0933-3657(02)00051-9 PMID:12234716

Breiman, L. (2001). Random forests. *Machine Learning, 45*(1), 5–32. doi:10.1023/A:1010933404324

Brijs, T., Swinnen, G., Vanhoof, K., & Wets, G. (1999, August). Using association rules for product assortment decisions: A case study. In *Proceedings of the fifth ACM SIGKDD international conference on Knowledge discovery and data mining* (pp. 254-260). ACM. doi:10.1145/312129.312241

Brijs, T., Goethals, B., Swinnen, G., Vanhoof, K., & Wets, G. (2000, August). A data mining framework for optimal product selection in retail supermarket data: the generalized PROFSET model. In *Proceedings of the sixth ACM SIGKDD international conference on Knowledge discovery and data mining* (pp. 300-304). ACM. doi:10.1145/347090.347156

Brossette, S. E., Sprague, A. P., Hardin, J. M., Waites, K. B., Jones, W. T., & Moser, S. A. (1998). Association rules and data mining in hospital infection control and public health surveillance. *Journal of the American Medical Informatics Association, 5*(4), 373–381. doi:10.1136/jamia.1998.0050373 PMID:9670134

Bucklin, R. E., & Sismeiro, C. (2003). A model of web site browsing behavior estimated on clickstream data. *JMR, Journal of Marketing Research, 40*(3), 249–267. doi:10.1509/jmkr.40.3.249.19241

Bultez, A., & Naert, P. (1988). SH.ARP: Shelf allocation for retailers' profit. *Marketing Science, 7*(3), 211–231. doi:10.1287/mksc.7.3.211

Burbidge, R., & Buxton, B. (2015). *An Introduction to Support Vector Machines for Data Mining.* Retrieved June 27, 2015, from http://www.cc.gatech.edu/classes/AY2008/cs7641_spring/handouts/yor12-introsvm.pdf

Buttle, F. (1984). Merchandising. *European Journal of Marketing, 18*(6/7), 104–123. doi:10.1108/EUM0000000004795

Campbell, J. Y., & Thompson, S. (2008). Predicting the Equity Premium Out of Sample: Can Anything Beat the Historical Average? *Review of Financial Studies*, *21*(4), 1509–1531. doi:10.1093/rfs/hhm055

Cao, Y., Xu, J., Liu, T. Y., Li, H., Huang, Y., & Hon, H. W. (2006, August). Adapting ranking SVM to document retrieval, In *Proceedings of the 29th annual international ACM SIGIR conference on Research and development in information retrieval* (pp. 186-193). ACM.

Cao, Z., Qin, T., Liu, T. Y., Tsai, M. F., & Li, H. (2007, June). Learning to rank: from pairwise approach to listwise approach. In *Proceedings of the 24th international conference on Machine learning* (pp. 129-136). ACM. doi:10.1145/1273496.1273513

Caponetto, R., Fortuna, L., Fazzino, S., & Xibilia, M. G. (2003). Chaotic sequences to improve the performance of evolutionary algorithms. *Evolutionary Computation. IEEE Transactions on*, *7*(3), 289–304.

Carreño, I. R., & Vuskovic, M. (2007). Wavelet Transform Moments for Feature Extraction from Temporal Signals. In *Proceedings of Informatics in Control, Automation and Robotics II* (pp. 235–242). Netherlands: Springer. doi:10.1007/978-1-4020-5626-0_28

Castaeda-Méndez, K., Mangan, K., & Lavery, A. M. (1998). The role and application of the balanced scorecard in healthcare quality management. *Journal for Healthcare Quality*, *20*(1), 10–13. doi:10.1111/j.1945-1474.1998.tb00243.x PMID:10177013

Castellani, B., & Castellani, J. (2003). Data mining: Qualitative analysis with health informatics data. *Qualitative Health Research*, *13*(7), 1005–1018. doi:10.1177/1049732303253523 PMID:14502965

Castelli, M., & Vanneschi, L. (2014). Genetic algorithm with variable neighborhood search for the optimal allocation of goods in shop shelves. *Operations Research Letters*, *42*(5), 355–360. doi:10.1016/j.orl.2014.06.002

Chae, Y. M., Ho, S. H., Cho, K. W., Lee, D. H., & Ji, S. H. (2001). Data mining approach to policy analysis in a health insurance domain. *International Journal of Medical Informatics*, *62*(2), 103–111. doi:10.1016/S1386-5056(01)00154-X PMID:11470613

Chae, Y. M., Kim, H. S., Tark, K. C., Park, H. J., & Ho, S. H. (2003). Analysis of healthcare quality indicator using data mining and decision support system. *Expert Systems with Applications*, *24*(2), 167–172. doi:10.1016/S0957-4174(02)00139-2

Chamodrakas, I., Batis, D., & Martakos, D. (2010). Supplier selection in electronic marketplaces using satisficing and fuzzy AHP. *Expert Systems with Applications*, *37*(1), 490–498. doi:10.1016/j.eswa.2009.05.043

Chan, C. C. (2008). Intelligent value-based customer segmentation method for campaign management: A case study of automobile retailer. *Expert Systems with Applications*, *34*(4), 2754–2762. doi:10.1016/j.eswa.2007.05.043

Chan, C. K., Chan, C. K., & Cheng, L. M. (2001). *Software Generation of Random Numbers by Using Neural Network. Artificial Neural Nets and Genetic Algorithms*. Springer. doi:10.1007/978-3-7091-6230-9_51

Chandramohan, A., Rao, M. V. C., & Arumugam, S. M. (2006). Two new and useful defuzzification methods based on root mean square value. Soft Computing-A Fusion Of Foundations. *Methodologies And Applications*, *10*(11), 1047–1059.

Changchien, S. W., & Lu, T. Z. (2001). Mining association rules procedure to support on-line recommendation by customers and products fragmentation. *Expert Systems with Applications*, *20*(4), 325–335. doi:10.1016/S0957-4174(01)00017-3

Chang, P. C., Fan, C. Y., & Lin, J. J. (2011). Monthly electricity demand forecasting based on a weighted evolving fuzzy neural network approach. *International Journal of Electrical Power & Energy Systems*, *33*(1), 17–27. doi:10.1016/j.ijepes.2010.08.008

Chan, N., Felix, T. S., Kumar, M. K., Tiwari, H. C., Lau, W., & Choy, K. L. (2008). Global supplier selection: A fuzzy-AHP approach. *International Journal of Production Research*, *46*(14), 3825–3857. doi:10.1080/00207540600787200

Chapelle, O., & Keerthi, S. S. (2010). Efficient algorithms for ranking with SVMs. *Information Retrieval Journal*, *13*(3), 201–215. doi:10.1007/s10791-009-9109-9

Charilas, D., Markaki, O., Nikitopoulos, D., & Theologou, M. (2008). Packet-switched network selection with the highest QoS in 4G networks. *Computer Networks*, *52*(1), 248–258. doi:10.1016/j.comnet.2007.09.005

Charilas, D., Panagopoulos, A., & Markaki, O. (2014). A unified network selection framework using principal component analysis and multi attribute decision making. *Wireless Personal Communications*, *74*(1), 147–165. doi:10.1007/s11277-012-0905-y

Chase, R., Aquilano, N., & Jacobs, R. (2001). *Operations management for competitive advantage*. New York: McGraw-Hill/Irwin.

Chee, T., Chan, L. K., Chuah, M. H., Tan, C. S., Wong, S. F., & Yeoh, W. (2009). Business intelligence systems: state-of-the-art review and contemporary applications. In *Symposium on Progress in Information & Technology*.

Che, J., Wang, J., & Tang, Y. (2012). Optimal training subset in a support vector regression electric load forecasting model. *Applied Soft Computing*, *12*(5), 1523–1531. doi:10.1016/j.asoc.2011.12.017

Chen, C. Y., & Ye, F. (2004). Particle swarm optimization algorithm and its application to clustering analysis. In *Networking, Sensing and Control, 2004 IEEE International Conference on* (Vol. 2, pp. 789-794). IEEE.

Chen, J., Wang, J., & Zelikovsky, A. (2011). Bioinformatics Research and Application. In *7th International Symposium, ISBRA 2011, Proceedings (Vol. 6674)*. Springer Science & Business Media.

Chen, B., Chang, M., & Lin, C. (2004). Load forecasting using support vector machines: A study on EUNITE competition 2001. *IEEE Transactions on Power Systems*, *19*(4), 1821–1830. doi:10.1109/TPWRS.2004.835679

Chen, C. T. (2000). Extensions of the TOPSIS for group decision-making under fuzzy environment. *Fuzzy Sets and Systems*, *114*(1), 1–9. doi:10.1016/S0165-0114(97)00377-1

Cheng W., McClain B.W., Kelly C. (1997). Artificial Neural Networks Make Their Mark as a Powerful Tool for Investors. *Review of Business,* 4 –9.

Cheng, C.-H., & Chen, Y.-S. (2009). Classifying the segmentation of customer value via RFM model and RS theory. *Expert Systems with Applications*, *36*(3), 4176–4184. doi:10.1016/j.eswa.2008.04.003

Chen, L. Y., & Wang, T. (2009). Optimizing Partners' Choice in IS/IT Outsourcing Process: The Strategic Decision of Fuzzy VIKOR. *Int. J. Produciton Economics*, *120*(1), 233–242. doi:10.1016/j.ijpe.2008.07.022

Chen, M. C., & Lin, C. P. (2007). A data mining approach to product assortment and shelf space allocation. *Expert Systems with Applications*, *32*(4), 976–986. doi:10.1016/j.eswa.2006.02.001

Chen, N., Lu, W., Yang, J., & Li, G. (2004). *Support vector machine in chemistry* (Vol. 11). Singapore: World Scientific.

Chen, S. T., Yu, D. C., & Moghaddamjo, A. R. (1992). Weather sensitive short-term load forecasting using nonfully connected artificial neural network. *Power Systems. IEEE Transactions on*, *7*(3), 1098–1105. doi:10.1109/26.142800

Chen, T. (2012). A collaborative fuzzy-neural approach for long-term load forecasting in Taiwan. *Computers & Industrial Engineering*, *63*(3), 663–670. doi:10.1016/j.cie.2011.06.003

Chen, Z. (2001). *Data Mining and Uncertain Reasoning: An Integrated Approach*. Wiley.

Chiu, C. (2002). A case-based customer classification approach for direct marketing. *Expert Systems with Applications*, *22*(2), 163–168. doi:10.1016/S0957-4174(01)00052-5

Chiu, C.-Y., Chen, Y.-F., Kuo, I., & Kun, H. C. (2009). An intelligent market segmentation system using k-means and particle swarm optimization. *Expert Systems with Applications*, *36*(3), 4558–4565. doi:10.1016/j.eswa.2008.05.029

Chow, T. W. S., & Leung, C. T. (1996b). Nonlinear autoregressive integrated neural network model for short-term load forecasting. In *Generation, transmission and distribution, IEE proceedings-* (Vol. 143, pp. 500-506). doi:10.1049/ip-gtd:19960600

Chow, T. W. S., & Leung, C. T. (1996a). Neural network based short-term load forecasting using weather compensation. *Power Systems. IEEE Transactions on*, *11*(4), 1736–1742.

Christiaanse, W. R. (1971). Short-term load forecasting using general exponential smoothing. *Power Apparatus and Systems, IEEE Transactions on*, (2), 900-911.

Chu, M. T., Shyu, J., Tzeng, G. H., & Khosla, R. (2007). Comparison Among Three Analytical Methods For Knowledge Communities Group Decision Analysis. *Expert Systems with Applications*, *33*(4), 1011–1024. doi:10.1016/j.eswa.2006.08.026

Ciaccio, E. J., Dunn, S. M., & Akay, M. (1993). Biosignal pattern recognition and interpretation systems, Methods for feature extraction and selection. *IEEE Engineering in Medicine and Biology Magazine*, *12*(4), 106–113. doi:10.1109/51.248173

Cicek, I., Pusane, A. E., & Dundar, G. (2014). A novel design method for discrete time chaos based true random number generators. *Integration, the VLSI Journal*, *47*(1), 38-47. doi:10.1016/j.vlsi.2013.06.003

Cil, I. (2012). Consumption universes based supermarket layout through association rule mining and multidimensional scaling. *Expert Systems with Applications*, *39*(10), 8611–8625. doi:10.1016/j.eswa.2012.01.192

Cios, K. J., & Moore, G. W. (2002). Uniqueness of medical data mining. *Artificial Intelligence in Medicine*, *26*(1), 1–24. doi:10.1016/S0933-3657(02)00049-0 PMID:12234714

CISKO. (2015). *İnternet servis sağlayıcılar*. Retrieved June 27, 2015, from http://www.cisco.com/web/TR/solutions/sp/segments/isp/isp_home.html

Conci, A., & Castro, E. M. M. (2002). Image mining by content. *Expert Systems with Applications*, *23*(4), 377–383. doi:10.1016/S0957-4174(02)00073-8

Corchado, J. M., Bajo, J., De Paz, Y., & Tapia, D. I. (2008). Intelligent environment for monitoring Alzheimer patients, agent technology for health care. *Decision Support Systems*, *44*(2), 382–396. doi:10.1016/j.dss.2007.04.008

Correa, E. S., Freitas, A. A., & Johnson, C. G. (2006, July). A new discrete particle swarm algorithm applied to attribute selection in a bioinformatics data set. In *Proceedings of the 8th annual conference on Genetic and evolutionary computation* (pp. 35-42). ACM. doi:10.1145/1143997.1144003

Corstjens, M., & Doyle, P. (1981). A model for optimizing retail space allocations. *Management Science*, *27*(7), 822–833. doi:10.1287/mnsc.27.7.822

Coulter, D. M., Bate, A., Meyboom, R. H., Lindquist, M., & Edwards, I. R. (2001). Antipsychotic drugs and heart muscle disorder in international pharmacovigilance: Data mining study. *BMJ (Clinical Research Ed.)*, *322*(7296), 1207–1209. doi:10.1136/bmj.322.7296.1207 PMID:11358771

Cox, K. (1964). The responsiveness of food sales to shelf space changes in supermarkets. *JMR, Journal of Marketing Research*, *1*(2), 63–67. doi:10.2307/3149924

Cox, K. K. (1970). The effect of shelf space upon sales of branded products. *JMR, Journal of Marketing Research*, *7*(1), 55–58. doi:10.2307/3149507

Crespo, F., & Weber, R. (2005). A methodology for dynamic data mining based on fuzzy clustering. *Fuzzy Sets and Systems*, *150*(2), 267–284. doi:10.1016/j.fss.2004.03.028

Cubillas, J. J., Ramos, M. I., Feito, F. R., & Ureña, T. (2014). An improvement in the appointment scheduling in primary health care centers using data mining. *Journal of Medical Systems*, *38*(8), 1–10. doi:10.1007/s10916-014-0089-y PMID:24964781

Cui, X., & Potok, T. E. (2005). Document clustering analysis based on hybrid PSO+K-means algorithm. *Journal of Computer Sciences*, 27-33.

Cui, X., Potok, T. E., & Palathingal, P. (2005), Document clustering using particle swarm optimization, *Proceedings of IEEEin Swarm Intelligence Symposium.*

Cui, X., Potok, T. E., & Palathingal, P. (2005, June). Document clustering using particle swarm optimization. In *Swarm Intelligence Symposium, 2005. SIS 2005.Proceedings 2005 IEEE* (pp. 185-191). IEEE.

Cui, H., & Ding, Y. (2015). Renormalization and conjugacy of piecewise linear Lorenz maps. *Advances in Mathematics*, *271*, 235–272. doi:10.1016/j.aim.2014.11.024

Cui, X., Gao, J., & Potok, T. E. (2006). A flocking based algorithm for document clustering analysis. *Journal of Systems Architecture*, *52*(8), 505–515. doi:10.1016/j.sysarc.2006.02.003

Curhan, R. C. (1972). The relationship between shelf space and unit sales in supermarkets. *JMR, Journal of Marketing Research*, *9*(4), 406–412. doi:10.2307/3149304

D'Angelo, G., & Marzolla, M. (2014). New trends in parallel and distributed simulation: From many-cores to Cloud Computing. *Simulation Modelling Practice and Theory*, *49*, 320–335. doi:10.1016/j.simpat.2014.06.007

Dash, R., Dash, P. K., & Bisoi, R. (2014). A self adaptive differential harmony search based optimized extreme learning machine for financial time series prediction. *Swarm and Evolutionary Computation*, *19*, 25–42. doi:10.1016/j.swevo.2014.07.003

Delen, D., Fuller, C., McCann, C., & Ray, D. (2009). Analysis of healthcare coverage: A data mining approach. *Expert Systems with Applications*, *36*(2), 995–1003. doi:10.1016/j.eswa.2007.10.041

Delen, D., Walker, G., & Kadam, A. (2005). Predicting breast cancer survivability: A comparison of three data mining methods. *Artificial Intelligence in Medicine*, *34*(2), 113–127. doi:10.1016/j.artmed.2004.07.002 PMID:15894176

Delesie, L., & Croes, L. (2000). Operations research and knowledge discovery: A data mining method applied to health care management. *International Transactions in Operational Research*, *7*(2), 159–170. doi:10.1111/j.1475-3995.2000.tb00192.x

Desarbo, W. S., Atalay, A. S., Lebaron, D., & Blanchard, S. J. (2008). Estimating multiple consumer segment ideal points from context-dependent survey data. *The Journal of Consumer Research*, *35*(1), 142–153. doi:10.1086/529534

Dey, N., & Kar, Á. (2015). Image mining framework and techniques: A review. *International Journal of Image Mining*, *1*(1), 45–64. doi:10.1504/IJIM.2015.070028

Dhalla, N. K., & Mahatoo, W. H. (1976). Expanding the scope of segmentation research. *Journal of Marketing*, *40*(2), 34–41. doi:10.2307/1251004

Diez, J., Coz, J. J., Luacez, O., & Bahamonde, A. (2008). Clustering people according to their preference criteria. *Expert Systems with Applications, 34*(2), 1274–1284. doi:10.1016/j.eswa.2006.12.005

Diwani, S. A., & Sam, A. (2014). Data Mining Awareness and Readiness in Healthcare Sector: A case of Tanzania. *Advances in Computer Science: an International Journal, 3*(1), 37–43.

Dolnicar, S. (2004). Beyond commonsense segmentation: A systematics of segmentation approaches in tourism. *Journal of Travel Research, 42*(3), 244–250. doi:10.1177/0047287503258830

Dolnicar, S., & Leisch, F. (2004). Segmenting markets by bagged clustering. *Australasian Marketing Journal, 12*(1), 51–65. doi:10.1016/S1441-3582(04)70088-9

dos Santos Coelho, L. (2009). Reliability and redundancy optimization by means of a chaotic differential evolution approach. *Chaos, Solitons, and Fractals, 41*(2), 594–602. doi:10.1016/j.chaos.2008.02.028

Douglas, A. P., Breipohl, A. M., Lee, F. N., & Adapa, R. (1998). The impacts of temperature forecast uncertainty on Bayesian load forecasting. *Power Systems. IEEE Transactions on, 13*(4), 1507–1513.

Draco, J., Petrowski, A., Siarry, P., & Taillard, E. (2006). *Metaheuristics for hard optimization: methods and case studies.* Springer Science & Business Media.

Dreze, X., Hoch, S. J., & Purk, M. E. (1995). Shelf management and space elasticity. *Journal of Retailing, 70*(4), 301–326. doi:10.1016/0022-4359(94)90002-7

Drucker, H., Burges, C. J. C., Kaufman, L., Smola, A., & Vapnik, V. (1997). Support vector regression machines. *Advances in Neural Information Processing Systems*, 155–161.

Duan, L., Street, W. N., & Xu, E. (2011). Healthcare information systems: Data mining methods in the creation of a clinical recommender system. *Enterprise Information Systems, 5*(2), 169–181. doi:10.1080/17517575.2010.541287

Dubois, D., & Padre, H. (1980). *Fuzzy Sets and Systems: Theory and Applications.* New York: Academic Press.

Dunn, J. C. (1974). Well-separated clusters and the optimal fuzzy partitions. *Journal of Cybernetics, 4*(1), 95–104. doi:10.1080/01969727408546059

D'Urso, P., Giovanni, L. D., Disegna, M., & Massari, R. (2013). Bagged clustering and its application to tourism market segmentation. *Expert Systems with Applications, 40*(12), 4944–4956. doi:10.1016/j.eswa.2013.03.005

Dutta, S., & Shekhar, S. (1988). Bond-rating: a Non-conservative Application of Neural Networks.*Proceedings of the IEEE International Conference on Neural Networks.* doi:10.1109/ICNN.1988.23958

Easton, J. F., Stephens, C. R., & Angelova, M. (2014). Risk factors and prediction of very short term versus short/intermediate term post-stroke mortality: A data mining approach. *Computers in Biology and Medicine, 54*, 199–210. doi:10.1016/j.compbiomed.2014.09.003 PMID:25303114

Eberhart, R. C., & Shi, Y. (2001). Tracking and optimizing dynamic systems with particle swarms. *Evolutionary Computation, 2001.Proceedings of the 2001 Congress on* (vol. 1, pp. 94-100) IEEE. doi:10.1109/CEC.2001.934376

Eberhart, R. C., & Kennedy, J. (1995, October). A new optimizer using particle swarm theory. In *Proceedings of the sixth international symposium on micro machine and human science* (Vol. 1, pp. 39-43). doi:10.1109/MHS.1995.494215

Eisend, M. (2014). Shelf space elasticity: A meta-analysis. *Journal of Retailing, 90*(2), 168–181. doi:10.1016/j.jretai.2013.03.003

Englehart, K., Hudgins, B., & Parker, P. A. (2001). A wavelet-based continuous classification scheme for multifunction myoelectric control. *IEEE Transactions on Bio-Medical Engineering, 48*(3), 302–311. doi:10.1109/10.914793 PMID:11327498

Englehart, K., Hudgins, B., Parker, P. A., & Stevenson, M. (1999). Classification of the myoelectric signal using time frequency based representations. *Medical Engineering & Physics, 21*(6-7), 431–438. doi:10.1016/S1350-4533(99)00066-1 PMID:10624739

Esnaf, Ş., Küçükdeniz, T., & Tunçbilek, N. (2014). Fuzzy C-Means Algorithm with Fixed Cluster Centers for Uncapacitated Facility Location Problems: Turkish Case Study. In Supply Chain Management Under Fuzziness (pp. 489-516). Springer Berlin Heidelberg.

Esnaf, S., & Kucukdeniz, T. (2009). A fuzzy clustering-based hybrid method for a multi-facility location problem. *Journal of Intelligent Manufacturing, 20*(2), 259–265. doi:10.1007/s10845-008-0233-y

Esnaf, S., & Küçükdeniz, T. (2013). Solving Uncapacitated Planar Multi-facility Location Problems by a Revised Weighted Fuzzy c-means Clustering Algorithm. *Multiple-Valued Logic and Soft Computing, 21*(1-2), 147–164.

Espinoza, M., Suykens, J., & De Moor, B. (2005). Load forecasting using fixed-size least squares support vector machines. *Computational Intelligence and Bioinspired Systems*, 488-527.

Espinoza, M., Suykens, J. A., & De Moor, B. (2006). Fixed-size least squares support vector machines: A large scale application in electrical load forecasting. *Computational Management Science, 3*(2), 113–129. doi:10.1007/s10287-005-0003-7

Essl, G. (2006). Circle maps as a simple oscillators for complex behavior: Ii. experiments. In *Proceedings of the International Conference on Digital Audio Effects (DAFx)*.

Evans, J. R., & Olson, D. L. (2007). *Statistics, data analysis, and decision modeling*. Pearson/Prentice Hall.

Fan, S., & Chen, L. (2006). Short-term load forecasting based on an adaptive hybrid method. *Power Systems. IEEE Transactions on, 21*(1), 392–401.

Farahani, R. Z., SteadieSeifi, M., & Asgari, N. (2010). Multiple criteria facility location problems: A survey. *Applied Mathematical Modelling, 34*(7), 1689–1709. doi:10.1016/j.apm.2009.10.005

Fayyad, U. M., Piatetsky-Shapiro, G., & Smyth, P. (1996). The KDD process for extracting useful knowledge from volumes of data. *Communications of the ACM, 39*(11), 27–41. doi:10.1145/240455.240464

Fazlollahtabar, H., Mahdavi, I., Ashoori, M. T., Kaviani, S., & Mahdavi-Amiri, N. (2011). A multi-objective decision-making process of supplier selection and order allocation for multi-period scheduling in an electronic market. *International Journal of Advanced Manufacturing Technology, 52*(9-12), 1039–1052. doi:10.1007/s00170-010-2800-6

Fish, K., Barnes, J., & Aiken, M. (1995). Artificial neural networks: A new methodology for industrial market segmentation. *Industrial Marketing Management, 24*(5), 432–438. doi:10.1016/0019-8501(95)00033-7

Fitöz, E. (2008). *Türkiye'de konut piyasasının belirleyicileri: Ampirik bir uygulama*. (Unpublished master thesis). Zonguldak Karaelmas University, Graduate School of Social Sciences.

Forsati, R., Keikha, A., & Shamsfard, M. (2015). An improved bee colony optimization algorithm with an application to document clustering. *Neurocomputing, 159*, 9–26. doi:10.1016/j.neucom.2015.02.048

Francois, M., Grosges, T., Barchiesi, D., & Erra, R. (2014). Pseudo-random number generator based on mixing of three chaotic maps. *Communications in Nonlinear Science and Numerical Simulation, 19*(4), 887–895. doi:10.1016/j.cnsns.2013.08.032

Frank, E., Hall, M., & Pfahringer, B. (2003). Locally weighted naive bayes. In *19th Conference in Uncertainty in Artificial Intelligence*.

Frawley, W., Piatetsky-Shapiro, G., & Matheus, C. (1991). Knowledge discovery in databases: An overview. In *Knowledge discovery in databases*. The AAAI Press.

Fridrich, J. (1998). Symmetric ciphers based on two-dimensional chaotic maps. *International Journal of Bifurcation and Chaos in Applied Sciences and Engineering, 8*(6), 1259–1284. doi:10.1142/S021812749800098X

Gajjar, T. Y., & Chauhan, N. C. (2012). A review on image mining frameworks and techniques. *International Journal of Computer Science and Information Technologies, 3*(3).

Gajjar, H. K., & Adil, G. K. (2010). A piecewise linearization for retail shelf space allocation problem and a local search heuristic. *Annals of Operations Research, 179*(1), 149–167. doi:10.1007/s10479-008-0455-6

Gajjar, H. K., & Adil, G. K. (2011). Heuristics for retail shelf space allocation problem with linear profit function. *International Journal of Retail & Distribution Management, 39*(2), 144–155. doi:10.1108/09590551111109094

Galvão, R. D. (2004). Uncapacitated facility location problems: Contributions. *Pesquisa Operacional, 24*(1), 7–38. doi:10.1590/S0101-74382004000100003

Gao, C., Bompard, E., Napoli, R., & Cheng, H. (2007). Price forecast in the competitive electricity market by support vector machine. *Physica A: Statistical Mechanics and its Applications, 382*(1), 98-113.

Gao, X., & Lu, Y. (2012). Automatic text clustering via particle swarm optimization. *International Journal of Digital Content Technology and its Applications, 6*(23), 12-21.

García-Pedrajas, N., & de Haro-García, A. (2012). Scaling up data mining algorithms: Review and taxonomy. *Progress in Artificial Intelligence, 1*(1), 71–87. doi:10.1007/s13748-011-0004-4

Garcia, R. C., Contreras, J., Van Akkeren, M., & Garcia, J. B. C. (2005). A GARCH forecasting model to predict day-ahead electricity prices. *Power Systems. IEEE Transactions on, 20*(2), 867–874.

Garg, G., Behl, S., & Singh, V. (2011). Assessment of non-parametric and parametric PSD estimation methods for automated epileptic seizure detection. *Journal of Computing, 3*, 160–166.

Garg, G., Singh, V., Gupta, J. R. P., & Mittal, A. P. (2012). Relative Wavelet Energy As A New Feature Extractor for Sleep Classification using EEG Signals. *International Journal of Biomedical Signal Processing, 2*, 75–79.

Garg, G., Singh, V., Gupta, J. R. P., & Mittal, A. P. (2012). Wrapper Based Wavelet Feature Optimization for EEG signals, *Springer. Biomedical Engineering Letters, 2*(1), 24–37. doi:10.1007/s13534-012-0044-0

Garg, G., Singh, V., Gupta, J. R. P., Mittal, A. P., & Chandra, S. (2011). Computer assisted automatic sleep scoring system using relative wavelet energy based neuro fuzzy model. *WSEAS Transaction on Biology & Biomedicine, 8*, 12–24.

Garg, G., Singh, V., Gupta, J. R. P., Mittal, A. P., & Chandra, S. (2011). Computer Assisted Automatic Sleep Scoring System Using Relative Wavelet Energy Based Neuro Fuzzy Model. *WSEAS Transaction on Biology and Biomedicine, 8*, 12–24.

Geismar, H. N., Dawande, M., Murthi, B. P. S., & Sriskandarajah, C. (2015). Maximizing Revenue Through Two-Dimensional Shelf-Space Allocation. *Production and Operations Management, 24*(7), 1148–1163. doi:10.1111/poms.12316

Gentle, J. E., Hardle, W., & Mori, Y. (Eds.). (2004). Handbook of Computational Statistics. Springer.

Ghaderi, A., Jabalameli, M. S., Barzinpour, F., & Rahmaniani, R. (2012). An efficient hybrid particle swarm optimization algorithm for solving the uncapacitated continuous location-allocation problem. *Networks and Spatial Economics*, *12*(3), 421–439. doi:10.1007/s11067-011-9162-y

Ghiassi, M., Zimbra, D. K., & Saidane, H. (2006). Medium term system load forecasting with a dynamic artificial neural network model. *Electric Power Systems Research*, *76*(5), 302–316. doi:10.1016/j.epsr.2005.06.010

Gholap, A., Naik, G., Joshi, A., & Rao, C. K. (2005, August). Content-based tissue image mining. In Computational Systems Bioinformatics Conference, 2005. Workshops and Poster Abstracts. IEEE (pp. 359-363). IEEE. doi:10.1109/CSBW.2005.45

Ghosh-Dastidar, S., Adeli, H., & Dadmehr, N. (2007). Mixed band wavelet-chaos-neural network methodology for epilepsy and epileptic seizure detection. *IEEE Transactions on Bio-Medical Engineering*, *54*(9), 1545–1551. doi:10.1109/TBME.2007.891945 PMID:17867346

Gilli, M., Maringer, D., & Schumann, E. (2011). Generating Random Numbers. In M.G.M. Schumann (Ed.), Numerical Methods and Optimization in Finance (pp. 119-158). San Diego, CA: Academic Press.

Gillis, N. (2014). The why and how of nonnegative matrix factorization. *Regularization, Optimization, Kernels, and Support Vector Machines*, *12*, 257.

Gilmore, R. (2015). Explosions in Lorenz maps. *Chaos, Solitons, and Fractals*, *76*, 130–140. doi:10.1016/j.chaos.2015.03.020

Gil-Saura, I., & Ruiz-Molina, M.-E. (2008). Customer segmentation based on commitment and ICT use. *Industrial Management & Data Systems*, *109*(2), 206–223. doi:10.1108/02635570910930109

Glover, F. (1986). Future paths for integer programming and links to artificial intelligence. *Computers & Operations Research*, *13*(5), 533–549. doi:10.1016/0305-0548(86)90048-1

Glover, F., & Kochenberger, G. A. (2003). *Handbook of metaheuristics Springer Science & Business Media.*

Gomes, H., Ribeiro, A., & Lobo, V. (2007). Location model for CCA-treated wood waste remediation units using GIS and clustering methods. *Environmental Modelling & Software*, *22*(12), 1788–1795. doi:10.1016/j.envsoft.2007.03.004

Gong, W., Li, D., Liu, X., Yue, J., & Fu, Z. (2007). Improved two-grade delayed particle swarm optimisation (TGDPSO) for inventory facility location for perishable food distribution centres in Beijing. New Zealand. *Journal of Agricultural Research*, *50*(5), 771–779.

Gonzalez, T. F. (2007). *Handbook of approximation algorithms and metaheuristics CRC Press.* doi:10.1201/9781420010749

Goodarzi, M., & Freitas, M. (2010). MIA-QSAR, PCA-ranking and least-squares support-vector machines in the accurate prediction of the activities of phosphodiesterase type 5 (PDE-5) inhibitors. *Molecular Simulation*, *36*(11), 871–877. doi:10.1080/08927022.2010.490261

Goyal, A., & Welch, I. (2008). A Comprehensive Look at the Empirical Performance of Equity Premium Prediction. *Review of Financial Studies*, *21*(4), 1455–1508. doi:10.1093/rfs/hhm014

Graham, R. L. (1995). *Handbook of combinatorics* (1st ed.). Elsevier.

Greenberg, M., & Mcdonald, S. S. (1989). Successful needs/benefits segmentation: A user's guide. *Journal of Consumer Marketing*, *6*(3), 29–36. doi:10.1108/EUM0000000002552

Greenwood, J., & Hercowitz, Z. (1991). The allocation of capital and time over the business cycle. *Journal of Political Economy*, *99*(6), 1188–1214. doi:10.1086/261797

Gu, F., Greensmith, J., Oates, R., & Aickelin, U. (2010). *Pca 4 dca: The application of principal component analysis to the dendritic cell algorithm.* arXiv preprint arXiv:1004.3460

Gun, A. N., & Badur, B. (2008, July). Assortment planning using data mining algorithms. In *Management of Engineering & Technology, 2008. PICMET 2008. Portland International Conference on* (pp. 2312-2322). IEEE. doi:10.1109/PICMET.2008.4599855

Guner, A. R., & Sevkli, M. (2008). A discrete particle swarm optimization algorithm for uncapacitated facility location problem. *Journal of Artificial Evolution and Applications*, *2008*, 10. doi:10.1155/2008/861512

Guneri, A. F., & Kuzu, A. (2009). Supplier selection by using a fuzzy approach in just-in-time: A case study. *International Journal of Computer Integrated Manufacturing*, *22*(8), 774–783. doi:10.1080/09511920902741075

Guo L., Rivero D., Seoane J. A., & Pazos A. (2009). Classification of EEG signals using relative wavelet energy and artificial neural networks. In *Proceeding of 1st ACM/SIGEVO Summit on Genetic and Eutionary Computation*, (pp. 177-184). ACM.

Guo, J., & Zhang, W. (2008). Selection of Suppliers Based on Rough Set Theory and VIKOR Algorithm. *Intelligent Information Technology Application Workshops. IITAW '08. International Symposium on*, (pp. 49 – 52).

Guo-Dong, L., Yamaguchi, D., & Nagai, M. (2007). A grey-based decision-making approach to the supplier selection problem. *Mathematical and Computer Modelling*, *46*(3-4), 573–581. doi:10.1016/j.mcm.2006.11.021

Guo-Dong, L., Yamaguchi, D., & Nagai, M. (2008). A grey-based rough decision-making approach to supplier selection. *International Journal of Advanced Manufacturing Technology*, *36*(9-10), 1032–1040. doi:10.1007/s00170-006-0910-y

Gustafson, D., & Kessel, W. (1978). Fuzzy clustering with a fuzzy covariance matrix. In *1978 IEEE conference on decision and control including the 17th symposium on adaptive processes* (No. 17, pp. 761-766). doi:10.1109/CDC.1978.268028

Gu, Y., & Hu, F. (2012). An intelligent forecasting method for short term electric power load based on partitioned support vector regression. In *2012 IEEE International Conference on Cyber Technology in Automation, Control, and Intelligent Systems (CYBER)*. doi:10.1109/CYBER.2012.6320044

Guyon, I., Weston, J., Barnhill, S., & Vapnik, V. (2002). Gene selection for cancer classification using support vector machines. *Machine Learning*, *46*(1/3), 389–422. doi:10.1023/A:1012487302797

Hadi-Vencheh, A. (2011). A new nonlinear model for multiple criteria supplier-selection problem. *International Journal of Computer Integrated Manufacturing*, *24*(1), 32–39. doi:10.1080/0951192X.2010.527372

Hagan, M. T., & Behr, S. M. (1987). The time series approach to short term load forecasting. *Power Systems. IEEE Transactions on*, *2*(3), 785–791.

Haida, T., & Muto, S. (1994). Regression based peak load forecasting using a transformation technique. *Power Systems. IEEE Transactions on*, *9*(4), 1788–1794.

Haley, R. I. (1968). Benefit segmentation: A decision-oriented research tool. *Journal of Marketing*, *32*(3), 30–35. doi:10.2307/1249759

Hamzaçebi, C. (2007). Forecasting of Turkey's net electricity energy consumption on sectoral bases. *Energy Policy*, *35*(3), 2009–2016. doi:10.1016/j.enpol.2006.03.014

Han, J., Kamber, M., & Pei, J. (2012). Data Mining: Concepts and Techniques (3rd ed.). Morgan Kaufmann.

Hansen, J. M., Raut, S., & Swami, S. (2010). Retail shelf allocation: A comparative analysis of heuristic and meta-heuristic approaches. *Journal of Retailing*, *86*(1), 94–105. doi:10.1016/j.jretai.2010.01.004

Hansen, P., & Heinsbroek, H. (1979). Product selection and space allocation in supermarkets. *European Journal of Operational Research*, *3*(6), 474–484. doi:10.1016/0377-2217(79)90030-4

Hariga, M. A., Al-Ahmari, A., & Mohamed, A. R. A. (2007). A joint optimisation model for inventory replenishment, product assortment, shelf space and display area allocation decisions. *European Journal of Operational Research*, *181*(1), 239–251. doi:10.1016/j.ejor.2006.06.025

Hartzmark, M. L. (1987). Returns to individual traders of futures: Aggregate results. *Journal of Political Economy*, *95*(6), 1292–1306. doi:10.1086/261516

Ha, S. H. (2007). Applying knowledge engineering techniques to customer analysis in the service industry. *Advanced Engineering Informatics*, *21*(3), 293–301. doi:10.1016/j.aei.2006.12.001

Ha, S. H., Bae, S. M., & Park, S. C. (2002). Customers time-variant purchase behavior and corresponding marketing strategies: An online retailer's case. *Computers & Industrial Engineering*, *43*(4), 801–820. doi:10.1016/S0360-8352(02)00141-9

Ha, S. H., & Park, S. C. (1998). Application of data mining tools to hotel data mart on the intranet for database marketing. *Expert Systems with Applications*, *15*(1), 1–31. doi:10.1016/S0957-4174(98)00008-6

Hashmi, Z. I., Cheah, Y. N., Hassan, S. Z., Lim, K. G., & Abidi, S. S. R. (2003). *Intelligent Agent Modeling and Generic Architecture Towards a Multi-Agent Healthcare Knowledge Management System* (pp. 941–944). ICWI.

Hastie, T., Tibshirani, R., Friedman, J., & Franklin, J. (2005). The elements of statistical learning: Data mining, inference and prediction. *The Mathematical Intelligencer*, *27*(2), 83–85. doi:10.1007/BF02985802

Hausdorff, J. M. (n.d.). *Gait in Aging and Disease Database*. Available on: http://physionet.org/physiobank/database/gaitdb/ doi:10.13026/C2C889

Haux, R., Ammenwerth, E., Herzog, W., & Knaup, P. (2002). Health care in the information society. A prognosis for the year 2013. *International Journal of Medical Informatics*, *66*(1), 3–21. doi:10.1016/S1386-5056(02)00030-8 PMID:12453552

Hein, A., Nee, O., Willemsen, D., Scheffold, T., Dogac, A., & Laleci, G. (2006). *SAPHIRE-Intelligent Healthcare Monitoring based on Semantic Interoperability Platform-The Homecare Scenario*. ECEH.

Hema, A., & Annasaro, E. (2013). A survey in need of image mining techniques. *International Journal of Advanced Research in Computer and Communication Engineering*, 2319-5940.

Heneghan, C. (n.d.). *St. Vincent's University Hospital / University College Dublin Sleep Apnea Database*. Available on: http://physionet.org/physiobank/database/ucddb/ doi:10.13026/C26C7D

Herbrich, R., Graepel, T., & Obermayer, K. (1999). Large margin rank boundaries for ordinal regression. *Advances in Neural Information Processing Systems*, 115–132.

Herngren, L., Goonetilleke, A., & Ayoko, G. A. (2006). Analysis of heavy metals in road-deposited sediments. *Analytica Chimica Acta*, *571*(2), 270–278. doi:10.1016/j.aca.2006.04.064 PMID:17723448

He, X. C., & Yung, N. H. (2008). Corner detector based on global and local curvature properties. *Optical Engineering (Redondo Beach, Calif.)*, *47*(5), 057008–057008. doi:10.1117/1.2931681

Hippert, H. S., Bunn, D. W., & Souza, R. C. (2005). Large neural networks for electricity load forecasting: Are they overfitted? *International Journal of Forecasting*, *21*(3), 425–434. doi:10.1016/j.ijforecast.2004.12.004

Hochbaum, D. S., Hsu, C. N., & Yang, Y. T. (2012). Ranking of multidimensional drug profiling data by fractional-adjusted bi-partitional scores. *Bioinformatics (Oxford, England)*, *28*(12), i106–i114. doi:10.1093/bioinformatics/bts232 PMID:22689749

Hoffman, K. C., & Wood, D. O. (1976). Energy system modeling and forecasting. *Annual Review of Energy*, *1*(1), 423-453.

Ho, K. L., Hsu, Y. Y., Chen, C. F., Lee, T. E., Liang, C. C., Lai, T. S., & Chen, K. K. (1990). Short term load forecasting of Taiwan power system using a knowledge-based expert system. *Power Systems. IEEE Transactions on*, *5*(4), 1214–1221.

Holmes, J. H., & Peek, K. (2007). Intelligent data analysis in biomedicine. *Journal of Biomedical Informatics*, *40*(6), 605–608. doi:10.1016/j.jbi.2007.10.001 PMID:17959422

Hong, W. C. (2009a). Electric load forecasting by support vector model. *Applied Mathematical Modelling*, *33*(5), 2444–2454. doi:10.1016/j.apm.2008.07.010

Hong, W. C. (2009b). Chaotic particle swarm optimization algorithm in a support vector regression electric load forecasting model. *Energy Conversion and Management*, *50*(1), 105–117. doi:10.1016/j.enconman.2008.08.031

Hong, W. C. (2009c). Hybrid evolutionary algorithms in a SVR-based electric load forecasting model. *International Journal of Electrical Power & Energy Systems*, *31*(7), 409–417. doi:10.1016/j.ijepes.2009.03.020

Hong, W. C. (2011). Electric load forecasting by seasonal recurrent SVR (support vector regression) with chaotic artificial bee colony algorithm. *Energy*, *36*(9), 5568–5578. doi:10.1016/j.energy.2011.07.015

Hong, W. C., Dong, Y., Zhang, W. Y., Chen, L. Y., & Panigrahi, B. K. (2013). Cyclic electric load forecasting by seasonal SVR with chaotic genetic algorithm. *International Journal of Electrical Power & Energy Systems*, *44*(1), 604–614. doi:10.1016/j.ijepes.2012.08.010

Hooshmand, R. A., Amooshahi, H., & Parastegari, M. (2013). A hybrid intelligent algorithm based short-term load forecasting approach. *International Journal of Electrical Power & Energy Systems*, *45*(1), 313–324. doi:10.1016/j.ijepes.2012.09.002

Hor, C. L., Watson, S. J., & Majithia, S. (2006, June). Daily load forecasting and maximum demand estimation using ARIMA and GARCH. In *Probabilistic Methods Applied to Power Systems, 2006. PMAPS 2006. International Conference on* (pp. 1-6). IEEE. doi:10.1109/PMAPS.2006.360237

Hor, C. L., Watson, S. J., & Majithia, S. (2005). Analyzing the impact of weather variables on monthly electricity demand. *Power Systems. IEEE Transactions on*, *20*(4), 2078–2085.

Hornik, K., Stinchcombe, M., & White, H. (1989). Multilayer Feedforward Networks are Universal Approximators. *Neural Networks*, *2*(5), 359–366. doi:10.1016/0893-6080(89)90020-8

Hruschka, H. (1986). Market definition and segmentation using fuzzy clustering methods. *International Journal of Research in Marketing*, *3*(2), 117–134. doi:10.1016/0167-8116(86)90015-7

Hruschka, H., Fettes, W., & Probst, M. (2004). Market segmentation by maximum likelihood clustering using choice elasticities. *European Journal of Operational Research*, *154*(3), 779–786. doi:10.1016/S0377-2217(02)00807-X

Hruschka, H., & Natter, M. (1999). Comparing performance of feed-forward neural nets and k-means for cluster-based market segmentation. *European Journal of Operational Research*, *114*(2), 346–353. doi:10.1016/S0377-2217(98)00170-2

Hsia, K. H., & Wu, J. H. (1998). A study on the data preprocessing in grey relational analysis. *J. Chinese Grey System Association*, *1*(1), 47–53.

Hsieh, N. (2004). An integrated data mining and behavioural scoring model for analysing bank customers. *Expert Systems with Applications*, *27*(4), 623–633. doi:10.1016/j.eswa.2004.06.007

Hsu, C. C., Wu, C. H., Chen, S. C., & Peng, K. L. (2006, January). Dynamically optimizing parameters in support vector regression: An application of electricity load forecasting. In *System Sciences, 2006. HICSS'06.Proceedings of the 39th Annual Hawaii International Conference on* (Vol. 2, pp. 30c-30c). IEEE.

Hsu, T., Chu, K., & Chan, H. (2000). *The fuzzy clustering on market segment*. The 9th IEEE Int. Conference on Fuzzy Systems.

Hsu, C. C., & Chen, C. Y. (2003). Regional load forecasting in Taiwan—applications of artificial neural networks. *Energy Conversion and Management*, *44*(12), 1941–1949. doi:10.1016/S0196-8904(02)00225-X

Hsu, L.-C., & Wang, C.-H. (2009). Forecasting integrated circuit output using multivariate grey model and grey relational analysis. *Expert Systems with Applications*, *36*(2), 1403–1409. doi:10.1016/j.eswa.2007.11.015

Hsu, S. C. (2012). The RFM-based institutional customers clustering: Case study of a digital content provider. *Information Technology Journal*, *11*(9), 1193–1201. doi:10.3923/itj.2012.1193.1201

Hsu, T. (2000). An application of fuzzy clustering in group-positioning analysis. *Proc. Natl. Sci*, *10*, 157–167.

Huang, S. J., & Shih, K. R. (2003). Short-term load forecasting via ARMA model identification including non-Gaussian process considerations. *Power Systems. IEEE Transactions on*, *18*(2), 673–679.

Huang, Y. K., Shieh, S. L., Jane, C. J., & Jheng, D. J. (2008). A new Grey Relation Analysis Applied to the Assert Allocation of stock portfolio. *Int. J. Computational Cognition*, *6*(3), 6–12.

Hubele, N. F., & Cheng, C. S. (1990). Identification of seasonal short-term load forecasting models using statistical decision functions. *Power Systems. IEEE Transactions on*, *5*(1), 40–45.

Hung, C., & Tsai, C.-F. (2008). Market segmentation based on hierarchical self-organizing map for markets of multimedia on demand. *Expert Systems with Applications*, *34*(1), 780–787. doi:10.1016/j.eswa.2006.10.012

Hung, Y. S., Chen, K. L. B., Yang, C. T., & Deng, G. F. (2013). Web usage mining for analysing elder self-care behavior patterns. *Expert Systems with Applications*, *40*(2), 775–783. doi:10.1016/j.eswa.2012.08.037

Hu, T., & Sheu, J. (2003). A fuzzy-based customer classification method for demand-responsive logistical distribution operations. *Fuzzy Sets and Systems*, *139*(2), 431–459. doi:10.1016/S0165-0114(02)00516-X

Hu, X., Wang, Z., & Ren, X. (2005). Classification of surface EMG signal using relative wavelet packet energy. *Computer Methods and Programs in Biomedicine*, *79*(3), 189–195. doi:10.1016/j.cmpb.2005.04.001 PMID:15913836

Hwang, H., Choi, B., & Lee, G. (2009). A genetic algorithm approach to an integrated problem of shelf space design and item allocation. *Computers & Industrial Engineering*, *56*(3), 809–820. doi:10.1016/j.cie.2008.09.012

Hwang, H., Choi, B., & Lee, M. J. (2005). A model for shelf space allocation and inventory control considering location and inventory level effects on demand. *International Journal of Production Economics*, *97*(2), 185–195. doi:10.1016/j.ijpe.2004.07.003

Hwang, H., Jung, T., & Suh, E. (2004). A LTV model and customer segmentation based on customer value: A case study on the wireless telecommunication industry. *Expert Systems with Applications*, *26*(2), 181–188. doi:10.1016/S0957-4174(03)00133-7

ICTA. (2012). *Electronic Communications Market in Turkey*. Retrieved June 27, 2015, from http://eng.btk.gov.tr/dosyalar/2012-3-English_25_12_12.pdf

Inamdar, N., Kaplan, R. S., Bower, M., & Reynolds, K. (2002). Applying the balanced scorecard in healthcare provider organizations. *Journal of Healthcare Management, 47*(3), 179–196. PMID:12055900

International Business Times AU. (n.d.). *What is Foreign Exchange?* Retrieved February 11, 2011 from http://au.ibtimes.com/forex

Irion, J., Al-Khayyal, F., & Lu, J. C. (2004). *A piecewise linearization framework for retail shelf space management models.* Academic Press.

Jabbour, K., Riveros, J. F. V., Landsbergen, D., & Meyer, W. (1988). ALFA: Automated load forecasting assistant. *Power Systems. IEEE Transactions on, 3*(3), 908–914.

Jacob, S. G., & Ramani, R. G. (2012). Data Mining in Clinical Data Sets: A Review. *International Journal of Applied Information Systems, 4*(6), 15–26. doi:10.5120/ijais12-450774

Jae-Hyeon, A., Sang-Pil, H., & Yung-Seop, L. (2006). Customer churn analysis: Churn determinants and mediation effects of partial defection in the Korean mobile telecommunications service industry. *Telecommunications Policy, 30*(10-11), 552–568. doi:10.1016/j.telpol.2006.09.006

Jahan, M. V., & Akbarzadeh, T. (2012). Hybrid local search algorithm via evolutionary avalanches for spin glass based portfolio selection. *Egyptian Informatics Journal, 13*(2), 65–73. doi:10.1016/j.eij.2012.04.002

Jain, A., & Satish, B. (2009, June). Clustering based short term load forecasting using support vector machines. In PowerTech, 2009 IEEE Bucharest (pp. 1-8). IEEE. doi:10.1109/PTC.2009.5282144

Jain, A. K., & Dubes, R. C. (1948). *Algorithms for clustering data.* Prentice Hall.

James, G., Witten, D., Hastie, T., & Tibshirani, R. (2014). *An introduction to statistical learning with applications in R.* New York: Springer.

Janssen, C. (2015). *Data Preprocessing.* Retrieved June 27, 2015, from http://www.techopedia.com/definition/14650/data-preprocessing

Ji, C., Zhang, Y., Gao, S., Yuan, P., & Li, Z. (2004, March). Particle swarm optimization for mobile ad hoc networks clustering. In *Networking, Sensing and Control, 2004 IEEE International Conference on* (Vol. 1, pp. 372-375). IEEE.

Jin, C. H., & Ryu, H. G. (2012). Performance evaluation of chaotic CDSK modulation system with different chaotic maps. *ICT Convergence (ICTC), 2012 International Conference on* (pp. 603-606) IEEE. doi:10.1109/ICTC.2012.6387115

Jin, M., Zhou, X., Zhang, Z. M., & Tentzeris, M. M. (2012). Short-term power load forecasting using grey correlation contest modeling. *Expert Systems with Applications, 39*(1), 773–779. doi:10.1016/j.eswa.2011.07.072

Joachims, T. (2009). *Support vector machines for ranking.* Retrieved May 10, 2015, from http://www.cs.cornell.edu/People/tj/svm_light/svm_rank.html

Joachims, T. (2002, July). Optimizing search engines using clickthrough data. In *Proceedings of the eighth ACM SIGKDD international conference on Knowledge discovery and data mining* (pp. 133-142). ACM. doi:10.1145/775047.775067

John, H. H. (1992). *Adaptation in natural and artificial systems: an introductory analysis with applications to biology, control, and artificial intelligence.* MIT Press.

Jonker, J., Piersma, N., & Poel, D. V. (2004). Joint optimization of customer segmentation and marketing policy to maximize long-term profitability. *Expert Systems with Applications, 27*(2), 159–168. doi:10.1016/j.eswa.2004.01.010

Joseph, C. N., & Wilson, A. (2014, November). Retrieval of images using data mining techniques. In *Contemporary Computing and Informatics (IC3I), 2014 International Conference on* (pp. 204-208). IEEE.

Juan, A. A., Faulin, J., Grasman, S. E., Rabe, M., & Figueira, G. (2015). A review of simheuristics: Extending metaheuristics to deal with stochastic combinatorial optimization problems. *Operations Research Perspectives, 2,* 62–72. doi:10.1016/j.orp.2015.03.001

Ju-Long, D. (1982). Control problems of grey systems. *Systems & Control Letters, 1*(5), 288–294. doi:10.1016/S0167-6911(82)80025-X

Kamal, N., Wiebe, S., Engbers, J. D. T., & Hill, M. D. (2014). Big data and visual analytics in health and medicine: From pipe dream to reality. *J Health Med Informat, 5,* e125.

Kandil, M. S., El-Debeiky, S. M., & Hasanien, N. E. (2002). Long-term load forecasting for fast developing utility using a knowledge-based expert system.*Power Systems. IEEE Transactions on, 17*(2), 491–496.

Kannan, A., Mohan, V., & Anbazhagan, N. (2010). Image clustering and retrieval using image mining techniques. In *IEEE International Conference on Computational Intelligence and Computing Research* (Vol. 2).

Kanso, A., & Smaoui, N. (2009). Logistic chaotic maps for binary numbers generations. *Chaos, Solitons, and Fractals, 40*(5), 2557–2568. doi:10.1016/j.chaos.2007.10.049

Karaboga, D. (2005). *An idea based on honey bee swarm for numerical optimization* (Vol. 200). Technical report-tr06. Erciyes University, Engineering Faculty, Computer Engineering Department.

Karaboga, D., & Akay, B. (2011). A modified artificial bee colony (ABC) algorithm for constrained optimization problems. *Applied Soft Computing, 11*(3), 3021–3031. doi:10.1016/j.asoc.2010.12.001

Karacor, A. G., Sivri, N., & Ucan, O. N. (2007). Maximum Stream Temperature Estimation of Degirmendere River Using Artificial Neural Network. *Journal of Scientific and Industrial Research, 66*(5), 363–366.

Karacor, G., & Denizhan, Y. (2004). Advantages of Hierarchical Organisation in Neural Networks. *International Journal Of Computing Anticipatory Systems, 16,* 48–60.

Kardiyen, F., & Orkcu, H. H. (2006). The Comparison of Principal Component Analysis and Data Envelopment Analysis in Ranking of Decision Making Units. *Gazi University Journal of Science, 19*(2), 127–133.

Kargi, B. (2013). Konut piyasası ve ekonomik büyüme ilişkisi: Türkiye üzerine zaman serileri analizi (2000-2012)[in Turkish]. *International Journal of Human Sciences, 10*(1), 897–892.

Karimi, H., Hosseini, S. M., & Jahan, M. V. (2013). On the combination of self-organized systems to generate pseudo-random numbers. *Information Sciences, 221,* 371–388. doi:10.1016/j.ins.2012.09.029

Karol, S., & Mangat, V. (2013). Evaluation of text document clustering approach based on particle swarm optimization. *Central European Journal of Computer Science, 3*(2), 69–90.

Karpak, B., Kumcu, E., & Kasuganti, R. R. (2001). Purchasing materials in the supply chain: Managing a multi-objective task. *European. Journal of Purchasing and Supply Management, 7*(1), 209–216. doi:10.1016/S0969-7012(01)00002-8

Kaufman, L., & Rousseeuw, P. J. (2005). *Finding groups in data: An Introduction to cluster analysis.* New York: John Wiley & Sons Inc.

Kaur, H., & Wasan, S. K. (2006). Empirical study on applications of data mining techniques in healthcare. *Journal of Computer Science, 2*(2), 194–200. doi:10.3844/jcssp.2006.194.200

Kaymak, U. & Setnes, M. (2000). *Extended fuzzy clustering algorithms*. ERIM Report Series Research in Management, No: ERS-2000-51-LIS, Rotterdam, Netherlands.

Kaymak, U. Fuzzy target selection using RFM variables. *Proceedings of Joint 9th IFSA World Congress and 20th NAFIPS Int. Conference*. doi:10.1109/NAFIPS.2001.944748

Kearns, J., & Manners, P. (2004). *The Profitability of Speculators in Currency Futures Markets*. Working Paper. Reserve Bank of Australia.

Keller, J. A., & Wiese, H. (2007). Period lengths of chaotic pseudo-random number generators.*Proceedings of the Fourth IASTED International Conference on Communication, Network and Information Security* (pp. 7-11). ACTA Press.

Kemp, B., Zwinderman, A. H., Tuk, B., Kamphuisen, H. A. C., & Oberyé, J. J. L. (2000). Analysis of a sleep-dependent neuronal feedback loop: The slow-wave microcontinuity of the EEG. *IEEE Transactions on Bio-Medical Engineering*, *47*(9), 1185–1194. doi:10.1109/10.867928 PMID:11008419

Kennedy, J., & Mendes, R. (2002). *Population structure and particle swarm performance*. Academic Press.

Keramati, A., & Ardabili, S. M. S. (2011). Churn analysis for an Iranian mobile operator. *Telecommunications Policy*, *35*(4), 344–356. doi:10.1016/j.telpol.2011.02.009

Kermanshahi, B., & Iwamiya, H. (2002). Up to year 2020 load forecasting using neural nets. *International Journal of Electrical Power & Energy Systems*, *24*(9), 789–797. doi:10.1016/S0142-0615(01)00086-2

Khadra, L., Al-Fahoum, A. S., & Al-Nashash, H. (1997). Detection of life-threatening cardiac arrhythmias using the wavelet transformation. *Medical & Biological Engineering & Computing*, *35*(6), 626–632. doi:10.1007/BF02510970 PMID:9538538

Kho, B. C. (1996). Time-varying Risk Premia, Volatility, and Technical Trading Rule Profits: Evidence from Foreign Currency Futures Markets. *Journal of Financial Economics*, *41*(2), 249–290. doi:10.1016/0304-405X(95)00861-8

Khosravi, A., Nahavandi, S., & Creighton, D. (2013). A neural network-GARCH-based method for construction of Prediction Intervals. *Electric Power Systems Research*, *96*, 185–193. doi:10.1016/j.epsr.2012.11.007

Khotanzad, A., Zhou, E., & Elragal, H. (2002). A neuro-fuzzy approach to short-term load forecasting in a price-sensitive environment. *Power Systems. IEEE Transactions on*, *17*(4), 1273–1282.

Khushaba, R. N., Kodagoa, S., Lal, S., & Dissanayake, G. (2011). Driver drowsiness classification using fuzzy wavelet packet based feature extraction algorithm. *IEEE Transactions on Bio-Medical Engineering*, *58*(1), 121–131. doi:10.1109/TBME.2010.2077291 PMID:20858575

Kiang, M. Y., Hu, M. Y., & Fisher, D. M. (2004). An extended self-organizing map network for market segmentation—a telecommunication example. *Decision Support Systems*, *42*(1), 36–47. doi:10.1016/j.dss.2004.09.012

Kim, S., Bok, J., & Ryu, H. G. (2013). Performance evaluation of DCSK system with chaotic maps. *Information Networking (ICOIN), 2013 International Conference on* (pp. 556-559). IEEE.

Kim, C. I., Yu, I. K., & Song, Y. H. (2002). Kohonen neural network and wavelet transform based approach to short-term load forecasting. *Electric Power Systems Research*, *63*(3), 169–176. doi:10.1016/S0378-7796(02)00097-4

Kim, J., Wei, S., & Ruys, H. (2003). Segmenting the market of western Australia senior tourists using artificial neural networks. *Tourism Management*, *24*(1), 25–34. doi:10.1016/S0261-5177(02)00050-X

Kim, K. H., Youn, H. S., & Kang, Y. C. (2000). Short-term load forecasting for special days in anomalous load conditions using neural networks and fuzzy inference method. *Power Systems. IEEE Transactions on*, *15*(2), 559–565.

Kim, K., & Ahn, H. (2008). A recommender system using GA *k*-means clustering in an online shopping market. *Expert Systems with Applications*, *34*(2), 1200–1209. doi:10.1016/j.eswa.2006.12.025

Kim, S.-Y., Jung, T.-S., Suh, E.-H., & Hwang, H.-S. (2006). Customer segmentation and strategy development based on customer lifetime value: A case study. *Expert Systems with Applications*, *31*(1), 101–107. doi:10.1016/j.eswa.2005.09.004

Kisioglu, P., & Topcu, Y. (2011). Applying Bayesian Belief Network approach to customer churn analysis: A case study on the telecom industry of Turkey. *Expert Systems with Applications*, *38*(6), 7151–7157. doi:10.1016/j.eswa.2010.12.045

Ko, C. N., & Lee, C. M. (2013). Short-term load forecasting using SVR (support vector regression)-based radial basis function neural network with dual extended Kalman filter. *Energy*, *49*, 413–422. doi:10.1016/j.energy.2012.11.015

Koh, H. C., & Tan, G. (2011). Data mining applications in healthcare. *Journal of Healthcare Information Management*, *19*(2), 65. PMID:15869215

Konstantinidi, E., & Skiadopoulos, G. (2011). Are VIX futures prices predictable? An empirical investigation. *International Journal of Forecasting*, *27*(2), 543–560. doi:10.1016/j.ijforecast.2009.11.004

Kotler, P. (2003). *Marketing management*. Prentice-Hall.

Kotsiantis, S., Kanellopoulos, D., & Pintelas, P. (2006). Data Preprocessing for Supervised Leaning. *International Journal of Computer Science*, *1*, 111–117.

Küçükdeniz, T. (2009). *Sürü Zekası Optimizasyon Yöntemi ve Tedarik Zinciri Yönetiminde Bir Uygulama*. (Doctoral Dissertation). İstanbul Üniversitesi Fen Bilimleri Enstitüsü.

Küçükdeniz, T., Baray, A., Ecerkale, K., & Esnaf, Ş. (2012). Integrated use of fuzzy c-means and convex programming for capacitated multi-facility location problem. *Expert Systems with Applications*, *39*(4), 4306–4314. doi:10.1016/j. eswa.2011.09.102

Küçükdeniz, T., & Esnaf, Ş. (2015). Data clustering by particle swarm optimization with the focal particles. In P. Pardalos, M. Pavone, G. M. Farinella, & V. Cutello (Eds.), Lecture Notes in Computer Science: Vol. 9432. *Machine Learning, Optimization, and Big Data* (pp. 280–292). Switzerland: Springer Publishing International; doi:10.1007/978-3-319-27926-8_25

Kulkarni, S., Simon, S. P., & Sundareswaran, K. (2013). A spiking neural network (SNN) forecast engine for short-term electrical load forecasting. *Applied Soft Computing*, *13*(8), 3628–3635. doi:10.1016/j.asoc.2013.04.007

Kumar, J., Shukla, S., Prakash, D., Mishra, P., & Kumar, S. (2011). Random Number Generator Using Various Techniques Through VHDL. *International Journal of Computer Applications in Engineering Sciences*, *1*.

Kumar, V. S., & Mohan, M. R. (2011). A genetic algorithm solution to the optimal short-term hydrothermal scheduling. *International Journal of Electrical Power & Energy Systems*, *33*(4), 827–835. doi:10.1016/j.ijepes.2010.11.008

Kuo, M. S., & Liang, G. S. (2011). Combining VIKOR with GRA techniques to evaluate service quality of airports under fuzzy environment. *Expert Systems with Applications*, *38*(3), 304–1312. doi:10.1016/j.eswa.2010.07.003

Kuo, R. J., an, Y., Wang, H., & Chung, W. (2006). Integration of self-organizing feature maps neural network and genetic K-means algorithm for market segmentation. *Expert Systems with Applications*, *30*(2), 313–324. doi:10.1016/j. eswa.2005.07.036

Kuo, R. J., Chang, K., & Chien, S. Y. (2004). Integration of self-organizing feature maps and generic algorithm-based clustering method for market segmentation. *Journal of Organizational Computing and Electronic Commerce*, *14*(1), 43–60. doi:10.1207/s15327744joce1401_3

Kuo, R. J., Ho, L. M., & Hu, C. M. (2002a). Cluster analysis in industrial market segmentation through artificial neural network. *Computers & Industrial Engineering*, *42*(2), 391–399. doi:10.1016/S0360-8352(02)00048-7

Kuo, R. J., Ho, L. M., & Hu, C. M. (2002b). And data mining for product recommendation based on customer lifetime value. *Information & Management*, *42*(3), 387-400.

Labib, A. W. (2011). A supplier selection model: A comparison of fuzzy logic and the analytic hierarchy process. *International Journal of Production Research*, *49*(21), 6287–6299. doi:10.1080/00207543.2010.531776

Lam M. (2003). Neural Network Techniques for Financial Performance Prediction: Integrating Fundamental and Technical Analysis. *Decision Support Systems*, *37*(2004), 567– 581.

Lavrač, N., Bohanec, M., Pur, A., Cestnik, B., Debeljak, M., & Kobler, A. (2007). Data mining and visualization for decision support and modeling of public health-care resources. *Journal of Biomedical Informatics*, *40*(4), 438–447. doi:10.1016/j.jbi.2006.10.003 PMID:17157076

Lee, L. P., & Wong, K. W. (2004). A random number generator based on elliptic curve operations. *Computers & Mathematics with Applications*, *47*(2-3), 217-226. doi:10.1016/S0898-1221(04)90018-1

Lee, C. S., & Wang, M. H. (2007). Ontology-based intelligent healthcare agent and its application to respiratory waveform recognition. *Expert Systems with Applications*, *33*(3), 606–619. doi:10.1016/j.eswa.2006.06.006

Leung, K. M. (2007). *k-Nearest Neighbor Algorithm for Classification*. Retrieved June 27, 2015, from http://cis.poly.edu/mleung/FRE7851/f07/k-NearestNeighbor.pdf

Levin, Y., & Ben-Israel, A. (2004). A heuristic method for large-scale multi-facility location problems. *Computers & Operations Research*, *31*(2), 257–272. doi:10.1016/S0305-0548(02)00191-0

Lewis, C. D. (1982). *Industrial and business forecasting methods: A practical guide to exponential smoothing and curve fitting*. London: Butterworth-Heinemann.

Li, N. (2011, January). Research on location of remanufacturing factory based on particle swarm optimization. In *Management Science and Industrial Engineering (MSIE), 2011 International Conference on* (pp. 1016-1019). IEEE.

Liang, C., Cheung, Y. M., & Wang, Y. (2007, August). A bi-objective model for shelf space allocation using a hybrid genetic algorithm. In *Neural Networks, 2007. IJCNN 2007. International Joint Conference on* (pp. 2460-2465). IEEE. doi:10.1109/IJCNN.2007.4371344

Liao, C. N., & Kao, H. P. (2011). An integrated fuzzy TOPSIS and MCGP approach to supplier selection in supply chain management. *Expert Systems with Applications*, *38*(9), 10803–10811. doi:10.1016/j.eswa.2011.02.031

Li, D., Chang, C., Chen, C., & Chen, W. (2012). Forecasting short-term electricity consumption using the adaptive grey-based approach – An Asian case. *Omega*, *40*(6), 767–773. doi:10.1016/j.omega.2011.07.007

Li, G. D., Yamaguchi, D., & Nagai, M. (2006). Application of improved grey prediction model to short term load forecasting. *Proceedings of International Conference on Electrical Engineering*, 1-6.

Li, H. (2011). A short introduction to learning to rank. *IEICE Transactions on Information and Systems*, *E94-D*(10), 1–9. doi:10.1587/transinf.E94.D.1854

Li, H. Z., Guo, S., Li, C. J., & Sun, J. Q. (2013). A hybrid annual power load forecasting model based on generalized regression neural network with fruit fly optimization algorithm. *Knowledge-Based Systems*, *37*, 378–387. doi:10.1016/j.knosys.2012.08.015

Li, L., Tang, H., Wu, Z., Gong, J., Gruidl, M., Zou, J., & Clark, R. A. (2004). Data mining techniques for cancer detection using serum proteomic profiling. *Artificial Intelligence in Medicine*, *32*(2), 71–83. doi:10.1016/j.artmed.2004.03.006 PMID:15364092

Lim, A., Rodrigues, B., Xiao, F., & Zhang, X. (2002). Adjusted network flow for the shelf-space allocation problem. In *Tools with Artificial Intelligence, 2002. (ICTAI 2002). Proceedings. 14th IEEE International Conference on* (pp. 224-229). IEEE. doi:10.1109/TAI.2002.1180808

Lim, A., Rodrigues, B., & Zhang, X. (2004). Metaheuristics with local search techniques for retail shelf-space optimization. *Management Science*, *50*(1), 117–131. doi:10.1287/mnsc.1030.0165

Liou, T. S., & Wang, M. J. (1992). Ranking fuzzy numbers with integral value. *Fuzzy Sets and Systems*, *50*(3), 247–255. doi:10.1016/0165-0114(92)90223-Q

Liu, S., & Lin, Y. (2006). *Grey information: theory and practical applications*. London: Springer Science & Business Media.

Lorenz, E. N. (1963). Deterministic nonperiodic flow. *Journal of the Atmospheric Sciences*, *20*(2), 130–141. doi:10.1175/1520-0469(1963)020<0130:DNF>2.0.CO;2

Lozano, S., Guerrero, F., Onieva, L., & Larraneta, J. (1998). Kohonen maps for solving a class of location-allocation problems. *European Journal of Operational Research*, *108*(1), 106–117. doi:10.1016/S0377-2217(97)00046-5

Lozi, R., & Taralova, I. (2014). From chaos to randomness via geometric undersampling. *ESAIM: Proceedings and Surveys, 46*, 177-195. Retrieved from EDP Sciences.

Lu, H.-C., & Yeh, M.-F. (1997). Some basic features of GM (1, 1) model (II). *Journal of Grey System*, *4*, 307–321.

Lu, I. J., Lin, S. J., & Lewis, C. (2008). Grey relation analysis of motor vehicular energy consumption in Taiwan. *Energy Policy*, *36*(7), 2556–2561. doi:10.1016/j.enpol.2008.03.015

Lu, K. C., & Yang, D. L. (2009). Image Processing and Image Mining using Decision Trees. *J. Inf. Sci. Eng.*, *25*(4), 989–1003.

Luke, S. (2009). *Essentials of Metaheuristics. A Set of Undergraduate Lecture Notes*. Zeroth Edition.

Machnik, Ł. (2007). A document clustering method based on ant algorithms. *Task Quarterly*, *11*(1-2), 87–102.

Madigan, E. A., & Curet, O. L. (2006). A data mining approach in home healthcare: Outcomes and service use. *BMC Health Services Research*, *6*(1), 18. doi:10.1186/1472-6963-6-18 PMID:16504115

Mahdavi, M., & Abolhassani, H. (2009). Harmony K-means algorithm for document clustering. *Data Mining and Knowledge Discovery*, *18*(3), 370–391. doi:10.1007/s10618-008-0123-0

Maini, R., & Aggarwal, H. (2009). Study and comparison of various image edge detection techniques. *International Journal of Image Processing, 3*(1), 1-11.

Mallat, S. G. (1989). A Theory for Multiresolution Signal Decomposition: The Wavelet Representation. *IEEE Transactions on Pattern Analysis and Machine Intelligence*, *11*(7), 674–693. doi:10.1109/34.192463

Mamlook, R., Badran, O., & Abdulhadi, E. (2009). A fuzzy inference model for short-term load forecasting. *Energy Policy*, *37*(4), 1239–1248. doi:10.1016/j.enpol.2008.10.051

Mandal, P., Senjyu, T., Urasaki, N., & Funabashi, T. (2006). A neural network based several-hour-ahead electric load forecasting using similar days approach. *International Journal of Electrical Power & Energy Systems*, *28*(6), 367–373. doi:10.1016/j.ijepes.2005.12.007

Manikandan, M. S., & Dandapat, S. (2007). Wavelet energy based diagnostic distortion measure for ECG. *Biomedical Signal Processing and Control*, *2*(2), 80–96. doi:10.1016/j.bspc.2007.05.001

Marton, K., Suciu, A., & Ignat, I. (2010). Randomness in digital cryptography: A survey. Romanian Journal of Information Science and Technology. *ROMJIST*, *13*(3), 219–240.

May, R. M. (1976). Simple mathematical models with very complicated dynamics. *Nature*, *261*(5560), 459–467. doi:10.1038/261459a0 PMID:934280

Mazanec, J. A. (1992). Classifying tourists into market segments: A neural network approach. *Journal of Travel & Tourism Marketing*, *1*(1), 39–59. doi:10.1300/J073v01n01_04

Mazanec, J. A. (2001). Neural market structure analysis: Novel topology-sensitive methodology. *European Journal of Marketing*, *35*(7/8), 894–914. doi:10.1108/EUM0000000005730

McGuire, M. (2011, August 26). *Computer Graphics Archive*. Retrieved September 16, 2015.

McIntyre, S. H., & Miller, C. M. (1999). The selection and pricing of retail assortments: An empirical approach. *Journal of Retailing*, *75*(3), 295–318. doi:10.1016/S0022-4359(99)00010-X

Mendel, J. (1995). Fuzzy logic systems for engineering: A tutorial. *Proceedings of the IEEE*, *83*(3), 345–377. doi:10.1109/5.364485

Mettler, T., & Vimarlund, V. (2009). Understanding business intelligence in the context of healthcare. *Health Informatics Journal*, *15*(3), 254–264. doi:10.1177/1460458209337446 PMID:19713399

Miller, C. M., Smith, S. A., McIntyre, S. H., & Achabal, D. D. (2010). Optimizing and evaluating retail assortments for infrequently purchased products. *Journal of Retailing*, *86*(2), 159–171. doi:10.1016/j.jretai.2010.02.004

Mirasgedis, S., Sarafidis, Y., Georgopoulou, E., Lalas, D. P., Moschovits, M., Karagiannis, F., & Papakonstantinou, D. (2006). Models for mid-term electricity demand forecasting incorporating weather influences. *Energy*, *31*(2), 208–227. doi:10.1016/j.energy.2005.02.016

Missaoui, R., & Palenichka, R. M. (2005, August). Effective image and video mining: an overview of model-based approaches. In *Proceedings of the 6th international workshop on Multimedia data mining: mining integrated media and complex data* (pp. 43-52). ACM. doi:10.1145/1133890.1133895

Mitra, S., Pal, S. K., & Mitra, P. (2002). Data mining in soft computing framework: A survey. *IEEE Transactions on Neural Networks*, *13*(1), 3–14. doi:10.1109/72.977258 PMID:18244404

Moghram, I., & Rahman, S. (1989). Analysis and evaluation of five short-term load forecasting techniques. *Power Systems. IEEE Transactions on*, *4*(4), 1484–1491.

Mohammadzadeh, N., & Safdar, İ, R., & Mohammadzadeh, F. (2014). Using intelligent data analysis in cancer care: Benefits and challenges. *Journal of Health Informatics in Developing Countries*, *8*(2).

Mohandes, M. (2002). Support vector machines for short-term electrical load forecasting. *International Journal of Energy Research*, *26*(4), 335–345. doi:10.1002/er.787

Mo, J., Kiang, M., Zou, P., & Li, Y. (2010). A two-stage clustering approach for multi-region segmentation. *Expert Systems with Applications*, *37*(10), 7120–7131. doi:10.1016/j.eswa.2010.03.003

Moody, G. B., & Mark, R. G. (2001). The impact of the MIT-BIH Arrhythmia Database. *IEEE Engineering in Medicine and Biology*, *20*(3), 45–50. doi:10.1109/51.932724 PMID:11446209

Mukhopadhyay, S., & Banerjee, S. (2012). Global optimization of an optical chaotic system by chaotic multi swarm particle swarm optimization. *Expert Systems with Applications*, *39*(1), 917–924. doi:10.1016/j.eswa.2011.07.089

Murray, C. C., Talukdar, D., & Gosavi, A. (2010). Joint optimization of product price, display orientation and shelf-space allocation in retail category management. *Journal of Retailing*, *86*(2), 125–136. doi:10.1016/j.jretai.2010.02.008

Myers, J. H., & Tauber, E. (1977). *Market structure analysis*. Chicago: American Marketing Association.

Nafari, M., & Shahrabi, J. (2010). A temporal data mining approach for shelf-space allocation with consideration of product price. *Expert Systems with Applications*, *37*(6), 4066–4072. doi:10.1016/j.eswa.2009.11.045

Nairn, A., & Berthon, P. (2003). Creating the customer: The influence of advertising on consumer market segments. *Journal of Business Ethics*, *42*(1), 83–99. doi:10.1023/A:1021620825950

Namboodiri, K. (1984). *Matrix algebra an introduction*. Sage University Papers.

Nardo, M., Saisana, M., Saltelli, A., Tarantola, S., Hoffmann, A., & Giovannini, E. (2008). *Handbook on constructing composite indicators: Methodology and user guide*. Paris: OECD publications.

Natter, M. (1999). Conditional market segmentation by neural networks: A monte-carlo study. *Journal of Retailing and Consumer Services*, *6*(4), 237–248. doi:10.1016/S0969-6989(98)00008-3

Neil, F. (n.d.). *Neuron*. Retrieved June 15, 2015 from http://vv.carleton.ca/~neil/neural/neuron-a.html

Nelson, D. (2008). *The Penguin dictionary of mathematics*. UK: Penguin.

NEOS Guide. (2015). *Companion Site to the NEOS Server*. Retrieved July 29, 2015. http://neos-guide.org/

NeuroSolutions. (n.d.). NeuroDimension Inc. Retrieved June 15, 2015 from www.nd.com

Nie, G., Rowe, W., Zhang, L., Tian, Y., & Shi, Y. (2011). Credit card churn forecasting by logistic regression and decision tree. *Expert Systems with Applications*, *38*(12), 15273–15285. doi:10.1016/j.eswa.2011.06.028

Niu, D. X., Li, W., Han, Z. H., & Yuan, X. E. (2008, October). Power Load Forecasting based on Improved Genetic Algorithm–GM (1, 1) Model. In *Natural Computation, 2008. ICNC'08. Fourth International Conference on* (Vol. 1, pp. 630-634). IEEE.

Niu, D., Wang, Y., & Wu, D. D. (2010). Power load forecasting using support vector machine and ant colony optimization. *Expert Systems with Applications*, *37*(3), 2531–2539. doi:10.1016/j.eswa.2009.08.019

Noble, B. (1967). *Applications of undergraduate mathematics in engineering*. New York: Macmillan.

Nydick, R. L., & Hill, R. P. (1992). Using the analytic hierarchy process to structure the supplier selection procedure. *Int. J. Purchasing and Materials Management*, *28*(2), 31–36.

Obenshain, M. K. (2004). Application of data mining techniques to healthcare data. *Infection Control*, *25*(08), 690–695. doi:10.1086/502460 PMID:15357163

Oh, J., & Kim, B. (2010). Prediction model for demands of the health meteorological information using a decision tree method. *Asian Nursing Research, 4*(3), 151-162.

Omran, M. G., Salman, A., & Engelbrecht, A. P. (2006). Dynamic clustering using particle swarm optimization with application in image segmentation. *Pattern Analysis & Applications*, *8*(4), 332–344. doi:10.1007/s10044-005-0015-5

Omran, M., Salman, A., & Engelbrecht, A. P. (2002, November). Image classification using particle swarm optimization. In *Proceedings of the 4th Asia-Pacific conference on simulated evolution and learning* (Vol. 1, pp. 18-22).

Onal, S. A., & Kilincci, O. (2011). Fuzzy AHP approach for supplier selection in a washing machine company. *Expert Systems with Applications, 38*(8), 9656–9664. doi:10.1016/j.eswa.2011.01.159

Onut, S., & Kara, S. S., & Isik, E. (2009). Long term supplier selection using a combined fuzzy MCDM approach: A case study for a telecommunication company. *Expert Systems with Applications, 36*(2), 3887–3895.

Opricovic, S. (1998). *Multi-Criteria Optimization of Civil Engineering Systems*. Belgrade: Faculty of Civil Engineering.

Opricovic, S., & Tzeng, G. H. (2004). Compromise solution by MCDM methods: A comparative analysis of VIKOR and TOPSIS. *European Journal of Operational Research, 156*(2), 445–455. doi:10.1016/S0377-2217(03)00020-1

ORACLE. (2015). *Classification*. Retrieved June 27, 2015, from http://docs.oracle.com/cd/B28359_01/datamine.111/b28129/classify.htm#i1005746

Ordonez, C., & Omiecinski, E. R. (1998). *Image mining: A new approach for data mining*. Academic Press.

Ordoobadi, S. M. (2009). Development of a supplier selection model using fuzzy logic. *Supply Chain Management. International Journal (Toronto, Ont.), 14*(4), 314–327.

Orr, M. (1996). *Introduction to Radial Basis Functions*, Retrieved June 15, 2015 from http://www.anc.ed.ac.uk/rbf/intro/intro.html

Osman, I. H., & Laporte, G. (1996). Metaheuristics: A bibliography. *Annals of Operations Research, 63*(5), 511–623. doi:10.1007/BF02125421

Ott, E. (1993). *Chaos in Dynamical Systems*. Cambridge University Press.

Ouenniche, J. (2011). *Unpublished lecture notes for design and operational management of supply chains of products and services*. Lecture at ESC Rennes School of Business.

Owczarczuk, M. (2010). Churn models for prepaid customers in the cellular telecommunication industry using large data marts. *Expert Systems with Applications, 37*(6), 4710–4712. doi:10.1016/j.eswa.2009.11.083

Ozcakar, N. (2015). *Unpublished lecture notes for production management at Istanbul University*.

Ozcan, T., & Esnaf, S. (2011, June). A heuristic approach based on artificial bee colony algorithm for retail shelf space optimization. In *Evolutionary Computation (CEC), 2011 IEEE Congress on* (pp. 95-101). IEEE. doi:10.1109/CEC.2011.5949604

Ozcan, T., Celebi, N., & Esnaf, S. (2011). Comparative analysis of multi-criteria decision making methodologies and implementation of a warehouse location selection problem. *Expert Systems with Applications, 38*(8), 9773–9779. doi:10.1016/j.eswa.2011.02.022

Ozcan, T., & Esnaf, S. (2013). A discrete constrained optimization using genetic algorithms for a bookstore layout. *International Journal of Computational Intelligence Systems, 6*(2), 261–278. doi:10.1080/18756891.2013.768447

Ozdagoglu, A. (2008). Tesis yeri seciminde farkli bir yaklasim: Bulanik analitik serim sureci [A different approach in facility location selection: Fuzzy analytical network process]. *Ataturk University Journal of Economics and Administrative Sciences, 22*(1).

Ozer, M. (2001). User segmentation of online music services using fuzzy clustering. *Omega, 29*(2), 193–206. doi:10.1016/S0305-0483(00)00042-6

Ozkok, B. A., & Tiryaki, F. (2011). A compensatory fuzzy approach to multi-objective linear supplier selection problem with multiple-item. *Expert Systems with Applications, 38*(9), 11363–11368. doi:10.1016/j.eswa.2011.03.004

Öztürk, N., & Fitöz, E. (2009). Türkiye'de konut piyasasının belirleyicileri: Ampirik bir uygulama. *ZKÜ Sosyal Bilimler Dergisi, 5*(10), 21-46. Available from http://ijmeb.org/index.php/zkesbe/article/view/197

Pai, P. F., & Hong, W. C. (2005a). Support vector machines with simulated annealing algorithms in electricity load forecasting. *Energy Conversion and Management, 46*(17), 2669–2688. doi:10.1016/j.enconman.2005.02.004

Pai, P. F., & Hong, W. C. (2005b). Forecasting regional electricity load based on recurrent support vector machines with genetic algorithms. *Electric Power Systems Research, 74*(3), 417–425. doi:10.1016/j.epsr.2005.01.006

Papadakis, S. E., Theocharis, J. B., Kiartzis, S. J., & Bakirtzis, A. G. (1998). A novel approach to short-term load forecasting using fuzzy neural networks. *Power Systems. IEEE Transactions on, 13*(2), 480–492.

Papalexopoulos, A. D., Hao, S., & Peng, T. M. (1994). An implementation of a neural network based load forecasting model for the EMS. *Power Systems. IEEE Transactions on, 9*(4), 1956–1962.

Papalexopoulos, A. D., & Hesterberg, T. C. (1990). A regression-based approach to short-term system load forecasting. *Power Systems. IEEE Transactions on, 5*(4), 1535–1547.

Parkpoom, S., Harrison, G. P., & Bialek, J. W. (2004, September). Climate change impacts on electricity demand. In *Universities Power Engineering Conference, 2004. UPEC 2004. 39th International* (Vol. 3, pp. 1342-1346). IEEE.

Peitgen, H. O., Jürgens, H., & Saupe, D. (2006). *Chaos and fractals: new frontiers of science.* Springer Science & Business Media.

Peltier, J. M., & Schribrowsky, J. A. (1997). The use of need-based segmentation for developing segment-specific direct marketing strategies. *Journal of Direct Marketing, 11*(4), 54–62. doi:10.1002/(SICI)1522-7138(199723)11:4<53::AID-DIR8>3.0.CO;2-V

Peng, T. M., Hubele, N. F., & Karady, G. G. (1992). Advancement in the application of neural networks for short-term load forecasting. *Power Systems. IEEE Transactions on, 7*(1), 250–257.

Penzel, T., Moody, G. B., Mark, R. G., Goldberger, A. L., & Peter, J. H. (2000). The Apnea-ECG Database. *Computers in Cardiology, 27*, 255–258.

Petroni, A., & Braglia, M. (2000). Vendor selection using principal component analysis. *The Journal of Supply Chain Management, 36*(1), 63–69. doi:10.1111/j.1745-493X.2000.tb00078.x

Phatak, S. C., & Rao, S. S. (1995). Logistic map: A possible random-number generator. *Physical Review E: Statistical Physics, Plasmas, Fluids, and Related Interdisciplinary Topics, 51*(4), 3670–3678. doi:10.1103/PhysRevE.51.3670 PMID:9963048

Phillips-Wren, G., Sharkey, P., & Dy, S. M. (2008). Mining lung cancer patient data to assess healthcare resource utilization. *Expert Systems with Applications, 35*(4), 1611–1619. doi:10.1016/j.eswa.2007.08.076

Pichette, L., & Rennison, L. (2011). *Extracting Information from the Business Outlook Survey: A Principal-Component Approach, Canadian Economic Analysis* [PDF document]. Retrieved from http://www.bankofcanada.ca/wp-content/uploads/2011/11/pichette.pdf

Pineno, C. J. (2002). The balanced scorecard: An incremental approach model to health care management. *Journal of Health Care Finance, 28*(4), 69–80. PMID:12148665

Piras, A., Germond, A., Buchenel, B., Imhof, K., & Jaccard, Y. (1996). Heterogeneous artificial neural network for short term electrical load forecasting. *Power Systems. IEEE Transactions on, 11*(1), 397–402.

Pivoluska, M., & Plesch, M. (2015). *Device Independent Random Number Generation.* arXiv:1502.06393

Potharst, R., Kaymak, U., & Pijls, W. (2001). *Neural networks for target selection in direct marketing.* ERIM Report Series Research in Management, No: ERS-2001-14-LIS, Rotterdam, Netherlands, March, 1-15.

Prasad, U. & Madhavi, S. (2012). Prediction of Churn Behavior of Bank Customers. *Business Intelligence Journal, 5*, 96-101.

Premalatha, K., & Natarajan, A. M. (2010a). A literature review on document clustering. *Information Technology Journal, 9*(5), 993–1002. doi:10.3923/itj.2010.993.1002

Premalatha, K., & Natarajan, A. M. (2010b). Hybrid PSO and GA models for Document Clustering. *Int. J. Advance. Soft Comput. Appl, 2*(3), 302–320.

Punj, G., & Stewart, D. W. (1983). Cluster analysis in marketing research: Review and suggestions for applications. *JMR, Journal of Marketing Research, 20*(2), 134–148. doi:10.2307/3151680

Pyle, D. (1999). *Data Preparation for Data Mining.* Los Altos, CA: Morgan Kaufmann Publishers.

Rafalski, E. (2002). Using data mining/data repository methods to identify marketing opportunities in health care. *Journal of Consumer Marketing, 19*(7), 607–613. doi:10.1108/07363760210451429

Raghupathi, W., & Raghupathi, V. (2014). Big data analytics in healthcare: Promise and potential. *Health Information Science and Systems, 2*(1), 3. doi:10.1186/2047-2501-2-3 PMID:25825667

Rahman, M. M., Khanam, R., & Xu, S. (2012). The factors affecting housing price in Hangzhou: An empirical analysis. *International Journal of Economic Perspectives, 6*(4), 57–66.

Rahman, S. (1990). Formulation and analysis of a rule-based short-term load forecasting algorithm. *Proceedings of the IEEE, 78*(5), 805–816. doi:10.1109/5.53400

Rahman, S., & Bhatnagar, R. (1988). An expert system based algorithm for short term load forecast. *Power Systems. IEEE Transactions on, 3*(2), 392–399.

Rajaraman, A., & Ullman, J. D. (2012). *Mining of massive datasets* (Vol. 77). Cambridge, UK: Cambridge University Press.

Ramaseshan, B., Achuthan, N. R., & Collinson, R. (2009). A retail category management model integrating shelf space and inventory levels. *Asia-Pacific Journal of Operational Research, 26*(04), 457–478. doi:10.1142/S0217595909002304

Reese, A. (2009). Random number generators in genetic algorithms for unconstrained and constrained optimization. Nonlinear Analysis: Theory. *Methods & Applications, 71*(12), e679–e692.

Reinelt, G. (1995). *Tsplib95. Interdisziplinäres Zentrum für Wissenschaftliches Rechnen.* Heidelberg, Germany: IWR.

Rencher, A. C. (2002). *Methods of multivariate analysis.* John Wiley & Sons. doi:10.1002/0471271357

ReVelle, C. S., & Eiselt, H. A. (2005). Location analysis: A synthesis and survey. *European Journal of Operational Research, 165*(1), 1–19. doi:10.1016/j.ejor.2003.11.032

Reyad, O., & Kotulski, Z. (2015). On Pseudo-Random Number Generators Using Elliptic Curves and Chaotic Systems. *Applications of Mathematics, 9*(1), 31–38.

Reyes, P. M., & Frazier, G. V. (2005). Initial Shelf Space Considerations at New Grocery Stores: An Allocation Problem With Product Switching and Substitution. *The International Entrepreneurship and Management Journal*, *1*(2), 183–202. doi:10.1007/s11365-005-1128-4

Reyes, P. M., & Frazier, G. V. (2007). Goal programming model for grocery shelf space allocation. *European Journal of Operational Research*, *181*(2), 634–644. doi:10.1016/j.ejor.2006.07.004

Reyes-Sierra, M., & Coello, C. C. (2006). Multi-objective particle swarm optimizers: A survey of the state-of-the-art. *International Journal of Computational Intelligence Research*, *2*(3), 287-308.

Roasoft Sample Size Calculator. (2015). Retrieved September 30, 2015, from http://www.raosoft.com/samplesize.html

Rogers, T. D., & Whitley, D. C. (1983). Chaos in the cubic mapping. *Mathematical Modelling*, *4*(1), 9–25. doi:10.1016/0270-0255(83)90030-1

Rosso, O. A., Martin, M. T., Figliola, A., Keller, K., & Plastino, A. (2006). EEG analysis using wavelet-based information tools. *Journal of Neuroscience Methods*, *153*(2), 163–182. doi:10.1016/j.jneumeth.2005.10.009 PMID:16675027

Rothlauf, F. (2011). Design of Modern Heuristics Principles and Application. Springer. doi:10.1007/978-3-540-72962-4

Rouse, M. (2013). *Churn Rate (Predictive Churn Modeling)*. Retrieved June 27, 2015, from http://searchcrm.techtarget.com/definition/churn-rate

Ruan, Q., Miao, L., & Zheng, Z. (2010, October). A novel clustering-based approach for the location of multi-logistics centers. In *Supply Chain Management and Information Systems (SCMIS), 2010 8th International Conference on* (pp. 1-5). IEEE.

Runkler, T. A. (1996). Extended Defuzzification Methods and Their Properties. *IEEE Transactions*, 694-700.

Russell, R. A., & Urban, T. L. (2010). The location and allocation of products and product families on retail shelves. *Annals of Operations Research*, *179*(1), 131–147. doi:10.1007/s10479-008-0450-y

Rutkove, S. (n.d.). *Examples of Electromyograms*. Available on: http://physionet.org/physiobank/database/emgdb/ doi:10.13026/C24S3D

Saaty, T. L. (1980). *The analytic hierarchy process*. New York: McGraw-Hill.

Saaty, T. L. (2003). Decision-making with the AHP: Why is the principal eigenvector necessary. *European Journal of Operational Research*, *145*(1), 85–91. doi:10.1016/S0377-2217(02)00227-8

Sæbø, J. I., Kossi, E. K., Titlestad, O. H., Tohouri, R. R., & Braa, J. (2011). Comparing strategies to integrate health information systems following a data warehouse approach in four countries. *Information Technology for Development*, *17*(1), 42–60. doi:10.1080/02681102.2010.511702

Salton, G., Wong, A., & Yang, C.-S. (1975). A vector space model for automatic indexing. *Communications of the ACM*, *18*(11), 613–620. doi:10.1145/361219.361220

Sanayei, A., Mousavi, S. F., & Yazdankhah, A. (2010). Group Decision Making Process For Supplier Selection With VIKOR Under Fuzzy Environment. *Expert Systems with Applications*, *37*(1), 24–30. doi:10.1016/j.eswa.2009.04.063

Santos, R. S., Malheiros, S. M. F., Cavalheiro, S., & De Oliveira, J. P. (2013). A data mining system for providing analytical information on brain tumors to public health decision makers. *Computer Methods and Programs in Biomedicine*, *109*(3), 269–282. doi:10.1016/j.cmpb.2012.10.010 PMID:23122302

Sari, B., Sen, T., & Kilic, S. E. (2008). AHP model for the selection of partner companies in virtual enterprises. *International Journal of Advanced Manufacturing Technology*, *38*(3-4), 367–376. doi:10.1007/s00170-007-1097-6

Scala, N., Rajgopal, J., Vargas, L., & Needy, K. (2014). *Using principal components analysis for aggregating judgments in the analytic hierarchy process*. International Symposium of the Analytic Hierarchy Process 2014, Washington, DC.

Senjyu, T., Takara, H., Uezato, K., & Funabashi, T. (2002). One-hour-ahead load forecasting using neural network. *Power Systems. IEEE Transactions on*, *17*(1), 113–118.

Serra, J., & Soille, P. (Eds.). (2012). *Mathematical morphology and its applications to image processing* (Vol. 2). Springer Science & Business Media.

Serrano, J., & Hoesli, M. (2010). Are Securitized Real Estate Returns more Predictable than Stock Returns? *The Journal of Real Estate Finance and Economics*, *41*(2), 170–192. doi:10.1007/s11146-008-9162-y

Sevkli, M., & Guner, A. R. (2006). A continuous particle swarm optimization algorithm for uncapacitated facility location problem. In *Ant colony optimization and swarm intelligence* (pp. 316–323). Springer Berlin Heidelberg. doi:10.1007/11839088_28

Sezgin, M. (2004). Survey over image thresholding techniques and quantitative performance evaluation. *Journal of Electronic Imaging*, *13*(1), 146–168. doi:10.1117/1.1631315

Shah, N., & Mahajan, S. (2012). Document Clustering: A Detailed Review. *International Journal of Applied Information Systems*, 2249-0868.

Sharma, A., & Lambert, D. M. (1994). Segmentation of markets based on customer service. *Int. Journal of Physical Distribution & Logistics Management*, *24*(4), 50–58. doi:10.1108/09600039410757649

She, Y. Y. (2006). *Real-time animation of walking and running using inverse kinematics*. (Doctoral dissertation). Concordia University.

Shepard, R. N. (1987). Toward a universal law of generalization for psychological science. *Science*, *237*(4820), 1317–1323. doi:10.1126/science.3629243 PMID:3629243

Shim, B., Choi, K., & Suh, Y. (2012). CRM strategies for a small-sized online shopping mall based on association rules and sequential patterns. *Expert Systems with Applications*, *39*(9), 7736–7742. doi:10.1016/j.eswa.2012.01.080

Shin, H. W., & Sohn, S. Y. (2004). Segmentation of stock trading customers according to potential value. *Expert Systems with Applications*, *27*(1), 27–33. doi:10.1016/j.eswa.2003.12.002

Shi, Y., & Eberhart, R. C. (1998, January). Parameter selection in particle swarm optimization. In *Evolutionary programming VII* (pp. 591–600). Springer Berlin Heidelberg. doi:10.1007/BFb0040810

Singh, Y. & Chauhan, A. S. (2009). Neural Networks in Data Mining. *Journal of Theoretical and Applied Information Technology*, 37-42.

Singhai, N., & Shandilya, S. K. (2010). A survey on: Content based image retrieval systems. *International Journal of Computers and Applications*, *4*(2), 22–26. doi:10.5120/802-1139

Smith, L. (2002). *A tutorial on principal components analysis* [PDF document]. Retrieved from http://www.cs.otago.ac.nz/cosc453/student_tutorials/principal_components.pdf

Smith, K. A., Willis, R. J., & Brooks, M. (2002). An analysis of customer retention and insurance claim patterns using data mining: A case study. *The Journal of the Operational Research Society*, *51*(5), 532–541. doi:10.1057/palgrave.jors.2600941

Smith, W. R. (1956). Product differentiation and market segmentation as an alternative marketing strategy. *Journal of Marketing*, *21*(1), 3–8. doi:10.2307/1247695

Soba, M. (2014). Banka yeri seçiminin Analitik Hiyerarsi Sureci ve Electre metodu ile belirlenmesi, Usak ilceleri ornegi[Determining the selection of the bank location through Analytical Hierarchy Process and Electre methods: The case of Usak towns]. *Mustafa Kemal University Journal of Graduate School of Social Sciences*, *11*(25), 459–473.

Solanki, A. V. (2014). Data Mining Techniques Using WEKA classification for Sickle Cell Disease. *International Journal of Computer Science and Information Technologies*, *5*(4), 5857–5860.

Song, Q., & Jamalipour, A. (2005). An adaptive quality-of-service network selection mechanism for heterogeneous mobile networks. *Wireless Communications and Mobile Computing*, *5*(6), 697–708. doi:10.1002/wcm.330

Song, Q., Shepperd, M., & Mair, C. (2005). Using grey relational analysis to predict software effort with small data sets.*11th IEEE International Software Metrics Symposium*. doi:10.1109/METRICS.2005.51

Souza, C., Omkar, S. N., & Senthilnath, J. (2012). Pickup and delivery problem using metaheuristics techniques. *Expert Systems with Applications*, *39*(1), 328–334. doi:10.1016/j.eswa.2011.07.022

Spruit, M., Vroon, R., & Batenburg, R. (2014). Towards healthcare business intelligence in long-term care: An explorative case study in the Netherlands. *Computers in Human Behavior*, *30*, 698–707.

Srinivas, K., Rani, B. K., & Govrdhan, A. (2010). Applications of data mining techniques in healthcare and prediction of heart attacks. *International Journal on Computer Science and Engineering*, *2*(02), 250–255.

Stevenson, W. (1996). *Production/Operations Management.* Irwin.

Strozzi, F., & Zaldivar, J. M. (2005). Non-linear Forecasting in High-frequency Financial Time Series. *Physica A*, *353*, 463–479. doi:10.1016/j.physa.2005.01.047

Subasi, A., & Gursoy, M. I. (2010). EEG Signal classification using PCA, ICA, LDA and support vector machine. *Expert Systems with Applications*, *37*(12), 8659–8666. doi:10.1016/j.eswa.2010.06.065

Su, C. T., Yang, C. H., Hsu, K. H., & Chiu, W. K. (2006). Data mining for the diagnosis of type II diabetes from three-dimensional body surface anthropometrical scanning data. *Computers & Mathematics with Applications (Oxford, England)*, *51*(6), 1075–1092. doi:10.1016/j.camwa.2005.08.034

Suh, E. H., Noh, K. C., & Suh, C. K. (1999). Customer list segmentation using the combined response model. *Expert Systems with Applications*, *17*(2), 89–97. doi:10.1016/S0957-4174(99)00026-3

Sule, D. R. (2001). *Logistics of facility location and allocation.* New York: CRC Press. doi:10.1201/9780203910405

Sun, S. (2009). An analysis on the conditions and methods of market segmentation. *International Journal of Business and Management*, *4*(2), 63–70. doi:10.5539/ijbm.v4n2p63

Szczepanski, J., Wajnryb, E., Amiga, J. M., Sanchez-Vives, M. V., & Slater, M. (2004). Biometric random number generators. *Computers & Security*, *23*(1), 77–84. doi:10.1016/S0167-4048(04)00064-1

Tahoun, M., Nagaty, K., & El-Arief, T. (2005, March). A robust content-based image retrieval system using multiple features representations. In Networking, Sensing and Control, 2005. Proceedings. 2005 IEEE (pp. 116-122). IEEE.

Taillard, É. D. (2003). Heuristic methods for large centroid clustering problems. *Journal of Heuristics*, *9*(1), 51–73. doi:10.1023/A:1021841728075

Talbi, E. G. (2009). Metaheuristics: from design to implementation (74th ed.). John Wiley & Sons.

Talbi, E.-G. (2009). *Metaheuristics from Design to Implementation*. Hoboken, NJ: John Wiley & Sons, Inc.

Tarczynski, T. (2011). Document Clustering-Concepts, Metrics and Algorithms. *International Journal of Electronics and Telecommunications, 57*(3), 271-277.

Tarokh, M. J., Shemshadi, A., Shirazi, H., & Toreihi, M. (2011). A fuzzy VIKOR method for supplier selection based on entropy measure for objective weighting. *Expert Systems with Applications, 38*(10), 12160–12167. doi:10.1016/j.eswa.2011.03.027

Taylor, J. W. (2008). An evaluation of methods for very short-term load forecasting using minute-by-minute British data. *International Journal of Forecasting, 24*(4), 645–658. doi:10.1016/j.ijforecast.2008.07.007

Taylor, J. W. (2010). Triple seasonal methods for short-term electricity demand forecasting. *European Journal of Operational Research, 204*(1), 139–152. doi:10.1016/j.ejor.2009.10.003

Taylor, J. W. (2012). Short-term load forecasting with exponentially weighted methods. *Power Systems. IEEE Transactions on, 27*(1), 458–464.

Taylor, J. W., & Buizza, R. (2002). Neural network load forecasting with weather ensemble predictions. *Power Systems. IEEE Transactions on, 17*(3), 626–632.

Taylor, J. W., & Buizza, R. (2003). Using weather ensemble predictions in electricity demand forecasting. *International Journal of Forecasting, 19*(1), 57–70. doi:10.1016/S0169-2070(01)00123-6

Taylor, J. W., & McSharry, P. E. (2007). Short-term load forecasting methods: An evaluation based on european data. *Power Systems. IEEE Transactions on, 22*(4), 2213–2219.

Taylor, S. J. (1992). Rewards Available to Currency Futures Speculators: Compensation for Risk or Evidence of Inefficient Pricing? *The Economic Record, 68*(Supplement), 105–116. doi:10.1111/j.1475-4932.1992.tb02298.x

Teisberg, T. J., Weiher, R. F., & Khotanzad, A. (2005). The economic value of temperature forecasts in electricity generation. *Bulletin of the American Meteorological Society, 86*(12), 1765–1771. doi:10.1175/BAMS-86-12-1765

Tektas, A., & Hortacsu, A. (2003). Karar vermede etkinliği artıran bir yöntem: Analitik hiyerarsi sureci ve magaza secimine uygulanmasi [A tool for effective decision making: Analytic hierarchy process and application to store location selection]. *Iktisat Isletme ve Finans, 18*(209), 52–61.

TELKODER. (2015). *İnternet Tabanlı Hizmetler (ITH/Ott) Elektronik haberleşme sektörüne etkisi ve düzenleme önerileri*. Retrieved June 27, 2015, from http://www.telkoder.org.tr/core/uploads/page/document/4840_130415306458648.pdf

Thomas Ng, S., Skitmore, M., & Wong, K. F. (2008). Using genetic algorithms and linear regression analysis for private housing demand forecast. *Building and Environment, 43*(6), 1171–1184. doi:10.1016/j.buildenv.2007.02.017

Tianchang, L., Zhiwei, Z., & Lin, Z. (2008). Evaluation and selection of suppliers in supply chain based on RST and VIKOR algorithm.*Control and Decision Conference, CCDC 2008*. doi:10.1109/CCDC.2008.4597658

Tien, T.-L. (2012). A research on the grey prediction model GM (1, n). *Applied Mathematics and Computation, 218*(9), 4903–4916. doi:10.1016/j.amc.2011.10.055

Timor, M. (2011). *Analitik hiyerarsi prosesi* [Analytical hierarchy process]. Istanbul: Turkmen Kitabevi.

Ting, S. L., Shum, C. C., Kwok, S. K., Tsang, A. H., & Lee, W. B. (2009). Data mining in biomedicine: Current applications and further directions for research. *Journal of Software Engineering and Applications, 2*(03), 150–159. doi:10.4236/jsea.2009.23022

Toloo, M., & Nalchigar, S. (2011). A new DEA method for supplier selection in presence of both cardinaland ordinal data. *Expert Systems with Applications*, *38*(12), 14726–14731. doi:10.1016/j.eswa.2011.05.008

Tsai, C. H., Chang, C. L., & Chen, L. (2003). Applying grey relational analysis to the vendor evaluation model. *Int. J. The Computer. The Internet and Management*, *11*(3), 45–53.

Tsai, C. Y., & Chiu, C. C. (2004). A purchase-based market segmentation methodology. *Expert Systems with Applications*, *27*(2), 265–276. doi:10.1016/j.eswa.2004.02.005

Tsai, C. Y., & Huang, S. H. (2015). A data mining approach to optimise shelf space allocation in consideration of customer purchase and moving behaviours. *International Journal of Production Research*, *53*(3), 850–866. doi:10.1080/00207543.2014.937011

Tsaur, R.-C. (2006). Forecasting analysis by fuzzy grey model GM (1, 1). *Journal of the Chinese Institute of Industrial Engineers*, *23*(5), 415–422. doi:10.1080/10170660609509337

Tseng, F. M., & Tzeng, G. H. (2002). A fuzzy seasonal ARIMA model for forecasting. *Fuzzy Sets and Systems*, *126*(3), 367–376. doi:10.1016/S0165-0114(01)00047-1

Tsiotsou, R. (2006). Using visit frequency to segment ski resorts customers. *Journal of Vacation Marketing*, *12*(1), 15–26. doi:10.1177/1356766706059029

Tsipourasemail, M. G., & Fotiadis, D. I. (2004). Automatic arrhythmia detection based on time and time–frequency analysis of heart rate variability. *Computer Methods and Programs in Biomedicine*, *74*(2), 95–108. doi:10.1016/S0169-2607(03)00079-8 PMID:15013592

Tsoi, K. H., Leung, K. H., & Leong, P. H. W. (2003). Compact FPGA-based true and pseudo random number generators. *Field-Programmable Custom Computing Machines, 2003. FCCM 2003. 11th Annual IEEE Symposium on* (pp. 51-61). IEEE.

Turban, E., Sharda, R., Delen, D., & King, D. (2011). *Business Intelligence: A Managerial Approach*. Academic Press.

Tynan, A. C., & Drayton, J. (1987). Market segmentation. *Journal of Marketing Management*, *1*(3), 301–335. doi:10.1080/0267257X.1987.9964020

Tzeng, G. H., Lin, C. W., & Opricovic, S. (2005). Multi- Criteria Analysis of Alternative-Fuel Buses for Public Transportation. *Energy Policy*, *33*(11), 1373–1383. doi:10.1016/j.enpol.2003.12.014

Tzeng, G., & Chiang, C. (1998). Applying possibility regression to grey model. *Journal of Grey System*, *1*(1), 19–31.

Uchida, A. (2012). *Optical communication with chaotic lasers: applications of nonlinear dynamics and synchronization*. John Wiley & Sons.

Uludag, A. S., & Deveci, M. E. (2013). Using the multi-criteria decision making methods in facility location selection problems and an application. *Abant Izzet Baysal University Graduate School of Social Sciences*, *13*(1), 257–287.

Urban, T. L. (1998). An inventory-theoretic approach to product assortment and shelf-space allocation. *Journal of Retailing*, *74*(1), 15–35. doi:10.1016/S0022-4359(99)80086-4

Uyan, M. (2013). GIS-based solar farms site selection using analytic hierarchy process (AHP) in Karapinar region, Konya/Turkey. *Renewable & Sustainable Energy Reviews*, *28*, 11–17. doi:10.1016/j.rser.2013.07.042

Vahdani, B., & Zandieh, M. (2010). Selecting suppliers using a new fuzzy multiple criteria decision model: The fuzzy balancing and ranking method. *International Journal of Production Research*, *48*(18), 5307–5326. doi:10.1080/00207540902933155

Van den Bergh, F., & Engelbrecht, A. P. (2004). A cooperative approach to particle swarm optimization. Evolutionary Computation. *IEEE Transactions on*, *8*(3), 225–239.

Van der Merwe, D. W., & Engelbrecht, A. P. (2003, December). Data clustering using particle swarm optimization. In Evolutionary Computation, 2003. CEC'03. The 2003 Congress on (Vol. 1, pp. 215-220). IEEE. doi:10.1109/CEC.2003.1299577

Vapnik, V. N., & Chervonenkis, A. J. (1974). *Theory of pattern recognition*. Academic Press.

Vellido, A., Lisboa, P. J., & Meehan, K. (1999). Segmentation of the online shopping market using neural networks. *Expert Systems with Applications*, *17*(4), 303–314. doi:10.1016/S0957-4174(99)00042-1

Vercellis, C. (2009). *Business Intelligence: Data Mining and Optimization for Decision Making*. Editorial John Wiley and Sons. doi:10.1002/9780470753866

Vermaak, J., & Botha, E. C. (1998). Recurrent neural networks for short-term load forecasting. *Power Systems. IEEE Transactions on*, *13*(1), 126–132.

Vesanto, J., & Alhoniemi, E. (2000). Clustering of the self-organizing map. *IEEE Transactions on Neural Networks*, *11*(3), 586–600. doi:10.1109/72.846731 PMID:18249787

Vidal, R., & Ravichandran, A. (2005, June). Optical flow estimation & segmentation of multiple moving dynamic textures. In *Computer Vision and Pattern Recognition, 2005. CVPR 2005. IEEE Computer Society Conference on* (Vol. 2, pp. 516-521). IEEE. doi:10.1109/CVPR.2005.263

Vinodh, S., Ramiya, R. A., & Gautham, S. G. (2011). Application of fuzzy analytic network process for supplier selection in a manufacturing organisation. *Expert Systems with Applications*, *38*(1), 272–280. doi:10.1016/j.eswa.2010.06.057

Voelker, K. E., Rakich, J. S., & French, G. R. (2001). The balanced scorecard in healthcare organizations: A performance measurement and strategic planning methodology. *Hospital Topics*, *79*(3), 13–24. doi:10.1080/00185860109597908 PMID:11794940

Voges, K., Pope, N., & Brown, M. (2003). A rough cluster analysis of shopping orientation data. In *ANZMAC Proceedings*.

Vučenović, D., Trivić, I., & Kos, D. (2015). *Intelligent data analysis – From data to knowledge*. Retrieved from http://www.astro.hr/s3/izvjestaji/s3pp2009/WebReport_IntelligentDataAnalysis.pdf

Wang, D., Wu, C. H., Ip, A., Wang, D., & Yan, Y. (2008, June). Parallel multi-population particle swarm optimization algorithm for the uncapacitated facility location problem using openMP. In *Evolutionary Computation, 2008. CEC 2008. (IEEE World Congress on Computational Intelligence). IEEE Congress on* (pp. 1214-1218). IEEE.

Wang, Q., Yu, S., Ding, W., & Leng, M. (2008). Generating high-quality random numbers by cellular automata with PSO. *Natural Computation, 2008. ICNC'08. Fourth International Conference on* (vol. 7, pp. 430-433). IEEE. doi:10.1109/ICNC.2008.560

Wang, C. (2004). Futures Trading Activity and Predictable Foreign Exchange Market Movements. *Journal of Banking & Finance*, *28*(5), 1023–1041. doi:10.1016/S0378-4266(03)00047-5

Wang, C. H. (2009). Outlier identification and market segmentation using kernel-based clustering techniques. *Expert Systems with Applications*, *36*(2), 3744–3750. doi:10.1016/j.eswa.2008.02.037

Wang, C., & Hsu, L. (2008). Using genetic algorithms grey theory to forecast high technology industrial output. *Applied Mathematics and Computation*, *195*(1), 256–263. doi:10.1016/j.amc.2007.04.080

Wang, G., Wang, Z., Chen, W., & Zhuang, J. (2006). Classification of surface EMG signals using optimal wavelet packet method based on Davies-Bouldin criterion. *Medical & Biological Engineering & Computing, 44*(10), 865–872. doi:10.1007/s11517-006-0100-y PMID:16951931

Wang, J. W., Cheng, C. H., & Kun-Cheng, H. (2009). Fuzzy hierarchical TOPSIS for supplier selection. *Applied Soft Computing, 9*(1), 377–386. doi:10.1016/j.asoc.2008.04.014

Wang, L., Ranjan, R., Kołodziej, J., Zomaya, A., & Alem, L. (2015). Software Tools and Techniques for Big Data Computing in Healthcare Clouds. *Future Generation Computer Systems, 43*, 38–39. doi:10.1016/j.future.2014.11.001

Wang, Q. P., Zhang, D. H., & Hu, H. Q. (2007). A method of Grey Incidence Analysis for Group Decision-Making under Fuzzy Information.*Proceedings of International Conference on Grey Systems and Intelligent Services.* doi:10.1109/GSIS.2007.4443263

Wasan, S. K., Bhatnagar, V., & Kaur, H. (2006). The impact of data mining techniques on medical diagnostics. *Data Science Journal, 5*, 119–126. doi:10.2481/dsj.5.119

Weber, C. A., Current, J. R., & Benton, W. C. (1991). Vendor selection criteria and methods. *European Journal of Operational Research, 50*(1), 2–18. doi:10.1016/0377-2217(91)90033-R

Weber, R. (1996). Customer segmentation for banks and insurance groups with fuzzy clustering techniques. In J. F. Baldwin (Ed.), *Fuzzy Logic*. New York: John Wiley & Sons.

Wedding, D. K. II, & Cios, K. J. (1996). Time series forecasting by combining RBF networks, certainty factors, and the Box-Jenkins model. *Neurocomputing, 10*(2), 149–168. doi:10.1016/0925-2312(95)00021-6

Wedel, M., & Kamakura, W. (2000). *Market segmentation: Conceptual and methodological foundations.* Norwell, MA: Kluwer Academic Publishing. doi:10.1007/978-1-4615-4651-1

Wedel, M., & Steenkamp, J. E. M. (1989). Fuzzy clusterwise regression approach to benefit segmentation. *International Journal of Research in Marketing, 6*(4), 241–258. doi:10.1016/0167-8116(89)90052-9

Wen, K. L. (2004). *Grey Systems: Modeling and Prediction.* YangSky Scientific Press.

Wilkie, W. L., & Cohen, J. B. (1977). *An overview of market segmentation: Behavioral concepts and research approaches.* Cambridge, MA: Marketing Science Institute.

Wilson, A. M., Thabane, L., & Holbrook, A. (2004). Application of data mining techniques in pharmacovigilance. *British Journal of Clinical Pharmacology, 57*(2), 127–134. doi:10.1046/j.1365-2125.2003.01968.x PMID:14748811

Wilson, J. N., & Ritter, G. X. (2000). *Handbook of computer vision algorithms in image algebra.* CRC Press.

Wind, Y. (1978). Issues and advances in segmentation research. *JMR, Journal of Marketing Research, 15*(3), 317–337. doi:10.2307/3150580

Wind, Y., & Lerner, D. (1979). On the measurement of purchase data: Surveys versus purchase diaries. *JMR, Journal of Marketing Research, 16*(1), 39–47. doi:10.2307/3150872

Wu, D. (2009). Supplier selection in a fuzzy group setting: A method using grey related analysis and Dempster–Shafer theory. *Expert Systems with Applications, 36*(5), 8892–8899. doi:10.1016/j.eswa.2008.11.010

Wu, H. H. (2002). A comparative study of using grey relational analysis in multiple attribute decision making problems. *Quality Engineering, 15*(2), 209–217. doi:10.1081/QEN-120015853

Wu, J. (2012). Cluster analysis and K-means clustering: An introduction. In *Advances in K-means Clustering* (pp. 1–16). Springer Berlin Heidelberg. doi:10.1007/978-3-642-29807-3_1

Wu, M., & Liu, Z. (2011). The supplier selection application based on two methods: VIKOR algorithm with entropy method and Fuzzy TOPSIS with vague sets method. *Int. J. Management Science and Engineering Management, 6*(2), 110–116.

Wu, R.-S., & Chou, P.-H. (2011). Customer segmentation of multiple category data in e-commerce using a soft-clustering approach. *Electronic Commerce Research and Applications, 10*(3), 331–341. doi:10.1016/j.elerap.2010.11.002

Wu, W.-Y., & Chen, S.-P. (2005). A prediction method using the grey model GMC (1, n) combined with the grey relational analysis: A case study on Internet access population forecast. *Applied Mathematics and Computation, 169*(1), 198–217. doi:10.1016/j.amc.2004.10.087

Xia, J., Evans, F. H., Spilsbury, K., Ciesielski, V., Arrowsmith, C., & Wright, G. (2010). Market segments based on the dominant movement patterns of tourists. *Tourism Management, 31*(4), 464–469. doi:10.1016/j.tourman.2009.04.013

Xia, M., & Wong, W. K. (2014). A seasonal discrete grey forecasting model for fashion retailing. *Knowledge-Based Systems, 57*, 119–126. doi:10.1016/j.knosys.2013.12.014

Xi, L., Muzhou, H., Lee, M. H., Li, J., Wei, D., Hai, H., & Wu, Y. (2014). A new constructive neural network method for noise processing and its application on stock market prediction. *Applied Soft Computing, 15*, 57–66. doi:10.1016/j.asoc.2013.10.013

Yadav, V., & Srinivasan, D. (2011). A SOM-based hybrid linear-neural model for short-term load forecasting. *Neurocomputing, 74*(17), 2874–2885. doi:10.1016/j.neucom.2011.03.039

Yang, C. C., & Chen, B. S. (2006). Supplier selection using combined analytical hierarchy process and grey relational analysis. *Journal of Manufacturing Technology Management, 17*(7), 926–941. doi:10.1108/17410380610688241

Yang, M. H. (2001). An efficient algorithm to allocate shelf space. *European Journal of Operational Research, 131*(1), 107–118. doi:10.1016/S0377-2217(99)00448-8

Yang, M. H., & Chen, W. C. (1999). A study on shelf space allocation and management. *International Journal of Production Economics, 60*, 309–317. doi:10.1016/S0925-5273(98)00134-0

Yang, X.-S. (2010). *Nature-Inspired Metaheuristic Algorithms*. Luniver Press.

Yankelovich, D. (1964). New criteria for market segmentation. *Harvard Business Review, 42*(2), 83–90.

Yankelovich, D., & Meer, D. (2006). Rediscovering market segmentation. *Harvard Business Review, 84*(2), 122–131. PMID:16485810

Yano, F., Shohdohji, T., & Toyoda, Y. (2008). Modification of hybridized particle swarm optimization algorithms applying to facility location problems. In *Proceedings of the 9th Asia Pacific Industrial Engineering & Management Systems Conference* (pp. 2278-2287).

Yao, A. W. L., Chi, S. C., & Chen, J. H. (2003). An improved grey based approach for electricity demand forecasting. *Electric Power Systems Research, 67*(3), 217–224. doi:10.1016/S0378-7796(03)00112-3

Yapıcıoğlu, H., Dozier, G., & Smith, A. E. (2004, June). Bi-criteria model for locating a semi-desirable facility on a plane using particle swarm optimization. In Evolutionary Computation, 2004. CEC2004. Congress on (Vol. 2, pp. 2328-2334). IEEE. doi:10.1109/CEC.2004.1331188

Yegnanarayana, B. (2009). *Artificial neural networks*. PHI Learning Pvt. Ltd.

Yoo, J., & Maddala, G. S. (1991). Risk Premia and Price Volatility in Futures Markets. *Journal of Futures Markets*, *11*(2), 165–177. doi:10.1002/fut.3990110204

Yuancheng, L., Tingjian, F., & Erkeng, Y. (2002, October). Short-term electrical load forecasting using least squares support vector machines. In *Power System Technology, 2002. Proceedings. PowerCon 2002. International Conference on* (Vol. 1, pp. 230-233). IEEE. doi:10.1109/ICPST.2002.1053540

Yucel, A., & Guneri, A. F. (2011). A weighted additive fuzzy programming approach for multi-criteria supplier selection. *Expert Systems with Applications*, *38*(5), 6281–6286. doi:10.1016/j.eswa.2010.11.086

Yu, H., & Kim, S. (2012). SVM Tutorial-Classification, Regression, and Ranking. In *Handbook of Natural Computing* (pp. 479–506). Springer Berlin Heidelberg. doi:10.1007/978-3-540-92910-9_15

Yu, L., Lai, K. K., & Wang, S. (2008). Multistage RBF neural network ensemble learning for exchange rates forecasting. *Neurocomputing*, *71*(16-18), 3295–3302. doi:10.1016/j.neucom.2008.04.029

Zadeh, L. A. (1965). Fuzzy Sets. *Information and Control*, *8*(3), 338–353. doi:10.1016/S0019-9958(65)90241-X

Zaki, M. J., & Meira, W. Jr. (2014). *Data mining and analysis: fundamental concepts and algorithms*. Cambridge University Press.

Zaw, M. M., & Mon, E. E. (2013). Web document clustering using cuckoo search clustering algorithm based on levy flight. *International Journal of Innovation and Applied Studies*, *4*(1), 182–188.

Zelman, W. N., Pink, G. H., & Matthias, C. B. (2003). Use of the balanced scorecard in health care. *Journal of Health Care Finance*, *29*(4), 1–16. PMID:12908650

ZENTUT. (2015). *Data mining applications*. Retrieved June 27, 2015, from http://www.zentut.com/data-mining/data-mining-applications/

Zhang, C., Ouyang, D., & Ning, J. (2010). An artificial bee colony approach for clustering. *Expert Systems with Applications*, *37*(7), 4761–4767. doi:10.1016/j.eswa.2009.11.003

Zhang, J., Hsu, W., & Lee, M. L. (2001). Image mining: Issues, frameworks and techniques. In *Proceedings of the 2nd ACM SIGKDD International Workshop on Multimedia Data Mining (MDM/KDD'01)*. University of Alberta.

Zhou, P., Ang, B. W., & Poh, K. L. (2006). A trigonometric grey prediction approach to forecasting electricity demand. *Energy*, *31*(14), 2839–2847. doi:10.1016/j.energy.2005.12.002

Zhuang, Z. Y., Churilov, L., Burstein, F., & Sikaris, K. (2009). Combining data mining and case-based reasoning for intelligent decision support for pathology ordering by general practitioners. *European Journal of Operational Research*, *195*(3), 662–675. doi:10.1016/j.ejor.2007.11.003

Žorž, G. F., Kavšek, G., Antolič, Ž. N., & Jager, F. (2008). A comparison of various linear and non-linear signal processing techniques to separate uterine EMG records of term and pre-term delivery groups. *Medical & Biological Engineering & Computing*, *46*(9), 911–922. doi:10.1007/s11517-008-0350-y PMID:18437439

Zufryden, F. S. (1986). A dynamic programming approach for product selection and supermarket shelf-space allocation. *The Journal of the Operational Research Society*, *37*(4), 413–422. doi:10.1057/jors.1986.69

Zunino, L., Tabak, B.M., Serinaldi, F., Zanin, M., Perez, D.G., & Rosso, O.A. (2010). Commodity Predictability Analysis with a Permutation Information Theory Approach. *Physica A*, *390*(2011), 876–890.

About the Contributors

Numan Çelebi received his B.S. degree in Electrical engineering from Istanbul Technical University and a M.S. degree in Electrical engineering from Sakarya University. He then earned his PhD degree in Industrial engineering with concentration rough set theory and inductive learning from Sakarya University. He worked as an assistant professor in the Department of Industrial engineering at the University of Istanbul about seven years. He also spent one and half year in the Department of Industrial and System Engineering at Auburn University in USA as a post-doctoral researcher funding by TUBITAK for research on metaheuristic algorithms and their applications. He currently serves as an Associate Professor for Sakarya University at the Department of Information System Engineering. His main research area is data mining and applications on rough set theory. His current research interest is the area of metaheuristic algorithms and their applications in computer science. Now he has started to become interested in applications metaheuristic strategies to make the encrypted information readable.

* * *

Alp Baray received his Ph.D degree on production management from Istanbul University in 1991. He is a member of Industrial Engineering Department in Istanbul University and still working as Professor. He has lots of experiences about the quality management and production planning in industries that especially produce metallurgical and plastic products. Baray, whose research interests are "Statistical Process Control" and "Optimization", published three books and many national and international research and conference papers.

Sinem Büyüksaatçı was born in Istanbul, Turkey, in 1984. She received her both B.Sc and M.Sc. degree on industrial engineering from Istanbul University, Istanbul, Turkey in 2006 and 2009 respectively. She attained her Ph.D degree recently in 2015. She is still working as a research assistant in Istanbul University, Industrial Engineering Department. Her research interests include optimization, metaheuristic algorithms, statistical quality control and design of experiments.

Halil Ibrahim Cebeci has been in University since 2002. He started his career as a research assistant and has been working in different departments including Informatics Department (2002-2005), and Distance Learning Implementation and Research Centre (2005-2011), Information Systems Engineering Department (2011-2013) of Sakarya University. He received a BSc degree from Istanbul University Industrial Engineering Department in 2002 and was awarded with a master and PhD degree in the same area in 2004 and 2011 from Sakarya University. During his PhD, he worked on mitigating the bullwhip effect in multi echelon supply chains with designing and implementing extended vendor managed inventory model within the context of information sharing. He works for Sakarya University Faculty of Management / Management Department. He has several research interests such as Supply Chain Management, Data Mining, Business Intelligence, Advanced Statistical Techniques and e-Learning. He has around 10 publications and attended several national and international conferences in these areas. He also has project experience in inter-disciplinary projects at national and EU-level.

Ismail Hakki Cedimoglu received his BSc (1982), MSc (1985) from Technical University of Istanbul in Industrial Engineering and PhD (1993) from Cranfield Institute of Technology in School of Industrial and Manufacturing Scince. His research interests are in manufacturing planning and control, artificial neural networks, enterprise resource planning systems and database management systems.

Ali Kemal Çelik was born in Kars, Turkey, in 1983. He studied Business Administration in Hacettepe University, Ankara, Turkey. He received his Master degree in Business Administration from Atatürk University, Erzurum, Turkey, where he continues studying Econometrics to receive a Doctoral degree. Since 2011, he is a research assistant at Atatürk University, Department of Quantitative Methods.

Mehmet Yahya Durak earned a B.S. degree both in Industrial Engineering and Business Administration at Istanbul Kültür University in 2012 and a M.S. degree in Industrial Engineering from Istanbul Technical University in 2015. In 2012, he joined as a Research Assistant in the Istanbul Kültür University Engineering Faculty at Industrial Engineering Department. His current research interests are Lean Thinking, Data Mining and Mathematical Programming.

Sakir Esnaf is presently working at the Istanbul University as a Professor in the Department of Industrial Engineering at the Faculty of Engineering and acting as the Chair of the Department. He graduated from the Department of Industrial Engineering at the Istanbul Technical University. He received his M.S. and Ph.D. Degrees in Production Management from the Istanbul University. He was a postdoctoral research fellow in the Department of Mechanical and Industrial Engineering at the University of Toronto, Canada. His current research topics are facility location applications of fuzzy clustering and metaheuristics, shelf space management and optimization in retailing, revenue management and dynamic pricing, health care operations management, and large scale optimization problems. He has several national and international research and conference papers published.

Miraç Eren is a Research Assistant Dr at Atatürk University.

Girisha Garg completed her doctorate from Netaji Subhas Institute of Technology, Delhi in 2013. Her areas of specialization are pattern recognition, wavelet transform and biomedical signal processing techniques.

Abdulkadir Hiziroglu has been in academia since 2001. He had worked in Informatics Department, Distance Education Centre, Industrial Engineering and Management Information Systems Departments of Sakarya University. He received his Bachelor and Master degrees in Industrial Engineering and he then pursued his PhD degree at Manchester Business School where he worked on designing and implementing a customer segmentation model using soft computing technologies within the framework of data mining and knowledge discovery. Currently, He works as an Associate Professor for Yildirim Beyazit University Management Information Systems Department in Ankara. He has several research interests such as soft computing/data mining applications in business and management, business intelligence and customer analytics, and e-learning. His publications have appeared in several journals including Expert Systems with Applications, Journal of Intelligent and Fuzzy Systems, Journal of Economic Studies, Journal of Marketing Analytics and International Journal of Fuzzy Systems Applications.

İbrahim Huseyni was born in 1979 in Silopi. He graduated from Atatürk University and has worked for Şırnak University since 2012.

Adil Gursel Karacor was born in 1969. He graduated from Istanbul Technical University, Istanbul, Turkey with a Bsc. in Computer and Control Engineering in 1995. He completed Msc. in Systems and Control Engineering at Bogazici University, Istanbul, Turkey in 2002. He is currently pursuing PhD. in Modeling and Design of Engineering Systems at Atilim University, Ankara Turkey, with thesis entitled: "Artificial Neural Network Based Decisive Prediction Models on High Frequency Financial Data". He worked as a tutor and research assistant at Turkish Air Force Academy for 9 years. He also worked for a total of 19 years as a research and development engineer at the Turkish Air Force. At present he works for Kuveytturk Participation Bank as Artificial Intelligence Team Leader. His research interest is mainly in Artificial Intelligence, Data Science, and predictive modeling. He is married with a 13 year old son.

Emel Şeyma Küçükaşcı is a research assistant in the Department of Industrial Engineering at Istanbul Commerce University, where she received a BS degree in Industrial Engineering, in 2010. She also received an MS degree in Industrial Engineering from Boğaziçi University, in 2013. She is currently a PhD student in the Department of Industrial Engineering at Boğaziçi University. Her research interests include metaheuristics and optimization in data mining.

Tarık Küçükdeniz is presently working at the Istanbul University as a Assistant Professor in the Department of Industrial Engineering at the Faculty of Engineering. He is graduated from the Department of Industrial Engineering at the Istanbul University. He received his M.S. and Ph.D. Degrees from the Industrial Engineering Department of Istanbul University.

Tuncay Özcan is an Assistant Professor in the Department of Industrial Engineering at the Istanbul University. His research interests include multi-criteria decision making, metaheuristics, data mining,forecasting, and shelf space management models for retailing. He has published in Expert Systems with Applications, International Journal of Computational Intelligence Systems and other journals.

Alper Ozpinar has obtained his PhD degree in Mechanical Engineering from Yildiz Technical University. He also holds an MS degree in Systems Engineering from Yeditepe University and BS degree in Chemical Engineering from Bogazici University, all located in Istanbul Turkey. His field of expertise include, application of various computer and information systems to different fields of engineering, especially energy, demand side management, environmental health and safety, renewable energy sources, industrial automation and control, automatic data collection systems, systems modeling and simulation. He has seventeen years of experience in computer and software applications last twelve years of which has been focused on environmental and energy field. Served as a consultant and project manager for government organizations like Ministry of Forestry and Environment, Greater Municipality of Istanbul moreover international companies like ABB, Toyota, Bosch, Siemens. He has also worked part time and full time as instructor at different universities and departments given courses related with Cloud Computing, Computer Networks, Programming with different programming languages such as ASP. NET, VB.NET, C++, Java, Numerical Analysis, Artificial Intelligence and Database Systems. He has a vast experience in artificial intelligence applications such as smart grids, artificial neural networks, artificial intelligence, fuzzy logic, genetic algorithm applications. He has worked on neural networks, energy applications, active and passive RFID tags, readers and controllers, RFID technology expert especially on electronic vehicle identification. He has developed numerous projects and software applications with MS Azure, MsAccess, Visual Basic, C# and ASP and VB.Net in Automative, Textiles, Services Sector, Health Sector and various fields of engineering. He is a full time Asst. Prof. Dr. in the Department of Mechatronics in Istanbul Commerce University.

Ihsan Hakan Selvi received his BSc (2001), MSc (2004) and PhD (2004) degrees in Industrial Engineering from Sakarya University. After completing his PhD, he worked as a postdoctoral researcher in the Intelligent System Center at University of Missouri Science and Technology. His main research interest are in the areas of manufacturing planning and control, cloud manufacturing and multi criteria decision making.

Funda H. Sezgin is currently a member in Industrial Engineering Department of the Istanbul University Engineering Faculty. She completed her B.Sc. in Econometrics Department of Istanbul University Economics Faculty, M.Sc. in Econometrics Department of Istanbul University Institute of Social Sciences, Ph.D. in Econometrics Department of Marmara University Institute of Social Sciences. She is married and has a daughter.

Vijander Singh received his B. Tech in Electrical Engineering from G.B. Pant University of Agriculture and Technology in Uttarakhand in 1995. He received M.E. degree in Electrical Engineering in 2000 and Ph. D in Electrical Engineering in 2007 from IIT Roorkee. He has published many papers in international journals and conferences. He has chaired many international conferences. More than 25 M.Tech theses have been completed under his guidance. At present he has eight Ph.D students under his supervision and 2 Ph.Ds are completed. He is working as Professor in Instrumentation and Control Engineering Division at Netaji Subhas Institute of Technology, New Delhi, affiliated to University of Delhi, Delhi. His areas of research are Process control, Biomedical Instrumentation, Artificial Intelligence and Image Processing.

Tugrul Tasci received his Ph.D. degree from Sakarya University, Turkey in Computer Engineering in 2014. Currently he is a researcher at Faculty of Computer and Information Sciences of the same university. His primary research interests include Bayesian filtering, optical motion tracking, image processing and computer vision. He also studies on information systems and educational technology.

Alper Tayalı is a Research Assistant in the Production Management Department at School of Business, Istanbul University. Having completed his Master of Arts on Production Management, he is pursuing a doctoral degree at the Quantitative Methods Department.

Seda Tolun is an Associate Professor in the Quantitative Methods Department at School of Business, Istanbul University. She has been a faculty member since 2002. She completed her Ph.D. at Istanbul University. She worked as a postdoctoral researcher in the Department of Engineering Science at the University of Auckland, New Zealand in 2009. Her research interests are, data mining and applications, game theory, and recently process mining. She teaches data mining, operations research, and project management courses both in the undergraduate and graduate level. Seda is the managing editor of the Journal of Istanbul Business School. She has been acting as the AACSB Coordinator of Istanbul University, School of Business and also the responsible for the Erasmus academic staff exchange program.

Orhan Torkul received his BSc (1982) from Technical University of Istanbul, MSc (1987) from Tecnical University of Yildiz both in Industrial Engineering and PhD (1993) from Cranfield Institute of Technology in School of Industrial and Manufacturing Scince. His research interests are in manufacturing planning and control, management information systems and enterprise resource planning systems.

İlayda Ülkü earned a B.S. degree in Industrial Engineering at Istanbul Kültür University in 2010 and a M.S. degree in Industrial Engineering from Galatasaray University in 2014. She has begun her Ph.D. studies in Industrial Engineering program at Marmara University in 2014. In 2010, she joined as a Research Assistant in the Istanbul Kültür University Engineering Faculty at Industrial Engineering Department. Her current research interests are Mathematical Programming, and Supply Chain Management.

Fadime Üney-Yüksektepe earned a B.S. degree in Chemical Engineering at Istanbul Technical University in 2003 and a M.S. degree in Industrial Engineering from Koç University in 2005. In 2009, she completed her Ph.D. studies in Industrial Engineering and Operations Management program at Koç University. In 2009, she joined the Istanbul Kültür University's Faculty of Engineering as Assistant Professor at Department of Industrial Engineering where she currently serves an Associate Professor. Her current research interests are Mathematical Programming, Data Mining, Healthcare Applications, Scheduling, and Supply Chain Management.

Index

Printed in the United States
By Bookmasters